Handbook of Psychology
in
Legal Contexts

Handbook of Psychology in Legal Contexts

Edited by
Ray Bull
University of Portsmouth, UK
and
David Carson
University of Southampton, UK

JOHN WILEY & SONS, LTD
Chichester • New York • Weinheim • Brisbane • Singapore • Toronto

Copyright © 1995 by   John Wiley & Sons Ltd,
Baffins Lane, Chichester,
West Sussex PO19 1UD, England

National   01243 779777
International (+44) 1243 779777
e-mail (for orders and customer service enquiries): cs-books@wiley.co.uk
Visit our Home Page on http://www.wiley.co.uk
or http://www.wiley. com

Reprinted December 1995
Published in paperback October 1999

Other Wiley Editorial Offices

John Wiley & Sons, Inc., 605 Third Avenue,
New York, NY 10158-0012, USA

WILEY-VCH GmbH, Pappelallee 3,
D-69469 Weinheim, Germany

Jacaranda Wiley Ltd, 33 Park Road, Milton,
Queensland 4064, Australia

John Wiley & Sons (Asia) Pte Ltd, 2 Clementi Loop #02-01,
Jin Xing Distripark, Singapore 129809

John Wiley & Sons (Canada) Ltd, 22 Worcester Road,
Rexdale, Ontario M9W 1L1, Canada

Library of Congress Cataloging-in-Publication Data

A catalogue record for this book is available from the Library of Congress

British Library Cataloguing in Publication Data

A catalogue record for this book is available from the British Library

ISBN 0-471-94182-4 (hbk)
0-471-49242-6 (pbk)

Printed and bound in Great Britain by Biddles Ltd, Guildford and King's Lynn
This book is printed on acid-free paper responsibly manufactured from sustainable forestry, in which at least two trees are planted for each one used for paper production.

Contents

About the Editors

Ray Bull
Department of Psychology, University of Portsmouth, King Charles Street, Portsmouth PO1 2ER, UK

David Carson
Faculty of Law, The University, Highfield, Southampton SO17 1BJ, UK

Ray Bull is professor and head of the Department of Psychology at the University of Portsmouth. He has published widely on topics at the interface of psychology and law, especially on witnessing. He is a founding co-editor (with David Carson) of the journal *Expert Evidence: The International Digest of Human Behaviour, Science and Law*. He is one of the very few research psychologists in Britain who has been allowed to give expert testimony in criminal trials on factors affecting witness testimony. Together with David Carson he acted as a consultant to Worldwide Pictures and the British Psychological Society regarding the 1994 video training package *Expert Testimony: Developing Witness Skills*.

David Carson is a senior lecturer in the Faculty of Law at the University of Southampton. In addition to courses for law undergraduates he teaches in several other faculties at the University. Any skills that he has, he believes, lie in 'bringing ideas together' in fresh frameworks and presentations. He tries to emphasise ways of preventing problems, for example preventing the misrepresentation of expert witnesses' evidence in court, and ways of presenting risk decisions so as to minimise the likelihood of litigation. He cannot meet the demand for continuing professional development courses from a wide range of disciplines. In 1992, with Professor Bull, he founded the international, quarterly, refereed journal *Expert Evidence*, which claims to be the most inter-disciplinary—in its subscribers, format and contents—of the law and behaviour science journals. In 1994 he established the Behavioural Science and Law Network as an agency for designing and providing courses and conferences at the interface between law and the behavioural sciences.

Contributors

Ramón Arce
University of Santiago de Compostela, Departamento de Psicología Social, 15106 Santiago de Compostela, Spain

Dean Bartlett
Department of Psychology, University of Southampton, Highfield, Southampton SO17 1BJ, UK

Ronald Blackburn
Research Unit, Ashworth Hospital, Maghull, Liverpool, L31 1HW, UK

Neil Brooks
Case Management Services, 17A Main Street, Balerno, Edinburgh EH14 7EQ, UK

David Canter
Department of Psychology, University of Liverpool, PO Box 147, Liverpool L69 3BX, UK

Isabel C.H. Clare
Department of Psychiatry, University of Cambridge, Douglas House, 18b Trumpington Road, Cambridge CB2 2AH, UK

Brian R. Clifford
Psychology Department, University of East London, Romford Road, London E15 4LZ, UK

Brian L. Cutler
Department of Psychology, Florida International University, North Miami Campus, FL33181, USA

Graham M. Davies
Department of Psychology, University of Leicester, University Road, Leicester LE1 7RH, UK

Hedy Red Dexter
Sociology Department, University of Northern Colorado, Greeley, CO 80639, USA

Ian Donald
Department of Psychology, University of Liverpool, PO Box 147, Liverpool L69 3BX, UK

David P. Farrington
Institute of Criminology, Cambridge University, 7 West Road, Cambridge CB3 9DT, UK

Gisli H. Gudjonsson
Reader in Forensic Psychology, Institute of Psychiatry, De Crespigny Park, Denmark Hill, London SE5 8AF, UK

S.D. Hart
Department of Psychology, Simon Fraser University, Burnaby, British Columbia, V5A 1S6, Canada

Bill Hebenton
School of Social Policy, Manchester University, Manchester M13 9PL, UK

Larry Heuer
Barnard College, Columbia University, 3009 Broadway, New York, NY 10027-6598, USA

Clive R. Hollin
School of Psychology, University of Birmingham, Edgbaston, Birmingham B15 2TT, UK

John Jackson
School of Law, Queen's University, Belfast BT7 1NN, UK

Rajvinder Kandola
Pearn Kandola, 76 Banbury Road, Oxford OX2 6JT, UK

Günter Köhnken
Institut für Psychologie, Universität Kiel, Olshausonstr 40, 24098 Kiel, Germany

Peter J. van Koppen
Netherlands Institute for the Study of Criminality and Law Enforcement, Witte Singel 103, 2313 AA Leiden, The Netherlands

Geoff Lindsay
Psychological Service, Sheffield LEA and Division of Education, University of Sheffield, 9 Newbould Lane, Sheffield S10 2PJ, UK

Jenny McEwan
Reader in Law, Department of Law, University of Keele, Keele, Staffordshire ST5 5BG, UK

Amina Memon
Department of Psychology, University of Southampton, Highfield, Southampton SO17 1BJ, UK

R.J. Menzies
Department of Criminology, Simon Fraser University, Burnaby, British Columbia, V5A 1S6, Canada

John A. Michon
Netherlands Institute for the Study of Criminality and Law Enforcement, Witte Singel 103, 2313 AA Leiden, The Netherlands

Glynis H. Murphy
Reader in Learning Disability, Tizard Centre, University of Kent, Canterbury, Kent CT2 7LZ, UK

Hans Nijboer
Faculteit der Rechtsgeleerdheid, Juuidiset Studieintram Hugo de Graat, University of Leiden, Postbus 9520, 2300 RA Leiden, Leiden, The Netherlands

Karl Nunkoosing
Department of Psychology, University of Portsmouth, King Charles Street, Portsmouth PO1 2ER, UK

R. Glynn Owens
Professor of Health Studies, Health Studies Research Division, Upper School, St David's Hospital, Bangor, Gwynedd LL57 4SL, UK

Francis J. Pakes
Netherlands Institute for the Study of Criminality and Law Enforcement, Witte Singel 103, 2313 AA Leiden, The Netherlands

Ken Pease
School of Human and Health Sciences, University of Huddersfield,
Queensgate, Huddersfield HD1 3DH, UK

Steven D. Penrod
Law School, 285 Law Center, University of Minnesota, 229 19th Avenue
South, Minneapolis, MN 55455, USA

Helen Carlton Smith
Head of Child and Adolescent Clinical Psychology Service, Bolton General
Hospital, Minerva Road, Farnworth, Bolton BL4 0JR, UK

Tracey Swaffer
Glenthorne Youth Treatment Centre, Kingsbury Road, Birmingham
B24 9SA, UK

Chrissie Verduyn
Head of Child and Adolescent Clinical Psychology Service, University
Hospital of South Manchester, Withington Hospital, West Didsbury,
Manchester M20 8LR, UK

C.D. Webster
Professor and Head of Department, Department of Psychology, Simon
Fraser University, Burnaby, British Columbia, V5A 1S6, Canada

A. Daniel Yarmey
Department of Psychology, University of Guelph, Guelph, Ontario,
N1G 2W1, Canada

Preface

This *Handbook's* origins lie in a discussion we had with Michael Coombs of John Wiley about a behavioural science and law journal. In the event the journal, full title *Expert Evidence: The International Digest of Human Behaviour Science and the Law*, came first. Jointly and severally, to use one of the few technical legal expressions in this volume, we have also been involved in organising, and continue to organise, inter-disciplinary conferences and courses including the establishment, in 1994, of the Behavioural Sciences and Law Network (currently organised out of Southampton University) and the Master's courses, at Portsmouth University, in criminal justice and child forensic studies. (The T-shirts and post-graduate degree will come in due course.)

We see the interaction of law and psychology (or psychology and law—it matters not) as a project which deserves to be tackled at several levels and in different ways. In this volume we have been fortunate to gain the contributions of many others involved at the interface between these disciplines. Without seeking to be different, just for the sake of being different, we have tried to assemble a range of innovative contributions demonstrating the variety and vitality of law and psychology. We have acknowledged, right from the start, that it is far from being a 'new' subject. Even if law and psychology conferences are relatively new, particularly in Europe, practising psychologists and lawyers have been interacting in courts and other fora for a long time. It is important not to take too narrow a focus. The book is designed, in part, to show how far we have come and how much more could be achieved.

Certainly more psychologists than lawyers have contributed to the book. That was planned, as well as inevitable. As an area of academic interest, many more psychologists than lawyers are involved. Psychologists have had to 'come to law' as they must practise within legal frameworks and tests. But it does not follow, particularly if the pragmatic needs of practitioners are considered, that lawyers are disinterested. A moment's thought about the problems in establishing, and proving, past facts will quickly establish the integral relevance of psychology to law and legal practice. But it has been difficult for both disciplines to make headway given their different orientations, methods and assumptions. A major goal of this handbook has been to ease the relationship, to encourage a mutual understanding of the other discipline and its adherents. Thus the loose framework has been for each section to be introduced by two more general chapters, one from a lawyer and one from a psychologist, before more detailed topics are addressed by specialists from that subject. Each chapter should be comprehensible to readers versed in the other discipline.

We anticipate that the *Handbook* will be used by practising lawyers when investigating whether a psychologist may have useful expert evidence to offer. But we must counsel that, despite the breadth of the topics considered in this volume, we have not been able to tackle all subjects. Psychology has much more to offer the courts than may be implied here.

Whilst many legal concepts are common or similar to different legal systems and traditions there are, of course, many differences of detail between the substantive law and procedure of each country. We have not tried to deny this problem but rather sought to concentrate upon key ideas and concepts. We have so much to learn from other countries' researches, laws, practices and experiences. Our contributors have not been trying to expound the law on particular discrete topics so much as demonstrating, sometimes through the medium of a particular country's law, the potential for further collaboration between the law and psychology.

We are very grateful to all our contributors, particularly for keeping, usually more than less, within word limits. They have had so much to say but so few words allowed. We hope that they are as happy with the final product as we are of their individual contributions. And we must, and readily do, thank Wendy Hudlass, of John Wiley & Sons, not least for avoiding chiding us too much for delays.

David Carson
Ray Bull
January, 1995

Part 1

Introduction: Interdisciplinary and Interprofessional

Chapter 1.1

Psychology in Legal Contexts: Idealism and Realism

David Carson
University of Southampton
and
Ray Bull
University of Portsmouth

One of us, at the start of his academic career, was warned against pursuing an interest in legal applications of psychology. It offered no future, it was said; it constituted a blind alley, good quality 'scientific' research would not be possible. The other was advised not to go too close to, or to cross, the boundary lines between law and other disciplines.

At the heart of law and psychology lies a conundrum. Both law and psychology, as has been so often noted, are concerned with human behaviour, understanding it, predicting it, influencing it (e.g. Saks and Hastie, 1978; Yarmey, 1979). Both have substantial theoretical foundations while also being profoundly practical, or applied, disciplines. But however relevant they may be to each other, the offspring of the relationship between psychology and law is still an infant and doubts are still cast upon its legitimacy. We have no doubts about the relevance of psychology to law and law to psychology. This handbook demonstrates the variety of ways in which psychology is already informing the law and legal system. (We may be criticised for leaving some topics out.) Indeed the handbook, surely, demolishes the often made claim that the relationship between law and psychology is all about, and only about, eye-witness testimony. This handbook also seeks to suggest further ways in which psychology may inform the content and practice of the law. It aims also to demonstrate the relative fecundity of this particular branch of behavioural sciences, and highlight the potential for further studies.

Psychology is inextricably bound up in the law and legal system. Questioning a witness about past events, for example, necessarily involves the psychology of memory. The law directly influences psychology; it determines how psychologists approach certain topics. The industrial psychologist, for example, advising about the existence or potential for discrimination in a firm's procedures and practices, must accommodate to, although may also go beyond, the law's concepts and tests. The issues are not the relevance of psychology and law to each other but the extent to which the law and legal system should, and are prepared, to embrace psychology and the extent to which psychologists should, and are prepared, to adapt their work to the needs and requirements of the legal system. The issues involve questions of principle as well as pragmatic considerations. That begins to explain why different positions are taken on the potential of law and psychology.

IDEALISM

It is very easy, and occasionally very proper, for both psychologists and lawyers to return to their roots, to their basics. Psychologists tend to emphasise the scientific origins and methodology of their discipline. Indeed several psychologists appear to 'retreat' into a scientific purism. They then tend to deny the possibility of collaboration or co-operation between law and psychology, although this can often be seen as a semantic dispute about the nature of co-operation. Many people, for example, have been critical of aspects of psychological research into eye-witness testimony. Any research study using university students as its subjects is automatically criticised. How can we be sure that other people, in real-life situations, would respond in the same way? We cannot be sure. However, again, it largely depends upon what is understood by 'sure'. Nevertheless, an emphasis upon scientific credibility and methodological rigour cannot be criticised.

The scientific orientation of psychology is used, by some lawyers, to question its relevance in legal contexts. Stone (1984), a judge in Scotland, contrasts psychologists' methodological emphasis upon controlling variables, associated with laboratory conditions, with lawyers' accumulated experience.

> Lawyers deal with living testimony every day. They acquire vast experience in this, but they do not carry out research into it. Psychologists on the other hand, carry out their research in controlled situations in their laboratories, but have no practical experience of the real subject of their inquiries in the courtroom. (Stone, 1984, p. 3)

King (1986) directly challenges psychologists' scientific credentials. He perceives 'a misguided campaign by psychologists to colonise the law' (p. 102). He condemns psychologists for avoiding criticism of their scientific methods by their criticising other disciplines for having less rigorous methods. He raises many important points, including the following. 'One cannot ... legitimately study individual social behaviour without also studying the social context in which such behaviour occurs' (p. 6). Psychology involves many issues of value; it is not a value-free enterprise in the same sense as are the natural sciences. It is not atheoretical; 'social psychologists who embark upon research equipped with methods and techniques, but with no theory are like hired guns' (p. 63). Its methods lead to an oversimplification of legal issues, restricting 'their analysis to what is observable and measurable ...' (p. 41; see also Twining, 1983). The legal system is wrongly treated, by pyschologists, as a closed system when there are many other factors which affect individual decisions. The meanings, or subjective accounts, that actors in the legal system give to their behaviour, tend to be ignored.

To the extent that these or other criticisms apply to particular psychological research they are good points. But they do not substantiate an argument that the development of law and psychology is either impossible or misconceived. King (1986, p. 101) may believe that 'the dream fostered by many psychologists working on legal issues or developing law and psychology into a scientific body of knowledge about human behaviour in legal contexts will never be realised', but that is, substantially if not entirely, a semantic dispute about the meaning of 'a scientific body of knowledge'. The lawyer's tendency to dichotomise is being demonstrated; it is either scientific or it is not scientific. But science is a process as well as a product. The goal is to make scientific statements, to be able to make predictions that will be fulfilled at all times, in all places. Occasionally that may be possible. But it is inappropriate to dismiss as 'unscientific' all statements that fall short of this state of scientific grace. For a variety of reasons, which King is right to list and to emphasise, research on human behaviour in legal contexts may always fall short of the ultimate standards in predictive accuracy. But that provides no excuse for not trying to develop and test theories about behaviour in such contexts, while always seeking greater degrees of predictive accuracy. It does, however, emphasise the importance of maintaining critical attitudes and developing standards and practices to ensure openness and honesty in the presentation of research data.

What is unwarranted is the total disregard of research findings, because they are perceived to be imperfect, and their substitution with inferences whose claim to authority, credibility and reliability, is an alleged 'common sense'. Stone (1984) sought to dismiss psychologists' criticisms:

> The fact is that this criticism of legal testimony is no more than a general impression formed in the artificial context of their experiments, which they seek to apply in a totally different situation. That is surely not entitled to any credit as a scientific conclusion. One may, therefore, reasonably prefer the general impression of those who actually work with the real material, namely the legal profession. (Stone, 1984, p. 6)

The reasoning adopted relies upon assertion and persuasion. The conclusion does not even flow, despite the cunning presence of 'therefore', from the dubious inference about imperfect criticisms. And, even if the conclusion was accepted, that we should prefer the general impressions of the legal profession, that would require a research study! What is the 'legal profession'? Solicitors, who do not appear in the courts, as well as barristers? Does it include judges? What about differential degrees of experience? How are 'general' impressions to be distinguished from others which might be too specific? We may be sure, given the nature of the problems, that the conclusions of that research project would be imperfect and could be described as 'unscientific', particularly by those who do not wish to take them into account.

It is dangerous to reify 'common sense' or to call it in aid of an argument (Meehl, 1989). It involves an assertion, rather than a demonstration, about how common is the perception. It necessarily involves abstracting a perception or generalisation from a context. It is a theory under a more attractive label. As such it deserves to be treated with suspicion until tested, for example, to determine how many share the impression. King (1986) might support such a proposition for he expressly praises psychological 'maxims', such as the uses that witnesses make of post-event information and children's appreciation of time.

> Even if these maxims may not be used to predict with any precision the outcome of specific cases or the results of particular policies, they are, nevertheless, able to change the way in which people, whether participants or observers, think about social events and behaviour within social institutions. This alone justifies the existence and *validity* of applicable social psychology as an admittedly ideological and culture-bound but none the less valuable body of knowledge. (King, 1986, p. 109, emphasis added)

These 'maxims' would seem to be psychologists' alternatives to judges' interpretations of 'common sense'. One difference is that the 'maxims' have been treated as hypotheses, tested and challenged to different degrees of rigour, and possibly reformulated in the light of challenges. Common-sense legal inferences, for example about the virtues of leading questions as a means of discovering liars and charlatans, are not subjected to a similar process. That is dangerous.

This helps to highlight some sources of the key problems between lawyers and psychologists. For some (including many psychologists) it is their explicit opinion, but for many others it is their implicit position; psychology on legal topics is fine, just so long as it stays outside the courts. Insights, say from research on memory, are fine and interesting. They may influence legislation. But the problem is their application in trial proceedings. In large measure the problem concerns the application to a particular case of a general statement, say about the effect on eye-witness reliability of a robber carrying a gun. But there is much more to it. In many other spheres of our lives, for example when we visit our doctors or cross a bridge, we readily accept that 'general' knowledge can and must be applied to individual (our) cases.

Considerable effort is expended in keeping 'scientific' knowledge out of courtrooms. Different jurisdictions have different rules (Freckelton, 1993) but there is a common concern about the nature or definition of the 'scientific' evidence which it is proposed should be admitted into or relied upon by our courts. The United States Supreme Court has, for example, adopted tests of 'science' and 'scientific methodology' which many scientists would recognise and accept (*Daubert v. Merrell Dow Pharmaceuticals, Inc.*, (113 S.Ct. 2786 (1993)). But that does not provide dichotomous answers. Rather it relies upon judges to make decisions of a kind that they may not be, as the Chief Justice suggested, competent to make. More significantly, rules of evidence exclude scientific, or expert, evidence on topics which are within the judge's or jury's competence to decide, or which are on the (ultimate) issue which the court must determine. How are courts to learn the limits of their knowledge, to learn that what they have assumed to be true may actually be false, to know when they are actually ignorant (in the non-pejorative sense) if the rules prevent them from discovering (Mackay and Colman, 1991)? If the concern related to the nature and quality of the scientific evidence, the same or similar rules would govern the use of expert evidence outside of the courts. Many decisions are taken prior to the case coming before a judge or jury. Indeed the analysis of the nature of the legal issue, and the assessment of chances of success which determine whether the case proceeds, will often depend upon scientific evidence. While its admissibility will be one consideration, should the case get to court, the rules regulating expert evidence do not apply outside of the court (Carson, 1992).

There is a dispute, the more complex because it is implicit rather than explicit, over the extent to which litigation ought to be a rational, strictly scientific, process. A range of studies may suggest, for example, that juries are inefficient and ineffective instruments for making reliable decisions about complex factual disputes. But it seems that juries are as important, if not more important, for what they are not, as for what they are. They are not judges. They are not experts. So it is difficult to criticise them, or other social institutions, for not achieving something which it is not clear is or was one of their objectives. The right of a defendant to try his or her luck with a jury, which is regularly considered to be more gullible, credulous or incompetent, rather than a professional judge, is jealously protected in many jurisdictions.

Law and lawyers are concerned with trying to achieve 'justice' and psychologists are seeking scientific truth. Both are worthy ideals. But both work within imperfect systems. It is not a case of perfect, or beyond criticism, law and legal system, and imperfect and thus inappropriate psychology. However shamelessly moderate and romantic it may sound it is clear that both disciplines, and their adherents, need to recognise that they can and should learn from each other, and co-operate openly, if always critically, if their goals are to be advanced. If the potential of law and psychology, which is self-evidently extensive, is to be achieved then the idealism must be tempered by realism. Unrealistic expectations are unhelpful, although perhaps not as damaging as unwillingness to consider the potential.

REALISM

If this handbook has a theory, and implicitly it must do, then it is that the wealth and breadth of practical applications of psychology in legal contexts deserves to be recognised and the potential for further benefits to the law and legal system appreciated. How that potential might best be achieved is, however, a major question. The answer must differ, to an extent, between different countries. Clearly the development of an academic base for law and psychology is most developed in the United States and Canada. But, without trying even to imply any comparative comment, it is also important to consider the degree of development at practitioner level. It is not just a question, for example, of which psychological topics are admissible as expert evidence, and the quality of that evidence, but also the frequency with which professional evidence on psychological evidence is admitted in practice, and many other issues such as the quality control exercised by professional bodies over that evidence. A law may permit certain expert evidence to be tendered, but there may not be present the psychologists able to give evidence of sufficient quality. Just as a legal system cannot appropriately be judged by concentrating upon the quality of its appeal courts' judgments, so the progress of psychological evidence cannot be judged by a few test cases.

Law and psychology may, through a focus upon similar issues, substantially be an international project. Of course, as this handbook may also demonstrate, particular national rules and procedures can too easily distract attention from the essentially similar problems and issues. However, the development of co-operation between lawyers and psychologists may be expected to differ nationally. It may be valuable to identify some of the differences. For example, there does appear, in the United States at least, to be a significant status differential. There appears to be an assumption that the role and task of legal psychology is to come to the aid of legal problems. The law and legal system is, substantially, taken as a given. Certainly there is a substantial reformist tradition but psychological research appears to be used to achieve the reforms dictated by, or the goals implicit in, the law and legal system. The legal agenda, or hegemony, is not challenged (Weiner and Hess, 1987; Kagehiro and Laufer, 1992). Psychological research has proven challenging of many legal assumtions and procedures but an 'alternative agenda' has not been pursued. By this we do not mean that a radical or political stance of opposition towards the law should be adopted. That might be appropriate if the argument was about ends, for example achieving particular law reform. However, this argument is about means. Instead of relatively piecemeal criticisms of law, psychologists and lawyers might construct alternative 'systems'. For example, extensive work has been undertaken, by psychologists and others, about factors which influence decision-making. A number of points, perhaps not of predictive purity, could be turned into good practice guidance. Why not construct a detailed alternative, normative, model to judicial decision-making? Law reform is not always the product of academic discourse and scientific proof, but rather the consequence of persuasion and appeal to different goals and values.

Therapeutic jurisprudence, associated principally with lawyers Wexler and Winick (e.g. Wexler, 1990; Wexler and Winick, 1991), is an example. Taking the deceptively simple framework of maintaining that the law, provided basic civil liberties are protected, ought to have therapeutic rather than anti-therapeutic outcomes, they have facilitated an extensive and growing body of work, regularly utilising psychological research or insights, that point the way to better laws and better practice. Indeed, Wexler (1993) argues that this new approach is related to major changes in legal scholarship flowing from:

> the recognition that legislatures and administrators, rather than judges, are today the primary lawmakers. ... To them, the law is an instrumentality designed to deal with a particular problem; law is successful if its results satisfactorily tackle the problem. ... Increasingly, in other words, the referent of legal analysis is social problems, not the body of law itself. ... The crucial task of the legal scholar, however, is not so much to generate data but rather to use data in framing recommendations and to suggest important and relevant lines of inquiry to social scientists. (Wexler, 1993, pp. 18–19)

Psychology may be much more successful in informing the law, and would be more efficient, if there were less emphasis upon contributions to individual trials. This might come in the form of King's (1986) 'maxims' or Wexler's focus on solving practical problems with which the law is involved. Outside of court there are not the same tensions about the proper balance between 'science' and 'law'. Inside courts the adversary system accentuates problems; why should a lawyer welcome expert evidence that will make it more difficult to win the case for his or her client? Why should judges or juries welcome expert evidence when its admission necessarily involves recognising that they are incompetent to decide that particular issue on their own? Inside court language and persuasive drama rule. Outside court there are many more opportunities for measured debate and discussion.

The focus needs to be broadened from 'law' to include procedure and professional practice standards. As this handbook demonstrates, psychologists are making a contribution to the legal system in many different ways and at many different stages of legal proceedings. An emphasis upon good practice, rather than premature 'solutions' or claims to have discovered the 'answer', has much to offer, for example in police procedures, in assessing dangerousness, in investigating educational problems. In order to protect their clients' best interests lawyers should be demanding adherence to best practice, codes and regular monitoring and revision of those practices. If greater assurances could be given about the quality and reliability of expert witnesses, for example through rigorous peer review and professional disciplinary procedures, then courts might be happier, given that they are impossibly placed to assess experts, to admit a wider range of expert evidence.

It is worth considering some implications of the increasing 'professional-isation' of pre-trial preparations, at least in the UK. Disputes over different kinds of evidence have, in recent years, sometimes led to controversy: identification, confessions, forensic evidence particularly traces of explosives. Sometimes the controversy leads to, or is associated with, an inquiry and official report. That leads to new ways of working which are seen, at least for some time, as having 'cured' the problem. A classic example involves allegations that police officers were falsifying suspects' confessions. That led to changes whereby in England and Wales the vast majority of confessions are recorded on audio-tape. This has led to a dramatic reduction in the number of allegations of false confessions. The defendant's lawyer may never listen to all of the tape and getting it transcribed is very expensive. Thus there is no automatic check on the veracity of the prosecution version of the confession. Nevertheless the new procedure is, justifiably, seen as a great improvement. But note what is happening. Because the court hears that a prescribed procedure was followed it finds that evidence implicitly credible. The court 'rubber stamps' such a confession unless there is a specific challenge to it.

Courts may be seen as a public, quality assurance procedure (Carson, 1990). The more that prescribed procedures are adopted and followed, the less there is for the court to do. There is nothing inherently wrong with this. Indeed, given that quality procedures are being investigated and applied, it is very beneficial. But it would be wise to acknowledge the process. Quality assurance mechanisms can become perfunctory procedures. If the role of the courts as a quality assurance agency, in the majority of cases, was recognised then it would become much easier to check that the courts keep performing that role successfully.

IDEALISM AND REALISM

The tensions between idealism and realism are very real in law and psychology. The dream is enticing; the problems are extensive. Nobody should be expected or asked to give up a critical attitude. But, equally, the potential benefits should lead everyone to analyse the source and nature of their criticisms.

These may best be investigated through the development of law and psychology courses, at undergraduate and postgraduate level. Such courses should not just involve the study of psychological researches on legal topics. They need to emphasise the different assumptions, goals, values and methods. From an appreciation of the differences some assimilation becomes possible.

Both disciplines, in their own different ways, are strong on analysis and values. Both are concerned about seeing principled and yet pragmatic change. We believe that much has already been achieved, not just in those topics that have attracted academic debate, and that there is no turning back. A willingness to recognise initially different ideals but a common concern for real improvements in justice and human advancement should provide the basis for the way forward.

We must hope so; otherwise those who advised us at the start of our careers will have been proved right.

REFERENCES

Carson, D. (1990). Reports to Court: a role in preventing decision errors. *Journal of Social Welfare Law*, 151–63.

Carson, D. (1992). Beyond the ultimate issue. In F. Lösel, D. Bender and T. Bliesener (Eds), *Psychology and Law: International Perspectives*. Berlin: de Gruyter.

Freckelton, I. (1993). Science and the legal culture. *Expert Evidence*, **2**, 3, 107–14.

Kagehiro, D.K. and Laufer, W.S. (Eds) (1992). *Handbook of Psychology and Law*. New York: Springer-Verlag.

King, M. (1986). *Psychology In and Out of Court: A Critical Examination of Legal Psychology*. Oxford: Pergamon.

Mackay, R.D. and Colman, A.M. (1991). Excluding expert evidence: a tale of ordinary folk and common experience. *Criminal Law Review*, 800–10.

Meehl, P.F. (1989). Law and the fireside inductions (with postscript): some reflections of a clinical psychologist. *Behavioral Sciences and the Law*, **7**, 4, 521–50.

Saks, M.J. and Hastie, R. (1978). *Social Psychology in Court*. New York: Van Nostrand Reinhold.

Stone, M. (1984). *Proof of Fact in Criminal Trials*. Edinburgh: W. Green & Son.

Twining, W. (1983). Identification and misidentification in legal process: redefining the problem. In S. Lloyd-Bostock and B. Clifford (Eds), *Evaluating Witness Evidence*. Chichester: Wiley.

Weiner, I.B. and Hess, A.K. (Eds) (1987). *Handbook of Forensic Psychology*. New York: Wiley.

Wexler, D.B. (1990). *Therapeutic Jurisprudence: The Law as a Therapeutic Agent*. Durham (NC): Carolina Academic Press.

Wexler, D.B. (1993). Therapeutic jurisprudence and changing conceptions of legal scholarship. *Behavioral Sciences and the Law*, **11**, 1, 17–29.

Wexler, D.B. and Winick, B.J. (1991). *Essays in Therapeutic Jurisprudence*. Durham, NC: Carolina Academic Press.

Yarmey, A.D. (1979). *The Psychology of Eyewitness Testimony*. New York: Free Press.

Chapter 1.2

Psychology's Premises, Methods and Values

Brian R. Clifford
University of East London

On the surface it would seem as if law and psychology share common concerns in that they are both trying to understand and predict human behaviour. In short, both law and psychology take human nature as their subject matter. However, beyond this commonality of focus, closer inspection would seem to reveal that the two disciplines appear to diverge at the levels of value, basic premises, their models, their approaches, their criteria of explanation and their methods.

Thus, while both psychology and substantive law, legal processes and jurisprudence all address assumptions about the causes and modifications of behaviour, about the process of perception, memory, recognition and decision making, and about how people think and feel, in the past mutual facilitation has been marked by its absence. Why is this?

Arguments have been made (e.g. Tapp, 1969) that while law is value-laden and subjective, relying upon tradition and precedent, psychology is value-free and objective, relying upon empirical research. Again, it has been asserted that law is a practical art, a system of rules, a means of social control, concerned with solving practical problems. Psychology, on the other hand, is a science, concerned with the description, explanation, understanding, prediction and control of human behaviour.

Haward (1979) talks of law as being an 'abattoir of sacred cows' for psychology, in so far as all the beliefs that psychologists are thought to hold dear are disputed by lawyers. Philosophically, the psychologist believes in some degree of determinism (or causality), whereas the lawyer believes in free will. Thus, while the psychologist tends to talk in terms of *causes of* behaviour the lawyer talks in terms of *reasons for* behaviour. The law conceives of people as freely and consciously controlling their own behaviour, choosing their actions and thus taking responsibility for them. As Bentley (1979) points out, consciousness and free will are axiomatic in legal theory. This does not sit well with psychology, which has a different explanatory framework.

At the level of theory construction and everyday practical activity, as Meehl (1977) points out, lawyers rely on common-sense generalisations about human behaviours, based upon speculation, introspection, intuition, reflection, culturally transmitted beliefs and personal anecdotal observation. Psychology, on the other hand, favours empirical research and, where feasible and ethically practicable, experimental (or at least systematic) testing. Thus, the proper place of common sense in the 'scheme of things' is a major battle ground: if psychology agrees with common sense, lawyers feel that nothing has been gained by their interaction with psychologists; if psychology disagrees, or produces counter-intuitive findings, lawyers prefer to run with common sense and intuition, perhaps because they believe that psychology's counter-factual assertions or propositions, masquerading as truth, may be nothing more than controversial or speculative theory, poorly corroborated by available evidence.

Like all caricatures, there is more than a grain of truth in this polarised stereotyping of law and psychology. But they are stereotypes none the less, and their truth values are called into question by the fact that in this century psychology has provided us with models, concepts and findings which have radically changed the way we think about people, frequently with implications for law, since law, legal procedures and discussions of law and jurisprudence all involve assumptions about the nature of human beings, their capacities and their behaviour. Psychological theory and research have influenced, *inter alia*, laws concerning discrimination, capital punishment, pornography, sexual behaviour, child abuse and the conditions under which individuals may not be held responsible for their actions (e.g. Tapp and Levine, 1977).

In other words, a case can certainly be mounted that scientific psychology has added to, clarified and, I would like to argue, possibly improved upon the common sense or naïve psychology on which law has proceeded in the past.

If this positive fertilisation is to continue and accelerate into mutually beneficial reciprocity, a clear understanding by lawyers of what psychology is, and is not, is required. It is the purpose of this chapter to begin this process by outlining the premises, methods and values of psychology.

PSYCHOLOGY'S PREMISES

Psychology claims to be both a theoretical science and at the same time an applied discipline, able to serve in the practical affairs of the world (Clifford, 1981). It makes this claim because, as a discipline, it sees itself as objective, empirical, eclectic and humane. Underpinning this self-perception is the acceptance of a number of premises.

Premise 1: Acceptance of the Scientific Method

Psychology accepts that science is but one approach to the discovery and ordering of knowledge. It is taken to be different from common sense, metaphysics, religion, magic, tradition, rationalism and phenomenology, not because of its subject matter, but because of its methodology. Psychology is unified and distinct because of its method or logic of discovery. Specific techniques vary between and within different sub-disciplines of psychology, but the basic method remains the same—careful, controlled observation, rational and constrained reasoning and the subjecting of theories to empirical test. Description is the empirical goal of psychology and explanation is the theoretical goal.

Premise 2: Acceptance of the Basic Assumptions of the Scientific Enterprise

The psychological approach is guided by assumptions that are unproven and unprovable. They are necessary prerequisites for the conduct of scientific discourse—they constitute the axiomatic substructure of psychology.

Nature is orderly and regular. Events do not occur haphazardly. Change itself displays patterns that can be understood. This belief applies to all people, conditions and phenomena.

We can know nature. This is an important axiom for psychology because it assumes that humans are just as much a part of nature as are other natural objects, and although they possess unique and distinctive characteristics they can yet be understood and explained by the same methods as all science. Individuals and groups exhibit sufficiently recurring, orderly and empirically demonstrable patterns as to be amenable to scientific study.

Nothing is self-evident. Claims for truth must be demonstrated objectively. Tradition, subjective belief and common sense are not sufficient for verification. Herein lies the sceptical and critical attitude of psychology.

Knowledge is acquired from the acquisition of experience. This emphasis on empirical knowledge is a counter to the belief that knowledge is innate in humans and that pure reason is sufficient to produce verifiable knowledge.

Premise 3: Acceptance of the Rules of Scientific Enquiry

The pre-theoretical axioms listed above break through to the surface when we examine the rules of science. These are many but the chief ones are as follows.

Use operational definitions. Operationism means that terms must be defined by the steps or operations used to measure them.

Generality. This means that discussion or statements need to be about abstract variables, not particular antecedent and consequent conditions. Thus, descriptions are stated in terms of variables, not the specific stimuli that exhibited these variables; for example, 'punishment', not a smack on the hand or a smack on the bottom.

Controlled observation. This allows tentative identification of why something happened, what caused it, under what conditions. The stress on this method is predicated upon the concept of causality. The argument is that, assuming causality, the surest way to uncover such causality is to hold constant all variables not under test while varying the variable that is under investigation (the independent variable), because variables that do not vary cannot explain changes in behaviour. Controlling variables is not the only way to discount a variable as the cause of change, but it is the most direct and certain. To lack control in this sense is to court the dreaded confound: where two variables vary together, making interpretation of their separate effects impossible.

Replication. To be replicable data must be reliable. If data are not reliable, then explanations are not either. Scientific statements are meant to apply to whole classes or populations of people, conditions or phenomena. Before generalisation can be accepted it must be shown to hold for an adequate sample drawn from the population of interest. Unless proper and sufficient replications are made, generalisations ought not to be made.

Parsimony. Psychologists should never produce a complicated or more abstract explanation unless all other, simpler, explanations have been experimentally ruled out.

Consistency. If two explanatory statements are contradictory then at least one of them must be false. The principle of consistency requires that an explanatory statement must not contradict any explanatory statement that has been confirmed.

Confirmation. Explanatory statements must admit of predictive statements and these statements must be verifiable/falsifiable.

Premise 4: Acceptance of the Generic Research Process

So far we have outlined the unwritten assumptions of the psychological method and we have detailed the discipline's operating ground rules for membership of the scientific club. Let us now see how psychologists actually progress, irrespective of their particular sub-discipline, at a fairly abstract level.

Scientific knowledge is knowledge provable by both reason and experience. That is, science operates in two distinct but interrelated worlds—the conceptual/theoretical and the observational/empirical. Logical validation and

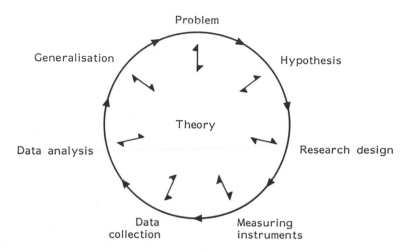

Figure 1.2.1

empirical verification are the criteria employed by science to evaluate claims to knowledge. So with psychology. Logic is concerned with valid reasoning but not empirical truth. Thus, while validity has to do with internal consistency, experience or empiricism has to do with approximations to truth. Both these ways of reasoning, and both aims or goals, are enshrined in the research process.

This research process has seven basic stages, as can be seen in Figure 1.2.1.

Problem formulation. The observation of a problem to be understood can come from anywhere or anyone. Problem formulation involves thinking about a problem and tentatively generating some possible explanations. These possible explanations are then converted into possible tests of their correctness. This is usually done in the form of hypotheses.

Hypotheses. Hypotheses represent refinements of ideas into testable propositions that can be, at least in principle, confirmed or falsified.

Research designs. The nature of the hypotheses generated and the embedding theory and experimentation that are known to be relevant to it will suggest how best to go about testing predictions. Different research methods and experimental designs each have their good and bad points. The selection of the appropriate design is as much an art as it is a science.

Measuring instruments. This is partly a function of operationalisation referred to above but, again, different questions will require different solutions in terms of which measures will be decided upon.

Data collection. Once again, decisions have to be made concerning the timing, duration, amount and nature of data to be collected. A basic issue, because of the reliance of experimental psychology on statistical analysis, is that the data should be quantifiable in some way, either initially or at least eventually. This is one of the areas where the psychologist and the psychiatrist can most clearly be differentiated. Unlike the psychologist, the psychiatrist is concerned to listen to the utterances of a person and then engage in interpretation of these utterances. However, when psychiatrists employ tests to aid their interpretation they are coming closer to the psychologist, because these tests will have involved standardisation on large numbers of people initially.

Data analyses. A huge number of statistical tests are potentially available to the psychologist, and a lawyer coming to psychology is likely to be mystified by this range. This is not a real issue, however, because the choice of appropriate statistical test is dictated by such things as the number of groups in the study, whether the conditions are related in some way or not, and the level of measurement of the dependent variable (see below). The number of types of different measurement one takes of any person in an experiment is also a deciding factor in what statistical tests should be used.

Generalisation. As was said above all psychologists wish to generalise their particular findings beyond the actual study conducted. Whether they can legitimately do so depends on a number of issues. Statistical analysis allows generalisation to other samples of the population from which the experimental sample was drawn, and the population of that sample *per se*. To the extent that the study reproduced the conditions of the situation to which the person wishes to generalise tentative generalisation is defensible. In general, the issue of extrapolation from known situations to unknown situations is a question of internal and external validity (see below).

Premise 5: Acceptance of the Aims of Science

The aims of science in general and psychology in particular are many and varied and shift at different stages in the maturity of the various sub-disciplines, and within a research programme's life cycle. However, with few exceptions, all psychologists would accept that they are concerned with describing, explaining, understanding, predicting and controlling particular processes and general behaviour repertoires.

These, then, are the premises upon which psychology operates. It believes that the scientific method is the most powerful calculus yet devised to produce verifiable and falsifiable knowledge. It has unwritten assumptions, unspoken rules of evidence and evaluation, and clearly marked stages of data gathering, theory construction and knowledge generation. It also has areas of uncertainty and controversy. The scientific method is believed by psychologists to be the royal road, but it is not without its pot holes—but these pot holes are troublesome, not terminal. Having looked at the premises, we can now move on to look at the methods that psychology employs.

METHODS OF PSYCHOLOGY

At the level of method all psychologists, of whatever persuasion, believe that observed behaviours and changes in behaviour are caused by something, whether they be external factors or internal factors such as limited processing capacity, attitudes, beliefs or values, or mere habit and conditioning. The application of research methods by psychology is concerned to establish just what causes what.

The True Experiment

The true experiment, defined as the random allocation of subjects (i.e. people) to experimental conditions and the manipulation of one or more independent variables, is believed to be the best way to disentangle cause and effect relationships. By randomly allocating people to experimental conditions any individual difference factors, due to the individuality of these different people, are spread throughout the experimental design and thus, while these human differences may dilute any real effects that are present, they will not distort the true effects. By varying only one or a few variables while holding all other conditions constant this allows fairly unambiguous delineation of cause and effect relationships.

The key feature of the experimental method involves careful manipulation or change of some aspect of a situation and observing the effects this change has on some behaviour or thought process of interest, in order to establish relationships. The event, condition or situation that is manipulated is called the independent variable (a variable being something that can assume different values—e.g. noise: high, medium or low), so called because it is under the control of the experimenter and independent of the people taking part in the experiment. The physical, psychological or social changes which are measured are called the dependent variable (because the changes depend on the values of the manipulated variable—e.g. increased, decreased or unchanged reasoning performance). Changes in the dependent variable are usually recorded as, or translated into, numbers to allow statistical procedures to be applied to them.

The basic experimental design involves two groups of people (subjects): the experimental group, which has the independent variable applied to or withheld from it, and the control group, which does not experience any experimental manipulation at all. This basic design can be, and usually is, greatly increased in complexity.

Usually an experiment involves taking measurements from each individual under each of the conditions of manipulation or treatment that they appear in. All these scores are then converted to a mean score (average) for the particular condition or group and then interpreted for correlation, difference or trend. Basic to this task is statistics: the discipline that deals with sampling data from a (theoretical) population of individuals and then drawing inferences about the population from the sample. Statistical tests are applied to the means of the different manipulated groups, and if numerical differences translate into statistically significant differences then this declares that the observed differences between the different groups are trustworthy and not due to chance factors. As such, they should generalise to other samples of the same population and the population as a whole.

There are a number of intrinsic but not insuperable problems in the true experiment as far as the law is concerned. First, in experimental analyses it is the *means* of the groups that are compared and, because of individual differences, it is possible that any one person in a particular group will be better or worse than the mean score would suggest. That is, group means may not represent the performance of any one individual in that group. This has the implication that, for example, a mean difference between adult and child witness groups, in favour of adults, may mask the fact that some children actually outperformed some adults.

A second problem is that significance is evaluated in terms of presence or absence, not size. But 'significance' does not equal 'importance'; it simply indicates that it is unlikely that the effect came about by chance. Most psychological research has not been analysed by the power statistics recommended by Cohen (1977; Cohen and Cohen, 1975) despite these being readily available and computationally simple. Thus we need to know not only that an effect is present, but whether it is large enough to matter for practical purposes.

Yet another issue raised concerning the experimental method is its artificiality. Rabbitt (1981) calls it a tenuous abstraction of real-life situations. This raises questions of internal and external validity. Internal validity refers to the degree to which we can be sure that variation in the dependent variable is due to manipulation of the independent variable. External validity refers to the extent to which the results of an experiment can be generalised to other situations, other subjects and other tasks. The problem is that, in general, as you increase one type of validity so you reduce the validity of the other. External validity is often talked about in terms of ecological validity, but the two are somewhat different. External validity refers to subject representativeness (can we extrapolate from rats to humans?), variable representativeness (do findings with 'white noise', which is known to cause arousal, generalise to the arousal present in rape situations?), and the setting representativeness of the study (do findings obtained from people watching a rape scene on a video recorder correspond to findings obtained from victims or witnesses actually involved in a real rape crime?). Only this last area of representativeness is concerned with ecological validity. However, when we consider problems of ecological validity we need to distinguish between realism and generalisability (Berkowitz and Donnerstein, 1982). Realism refers to whether the experimental setting bears a resemblance to the real world. A key question is the importance of the mundane realism (Clifford, 1978). If we can be sure that the psychological processes are the same in the contrived situation as in the real world, then the degree of realism is not a real threat to external validity. The ability of an experiment's results to generalise to other situations is more important than their superficial resemblance to the real world. Additionally, surface realism does not guarantee an increase in generalisability (Banaji and Crowder, 1989; Crowder, 1993). Thus it is generalisability rather than surface realism that determines whether a study is ecologically valid (Elmes, Kantowitz and Roediger III, 1992).

Despite all these objections the experimental method is still the linchpin of the psychological endeavour. This is so because, despite its acknowledged weaknesses, the true experiment is still the best method of ascertaining knowledge in situations where it is practical and ethical to conduct such a study. All the other research methods available, and used by the psychologist, have their own problems which, on balance, are more problematic than the experimental method.

However, in certain situations the true experiment is not available as an option and other methods must be adopted, as described below.

Case Studies

Case study research can be of two types: archival case histories or case studies proper. In the first, a researcher surveys the case records of many people, trying to discern trends or patterns. Such study can provide important descriptive information but not much else. The second type of case study involves longitudinal studies of single subjects over time with many observations being made. There are several problems with this type of research: there is no adequate baseline against which to compare change; because they are idiographic (based upon one person), generalisation is problematic; because variables are hopelessly confounded, causality cannot be unambiguously ascribed. Thus, the most we can have are interesting hypotheses.

Naturalistic Observation Studies

These are frequently referred to as field studies. Here humans are observed in their natural habitats. The major problems are what and how to observe. Choice of observational units may entail theory that has not been made explicit. How to measure will involve sampling of behaviours, and decisions over whether to measure frequency, rate, magnitude, duration or latency (i.e. period before onset) of behaviour will also have to be made. The biggest drawback to this form of research is that you are at the mercy of events. If the event of interest does happen then other things may be happening at the same time, either seen or not seen by the researcher. If this is the case, then again we have major problems of ascribing causality. To the extent that these methods cannot ascribe causality, then this type of research is merely illustrative, descriptive, interesting or suggestive.

Correlational Studies

These types of study look for relationships between two or more factors or variables, at least one of which is not controlled by the researcher. The correlational approach has been a valuable tool in the history of psychology, especially in the fields of personality, social and intellectual development. It is mainly used when manipulation is impossible or impractical. Multiple regression or factor analysis, in which many variables are inter-correlated, have frequently been employed with this type of method to determine the presence or importance of relevant clusters of common factors or correlations.

The problem with correlational studies is that correlation does not mean causation. All that a correlation study can show is one of two things: if there is no correlation then there can be no causal relationship between or among the variables being investigated; if, however, there is a statistically significant correlation between or among variables, causation cannot be deduced. This is because of the possibility of a mediating, but undetected, truly causal variable being present. Thus, a significant correlation can only be suggestive of causality, never definitively so.

Quasi Experimental Designs

Here we can directly manipulate the independent variable but we cannot randomly allocate subjects to experimental conditions. Because such designs are always dealing with intact groups (i.e. pre-existing different groups of people) within specific experimental conditions, causality is always problematical because other factors could be acting as confounds between these intact groups, falsely 'suggesting' that the independent variable is having an effect.

Questionnaire Research

This is a popular methodology of social psychologists. It can produce a huge amount of data on a wide range of issues in a short space of time. However, it has several difficulties and disadvantages. The questions asked have to be very carefully composed, the responses have to be considered in terms of the level of measurement that they will yield, and not everyone returns their questionnaire. This immediately causes problems of sampling and the possible distorted results that may eventuate from a self-selected sample. There is no check possible that the respondent filled out the questionnaire in the way it was hoped they would—or even that they, rather than someone else, filled it out. As such, this methodology is suggestive but never definitive.

Qualitative Research

This approach is used by social psychologists and by developmentalists who explain behaviour by underlying changes in structures and mechanisms that are related to age. The data sought are qualitative rather than quantitative, and are concerned with the feelings, concepts and imagery that people have about the issue under investigation. This type of research is being strengthened by the development of discourse analysis, and other quasi-quantifiable techniques such as Q sort, which gets people to sort a large number of statements into a rank order and then proceeds to interpret the groupings or cluster of *respondents* giving similar rank orderings. Thus, Q sort scales people, not items, and this analysis is aided by computerised statistical programs.

Statistical Methods

All the above research methodologies try to exercise some sort of experimental control over the responses of interest. It is, however, also possible to exercise statistical control. The major statistical technique is multiple regression. This technique is employed by those who accept that all behaviour is multi-determined and complex. Multiple regression assumes independent variables are correlated but that it is possible to separate out the individual and joint contribution of any factor to any dependent variable of interest. Thus, the contribution of age, sex, birth position, economic status, amount of television watched, previous offending, racial type, and so on, could all be looked at together in multiple regression analysis and the individual *and* collective contribution of each of these variables to, for example, delinquent behaviour could be assessed. There are other equally powerful statistical techniques that psychologists are increasingly employing as an alternative to tight experimental control over variables, especially where such control is difficult or unethical.

These then are the many and varied techniques that psychologists have at their disposal. The technique chosen will always be that which gives greatest control over variance (variability within subjects and between experimental conditions) and sources of error. Thus the methodology eventually chosen for use will be that which maximises induced variance, minimises error variance and controls extraneous variance, as far as the situation allows.

Having said this, however, a sensible approach that should be adopted by any psychologist who knows that his or her findings are going to be applied, or may be applied at some future date, is to validate initial findings by convergent operations. That is, attempt to obtain the same findings despite using several different methodologies, tasks and experimental populations. In addition, while it is true that the research method is a question of logic and not of location, ecological validity dictates that different situations of mundane realism be sampled also. Replication is the backbone of science and unless and until replications, replications with refinements, and conceptual replications have been undertaken no psychologists worth their salt would allow their results to go forward as solid and thus pertinent to practical issues.

VALUES IN PSYCHOLOGY

I began by arguing that psychologists comprise a wide range of specialisms. It was not always so. As psychology evolved from the 1890s onwards and established itself as an empirical science being based on systematic observation rather than reason alone, it developed and separated into a small number of loosely coherent schools best characterised by busy confusions with occasional transient clear directions. Such schools declined after the 1940s and this way of looking at psychology is no longer profitable. Their influence lives on but the organisation of psychology is now along different lines, and may best be conceived of in terms of perspectives, fields of interest or domains of operations or specialisms. That is, different groups believe that their particular approach offers the best value in understanding human beings.

It is with different perspectives, fields of interest or specialisms, rather than adherents to grand schools of psychology that lawyers will most likely interact. It is important to appreciate, however, that these different perspectives are not mutually exclusive and may represent merely a different focus on different aspects of the same complex phenomenon.

Many psychologists classify themselves as biological psychologists, psycho-physiologists, psychobiologists or neuropsychologists. Their basic assumption is that all psychological events correspond to some activity in the brain. The main concern is to explain psychological phenomena by means of brain sites or tissues, neurotransmitters, or hormonal activity stimulated by brain activity. Thus they will be interested, for example, in how hormones influence mood and behaviour, what areas of the brain control speech or reasoning and how brain damage or injury can cause the loss of these faculties, or how drugs can influence rational behaviour. Their major methods will be experimental, allied to invasive and increasingly non-invasive brain techniques.

Behavioural psychologists will not invoke neurophysiological structures in the brain to account for behaviour; nor will they seek to recruit mentalistic concepts. They will be concerned to explain functional relations between stimulus and response by making recourse to rewards and punishment, and their scheduling (their consistent or inconsistent application). Their major methods will be experimental and learning paradigms. Behavioural psychologists could be relevant to legal concerns by explaining the causes of crime and the roots of particular behaviours, to the concept of *mens rea* and to issues of punishment and rehabilitation programmes.

Cognitive psychologists are concerned with the higher mental processes of perception, memory, thinking and decision making. Thus, they will explain overt behaviour by recourse to cognitive mechanisms and processes. A key explanatory framework will involve information processing whereby incoming information is processed in a variety of ways—it is selected, transformed, translated, compared and contrasted with information and every-day world knowledge already in memory. Their methods will be almost exclusively experimental. These psychologists have already had a great deal of contact with the criminal justice system in the fields of witnessing, confessions and jury decision making.

A psychoanalytically orientated psychologist will have imbibed the views of the psychoanalytic school of Freud and his followers and will argue that much of our behaviour stems from unconscious processes. Unconscious motives rather than rational reasons are sought for all behaviours under this perspective. Their methods will involve case histories and talking-through. This involves allowing patients/clients to talk freely about their lives in order to facilitate the bringing to the surface of deep-seated blocks, and bound and free-floating anxieties. The analysis of dreams could also play a part in uncovering hidden motives for behaviour. These psychologists will be concerned with dangerousness, aggressive behaviour, the way trauma can have deep and lasting effects, and all cases involving mental or behavioural abnormality. All these behaviours, however, can also be explained outwith the psychoanalytic domain. Psychoanalytic psychologists are found within the developmental, clinical and educational specialisms to be discussed below.

Developmentalists concern themselves mainly with the evolutionary 'staged' aspects of development from birth to old age. They will be interested in such things as separation, attachment and bonding issues, and cognitive abilities that impact on, for example, competency to testify. All these issues are central concerns of the law in so far as it relates to children. Their methods will be eclectic and involve observation, survey, experimental and case history.

Personality psychologists are concerned with the uniqueness of persons, whether as a member of an identifiable type or group or as an individual. They continuously debate whether the nomothetic approach—which tries to establish the major dimensions of personality on which people may differ but which are present to some degree in everyone—or the idiographic approach—which seeks to establish the uniqueness of an individual's personality—is the better way fully to understand personality. That is, whether we should treat everyone as unique, thus ruling out the possibility of predicting their behaviour, but gaining a richer insight into their unique traits, or view each person as a constellation of known traits and thus somewhat predictable in known situations. Their methods will involve personality questionnaires, repertory grids, observation and correlational studies.

Clinical and counselling psychologists share the same focus but are differently trained. Clinical psychologists are not medically trained (as psychiatrists are), but they do deal with abnormal and psychiatric behaviour of all types. Counselling psychologists, while often concerned with abnormal behaviour, tend to be concerned with less severe forms of abnormality. However, because both are engaged in the application of psychological principles at the point of breakdown, and with the diagnosis and treatment of emotional and behavioural problems, they will be concerned with mental illness, drug addiction, marital and family conflicts and, especially counselling psychologists, less serious adjustment problems. As mentioned above, clinical psychologists may have a psychoanalytic orientation but, especially in the UK, the behaviouristic, cognitive and personality approach is also widely present.

Educational psychologists usually deal with individual children who have emotional or learning problems and thus could have an important role to play in several areas of the law as it relates to children. Their methods will involve psychometric testing, observation and case histories.

From the above it is likely that when a lawyer comes to the discipline of psychology he or she may be excused for exclaiming 'what discipline?'. So what is it that binds these disparate activities together? What principle brings about coherence? The answer is that, whatever the nature of activity being investigated, there is always a level of analysis beyond the 'what' level. This deeper level asks the question 'how' and 'why'. These questions are the focus of all professionals who called themselves psychologists, and it is the nature of the answers to these questions which cause the 'bewildering confederacy' of psychology to cohere, despite their very different methods of enquiry concerning the addressing of these questions.

This broad-stroke insight into what psychology is and is not should help you appreciate and understand what is to follow in subsequent chapters of this volume. The assumptions and working methods of a wide variety of psychologists have been outlined and the core relevance of psychology to law as a discipline, and as a body of professionals, has at least been hinted at.

REFERENCES

Banaji, M.R.. and Crowder, R.G. (1989). The bancruptcy of everyday memory. *American Psychologist*, **44**, 1185–93.
Bentley, D. (1979). The infant and the dream: psychology and the law. In

D.P. Farrington, K. Hawkins and S. Lloyd-Bostock (Eds), *Psychology, Law and Legal Processes*. London: Macmillan.

Berkowitz, L. and Donnerstein, E. (1982). External validity is more than skin deep. *American Psychologist*, **37**, 245–57.

Clifford, B.R. (1978). A critique of eyewitness research. In M.M. Gruneberg, P.E. Morris and R.N. Sykes (Eds), *Practical Aspects of Memory*. London: Academic Press.

Clifford, B.R. (1981). Towards a more realistic appraisal of the psychology of testimony. In S. Lloyd-Bostock (Ed.), *Psychology in Legal Context: Applications and Limitations*. London: Macmillan.

Cohen, J. (1977). *Statistical Power Analysis for Behavioural Sciences*. Hillsdale, NJ: Lawrence Erlbaum.

Cohen, J. and Cohen, P. (1975). *Applied Multiple Regression/Correlation Analysis for the Behavioural Sciences*. Hillsdale, NJ: Lawrence Erlbaum.

Crowder, R.G. (1993). Commentry: faith and skepticism in memory research. In G.M. Davies and R.H. Logie (Eds), *Memory in Everyday Life*. Amsterdam: Elsevier Science Publishers.

Elmes, D.G., Kantowitz, B.H. and Roediger III, H.L. (1992). *Research Methods in Psychology* (4th edn). St Pauls: West Publishing.

Haward, L.R.C. (1979). The psychologist as expert witness. In D.P. Farrington, K. Hawkins, and S. Lloyd-Bostock (Eds), *Psychology, Law and Legal Processes*. London: Macmillan.

Meehl, P.E. (1977). Law and the fireside inductions: some reflections of a clinical psychologist. In J.L. Tapp and F.J. Levine (Eds), *Law, Justice and the Individual in Society*. New York: Holt Rinehart & Winston.

Rabbitt, P. (1981). Applying human experimental psychology to legal questions about evidence. In S. Lloyd-Bostock (Ed.), *Psychology in Legal Contexts: Applications and Limitations*. London: Macmillan.

Tapp, J.L. (1969). Psychology and the law: the dilemma. *Psychology Today*, **11**, 16–22.

Tapp, J.L. and Levine, F.J. (1977). *Law, Justice and the Individual in Society*. New York: Holt, Rinehart & Winston.

Chapter 1.3

Law's Premises, Methods and Values

David Carson
University of Southampton

It cannot, meaningfully, be claimed that the study of law has a longer history than the study of behaviour. However, the formalised study of law, in universities and similar institutions, certainly has a much longer history than the study of psychology. Closely associated with this is the differential role, significance and appeal of tradition, plus the differential distribution of status, between the two disciplines and professions. Generally speaking, the law, its study and practice, is perceived as a more socially prestigious activity. Even in the allegedly more egalitarian USA, law professors are paid on higher scales than their other non-medical colleagues. It is proclaimed to be a success or advance when some psychologists are appointed to law departments (Melton, Monahan and Saks, 1987; Lösel, 1992). Why should we not seek the appointment of lawyers in psychology departments? Indeed, particularly in some continental European countries, the prestige and perceived power of lawyers, practising and academic, is considered to be an obstacle to the development of work in law and psychology. (Unfortunately neither of these 'problems', higher pay and social esteem, are experienced by academic lawyers in the UK!)

Tradition is important to lawyers. It is observable not just in the continued use of outdated courtroom clothes and modes of address. Such clothes and terminology would, surely, lead to rich laughter were not lawyers, aided and abetted by media representations, so successful in maintaining a hegemony of ideas and assumptions held by members of the public (Bankowski and Mungham, 1976). These particular customs may be most dramatic in the UK but they exist in most jurisdictions. Superficially such traditions might appear relatively unimportant, indeed endearing. However, the uncritical manner in which they are justified is significant. For example, it is often asserted that a formal and dignified atmosphere in a courtroom, with witnesses in awe of the setting and *dramatis personae*, is an aid to truth-telling by witnesses. The

Handbook of Psychology in Legal Contexts
Edited by R. Bull and D. Carson. © 1995 John Wiley & Sons Ltd

failure to consider it necessary to question or to test such propositions is very significant. But much more significant are lawyers' traditional and 'working' modes of thought. Here, it is submitted, is the source of many of the past, present and future problems for co-operation and collaboration between lawyers and psychologists. This chapter will try to draw out a number of the values, premises and working methods of lawyers that could cause problems for the inter-disciplinary development of law and psychology.

LAWYERS' SEARCH FOR JUSTICE

The long tradition of scholarship in law has, naturally, led to a substantial body of legal philosophy wherein some basic questions about the nature, purpose and role of law have been posed. The breadth, and depth, of this work, and its reflection in legal education which helps to socialise future generations of lawyers, begins to explain lawyers' relative lack of interest in behavioural science topics. The detailed content of the different theories and positions, regarding the nature of law and justice, can be discovered from most student texts. Here the purpose is to highlight features of lawyers' reasoning. A common theme is the essence of law and justice.

For many people there are certain 'truths', revealed in different ways. For example, different countries' constitutions declare certain propositions to be beyond challenge, inalienable. The Constitution of the USA declares certain truths to be self-evident. Certain propositions, for example that a constitution is a manifestation of the will of the people, defy empirical verification. Doubtless such a test was never envisaged. The appeal of the declaration is to senses other than reason. Arguably similar are the declarations of basic rights, such as the European Convention on Human Rights. They gain 'legal' authority, so as to become enforceable, if and when they are adopted by a legislature. But they also have an appeal and authority arising from their reference to apparently universal principles, applicable at all times and in all countries. Not surprisingly many lawyers are keen to encourage the articulation of such statements. Sometimes the 'intellectual power' or authority of the document arises from 'reason'; it is asserted to be self-evident, for example, that continued use of the world's natural resources, on current scales, is unsustainable. At other times their power arises from sympathy with the implicit values or philosophy, which may be religious in character.

If there are 'basic truths' then, the argument runs, they cannot be overridden by any other laws. Many lawyers share the widespread belief that there are certain 'natural' or fundamental laws. Even the young Karl Marx, for instance, argued that:

> Laws are not rules that repress freedom any more than the law of gravity is a law that represses movement ... laws are rather positive lights, general norms,

in which freedom has obtained an impersonal, theoretical existence that is independent of any arbitrary individual. Its law book is a people's bible of freedom. (McLellan, 1976)

If laws have essential characteristics, then individual rules and laws can be judged against them. If these features can be discovered then appeal or constitutional courts may use them to invalidate offending 'laws' and prevent governments from exceeding their proper jurisdiction.

Others insist that the defining characteristics of a law is the process by which it was enacted. If it followed the pre-stated procedure then, irrespective of its contents, it is a valid law. It involves adopting a positivistic theory of knowledge similar to that called in aid by empiricists. The only laws that exist are those that have been stated by a legislature or which arise from another accepted source such as, in a common law system, judges' decisions. It facilitates the drawing of a distinction between law and politics, between the study or application of rules and the approval or disapproval of their contents. Just as some scientists argue when working in areas which have military applications that they do not involve approval of militaristic values, so working on or applying any law is not perceived by these lawyers to be a political activity. Being a lawyer is associated with being a technician, a value-free activity. Law reform, perhaps more so in the UK than the USA, is perceived by these lawyers as being an 'after-hours' activity.

Law as a Value-free Activity

This law versus politics dichotomy is an important point for the future of law and psychology. A psychologist, for example, would regard the adoption of a new, improved, procedure or test, say for assessing a feature of a client, as a natural and necessary part of the job. For psychologists, as others, challenging and improving the content of and way in which the job is performed is an integral part of the task. However, the practising lawyer must keep using the law for so long as it is the law and whatever his or her opinion of it may be. There may be a consensus that the law is inappropriate, outdated or bad, but the lawyer, as technician, must keep using it, working to it. Of course if the lawyer has a new tactic for questioning witnesses, drafting contracts, avoiding or minimising a client's tax liability, then he or she must be expected to use it. But the law, itself, is seen and treated as a 'given'. Psychology is not given in any similar sense, however well established certain propositions may be.

Lawyers, for example, might agree that the examination of child witnesses in open court can traumatise them, is inefficient in generating information about and provides a poor guide as to their credibility (Spencer and Flin, 1993; Graffam Walker, 1994). But they have to operate within that system, until it is changed. If they are representing an alleged child abuser then they must be expected to take advantage of the opportunities that the system offers for undermining the accusing child's credibility. They will utilise their belief in the law as a neutral 'technology', will argue that they are only doing their job which, in the context of the system, is non-political. If it is in their client's interests to have separate trials, then they must be expected; indeed, in the terms of the system they are operating, they should be praised when they achieve this, even if it means that one jury fails to get a full picture of the case against the defendant.

Note the extent to which law involves a culture of criticism. Trials, civil or criminal, usually only involve two sides and two sets of lawyers. A base-rate probability of 50 per cent failure in trials has to be managed by the lawyers themselves and rationalised to their clients. Appeals against judges' decisions are not rare events but rather are structured into the legal system. Is there any other occupation which so regularly and systematically encourages criticism via appeals? Whilst an appeal court's criticisms may be couched in polite and circumspect language it is performed in public and involves disagreeing with at least one judge or a trial lawyer. Thus lawyers may reasonably feel, and argue, that the legal system is open and accountable in a way that few other occupations are. The argument is not that they become blasé about criticism but that further criticism may be considered inappropriate or misguided.

Challenging other lawyers, fighting with words and arguments, is part of the art and the skills of being a lawyer (Evans, 1983). Further, not taking those challenges and criticisms to heart, not letting what is said in court affect personal feelings and relationships is also a prized quality. It is professional for lawyers to challenge each other vigorously and then, just as if a switch had been pressed, once the trial is decided or adjourned, to be open and friendly to professional colleagues. To prevent this antagonism, challenge and criticism from undermining self-esteem and self-justification, lawyers need to be able to rationalise their work. Such beliefs as the duty upon lawyers (indeed the requirement of justice), to do their very best for their client, even if they believe their client to be guilty of a heinous crime (but do not actually know him or her to be guilty) need to be firmly believed in if the defence lawyer is not to feel guilty for being successful in a criminal defence.

Thus, it is submitted, lawyers should be expected to be, at the very least, wary or biased against reform proposals which threaten to undermine their self-justifications. Lawyers, like everyone else, need to be able to rationalise or justify their behaviour. It should not be surprising that they are antagonistic to other disciplines which criticise them even when they are operating existing law. Such criticisms are liable to be considered misconceived or misinformed. A great deal is at stake for lawyers. For example, an inter-disciplinary committee drew attention to 'the wide-ranging challenge to traditional notions of evidence posed by the advance in psychology' but, nevertheless, went on to make recommendations which it felt would not be too extreme for practising lawyers (Oddie, 1991).

Related to this, it is submitted, is the tendency for lawyers not to be satisfied by criticism of a law, practice or procedure. Criticism of an existing provision is insufficient; they like to see alternatives posed and assessed. So it is not enough to criticise current law and practice, say on the questioning of child witnesses. An alternative must be suggested so that it can be compared to see if it is preferable. Of course a lot of value judgements are involved in determining what constitutes 'better' and these issues are frequently left unstated. Lawyers' 'research' papers, on law reform topics, often involve the outline of an alternative system with a suggestion that it would be preferable. Editors and referees of law journals rarely require that the value judgement issues are made explicit or that criticisms or assertions are empirically verified.

Lawyers, particularly in the UK, are able to promote law reform with remarkable ease. The Law Commission for England and Wales is chaired by a senior judge, and has practising and academic lawyers as members. There appears to be no perceived need for, or value in having, a commissioner with a background in the behavioural sciences or skilled in assessing research methodology. Papers, authored jointly by a psychologist and a lawyer and conforming to the methods and expectations of both audiences, might be more successful in impressing lawyers and politicians into making changes.

Law in Practice

One rebellion against the positivistic emphasis upon the 'law in books' is the realist tradition. Does it matter what the law in the books is, if it is not applied in practice? The 'real' law, realists would argue, concerns what judges and other law enforcement agencies actually do. Note that, in this approach, the contribution of other legal decision-makers is recognised. If the police operate a 10 per cent margin on speeding offences then the maximum on this road is not 50 but 55 miles per hour. Law students should be taught not what the books say ought to happen but what the research and experience indicates actually happens. Fear of having your name printed in a newspaper may be a more effective disincentive to the commission of crime than standard punishments. The judge's mood may be a more reliable and significant factor in predicting his or her decisions than the precedent decisions. Legal skills concern the ability to predict the decisions of judges and others.

The realist emphasis on prediction supports an interest in the social and behavioural sciences as they aid the description and analysis of law officials' behaviour. This, it may be argued, has been a major influence upon the development of law and psychology in North America (Monahan and Walker, 1994). It may also in part explain the relative lack of development of law and psychology in the UK as the realist approach has much stronger associations with the USA than the UK. It may also involve a reflection of the different arrangements for legal education. In the UK most new lawyers take a three-year law degree as soon as they have left school, followed by professional training. Thus they can become practising lawyers without having studied any social or behavioural sciences other than that studied at school up to the age of 18. In the USA law is a postgraduate subject so that law students will already have studied other subjects at university as part of their Bachelor's degree. These will often include psychology.

While law schools are still dominated by 'black letter' lawyers, whose primary interest is in the collation, analysis and restatement of verbally formulated rules, virtually all will have some staff interested in socio-legal studies. Indeed the character of a law school can, substantially, be determined by the proportion swearing allegiance to a socio-legal approach to research and/or teaching. Many lawyers would characterise socio-legal studies as including an interest in the psychological implications of law (e.g. Lloyd-Bostock, 1981). It would be seen as a sub-set of the wider concept which would include politics (e.g. Podmore, 1977), history, anthropology (e.g. Snyder, 1981), economics (e.g. Veljanovski, 1980), indeed linguistics (e.g. Goodrich, 1984), geography (e.g. Economides, Blacksell and Watkins, 1986) and psychiatry (e.g. Fennell, 1986) as well as the sociology of law (e.g. Cotterrell, 1986). However, the vast majority of those lawyers interested in socio-legal studies, at least in the UK, are interested in the sociological and political rather than the psychological implications of law. The interest is in social theories and explanations rather than individualistic.

The interpretativist epistemologies implicit in realist and socio-legal approaches to law is important. The law is not perceived as politically neutral or independent of observation and choice. All actors, including judges, are making choices although they may be circumscribed. Interpreting and applying the law is neither a mechanical nor a neutral activity. Factual situations are ambiguous and have to be constructed and interpreted.

Note, however, that law schools and legal education remains dominated by cognitive studies of information. Research findings, say on eye-witness testimony, may find their way into 'liberal' texts on evidence. But, despite the realist and socio-legal movements, the emphasis remains upon rule, rather than fact, finding. The bulk of a practising lawyer's time and effort will be spent in determining the facts rather than the law; but this is still not reflected in legal education or law books (for an exception, see Anderson and Twining, 1991). Emphasis upon practical skills, other than appeal court argument, is a relatively novel development in legal education, especially in the UK (Macfarlane, 1992). Why are lawyers not being taught how to interview witnesses and clients in a manner which will produce plenty of reliable information for them? In straightforward terms of gaining instrumental skills lawyers could learn much from psychologists, even if the limits of current knowledge, and need for further research, kept being emphasised.

The socio-legal movement is related to interests in criminology and concern over criminal justice issues. In this context it is also noteworthy that psychologists have been prominent in the current reaction against the 'nothing works' school of thought about crime and recidivism (e.g. Blackburn, 1993). This, particularly given lawyers' interest in being able to recommend positive alternatives to custodial sentences, for individual clients, should provide another means whereby psychologists' contributions are demonstrated to be of instrumental value to lawyers (Berry, 1993).

Then, flowing from but involving a recognition of the perceived inadequacies of the realist and socio-legal approaches (Kelman, 1987), recent decades have demonstrated a growing interest in critical legal studies which:

> draws heavily on the radical political culture of the period since the 1960s. It asserts the inescapability of commitment and rejects the aspiration of the preceding intellectual climate's search for value neutrality. ... Critical legal studies seeks to provide an environment in which radical and committed scholarship can thrive in diversity with no aspiration to lay down a 'correct' theory or method. (Fitzpatrick and Hunt, 1987, p. 1)

This is a full-frontal assault upon the belief that law and politics, and all other normative systems, are separate entities which can and should be kept separate. Obviously it causes problems for many more-traditional lawyers. It also involves a fundamental attack on the perceived hierarchical and indoctrinating nature of legal education (e.g. Kennedy, 1982). Critical approaches to legal education would encourage students to observe the ideological nature of law and how it is just one system of ought statements among many others, although it has achieved much greater power substantially by obfuscating the nature of the interests being protected.

Because it stresses the absence of value neutrality and the necessarily political nature of the manner in which social and other problems that may be the subject of research are perceived, there would appear to be little opportunity for collaboration between psychologists and lawyers if a critical law framework was involved. Critical legal theory can be very negative and nihilistic; there is no such thing as 'truth' so why search for it? But, it is submitted, this is not necessarily the case. Critical theory professes to be very democratic, seeking to involve people in real decision-making, and it requires that the value assumptions, in so far as people are aware of them, are explicit, are 'up front' (see Kairys, 1982). Are these not values and objectives with which many others can identify? Working with, say, a prisoner or patient, many of the value assumptions could be made explicit and the client involved more in the choices available, recognising of course both that the service provider may not be able to allow certain choices, for example releasing a prisoner, and that many choices, and the ability to choose, will be artificial or false in that there is rarely full and complete freedom of choice. Through its denial of 'objective truths' critical law theory could also prove valuable in reminding both psychologists and lawyers that research is immanent, is always developing. In these senses critical legal theory can prove a valuable corrective although it must be recognised that most, if not all, critical law scholars would condemn this attempt to abstract a few key ideas into the beginnings of a method.

REASONABLE REASONING

This, necessarily selective and all too superficial, review of the range of ideas or schools of thought within jurisprudence or legal philosophy should have indicated the breadth and diversity of views and approaches that exist. It would be very misguided to think of lawyers as being less diverse in their assumptions and methods than are other disciplines. The discussion also, hopefully, indicated a number of ways in which particular positions, within this diversity, could facilitate or hinder developments with psychology. To this should be added a brief description of some characteristics of lawyers' practical reasoning. Aubert (1963), for example, has outlined a number of characteristics which has led others (Campbell, 1974) to argue that effective collaboration is unlikely. However, it will be argued, these characteristics arise out of the courtroom focus of some lawyers which is, substantially, just a stereotypical image of lawyers' work.

Lawyers, for example, tend to dichotomise. Both concepts and facts (to indulge in a dichotomy) are pressed into categories, particularly alternatives. It is one thing, although dangerous in many senses, for people to be pressed into categories such as 'mentally disordered' or not, criminal damage or not, but it extends right through to reasonable or unreasonable behaviour. Lawyers, and the law, have great difficulty with relative concepts. However, this mirrors the reasoning of many other groups of people and is perfectly understandable given the legal task of fitting facts into legal categories. Lawyers, it is argued, focus on past events, while 'proper' scientists are trying to make accurate predictions about the future. This is true in that lawyers have to find, from past events, facts which will permit a particular conclusion to their case. They have to do this for legal ends. But it is not, really, different from other disciplines. Psychologists also examine the past, for example a client's past history of violence, in order to make decisions for the future.

Lawyers concentrate upon the particular case, their client's, while others, for example psychologists researching the dangerousness of mentally disordered offenders, are trying to make generalised comments. Again the argument is not really valid. Yes, a lawyer has to try and get a particular outcome for a particular client. Similarly a psychologist will search the literature on the topic or about similar cases in order to help a particular client. The distinctions that ought to be being made are between lawyers generally and those in practice, who must work with the system, just as a distinction would be drawn between the research psychologist's motivation to make general comments about, for example, the recoverability of forgotten memories and the practitioner psychologist who is concerned with helping an individual client.

Working in courts is only one of many actual, and potential, roles for lawyers. When they appear in court they must, naturally enough, manipulate (which need not be interpreted as a critical term) the system. When operating in that mode such characteristic forms of reasoning must be expected. But it does not follow that such reasoning is utilised in other contexts. Lawyers, not just critical theory lawyers, can recognise the relativity of many concepts. The important variable is the closeness of the individual lawyer to practical applications of the law.

Other characteristics of lawyers' reasoning may be more important in practice. For example, there is the emphasis upon persuasion rather than deductive or inductive logic (Hart, 1963). The oral tradition of the law has been significant. That a proposition sounds reasonable, with or without the suggestive power of being labelled 'reasonable', is regularly accepted as a justification for a decision. It does not, for example, sound reasonable to most lawyers that the Blue Taxi Company should pay compensation to the victim of an accident just because the victim is certain that it was a taxi, but cannot recall whether it was blue or green, and the Blue Taxi Company owns 80 per cent of the taxis in that remote town to the Green Taxi Firm's 20 per cent. However, add one more piece of particularistic evidence, suggestive that it was a blue taxi, and now most lawyers will find the conclusion reasonable, on the available evidence.

The tendency of lawyers to reify goes beyond the use of colourful language. Many lawyers treat concepts as if they actually exist. For example the 'rule of law' is a neat phrase for articulating a system whereby pre-stated rules determine officials', including judges', behaviour. It is seen as preferable to a system where, for example, there is dependence upon the goodwill and discretion of someone to make decisions which need not follow any rule or other pattern. But it is just an idea, a preference. However, as with other examples, many lawyers can be heard treating the expression as if it actually referred to something concrete. 'Justice' is an ideal or aspiration and yet we are used to hearing and seeing it referred to as a distinct entity, indeed sometimes as having a corporeal form and gender. This kind of reification is dangerous because it closes off debate about the concept. What is the essence of justice? Why should it be blind? Does it include a requirement of equal opportunity, the equal distribution of or access to resources, or does it only refer to procedural requirements? The meaning of such concepts and ideas is not beyond debate but their articulation in a reified manner puts them beyond debate. This may be done deliberately or otherwise.

And lawyers seem to use 'time' in a distinctive manner. Progress appears to be treated as if it was simply linear. Of course it is, in the sense that days, weeks and months pass. But other disciplines, and practitioners with clients, are more likely to emphasise the significance rather than the mere passage of time. The expression 'day in court' is very significant to lawyers. Cases, witnesses, clients are prepared for the 'day in court' even though the vast majority of civil cases are settled before any trial and the vast majority of prosecutions lead to admission of guilt so that a full trial is unnecessary. The day in court becomes a focal point, not just for planning purposes. The expectation is that the court will be able to deal with all the conflicting issues and establish a clear sense of direction; problems and controversy in, solution out. But 'real' life is not entirely like that. In many jurisdictions judges have, effectively, had sentencing powers (a time component) taken away from them. They may pronounce a five-year sentence. Doubtless that has an immediate effect (not just upon the media) but many, particularly those with a previous criminal history, will quickly calculate, for example, earliest dates upon which early release might be sought. The release of prisoners and patients from conditions of detention depends, although there are usually formal maximum terms, largely upon the individual's preparedness and motivation, as well as the availability of resources for community supervision. The simple linear approach to time leaves out the significance of opportunities. The finding that children's conception of time is different from that of adults (Goldstein, Freud and Solnit, 1973) has generally been learnt. Trials are expedited, although arguably still not enough. But are courts in a position to seize, or ensure that others seize, the opportunities that flow into, and possibly out of, every child's life? The nature of a problem, particularly from a child's perspective, can change dramatically over a comparatively short period of time.

CONCLUSION

As many have remarked, it is strange that two disciplines and professions, with such common interests, have not collaborated more productively. This chapter has tried to suggest that some of the reasons lie in their different approaches and assumptions. Can co-operation be expected whenever there are major differences between lawyers, when there is no orthodoxy about the nature of law? Yes, it is submitted, if a number of things are always remembered. Among these are the observation that lawyers serve at least two goals, making the present system 'work' for their clients (even if those are just law students) and the much broader notion of fair and efficient law (or justice). Law, like psychology, is always developing, moving. This comment does not just refer to changes in the content of the law but ideas about law generally. Collaboration focused upon change, it is submitted, would prove an important way forward.

REFERENCES

Anderson, T. and Twining, W. (1991). *Analysis of Evidence: How to do Things with Facts.* London: Weidenfeld & Nicholson.

Aubert, V. (1963). The structure of legal thinking. In *Legal Essays: A Tribute to Fride Castberg on the occasion of his 70th birthday.* Boston: Universitetsforlaget.

Bankowski, Z. and Mungham, G. (1976). *Images of Law.* London: Routledge.

Berry, M. (Convenor) (1993). *Psychology and Antisocial Behaviour.* Leicester: British Psychological Society.

Blackburn, R. (1993). *The Psychology of Criminal Conduct.* Chichester: John Wiley.

Campbell, C. (1974). Legal thought and juristic values. *British Journal of Law and Society,* **1**, 1, 13–31.

Cotterrell, R. (1986). Law and sociology. *Journal of Law and Society,* **13**, 1, 9–34.

Economides, K., Blacksell, M. and Watkins, C. (1986). Law and geography. *Journal of Law and Society,* **13**, 2, 161–82.

Evans, K. (1983). *Advocacy at the Bar: A Beginner's Guide.* London: Financial Training Press.

Fennell, P. (1986). Law and psychiatry. *Journal of Law and Society,* **13**, 1, 35–65.

Fitzpatrick, P. and Hunt, A. (1987). Critical legal studies: an introduction. *Journal of Law and Society,* **14**, 1, 1–3.

Goldstein, J., Freud, A. and Solnit, A.J. (1973). *Beyond the Best Interests of the Child.* New York: Free Press.

Goodrich, P. (1984). Law and language. *Journal of Law and Society,* **11**, 2, 173–206.

Graffam Walker, A. (1994). *Handbook on Questioning Children: A Linguistic Perspective.* Washington, DC: ABA.

Hart, H.L.A. (1963). Introduction. In C. Perelman (Ed.), *The Idea of Justice and the Problem of Argument.* London: Routledge.

Kairys, D. (1982). Introduction. In D. Kairys (Ed.), *The Politics of Law: A Progressive Critique.* New York: Pantheon.

Kelman, M. (1987). *A Guide to Critical Legal Studies.* Cambridge, MA: Harvard University Press.

Kennedy, D. (1982). Legal education as training for hierarchy. In D. Kairys (Ed.), *The Politics of Law: A Progressive Critique.* New York: Pantheon.

Lloyd-Bostock, S. (1981). Psychology and the law. *British Journal of Law and Society,* **8**, 1, 1–28.

Lösel, F. (1992). Psychology and law: overtures, crescendos, and reprises. In F. Lösel, D. Bender and T. Bliesener (Eds), *Psychology and Law: International Perspectives.* Berlin: Walter de Gruyter.

Macfarlane, J. (1992). Look before you leap: knowledge and learning in legal skills education. *Journal of Law and Society,* **19**, 3, 293–319.

McLellan, D. (1976). *Karl Marx: His Life and Thought.* St Albans, UK: Paladin.

Melton, G.B., Monahan, J. and Saks, M.J. (1987). Psychologists as law professors. *American Psychologist,* 502–9.

Monahan, J. and Walker, L. (1994). *Social Sciences and the Law: Cases and Materials.* Westbury, NY: Foundation Press.

Oddie, C. (Chair) (1991). *Science and the Administration of Justice.* London: Justice.

Podmore, D. (1977). Lawyers and politics. *British Journal of Law and Society,* **4**, 2, 155–85.

Snyder, F.G. (1981). Anthropology, dispute processes and law. *British Journal of Law and Society,* **8**, 2, 141–80.

Spencer, J.R. and Flin, R. (1993). *The Evidence of Children: The Law and the Psychology* (2nd edn). London: Blackstone.

Veljanovski, C.G. (1980). The economic approach to law. *British Journal of Law and Society*, **7**, 2, 158–93.

Part 2

Individualism: Psychology's Support for Individuals

Individualism: Its Importance in Law and Psychology

David Carson
University of Southampton

A shared feature of the law, and of psychology, is a focus upon the individual, yet the social influences upon our behaviour are extensive. We experience life in and through groups and social institutions. Social interactions permeate every facet of our lives, from talking to uncomprehending, yet appreciative, babies to complex rituals at burials. This observation is uncontroversial, trite even. And yet both psychology and law focus primarily upon the individual.

INDIVIDUAL CLIENTS WITH SOCIAL PROBLEMS

Of course, there is a sub-discipline: social psychology. The behaviour of groups, such as juries, is a subject of important research. Yet the focus of psychologists' work, reflected again in this handbook, is largely upon individuals. That is not to deny that social factors are often adopted in analyses of individuals' behaviour or that the medium of providing practical help is not often groups. This is just to query the aptness of the balance.

The law recognises non-human entities, such as partnerships and companies, yet the focus remains on the individual. The language of individualism is significant. We speak of corporate bodies having a 'legal personality', of company directors being the head or brains of the organisation. That a company cannot be imprisoned because it does not have a body, although it can be fined (Law Commission, 1994), reinforces the significance of the human analogy. The concern is for 'human rights', for the 'rights of the individual'. Of course there are exceptions. Ireland's constitution, for example, gives the family a special status although that might, in practice, just empower the parents. And there are calls for the rights of native people, such as aborigines. Again, the point is about the focus rather than an explicit categorical distinction.

Handbook of Psychology in Legal Contexts
Edited by R. Bull and D. Carson. © 1995 John Wiley & Sons Ltd

Is the point significant? Should it be surprising that the two disciplines focus upon individualism when their clients are individuals? (Lawyers' corporate clients are instructed by individuals.) Yes, it is significant in the sense that the source of practitioners' clienteles ought to have no bearing upon the content and methodology of the discipline. If social class is a highly determining factor in, say, learning or committing crime, then should so much time and effort be put into individualistic interventions? No, it is not significant in the sense that individualism is highly prized, at least in Western societies. Law and the practice of psychology may be seen as reinforcing a social value, and in turn being reinforced. Democracy involves each individual having an equal vote, on specified issues at specified times, even though the distribution of power and influence is, otherwise, very unequal.

Does it matter? Should we be concerned that the primary focus of psychology and law is on the individual rather than upon the group? Yes, in that inappropriate analyses and strategies may be being developed. The reason why women are under-represented in the better-paid echelons of many workforces may be a large number of individual acts of sexual discrimination. However, structural and social explanation are likely to have more explanatory power. But even if such an individualistic analysis were appropriate, is it efficient for the law to adopt such a strategy, a large number of individual court actions? Procedures allowing people with similar legal complaints, such as the effects of a drug or a particular disaster, to come together in one test case rather than a lot of separate actions, may have been and may yet be further improved. But should not the problem be recognised as 'social', as structural, to do with social institutions, perceptions, values, practices? Consider when a large number of the customers of a company or utility default in their debts. Each individual may have a different explanation for defaulting. Individualism promises them their 'day in court' even though the actual process may more closely resemble a conveyor-belt in a factory (see, generally, Cotterrell, 1984, and sources cited therein). Perhaps 'the system' ought to be inquiring why there are so many defaults, inquiring into possible structural problems. It needs to be remembered that legal systems would collapse if all those individuals legally eligible to bring legal actions took up the opportunity.

Individualism carries with it many powerful political values. But it can also diminish individuals' power. Each person injured when tripping upon a city authority's pavements (sidewalks) may have a legal claim. But they might be more effective in getting things changed if they acted as a group, relied upon their numbers. Political power lies in the group. Individualisation diminishes that power (Morris, 1973). The point is more significant in relation to such allegations as discrimination. Individualism discourages systemic analyses.

How should psychologists operate within this 'individual versus social' debate when involved in a legal context? They are pressed into aiding individual cases whilst drawing upon 'social knowledge'. The forensic psychologist is asked to make a prediction about the dangerousness of an individual patient or prisoner. Actuarial data provide a major source, some would argue the only appropriate source of information (for example, see Faust and Ziskin, 1988, but also, to the contrary, Hoge and Grisso, 1992). The psychologist might wish to predict by referring to proportions of patients or prisoners sharing certain characteristics with the individual litigant. But the legal process specifies the individual. The task is to make information about, say, 80 per cent of similar people relevant to a particular individual when the psychologist must always admit that he or she cannot be sure that the client is not among the 20 per cent. The educational psychologist undertakes an individual assessment of a pupil. That may lead him or her to make suggestions about specific interventions to help the child. But the psychologist's control or influence over the physical or social resources available is limited.

LEGAL ACTION BY AND FOR GROUPS

It is not just that the law values individuality but that it has reflected antipathy, at least in England and Wales, to collective action. The act of people combining together to make demands for better working conditions was particularly feared (Pelling, 1963). Group behaviour, 'the mob', was considered particularly dangerous. It was perceived as less predictable than the patterns of individuals' acts. In the common law a conspiracy is both a crime and a civil wrong. It involves two or more legally responsible people agreeing to do something unlawful (which need not be 'illegal', which would involve a crime) or to do something lawful in an unlawful manner. (Married couples have been treated, rather romantically, as one person for these purposes.) Until relatively recently in England and Wales it was, and to a much more limited extent still is, a criminal conspiracy for two or more people to agree to do something which would not be a crime if it was committed by only one person (see, for example, Smith and Hogan, 1992). Agreement was sufficient; they did not have to carry out the agreed behaviour, although it could be difficult to prove the existence of an agreement without some joint action. The fact of two or more people acting together seemed to balance out the requirement that they had to agree to commit an existing crime. For example, an individual who 'corrupts public morality' could only be guilty if he or she committed a specific, pre-stated, offence. But if he or she agreed to do something which would corrupt public morality, with at least one other, then a crime has been committed at the time of agreement.

Lawyers must work with individuals rather than groups, it can be argued, because they would otherwise be engaging in politics. How are the rights and interests of people with dyslexia, for example, to be advanced? Individual cases can be brought before tribunals and courts. Selective test cases can be appealed to the highest courts to try and produce precedents that will influence the settlement of other individual cases (Chasty and Friel, 1991). (These are also the roles for which lawyers can be remunerated under schemes for helping those without adequate means to pay legal costs.) Going beyond those roles can be seen as 'political', as trying to change the law rather than to apply it.

But who is entitled to determine what the appropriate limits of lawyers' assistance are? Current definitions have more to do with traditional, and remunerated, methods of working than with any inherent limits. Lawyers working within services provided under the 'War on Poverty' in the United States in the 1960s were required to undertake community education and community action roles as well as providing the more traditional legal services for their clients (Society of Labour Lawyers, 1968). Teaching people about the law may prevent many more disputes than a few test-case precedents. It could also encourage more people to become clients of legal services and influence their attitudes towards the law and legal services. If people do not know that they have a legal problem they do not know that it can be resolved by relying upon the law. Community action may be the most effective, and efficient, way of helping groups of people (for example, those who are dyslexic).

PROTECTING INDIVIDUALS' BROADER INTERESTS

Lawyers should consider new ways of providing services which seek to protect their clients' 'social' rights and interests. Too often the law has to serve as a 'peg' for a lawyer's intervention. For example, lawyers clearly have a role when allegedly mentally disordered people are detained in a hospital. They also have a role concerning their discharge. But should that be the limit of their role? They could be involved in issues about consent to treatment but these are likely only to be exceptional cases in England and Wales (*In re C., (Adult: Refusal of Treatment)* [1994] 1 W.L.R. 290) because the relevant legislation (Mental Health Act 1983) does not, unlike with objections to detention, specify a hearing. They could develop roles, for example, to ensure that their clients are actively treated, that a sequence of appropriate risk decisions are taken with a view to the client's progressive independence. Such developments are taking place in the United States within the inter-disciplinary framework of therapeutic jurisprudence (see Wexler, 1993, and the many sources cited therein). Psychologists could help lawyers to develop such roles. It is interesting that whereas 'advocacy' has historically been associated with lawyers (also sometimes known as 'advocates'), the term has gained a much broader meaning, in long-term health and social care services in the UK, as referring to the articulation and promotion of the broad interests of patients and clients, and is not just associated with lawyers (for example, Sang and O'Brien, 1984). Lawyers might be able to reclaim the title if they did not pay such exclusive regard to the strictly legal interests of their individual clients.

Inter-disciplinary co-operation, involving a broader approach, is urgently required on assessments of risk and dangerousness. Psychologists and others can be asked to assist in assessing the dangerousness of a prisoner, the risk involved in discharging a mentally disordered patient or in returning a child to formerly abusive parents. Traditional approaches have concentrated upon analyses of the individuals involved (e.g. Floud and Warren, 1981) although situational factors, the circumstances in which the risk decision would take place, are increasingly being taken into account (e.g. Bedford, 1987). It is, now, being recognised that the focus must be broadened to include analysis of the decision-making process (Steadman et al., 1993a, b) and its management (Carson, 1990). Lawyers need, *inter alia*, to examine the risk decisions that are not taken as well as those that are taken, success rates as well as failures, the quality of the decision-making process, the quality of the data used to make assessments. They also need to look at the extent to which those who implement the risk decisions are helped to manage it and are supported, such as in a continuous learning cycle, by their managers. These are, eminently, areas for practical co-operation with psychologists. They flow from broadening the perspective from individuals.

In developing a wider role lawyers could work profitably with psychologists adopting a greater emphasis upon group behaviour. For example, they could help to identify behaviour associated with discrimination or harassment, not just identifying acts but also the accommodation to it. They could also encourage greater emphasis upon prevention. For example, divorce and related work is a staple of many a practising lawyer's diet. They are involved at the marriage contract's ending. Could they not also be involved at the start, helping the parties to agree a detailed marriage or cohabitation contract? Yes, this is already done in a few cases, but primarily with regard to property issues. It need not be so limited.

Psychologists' skills, in analysing behaviour and in helping individuals to control and change it, could be married with lawyers' skills in encouraging specificity and preparation for future contingencies. Their clients could be helped to think through the nature and quality of the relationship they wish to have. They could come to at least provisional agreements on issues which are known to cause problems in many relationships, for example child care, and what is to happen when certain issues arise, such as when one partner is offered an attractive job that would involve moving. They could articulate some governing principles, for example how major expenditure decisions are to be taken.

OPERATIONALISING INDIVIDUALITY

Many reject such suggestions because they are too impersonal. But they could empower people in a very practical manner, they would enhance individuality. Individuals' preferences and values would be articulated in advance allowing understanding and explicit negotiation. How important is sexual fidelity to *these* particular people? How do they wish to operationalise their belief that each of their careers is equally important? It would enhance individuality and choice whilst reducing the likelihood of one partner being submissive. Such a contract would have to be open to change as relationships, personalities and opportunities develop. But provision for managing that change could be incorporated into the 'contract'. Disputes are to be expected but the agreement could include procedures for early settlement and management. Of course, like any contract, the parties might choose not to use it, might not need to use it, or one might totally disregard it. But, again like any contract, it is an aid to relationships. Breaches can be discouraged but not entirely prevented. Given the importance of that relationship, particularly if children are involved, and the growing frequency of matrimonial breakdowns, such aids are socially as well as individually important. It is not a question of finding new areas of work for lawyers and psychologists, but rather asking whether there might not be very different ways of providing services that could *prevent* many of the traumatic pathologies that they now have to deal with.

Preparing pre-marital contracts encourages the parties to appreciate what they will be consenting to, should they decide to make the agreement. Consent is a key feature of individuality. It is a key feature of the law. Physical contacts, which would otherwise be crimes or civil wrongs such as assault and battery, become lawful if the person contacted was able to, and did give, his or her consent. Rape, for example, involves sexual intercourse without consent. Someone may be provided with excellent medical treatment but, if it was not consented to by someone entitled to withhold that consent, then there was a trespass (*Sidaway v. Board of Governors of the Bethlem Royal and the Maudsley Hospital*, [1985] 2 W.L.R. 480).

The legal meaning of 'consent' is, therefore, very important. It is also quite controversial. One issue concerns how informed the consent must be. Can someone consent to treatment if he or she does not know what the risks are? The question has, effectively, been dichotomised into whether the consent needs to be 'informed' or not? The law in the USA (*Canterbury v. Spence* 464 F Ed 772 (DC, 1972, as amended by most State legislatures)) and Canada (*Reibl v. Hughes*, (1980) 114 D.L.R. (3d) 1) is often portrayed as requiring 'informed' consent, but that is an exaggeration. Obviously 'informed' must always be a matter of degree. The issue is whether the standard should be specified by patients, hence the 'prudent patient' test articulated in parts of North America, or by professionals, as in the UK and most US states. In *Sidaway* (above) the House of Lords imported the standard of care, in the law of negligence, into the law of consent. Would a responsible body of co-professionals support giving that amount of information?

As so often occurs with the law, the emphasis upon one issue—in this case the amount of information required, deflects attention from other issues which can be as or more important. For example, the *Sidaway* decision made it clear that doctors must not give patients false information but did not appear to oblige them to answer all questions (Mason and McCall Smith, 1991), a position which has been confirmed (*Moyes v. Lothian Health Board*, [1990] 1 Med L.R. 463). Failure to give information can give patients false impressions. The decision emphasised that the duty is owed to individual patients, so different abilities to comprehend and manage the information must be taken into account. Clearly the ability to comprehend the information, particularly when as in the context of treatment it can be very complex, is critical if consent is to be meaningful. But relatively little has been done to develop practical tests or communication aids. How are patients, whose illness will often make it even more difficult, to cope with often complex information? The presentation of information in a fair and yet comprehensible manner for people to take decisions upon it is a skill separate from knowledge of the information. Standards in presenting information need to be articulated. Clearly there is an important role here for psychologists. They have undertaken important work on other kinds of statements, for example the comprehensibility of the warning given to those whom the police suspect of having committed a crime (Clare and Gudjonsson, 1992). Complex information can be broken down and formed into component parts to enable decision-makers to be better prepared. Lawyers could look to psychologists for help in constructing standards by which those providing information are judged both by the amount of information they provide and the effective empowering, rather than disabling such as by over-powering, of decision-makers.

Another problem with 'consent' is the extent to which is assumes assent. The idea of 'desire' or 'wish' fits within the meaning of 'consent' quite easily. But, often, we are asked to consent to things that we do not 'really' want. In one (intellectual rather than emotional) sense we want the surgery we know we need. But we would much rather not have to be operated upon. Is 'consent' entirely cognitive? Force and fraud, about the nature of the act, vitiate consent (Smith and Hogan, 1992). But what degrees and kinds of pressure ought to be inconsistent with consent? The issue is particularly important in rape and other sexual assaults. A sequence of past acts may be described as 'seduction' because, whilst there was no willingness at the start of the sequence there was consent at the end, which was obtained without physical force. We do not examine the sequence of acts, just the state of mind at the final act. The individual's reasons for consenting (always in the absence of force or fraud about what the act involves) are irrelevant.

Such an interpretation of 'consent' is a triumph for individualism. Social factors seem to get lost. A woman consents to sexual intercourse with a man in return for a cigarette. She consented. Why should we impose our values upon her? Think where it would end if we interfered with decisions that we did not think were wise? However, add some further information to this story. The woman has a learning disability. Now responses are likely to change. That makes a significant difference. We begin to assume that she lacked capacity to make a meaningful decision and/or that she was somehow tricked. Both of those approaches could produce the legal conclusion that she did not actually consent. But why do we take this approach of stigmatising certain people's consent rather than challenging the nature of 'consent' generally? Whose interests are advanced by the present, admittedly generally unquestioned, understanding of the meaning of 'consent'?

An alternative approach would emphasise assent, that is comprehending approval. Certain features of certain relationships raise the suggestion of exploitation. Frequently these will be manifestations of power, in its different forms. There is the strong and the weak, the old and experienced with the young and possibly naïve, the rich and powerful with the poor and dependent, the assertive and the unassertive. These are structural features of relationships with social significance in that they relate to the differences in ability to achieve wishes. If we examined 'consent' in the reality of these social relationships then we could recognise an obligation upon the more powerful person to be able to prove a robust, genuinely individual, assent (Carson, 1994). It is perfectly possible, for example, for a sexual relationship between one person with a learning disability and another without, to be rich, mutual and fulfilling. But there are particular dangers with such and many other kinds of relationships. A recognition of the social features involved when consent issues arise could, ironically, give it a more individual meaning.

DEMONSTRATING INDIVIDUALITY

Greater use could be made of functional tests. A woman's intelligence or 'intellectual age', for example, tells us very little about her ability to consent or her ability to manage her fertility. Yet such evidence has been prominent in legal decisions concerned with whether and when women with learning disabilities can be sterilised without their consent (see, for example, *In re F*, [1989] 2 W.L.R. 1063). Expert evidence which refers to standardised measures of highly conceptualised facets of human experience, such as intelligence and suggestibility, certainly has an important place. It also tends to re-enforce the image of that discipline's special knowledge base and that profession's skills. But evidence about what an individual has done, whether under natural or test conditions, is also important. Both kinds of evidence lead to inferences being drawn by the courts. Someone with that level of intelligence is likely to be considered to be unlikely (or likely) to be able to perform that act. Someone who was able to do that is likely to be able to achieve this. The issue is the appropriateness of the inference.

Functional tests add another perspective. If someone, who subsequently becomes a police suspect, demonstrated fear and avoidance of stressful circumstances in the past then it may be appropriate to infer repetition in similar circumstances. More naturalistic tests could help all concerned. For example, how are psychologists and others to be expected to make high-quality predictions of a long-term prisoner's dangerousness when he or she is detained in circumstances that discourage testing? Many male prisoners, for example, have problems in relating to women in an appropriate manner. How is anyone to test the success of any programme in the artificial single sex setting of a prison? If there is a desire to reduce the danger to the public and the likelihood of their clients re-offending then lawyers ought to support measures to increase the range and frequency of pre-discharge testing in relatively natural settings. In other contexts Haward (1981) developed a number of special experiments to test specific questions that had arisen before the courts, for example testing whether children with learning disabilities were poorer cyclists than other children. Whilst courts will still have to infer from such studies they are much more directly relevant to the issue that the court must decide.

Functional tests could be particularly valuable when the legal issue is an individual's capacity—for example, capacity to consent or to manage his or her property. If someone proposes to make a foolish decision, according to our values, there is a tendency (which is certainly not automatic) to infer that the individual lacked capacity to make that decision and, perhaps, is also mentally disordered. Equally there is a similar tendency to assume that if someone has a serious disability then he or she lacks capacity. But the tests are supposed to be separate and psychological research has challenged such assumptions (see Grisso and Appelbaum, 1991, and further forthcoming studies by these authors). The readiness with which these assumptions and inferences are made question the law's proclaimed emphasis upon individualism. Functional tests that require investigation into the competencies that the individual has demonstrated in the past could be useful.

Capacity is dynamic, interactive and affected by environmental factors (Anderer et al., 1990). It depends upon the input of others, such as carers, as well as the possibly incapacitated person. For example, the information necessary for making a decision can be communicated and explained in simple or complex terms, structured into sub-decisions for easier comprehension or left as amorphous information liable to overwhelm a large proportion of people, whether or not they have disabilities. The law could focus upon the efforts that others made to enable people to make legal decisions, instead of focusing upon their disabilities and problems (Carson, 1993).

The law could also focus more upon the practical problems and less upon the 'diagnostic' categories. The rationale for taking over responsibility for managing someone's property is that they are incapable of making rational decisions about it. In order to protect them we take over responsibility. It is likely that the vast majority of people treated in this way will have a mental illness or learning disability. The illness or disability will contribute—in part because the absence of enabling services will also be a cause—to those problems. But legal systems usually add, as an additional requirement to incapacity, the existence of such a disability. It is not enough that an individual is incapable of managing his or her property and affairs. He or she must be incapable because of the disability. In practice this permits a 'conceptual slide' or inference from the existence of disability to an assumption of incapacity. In practice it is too easy to conclude that someone is disabled and so, therefore, deserves to have decisions made for him or her. Unfortunately it appears that law reform in England and Wales will adopt the traditional approach of articulating tests of disability and incapacity (Law Commission, 1993). An objective is to ensure that people who do not have disabilities are not treated as incompetent. But why, if the problem is incapacity, should this be a problem?

INDIVIDUALISM FOR MINORITIES

The law and legal practice value individualism. In practice, however, especially where groups of minorities are distinguishable, there is a tendency, which law and legal practice encourages, to infer from perceived group characteristics to individuals. It may be an efficient means of making decisions about individuals but it distracts from their individuality. This chapter has not challenged the virtues of individualism but has questioned its application in practice. There is, it is submitted, considerable potential for lawyers and psychologists to work co-operatively in ensuring that the values of individual distinctiveness are maximised whilst the reality of social contexts is not inappropriately ignored.

REFERENCES

Anderer, S.J., Coleman, N.A., Lichtenstein, E.C. and Parry, J.W. (Eds) (1990). *Determining Competency in Guardianship Proceedings.* Washington: ABA.

Bedford, A. (1987). *Child Abuse and Risk.* London: NSPCC.

Carson, D. (1990). From risk policies to risk strategies. In D. Carson (Ed.), *Risk-taking in Mental Disorder: Analyses, Policies and Practical Strategies.* Chichester: SLE Publications.

Carson, D. (1993). Disabling progress: the Law Commission's proposals on mentally incapacitated adults' decision-making. *Journal of Social Welfare and Family Law,* 304–20.

Carson, D. (1994). The law's contribution to protecting people with learning disabilities from physical and sexual abuse. In J. Harris and A. Craft (Eds), *People With Learning Disabilities at Risk of Physical or Sexual Abuse.* Kidderminster: British Institute of Learning Disabilities.

Chasty, H. and Friel, J. (1991). *Children with Special Needs: Assessment, Law and Practice—Caught in the Act.* London: Jessica Kingsley.

Clare, I. and Gudjonsson, G. (1992). *Devising and Piloting an Experimental Version of the Notice to Detained Persons.* London: HMSO. (Research Study No. 7 for the Royal Commission on Criminal Justice.)

Cotterrell, R. (1984). *The Sociology of Law: An Introduction.* London: Butterworth.

Faust, D. and Ziskin, J. (1988). The expert witness in psychology and psychiatry. *Science*, **241,** 31–5.

Floud, J. and Warren, W. (1981). *Dangerousness and Criminal Justice*. London: Heinemann.

Grisso, T. and Appelbaum, P.S. (1991). Mentally-ill and non-mentally-ill patients' abilities to understand informed consent disclosures for medication. *Law and Human Behavior*, **15**, 4, 377–88.

Haward, L.R.C. (1981). *Forensic Psychology*. London: Batsford.

Hoge, S.K. and Grisso, T. (1992). Accuracy and expert testimony. *Bulletin of the American Academy of Psychiatry and Law*, **20**, 67–76.

Law Commission (1993). *Mentally Incapacitated Adults and Decision-making: A New Jurisdiction*. London: HMSO. (Consultation paper No. 128.)

Law Commission (1994). *Involuntary Manslaughter: A Consultation Paper*. London: HMSO. (Law Commission consultation paper No. 135.)

Mason, J.K. and McCall Smith, R.A. (1991). *Law and Medical Ethics* (3rd edn). London: Butterworth.

Morris, P. (1973). A sociological approach to research in legal services. In P. Morris, R. White and P. Lewis (Eds), *Social Needs and Legal Action*. London: Martin Robertson.

Pelling, H. (1963). *A History of British Trade Unionism*. Harmondsworth: Penguin.

Sang, B. and O'Brien, J. (1984). *Advocacy: The UK and American Experiences*. London: King's Fund.

Smith, J.C. and Hogan, B. (1992). *Criminal Law* (7th edn). London: Butterworth.

Society of Labour Lawyers (1968). *Justice for All*. London: Fabian Society.

Steadman, H.J., Monahan, J., Clark Robbins, P., Appelbaum, P., Grisso, T., Klassen, D., Mulvey, E.P. and Roth, L. (1993a). From dangerousness to risk assessment: implications for appropriate risk strategies. In S. Hodgins (Ed.), *Mental Disorder and Crime*. Newbury Park: Sage.

Steadman, H.J., Monahan, J., Appelbaum, P.S., Grisso, T., Mulvey, E.P., Roth, L.H., Clark Robbins, P. and Klassen, D. (1993b). Designing a new generation of risk assessment research. In J. Monahan and H.J. Steadman (Eds), *Violence and Mental Disorder: Developments in Risk Assessment*. Chicago: University of Chicago Press.

Wexler, D. (1993). New directions in therapeutic jurisprudence: breaking the bonds of conventional mental health scholarship. *New York Law School Journal of Human Rights*, **10**, 3, 759–76.

Chapter 2.2

Psychology and Assessment

Gisli H. Gudjonsson
Institute of Psychiatry, London

INTRODUCTION

Haward (1981) defines forensic psychology as 'that branch of applied psychology which is concerned with the collection, examination and presentation of evidence for judicial purposes' (p. 21). However, the term 'forensic psychology' is used more broadly by some American writers (e.g. Weiner and Hess, 1987), who view this speciality as any 'professional practice' and 'research endeavour' where psychology and the law interact.

In practice, there is often an overlap between the application of psychological techniques to the individual case and the impact of research findings in influencing legal structure, procedures and court of appeal decisions. Both are important and relevant to psychological assessment within legal contexts.

This chapter discusses the nature, role, validity and legal impact of psychological assessment within the context of the law. Since psychologists began to enter the courtroom about a century ago (Gudjonsson, 1991) a number of different assessment techniques have been developed to evaluate the individual case in many different legal contexts. These are typically based on scientific principles and empirical research and have established an important 'power base' for psychologists, because they provide psychologists with certain tools that can often be applied in a rather unique way to a variety of forensic problems, both civil and criminal (Haward, 1981; Grisso, 1986; Gudjonsson, 1992a). In recent years much greater emphasis has been placed on demonstrating the validity of these techniques by empirical research, before their general forensic use is recommended (Golding, 1992).

Handbook of Psychology in Legal Contexts
Edited by R. Bull and D. Carson. © 1995 John Wiley & Sons Ltd

PSYCHOLOGY AND THE LAW

Golding (1992) argues that the structure of both civil and criminal law 'is based, in part, upon a variety of theories and expectations of human behaviour, perception, intentionality, and judgement. As a consequence, social scientists, in general, and psychologists, in particular, are called upon, with increasing frequency, to offer expert evidence at various stages of adjudicatory and legislative process' (p. 253).

Haney (1980) wrote that 'law represents a powerful and entrenched structure and that psychological methods and data are for the most part assimilated into it' (p. 54). The legal structure, Haney believed, could be changed as a result of improved psychological knowledge and empirical data. Of fundamental importance here are the impact of: (a) empirical research findings; and (b) the application of psychological techniques to the collection, examination and presentation of evidence at judicial proceedings.

As far as empirical research and standardised psychological procedures are concerned, there are numerous examples of the ways in which research findings have influenced legal structures, procedures and case law (for a review of the impact on the American legal system, see Haney, 1993). For example, research into eye-witness testimony has influenced the ways in which eye-witness identification evidence is dealt with in some jurisdictions (Loftus, 1991). Research into the prediction of dangerousness (e.g. Monahan, 1981, 1984, 1988) has made the civil and criminal courts more cautious in their evaluation of experts' predictions of dangerousness. Empirical studies into forensic hypnosis and lie detection have highlighted problems which have made the courts more careful about accepting such evidence (Morris, 1990).

The impact of research on legal development can also be seen in Great Britain (Lloyd-Bostock, 1988). For example, empirical research influenced the development of the Codes of Practice under the Police and Criminal Evidence Act 1984 (Irving, 1990). Similarly, the recent report by the Royal Commission on Criminal Justice (1993), was heavily influenced in its recommendations about legal reform by empirical research findings in psychology and related sciences.

In terms of the impact on court decisions, including the court of appeal, psychological evidence has gained increased recognition and acceptance in Great Britain in a number of different cases (Gudjonsson, 1992a, b). For example, the judgment of the Court of Appeal on 5 December 1991, in the case of *Regina v. Raghip* (Law Report, the *Independent*, 6 December 1991) has had major implications for the admissibility of psychological evidence. The judges made a ruling which has widened the criteria for psychological evidence. First, psychological evidence is now seen as important in its own right, rather than relying on medical criteria for admissibility. Secondly, even if defendants have an IQ above the cut-off point of 70 (i.e. 'borderline') the psychological evidence is still admissible. Thirdly, evidence of psychological characteristics, such as suggestibility, was accepted by the Court of Appeal as important and admissible. Finally, psychological evidence was viewed by the judges as being valuable even though the jury had ample opportunity to observe the defendant testifying in court.

The legal acceptance of the diagnosis of post-traumatic stress disorder (PTSD), has had a major impact on both civil and criminal jurisprudence (Stone, 1993). The identification of PTSD symptoms forms the basis for defining psychological injury in civil (compensation) cases as well as mitigating sentences in criminal cases.

Of particular legal importance in Great Britain was the judgment in the ten test cases involving passengers on a ferry which capsized off Zeebrugge in March 1987. The test cases went for arbitration in February 1989, and for the first time in Great Britain PTSD became recognised as a legitimate condition for compensation (*Daily Mail*, 29 April 1989, p. 2). In addition, the judgment emphasised that disaster victims may be left 'vulnerable' to the risk of further illness and that this must be taken into consideration when awarding damages.

THE PSYCHOLOGICAL ASSESSMENT

Psychological assessment can be applied to a wide range of human functions and behaviour which are relevant to civil and criminal legal issues. These including: intellectual abilities (Wechsler, 1981), social functioning (Doll, 1965), neuropsychological status (Lezak, 1983; Martell, 1992), personality (Hathaway and McKinley, 1943; Eysenck and Eysenck, 1975; Pope, Butcher and Seelen, 1993), the competence and reliability of a witness in a criminal trial (Gudjonsson and Gunn, 1982), interrogative suggestibility and disputed confessions (Gudjonsson, 1992a), moral development and reasoning (Piaget, 1959; Kohlberg, 1976; Kohlberg and Candee, 1984), blood injury phobia (Gudjonsson and Sartory, 1983), post-traumatic stress disorder (Stone, 1993), the prediction of dangerousness (Monahan, 1981), attitudes of offenders towards their crime (Gudjonsson, 1984; Gudjonsson and Singh, 1989), sexual problems (Salter, 1988), anger problems (Novaco, 1975), deception (Gale, 1988), and malingering (Gudjonsson and Shackleton, 1986; Rogers, 1988).

Many of the above types of assessment would require the psychologist to be trained in clinical psychology.

There are different methods and techniques available for carrying out a psychological assessment. These depend primarily upon the nature of the assessment, the theoretical orientation, experience and preference of the psychologist, and the types of legal issue to be addressed. However, any comprehensive assessment typically consists of the following: (1) an interview of the person being assessed, and whenever possible, an interview of informants, which can be used to corroborate the 'client's' account and perhaps add to it; (2) behavioural observations of the 'client'; (3) biographical data and previous records; and (4) psychological testing and 'experimentation'. Therefore, 'testing' is only one of the techniques utilised by psychologists when conducting an assessment concerning a particular legal issue and its use is not without professional controversy (Heilbrun, 1992). According to Heilbrun, legal advocates are more interested in the test's 'relevance' when considering the admissibility of the expert's testimony than its 'accuracy' as a scientific tool. Nevertheless, the concepts of 'reliability' and 'validity' are crucial to the scientific acceptability of psychological tests (Anastasi, 1976; Matarazzo, 1990; Heilbrun, 1992).

The main impetus behind the development of psychological tests has been the need to identify and classify psychological deficits and vulnerability, which is commonly referred to in legal settings as 'incompetency' (Grisso, 1986), 'incapacity' (Law Commission Consultation Paper, 1993a, b, c), or 'vulnerabilities' (Metropolitan Police, 1991; Gudjonsson et al., 1993).

A test is 'a systematic procedure for observing behaviour and describing it with the aid of numerical scales or fixed categories' (Cronbach, 1984, p. 26). The basic function of psychological tests is objectively to measure differences between individuals or between the reactions of an individual on different occasions (Anastasi, 1976). Most standardised tests have some form of norms for different populations (e.g. normal subjects, psychiatric patients, offenders). The norms are used to evaluate the individual's performance in relation to a particular reference group. These can be expressed in various ways, including percentile ranks, which are expressed in terms of the percentage of persons in the standardisation groups who fall below or above a given raw score. For example, a score is generally said to fall outside the 'normal range' (i.e. it is abnormal) when found in fewer than 5 per cent or more than 95 per cent of the normative population, respectively. This corresponds to the 5th and 95th percentile rank. For example, an IQ score of 75 represents the bottom 5 per cent of the general population (5th percentile rank), whereas an IQ score of 125 represents the top 5per cent of the population (95th percentile rank).

Little is known about the extent to which psychological tests are used in forensic assessment. Forensic psychiatrists almost invariably base their assessment on a clinical interview and they do not, on the whole, have the necessary training or expertise for administering psychological tests. Clinical psychologists, on the other hand, have the advantage of being able to use standardised psychological tests for measuring functional skills and deficits, personality and mental status. This means that their evidence is generally more factually based than the evidence of psychiatrists who rely almost exclusively on an opinion.

Gudjonsson (1985), in his survey of members of the British Psychological Society, found that 96 per cent of the psychologists studied said they generally used psychological tests when carrying out a forensic assessment. The most common tests used were those that focused on functional strengths and deficits, such as the Wechsler Adult Intelligence Scale and various neuropsychological tests. A small minority (9 per cent), said that they most commonly used personality tests, including the Minnesota Multiphasic Personalty Inventory (MMPI; Hathaway and McKinley, 1943) and the Eysenck Personality Questionnaire (EPQ; Eysenck and Eysenck, 1975). In spite of the large proportion of psychologists who generally used psychological tests in their forensic assessment, most also relied on behavioural assessment and interview data. Therefore, although psychological tests are commonly applied when conducting a forensic assessment, they typically form only a part of the overall assessment.

The extent to which psychological tests are used in a forensic assessment will depend on the practice and orientation of the individual psychologist concerned. However, it also depends on the instructions received from the referral agent and the nature of the problem to be assessed. For example, subjects referred specifically for assessment of intellectual functioning or neuropsychological status would invariably need to be tested, whereas in child custody cases the psychological assessment is typically heavily dependant on information obtained by interviews and observations (Keilin and Bloom, 1986). Where the instruction given by the referral agent is not clear the psychologist will need to clarify the purpose of the assessment verbally or in writing. It is often useful to know the legal issues involved in a given case so that the psychological assessment can be planned accordingly.

Heilbrun (1992) provides useful guidelines for the use of psychological testing in forensic assessment. These include:

1. The test used should be adequately documented and reviewed in the scientific literature and needs to contain a manual describing the test's development, psychometric properties, and procedure.

2. The reliability of the test chosen should be considered carefully. 'Reliability' refers to the consistency of scores, for example, when people are tested on different occasions, or when they are rated by more than one observer. Knowing the reliability of a test is important, because it gives an indication of the stability of the test and it is used to calculate the 'error of measurement' of a single score from a test (i.e. it gives an indication of the band of error surrounding the person's 'true' score on a given test).

3. The test chosen must be relevant to the legal issue addressed, or the psychological construct underlying the legal issue. Preferably, relevance

should be supported by published validation research, although on occasions justification for using a particular test may be made on theoretical grounds.

'Validity' refers to the extent to which a particular test actually measures what it purports to measure, and how well it does so (Anastasi, 1976). It therefore provides an indication of how well a test fulfils its function as well as telling us what precisely the test measures. There are various ways of determining the validity of a test, but it is usually judged against an independent criterion (other observable facts).

4. The standard administration recommended in the test's manual should be used, which normally requires a quiet and distraction-free testing environment.

5. The findings from a particular test should not be applied towards a purpose for which the test was not developed (e.g. making inferences about suggestibility from the results of IQ tests). Interpretation of the results should be guided by population and situation specificity; that is, the closer the individual 'fits' the population and situation of those described in the validation studies, the greater the confidence one can express in the applicability of the results. Many tests used in forensic practice were standardised on non-forensic populations, which may make the generalisation of the results difficult.

6. There is considerable controversy in the literature about clinical versus statistical predictions (e.g. Meehl, 1954; Sawyer, 1966). Using a combination of results from clinical tests and actuarial data is preferable. Of course, very much depends on the type of assessment being carried out, and the circumstances under which the test is administered. For example, many clinical judgements of intellectual skills and suggestibility traits are often grossly wrong (Gudjonsson, 1992a), and objective measurements would give more valid information than clinical judgements. Conversely, a clinical interview is often essential for assessing the person's current or past mental state and this may be supplemented by objective tests, such as the General Health Questionnaire (Goldberg, 1981) and the Beck Depression Inventory (Beck and Steer, 1987).

7. When interpreting the results from tests it is important that the 'forensic' psychologist is sensitive to behaviours ('response style') that have a bearing on the validity of the results (e.g. defensiveness, evasiveness, denial, and malingering).

Heilbrun (1992) makes the point that psychological testing should be viewed as a part of hypothesis testing. He states: 'Psychological testing can serve as one source of information that can both formulate and confirm or disconfirm hypotheses about psychological constructs relevant to legal issues, but there are others as well: history, medical testing, interview data, and third-party observations of behaviour can all be used for these purposes' (p. 268). Once the hypotheses have been formulated they need to be tested by objective means. This view is supported by Pope, Butcher and Seelen (1993), in their recommendation of the forensic use of the MMPI, which is the most widely used and researched personality test ever developed.

The results from a psychological assessment have to be interpreted within the context of a given legal issue. This is often a difficult task to do, because psychological data are not directly applicable to legal concepts and arguments and should never be interpreted in isolation from other facts.

Grisso (1986) discusses in detail different types of 'legal competencies' (e.g. 'competency to stand trial', 'criminal responsibility', 'parental competency', 'competency to care for self or property', 'testamentary competency', and 'competency to consent to treatment') and argues that each type of competency refers to different capacities, individuals, and circumstances. According to Grisso, legal competency focuses on the 'individual's functional abilities, behaviours, or capacities' and these are 'related to, but distinct from, psychiatric diagnosis or conclusions about intellectual abilities and personality traits' (p. 15). Grisso provides a conceptual model for assessments of competencies, which focuses on guiding the collection of reliable case data, the use of empirical research to interpret data, and the development of new research, whilst advising that psychologists should be cautious about inferring legal concepts from psychological data. The purpose of the model is to increase the relevance of forensic assessment and improve its legal and scientific credibility. The central features of his conceptual framwork are: (1) the measurement of functional abilities; (2) the relevance of the functional abilities assessed to contexts of legal competency; (3) the type of 'causal inferences' that can be drawn about the relationship between the functional deficits and legal competency; (4) the degree to which the functional ability or deficit interacts with the demand characteristics of the situation; and (5) that legal competency constructs are 'judgemental' (i.e. they require legal or moral evaluation that the person-situation incongruency is sufficient to warrant a finding of incompetency) and 'dispositional' (i.e. the finding of incompetency authorises a particular legal response).

THE ROLES OF THE FORENSIC PSYCHOLOGIST

Haward (1981, 1990) describes in detail four main roles of psychologists in judicial proceedings. These roles are referred to by Haward as 'experimental', 'clinical', 'actuarial' and 'advisory' roles. The roles are relevant to both civil and criminal proceedings and direct the psychologist concerning the kind of assessment that is relevant to the legal issue in a particular case.

In the experimental role, psychologists perform a unique function which is generally outside the expertise of forensic psychiatrists. Because in this role human behaviour is studied by experimentation rather than by a clinical interview, it requires the ability and knowledge to apply psychological principles and techniques to unique forensic problems. On occasions it involves devising experiments, both in civil and criminal cases. Haward (1981) discusses the forensic importance of experiments into perception and memory. This kind of evidence falls into two distinct groups. First, general evidence about scientific findings concerning the limitations of human memory and its fallibility, particularly in relation to eye-witness identification evidence (Loftus, 1979). This kind of expert evidence, which is commonly presented in the courts in the United States, has usually been ruled inadmissible in Britain (Davies, 1983), but has recently been admitted in at least two criminal trials (Bull, 1993—personal comunication). This relates to the fact that British Courts are reluctant to admit evidence of a general nature that does not directly focus on abnormality in the personality or mental state of the defendant. The second type of scientific evidence, which is routinely admissible in the British courts, relates to experiments directly relevant to the individual case (e.g. Gudjonsson and Sartory, 1983).

The clinical role, which is the most common role, is most appropriately fulfilled by chartered clinical psychologists. It overlaps, to a certain extent, with the role fulfilled by forensic psychiatrists. Here the psychologist interviews a client and carries out the required assessment, which may include extensive psychometric testing (e.g. the administration of tests of intelligence, neuropsychological functioning, mental state, personality) and behavioural data (Gudjonsson, 1985). The nature of the assessment will, of course, depend upon the instruction of the referral agent and the type of problem being assessed. Clients may need to be assessed on more than one occasion. In addition, whenever possible and appropriate, informants should be consulted for providing corroboration and further information. Previous reports, including school reports and psychological and psychiatric assessments, should be obtained whenever they are likely to be relevant to the present assessment.

The actuarial role refers to the application of statistical probabilities to events and behaviour. This role is commonly used by statisticians and other scientists, including psychologists, when interpreting observational and behavioural data. The type of probabilities and observational data analysed by psychologists may include estimating the probability that a person with a given psychological deficit could earn a living or live independently in the community (Haward, 1981).

The advisory role generally consists of psychologists advising counsel about what questions to ask when cross-examining psychologists who are testifying for the other side. For example, the prosecuting counsel may request that a psychologist sits behind her or him in court to advise on cross-examining the defence psychologist. Reports by psychologists are increasingly being subjected to peer review by an expert for the other side. That expert may have carefully studied the psychological report and, in addition, may have carried out an assessment of the defendant.

Having another psychologist in court evaluating one's testimony has been reported to increase the stress experienced when psychologists testify (Gudjonsson, 1985). Sometimes there is considerable disagreement between the opinions of psychology experts and this may result in lengthy and stressful cross-examination (Tunstall et al., 1982). When preparing a court report psychologists should always assume that their report will be subjected to a careful peer review by the other side. Even if it is not, lawyers are becoming increasingly familiar with psychological testimony and are able to ask some very searching questions. The psychologist must be thoroughly familiar with the development and validation of the instruments and tests used.

CONCLUSIONS

Psychological explanations of human behaviour and motivation often form an important part of civil and criminal proceedings. For this reason psychologists are increasingly being instructed to conduct psychological assessments in a variety of legal contexts. Their assessment techniques are typically based on scientific principles and empirical research, which provides them with tools that can be applied in a unique way to a variety of forensic problems. Their assessments in legal contexts differ in some important respects from those found in general clinical practice, the main problem being the limit to which standard psychological techniques can be directly applied to address legal concepts and issues. However, psychological assessments in individual cases, and empirical research data bases, are often relevant to legal issues and have in recent years greatly influenced legal structures, procedures and case law.

REFERENCES

Anasatsi, A. (1976). *Psychologcal Testing* (4th edn). New York: Macmillan.

Beck, A.T. and Steer, R.A. (1987). *Beck Depression Inventory. Manual.* New York: The Psychological Corporation Harcourt Brace Jovanovich.

Cronbach, L.J. (1984). *Essentials of Psychological Testing* (4th edn). New York: HarperCollins.

Davies, G.M. (1983). The legal importance of psychological research in eyewitness testimony. British and American experiences. *Journal of the Forensic Science Society*, **24**, 165–75.

Doll, E.A. (1965). Vineland Social Maturity Scale: *Manual of Directions.* Minneapolis: American Guidance Service.

Eysenck, H.J. and Eysenck, S.B.G. (1975). *Manual of the Eysenck Personality Questionnaire*. London: Hodder & Stoughton.

Gale, A. (Ed.) (1988). *The Polygraph Test. Truth, Lies and Science*. London: Sage.

Goldberg, D. (1981). *The General Health Questionnaire* (GHQ28). Windsor: NFER-Nelson.

Golding, S.L. (1992). Increasing the reliability, validity, and relevance of psychological expert evidence. *Law and Human Behavior*, **16**, 253–6.

Grisso, T. (1986). *Evaluating Competencies. Forensic Assessments and Instruments*. New York: Plenum Press.

Gudjonsson, G.H. (1984). Attribution of blame for criminal acts and its relationship with personality. *Personality and Individual Differences*, **5**, 53–8.

Gudjonsson, G.H. (1985). Psychological evidence in court: results from the BPS survey. *Bulletin of the British Psychological Society*, **38**, 327–30.

Gudjonsson, G.H. (1991). Forensic psychology: the first century. *Journal of Forensic Psychiatry*, **2**, 129–31.

Gudjonsson, G.H. (1992a). *The Psychology of Interrogation, Confessions and Testimony*. Chichester: John Wiley.

Gudjonsson, G.H. (1992b). The admissibility of expert psychological and psychiatric evidence in England and Wales. *Criminal Behaviour and Mental Health*, **2**, 245–52.

Gudjonsson, G.H. and Gunn, J. (1982). The competence and reliability of a witness in a criminal court. *British Journal of Psychiatry*, **141**, 624–7.

Gudjonsson, G.H. and Sartory, G. (1983). Blood-injury phobia: a 'reasonable excuse' for failing to give a specimen in a case of suspected drunken driving. *Journal of the Forensic Science Society*, **23**, 197–201.

Gudjonsson, G.H. and Shackleton, H. (1986). The pattern of scores on Raven's Matrices during 'faking bad' and 'non-faking' performance. *British Journal of Clinical Psychology*, **25**, 35–41.

Gudjonsson, G.H. and Singh, K.K. (1989). The revised Gudjonsson Blame Attribution Inventory. *Personality and Individual Differences*, **10**, 67–70.

Gudjonsson, G.H., Clare, I., Rutter, S. and Pearse, J. (1993*). Persons at Risk During Interviews in Police Custody: The Identification of Vulnerabilities*. Royal Commission on Criminal Justice. London: HMSO.

Haney, C. (1980). Psychology and legal change. On the limits of a factual jurisprudence. *Law and Human Behavior*, **6**, 191–235.

Haney, C. (1993). Psychology and legal change. *Law and Human Behavior*, **17**, 371–98.

Hathaway, S.R. and McKinley, J.C. (1943). *Manual for Administering and Scoring the MMPI*. Minneapolis: University of Minnesota Press.

Haward, L.R.C. (1981). *Forensic Psychology*. London: Batsford.

Haward, L.R.C. (1990). *A Dictionary of Forensic Psychology*. Chichester: MediLaw/Barry Rose.

Heilbrun, K. (1992). The role of psychological testing in forensic assessment. *Law and Human Behaviour*, **16**, 257–72.

Irving, B. (1990). The codes of practice under the Police and Criminal Evidence Act 1984. In R. Bluglass and P. Bowden (Eds), *Principles and Practice of Forensic Psychiatry*. London: Churchill Livingstone, pp. 151–9.

Keilin, W.G. and Bloom, L.J. (1986). Child custody evaluation practices: a survey of experienced professionals. *Professional Psychology: Research and Practice*, **17**, 338–46.

Kohlberg, L. (1976). Moral stages and moralisation: the cognitive-developmental approach. In T. Lichona (Ed.), *Moral Development and Behavior.* New York: Holt, Rinehart & Winston.

Kohlberg, L. and Candee, D. (1984). The relationship of moral judgment to moral action. In W. M. Kurtines and J.W. Gewirtz (Eds), *Morality, Moral Behavior, and Moral Development.* Chichester: John Wiley.

Law Commission Consultation Paper (1993a*). Mentally Incapacitated Adults and Decision-Making: A New Jurisdiction.* London: HMSO. (Papers No. 128.)

Law Commission Consultation Paper (1993b). *Mentally Incapacitated Adults and Decision-Making: Medical Treatment and Research.* London: HMSO. (Papers No. 129.)

Law Commission Consultation Paper (1993c). *Mentally Incapacitated and Other Vulnerable Adults: Public Law Protection.* London: HMSO. (Papers No. 130.)

Lezak, M.D. (1983). *Neuropsychological Assessment* (2nd edn). Oxford: Oxford University Press.

Loftus, E. (1979). *Eyewitness Testimony.* London: Harvard University Press.

Loftus, E. (1991). Resolving legal questions with psychological data. *American Psychologist,* **46**, 1046–8.

Lloyd-Bostock, S.M.A. (1988). *Law in Practice. Applications of Psychology to Legal Decision Making and Legal Skills.* Leicester: British Psychological Society.

Martell, D.A. (1992). Forensic neuropsychology and the criminal law. *Law and Human Behavior,* **16**, 313–36.

Matarazzo, J.D. (1990). Psychologcal assessment versus psychological testing: validation from Binet to the school, clinic, and the courtroom. *American Psychologist,* **45**, 999–1017.

Meehl, P.E. (1954). *Clinical Versus Statistical Predictions.* Minneapolis: University of Minnesota Press.

Metropolitan Police (1991). *A Change of PACE. A Guide to the Changes to the Codes of Practice.* London: New Scotland Yard.

Monahan, J. (1981). *Predicting Violent Behavior: An Assessment of Clinical Techniques.* Beverly Hills: Sage.

Monahan, J. (1984). The prediction of violent behavior: toward a secondary generation of theory and policy. *American Journal of Psychiatry,* **141**, 10–15.

Monahan, J. (1988). Risk assessment of violence among the mentally disordered: generating useful knowledge. *International Journal of Law and Psychiatry,* **11**, 249–57.

Morris, R.A. (1990). The admissibility of evidence derived from hypnosis and polygraph. In D.C. Raskin (Ed.), *Psychological Methods in Criminal Investigation and Evidence.* New York: Springer, pp. 333–76.

Novaco, R.W. (1975). *Anger Control: The Development and Evaluation of an Experimental Treatment.* Lexington, MA: Heath.

Piaget, J. (1959). *Language and Thought of the Child.* London: Routledge & Kegan Paul.

Pope, H.S., Butcher, J.N. and Seelen, J. (1993). *The MMPI, MMPi-2 and MMPI-A in Court. A Prectical Guide for Expert Witnesses and Attorneys.* Washington, DC: American Psychological Association.

Rogers, R. (Ed.) (1988). *Clinical Assessment of Malingering and Deception.* New York: Guilford Press.

Royal Commission on Criminal Justice (1993). Report. London: HMSO.

Salter, A. (1988). *Treating Child Sex Offenders and Victims. A Practical Guide.* London: Sage.

Sawyer, J. (1966). Measurement and prediction, clinical and statistical. *Psychological Bulletin*, **66**, 178–200.

Stone, A.A. (1993). Post-traumatic stress disorder and the law: critical review of the new frontier. *Bulletin of the American Academy of Psychiatry and Law*, **21**, 23–36.

Tunstall, O., Gudjonsson, G., Eysenck, H. and Haward, L. (1982). Professional issues arising from psychological evidence presented in court. *Bulletin of the British Psychological Society*, **35**, 329–31.

Wechsler, D. (1981). *WAIS-R Manual. Wechsler Adult Intelligence Scale-Revised.* New York: Psychological Corporation.

Weiner, I.B. and Hess, A.K. (1987). *Handbook of Forensic Psychology.* New York: John Wiley.

Children, Assessment and Education

Geoff Lindsay
University of Sheffield

Professional psychologists working with children may be qualified in different specialisms. In the UK the main group comprise educational psychologists (about 2000) with over 300 clinical psychologists also specialising in childbased work. The situation is similar in the USA where the main group is school psychologists, but clinical and counselling psychologists also make a major contribution. In the rest of Europe the situation is more fluid as some countries (e.g. France) have a similar arrangement, while in others psychologists undertake a training which qualifies them as child psychologists.

Thus there are structural differences in the way that psychology is delivered to children. In this chapter the focus will be on psychological work with children in relation to the education system and its legal context, and hence on the practice of educational or school psychologists. It should be noted, however, that in the UK and many other countries educational psychologists have a wider brief relating to the legal contexts, including child abuse, custody disputes, delinquency, compensation following injury, and work with families, involving both assessment and intervention. The main interface between educational psychologists and the legal system, in terms of education, concerns the identification of children with special educational needs, the assessment of those needs, and the provision made by local educational authorities (LEAs), school districts, or schools themselves. Consequently a description will be given of the relevant legislation in the UK and reference will be made to that of other countries, including the USA.

CERTIFICATION

The position regarding legal registration of psychologists varies from one country to another. A survey of 54 developed and developing countries, conducted by Oakland and Cunningham (1992), found that the qualifications required to practise varied, with 28 per cent requiring an undergraduate degree, 24 per cent a Master's degree and one country demanding a doctoral degree as minimum entry. School (educational) psychologists were required to be licensed to practice in 49 per cent of the countries surveyed, but while this was the case in 63 per cent of countries with high gross national product (GNP), only 35 per cent of low GNP countries had this requirement. There are also variations within countries. For example, within the USA, local, State administered certification systems operate, linking under the aegis of the American Association of State Psychology Boards.

The major legislation that governs the assessment of children by educational psychologists in England and Wales has been the Education Act 1981. This legislation was devised following the Warnock Report (Department of Education and Science, 1978). For the first time educational psychologists were specifically mentioned as necessary in the assessment of children. This Act is replaced by Section III of the Education Act 1993 whose new provisions were given effect in 1994. In the USA the comparable federal legislation is the Education for All Handicapped Children Act 1975 (Public Law 94-142), which requires that a child with special educational needs be assessed and that an Individualised Education Program be drawn up and reviewed.

Educational psychologists were not mentioned specifically in the Education Act 1981, and this remains the case also with the 1993 Act. Rather, the Education (Special Educational Needs) Regulations (S.I. 1994 No. 1047) specify, among other matters, that the local educational authority *must* seek educational, medical and psychological advice for the purposes of making an assessment under the 1993 Act, and *may* seek other advice. The regulation concerning the provision of psychological advice is regulated by employment rather than qualification. This may be compared with the regulations concerning the provision of medical or educational advice. The former must be sought from 'a fully registered medical practitioner' (para. 8 of the Regulations, SI 1994 No 1047). The difficulty for educational psychologists is that there are no comparable regulations to those concerning medical practitioners. In 1987, the Privy Council approved the setting up of a Register of Chartered Psychologists which is administered by the British Psychological Society (1993) but this is a voluntary register and many educational psychologists have chosen not to subscribe, and hence are not subject to the accompanying disciplinary procedures.

INDEPENDENCE

Parents and lawyers are entitled to expect an independent professional opinion from an educational psychologist. In practice there are some difficulties. If the psychologist is employed by the local education authority or school board, will his or her advice be slanted to favour the employer? On the other hand, if the employer is the parent direct, or through a lawyer, will advice be slanted to favour the parent's wishes? It must be recognised that these are real and often subtle influences. Psychologists who are members of professional bodies, such as the British Psychological Society or the American Psychological Association, are subject to codes of conduct, backed up by disciplinary procedures. These certainly help to ensure high standards, but recent research by Pope and Vetter (1992) and Lindsay and Colley (1993) has revealed that such psychologists may still face significant ethical dilemmas.

Recent legislation in the UK, where state schools can opt to be funded directly from Government rather than via a local education authority, has led to fears that psychological services will not be available or that the independence of educational psychologists could be threatened by the demands of the market-place. For example, if a school paid for the psychologist would there be subtle, or even vigorous pressure on her/him? Would a headteacher expect the educational psychologist to find a child as having special educational needs, in order to gain extra resources for the school? In addition, would the following observation by the House of Commons Committee (1993, para. 22) pertain: 'If support services are no longer free at the point of delivery and schools have to pay for them, they might choose not to buy them'? In the event the government decided to make the psychological service a mandatory exception when LEA finances are calculated. Consequently the LEA retains the finance centrally to fund its psychological service, rather than delegating it to schools.

The experience of educational psychologists in other countries is varied, given the range of systems for providing such a service. In some countries the service is private, or provided by the social welfare agency. In others the service is rudimentary (for reviews see Saigh and Oakland, 1989; Oakland and Cunningham, 1992). But the fundamental issue of independence of the professional psychologist is common. This can never be absolute, but some systems are less supportive than others, and it should be noted that these difficult situations are not simply found in Eastern Europe, but rather that there are challenges to independence to be found in all political systems.

ASSESSMENT OF CHILDREN'S SPECIAL EDUCATIONAL NEEDS

Before placing the psychological assessment process within a legal context, the nature of assessment itself will be discussed. The rationale for a psychological assessment in this context is to understand better a child's functioning in order to improve his or her development. The child is the client that the psychologist is serving. However, in practice, owing to age or level and type of impairment, the parent or legal guardian of the child has a key role. It is this person who must agree to the assessment, on behalf of the child, and take responsibility for implementing the recommendations which arise.

Psychologists offer services to a wide range of children and their families and it is only a small number who become subject to the legislation regarding formal assessments in the UK, or comparable legislation elsewhere. In practice children will cause different levels of concern, and consequently will receive varying types and intensity of assessment and monitoring by teachers and other professionals. The educational psychologist is likely to be involved with only a minority of these children, in some cases giving general advice to teachers and parents, while in a small number of instances more particular assessments will be carried out. Also, the educational psychologist is likely to advocate and will want to evaluate the effects of interventions by, and in conjunction with, teachers and parents.

As a result of such practice it will be possible to make more informed judgements as to which children have needs which are likely to require a decision by the LEA, school board or appropriate authority on whether to undertake an assessment to decide upon a statement of special educational needs, or equivalent. Consequently, using the UK example, the *formal* assessment, under the 1993 Act will be integrated with the *informal* stages. In the experience of the present author this leads to a more satisfactory process as the psychologist works collaboratively with parents, and indeed the child, and helps them to see the nature of the child's difficulties (or in some cases the lack of significant problems) in a gradual and supportive manner.

A psychological assessment will have several characteristics. First, it will be *problem related*, that is the exact content will depend on the nature of the problem referred, and hypotheses formulated on the prior information. Second, it will follow a *sequential strategy* and the nature of the assessment will be modified as hypotheses are tested and reformulated. Third, the assessment will make use of a *variety of measures and techniques*. These include standardised tests of cognitive ability or attainment, observation of the child in a naturalistic setting, self-report scales and personality inventories, and the structured interview. Fourth, the advice produced may be directed at specific, microlevel concerns (for example, a dynamic 'assessment through teaching' approach— e.g. Pearson and Lindsay, 1986—in order to develop a teaching programme) or major longterm issues at the macrolevel (for example, school placement). If the assessment is being undertaken at the request of a lawyer it may also provide the basis of a critique of an earlier assessment or of decisions made about the child.

The educational psychologist who assesses a child for the purposes of providing advice under legislation is likely to follow a general set of guidelines, to ensure a degree of consistency of practice, both with respect to the areas of investigation and reporting upon them. In some places the methods used (e.g. specific tests) may also be specified, but this is not the case in the UK. Thus a parent or lawyer acting on behalf of a child can expect an educational psychologist to use professional judgement to determine the method of enquiry, but within a framework which indicates the issue(s) to be investigated. These might include the child's general level of intellectual functioning. This might be relevant if the appropriateness of the curriculum or a school placement outside mainstream education is being considered. Specific learning difficulties/dyslexia will be examined by analysis of the child's different cognitive skills and their relationship with school attainments. Discrepancies and specific cognitive difficulties or impairments may be relevant to the type of education a child receives, or whether the child receives special arrangements at times of examinations (e.g. a reader of questions, extra time, ignoring spelling errors or allowing electronic spellcheckers).

In other cases the necessary focus may be on the child's emotional and behavioural development. Here the assessment may include cognitive factors but will concentrate more on the child's personality, self-esteem, and interactions with other children and adults. It is also common practice for many psychologists to assess not only the child but the learning environments (school, family) and the interactions between the various factors. For example, a child may have high general intellectual ability but a family environment that is stifling development. Another child may be underachieving because of the school, rather than his or her own intrinsic disabilities.

ASSESSMENT UNDER THE EDUCATION ACT 1993

The 1981 Act was a landmark, in the same way as was the Warnock Report (Department of Education and Science, 1978), as it was the first comprehensive legislation for all children with special educational needs. The 1993 Act is a wideranging piece of legislation which covers matters in addition to special educational needs. However, this will now be the primary legislation, in conjunction with what remains of the Education Act 1944. It is Part III of this Act which is concerned with special educational needs.

Section 165 of the Education Act 1993 imposes a general duty on LEAs to identify children with special educational needs and section 167 specifies the criteria determining that the LEA shall make an assessment of a child's educational needs. It is the local educational authority which has the duty to carry out assessments of children under the 1993 Act. This duty must be exercised when a child is considered to have special educational needs arising from a 'learning difficulty', which is defined in section 156.

The Act lays duties on the LEA to make and maintain a statement of special educational needs if, as a result of the assessment and representations by the parent, the LEA decides that it is necessary 'for the LEA to determine the special educational provision which any learning difficulty he may have calls for' (SS.168 (1)). The LEA must also review the progress of children with statements of special educational needs (S.172).

Parents may appeal against the LEA not making an assessment (S.173); not making a statement, following an assessment (S.169); the contents of the statement, including the psychological, or other, advice (S.170). Guidance on the form of assessments is currently limited to that enclosed in Schedule 9 of the Act. Paragraph 2 (2) specifies that psychological advice must be sought, and paragraph 3 (1) states that regulations will be drawn up which may specify 'the manner in which assessments are to be conducted', including the time in which such assessments should be carried out. This Schedule also states that a parent 'may be present at the examination if he so desires'.

Guidance on the conduct of a formal assessment under the Education Act 1993 is also provided in the Code of Practice. However, the decision whether or not to carry out a formal assessment will be made by the LEA when the child's abilities are considered against the criteria set. Educational psychologists will therefore make an important contribution to this stage of the process by providing information on the child's developmental progress and difficulties.

ASSESSMENT—THE IMPACT OF LEGISLATION

We have seen that the legislation that most affects the practice of educational psychologists in the UK does so indirectly by the duties and responsibilities placed upon their major employer, the LEA. There is no primary legislation that specifies, say, what a psychological assessment should comprise. The situation is different elsewhere. The USA, for example, has rulings on the use of particular types of assessments, especially the use of intelligence tests with children from minority groups. In their review, Bersoff and Hofer (1990) claim that 'the practice of school psychology has become highly regulated' (p. 937).

The situation in the UK appears to be rather different. In their review of 11 cases which had gone to judicial review in the courts, concerning assessment under the Education Act 1981, Denman and Lunt (1993) indicate that all the cases were essentially concerned with the decisions of the relevant LEAs with respect to the making of a statement, or the decision whether to carry out an assessment. In no case reviewed was the main issue one of direct concern regarding the nature of the educational psychologists' assessment, either its content, procedure or the opinions which were derived by the psychologists themselves. Parents have also been able, under the 1981 Act, to appeal to a tribunal, (under the 1980 Education Act), to the Secretary of State, and to the local government Ombudsman if they have been dissatisfied. The 1993 Act institutes a new Special Educational Needs Tribunal (SS.177–181). It is at the local tribunal that educational psychologists may first have their practice examined and criticised, or may act on behalf of a child and parent.

The other issues concerning educational psychologists following the 1993 Act are very similar to those which arose from the 1981 Act, whose operation gradually gave rise to more and more concerns, which have been explored in a number of texts covering the field of special educational needs (e.g. Norwich, 1990); by the Audit Commission (1992a, b); and by Select Committees of Members of Parliament (House of Commons, 1987, 1993). The concerns have covered various aspects of the working of that Act, and its underlying philosophy. One issue for educational psychologists is largely practical, concerning the ability of psychological services to assess the numbers of children referred. The Code of Practice (Department for Education, 1994) requires that the assessment and making of a statement be completed in six months and that the assessment phase should be only ten weeks. As the Audit Commission (1992a) reported that the median time taken to complete an assessment and write a statement by the 12 LEAs studied was 12 months, it is clear that to meet such targets more resources including educational psychologists will be needed. Similarly in the USA there has been much debate (e.g. Henderson, 1993) concerning the operation of Public Law 94–142, both in terms of procedures and outcomes for the children concerned.

ASSESSMENT—PSYCHOLOGICAL ISSUES

A more substantial issue for educational psychologists lies at the heart of the legislation described here, namely the concept of a 'learning difficulty', as defined by section 156(2) of the Education Act 1993. What is 'a significantly greater difficulty in learning than the majority of children of his age'? The two reports from the House of Commons (1987; 1993) expressed concern about the basic definition of 'learning difficulties' and hence of special educational needs. In particular the 1987 report highlighted the problems inherent in a relativistic definition whereby a child's special educational needs are determined not only by his or her own inherent profile of abilities and disabilities, but also by the nature of the provision generally available. Furthermore, the accompanying guidance to the 1981 Act, in particular Circular 1/83 (Department of Education and Science, 1983), stressed that the population of children who might have special educational needs at some stage of their schooling was not the 2 per cent who were expected to receive statements following assessments under the Act, but a much larger group—about 20 per cent in all. Consequently the reports of the House of Commons Education, Science and Arts Committee argued that there was a need for more guidance. In their second report the Committee go on to make the following recommendation:

> We recommend that the DfE (Department for Education) should ensure that the Code of Practice includes guidelines and criteria to assist parents, schools and LEAs to determine the levels of need for which statutory assessment procedures should be initiated. (House of Commons, 1993, para. 16).

But educational psychologists are not called upon, under this legislation, to decide these matters. Their task is to carry out assessments which enable the child's profile of capabilities and disabilities to be identified; to recommend what should be the educational aims for the child; and to advise on the provision necessary to meet these needs. In making these assessments, educational psychologists must try to distinguish any difficulties in learning that arise from the child having English as a second language.

Leaving aside the issue of second language, it is still possible to propose different forms of learning difficulty. First, consider a child who has had a very disadvantaged early history, aged 10 with little exposure to quality learning experiences. Such a child is likely to find the learning of reading and other educational tasks problematic and to be educationally retarded (e.g. Davie, Butler and Goldstein, 1972; Snow et al., 1991). Consider secondly a child who has suffered a brain injury resulting in impaired cognitive abilities in some, but not all, areas of skill development. Finally, consider a child who has a general intellectual impairment resulting from a genetic disorder.

Should each of these children be deemed to have a learning difficulty as defined by the 1993 Act? The distinction to be made here is between the wider group of children (the '20 per cent') who are considered to have special educational needs at some time in their lives, and the smaller group for whom an authority should make a statement because they require special educational provision, as defined in section 156 of the 1993 Act. There are several related but different factors: the prevalence of the problem; the presenting difficulties; the aetiology; and the severity. These raise different assessment issues. For example, questions of prevalence and severity are essentially normative issues, while aetiology and the nature of the presenting problems are diagnostic. The educational psychologist is therefore required to undertake assessments which address all of these concerns, using normative and criterion-referenced measures, assessing task-related functioning, cognitive processes, inter-personal behaviour and emotional development.

The assessment of young children poses additional difficulties as they are often not amenable to standardised testing procedures, and are also going through a period which may be characterised by rapid cognitive growth. Hence an assessment of a child at preschool on a standardised test of intelligence is a less reliable predictor of later performance on such instruments given at junior or secondary stages of schooling (e.g. Hindley and Owen, 1978). Moffitt et al. (1993) have argued that such variations in IQ over time are primarily a result of test error rather than actual cognitive changes; however, there are some children for whom the latter is indeed the case, as their research indicates. This might be a small group in total, but may be overrepresented among the children who are assessed under the 1993 Act, or comparable legislation in other countries.

EDUCATIONAL PSYCHOLOGISTS AND LAWYERS

The preceding discussion indicates that, although the practice of educational psychologists may be governed by statute, as in the case of the UK, there may at present be relatively little interaction with lawyers. This situation varies from one country to another and depends on many factors including the tendency to resort to litigation and the nature of the law relating to education itself. Accordingly there is relatively little experience of educational psychologists and lawyers working together. But there are signs that this is changing in some countries, including the UK. What, therefore, should a lawyer reasonably expect of an educational psychologist?

The tradition described above is one where the psychologist attempts to provide a detailed analysis of a child's difficulties and then makes recommendations designed to address these. In the forensic situation, of course, this detached objectivity may be challenged if the psychologist is acting for the child against another party, usually the school or school authority. Objectivity is a common issue throughout this book, but is particularly significant here as it represents a new challenge to educational psychologists in many countries. In terms of education, the psychologist is most likely to be called upon by a lawyer when a parent is challenging a decision regarding her or his child's disability or special educational needs. This may take one of several forms. The parent may challenge the suggestion that the child has a disability or special needs. On the other hand the parent may argue that the child does have such needs and that these are not recognised, or that the provision proposed is not acceptable. There may also be challenges to the process undertaken by the authority in question.

A lawyer acting on behalf of a child and parents in such cases may seek the opinion of an educational psychologist. In such cases the psychologist may assess or reassess the child and provide an alternative opinion on the child's status and needs. The exact nature of the assessment will depend upon the specified areas of dispute, but could include any aspect of the child's psychoeducational development. It is likely to include an interview with the child and parents, which will include a detailed assessment of the child's attributes relevant to the issue at hand. Ideally there should also be an assessment of the natural learning environment, normally a school, in order to evaluate the degree to which the child's needs are being met. Thus a full assessment should be of a child in context, not simply of the child alone.

Following such an assessment the psychologist will offer an opinion relative to the legal concern. This may address whether the child does indeed have special educational needs; whether an assessment should be undertaken under relevant legislation; what provision is appropriate, and whether that provided or planned for the child is suitable; and whether the procedures previously followed have been appropriate from a psychological point of view. A psychologist may be asked to offer an opinion on the practice of other psychologists, including their methods of assessment or the soundness of their judgements. A lawyer should not necessarily expect all psychological reports to follow the same format, but they should address the issues of concern in a thorough and analytic manner. Evidence should be clearly distinguished from the psychologist's opinion as in any expert report. Lawyers should also be wary of 'overkill' where a psychologist uses large numbers of tests and provides a report of inordinate length. As with all expert investigations the assessment should be reliable, valid and relevant, and the lawyer will desire an indication of the degree to which the evidence being challenged, or that being provided, meets these criterla.

An Example

A child is thought by the parents to have specific learning difficulties. The authority has refused to accept this or to make extra provision. In such a case the educational psychologist is likely to assess, as a minimum, the child's cognitive abilities and educational attainments. One issue will be whether the child's attainments are significantly discrepant from those that would be expected of a child of that age and general level of intelligence. A standard test of general cognitive ability, such as the Wechsler Intelligence Scale for Children—3rd Edition (Wechsler, 1992) or the British Abilities Scales (Elliott, Murray and Pearson, 1983) together with tests of reading and spelling are likely to form the core of an assessment. Analysis of the child's profile may be undertaken to explore specific areas of cognitive development, particularly memory, in more detail using other standardised tests or specially created mini-experiments based upon the child's current level of functioning and the tasks he or she is expected to undertake in school. In addition the psychologist will want to gain a view of the child's self-esteem, social skills and interests, friendships, and perceptions of his or her life situation, both in terms of education and the family. Ideally the educational psychologist will also observe the child in class and interview relevant teachers.

The information so gained will enable the psychologist to form an opinion on the nature of the child's difficulties if they exist, for in some cases the child's progress will be considered normal. Assuming the psychologist considers the child to have significant problems, an opinion will be given on their nature, including the degree of severity and likely persistence. Finally the educational psychologist will offer an opinion on suitable intervention. In making these comments the psychologist may challenge the views of others, presenting different data or opinions.

As discussed elsewhere in this volume, the nature of a psychological opinion can rarely, if ever, be absolute. For example, there is not a uniformity of opinion within the profession on the use of different assessment techniques. There is also debate on the level of a child's learning difficulties or other disabilities which should trigger extra provision. A lawyer acting for a parent should consider the same factors as with any expert witness: expertise and competence, professional standing and integrity. Registration with the appropriate body (e.g. a State board in the USA or as a chartered psychologist in the UK) is another relevant factor as this ensures not only that the person is qualified but that she or he is also subject to the profession's disciplinary procedures.

CONCLUDING COMMENT

This chapter has focused on educational assessment, and in particular the assessment of special educational needs. In the UK educational psychologists may also be called upon to advise on whether the requirements of the National Curriculum (for what should be taught in schools) should be amended, or removed, in the case of particular children, under the Education Reform Act 1988, sections 17–19. This currently is not a frequent activity unless it is part of the assessment and review procedures for children on statements. The ever-changing proposals for the content and implementation of the National Curriculum (e.g. Dearing, 1993) make it difficult to comment on the likelihood of further developments

The Children Act 1989 (which includes powers to intervene in families) also has important implications for educational psychologists in their other work with children and young people. This is still relatively newly implemented legislation and its full impact on the education service, and on educational psychologists has yet to be felt. There are some problems of interpretation, particularly in the concept of 'children in need', which overlaps with, but is not synonymous with, special educational needs. Educational psychologists have no direct statutory duties under this Act, but in their professional practice will contribute to processes which derive from it, particularly child protection.

Educational Psychologists in many countries also work with school systems, in addition to direct practice with children (e.g. Lindsay and Miller, 1991; Saigh and Oakland, 1989). This includes acting as advisers to the LEA, school district or school. For example, educational psychologists may advise on the authority's implementation of its general responsibilities under the 1993 Act, including the development of guidelines for assessment. Such guidelines can be developed to reflect psychological principles, as well as the requirements of the legislation. This is not to suggest that the task is easy, as Reynolds (1990) has shown in his review of practice in the USA. Also, the task is not only one of developing guidelines. Educational psychologists may also be involved in the training of teachers in the implementation of the system; as well as providing advice and guidance to parents. Thus the most common examples of practice for educational psychologists in most countries are in implementing the law and trying to ensure that this is done to the benefit of children with special educational needs, rather than acting on behalf of children and parents challenging such implementation.

However, the evidence from many countries suggests that the practice of educational psychologists will become more concerned with the law, either by the development of legislation regulating the assessment process, leading to psychologists acing as expert witnesses on behalf of the child and parent, or because of an increase in litigation requiring psychologists to justify their actions. In either case educational psychology and the law will develop a closer working relationship.

REFERENCES

Audit Commission and Her Majesty's Inspectors (1992a). *Getting in on the Act: Provision for Pupils with Special Educational Needs. The National Picture.* London: HMSO.

Audit Commission and Her Majesty's Inspectors (1992b). *Getting the Act Together: Provision for Pupils with Special Educational Needs.* London: HMSO.

Bersoff, D.N and Hofer, P.T. (1990). The legal regulation of school psychology. In T.B. Gutkin and C.R. Reynolds (Eds), *The Handbook of School Psychology.* New York: John Wiley.

British Psychological Society (1993). *The Register of Chartered Psychologists.* Leicester: British Psychological Society.

Davie, R., Butler, N. and Goldstein, H. (1972). *From Birth to Seven.* London: Longman.

Dearing, R. (1993). *The National Curriculum and its Assessment: Interim Report.* York: National Curriculum Council, and London: School Examinations and Assessment Council.

Denman, R. and Lunt, I. (1993). Getting the Act together: some implications for EPs of cases of judicial review. *Educational Psychology in Practice,* **9**, 9–16.

Department for Education (1994). *Code of Practice on the Identification and Assessment of Special Educational Needs.* London: Department for Education.

Department of Education and Science (1978). *Special Educational Needs: Report of the Warnock Committee.* London: HMSO.

Department of Education and Science (1983). *Circular 1/83: Assessments and Statements of Special Educational Needs.* London: HMSO.

Elliott, C.D., Murray, D.J. and Pearson, L.S. (1983). *British Ability Scales.* Windsor: NFER-Nelson.

Henderson, R.A. (1993). What is this 'Least Restrictive Environment' in the United States? In R. Slee (Ed.), *Is There a Desk With My Name On It?* London: Falmer Press.

Hindley, C.B. and Owen, C.F. (1978). The extent of individual changes in IQ for ages between 6 months and 17 years in a British longitudinal study. *Journal of Child Psychology and Psychiatry,* **19**, 329–50.

House of Commons (1987). *Special Educational Needs: Implications of the Education Act 1981. Third Report from the Education, Science and Arts Committee Session 1986–87.* London: HMSO.

House of Commons (1993). *Meeting Special Educational Needs Statements of Needs and Provision. Education Committee Third Report Session 1992–93.* London: HMSO.

Lindsay, G. and Colley, A. (1993). Ethical dilemmas of members of the British Psychological Society. Paper presented at the London Conference of the British Psychological Society, London, December.

Lindsay, G and Miller, A. (1991). *Psychological Services for Primary Schools.* Harlow: Longman.

Moffitt, T.E., Caspi, A., Harkness, A.R. and Silva, P.A. (1993). The natural history of change in intellectual performance: Who changes? How much? Is it meaningful? *Journal of Child Psychology and Psychiatry,* **34**, 455–506.

Norwich, B. (1990). *Reappraising Special Needs Education.* London: Cassell.

Oakland, T.D. and Cunningham, J.L. (1992). A survey of school psychology in developed and developing countries. *School Psychology International,* **13**, 99–130.

Pearson, L. and Lindsay, G. (1986). *Special Needs in the Primary School.* Windsor: NFER-Nelson.

Pope, K.S. and Vetter, V.A. (1992). Ethical dilemmas encountered by members of the American Psychological Association. *American Psychologist,* **47**, 397–411.

Reynolds, C.R. (1990). Conceptual and technical problems in learning disability diagnosis. In C.R. Reynolds and R.W. Kamphaus (Eds), *Handbook of Psychological and Educational Assessment of Children: Intelligence and Achievement.* New York: The Guilford Press.

Saigh, P.A. and Oakland, T.D. (1989). *International Perspectives on Psychology in the Schools.* Hillsdale, NJ: Lawrence Erlbaum.

Snow, C.E., Barnes, W.S., Chandler, J., Goodman, I.F. and Hemphill, L. (1991). *Unfulfilled Expectations: Home and School Influences on Literacy.* London: Harvard University Press.

United States Congress, Senate (1975). *Education for All Handicapped Children Act.*

Wechsler, D. (1992). *Wechsler Intelligence Scale for Children* (3rd edn). Sidcup: Psychological Corporation.

Children and Clinical Assessments

Chrissie Verduyn
University Hospital of South Manchester
and
Helen Carlton Smith
Bolton General Hospital

PSYCHOLOGICAL PROBLEMS IN CHILDHOOD

Population surveys of psychological disorder in childhood and adolescence consistently indicate a prevalence of 10 to 15 per cent. Various classification systems for childhood problems exist. These have in common a basic distinction between disorders which manifest themselves with overt distress (that is, emotional disorders) and those where the major problem lies in unacceptable behaviour (that is, conduct disorders). These two categories of problem account for at least 90 per cent of childhood disorder. Other much rarer disorders include childhood psychoses and autism.

THE WORK OF THE CHILD CLINICAL PSYCHOLOGIST

About 20 per cent of clinical psychologists work primarily with children, adolescents and their families. They work from community and hospital settings, such as clinical psychology departments, in and out-patient paediatric facilities, child development centres, child and adolescent psychiatric units, social services day nurseries and general practice surgeries. The majority of clinical psychology departments provide a service specifically for children and adolescents and larger departments or districts with specialist paediatric units may have several child clinical psychologists. Some are based within a multi-disciplinary resource such as a child development centre or child psychiatric unit and take the majority of referrals from there. Local circumstances will inevitably have influenced the pattern of service delivery within a specific area.

Almost all child clinical psychologists take direct referrals (typically medical), but some will accept referrals from health visitors, social workers, guardians *ad litem*, educational psychologists and other non-medical professionals. Work related to provision of a clinical opinion for a legal decision may have come from any of these sources.

Children are referred with a wide range of problems. These include common disorders such as bed-wetting, sleeping and feeding difficulties (and other behavioural problems) and psychosomatic disorders such as headaches or abdominal pain. Children with specific or generalised developmental disorders or with problems associated with chronic physical illness such as diabetes may be referred, particularly if there are associated emotional or behavioural problems. Common reasons for referral of adolescents include depression or relationship difficulties with parents or peers.

Child clinical psychologists may work with the individual child and his or her parents or family, with the child as an in-patient or in other contexts such as nursery or school. In addition they often advise other professionals on the management of a child's difficulties and take part in the development of policy or training for children's services.

In general clinical practice, child clinical psychologists will routinely deal with issues regarding client confidentiality and consent to treatment. Child protection issues will be involved in some cases and some children, often those referred by social services departments, will be involved in 'official' proceedings (e.g. in England and Wales under the Children Act, 1989). Children may be referred during or following matrimonial proceedings with a parent seeking support on an issue of contact or residence. Further discussion of these areas is provided in this chapter. Child clinical psychologists may be involved in assessment and management of a child following trauma where information regarding the sequelae of a head injury or road traffic accident is sought with a view to compensation.

Involvement in criminal proceedings is less common, although child clinical psychologists sometimes provide a service to social work teams and courts by identifying psychological issues and possible treatment of young offenders. Psychologists may also provide reports regarding trauma suffered by victims of criminal injuries.

FRAMEWORKS FOR UNDERSTANDING CHILDREN'S PSYCHOLOGICAL PROBLEMS

There is no single theoretical model which accounts for the development of all psychological problems in childhood. Problems are conceptualised as multifactorial in origin and a range of aspects of the child's individual development, family and life context needs to be considered in assessment. The following frameworks guide the assessment process and method of intervention.

Biological and Developmental Considerations

The normal sequence of physical and psychological maturation from the point of conception is the background against which any difficulties will emerge. Aspects of development will influence not only vulnerability to psychological difficulties but also how such difficulties may be manifest.

Vulnerability factors include genetic predisposition and adverse pre- and perinatal influences such as neonatal seizures following an abnormal birth. Impairment or delay in any one area of function may compromise psychological development in other domains. For instance, children with language delay may experience difficulty in expressing their needs or wishes verbally. Under these circumstances it is not unusual to see an escalation or persistence of behaviours of frustration such as temper tantrums.

Both the child's age and stage of development are important in evaluating whether or not a specific behaviour is normal. For instance bed-wetting cannot be considered abnormal without knowledge of the child's age (normal at age five, rare at age 11), and developmental level (in a child with general developmental delay bed-wetting at age nine might be consistent with progress in all areas).

Gender

Boys outnumber girls in both general population and clinic samples for presence of psychological problems during early and middle childhood, although by adolescence the proportion is roughly equal. It is common for distress in childhood to be indicated by behaviour more usually seen in a younger child. Common examples of this include bed-wetting of a normally dry child under acute stress or an increase in clinginess and reluctance to separate from a parent. Such changes are normal if transitory and with a clear stressor, but if persistent may require expert intervention.

Ill Health

There is an increased risk of psychological disorder in children with physical handicap or chronic physical illness. This is not solely a direct result of the disease or impairment although the higher rates of psychological disorder in children with brain injury, inherited or acquired, often involve both direct and indirect effects.

Temperament

Temperament refers to a characteristic behavioural style—the 'how' rather than the 'what' of behaviour. Temperamental differences between children are present virtually from birth and persist throughout development. About 5 per cent of children are temperamentally 'difficult'. Their characteristics include being highly reactive, difficult to pacify, irritable and overactive. There is now a substantial body of evidence that such children are more likely to develop behavioural problems. The mechanism for problem development may involve the inevitably greater level of challenge to parents that these children present. That is, parents finding it difficult to gain a positive response to their attempts to insititute appropriate routines may tend towards negative or inconsistent approaches to child management. In addition intrinsic factors may play a part (Thomas and Chess, 1982).

Family Life

Development of psychological problems in childhood has been associated consistently with a number of family factors. These include family size, ordinal position, parental mental illness, parental criminality. Wider psychosocial stresses on the family such as unemployment, poor housing and overcrowding increase risks of problem development in children. Of particular importance in children's development is the quality of family relationships. This has been most consistently demonstrated in relation to the negative effects on children of marital discord (Emery, 1982).

Family systems theorists emphasise the importance of family relationships in the presentation of a child as problematic. In this theoretical approach it is the family as a whole which is viewed as dysfunctional, with one member being presented as symptomatic of a problem in communication and relationships. For instance, a child may become the focus between warring parents. Systems theorists consider that to understand family functioning the stage of development of the family, its intergenerational and historical aspects, and the present structure and pattern of communication in the family need to be assessed.

Attachment

The relationship which has received most attention regarding the promotion of healthy psychological development is that of mother and child, with the work of Bowlby (1953) being a particularly important influence. The mother–child relationship forms the basis of psychoanalytic theories of development and has influenced ethological approaches, most notably through the debate over critical periods for attachment. Healthy emotional development is associated with a secure attachment to a parent or carer. From this base, children are able to develop confident, independent relationships outside the family based on a positive sense of self-esteem. While the dimensions of the concept of attachment have been much debated in the theoretical literature (Herbert, Sluckin and Sluckin, 1983) its practical applications in understanding clinical problems are undisputed.

Learning

Cognitive-behavioural theories address the processes of development through consideration of the processes involved in learning (Herbert, 1994). Behavioural theorists, such as Skinner, described processes of operant conditioning whereby specific behaviours occur in response to a stimulus and, if reinforced, are repeated if that stimulus recurs. Social learning theorists place, in addition, emphasis on the learning potential of the observation of the reinforcement of others. Cognitive theorists take into account the role of thoughts and emotions in mediating learning and in the development of self-esteem and a sense of personal mastery.

Impact of Life Events

Life events affect the child both directly, for instance if a child is a victim in a road traffic accident, and indirectly through the influence that events have on the family as a whole, for instance a grandmother's illness may decrease a mother's availability, an accident to one child may cause more fearful parents to be more protective of siblings. Chronic adversities, such as parental separation, or frequent events, such as a succession of moves of home, are associated with increased risk of psychological disorder.

Coping and Resilience

During the 1980s, influenced specifically by the work of Rutter (1990), there was a a shift in emphasis from factors which predispose to disorder to processes which protect children in adversity and promote coping. The concept of resilience has received increasing attention. Studies of stress-resistant children indicate the importance of supportive family and social networks and positive self-esteem. It has been shown consistently that girls are more resilient than boys (Garmezy, 1985).

Continuities into Adult Life

It is self-evident that if all childhood disorder were transitory in nature there would be no need for the employment of professionals working in the field of child and adolescent mental health. Research studies which examine outcome into adulthood are methodologically complex, costly and present numerous practical difficulties. The available evidence demonstrates continuities into adulthood of several disorders including anxiety and depression (Harrington, Fudge and Rutter, 1990). Conduct disorder in childhood is associated with antisocial and personality disorders in adulthood (Robins, 1991).

CLINICAL PSYCHOLOGY ASSESSMENT AND THE CHILDREN ACT

In England and Wales the Children Act, 1989 covers all aspects of law relating to child care. In this Act, two key areas of definition in relation to assessment are those of 'children in need' and of 'significant harm'.

The Act defines a child as in need if:

(a) he is unlikely to achieve or maintain, or have the opportunity of achieving or maintaining a reasonable standard of health or development without the provision for him of services by a local authority.

(b) his health or development is likely to be significantly impaired, or further impaired, without the provision for him of such services; or

(c) he is disabled. (The Children Act, 1989, s.17(10))

A child is disabled if 'he is blind, deaf, or dumb or suffers from mental disorder of any kind or is substantially and permanently handicapped by illness, injury or congenital deformity or such other disability as may be prescribed' (The Children Act, 1989, s. 17(11)).

A clinical psychologist is qualified to contribute to the multidisciplinary assessment, identifying a child as in need, and the provision required particularly if there are concerns about social, emotional and cognitive development.

In relation to child protection, clinical psychologists may be involved in identifying children who have been or are at risk of abuse. More commonly, assessment may relate to identifying significant harm. Section 31(10) states: 'Where the question of whether harm suffered by the child is significant turns on the child's health or development, his health or development shall be compared with that which could reasonably be expected of a similar child.' A further area of assessment may involve the child's ability to express an independent opinion, to understand consequences or to consent to treatment.

THE ASSESSMENT PROCESS
Purposes of Assessment

A referral for psychological assessment should provide clear, unambiguous information regarding its context and purpose. The assessment process will in part be dictated by the nature of the questions asked of the psychologist and the purposes for which any information will be used. Many children referred to clinical psychologists will have concerned parents who have themselves sought assistance on the child's behalf. Difficulties in assessment most commonly arise when agencies (other than the parent) have identified a problem and sought the assistance of the psychologist in clarification and identification of a course of action. In these situations it may be helpful to consider the agency making the referral as the client rather than the parent(s) and child. The first stage of assessment may then consist of negotiation with that agency regarding the aims of the assessment. Ethical issues, including the family's understanding of the purpose and nature of assessment and confidentiality regarding the information they give, must be clarified before assessment commences. In general parents are seen as responsible for giving consent to treatment on behalf of their children but consent is often sought directly from adolescents.

Sources of Information

Children almost always present to services because an adult has identified a problem. Further, much of the information required in assessments will be obtained from parents and others expressing concern. Communication with the child is therefore essential in order to obtain his or her point of view about any difficulties. It also involves gaining an appreciation of the child's thoughts and feelings and some understanding of his or her inner world. This is of particular importance during adolescence where young people may well prefer to express their private thoughts in the absence of their parents. Some symptoms, for instance of depression or suicidal thoughts, may only be accessed by skilled individual interview.

Children's behaviour can be highly context dependent. A child who presents constant challenges to the stressed parent may be a model of conformity during interviews or in the structured environment of school. A full assessment will encompass several areas of the child's functioning in order to gain an understanding of his/her difficulties and competencies.

A range of methods may be used to access information including observation in real-life settings, observations of interactions between family members, as well as formal interview.

The clinical interview is the basis for assessment. Its functions are multiple including engaging parents and child in a therapeutic relationship with the clinician and commencing intervention as well as information-gathering. The nature of the questions to be addressed by the assessment may dictate the form of interview. The style of an investigative interview (when, for instance, a social worker rather than the parents has identified difficulties) will differ from that where assessment is the pre-cursor to a joint formulation of the problem with parents followed by an agreed plan for intervention. In some cases a need for treatment may be identified but therapy cannot be commenced because of litigation pending. This requires careful management if the beneficial relationship developed in assessment is not to be lost.

Domains of information sought include problem definition, the child's personal and developmental history, family background and relationships, and details of significant events. Observations made during the interview supplement facts and are of particular value in assessing emotional significance, relationship quality and motivation for change. Inevitably much information will be provided by parents but the presence of the child during the interview allows for observation of parent–child relationships and, particularly with younger children, enables some rapport to be developed by the interviewer in the presence of trusted adults prior to any interview of the child alone. Many practitioners prefer to have children present throughout, interviewing parents alone only when necessary to explore sensitive areas (such as the quality of marital relationship) where the child's presence would be inappropriate. Some semi-structured interview methods exist for interviews with parents and children which provide explicit guidelines and scoring systems for responses. These are used principally for research purposes, for instance Kiddie SADS (Ambrosini, 1989).

Use of Standardised Assessments

Various formal psychometric measures can be used to supplement information obtained by other means. These are often used to assess specific problem areas, including severity, and as a basis for measuring change. Others identify the level of a specific symptom, for instance Children's Depression Inventory (Kovacs, 1981), Children's Manifest Anxiety Scale (Reynolds and Richmond, 1978) and they can be used successfully to establish change in symptoms following intervention. Some checklists are intended to screen for the presence of disorder and are not designed to measure change.

A further group of measures assess functioning or competence in specific areas, for instance, self-esteem (Coopersmith, 1986), social maturity (Sparrow, Balla and Cicchelti, 1986). These are standardised on large populations and scores must be interpreted in relation to the population on which the test was developed.

In addition there are various assessment techniques that use a standardised presentation, in which the results are obtained not as a score that can be compared to test norms, but which are considered according to more general criteria. Such tests have been developed in areas relating to relationships and emotional development, for instance the Family Relations Test (Bene and Anthony, 1978) and they are designed to provide an insight into the child's inner world.

The techniques of assessment historically most associated with psychology are those designed to assess cognitive functioning. When there is suspicion of developmental delay, either general or specific, in young children, a test such as the Griffiths (Griffiths, 1976) provides age equivalent scores for the child's performance in areas of motor, language and social functioning. In older children testing is commonly to explore intellectual functioning in relation to educational performance. Tests of intelligence, such as Wechsler Intelligence Scales for Children-III (Wechsler, Golombok and Rust, 1992) and British Ability Scales (Elliott, Murray and Pearson, 1983), can be used in conjunction with tests which produce scores for attainment at reading, spelling and numeracy. Where specific cognitive deficits are suspected, for instance in memory functioning following a head injury, diagnostic tests are available.

Tests of cognitive functioning may be used at intervals in order to assess the impact of remedial intervention with children with developmental delay.

Problem-based assessment may include use of descriptive observational measures designed to assess the frequency and context of a specific behaviour. Parents or carers are often requested to keep a systematic record over a period of time. Such measures may be designed by the clinician specifically for that child and may include simple recording (for instance of the daily occurrence of daytime or bed-wetting) or sampling the occurrence of a behaviour over a specified time of day, or involve more detailed recording of the antecedents and consequences of problem behaviours such as temper tantrums. Such measures are characteristic of behavioural interventions with children's problems and are used to monitor change throughout a treatment programme. Standardised observational measures can be used in some circumstances, for instance the Strange Situation Procedure (Ainsworth, Blehar and Waters, 1978) which is used to assess mother–child attachment.

INTERVENTION

Child clinical psychologists are typically involved in helping a child with psychological problems by acting both directly with the child and family and, on the child's behalf, with other carers or professionals. At the conclusion of assessment a formulation of the child's or family's problem will have been developed. This includes a clear definition of the problem and an explanation in terms of past and present factors which have a bearing on its development and persistence. The formulation will be outlined to parents and child and on the basis of this a programme of intervention designed. It is common for an informal contract with the parents to be established; defining the treatment process, the number of sessions with the psychologist, frequency of review of progress, involvement with school or other agencies and expectations for change by the parents.

A formulation represents a hypothesis regarding the problem and the child in his or her family and life context. Although intervention may begin, the process of assessment and evaluation continues throughout treatment. New information may come to light, lack of progress may lead to re-appraisal and to a different understanding of the basis of difficulties. Assessment and intervention are inextricably interwoven, in a sense intervention beginning at the first meeting with the family and assessment continuing throughout the treatment process.

Effective intervention requires the family's understanding of the treatment process, albeit not necessarily at the level of sophistication of the therapist. Motivation to attempt the task of change is an essential prerequisite.

Clinical psychologists may be involved in providing a psychological perspective to other professionals working with the child and family. This may involve implementing a programme of treatment outside the home, for instance discussing with the child's teacher the management of episodes of soiling in the classroom, or consultation regarding a particular strategy such as how a residential social worker might approach a discussion of episodes of self-harm with an adolescent in care.

Behavioural Interventions

Behavioural methods are based on learning theory as an explanation of human behaviour. They can broadly be divided into techniques which develop a particular skill or train a new behaviour and those which increase the frequency of a desired behaviour whilst diminishing the frequency of an undesired behaviour. Examples of the first type of technique might include toilet training an incontinent child or teaching a developmentally delayed child to dress unaided. Examples of the second include increasing compliance with instructions and reducing temper outbursts with an active challenging five year old, or advising on managing settling and night waking problems in a two year old.

Careful assessment and baseline observational measures will have led to a problem formulation which identifies the setting conditions for the behaviour, the factors reinforcing the problem behaviour, goals for change and reinforcement which can be used to promote the desired behaviour. The most effective reinforcers in almost all cases involve adult attention in play, chosen activities or simply in praising the child's efforts. Various methods may be used to formalise this attention, for instance small rewards or stars on a chart to denote the child's achievement. Reinforcement needs to be identified for each individual child taking into account the family's circumstances. There has generally been an overreliance on star charts with children too young to understand their symbolic relevance to the problem.

Positive reinforcement is the commonest behavioural method of increasing desired behaviour—used in conjunction with shaping up a new behaviour or showing a child what is required. A range of methods can be applied to decrease unwanted behaviour. Removing reinforcement, commonly by ignoring a behaviour, is the commonest. In behavioural terms, the behaviour is likely first to increase in frequency. This may make ignoring it unsafe or impossible. Formalised procedures such as time-out may be used. This involves 'shaping up' the child to accept temporary removal from a situation and from adult attention, for instance by sitting unoccupied in a particular chair for several minutes. Other techniques include rewarding a child for behaviour which is incompatible with the undesired behaviour, or changing the stimulus for the behaviour, for instance by distracting a child into play when a temper tantrum is beginning. It is generally found that reward-based strategies designed to shape up and encourage desired behaviour are more effective than approaches involving withdrawal of privileges or applying sanctions. It is especially important that parents do not withhold essential aspects of care (such as love, affection, food, etc.) in an attempt to decrease their child's problem behaviour.

In general, behavioural interventions are implemented by training parents to use positive techniques with their child. Clarity and consistency in application are very important. Problem behaviours are generally tackled one at a time, and the emphasis is on building up prosocial behaviours. Parents maintain records and progress is reviewed, often weekly and any additional changes made in the programme on the basis of progress. Programmes often proceed step-wise and may be implemented in a range of settings.

Parent training groups have been used with common problems such as sleep disorders in preschool children. These methods often have a high level of face validity to parents but rely on motivation to change patterns of habitual behaviour on the part of parents as well as children. Interventions are planned to fade, once effective, such that change is maintained in the long term.

Evidence of the effectiveness of behavioural interventions has been demonstrated with a range of childhood problems including preschool behaviour problems, day and night-time wetting, soiling and conduct disorders in middle childhood (Herbert, 1994). Interventions vary in level of intensity, from those where there is live intervention by observers during the child's play with a parent (Parent–Child Game: Forehand and McMahon, 1981) to groups for parents using video modelling and discussion (Webster-Stratton, 1991).

Cognitive Behavioural Interventions

With many children referred to child clinical psychologists it is not a specific behaviour which is identified as problematic, rather problems which are emotional in nature such as anxiety or low self-esteem. An anxious child who is identified as underconfident and reluctant to separate from parents because of an excessive need for reassurance or a disproportionate fear, cannot be treated as a behaviour problem at bedtime without addressing the child's emotions and coping style. Cognitive techniques include teaching the child methods of challenging anxious thoughts, relaxing, recognising emotional states and their precipitants and replacing these with thoughts relating to coping. Parents are likely to be coached in supporting the child in using the techniques and in not unwittingly encouraging anxiety by over-reassurance or over-involvement. Techniques of cognitive therapy developed with depressed adult clients (Beck et al., 1979) may similarly be used to assist the depressed child or adolescent in understanding and challenging negative thoughts associated with low mood and increasing activities which develop a sense of competence and self-esteem.

Cognitive-behavioural techniques are also applied in work with individual children with deficits or disturbances in social behaviour. For instance, aggressive children may have social skills deficits and difficulties in impulse control which can be helped. Children can be taught techniques of creative problem-solving to help approach difficult situations more effectively. Such skills are often coached and practised in role-playing situations. Group work using these techniques may be offered, particularly for adolescents.

Techniques of cognitive behaviour therapy have been less rigorously researched with children than have other behavioural methods. However, there is promising evidence of their effectiveness in emotional disorders, social skills problems and with some impulsive and aggressive children and adolescents (Kendall, 1991). Outcome studies have identified the applicability of these techniques both with individuals and groups.

Behavioural and cognitive-behavioural methods have been criticised for ignoring the wider family context of childhood problems. These techniques should be used in conjunction with a supportive approach to family problems. In addition the skilled therapist will use observations of family interaction in applying techniques (for instance, working to include an under-involved father in sessions). Changes in behaviour allow for changes in attitude, both in parents' sense of their own competence and in the more positive relationship possible with a child whose behaviour is under his or her own and their parents' control. Another common criticism, that these methods involve 'bribery' or 'indoctrination', fails to account for the child's choices within the situation, when existing skills or strategies are utilised and developed as constructively as possible.

Family Therapy

Applications of family therapy are not limited to childhood problems. Increasingly psychological difficulties throughout the life span are assisted by this therapeutic approach which has developed rapidly since the 1970s. The referred patient is usually seen, from the onset, together with all family members living at home.

Family therapists frequently work in teams; one member working face-to-face with the family and others observing or acting in a consultative capacity. This approach is justified on the basis that working with a whole family in an objective manner requires the balance and creativity provided by more independent observers whose additional observations supplement those of the therapist who is more preoccupied by the process of interviewing. In some clinics one-way screens are used to make the observers less obtrusive although, for ethical reasons, the family members always have to consent to the team's presence. Teams are often multi-disciplinary.

Family therapy is derived from a systemic approach to understanding problem development and persistence. For obvious resource reasons, most clinicians in the UK who work from a systemic perspective in typical National Health Service practice will only spend a small proportion of their time working in teams with entire families and hence these interventions tend to be applied in complex cases where issues of relationships, communication and problem-solving require to be tackled within a family. It is not unusual for such work to be conducted with clients where child protection is a factor and a particularly thorough understanding is required. Family assessment can be undertaken from a systemic perspective and the opportunity to observe family interactions can provide useful information in understanding the presenting difficulties.

Techniques of family therapy involve eliciting customary patterns of communication and placing these in the context of the family's history, attitudes and relationships. The family will be encouraged to listen to each other's points of view, discuss different expectations and beliefs, consider the impact of various events or myths on the family and try out different ways of behaving in relation to each other. Family therapists have been much interested and exercised in tackling issues relating to gender and power within families and with ethical issues in treatment (Jones, 1993). Family approaches are often used with adolescent problems including anorexia and for problems where relationships and life events (for instance, divorce or reconstitution of the family) have played a role in problem development.

There have been numerous research studies assessing the effectiveness of family therapy. The available research outcome literature supports applying such methods with children with, by conventional classification, psycho-somatic disorders, anorexia, school refusal and many emotional and behavioural problems in adolescence (Jenkins, 1990).

Marital therapy is rarely practised by child clinical psychologists who are likely to refer couples requiring this on to adult services or voluntary agencies. It is, however, not unusual, whilst considering the relationship between marital disorder and childhood disorder, for child psychologists to work with parents regarding issues of mutual support, expectations and conflict management in relation to children's problems. This may, of course, involve working indirectly on marital problems which are not presented overtly. Similarly, working on a marital relationship may be one aspect of family therapy.

A developing area of particular relevance in child protection is that of therapies which work on improving parent–child (or carer–child) relationships. These have developed largely from two different theoretical perspectives but are increasingly finding a place in the range of therapies used by child clinical psychologists. One model of intervention—that of the 'parent–child game'—has developed from the behavioural management of problems in controlling and rewarding a child's behaviour by parents (Forehand and McMahon, 1981). Techniques such as live observation of typical situations with direct instructions to the parent about how to respond, sometimes using 'bug-in-the-ear' radio devices, are used in this intensive approach (Jenner, 1992).

The other framework guiding this type of work is that of attachment theory. Here problems are framed according to classification of the child's attachment behaviour and, often, the mother's own attachment history. Work focusses on helping the parents or carers to act as the responsible carers, understand the child's reactions, take control of situations to promote the child's sense of security and allow themselves to enjoy their child. In sum, by increasing intimacy with and sensitivity to the child, this can repair relationships which have been damaged.

An important component in both the above approaches is helping the parents or carers learn to play with the child and, hence, assisting the child's acquisition of play skills and prosocial behaviour. Similar methods have been developed for carers of children who are fostered or adopted, most notably by Fahlberg (1988). As yet the literature on effectiveness is scant, although applications of these techniques both in individual pairs and in groups is increasing.

Individual Therapy with Children

Individual therapy with children takes place from a wide range of theoretical perspectives. Cognitive and cognitive-behavioural approaches have already been described. A range of psychodynamic approaches provide the basis for individual work with children. Most involve play, and much of what is termed play therapy has features in common with child psychotherapy. These approaches focus on elaborating the child's inner experience including areas of which he or she may be unaware. The relationship with the therapist as a trusted adult is viewed as a vital component in the process of change. The therapist may encourage the use of expressive aids such as toys or art materials either to communicate or, more directively, to interpret or reflect back to the child the unconscious themes from the play.

Most individual therapy with children will be supported by another professional working with the child's parents. Sessions occur weekly at least. Some psychodynamic therapists may see children three to five times weekly although this is very rare in National Health Service settings in the UK. Work with adolescents applies similar principles, but usually incorporates verbal communication rather than using just play. Therapists may be from a range of professional backgrounds and those practising exclusively using individual therapy will almost invariably work as part of a multi-disciplinary team. It is more common for child clinical psychologists to work from cognitive-behavioural or family systems perspectives, but many of the methods of play assessment and use of communication with young children now used by child psychologists have been drawn from techniques developed within/by child psychotherapy.

The traditional reluctance of therapists working from a psychodynamic perspective to address issues of effectiveness has changed over recent years. Interpretation of research is often, however, confounded by methodological flaws and more recent research has been more creative in methods of assessing outcome. A relatively recent review (Barnett, Docherty and Franmett, 1991) described the few studies suggesting the effectiveness of child psychotherapy. In evaluating this it should be borne in mind that in normal clinical practice individual therapy is likely to represent one part of a therapeutic package with a range of components.

Clinical Practice and the Courts

Most child clinical psychologists encounter issues central to forensic child clinical psychology during training. Involvement in court work in everyday practice is rare, anxiety about unfamiliar court processes tends to lead to a preoccupation with learning court craft. Dialogue is needed in order that child clinical psychologists may develop greater understanding of legal processes and lawyers come to understand better the questions with which clinical psychologists can assist.

REFERENCES

Ainsworth, M.D.S., Blehar, M.C. and Waters, E. (1978). *Patterns of Attachment: A Psychological Study of the Strange Situation.* Hillside, NJ: Lawrence Erlbaum.

Ambrosini, P.J. (1989). Third revised edition of the K-SADS. Department of Psychiatry, Medical College of Pennsylavia, Philadelphia, PA.

Barnett, R.J., Docherty, J.P. and Franmett, G.M. (1991). A review of child psychotherapy research since 1963. *Journal of the American Academy of Child & Adolescent Psychiatry,* **30**, 1–14.

Beck, A.T., Rush A.J., Shaw B.F. and Emery, G. (1979). *Cognitive Therapy of Depression.* New York: Guilford Press.

Bene, E. and Anthony, J. (1978). *Manual for the Children's Version of the Family Relations Test.* Windsor: NFER-Nelson.

Bowlby, J. (1953). *Child Care and the Growth of Love.* Harmondsworth: Pelican.

Coopersmith, S. (1986). *Self Esteem Inventories.* Palo Alto, CA: Consulting Psychologists Press.

Elliott, C.D., Murray, D.J. and Pearson, L.S. (1983). *British Ability Scales*. Reading, Berks: NFER-Nelson.

Emery, R.E. (1982). Interparental conflict and the children of discord and divorce. *Psychological Bulletin*, **92**, 310–30.

Fahlberg, V. (1988). *Fitting the Pieces Together*. London: British Agencies for Adoption and Fostering.

Forehand, R.L. and McMahon, R.J. (1981). *Helping the Noncompliant Child. A Clinician's Guide to Parent Training*. New York: Guilford Press.

Garmezy, N. (1985). Stress-resistant children—the search for protective factors. In *Recent Advances in Developmental Psychopathology*. Chichester: Wiley.

Griffiths, R. (1976). *The Abilities of Babies*. Thetford: Lowe & Brydone.

Harrington, R.C., Fudge, H. and Rutter, M. (1990). Adult outcome of childhood and adolescent depression 1. Psychiatric status. *Archives of General Psychiatry*, **47**, 465–73.

Herbert, M. (1994). Behavioural methods. In M. Rutter, L. Hersov and E. Taylor (Eds), *Child and Adolescent Psychiatry. Modern Approaches* (3rd edn). Oxford: Blackwell.

Herbert, M., Sluckin, A. and Sluckin, W. (1983). *Maternal Bonding*. Oxford: Blackwell.

Jenkins, H. (1990). Family therapy developments in thinking and practice. *Journal of Child Psychology and Psychiatry*, **31**, 1015–26.

Jenner, S. (1992). The assessment and treatment of parenting skills and deficits: within the framework of child protection. *ACPP Newsletter*, **14**, 228–33.

Jones, E. (1993). *Family Systems Therapy Developments in the Milan-systemic Therapies*. Chichester: Wiley.

Kendall, P.C. (Ed.) (1991). *Child and Adolescent Therapy. Cognitive-behavioural Procedures*. London: Guilford.

Kovacs, M. (1981). Rating scales to assess depression in school aged children. *Acta Paedopsychiatria*, **46**, 305–15.

Reynolds, C.R. and Richmond, B.O. (1978). 'What I think and feel': a revised measure of children's manifest anxiety. *Journal of Abnormal Child Psychology*, **6**, 271–80.

Robins, L.N. (1991). Conduct disorder. *Journal of Child Psychology and Psychiatry*, **32**, 193–212.

Rutter, M. (1990). Psychosocial resilience and protective mechanisms. In J. Rolfe, A.S. Maston and D. Cicchetti (Eds), *Risk and Protective Factors in the Development of Psychopathology*. Cambridge: Cambridge University Press.

Sparrow, S., Balla, D. and Cicchelti, D. (1986). *Vineland Adaptive Behaviour Scales: Reading*. Windsor: NFER.

Thomas, A. and Chess, S. (1982). Temperament and follow-up to adulthood. In R. Porter and G.M. Collins (Eds), *Temperamental Differences in Infants and Young Children*. London: Pitman.

Webster-Stratton, C. (1991). Strategies for helping families with conduct disordered children. *Journal of Child Psychology and Psychiatry*, **32**, 1047–62.

Wechsler, D., Golombok, S. and Rust, J. (1992). *Wechsler Intelligence Scale for Children—Third Edition, UK*. Sidcup, Kent: Psychological Corporation/Harcourt Brace.

Chapter 2.5

Adults' Capacity to Make Decisions Affecting the Person: Psychologists' Contribution

Glynis H. Murphy
University of Kent
and
Isabel C.H. Clare
University of Cambridge

INTRODUCTION

There are a variety of situations and conditions in which an individual's ability to make decisions affecting the person, including legally significant decisions, may be impaired. Varying terminology is used in legal contexts to describe this decision-making ability; it will be referred to here as 'capacity'.

Psychologists' contribution to the determination of adults' capacity has been dominated by two approaches: diagnostic and functional. A diagnostic approach, adopted from psychiatry, involves inferences based on identification of an individual as a member of a population known from clinical experience or experimental evidence to have some abnormality or impairment of functioning relative to the general population, as a result of which clinical treatment or support is likely to be needed. The populations involved include individuals with psychiatric disorders such as a 'mental illness' (e.g. 'schizophrenia', or 'severe' or 'major' depression) and/or deficits in their intellectual ability and general functioning, such as those associated with 'dementia' or a 'learning disability' (previously known in the UK as 'mental handicap' and currently referred to as 'mental retardation' or 'developmental disabilities' in the USA). The diagnostic approach has been subject to considerable criticism by lawyers, at least in the USA (for a summary of the main arguments see Grisso, 1986,

Handbook of Psychology in Legal Contexts
Edited by R. Bull and D. Carson. © 1995 John Wiley & Sons Ltd

p. 8 ff.). One of the most salient objections, according to Grisso's summary, has been of irrelevance, on the grounds that reference to a diagnosis, or even to the difficulties it summarises, provides no direct information about the capacity of a specific individual within a particular legal context.

In contrast, a functional approach, exemplified by the pioneering work of Grisso, is based on establishing (i) a person's 'functional abilities, behaviors or capacities' (Grisso, 1986, p. 15), that is, what he or she understands, knows, believes, or can do that is *directly* relevant to the legal context at issue (such as capacity to manage the role of defendant in a trial), and (ii) the extent to which these functional abilities meet the demands of a particular situation within a given legal context (e.g. within the context 'trials', a brief and simple trial versus one that is likely to be lengthy and involve complex issues). In contrast with the diagnostic approach, which focuses exclusively on the person, the functional approach emphasises that capacity reflects the *interaction* between a person's functional abilities and a given situation. The implication is that, before making any declaration of incapacity, consideration needs to be given to whether it would be possible to (a) improve the person's relevant functional abilities (such as by ensuring that he or she is offered training or additional support), and/or (b) simplify or otherwise amend the situation.

Whilst a functional approach rejects the making of inferences about an individual's capacity on the basis of his or her diagnostic label, it does not suggest that evidence concerning the difficulties of identified populations requiring clinical treatment and support is irrelevant. Instead, as Grisso (1986, p. 30) notes, evidence about the population of which the individual is a member is a source of 'supplemental data with which to assist courts in addressing causal, predictive, and remediation questions about ... functional abilities'. The purpose of this chapter is two-fold. First, to provide an introduction to some of these 'supplemental data' through an overview of the psychological functioning of three populations which are frequently involved in determinations of capacity: people with (a) learning disabilities, (b) mental illness, and (c) dementia. The second purpose is to consider some of the issues and specific tests which psychologists, and others adopting a psychological perspective, may take into account in a functional assessment of capacity, using three illustrative contexts: consent to treatment, consent to sexual intimacy, and capacity to parent.

PSYCHOLOGICAL FUNCTIONING IN PEOPLE WITH LEARNING DISABILITIES, MENTAL ILLNESS AND DEMENTIA

Definitions of 'learning disabilities' and 'mental illness' continue to be debated. For the moment, there is agreement that learning disabilities (or its equivalent) should be defined as a developmental difficulty involving significant impairments of intellectual and social functioning or adaptive behaviour (Grossman, 1983; BPS (British Psychological Society), 1991; Luckasson et al., 1992). Although the meaning of 'mental illness' is often unclear, in practice, the term seems to be restricted to the subset of psychiatric disorders or mental health problems which are associated, normally transiently, with abnormal psychological phenomena (or 'psychotic symptoms') such as hallucinations ('hearing voices'), delusions ('irrational' beliefs) and disordered thinking. These phenomena are most frequent among persons with a diagnosis of schizophrenia or affective disorder (such as mania, severe depression, or manic-depression—for details of the clinical features of these conditions, see Gelder, Gath, and Mayou, 1989). About 40 per cent of people who experience a single episode of mental illness recover fully. Most of the remainder make at least a partial recovery, although they may continue to need treatment and support at times; only a small minority require assistance for almost all their lives (Kuipers and Bebbington, 1987). 'Dementia' usually occurs after a period of normal functioning and involves 'the global impairment of higher cortical functions' (Royal College of Physicians, 1981), and affects memory, thoughts, language, emotion, personality and behaviour, and motor and sensory abilities. It may arise from a number of underlying conditions, although the most frequent causes of dementia in 'elderly' people (i.e. persons aged 65 years or more), such as Alzheimer's disease (the commonest form in this group), are progressive and irreversible (for details of different types of dementia see Lishman, 1987).

However, each of the broad diagnostic labels being used here refers to a heterogeneous population, and the variation between different individuals within the same group can hardly be over-stated. Within each group, there are many individuals who resemble the general population much more than they do other persons with the same diagnosis. For example, among the group with learning disabilities, the overwhelming majority (80 per cent; Gelder, Gath and Mayou, 1989) have mild learning disabilities: their difficulties are likely to be subtle and would not easily be recognised. In contrast, a very small proportion (1 per cent; Gelder, Gath and Mayou, 1989) are people with profound learning disabilities: persons in this group are unlikely to be able to use verbal language or to carry out simple tasks of everyday living (such as cooking) without support (Hogg and Sebba, 1986). In addition to this inter-individual variation, there may be major intra-individual fluctuations over time, arising from changes in the person's clinical state.

Theoretical analyses (e.g. Tepper and Elwork, 1984; Grisso and Appelbaum, 1991; Law Commission, 1993a) have suggested that legal decision-making involves at least three main stages: (a) understanding the nature of the choice to be made, (b) making the decision, and (c) conveying the decision to others. This framework indicates the areas of psychological functioning which may be relevant in providing 'supplemental data'. These areas will be discussed under two main headings: cognitive and social.

Cognitive Functioning

Overall Intellectual Ability

By definition, the intellectual ability of people with learning disabilities or dementia is impaired. Similarly, overall intellectual impairment often accompanies serious mental illness (e.g. acute schizophrenia, Hemsley, 1988), at least whilst there is evidence of psychotic symptoms. More lasting impairments are often evident in people who continue to require treatment and support (e.g. people with chronic schizophrenia, Nelson et al., 1990).

Surprisingly, the relationship between impaired intellectual ability and any aspect of legally significant decision-making has rarely been examined. Where preliminary investigations have been carried out (Grisso and Appelbaum, 1991; Rosenfeld, Turkheimer and Gardner, 1992), it has appeared that, even within a group of persons with a single diagnosis, decision-making cannot always be predicted on the basis of one or more sub-tests of a widely used global measure of overall ability (the Wechsler Adult Intelligence Scales-Revised, WAIS-R, Wechsler, 1981). One reason may be that each sub-test normally reflects a variety of skills, including abstract ability, concentration, motivation and educational background (Lezak, 1983) so that similar scores, even on a single sub-test and in people with the same diagnosis, may reflect different underlying patterns of skills and difficulties. As a result, overall intellectual ability is a poor predictor of decision-making. Nevertheless, information about overall ability and detailed analysis of the responses to the specific tasks involved in each sub-test provide useful starting points for an exploration of an individual's difficulties.

Memory

It would be expected that memory would be involved in decision-making. Memory problems are most evident in people with dementia (Morris, 1991; Wilcock and Jacoby, 1991), where they are often the first indicator of the onset of the condition. Given that, in people of below average intellectual ability, memory and intelligence are related (Gudjonsson, 1988), it is not surprising that there is also evidence of memory problems in people with learning disabilities (Tully and Cahill, 1984; Clare and Gudjonsson, 1993). Similarly, some problems in memory have been noted among people with a mental illness (acute and chronic schizophrenia—Cutting, 1985; severe depression—McAllister, 1981).

However, the term 'memory' summarises complex processes, involving the acquisition, retention and retrieval of information (Loftus, 1979). Acquisition refers to a process involving the perception of the material by a sensory register, where it is retained for a very brief period, before being transferred to working memory (Baddeley, 1986). The material is stored for only so long as it receives attention in the form of rehearsal or other conscious routines. It is related to current knowledge of the world imported from long-term memory before passing to long-term, more permanent, memory. Retention refers to the period of time between encoding and recollection, whilst retrieval involves the person bringing the information from short-term or long-term memory back into awareness.

Memory problems may therefore reflect one or a number of difficulties at different stages: for example, inadequate rehearsal in working memory—itself arising from a variety of factors—leading to a loss of the material before it reaches long-term memory (severe learning disabilities—Hulme and MacKenzie, 1992; schizophrenia—Nuechterlein and Dawson, 1984; depression—McAllister, 1981), inefficient encoding from working memory into long-term memory (dementia—Morris, 1991), and inadequate retrieval strategies (schizophrenia—Cutting, 1985). Detailed knowledge of the probable causes and location of memory difficulties in different groups of persons suggests possible remedial strategies.

Problem-solving

Intuitively, decision-making seems related to problem-solving. Difficulties in solving problems in everyday life, many of which involve the assessment of social consequences, are often among the most striking clinical indicators of learning disabilities, dementia and mental illness. Such everyday problem-solving forms much of the content of the most widely used measure (the Vineland Adaptive Behavior Scales—Sparrow, Balla, and Cicchetti, 1984) for the assessment of social functioning or adaptive behaviour in people with learning disabilities (recommended in the UK for this purpose by the BPS, 1991). Experimental evidence, from tasks rather unrelated to everyday life, seems consistent with clinical observations: for example, people with learning disabilities have difficulties in applying previously learned strategies spontaneously or generating novel strategies (Ferretti and Cavalier, 1991). Similarly, Pishkin and Bourne (1981, cited in Cutting, 1985, p. 327) found that, compared with the general population, people with a diagnosis of chronic schizophrenia had deficits in generating problem-solving strategies spontaneously, although they could apply rules which they had previously learned.

These difficulties are not surprising given that it is believed (Weisberg, 1980) that problem-solving involves memory and thinking processes. Impairments in memory in each of the three groups have already been mentioned (see above) and there is also evidence of disordered or disorganised thinking. These include concreteness and difficulty in abstracting the significance from examples (learning disabilities and dementia—Lezak, 1983; chronic schizophrenia—Cutting, 1985), problems in completing one train of thought before experiencing interruptions by another (mania and acute schizophrenia—Gelder, Gath and Mayou, 1989), and repetitive, negative, ruminations about the self, the world, and the future (depression—Beck et al., 1979).

Despite this evidence for difficulties in problem-solving, there has been little investigation of the extent to which people with learning disabilities, mental illness, or dementia have deficits in making the individual decisions which contribute to the solution of more complex problems. A few studies (e.g. Radford, Mann, and Kalucy, 1986; Garety, Hemsley, and Wessely, 1991; Rosenfeld, Turkheimer and Gardner, 1992) have examined decision-making using simple, concrete, and probably familiar, experimental tasks with people with diagnosed mental illness who had been admitted to hospital. Although some participants—generally those with the most severe symptomatology—experienced difficulties, decision-making was not necessarily impaired compared with the general population. Although the results are limited, they imply that breaking problems down into smaller segments may be helpful.

Verbal Language and Reading

Many decisions involve understanding and expressing verbal language. In learning disabilities, language is often impaired to a greater extent than non-verbal skills (Clements, 1987), particularly in people with the social impairments characteristic of autism (for a description of autism, see Baron-Cohen and Bolton, 1993). However, there is often a discrepancy between the two aspects of language, with understanding more developed than expression (Clements, 1987). A significant minority of people with severe learning disabilities have no expressive language (Mittler and Preddy, 1981), and are reliant on other forms of communication, such as sign language (Kiernan, 1985), or the questionnable assistance of facilitated communication (Biklen, 1990) where a helper physically assists a person to point to letters to spell out messages. In people with Alzheimer's Disease, understanding is impaired at a much earlier stage than expression, although even near the start of the condition there is difficulty in retrieving specific words (anomia), leading to problems speaking precisely. In addition, there is a loss of ability to use language as a means to interact with other people (Morris, 1991; for a detailed review see Morris, 1993). Problems related to language are also frequent in some groups of persons with diagnosed mental illness: for example, people with the psychotic symptoms associated with schizophrenia frequently have difficulty in communicating complex meanings clearly to others (Cutting, 1985). In addition, they may fail to understand the meaning of words in context (Cutting, 1985). However, these difficulties are not a simple function of the person's diagnosis: among people admitted to psychiatric hospital with a diagnosis of schizophrenia or depression, they appear, at least in part, to reflect the severity of the individual's symptomatology (Grisso and Appelbaum, 1991). The relevance or familiarity of the material may also be important: in the same study, psychiatric 'patients' generally demonstrated better understanding of information when it related to their own mental illness than when it concerned medical conditions which they had not experienced.

In addition to problems relating to verbal language, people with learning disabilities often have difficulties in reading words (e.g. Carr, 1988) and, even more commonly, in understanding the meaning of what they have read. In people with dementia, the ability to read words is commonly retained, at least during the early stages. As a result, it is possible to use a test involving reading aloud unusual words (the National Adult Reading Test, NART; Nelson, 1982) to estimate pre-morbid intellectual functioning (Morris, 1991). However, given their verbal comprehension difficulties, it is not surprising that they also have some problems in understanding written material (Woods and Britton, 1985). A similar discrepancy between the ability to read words, which is retained at a pre-morbid level (Dalby and Williams, 1986), and understanding of what is read seems likely in people with recurrent episodes of schizophrenia.

Overall, these findings suggest that people in the three groups under consideration will often have difficulties in dealing with the verbal and written means by which information about decisions is normally conveyed, and that alternative means of communication may often be required.

Acquiescence and Interrogative Suggestibility

In addition to verbal and language skills, it seems likely that decision-making will be affected by the extent to which a person is able to express his or her own views, rather than those indicated to him or her, albeit inadvertently, by other people. Among the psychological characteristics which may be involved are acquiescence and interrogative suggestibility, both of which can be assessed using standardised tests (for a full review see Gudjonsson, 1992). Acquiescence refers to a person's tendency to answer closed 'yes' or 'no' questions affirmatively, regardless of their content. High acquiescence is more common among people with low intellectual ability (Sigelman et al., 1981; Gudjonsson, 1986, 1990; Clare and Gudjonsson, 1993), so that people with severe learning disabilities are particularly vulnerable. Given the relationship with intellectual ability, it would be expected that people with dementia would also be at increased risk of acquiescence, as would at least some groups of people with a mental illness (for example, people with the overall intellectual impairments associated with chronic schizophrenia, Nelson et al., 1990).

Interrogative suggestibility comprises two main aspects: the tendency to be (mis)led by leading questions, and the tendency to shift initial answers in response to negative feedback. People with (mild) learning disabilities are much more suggestible than their average intellectual ability counterparts, because of their vulnerability to leading questions (Clare and Gudjonsson, 1993). On theoretical grounds, it would be expected that people with a mental illness or dementia would be more susceptible to both aspects of suggestibility (see Gudjonsson, 1992). However, it is clear that the suggestibility of specific vulnerable groups must be assessed directly, rather than on the basis of supposed similarities in, for example, intellectual ability (Clare and Gudjonsson, 1993).

The known and putative difficulties of people in all three groups in conveying their own views draws attention to the need to consider the way in which decisions are presented to, and requested of, them.

Social

In addition to the impact of deficits in their cognitive functioning, the psychological functioning of people with learning disabilities, mental illness, and dementia is likely to be impaired by social difficulties. These may be of two types: (i) primary impairments, which define or are associated with the condition itself (for example, the change in personality, often affecting attention to personal hygiene, social skills, emotional control, and sensitivity to others, found in dementia—Wilcock and Jacoby, 1991), and (ii) social disadvantages, which arise as a consequence of the person's difficulties and need for support. These disadvantages include poverty, limited opportunities for a wide range of experiences, isolation from others and loneliness (learning disabilities, Murphy, 1992), and low status in society (illustrated by a sobering survey of attitudes among the general population to people with learning disabilities—MENCAP, 1992).

Recently, there has also been increasing attention to the experiences of people with learning disabilities, mental illness, and dementia of different forms of abuse by others, ranging from inequalities in treatment (for details relating to women in mental health services, see Williams et al., 1993) and neglect, to financial, verbal, physical and sexual, abuse. The prevalence of different forms of abuse of the three populations is unclear, and reported rates vary greatly. In part, this is likely to reflect the use of different definitions of abuse and variation in the ways in which the populations are defined (for discussion of these issues in relation to sexual abuse (non-consenting sexual acts) with people with learning disabilities see Brown and Turk, 1992). Furthermore, the likelihood of sexual, and other, abuse coming to light in people with disabilities is much lower than for the general population (James, 1988, cited in Tharinger, Horton and Millea, 1990) because, for example, of communication difficulties (Tharinger, Horton and Millea, 1990) or embarassment (elderly people, Fisk, 1991). As a result, most prevalence or incidence rates are likely to be gross under-estimates. Given the methodological difficulties, it is not surprising that reported rates have varied widely (for example, for sexual abuse of people with learning disabilities: 25 per cent—Chamberlain et al., 1984; 8 per cent—Buchanan and Wilkins, 1991; around 4 per cent—Cooke, 1990). Nevertheless the figures are consistent in indicating a significant problem. Similarly, whilst the prevalence of sexual and other abuse among people with dementia is uncertain, the rate of 4 per cent often cited for abuse of the ordinary elderly population is likely to be an underestimate, particularly since physical or mental frailty appears to be a risk factor (see review by Fisk, 1991). Among women with a variety of mental health problems (including mental illness) it now seems that, in addition to a high proportion having a history of major physical or sexual abuse prior to the onset of their difficulties (Jacobson and Richardson, 1987; Copperman, unpublished M.Sc. thesis, 1991, quoted in Copperman and Burrowes, 1992), a significant minority experience sexual abuse during admission to hospital for treatment (Nibert, Cooper and Crossmaker, 1989). The available data indicate consistently that a very substantial proportion of abuse of all three groups is carried out by people with some presumed 'caring' relationship to the victim, including family members (learning disabilities, Sobsey, 1994; elderly persons, Decalmer, 1993), 'friends' (learning disabilities—Sobsey, 1994; elderly persons—Decalmer and Marriott, 1993) or paid carers (learning disabilities—Sobsey, 1994; women with mental illness—Nibert, Cooper and Crossmaker, 1989; elderly persons—Fisk, 1991).

The main impact of these experiences of social disadvantage is that people with learning disabilities, mental illness, or dementia will often have an inadequate, or grossly distorted, experience of the context in which a decision is to be made. Even when this is not the case, the low self-esteem which often accompanies social disadvantage places individuals in each of the three groups at increased risk of compliance. Compliance, which is related to suggestibility (Gudjonsson, 1990), refers to a person's tendency to 'go along with propositions, requests or instructions for some immediate instrumental gain' (Gudjonsson, 1992, p. 137), regardless of his or her own private views. Awareness of the possibility of compliant responding draws attention to the need to consider the realities of the relationship between the persons presenting or requesting decisions, and the decision-maker.

Summary

While the heterogeneity of the populations means that impaired decision-making should not be assumed, individuals with learning disabilities, mental illness and dementia are at increased risk of experiencing difficulties. However, the possible difficulties are multiple and complex, and need careful individual assessment.

SPECIFIC DECISIONS AND TESTS OF CAPACITY

Consent to Treatment

In English (England and Wales) law and in the USA, for treatment to be lawful patients must consent to treatment, except under particular conditions and circumstances. For adults, this consent must be provided by the person receiving the treatment. With the exception of certain circumstances (see below), an individual has an absolute right to refuse treatment, even if his or her decision seems unreasonable to others. While most discussions of consent to treatment focus on medical treatment (which is usually taken to include nursing and rehabilitation under medical supervision, section 145, Mental

Health Act 1983), other treatments can also interfere with people's rights and have been the subject of controversy from time to time (Wexler, 1973; Repp and Singh, 1990; Murphy, 1993).

In practice, many people with learning disabilities (particularly mild learning disabilities), mental illness or dementia are not in touch with the relevant services. As a result, they may not be offered treatment which they deserve and thus their consent to treatment may not be sought. For those who are in contact with services, however, assumptions may be made about incapacity on the basis of their diagnosis, despite consistent research evidence showing that, at least for some people with schizophrenia or depression (Roth et al., 1982; Grisso and Appelbaum, 1991) or learning disabilities (Morris, Niederbuhl and Mahr, 1993), this is unwarranted. However, there may also be occasions on which people with disabilities are offered treatment and consent to it without having understood fully what is involved. Their consent may be assumed to be valid simply because the decision seems sensible to a medical practitioner or another powerful professional.

In English law, an individual is required only to understand the issue to which he or she is consenting 'in broad terms'. The vagueness of this may help preserve the autonomy of people with learning disabilities, mental illness, or dementia. However, precisely how consent should be established is unclear. Health care professionals in England and Wales have some responsibility to provide adequate information for consent (see the cases of *Bolam v. Friern Hospital Management Committee* [1957] 2 All ER 118) and *Sidaway v. Bethlem Royal Hospital Governors* [1985] 1 All ER 643) but there is no requirement, as yet, for medical practitioners and others to provide a warning of a risk which a 'prudent patient' would consider significant (Lord Scarman's suggestion in the *Sidaway* case). Instead, they merely have to act 'in accordance with a practice accepted at the time as proper by a responsible body of medical opinion skilled in the particular form of treatment in question' (Gunn, 1985; Mackay, 1990).

In parts of the USA, people have to give 'informed consent' to treatment. This requires knowledge of the information relevant to a treatment decision, voluntarily exercising choice and having the capacity to make the decision (Grisso, 1986). The 'knowledge' element is stringent and clearly defined (for details see Grisso, 1986, chapter 10). In contrast, the 'capacity' element is unclear and Grisso (1986) has pointed out that several interpretations are possible. Following the proposal that 'capacity' should include only the general ability to understand factual information, rather than an actual understanding of the facts in a particular case (Grisso, 1986), a few measures, designed for research purposes, have been developed on this basis: the individual is presented with hypothetical information on disorders and possible treatments, and the person's capacity to understand the information, weigh the risks and benefits, and appreciate the consequences is assessed. Other tests (e.g. Roth et al., 1982), also designed for research purposes, are more specific. An example of each type is outlined below.

Grisso and Applebaum (1991) developed a procedure (originally called the MUD, Measuring Understanding of Disclosure; now known as the UTD, Understanding Treatment Disclosures) for assessing the understanding of hypothetical information about people admitted to hospital with a diagnosis of schizophrenia or depression. Participants were presented, verbally, with two 'disclosures' (relating to their diagnosis and one of two medical disorders). Each disclosure consisted of five paragraphs of information relating to the disorder, its symptoms, commonly prescribed medication, the benefits and side-effects of the medication, and alternative treatments. Assessment of participants' understanding was tested in three ways: (i) uninterrupted disclosure, where standardised questions were asked after the information was presented to elicit the participant's paraphrased recall of all the material, (ii) single unit disclosure, where questions to elicit paraphrased recall followed each paragraph and (iii) single unit recognition, where each paragraph was again taken separately and the participant was asked to identify which of four statements were the same as, and which different from, the information which was presented. An up-dated version of the procedure, which has been amended for the single unit disclosure (so that this now includes a recognition part), and clear criteria for scoring, is presented in the manual (Grisso and Appelbaum, 1992[1]). Research data in the manual indicate that, when administered and scored by trained researchers, the inter-rater reliability of the scoring system is satisfactory.

As Grisso and Appelbaum (1991, 1992) point out, the relationship between scores on any part of this measure and capacity or incapacity to consent at any point in time is not known, meaning that it would be quite illegitimate to attempt to draw any legal or psychological conclusions from a person's performance on the UTD. Nevertheless, it does provide a clear, standardised, procedure which could form part of an assessment of consent to treatment. Moreover, although the content of the disclosure information may be contentious (some would argue that it is too medically oriented), the simple language, which has been subjected to a 'reading ease' procedure, could serve as a model for clinicians providing information to users of their services.

Grisso and Appelbaum (1991) found a tendency for both the participants with diagnoses of mental illness, and control groups of general hospital patients, to demonstrate better understanding on single-unit than on uninterrupted disclosure tasks. This suggests that complex information is universally difficult to deal with and is consistent with the results of an earlier study, by Roth et al. (1982). Roth and her colleagues examined capacity to consent to electro-convulsive therapy (ECT) amongst persons being offered this treatment in one psychiatric hospital. After answering standardised written questions regarding their understanding of the information about ECT given on a standard hospital consent form, participants received a semi-structured interview during which the procedures were explained more simply, and understanding was reassessed. The interviews were video-taped and rated by experts with no knowledge of participants' scores on the earlier test. The raters judged as competent all of those who gained high scores (indicative of competence) on the standardised written questions. However, almost half of those persons who had obtained scores below 50% on the earlier test (and therefore appeared incompetent) were judged 'likely competent' on the basis of their video-taped responses following the simplified explanation.

Recently, a variation of the hypothetical information procedure has been used with people with learning disabilities. Morris, Niederbuhl and Mahr (1993) designed three hypothetical treatment dilemmas (concerning consent to behavioural treatment, surgery, and psychotropic medication) and presented one example of each to adults of average intellectual ability and to adults with mild or moderate learning disabilities. Interviews were then carried out using probe questions (and follow-up questions as necessary) regarding understanding of different aspects of the treatment and its alternatives. The results indicated that some of the tasks involved in capacity to consent are more difficult than others: for example, participants (including those without learning disabilities) found it much easier to understand the nature of the treatment than their rights and choices in relation to it. Similar variation in the difficulty of different tasks relating to consent to treatment was found in an earlier study (Weithorn and Campbell, 1982), involving children of nine years of age: the children were as able as adults to select 'reasonable' choices (derived from the views of experts) regarding treatment dilemmas, but were less able than teenagers (aged 14 years) or adults to recall all the relevant factual information.

In summary, these studies suggest that, as would be expected from the overview of psychological functioning (see above), capacity to consent is likely to depend on at least the manner in which information is presented and tested, and the complexity of the task required.

When Consent is Not Required

A controversial issue concerns the provision of medical treatment for adults who are unable or unwilling to consent. For example, at present, in England and Wales, there is no clear procedure—except through the Mental Health Act 1983 (which authorises only treatment for people with a mental disorder) or in exceptional circumstances, involving either 'necessity' (the meaning of which is unclear, according to Mackay, 1990) or 'emergency'—since parents and/or carers cannot legally consent to treatment in place of an adult. It has been asserted that this difficulty means that doctors and dentists may refuse to carry out treatment with some people because of uncertainties about its lawfulness (MENCAP, 1989). Nevertheless, it is clear that treatment of a questionable kind sometimes does take place when the recipient has little power (e.g. in 1987, it was reported that, in England, about 90 sterilisations a year were performed on women under 19 years of age, Dyer, 1987). In England and Wales, these dilemmas have been highlighted by several cases regarding girls and women with learning disabilities.

In the first case (*Re D* [1976] 1 All ER 326), the mother, general practitioner (local physician), paediatrician and gynaecologist of a girl aged 11 years, with Soto's syndrome, proposed that she be sterilised. However, the Court ruled that sterilisation would be unlawful since it was being proposed for non-therapeutic reasons, was not in the girl's best interests and would prevent her from exercising her basic human right to reproduce. In a second case, 'Jeanette' (*Re B* [1987] 2 All ER 206), the Court considered whether a young woman who was 17 years old and had a severe learning disability, could be sterilised when she was believed to be unable to consent to it herself. Sterilisation was authorised on the debatable grounds that it was a relatively minor operation with a few side effects and would provide a high degree of protection from pregnancy. However, it was also stated that no sterilisation would be authorised for eugenic or social purposes. In a third case (*Re F* [1990] 2 A.C.1), sterilisation was sought for a woman aged 35 years, who had a severe learning disability, was living in an institution, and had an active sexual relationship with a man who also lived in the hospital and had a severe learning disability. In this case, the House of Lords (the supreme appeal court in the UK) ruled that those providing treatment for someone unable to consent would not be subject to accusations of unlawful action, provided that they acted in the person's best interests and in accordance with a responsible and competent body of relevant professional opinion.

With regard to both *Re B* and *Re F*, however, it has been argued (e.g. Baum, 1994) that sterilisation was undertaken far too lightly. In the case of *Re B*, there was no current, active sexual relationship; and the nature of the sexual activity in *Re F* was not clearly established. In addition, certain forms of contraception were dismissed very readily (and seem not to have been considered at all for the male partner in *Re F*). Moreover, little attention was given to the possibility of a period of sex education for the women (both had communication difficulties but a level of comprehension that might have made basic sex education feasible) which may have assisted them to become sufficiently aware of the relevant issues to become capable of consent. Recently, a practice note from the Offical Solicitor (who has special responsibility for protecting the legal interests of people with disabilities) has proposed that some of these issues should be attended to in future applications to the Court (Practice Note (Official Solicitor), 1993). In addition, in neither *Re B* nor *Re F* did the courts seem concerned about the women having sexual relationships (see below) and their attendant risks (e.g. exploitation or sexually transmitted diseases) but only about the possibility of pregnancy and the production of children, suggesting that the decisions may, in part, have been motivated by eugenic considerations.

It has been argued (MENCAP, 1989) that resorting to the High Court for treatment decisions for those deemed unable to consent to treatment is unnecessarily costly and time-consuming and that a more appropriate procedure is needed. Subsequently, in England and Wales, the Law Commission has made suggestions for the English legal system (Law Commission, 1993a). It has suggested that a person should normally be presumed to have the capacity to consent to treatment. However, for those deemed incapable of making a particular decision, a new procedure has been proposed, by which a 'treatment provider' would be given a statutory authority to carry out treatment to safeguard and promote the best interests of the person, after consultation with the nearest relative. Certain forms of treatment (e.g. sterilisation, tissue donation, withdrawal of nutrition and hydration, and possibly abortion and participation in medical research) would require referral to a judicial forum for approval before being implemented. This forum would have the power to appoint medical treatment proxies to ensure that its orders were carried out. These proposals, which seem likely to lead to medical paternalism given the power proposed for the treatment provider, have been criticised in detail by Carson (1993). Carson has proposed a sensible alternative approach: a declaration that someone is incapacitated should automatically prompt an inquiry during which the treatment provider and carers would be obliged to demonstrate (for example, by showing a videotape of their practice) that they had adopted a functional approach to determining the person's capacity (see Introduction, p. 97 above). In practice, adopting this approach might involve breaking the relevant information down into small segments, teaching it on a number of occasions over a period of time so that it became familiar, and employing communication and memory aids (such as pictorial representations, augmentative communication systems, etc.) to help the individual to retain the material and communicate his or her decision.

Other countries have approached consent to treatment for persons who are incapacitated by appointing guardians but, in some ways, this has not been satisfactory (Carson, 1991; Law Commission, 1993a). In the USA, for example, where the majority of guardians are appointed for elderly persons, there are great variations between States in the definitions of capacity, types of capacity decisions possible (for example, some States will provide only categorical decisions about capacity or incapacity, while others accept the concept of limited capacity), the extent to which the person is represented in hearings and the provisions for review (Grisso, 1986). A better solution, perhaps, is that adopted in Sweden, where special representatives (social workers), independent of carers and treatment providers, assist persons with difficulties to make decisions, without removing capacity from them.

Consent to Sexual Intimacy

Particularly during the last part of the previous century, and the first half of this one (Showalter, 1985), there was a great deal of concern in the UK, USA and elsewhere about the sexual reproduction of a number of groups, including people with learning disabilities or a mental illness, who were deemed to be 'unfit' (see Showalter, 1985, p. 110). Reflecting this concern, 'patients' in psychiatric and 'mental handicap' hospitals were very strongly discouraged from having sexual relationships (although illicit and abusive sexual activities were far from unknown). For example, wards were segregated by sex, and no contraceptive or sexual advice was offered, even in long-stay hospitals. The advent of the normalisation movement (Nirje, 1980; Wolfensberger, 1980, 1983; Emerson, 1992) radically changed views about the opportunities which should be offered to people with learning disabilities, providing a new emphasis on age-appropriate and culturally normative experiences. There was a recognition that sex education should be offered (Craft and Craft, 1983; Murphy, Coleman and Abel, 1983) and, increasingly, a move to more ordinary living conditions in the community. Similar deinstitutionalisation has taken place in regard to people with a diagnosed mental illness, and hospitals themselves have become less prohibitive about sexual matters: most wards now contain men and women so that, in general, there is a greater freedom for people to have heterosexual relationships, at least (in the UK, homosexual, and lesbian (Williams et al., 1993), relationships are still strongly discouraged in services for people with learning disabilities or mental illness).

Most countries have laws to protect people from unwanted sexual encounters and there are often added protections for those who are regarded as unable to consent (such as men and women with severe learning disabilities; for the relevant law, see Gunn, 1991). However, at least in English law, with these very few exceptions, everyone above a certain age can consent to sexual activity and the law normally only becomes involved where it is reported that a person did not consent. The *reason* why consent is given is not considered relevant in law, enabling people to consent to sex for all sorts of reasons including sexual gratification, affection, duty, money, physical closeness, physical comfort or fear. As a result, in cases where a man or woman has consented to sexual activities for a small gift, such as a cigarette, there can be no grounds for prosecution, even though others may feel that he or she has been exploited.

Through their cognitive and social disadvantages, people with learning disabilities, a mental illness, or dementia may be at increased risk of sexual exploitation, and a number of groups have recently become concerned about how better to provide them with protection, without wishing to remove their right to consenting sexual relationships. Copperman and Burrowes (1992), for example, have recently argued that mixed sex wards in psychiatric hospitals place women with mental illness or other mental health problems at risk of sexual abuse and that single sex provision should therefore be available. A similar argument might be made for women with learning disabilities living in hospital or community services.

Precisely what constitutes 'consent' to sexual activity is unclear. In the USA and most European countries, there is no requirement that someone engaging in sexual activity should exercise 'informed consent' of the kind required for medical treatment (i.e. to be informed and to choose voluntarily). As a result, there seems to be no need, in law, for a person to demonstrate that he or she understands the nature of sexual activity, its benefits and risks and the alternatives to sexual activity. If there were such requirements, people would presumably need to understand and differentiate between sexual intercourse, masturbation and procreation. They would also need to understand the risks of pregnancy and sexually transmitted diseases, particularly HIV. In addition, they would need an understanding of alternative forms of contraception and of how to gain the benefits of sexual behaviour by other means (for example, if they are going to engage in sexual intercourse for material objects, they need to know how else these objects might be obtained). Realistically, to make a voluntary choice, many people would also need assertiveness training, so that they did not simply submit to sexual activity because of compliance. In fact, very few staff, at least among those working in services for people with learning disabilities and mental illness, would consider these factors. Rather, staff tend to consider themselves 'enlightened' in allowing sexual intercourse between people with disabilities, without really considering the potential of one person to abuse the other.

Recently, a number of local guidelines on personal and sexual relationships have been drawn up by and for staff in residential and day care facilities for people with learning disabilities (Booth and Booth, 1992). Most of the guidelines assert that such persons have the same right to sexual expression as people without disabilities but that they also have a right to be protected from abuse and exploitation; these points do not seem controversial. Some guidelines are then mainly concerned with procedures to be followed when abuse comes to light but provide no guidance on what constitutes consent. Others (such as the ones drafted by the Social Services Department of the London Borough of Southwark but revised very extensively prior to implementation[2]) have included the assertion that proper consent has to include an understanding of the nature of sexual acts, the inappropriateness of certain kinds of sexual behaviour (e.g. incest), the 'value' of sexual acts (e.g. that exchanging sex for one cigarette would not be regarded as wise by many people), possible consequences of sexual behaviour (such as pregnancy and sexually transmitted diseases), whether pressure from a family member or staff member was involved, whether the use of (or threat of use of) force, weapon or injury to the person occurred, and whether there was a power imbalance which made witholding consent difficult for the 'weaker' person. The Southwark guidelines suggest that where it is difficult to be sure whether their consent is valid, services should look to see whether the two people actively seek each other out, spend time together, share leisure activities and restrict activities with other partners.

In the UK, the Law Commission (England and Wales) has recently considered the issue of making decisions for those who may not be able to do so themselves. It has recommended that a person be considered to be unable to take a decision if he or she does not understand 'an explanation in broad terms and simple language ... including information about the reasonably foreseeable consequences of taking or failing to take it' (Law Commission, 1993b, p. 28), or cannot 'retain the information for long enough to take an effective decision' (Law Commission, 1993b, p. 28) or is unable 'because of mental disorder to make a true choice' despite understanding the information (Law Commission, 1993b, p. 28). This recommendation, which, arguably (see Carson, 1993) is based, in part, on a model of decision-making which may be employed by few of the general population, is almost as stringent as the test of consent in Southwark's draft guidelines. The Law Commission has proposed that many carers be enabled to make many decisions for their relatives or users of their services but, in so doing, have to act in the best interests of the person, taking into account his or her past and present wishes and feelings, the need to encourage the the individual to participate in making the decision, and adopting the least restrictive alternative as far as possible (Law Commission, 1993b). However, decisions about a service user's sexual relationships, as well as those relating to the marriage and adoption of children, would not be included among the increased decision-making powers of carers, on the basis that these decisions 'must be taken personally' (Law Commission, 1993b, p. 69).

In practice, where a sexual relationship involving a person who is believed to have a learning disability, a mental illness, or dementia, has begun or appears imminent, then it is suggested that families, carers and professionals should consider the following issues:

- Is there a major imbalance of power between the two persons (for example, one physically frail or subservient partner)? If so, then there is a much greater risk of an abusive relationship.

- Is the sexual relationship rewarding in itself or is one person offering inducements to the other (such as cigarettes or car rides)? If tangible inducements are always given by one partner to the other, there is a far greater risk of the relationship being abusive.

- If the relationship is heterosexual, do both partners understand (at least) that pregnancy can result from sexual intercourse?

- Where the relationship is heterosexual, do both know what contraception means and how to use methods of contraception?

- Do both partners understand that there is a risk of sexually transmitted diseases, particularly when the sexual activity includes oral, vaginal, or anal penetration, and know how to engage in safer sex?

- If pregnancy is a possibility, have both people been given adequate access to genetic counselling and have they been informed and understood issues relating to parenting (including the reality that fostering may be required)?

In some cases, where the answer to any of these questions is 'No', then one or both persons may need counselling and/or sex education, possibly with assertiveness training if the relationship appears exploitative. There are a number of sex education packages available for people with learning disabilities (Craft and Brown, 1994), including both slide and pictorial packages, many of which can be employed in either group or individual training (e.g. Kempton, 1988; McCarthy and Thompson, 1993). Most of these would also be appropriate for other adults who may be more vulnerable than the general population. It may be necessary to assess a person's understanding both before and after the training and ideally this ought to be done in a standard way, using the same questions each time, to see what the person has gained from the training. There are a number of tests of sexual knowledge available for this kind of assessment, some of which include questions about social interactional issues (as well as sexual facts) and have been designed specifically for a particular population (e.g. Fischer, Krajicek and Borthick, 1973; Wish, McCombs and Edmonson, 1979; Bender et al., 1983). If the two people appear not to be able to understand or retain information from the sex education sessions, even though pictorial, signed and other forms of communication have been used, then informed consent may not be possible. Many carers, however, would still consider that the couple had a right to be sexual (Craft and Brown, 1994) if it appeared that they had a genuine affection for each other and there was no clear evidence of exploitation. In such circumstances, it may be possible for carers to assist the couple in obtaining protection from any risk of pregnancy; however, limiting the risk of sexually transmitted diseases is much more problematic (practical guidance on this issue is given by McCarthy and Thompson, 1994). In the absence of apparent affection between the two people, some carers would argue that a sexual relationship should be discouraged if informed consent is not possible (see the draft Southwark guidelines above) and this may mean that some people have less likelihood of establishing a sexual relationship (for example, people with autism are unlikely to display affectionate behaviour in a normal way). Meanwhile, Carson (1994) has argued that what is needed is a change in the law, creating a new offence of serious exploitation of a person with a 'mental disorder', as defined in Section 1 of the Mental Health Act 1983. This would provide some legal recourse for vulnerable persons (and might serve some protective role, through serving as a deterrent to potential abusers) but enable even those with severe learning disabilities to engage in non-exploitative sexual relationships.

Capacity to Parent

Assertions that people with learning disabilities, or mental illness or other mental health needs, are inadequate, feckless, parents have a long history

(Rutter, 1966; Murphy, Coleman and Abel, 1983; Rutter and Quinton, 1984; Dowdney and Skuse, 1993; Tymchuk and Andron, 1994). Indeed, the presence of these conditions in mothers (arguably, rather different standards are used to evaluate fathers, see Chesler, 1991) has often been regarded as sufficient justification for the removal of their children (for example, USA, see Grisso, 1986, p. 191). In fact, the available evidence indicates that, contrary to popular and historical views, the families of people with learning disabilities are generally smaller than average (Murphy, Coleman and Abel, 1983; Tymchuk and Andron, 1990), and the children are likely to be less disabled than their parents, possibly because of a regression towards average intellectual ability (Murphy, Coleman and Abel, 1983; Gath, 1988). Although there is conflict between the conclusions of different studies (see review by Dowdney and Skuse, 1993), it seems that many people with learning disabilities are satisfactory parents, especially if sufficient training in parenting skills is available, together with flexible day-to-day support, which is maintained over time (Feldman et al., 1986; Tymchuk, Andron and Bavolek, 1990; Tymchuk and Andron, 1992; Dowdney and Skuse, 1993). Similarly, it now appears that, even for the children of parents with a diagnosed mental illness, the outcome need not necessarily be negative, but depends, for example, on whether the parents' difficulties pre- or post-date the child's birth (Melhuish, Gambles and Kumar, 1988), the treatment available to them, and the extent of the difficulties. In a study of the children of parents requiring psychiatric support, Rutter and Quinton (1984) found that, in two-thirds, emotional or behavioural difficulties were only transient. In addition, there is evidence that, despite suffering from depression, many mothers manage to preserve the quality of their relationship, and interaction, with their child (Pound et al., 1985; Goodman and Brumley, 1990; for an opposing view see Meadows, 1993). Overall, it appears that deleterious outcomes for children of parents with a mental illness or other, less serious, mental health needs may not result directly from the condition but instead from disturbances in psychosocial functioning within the family (Rutter, 1990), such as those associated with pervasive parental interpersonal problems.

Nevertheless, it has to be acknowledged that (i) children from families where one or both parents have learning disabilities or a diagnosed mental illness or other mental health needs are at greater *risk* of developing difficulties, (ii) particular parental characteristics predict particular problems for at least *some* of the children (e.g. Milner and Chilamkurti, 1991), and (iii) risk factors are sometimes multiplicative, rather than just additive, in their effects. It has been found, for example, that children experiencing four or more risk factors (maternal mental health needs, paternal criminal record, severe marital discord, low social status, large family size, placement in local authority care) have a 1:5 chance of developing a psychiatric disorder; in contrast, those experiencing only two or three risk factors have only a 1:16 chance (Rutter, 1987). Similarly, an increased number of risk factors (including poor maternal education, large family size, high maternal anxiety, stressful life events, and low positive interactions with the child) leads to poorer cognitive and socio-emotional outcomes in the children of mothers with a diagnosis of schizophrenia (Sameroff and Seiffer, 1990). Overall, it seems that, while many children thrive in families where one or both parents have learning disabilities, or a mental illness or other mental health needs, the proportion having problems is higher than in families where the parents do not have such difficulties.

In the fields of child development and child psychology and psychiatry, there has been an enormous amount of research into parenting among the general population, particularly into those factors related to cognitive and social development, and child abuse and neglect (see, for example, Macoby and Martin, 1983; Milner, 1991, 1992, 1993a; Garmezy and Masten, 1994; Skuse and Bentovim, 1994; Smith and Bentovim, 1994).

Some of the factors which increase the likelihood of adequate parenting are known: they include the parents themselves having an early history of being adequately cared for, an absence of parental or child medical disorders, an absence of parental challenging behaviour or criminal convictions, good parental emotional health, good family support, the existence of sufficient reading skills to be able to cope with common food and medicine labels and simple instructional leaflets, and participation in parenting programmes where these are offered (Murphy, Coleman and Abel, 1983; Tymchuk and Andron, 1990; Tymchuk, 1992; Garmezy and Masten, 1994).

Much of the research in child development and child psychology and psychiatry has sought to find stable characteristics of parents which will predict development or behaviour in the children (Macoby and Martin, 1983), and to this end, numerous measures, investigating different aspects of parenting, have been developed. However, although it has been agreed that certain gross indices (such as the level of intellectual ability) are not good predictors of adequate parenting ability, there is no well-co-ordinated and carefully evaluated set of measures. Instead, a plethora of different measures are used to consider some or many aspects of at least the following areas (Clausen, 1968, p. 141, cited in Grisso, 1986):

• provision of nurturance and physical care

• training and channeling of physiological needs in toilet training, weaning, provision of solid foods, etc.

• teaching and skill training in language, perceptual skills, physical skills, self-care skills in order to facilitate care and ensure safety

• orienting the child to his or her immediate world of kin, neighbourhood, community and society, and to his or her own feelings

- transmitting cultural and subcultural goals and values and motivating the child to accept them as his or her own

- promoting interpersonal skills, motives, and modes of feeling and behaving in relation to others

- guiding, correcting and helping the child formulate his or her own goals and plan his or her own activities.

In addition to the variation in the scope of different measures, there is diversity in the manner in which information is collected (Macoby and Martin, 1983). However, most of the measures are completed with the parent(s) in a clinic setting, in the absence of their children. As a result, the home environment and parental behaviour towards the children may never be seen. This is a serious problem which has sometimes been addressed as part of the determination of the validity of the instruments. Nevertheless, as Grisso (1986) has commented, the data on the validity of the measures are often extremely poor. Only a few measures, such as the Moos Family Environment Scale (Moos and Moos, 1984) and the Bradley and Caldwell HOME inventory (Bradley and Caldwell, 1979) are completed in the home, or involve direct observational measures of the parent's actual behaviour with his or her children (e.g. the Mother's Project Rating Scales of Mother–Child Interaction; Clark et al., 1980).

Three types of measures are examined in more detail below in order to illustrate the information which can be provided by these assessments. The first type examines parental attitudes, using ratings of the extent of agreement with a series of statements. Many of these measures (for example, the Parental Attitude Research Instrument of Schaefer and Bell, 1958; the Mother–Child Relationship Evaluation of Roth, 1980; the Parent Attitude Survey of Hereford, 1963) attempt to cover a broad spectrum of parenting behaviours (see Grisso, 1986) but some are more specific, such as the Child Abuse Potential Inventory (Milner, 1986), which may be particularly useful in assessing a crucial aspect of parenting.

The Child Abuse Potential Inventory is based on a cognitive theory of physical abuse (Milner, 1993b) and was developed specifically to screen parents suspected of this form of abuse. The scale, which has been used in a legal context to assess competency to parent, consists of 160 written items, such as 'Children should never be bad', to which parents have to either agree or disagree. The ratings on 77 items are used for the abuse score, while other items make up the lie scale, random response scale and inconsistency scale scores. The scale is very successful in discriminating between parents who have or do not have a history of physically abusing their children (Milner and Wimberly, 1980) although, like many other measures, it is a poor predictor of future behaviour (in this case, because of a high false positive rate, so that some parents are identified as abusers who do not subsequently engage in this behaviour).

The second type of measure involves asking children within a family to rate their parents' behaviour. Intermediate between this type, and the first, are a few questionnaires which have been designed to be given to children and their parents: each rates whether or not the parents display various behaviours and the results for the parents and children can then be compared (e.g. the Parent–Child Relationship measure, the Parent Discipline Behaviour measure and the Expression of Affection measure—Hetherington and Clingempeel, 1992). More numerous, however, are the scales which simply examine the child's view, such as the inventory of Children's Reports of Parental Behaviour (Schaefer, 1965), which has been used to assess competency to parent, and is reviewed in detail by Grisso (1986, pp. 207–15). This measure involves presenting the child (either in writing, or orally) with a series of items (56 in the short version) such as 'My mother/father often speaks of the good things I do'. The child's task is to rate each item as like/somewhat like/not like his or her mother and father, separately. The items are scored and contribute to three dimensions which purport to measure the parent's degree of acceptance versus rejection, psychological autonomy versus psychological control, and firm versus lax discipline. There is evidence that the measure has some validity, at least for older children: for example, 'delinquent' young people rated their parents as low on positive involvement, high on hostile detachment and inconsistent in discipline (as would be expected from other research on delinquency). However, although the scores (and standard deviations) for the three factors for various groups of children have been published, there are no normative data stratified by, for example, age, sex, ethnic or cultural background, with which the responses of a particular individual child could be compared.

The third type of measure involves direct observations of parents' behaviour towards the child. The observations sometimes take place in the home (for example, the HOME—Bradley and Caldwell, 1979), and sometimes in a clinic or laboratory setting (e.g. the Mother's Project Rating Scale of Mother–Child Interaction). The HOME inventory (Home Observation for Measurement of the Environment) was initially intended for very young children (under three years) but later versions were developed for older children (e.g. Bradley and Caldwell, 1979; Bradley et al., 1992). In the version for younger children, there are 45 items arranged in six sub-scales, some of which are rated from interviews with the main care-giver and some from observations of physical or psychological aspects of the home environment. The six sub-scales are: Emotional and Verbal Responsivity of Mother, Avoidance of Restriction and Punishment, Organisation of Physical and Temporal Environment, Provision of Appropriate Play Materials, Maternal Involvement with Child, Opportunities for Variety in Daily Stimulation. Examples of items rated through interview include: 'When mother is away, care is provided by one of three regular substitutes' (from the Organisation of Physical and Temporal Environment sub-scale), and 'Family visits or receives visits from relatives' (from the Opportunities for Variety in Daily Stimulation sub-scale). Examples of items rated through observations include: 'Mother caresses or kisses child at least once during visit' (from the Emotional and Verbal Responsivity sub-scale) and 'Mother provides toys or interesting activities for child during interview' (from the Provision of Appropriate Play Materials sub-scale). The versions for older children are in a similar format but divided into somewhat different sub-scales (see Bradley, 1985; Bradley et al., 1992). Numerous studies employing the HOME inventory have shown that it discriminates well between families where it has already been established that the children have difficulties, such as developmental delays, malnutrition, failure-to-thrive, and a variety of other conditions, and comparison families (although its predictive validity has not been established). The availability of normative data on various samples of families, including some from ethnic minority backgrounds, means that families can be assessed as within or outside the normal range for parenting (Bradley, 1985).

In contrast with the HOME, the Mother's Project Rating Scale of Mother–Child Interaction (Clark et al., 1980) is entirely observation-based. The mother is provided with some toys and asked to play with the child as she would at home. The five-minute play session is then video-taped and rated according to a 53-item scale, covering tone of voice, mood and expressed affect of the mother, and behaviour, mood and affect of the child, with some ratings also of the interactional mutuality of the dyad. Given (i) the well-established complex relationship between attitudes and behaviour (e.g. Warren and Jahoda, 1973), (ii) the difficulties which at least some parents would have in completing some of the parental questionnaires, and (iii) that children vary a great deal in the extent to which they require different parenting abilities so that the competence of a particular parent may be very dependent on the nature of the child for whom they are caring, direct observation of this sort seems essential, wherever possible.

People with learning disabilities or mental illness who are not in touch with services may become parents without anyone raising the issue of capacity. Where an assessment of a person's ability to parent is needed in advance of a baby being born, which is sometimes the case with people in contact with services, there may be relatively little choice of suitable measures. In such situations, the most that can be achieved at present is to measure the potential parents' child-rearing attitudes, their knowledge of safety issues, and perhaps try to gain gross information about their general child-interaction skills from observation of their behaviour with children. However, where the issue arises later, for example, because of fears that a child may have been abused, it would be possible to employ a variety of measures to examine whether the person is able to display adequate parenting skills, using direct observation of child–parent interaction, measures of the child's reporting of parental behaviour and measures of parents' attitudes, and of the congruence between them. One of the difficulties, however, is to decide how good is good enough (Grisso, 1986). If parents were clearly displaying unacceptable ignorance (such as saying it would be safe to leave a three-month-old baby in the bath while answering the doorbell), then it would be agreed by most professional and lay people that extra parent training, at the very least, would be required. However, if a person simply scores somewhat less well on particular attitude scales, then it is far more difficult to determine whether the individual has the capacity to parent that particular child or whether she (and it is usually the skills of the mother which are in question) is in need of extra training (and, if so, how much training) and support. Such a decision needs to be made with reference to normative data for parents of the same ethnic and cultural background (for example, taking scores more than two standard deviations below the mean as indicating that further training was warranted).

The provision of training and support for people who may have difficulties in parenting is a growing specialty. Health services for adults with mental health needs are increasingly recognising the importance of preventive interventions for families where one member has mental health needs (Beardslee, 1990), and, in places, services for adults with learning disabilities are developing exemplary parental support programmes (Tymchuk and Andron, 1994). However, at present, as Tymchuk and Andron (1994) comment, the current services offered in most parts of the USA are patchy and ill-organised; those available in the UK and many other countries are probably even worse.

CONCLUSIONS

Two major conclusions may be drawn from the material presented in this chapter. First, it appears from research carried out by psychologists, and by others with a psychological perspective, that the factors involved in adults' decision-making are very complex: any particular decision is likely to reflect an interaction between, at the least, the individual's cognitive skills and assertiveness, his or her knowledge and experience of the background to the decision, the way in which information about the decision is presented and sought, the specific tasks relating to the decision, and the nature of the relationship between the presenter and the decision-maker. The implication of this complexity is that an approach to assessment based simply on diagnosis is quite inadequate, and that the criticisms to which it has been subjected (see the introduction to this chapter) are justified. Instead, lawyers should expect that, when psychologists are involved in the determination of the capacity of a specific individual within a particular legal context, they will provide the detailed information which is demanded by a functional approach. Included in this should be evidence that the psychological literature on the increased likelihood of different difficulties within identified populations has been used to attempt to locate the source(s) of any discrepancy between the person's abilities and a given situation, and that an effort has been made to provide appropriate remedial strategies, as far as possible.

Unfortunately, the second general conclusion, highlighted by a consideration of the three specific contexts, is that the contribution which psychologists may make to the above task may be rather limited, at present. A functional approach to the determination of capacity remains underdeveloped, at least in the UK. For a number of legal contexts, there are few standardised and agreed psychological measures which permit assessment of the functional abilities of particular individuals (particularly those whose functioning differs markedly from that of the general population) and the extent to which these meet the demands of a given situation. In part, at least, this deficiency reflects uncertainties about the meaning of some of the legal definitions relating to capacity. As a result, it is often difficult to conceptualise the functional abilities which might be relevant, let alone design assessment measures which fulfil scientific standards of reliability and validity (see Gudjonsson, chapter 2.2). A task for the future is for psychologists to work closely with lawyers (along the lines suggested by Grisso, 1986, pp. 345 ff.) to enable this area of work to develop.

ACKNOWLEDGEMENTS

We are grateful to Professor David Hemsley and Dr Robin Morris, Psychology Department, Institute of Psychiatry, University of London, and to Ms Michelle McCarthy, Tizard Centre, University of Kent, for their helpful comments on various sections of this chapter.

NOTES

1. Grisso, T. and Appelbaum, P. (1992). Manual for Understanding Treatment Disclosures. Available from Dr. T. Grisso, Professor of Psychiatry (Clinical Psychology), Department of Psychiatry, University of Massachussetts Medical Center, 55, Lake Avenue North, Worcester, MA 01655, U.S.A.

2. Southwark Social Services (1991/2). Draft guidelines for dealing with sexual abuse of adults with learning difficulties, London Borough of Southwark.

REFERENCES

Baddeley, A.D. (1986). *Working Memory*. Oxford: Oxford University Press.
Baron-Cohen, S. and Bolton, P. (1993). *Autism: The Facts*. Oxford: Oxford University Press.
Baum, S. (1994). Interventions with a pregnant woman with severe learning

disabilities: a case example. In A. Craft (Ed.), *Practice Issues in Sexuality and Learning Disabilities*. London: Routledge, pp. 217–36.

Beardslee, W.R. (1990). Development of a preventive intervention for families in which parents have serious affective disorder. In G.I. Keitner (Ed.), *Depression and Families: Impact and Treatment*. Washington, DC: American Psychiatric Press, pp. 101–20.

Beck, A.T., Rush, A.J., Shaw, B.F. and Emery, G. (1979). *Cognitive Therapy of Depression*. New York: The Guilford Press.

Bender, M., Aitman, J.B., Biggs S.J. and Haug, U. (1983). Initial findings concerning a sexual knowledge questionnaire. *Mental Handicap*, **11**, 168–9.

Biklen, D. (1990). Communication unfound: autism and praxis. *Harvard Educational Review*, **60**, 291–314.

Booth, T. and Booth, W. (1992). Practice in sexuality. *Mental Handicap*, **20**, 64–9.

Bradley, R.H. (1985). The HOME Inventory: rationale and research. In J.E. Stevenson (Ed.), *Recent Research in Developmental Psychopathology*. Oxford: Pergamon Press, pp. 191–202.

Bradley, R.H. and Caldwell, B. (1979). Home observation for the measure of the environment: a revision of the pre-school scale. *American Journal of Mental Deficiency*, **84**, 235–44.

Bradley, R.H., Caldwell, B.M., Brisky, J., Magee, M. and Whiteside, L. (1992). The HOME inventory: a new scale for families of pre- and early adolescent children with disabilities. *Research in Developmental Disabilities,* **13**, 313–33.

Brahams, D. (1987). Court of Appeal agrees to the sterilisation of 17-year-old mentally handicapped girl under wardship jurisdiction. *The Lancet*, i, 757–8.

British Psychological Society (1991). *Mental Impairment and Severe Mental Impairment: A Search for Definitions*. Leicester: British Psychological Society.

Brown, H. and Turk, V. (1992). Defining sexual abuse as it affects adults with learning disabilities. *Mental Handicap*, **20**, 44–55.

Buchanan, A. and Wilkins, R. (1991). Sexual abuse of the mentally handicapped: difficulties in establishing prevalence. *Psychiatric Bulletin*, **15**, 601–5.

Carr, J. (1988). Six weeks to twenty-one years old: a longitudinal study of children with Down's Syndrome and their families. *Journal of Child Psychology and Psychiatry*, **29**, 407–31.

Carson, D. (1991). Clarifying the law on mental responsibility. *Health Service Journal*, 16 May, 14–5.

Carson, D. (1993). Disabling progress: The Law Commission's proposals on mentally incapacitated adults' decision-making. *Journal of Social Welfare and Family Law*, **5**, 304–20.

Carson, D. (1994). The law's contribution to protecting people with learning disabilities from physical and sexual abuse. In J. Harris and A. Craft (Eds), *People with Learning Disabilities at Risk of Physical or Sexual Abuse*. Kidderminster: BILD Publications (BILD Seminar Papers, No. 4), pp. 133–43.

Chamberlain, A., Rauh, J., Passer, A., McGrath, M. and Burket, R. (1984). Issues in fertility control for mentally retarded female adolescents. I: Sexual activity, sexual abuse and contraception. *Pediatrics*, **73**, 445–50.

Chesler, P. (1991). Mothers on trial: the custodial vulnerability of women. *Feminism and Psychology*, **1,** 3, 409–26.

Clare, I.C.H. and Gudjonsson, G.H. (1993). Interrogative suggestibility, confabulation, and acquiescence in people with mild learning disabilities (mental handicap): implications for reliability during police interrogations. *British Journal of Clinical Psychology*, **32**, 295–301.

Clark, R., Musick, J., Stott, S. and Klehr, K. (1980). *The Mother's Project Rating Scales of Mother–Child Interaction*. Madison, Wisconsin: Dept. of Psychiatry, University of Wisconsin Medical School.

Clausen, J. (1968). Perspectives in childhood socialization. In J. Clausen (Ed.), *Socialization and Society*. Boston, MA: Little, Brown, pp. 130–81.

Clements, J. (1987). *Severe Learning Disability and Psychological Handicap*. Chichester: John Wiley.

Copperman, J. and Burrowes, F. (1992). Reducing the risk of assault. *Nursing Times*, **88**, 64–5.

Cooke, L.B. (1990). Abuse of mentally handicapped adults. *Psychiatric Bulletin*, **14**, 608–9.

Craft, A. and Brown, H. (1994). Personal relationships and sexuality: the staff role. In A. Craft (Ed.), *Practice Issues in Sexuality and Learning Disabilities*. London: Routledge, pp. 1–22.

Craft, A. and Craft, M. (1983). *Sex Education and Counselling for Mentally Handicapped People*. Tunbridge Wells, UK: Costello.

Cutting, J. (1985). *The Psychology of Schizophrenia*. Edinburgh: Churchill Livingstone.

Dalby, J.T. and Williams, R. (1986). Preserved reading and spelling ability in psychiatric disorders. *Psychological Medicine*, **16**, 171–5.

Decalmer, P. (1993). Clinical presentation. In P. Decalmer and F. Glendenning (Eds), *The Mistreatment of Elderly People*. London: Sage, pp. 35–61.

Decalmer, P. and Marriott, A. (1993). The multi-disciplinary assessment of clients and patients. In P. Decalmer and F. Glendenning (Eds), *The Mistreatment of Elderly People*. London: Sage, pp. 117–35.

Dowdney, L. and Skuse, D. (1993). Parenting provided by adults with mental retardation. *Journal of Child Psychology and Psychiatry*, **34**, 25–47.

Dyer, C. (1987). Sterilisation of mentally handicapped woman. *British Medical Journal*, **294**, 825.

Emerson, E. (1992). What is normalisation? In H. Brown and H. Smith (Eds), *Normalisation: A Reader for the Nineties*. London: Routledge, pp. 1–18.

Feldman, M., Towns, F., Betel, J., Case L., Rincover, A. and Rubino, C. (1986). Parent education project II: Increasing stimulating interactions of developmentally handicapped mothers. *Journal of Applied Behaviour Analysis*, **19**, 23–37.

Ferretti, R.P. and Cavalier, A.R. (1991). Constraints on the problem solving of persons with mental retardation. In N.W. Bray (Ed.), *International Review of Research in Mental Retardation*, **17**. London: Academic Press, pp. 153–92.

Fischer, H.L., Krajicek, M.J. and Borthick, W.A. (1973). *Sex Education for the Developmentally Disabled: A Guide for Parents Teachers and Professionals*. Baltimore, Maryland: University Park Press.

Fisk, J. (1991). Abuse of the elderly. In R. Jacoby and C. Oppenheimer (Eds), *Psychiatry in the Elderly*. Oxford: Oxford University Press, pp. 901–14.

Frith, U. (1989). *Autism: Explaining the Enigma*. Oxford: Basil Blackwell.

Garety, P.A., Hemsley, D.R. and Wessely, S. (1991). Reasoning in deluded schizophrenic and paranoid patients. *Journal of Nervous and Mental Disease*, **179**, 194–201.

Garmezy, N. and Masten, A.S. (1994). Chronic adversities. In M. Rutter, E. Taylor and

L. Hersov (Eds), *Child and Adolescent Psychiatry: Modern Approaches*. Oxford: Basil Blackwell, pp 191–208.

Gath, A. (1988). Mentally handicapped people as parents. *Journal of Child Psychology and Psychiatry*, **29**, 739–44.

Gelder, M., Gath, D. and Mayou, R. (1989). *Oxford Textbook of Psychiatry* (2nd edn). Oxford: Oxford University Press.

Goodman, S.H. and Brumley, H.E. (1990). Schizophrenic and depressed mothers: relational deficits in parenting. *Developmental Psychology*, **26**, 31–9.

Grisso, T. (1986). *Evaluating Competencies: Forensic Assessments and Instruments*. New York: Plenum Press.

Grisso, T. and Appelbaum, P. (1991). Mentally ill and non-mentally ill patients abilities to understand informed consent disclosures for medication. *Law and Human Behaviour*, **15**, 377–88.

Grossman, H.J. (1983). *Classification in Mental Retardation*. Washington, DC: American Association on Mental Deficiency.

Gudjonsson, G.H. (1986). The relationship between interrogative suggestibility and acquiesccence: empirical findings and theoretical implications. *Personality and Individual Differences*, **7**, 195–9.

Gudjonsson, G.H. (1988). The relationship of intelligence and memory to interrogative suggestibility: the importance of range effects. *British Journal of Clinical Psychology*, **27**, 185–7.

Gudjonsson, G.H. (1990). The relationship of intellectual skills to suggestibility, compliance and acquiescence. *Personality and Individual Differences*, **11**, 227–31.

Gudjonsson, G.H. (1992). *The Psychology of Interrogations, Confessions and Testimony*. Chichester: John Wiley.

Gunn, M.J. (1985). The law and mental handicap: 3 The Mental Health Act, 1983—consent to treatment. *Mental Handicap*, **13**, 70–2.

Gunn, M.J. (1991). *Sex and the Law: A Brief Guide for Staff Working with People with Learning Difficulties* (3rd edn). London: Family Planning Association.

Hemsley, D.R. (1988). Psychological models of schizophrenia. In E. Miller and P.J. Cooper (Eds), *Adult Abnormal Psychology*. Edinburgh: Churchill Livingstone, pp. 101–27.

Hereford, C. (1963). *Changing Parental Attitudes through Group Discussion*. Austin, Texas: University of Texas Press.

Hetherington, E.M. and Clingempeel, W.G. (1992). Coping with marital transitions: a family systems perspective. *Monographs for the Society for Research in Child Development*, **57**.

Hogg, J. and Sebba, J. (1986). *Profound Retardation and Multiple Impairment*, 1, *Development and Learning*. London: Croom Helm.

Hulme, C. and MacKenzie, S. (1992). *Working Memory and Severe Learning Difficulties*. Hove, UK: Lawrence Erlbaum.

Jacobson, A. and Richardson, B. (1987). Assault experience of 100 psychiatric inpatients. Evidence of the need for routine inquiry. *American Journal of Psychiatry*, **144**, 908–13.

James, S.K. (1988). Sexual abuse of the handicapped. Paper presented at the Deaf/Blind/Multiply Handicapped Conference, Austin, Texas.

Kempton, W. (1988). *Life Horizons I and II: Sex Education for Persons with Special Needs*. Santa Monica, CA: James Stanfield & Company.

Kiernan, C. (1985). Communication. In A.M. Clarke, A.D.B. Clarke and J.M. Berg

(Eds), *Mental Deficiency: The Changing Outlook* (4th edn). London: Methuen, pp. 584–638.

Kolvin, I., Miller, F.J.W., Fleeting, M. and Kolvin, P.A. (1988). Social and parenting factors affecting criminal offence rates (findings from the Newcastle Thousand Families Study, 1947–1980). *British Journal of Psychiatry*, **152**, 80–90.

Kuipers, E. and Bebbington, P. (1987). *Living with Mental Illness: A Book for Relatives and Friends*. London: Souvenir Press.

Law Commission (1993a). *Mentally Incapacitated Adults and Decision-Making*. London: HMSO. (Consultation Paper, No. 129.)

Law Commission (1993b). *Mentally Incapacitated Adults and Decision-Making. A New Jurisdiction*. London: HMSO. (Consultation Paper, No. 128.)

Lezak, M.D. (1983). *Neuropsychological Assessment* (2nd edn). New York: Oxford University Press.

Lishman, W.A. (1987). *Organic Psychiatry* (2nd edn). Oxford: Blackwell Scientific Publications.

Loftus, E.F. (1979). *Eyewitness Testimony*. New York: Harvard University Press.

Luckasson, R., Coulter, D.L., Polloway, E.A., Reiss, S., Schalock, R.L., Snell, M.E., Spitalnik, D.M. and Stark, J.A. (1992). *Mental Retardation: Definition, Classification, and Systems of Supports*. Washington. DC: American Association on Mental Retardation.

McAllister, T.W. (1981). Cognitive functioning in the affective disorders. *Comprehensive Psychiatry*, **22**, 572–86.

McCarthy, M. and Thompson, D. (1993). *Sex and the 3 Rs: Rights, Responsibilities and Risks*. Hove, UK: Pavilion Publishing.

McCarthy, M. and Thompson, D. (1994). HIV/AIDS and safer sex work with people with learning disabilities. In A. Craft (Ed.), *Practice Issues in Sexuality and Learning Disabilities*. London: Routledge, pp. 186–201.

Mackay, R. (1990). Consent to treatment. In R. Bluglass and P. Bowden (Eds), *Principles and Practice of Forensic Psychiatry*. Edinburgh: Churchill Livingstone, pp. 1149–62.

Macoby, E.E. and Martin, J.A. (1983). Socialisation in the context of the family: parent–child interaction. In E.M. Hetherington (Ed.), *Handbook of Child Psychology, Vol. IV: Socialisation, Personality and Social Development*. New York: John Wiley, pp. 1–102.

Meadows, S. (1993). *The Child as Thinker*. London: Routledge.

Melhuish, E.C., Gambles, C. and Kumar, R. (1988). Maternal mental illness and the mother–infant relationship. In R. Kumar and I.F. Brockington (Eds), *Motherhood and Mental Illness: 2 Causes and Consequences*. London: Wright, pp. 191–211.

MENCAP (1989). *Competency and Consent to Medical Treatment*. London: MENCAP.

MENCAP (1992, unpublished). A survey of attitudes towards people with a mental handicap. London: MENCAP.

Milner, J.S. (1986). *The Child Abuse Potential Inventory: Manual* (2nd edn). Webster, North Carolina: Psytec Corporation.

Milner, J.S. (1991). Introduction: Current perspectives on physical child abuse. In special issue on child physical abuse, J.S. Milner (Ed.), *Criminal Justice and Behaviour*, **18**, 4–7.

Milner, J.S. (1992). Introduction: Sexual child abuse: theory, assessment and treatment. In special issue on child sexual abuse, J.S. Milner (Ed.), *Criminal Justice and Behaviour,* **19**, 4–7.

Milner, J.S. (1993a). Introduction: Child neglect: theory, research and intervention. In special issue on child neglect, J.S. Milner (Ed.), *Criminal Justice and Behaviour,* **20**, 4–7.

Milner, J.S. (Ed.) (1993b). Social information processing and physical child abuse. *Clinical Psychology Review*, **13**, 275–94.

Milner, J.S. and Chilamkurti, C. (1991). Physical child abuse perpetrator characteristics: a review of the literature. *Journal of Interpersonal Violence*, **6**, 345–66.

Milner, J.S. and Wimberley, R. (1980). Prediction and explanation of child abuse. *Journal of Clinical Psychology*, **36**, 875–84.

Mittler, P. and Preddy, D. (1981). Mentally handicapped pupils and school leavers: a survey in North-West England. In B. Cooper (Ed.), *Assessing the Handicaps and Needs of Mentally Retarded Children.* London: Academic Press, pp. 33–51.

Moos, R.H. and Moos, B.S. (1984). *Family Environment Scale Manual.* Palo Alto, California: Consulting Psychologists' Press.

Morris, C.D., Niederbuhl, J.M. and Mahr, J.M. (1993). Determining the capability of individuals with mental retardation to give informed consent. *American Journal on Mental Retardation*, **98**, 263–72.

Morris, R.G. (1991). Cognition and ageing. In R. Jacoby and C. Oppenheimer (Eds), *Psychiatry in the Elderly.* Oxford: Oxford University Press, pp. 58–88.

Morris, R.G. (1993). Language dysfunction in dementia. In J.M.Y. Simpson (Ed.), *The Encyclopedia of Language and Linguistics.* Aberdeen: Pergamon and Aberdeen University Press, pp. 1067–8.

Murphy, G.H. (1992). Community adjustment, social integration, work and social competence for people with intellectual disabilities or mental retardation. *Current Opinion in Psychiatry*, **5**, 831–5.

Murphy, G.H. (1993). The use of aversive stimuli in treatment: the issue of consent. *Journal of Intellectual Disability Research,* **37**, 211–9.

Murphy, W.D., Coleman, E.M. and Abel, G.G. (1983). Human sexuality in the mentally retarded. In J.L. Matson and F. Andrasik (Eds), *Treatment Issues and Innovations in Mental Retardation,* pp. 581–642. New York: Plenum Press.

Nelson, H.E. (1982). *The National Adult Reading Test.* Windsor, UK: NFER-Nelson.

Nelson, H.E., Pantelis, C., Carruthers, K., Speller, J., Baxendale, S. and Barnes, T.R.E. (1990). Cognitive functioning and symptomatology in chronic schizophrenia. *Psychological Medicine*, **20**, 357–65.

Nibert, D., Cooper, C. and Crossmaker, M. (1989). Assaults against residents of a psychiatric institution. *Journal of Interpersonal Violence*, **4**, 343–9.

Nirje, B. (1980). The normalisation principle. In R.J. Flynn and Nitsch, K.E. (Eds), *Normalisation, Social Integration and Community Services.* Austin, Texas: Pro-ed., pp. 71–116.

Nuechterlein, K.H. and Dawson, M.E. (1984). Information processing and attentional functioning in the developmental course of schizophrenic disorders. *Schizophrenia Bulletin*, **10**, 160–203.

Pishkin, V. and Bourne, L.E. (1981). Abstraction and the use of available information by schizophrenic and normal individuals. *Journal of Abnormal Psychology*, **90**, 197–203.

Pound, A., Cox, A., Puckering, C. and Mills, M. (1985). The impact of maternal depression on young children. In J.E. Stevenson (Ed.), *Recent Research in Developmental Psychopathology.* Oxford: Pergamon Press, pp. 3–17.

Practice Note (Official Solicitor) (1993). Sterilisation. *New Law Journal*, **143**, 1067.

Radford, M.H., Mann, L. and Kalucy, R.S. (1986). Psychiatric disturbance and decision-making. *Australian and New Zealand Journal of Psychiatry*, **20**, 210–17.

Repp, A. and Singh, N. (1990). *Perspectives on the Use of Non-Aversive and Aversive Interventions for Persons with Developmental Disabilities*. DeKalb, IL: Sycamore Press.

Rosenfeld, B., Turkheimer, E. and Gardner, W. (1992). Decision making in a schizophrenic population. *Law and Human Behavior*, **16**, 651–61.

Roth, L.H., Lidz, C.W., Meisel, A., Soloff, P.H., Kaufman, K., Spiker, D.G. and Foster, F.G. (1982). Competency to decide about treatment or research: an overview of some empirical data. *International Journal of Law and Psychiatry*, **5**, 29–50.

Roth, R.M. (1980). *The Mother–Child Relationship Evaluation: Manual*. Los Angeles: Western Psychological Services.

Royal College of Physicians (1981). Organic mental impairment in the elderly: implications for research, education and the provision of services, report of the Royal College of Physicians by the College Committee on Geriatrics. *Journal of the Royal College of Physicians of London*, **15**, 141–67.

Rutter, M. (1966). *Children of Sick Parents: An Environmental and Psychiatric Study*. Maudsley Monograph, No. 16, Oxford: Oxford University Press.

Rutter, M. (1987). Psychosocial resilience and protective mechanisms. *American Journal of Orthopsychiatry*, **57**, 316–31.

Rutter, M. (1990). Commentary: some focus and process considerations regarding the effects of maternal depression on children. *Developmental Psychology*, **26**, 60–7.

Rutter, M. and Quinton, D. (1984). Parental psychiatric disorder: effects on children. *Psychological Medicine*, **14**, 853–80.

Sameroff, A.J. and Seifer, R. (1990). Early contributors to developmental risk. In J. Rolf, A.S. Masten, D. Cicchetti, K.H. Neuchterlein and S. Weintraub (Eds), *Risk and Protective Factors in the Development of Psychopathology*. Cambridge: Cambridge University Press, pp. 52–66.

Schaefer, E. (1965). Children's reports of parental behaviour: an inventory. *Child Development*, **36**, 417–23.

Schaefer, E. and Bell, R. (1958). Development of a parental attitude research instrument. *Child Development*, **29**, 339–61.

Showalter, E. (1985). *The Female Malady: Women, Madness and English Culture, 1830–1980*. London: Virago.

Sigelman, C.K., Budd, E.D., Spanhel, C.L. and Schoenrock, C.J. (1981). When in doubt, say yes: acquiescence in interviews with mentally retarded persons. *Mental Retardation*, **19**, 53–8.

Skuse, D. and Bentovim, A. (1994). Physical and emotional maltreatment. In M. Rutter, E. Taylor and L. Hersov (Eds), *Child and Adolescent Psychiatry: Modern Approaches*. Oxford: Blackwell, pp. 209–29.

Smith, M. and Bentovim, A. (1994). Sexual abuse. In M. Rutter, E. Taylor and L. Hersov (Eds), *Child and Adolescent Psychiatry: Modern Approaches*. Oxford: Blackwell, pp. 230–51.

Sobsey, D. (1994). Sexual abuse of individuals with intellectual disability. In A. Craft (Ed.), *Practice Issues in Sexuality and Learning Disabilities*. London: Routledge, pp. 93–115.

Sparrow, S.S., Balla, D.A. and Cicchetti, D.V. (1984). *Vineland Adaptive Behavior Scales* (Interview Edition–Survey Form). Circle Pines, Minnesota: American Guidance Association.

Tepper, A.M. and Elwork, A. (1984). Competence to consent to treatment as a psycholegal construct. *Law and Human Behavior*, **8**, 205–23.

Tharinger, D., Horton, C.B. and Millea, S. (1990). Sexual abuse and exploitation of children and adults with mental retardation and other handicaps. *Child Abuse and Neglect*, **14**, 301–12.

Tully, B. and Cahill, D. (1984). *Police Interviewing of the Mentally Handicapped.* London: The Police Foundation.

Tymchuk, A. (1992). Predicting adequacy of parenting by persons with mental retardation. *Child Abuse and Neglect*, **16**, 165–78.

Tymchuk, A. and Andron, L. (1990). Mothers with mental retardation who do or do not abuse or neglect their children. *Child Abuse and Neglect*, **14**, 313–23.

Tymchuk, A. and Andron, L. (1992). Project Parenting: child interactional training with mothers who are mentally handicapped. *Mental Handicap Research*, **5**, 4–32.

Tymchuk, A. and Andron, L. (1994). Rationale, approaches, results and resource implications of programmes to enhance parenting skills of people with learning disabilities. In A. Craft (Ed.), *Practice Issues in Sexuality and Learning Disabilties*. London: Routledge, pp. 202–16.

Tymchuk, A., Andron, L. and Bavolek, S. (1990). *Nurturing Programme for Parents with Developmental Disabilties and their Children.* Park City: Family Development Resources.

Warren, N. and Jahoda, M. (1973). *Attitudes: Selected Readings* (2nd edn). Harmondsworth: Penguin.

Wechsler, D. (1981). *Manual for the Wechsler Adult Intelligence Scale-Revised (WAIS-R).* New York: The Psychological Corporation.

Weisberg, R.W. (1980). *Memory, Thought, and Behaviour.* New York: Oxford University Press.

Weithorn, L.A. and Campbell, S.B. (1982). The competency of children and adolescents to make informed treatment decisions. *Child Development*, **53**, 1589–98.

Wexler, D.B. (1973). Token and taboo: behaviour modification, token economies and the law. *California Law Review*, **61**, 81–109.

Wilcock, G. and Jacoby, R. (1991). Alzheimer's Disease. In R. Jacoby and C. Oppenheimer (Eds), *Psychiatry in the Elderly*. Oxford: Oxford University Press, pp. 586–605.

Williams, J., Watson, G., Smith, H., Copperman, J. and Wood, D. (1993). *Purchasing Effective Mental Health Services for Women: A Framework for Action.* London: MIND Publications.

Wish, J., McCombs, K.F. and Edmonson, B. (1979). *Manual for the Socio-Sexual Knowledge and Attitudes Test.* Chicago: Stoelting Corporation.

Wolfensberger, W. (1980). The definition of normalisation. In R.J. Flynn and K.E. Nitsch (Eds), *Normalisation, Social Integration and Community Services*. Austin, Texas: Pro-ed, pp. 71–116.

Wolfensberger, W. (1983). Social role valorisation: a proposed new term for the principle of normalisation. *Mental Retardation*, **21**, 234–9.

Woods, R.T. and Britton, P.G. (1985). *Clinical Psychology With the Elderly.* London: Croom Helm.

Chapter 2.6

Mental Health: Psychology's Contribution to Diagnosis, Assessment and Treatment

Clive R. Hollin
University of Birmingham & The Youth Treatment Service
and
Tracey Swaffer
The Youth Treatment Service

DEFINITION AND ASSESSMENT

The mental health of an offender is of paramount importance legally, practically, and theoretically (Baker 1993; Hodgins, 1993; Howells and Hollin, 1993; Whitehead, 1983). Those offenders who are judged to be of sound mental health and responsible for their actions will be dealt with under criminal law and so face the penalties under the criminal justice system. On the other hand, offenders deemed not to be of sound mental health (i.e. deemed to have a mental disorder) may be subject to mental health legislation and appropriate treatment services should be provided.

While the principle is easily stated, the issue of definition is not so straightforward: what are the rules by which decisions can be made concerning mental health, competence and responsibility? (There are in addition other conceptual issues that will not be addressed here: these include, for example, the debate about the very concept of mental events (e.g. Hayes and Brownstein, 1987); the usefulness of the term 'mental disorder' (e.g. Wakefield, 1992); and the controversy over the mythical status of mental illness (e.g. Szasz, 1974).)

Legal systems across the world approach the definitional issue in different ways. In England and Wales, for example, the Mental Health Act 1983 seeks to define those people who are categorised as mentally disordered. Essentially, the 1983 Act divides the concept of mental disorder into four categories: that is, mental disorder refers to 'mental illness, arrested or incomplete development of the mind, psychopathic disorder and any other disorder or disability of mind' (s. 1(2)). In practice the first three of these categories—mental illness, learning disability (i.e. arrested or incomplete development of the mind, itself subdivided into impairment and severe impairment), and psychopathic disorder—assumes the greatest importance. Given the universality of the issues, these three manifestations of mental disorder provide a convenient illustrative vehicle with respect to the complexities of assessment.

Mental Illness

While the 1983 Act is less than exact in specifying what is meant by the term mental illness (Ashworth and Gostin, 1985), in practice mental illness includes a range of diagnostic categories including psychoses, affective disorders and, exceptionally, anxiety states. Further, even within one class of mental illness there will be a range of possibilities: for example, schizophrenia encompasses disturbances of thought, perception, affect, and motor disorder. In reaching a diagnostic decision, clinicians will therefore use accepted criteria as defined in diagnostic manuals such as the *Diagnostic and Statistical Manual of Mental Disorders* (DSM-IV; American Psychiatric Association, 1994) or the *International Classification of Diseases* (ICD-10; Sartorius et al., 1988). Thus, to classify an offender as mentally ill, the symptoms as described in a given classification system would need to be monitored, and considered alongside indices such as family history, case notes, interviews, and responses to medication.

Learning Disability

Traditionally referred to as 'subnormal', 'mentally retarded', or 'mentally handicapped', the term 'learning disability' is currently preferred in many countries. The Mental Health Act 1983 refers to 'arrested or incomplete development of mind which includes ... impairment of intelligence and social functioning'. While the Act distinguishes 'severe' and 'significant' mental impairment, these terms are not defined (Ashworth and Gostin, 1985).

The assessment of learning disability will almost certainly include an assessment of intelligence. There are several standard IQ tests, although the Wechsler Adult Intelligence Scale (WAIS-R; Wechsler, 1981) and the Wechsler Intelligence Scale for Children (WISC-III; Wechsler, 1992) are perhaps the most widely used. Given variations in the scoring and interpretation of different IQ tests, it is not possible to define a 'legal level' of intellectual disability. In the field of intelligence testing an IQ score below 70 points on the WAIS-R begins to define significantly below-average levels of intellectual functioning. While the WAIS-R can help in making relatively fine distinctions in intellectual functioning, this power very much diminishes as IQ scores fall below 20–30 points. Indeed, many clinicians prefer to use an IQ band, such as 'average' or 'borderline', rather than presenting scores.

It would be unwise for courts to make judgments on the basis of IQ score alone. In clinical practice the assessment of disability should include an assessment of social functioning (e.g. Vineland Adaptation Scales; Sparrow, Ballo and Cicchetti, 1984). Social functioning ranges from the ability to perform simple tasks such as tying shoe-laces, to complex social interaction skills such as holding a conversation. The importance of the assessment of social functioning is illustrated in a study reported by Denkowski and Denkowski (1985), which looked at the prevalence of inmates with learning disability in the prisons of 20 states in the USA. Their figures on individually tested prisoners showed that 2.25 per cent. of prisoners were classified as learning disabled in states that relied solely on IQ testing. However, in five states where IQ *and* adaptive behaviour were assessed the percentage of learning disabled prisoners was 1.28 per cent. Clearly the decision regarding classification of offenders is significantly affected by the level and sophistication of the assessment procedure.

Psychopathic Disorder

As Hare, Strachan and Forth (1993) note, terms such as psychopath, sociopath, and antisocial personality disorder have all been used to refer to a particular type of violent offender. For example, in England and Wales the Mental Health Act 1983 defines 'psychopathic disorder' as 'a persistent disorder or disability of mind (whether or not including significant impairment of intelligence) which results in abnormally aggressive or seriously irresponsible conduct' (s. 1(2)).

The notion of psychopathy is troublesome on several fronts. Several commentators have questioned both the theoretical and psychiatric validity of the very idea of psychopathy (Howells, 1982; Grounds, 1987). This conceptual controversy is not helped by the lack of firm assessment criteria: for example, Blackburn (1993a) lists no fewer than five different ways of measuring psychopathy. In essence, however, there are two conflicting approaches to assessment (Thomas-Peter, 1992): one based on the use of standardised personality scales, the other relying on a checklist specifically designed to measure psychopathy.

The former approach is exemplified by the work of Blackburn (1971, 1986) using personality profiles generated by standardised personality tests such as the Minnesota Multiphasic Personality Inventory (MMPI; Hathaway, and McKinley, 1990). Blackburn suggests that there are two factors inherent in psychopathy: belligerence, including impulsivity and hostility; and withdrawal, referring to social isolation and low self-esteem. Further, Blackburn has identified two types of psychopath: primary and secondary psychopaths, who both score highly on the belligerence factor, but at opposite extremes of the withdrawal factor.

The second approach to assessment is, simply, based on refined measurement of factors deemed in clinical observation to be important diagnostic criteria (Cleckley, 1964; Lykken, 1957). More recently, Hare has developed a psychometrically sound assessment instrument, the Revised Psychopathy Checklist (PCL-R; Hare, 1991). The items from the PCL-R are shown in Table 2.6.1. Each item is scored on a 3-point scale, with information gathered from both files and interview: as Hare et al. (1993) note, 'PCL-R scores range from 0 to 40 ... For research purposes a cutoff score of 30 ... has proven useful for the diagnosis of psychopathy' (p. 167).

Table 2.6.1   Items in the Hare Psychopathy Checklist-Revised (PCL-R)

Item	
1	Glibness/superficial charm[a]
2	Grandiose sense of self worth[a]
3	Need for stimulation/proneness to boredom[b]
4	Pathological lying[a]
5	Conning/manipulative[a]
6	Lack of remorse or guilt[a]
7	Shallow affect[a]
8	Callous/lack of empathy[a]
9	Parasitic life style[b]
10	Poor behavioural controls[b]
11	Promiscuous sexual behaviour
12	Early behaviour problems[b]
13	Lack of realistic, long-term goals[b]
14	Impulsivity[b]
15	Irresponsibility[b]
16	Failure to accept responsibility for actions[a]
17	Many short-term marital relationships
18	Juvenile delinquency[b]
19	Revocation of conditional release[b]
20	Criminal versatility

Source: Hare (1991)
a   Loads on Factor 1 [callous, remorseless use of other people]
b   Loads on Factor 2 [chronically unstable and antisocial life style]

Factor analytic studies of the PCL-R have suggested two essential components to psychopathy (Harpur, Hakstian and Hare, 1988; Hare et al., 1990). The first factor reflects a selfish, callous and remorseless use of other people; the second, a chronically unstable and antisocial life style.

In summary, strong cases can be made for both approaches to the assessment of psychopathy: both have strong empirical backing and both have made theoretical contributions to understanding of severely antisocial behaviour. The major practical problem is that when administered to the same group of offenders, the two assessment methods do not result in exact agreement about which offenders display psychopathy (Harpur, Hare and Hakstian, 1989). In practice, forensic specialists tend to focus on specific features such as a failure to learn from experience, a lack of control over impulses, and chronic levels of antisocial behaviour as important indications of psychopathy (Davies and Feldman, 1981).

Other Aspects of Mental Health and Psychological Functioning

While for most legal purposes assessment of mental health will focus on the main types of disorder as detailed above, there are other aspects of psychological functioning for which assessment is sometimes needed. In truth this is a long list, including, for example, the recognised clinical states of anxiety, depression, organic dysfunction, and alcohol and drug dependency. There is a vast array of assessment material for each of these clinical conditions. The choice of assessment will depend on both the individual practitioner and the diagnostic system being followed. However, besides these clinical assessments, there are also several rather more criminological assessments of interest. These criminological areas include assessment of suggestibility, competence and dangerousness.

Suggestibility

It is the case that when accused of a criminal act some people make a false confession. While false confessions can be made voluntarily, they can also be the consequence of coercive police interviewing. Gudjonsson (1992) makes the distinction between two types of coerced false confession: a coerced-compliant false confession is made when the suspect admits to a crime that they know they did not commit; a coerced-internalised false confession occurs when the suspect, either temporarily or permanently, comes wrongly to believe during the process of interrogation that he or she did commit the crime.

There are obvious reasons why an individual would make a coerced-compliant confession; plainly the confession would stop the interrogation. The coerced-internalised false confession is less easily understood, but is thought to be associated with the individual's level of suggestibility. In this context, the term suggestibility is used to refer to a readiness by some individuals to absorb into their memory details provided from an extraneous source. Assessment of an individual's interrogative suggestibility is becoming a part of many forensic psychology reports.

Gudjonsson (1984, 1987) has developed a set of suggestibility scales, used in an interview, for forensic assessment purposes. Research with these scales has shown both their practical applicability and their potential for uncovering links between suggestibility and other aspects of psychological functioning (Gudjonnson, 1992). As can be seen from Table 2.6.2, several psychological factors, some already discussed above, are known to interact with levels of suggestibility. It seems likely that assessments of suggestibility would be informed by additional assessments of these factors.

Table 2.6.2   Psychological correlates of suggestibility

Psychological factor	Relationship with suggestibility
Acquiescence	Positive
Anxiety	Positive
Assertiveness	Negative
Facilitative Coping Style	Negative
Fear of Negative Evaluation	Positive
High Expectation of Accuracy	Positive
Intelligence	Negative
Memory Ability	Negative
Self-Esteem	Negative
Social Desirability	Positive

Note: A positive correlation indicates a direct relationship: for example, high anxiety predicts high suggestibility, and low anxiety predicts low suggestibility. A negative correlation predicts an inverse relationship: for example, high intelligence predicts low suggestibility, and low intelligence predicts high suggestibility.

Competency

While exact laws and definitions vary across different criminal justice systems, there is a general assumption that for justice to be done a defendant should be competent to stand trial. As Roesch and Golding (1987) note, the level of competency should be considered in terms of the complexity of the trial and the demands placed on the defendant. The assessment of competency is therefore of fundamental legal importance and must be distinguished from assessment of mental health *per se*. In practice, the assessment of competency in legal settings is comparatively rare in the UK compared with the USA.

It is important to state that competency is not automatically assumed to be in question if an individual is diagnosed as having a mental health problem. As Nicholson and Kugler (1991) highlight, neither severe mental illness nor mental impairment in and of themselves render an individual unfit for trial. The critical issue is whether an existing disorder, dysfunction, or deficiency impairs an individual's ability to understand his or her legal position. However, as Nicholson and Kugler (1991) also point out, defendants who receive a diagnosis showing a severe psychiatric disorder are more likely to be judged incompetent to stand trial.

As well as standard psychometric tests (e.g. IQ tests) there are several specifically designed forensic tests that have been used to assess competency: these include the Competency Screening Test (Lipsitt, Lelos and McGarry, 1971); the Competency Assessment Instrument (McGarry et al., 1973); and the Interdisciplinary Fitness Interview (Golding, Roesch and Schreiber, 1984). Nicholson and Kugler (1991) report that standard psychometric tests showed significant but small correlations with findings of competency tests. Assessment decisions are therefore typically based on the defendant performance on tests designed to assess legally relevant functional abilities. However, besides test findings, other factors such as age, gender, race, and legal history also show reliable correlations with competency decisions. Overall, a multitude of factors are involved in assessment of competency: some of these are clearly psychological in nature, while others appear to be more of a social judgement.

Dangerousness

The assessment of dangerousness is subtly different from other assessments. The types of assessment noted above all seek to make a statement about current psychological functioning. However, the assessment of dangerousness extends the debate into new realms. As Blackburn (1993b) points out, assessment of dangerousness has two components: (a) given certain conditions, does the individual in question display a tendency to behave violently?; (b) will the individual behave dangerously in the future? Thus, as well as assessment of current functioning, there is also an attempt to *predict* an individual's future behaviour. Assessment of the setting conditions related to a tendency to violent behaviour is a manageable task. Prediction, on the other hand, is an altogether more daunting task.

Assessments of dangerousness typically include a range of factors, including the individual's history, psychological indices such as anger disturbance, social setting and other environmental factors (Mulvey and Lidz, 1993). As might be expected with such a difficult task as predicting behaviour, a large and at times contradictory literature has evolved (e.g. Monahan, 1981, 1984; Prins, 1986; Litwack and Schlesinger, 1987; Pollock, McBain and Webster, 1989; Monahan and Steadman, 1994).

TREATMENT OF THE MENTALLY DISORDERED OFFENDER

There is a general acceptance of the principle that mentally disordered offenders should have rights of access to the same range of health provision as other members of society (e.g. Department of Health and the Home Office, 1992). What does differ, however, is the context in which these mental health services are delivered. Before looking directly at the treatment of the mentally disordered offender, it is worthwhile considering briefly the types of setting in which treatment takes place.

Treatment Settings

Acknowledging variations across countries, the range of settings in Great Britain is typical. Treatment for the mentally disordered offender is offered in psychiatric hospitals (usually in locked wards), special hospitals, regional secure units, some prisons, and in community facilities organised by both social services and the probation service (Prins, 1993).

Locked wards in psychiatric units may cater for offenders on both short-term and long-term bases. The treatment regime in such units is likely to be based on a traditional medical approach, involving medication and nursing care. A recent report by The British Psychological Society (BPS) suggested that offenders in locked wards have little contact with psychologists (BPS, 1993). Psychologists are, however, more prominent within the special hospital services. The special hospitals, rather like state hospitals in the United States, are provided for individuals who are both subject to mental health legislation and, because of their danger to the public and their violent and criminal acts, must be treated in secure conditions. Special hospitals are expected to admit all categories of mentally disordered offenders. The special hospitals may provide a long-term residential facility for some individuals, although those who no longer meet the admission criteria can be released back to the community sometimes via regional secure units (RSUs).

The RSUs were established in England in the 1980s to provide a placement for mentally disordered offenders who, because of their difficult behaviour, could not be managed in open psychiatric settings. The broad plan is that offenders will remain at an RSU for about two years before moving into more open, sometimes community, settings. There is a reasonable level of provision of psychological services within the RSUs. As noted above, the special hospitals may use RSUs as 'halfway houses' for clients returning to the community. Finally, some prisons have a hospital wing or annex that caters for mentally disordered offenders. These prison facilities are staffed by trained prison officers and members of the prison psychiatric services: psychologists may have a marginal role to play. In addition, there are a few prisons, such as Grendon Underwood Prison in England, that function as therapeutically orientated institutions. These prisons may be for offenders who show a mental disorder or whose offences suggest an element of psychiatric morbidity. With the involvement of psychologists, offenders are offered a range of therapies aimed at their eventual rehabilitation to the community.

Provisions within the community range from hostels to day support centres, typically run by organisations funded by charities or through either central government or local government grants. In addition, probation services, social services, and health services will offer support and assistance, including outpatient facilities. Many mentally disordered offenders are encouraged to use these provisions when returning to the community after a period in one of the other resources noted above. However, the stability and availability of such resources are dependent upon both the public and political attitudes of the time, and well-funded community support is not guaranteed (Prins, 1993).

Treatment Regimes

Before discussing the treatment regimes for mentally disordered offenders, it is appropriate to touch on some of the ethical issues involved. As Webster, Hucker and Grossman (1993) point out, the whole issue of treatment has to do with decision-making and judgements by lots of different people who are working to different agendas. In other words, while the primary concern of clinicians is the welfare and clinical interest of their patients, there is also a criminological agenda such that, whatever the clinical need, there are pressures on the clinician to protect the public, and to consider the political issues of retribution often demanded by society. In such circumstances the normal rules of client confidentiality are often not applicable and satisfactory clinical, legal, and administrative arrangements must be made. These arrangements must be acceptable to administrators, clinicians, and offenders (or their guardians), in total a far from simple task (Shah, 1993). In addition, there are profound legal and practical problems of sustaining a psychological treatment should an offender refuse to accept a given treatment regime. Yet further, even when treatment is possible, the restrictions of security, institutional demands, and lack of resources and trained staff may not be conducive to treatment. None the less, treatment programmes are delivered. The following sections give a brief overview of treatment interventions for the three major groups of mentally disordered offenders noted above (i.e. the mentally ill, those with learning disabilities, the psychopathic).

The Mentally Ill Offender

Several recent publications have looked at the provision of services for the mentally ill offender (Hallux, 1987; Kerr and Rosh, 1987; Rice et al., 1990; Webster, Hucker and Grossman, 1993). It is evident that mentally ill offenders are likely to be treated with medication, for example the positive symptoms of schizophrenia are often alleviated by appropriate pharmacological management. However, not all clients will respond to medication, and it may be that medication is more successful when accompanied by some form of psychological therapy.

Most therapeutic approaches and techniques can be used either with or without accompanying medication. For example, behaviour change programmes, such as contingency management and social skills training, with mentally ill offenders may focus on remedying behavioural deficits or reducing disruptive institutional behaviour (e.g. Machan and Streveler, 1990).

The Offender with Learning Disabilities

Despite a substantial literature on the relationship between learning disability and criminal behaviour (Day, 1993; Waldie and Spreen, 1993), Cullen (1993) notes that there is a lack of programmes for offenders with a learning disability. The programmes reported in the literature tend to blend an amalgam of styles and approaches to treatment, including skills acquisition, contingency management, counselling, group therapy, and psychotherapy (Denkowski and Denkowski, 1985; Day, 1988; Swanson and Garwick, 1990). Cullen (1993) recommends a constructional treatment approach for this offender group, with a focus on the acquisition of self-regulation and self-management skills. As Cullen notes, such programmes do require a degree of environmental control, therefore programmes must work towards generalisation of treatment gains to maintain progress once the offender returns to the community.

The Psychopathic Offender

It is perhaps somewhat paradoxical that the type of offender that has generated the greatest conceptual and diagnostic controversy should have attracted the greatest attention from clinicians. Despite the traditional view that the psychopathic offender is 'untreatable' there is a substantial treatment literature for this type of offender (Blackburn, 1993a, b).

As Blackburn notes, psychopharmacological interventions have not fared well with this group of offenders, either in terms of reducing violence or facilitating skills training. A similarly pessimistic outcome is found with individual and group psychotherapy. While there are some studies showing successful psychotherapeutic intervention, Blackburn suggests that the quality of the outcome data and length of follow-up are not always wholly satisfactory. There are limited signs of success for a therapeutic community approach to the treatment of psychopaths. The critical point in such interventions is the need to identify both the successful ingredients of a therapeutic community (Wexler, Falkin and Lipton, 1990), and the personal characteristics of those offenders most likely to benefit from such a regime.

As Blackburn notes, the development of behavioural treatment for psychopathic offenders has moved from operant-based methods, such as the token economy (Cavior and Schmidt, 1978); through skill acquisition programmes (Howells, 1976); to cognitive-behavioural methods, such as self-control training (Stermac, 1986); and finally to multimodal programmes incorporating a range of techniques and approaches (Grounds et al., 1987). The broad picture that emerges from the literature is that, by and large, the interventions are relatively successful in bringing about clinical change: there is, however, a tendency for high dropout rates with this offender group. However, in terms of criminological outcome, i.e. reduced offending, there is little in the way of substantial outcome data.

CONCLUDING REMARKS

The debate concerning an appropriate legislative system for the mentally disordered offender has a long and complex history. That debate has led to the intricacies of the current legal and administrative system, with an associated network of hospital and community services to cater for the needs of the mentally disordered offender. Psychologists have played a role in contributing to the debate on assessment and diagnosis. In addition, psychologists have played a practical role in the design of assessment tools, as witnessed by the availability of standardised psychometric tests for areas as diverse as competency to stand trial, interrogative suggestibility, and psychopathy. Yet further, psychologists have contributed to multidisciplinary research that considers the general effectiveness of services for the mentally disordered offender (e.g. MacCulloch et al., 1993). It is clear therefore that on this topic psychology has much to contribute both now and in the future. Indeed, a British Psychological Society Report on *Psychology and Antisocial Behaviour* contained no fewer than 49 recommendations intended to expand and enhance the role of psychologists in this field. It appears that when it comes to assessment, conceptual debate, diagnosis, and system outcome research, psychologists are playing a full role alongside other professional groups. However, if the effectiveness of clinical treatment component of the mental health services is considered, a different picture emerges.

While the lack of psychological expertise in some services, perhaps especially community services, is of concern, the lack of specific knowledge about the effectiveness of clinical interventions is more than disconcerting. With regard to offenders with learning disabilities, Cullen (1993) notes that 'there are remarkably few programmes which are specifically aimed at learning-disabled offenders' (p. 149). Similarly, Blackburn (1993b) makes the point that 'We do not as yet know which disorders within the heterogeneous category of psychopathic disorder or "antisocial personalities" respond to which interventions, and until clinically relevant discriminations are made within this group, practice will remain in a theoretical vacuum' (p. 203). Webster, Hucker and Grossman (1993) are a little more optimistic with respect to the mentally ill offender: 'Although the specific effectiveness of most generally-available treatment programmes is unknown, it is fair to say that several strong methods are at hand and that the means to evaluate these ventures are available' (p. 104). Indeed, it is true that theoretical research on the nature of the relationship between mental illness and criminal behaviour is moving apace (Monahan, 1992; Taylor et al., 1993). None the less, the general picture is one of a lack of knowledge about the clinical effectiveness of specific programmes for mentally disordered offenders. While it is undoubtably true that successful treatment programmes have been conducted, the issue remains of which interventions, delivered under what conditions, work best for which groups of mentally disordered offenders.

In seeking answers to these questions there is much to be taken from recent advances elsewhere in the research literature. It is now clear from the many meta-analysis studies that a great deal is known about the effectiveness of different treatments in different settings for a range of mental health problems (Lipsey and Wilson, 1993). It is also established, again by meta-analysis, which behaviour change methods have the greatest chance of impacting on criminal behaviour (Gendreau and Andrews, 1990; Lipsey, 1992). The next steps in designing clinical services for the mentally disordered offender may benefit from setting a clinical research agenda based on what is known to be effective in the treatment of mental disorder and in lowering offending.

ACKNOWLEDGEMENT

We would like to thank Ron Blackburn for his helpful comments on an earlier draft of this chapter.

REFERENCES

American Psychiatric Association (1994). *Diagnostic and Statistical Manual of Mental Disorders* (4th edn). Washington, DC: American Psychiatric Association.

Ashworth, A. and Gostin, L. (1985). Mentally disordered offenders and the sentencing process. In L. Gostin (Ed.), *Secure Provision*. London: Tavistock, pp. 72–86.

Baker, E. (1993). The social and legal framework. In K. Howells and C.R. Hollin (Eds), *Clinical Approaches to the Mentally Disordered Offender*. Chichester: John Wiley, pp. 9–34.

Blackburn, R. (1971). Personality types among abnormal homicides. *British Journal of Criminology*, **11**, 14–31.

Blackburn, R. (1986). Patterns of personality deviation among violent offenders. *British Journal of Criminology*, **26**, 254–69.

Blackburn, R. (1993a). Clinical programmes with Psychopaths. In K. Howells and C.R. Hollin (Eds), *Clinical Approaches to the Mentally Disordered Offender*. Chichester: John Wiley, pp. 179–210.

Blackburn, R. (1993b). *The Psychology of Criminal Conduct: Theory, Research and Practice*. Chichester: John Wiley.

(BPS) British Psychological Society (1993). *Psychology and Antisocial Behaviour*. Leciester: BPS.

Cavior, H.E. and Schmidt, A.A. (1978). Test of the effectiveness of a differential treatment strategy at the Robert F. Kennedy Centre. *Criminal Justice and Behavior*, **5**, 131–9.

Cleckley, H. (1964). *The Mask of Sanity* (4th edn). St Louis: Mosby.

Cullen, C. (1993). The treatment of people with learning disabilities who offend. In K. Howells and C.R. Hollin (Eds), *Clinical Approaches to the Mentally Disordered Offender*. Chichester: John Wiley, pp. 145–64.

Davies, W. and Feldman, P. (1981). The diagnosis of psychopathy by forensic specialists. *British Journal of Psychiatry*, **138**, 329–31.

Day, K. (1988). A hospital based treatment programme for male mentally handicapped offenders. *British Journal of Psychiatry*, **153**, 635–44.

Day, K. (1993). Crime and mental retardation: a review. In K. Howells and C.R. Hollin (Eds), *Clinical Approaches to the Mentally Disordered Offender*. Chichester: John Wiley, pp. 111–44.

Denkowski, G. and Denkowski, K.M. (1985). Community based residential treatment of the mentally retarded adolescent offender: Phase I, reduction of aggressive behaviour. *Journal of Community Psychology*, **13**, 299–305.

Department of Health and the Home Office (1992). Review of health and social service for mentally disordered offenders and others requiring similar services (the 'Reed' Committee, a series of papers). London: Department of Health and Home Office.

Gendreau, P. and Andrews, D.A. (1990). What the meta-analyses of the offender treatment literature tell us about 'What Works'. *Canadian Journal of Criminology*, **32**, 173–84.

Golding, S.L., Roesch, R. and Schreiber, J. (1984). Assessment and conceptualization of competency to stand trial: preliminary data on the interdisciplinary fitness interview. *Law and Human Behavior*, **8**, 321–34.

Grounds, A.T. (1987). Detention of psychopathic disorder patients in special hospitals: critical issues. *British Journal of Psychiatry*, **151**, 474–8.

Grounds, A.T., Quayle, M.T., France, J., Brett, T., Cox, M. and Hamilton, J.R. (1987). A unit for psychopathic disorder patients in Broadmoor Hospital. *Medicine Science and The Law*, **27**, 21–31.

Gudjonsson, G.H. (1984). A new scale of interrogative suggestibility. *Personality and Individual Differences*, **5**, 303–14.

Gudjonsson, G.H. (1987). A parallel form of the Gudjonsson Suggestibility Scale. *British Journal of Clinical Psychology*, **26**, 215–21.

Gudjonsson, G.H. (1992). *The Psychology of Interrogations, Confessions and Testimony*. Chichester: John Wiley.

Hallux, S. (1987). *The Mentally Disordered Offender*. Washington, DC: American Psychiatric Press.

Hare, R.D. (1991). *The Hare Psychopathy Checklist-Revised*. Toronto: Multi-Health Systems.

Hare, R.D., Harpur, T.J., Hakstian, A.R., Forth, A.E., Hart, S.D. and Newman, J.P. (1990). The Revised Psychopathy Checklist: reliability and factor structure. *Psychological Assessment: A Journal of Consulting and Clinical Psychology*, **2**, 338–41.

Hare, R.D., Strachan, C.E. and Forth, A.E. (1993). Psychopathy and crime: a review. In K. Howells and C.R. Hollin (Eds), *Clinical Approaches to The Mentally Disordered Offender*. Chichester: John Wiley, pp. 165–78.

Harpur, T.J., Hakstian, A.R. and Hare, R.D. (1988). Factor structure of the Psychopathy Checklist. *Journal of Consulting and Clinical Psychology*, **56**, 710–14.

Harpur, T.J., Hare, R.D. and Hakstian, A.R. (1989). Two-factor conceptualization of psychopath: construct validation and assessment implications. *Psychological Assessment: A Journal of Consulting and Clinical Psychology*, **1**, 6–17.

Hathaway, S. and McKinley, J. (1990). *MMPI* (2nd edn). Windsor, Berkshire: NFER-Nelson.

Hayes, S. and Brownstein, A. (1987). Mentalism, private events, and scientific explanation: a defense of B.F. Skinner's view. In S. Modgil and C. Modgil (Eds), *B. F. Skinner: Consensus and Controversy*. New York: Falmer Press, pp. 207–18.

Hodgins, S. (Ed.) (1993). *Mental Disorder and Crime*. Newbury Park, CA: Sage.

Howells, K. (1976). Interpersonal aggression. *International Journal of Criminology and Penology*, **4**, 319–30.

Howells, K. (1982). Mental disorder and violent crime. In P. Feldman (Ed.), *Developments in the Study of Criminal Behaviour. Vol. 2: Violence*. Chichester: John Wiley, pp. 163–200.

Howells, K. and Hollin, C.R. (Eds) (1993). *Clinical Approaches to the Mentally Disordered Offender*. Chichester: John Wiley.

HMSO (1983). *The Mental Health Act*. HMSO: London.

Kerr, C.A. and Rosh, J.A. (1987). Survey of facilities and programs for mentally disordered offenders. National Institute of Mental Health and Human Services, DHHS Publication No (Adm) 86–1493.

Lipsitt, P.D., Lelos, D. and McGarry, A.L. (1971). Competency for trial: a screening instrument. *American Journal of Psychiatry*, **139**, 105–9.

Lipsey, M.W. (1992). Juvenile delinquency treatment: a meta-analytic inquiry into the variability of effects. In T.D. Cook, H. Cooper, D.S. Cordray, H. Hartmann, L.V. Hedges, R.J. Light, T.A. Louis, and F. Mosteller (Eds), *Meta-analysis for Explanation: A Casebook*. New York: Russell Sage Foundation, pp. 83–127.

Lipsey, M.W. and Wilson, D.B. (1993). The efficacy of psychological, educational, and behavioral treatment: confirmation from meta-analysis. *American Psychologist*, **48**, 1181–209.

Litwack, T.R. and Schlesinger, L.B. (1987). Assessing and predicting violence: research, law and applications. In I.B. Wiener and A.K. Hess (Eds), *Handbook of Forensic Psychology*. New York: John Wiley, pp. 205–57.

Lykken, D.T. (1957). A study of anxiety in the sociopathic personality. *Journal of Abnormal and Social Psychology*, **55**, 6–10.

MacCulloch, M., Bailey, J., Jones, C. and Hunter, C. (1993). Nineteen male serious offenders who were discharged from a special hospital: II. Illustrated clinical issues. *Journal of Forensic Psychiatry*, **4**, 451–69.

Machan, S.J. and Streveler, A. (1990). Social and independent living skills for psychiatric patients in a prison setting. *Behavior Modification*, **14**, 490–518.

McGarry, A.L., Curran, W.J., Lipsett, P.D., Lelos, D., Schwitzgebel, R. and Rosenberg, A.H. (1973). *Competency to Stand Trial and Mental Illness*. Washington, DC: US Government Printing Office.

Monahan, J. (1981). *Predicting Violent Behavior: An Assessment of Clinical Techniques*. Newbury Park, CA: Sage.

Monahan, J. (1984). The prediction of violent behavior: toward a second generation of theory and practice. *American Journal of Psychiatry*, **141**, 10–15.

Monahan, J. (1992). Mental disorder and violent behaviour: perceptions and evidence. *American Psychologist*, **47**, 511–21.

Monahan, J. and Steadman, H.J. (Eds) (1994). *Mental Disorder: Developments in Risk Assessment*. Chicago: The University of Chicago Press.

Mulvey, E.P. and Lidz, C.W. (1993). Measuring patient violence in dangerousness research. *Law and Human Behavior*, **17**, 277–88.

Nicholson, R.A. and Kugler, K.E. (1991). Competent and incompetent criminal defendants: a quantitative review of comparative research. *Psychological Bulletin*, **10**, 355–70.

Pollock, N., McBain, I. and Webster, C.D. (1989). Clinical decision making and the assessment of dangerousness. In K. Howells and C.R. Hollin (Eds), *Clinical Approaches to Violence*. Chichester: John Wiley, pp. 89–118.

Prins, H. (1986). *Dangerous Behaviour, The Law and Mental Disorder*. London: Tavistock.

Prins, H. (1993). Service provision and facilities for the mentally disordered offender. In K. Howells and C.R. Hollin (Eds), *Clinical Approaches to the Mentally Disordered Offender*. Chichester: John Wiley, pp. 35–70.

Rice, M.E., Harris, G.T., Quinsey, V.L. and Cyr, M. (1990). Planning treatment programs in secure psychiatric facilities. In D.N. Weisstub (Eds), *Law and Mental Health: International Perspectives*, 5. New York: Pergamon, pp. 162–230.

Roesch, R. and Golding, S.L. (1987). Defining and assessing competency to stand trial. In I.B. Weiner and A.K. Hess (Eds), *Handbook of Forensic Psychology*. New York: John Wiley, pp. 378–94.

Sartorius, N., Jablensky, A., Cooper, J.E. and Burke, J.D. (Eds) (1988). Psychiatric classification in an international perspective. *British Journal of Psychiatry*, Supplement No. 1, 152.

Shah, S.A. (1993). A clinical approach to the mentally disordered offender: an overview and some major issues. In K. Howells and C.R. Hollin (Eds), *Clinical Approaches to the Mentally Disordered Offender*. Chichester: John Wiley, pp. 211–36.

Stermac, L.E. (1986). Anger control treatment for forensic patients. *Journal of Interpersonal Violence*, **1**, 446–57.

Sparrow, S.S., Ballo, D.A. and Cicchetti, D.V. (1984). *Vineland Adaptive Behavior Scales*. Circle Pines, MN: American Guidance Service.

Swanson, C.K. and Garwick, G.B. (1990). Treatment for low functioning sex offenders: group therapy and inter-agency coordination. *Mental Retardation*, **28**, 155–61.

Szasz, T.S. (1974). *The Myth of Mental Illness: Foundations of a Theory of Personal Conduct*. New York: Harper & Row.

Taylor, P.T., Garety, P., Buchanan, A., Reed, A., Wessely, S., Ray, K., Dunn, G. and Grubin, D. (1993). Delusions and violence. In J. Monahan and H.J. Steadman (Eds), *Violence and Mental Disorder: Developments and Risk Assessment*. Chicago: The University of Chicago Press, pp. 161–82.

Thomas-Peter, B.A. (1992). The classification of psychopathy: a review of the Hare vs Blackburn debate. *Personality and Individual Differences*, **13**, 337–42.

Wakefield, J.C. (1992). The concept of mental disorder: on the boundary between biological facts and social values. *American Psychologist*, **47**, 373–88.

Waldie, K. and Spreen, O. (1993). The relationship between learning disabilities and persisting delinquency. *Journal of Learning Disabilities*, **26**, 417–23.

Webster, C.D., Hucker, S.J. and Grossman, M.G. (1993). Clinical programmes for mentally ill offenders. In K. Howells and C.R. Hollin (Eds), *Clinical Approaches to the Mentally Disordered Offender*. Chichester: John Wiley, pp. 87–110.

Wechsler, D. (1981). *Wechsler Adult Intelligence Scale-Revised*. New York: Psychological Corporation.

Wechsler, D. (1992). *Wechsler Intelligence Scale for Children-III*. New York: NFER.

Wexler, H.K., Falkin, G.P. and Lipton, D.S. (1990). Outcome evaluation of a prison therapeutic community for substance abuse treatment. *Criminal Justice and Behavior,* **17**, 71-92.

Whitehead, T. (1983). *Mental Illness and the Law* (2nd edn). Oxford: Blackwell.

Learning Disability: Psychology's Contribution to Diagnosis, Assessment and Treatment

Karl Nunkoosing
University of Portsmouth

INTRODUCTION

As our understanding of the nature, causes and consequences of learning disability improves and our consciousness about the social situations of people with disabilities is raised, we continue to seek terms and definitions of learning disability that are both technically correct and do not impose negative imagery or insult people. Thus the multiplicity of terms—such as intellectual disability, mental retardation, learning disability, learning difficulty, developmental disability—that can be found in English language professional and academic publications is at times confusing, but stands as a reflection of both our growing knowledge and increased sensitivity.

The law and legal procedures also have to reflect the progress that has taken place in our greater understanding of learning disability, its consequences for the individual and in the social changes leading to the emergence of the self advocacy movement. The person with a learning disability should be able to expect that the law would protect his or her rights to self determination, to freedom from unnecessary constraints and of access to effective support and appropriate services. Moveover, people with learning disability also constitute a group that is vulnerable to exploitation. In this regard, the law is expected to protect the individual from abuse and exploitation and to provide explicit guidance about the duty of care on those who provide professional assistance to citizens with learning disability.

Handbook of Psychology in Legal Contexts
Edited by R. Bull and D. Carson. © 1995 John Wiley & Sons Ltd

Advocacy organisations, which have been a major impetus in our greater understanding of the life situations of people who experience learning disability, would prefer that we do not use any label that brings negative attention to people who experience learning disability. Through such organisations people with learning disabilities, and their families and friends have challenged the professional community to search for an appropriate definition of learning disability. The American Association on Mental Retardation (AAMR) has revised its widely used 1983 definition (Grossman, 1983) in order to reflect more contemporary knowledge about the nature, causes and consequences of learning disability and to reflect contemporary practices about the support that people require to make full use of their citizenship rights.

DEFINITION OF LEARNING DISABILITY

Mental Retardation refers to substantial limitations in present functioning. It is characterized by significant subaverage intellectual functioning, existing concurrently with related limitations in two or more of the following applicable adaptive skill areas: communication, selfcare, home living, social skills, community use, self direction, health and safety, functional academics, leisure and work. Mental retardation manifests before age 18. (AAMR, 1992)

'Substantial limitation in present functioning' refers to the difficulty that the person might experience in learning and in the performance of certain daily skills and these are due to limitations in conceptual, practical and social intelligence. As in Grossman's (1983) definition, sub-average intellectual functioning is interpreted in terms of an 'IQ standard score of 70 to 75 or below' (p. 11). The intellectual limitation is accompanied by, and is related to, limitations in adaptive skills. Such limitations should not arise from the person's culture or language, nor from sensory or motor limitation. Because limitation in intellectual functioning alone is not sufficient for a diagnosis of learning disability, limitations of adaptive skills in at least two areas that are important to life functioning must also be demonstrated as indicators of generalised limitations, as well as providing a safeguard against the probability of measurement error in the assessment of intellectual functioning. The age of onset before the age of 18, represents the age that, traditionally in Western societies, the individual is expected to assume adult roles. It is also related to a number of significant legal tests of capacity.

Attention is drawn to four assumptions that are considered central to the application of this definition:

1. The validity of an assessment is dependent upon the extent to which it considers factors such as the individual's culture, language, communication and behaviour.

2. The assessment of the individual's adaptive skills should be made in the context of his or her community environment and in relation to community members of similar age. The determination of the individual's limitation in adaptive skills should also determine the support and services that the individual will need for continued personal growth and development.

3. Having a learning disability does not mean that the person is seen only in terms of limitations in ability. The person with a learning disability often possesses strengths in adaptive skills, physical and social capabilities independent of the skills limitations that relate directly to the learning disability.

4. Most people with learning disability will improve in their general functioning, independence, productivity and community integration when provided with appropriate and effective support and services. Some individuals will need lifelong support, whilst for others it may only be needed intermittently. Where the individual does not demonstrate significant improvement it is necessary to determine whether this is due to the quality, effectiveness, and appropriateness of the support and services that are currently available to the person.

This variability over time has legal implications. For example, decisions made about a person's capacity should not stand for all time, as this may change as the person develops. Thus it may not be appropriate for people to be placed on guardianship, or have their property subjected to the Court of Protection (Mental Health Act, 1983) for the whole of their lives. There is also a need to be clear about the extent that service providers could be held responsible in instances where a service user does not demonstrate significant improvement.

This up-to-date definition reflects changes in our understanding of learning disability and differs from past definitions in many significant ways. First, it emphasises the need to define systems of support for the individual as part of the assessment process. Secondly, learning disability is not considered to be an absolute trait; learning disability results from an interaction between the individual and his or her environment. Learning disability is seen as a state in which adaptive and intellectual functioning interact in specific ways, consequently appropriate support and services can significantly influence this state. Thirdly, the identification of the adaptive skill areas essential for successful life functioning will provide guidance about the nature and quality of support that the individual might need. The usefulness does not necessarily mean that there is clear consensus about what constitutes an appropriate definition of learning disability. The implication of this in the legal context is that until the above definition becomes established, the law may well have to operate on the basis of its existing definition of learning disability. In the UK, for example, the Mental Health Act 1983 relies on definitions of 'mental disorder' and 'mental impairment' to include both learning disability and mental illness. In this context '"mental disorder" means mental illness, arrested or incomplete development of mind, psychopathic disorder and any other disorder or disability of mind' (Mental Health Act, 1983, s. 5.1). The law will have a significant role to play in the general acceptance of these new assumptions about the consequences of being diagnosed as having a learning disability and the nature of this disability.

AN ALTERNATIVE DEFINITION

Because learning disability does not constitute a homogeneous group of difficulties (Hooper and Willis, 1989), there are other conceptual definitions of it. Those who prefer categorical definitions, such as Zigler and Hodapp (1986), have argued that social adaptation is a vague concept that is difficult to measure and thus should be excluded from definitions of learning disability. Dockrell and McShane (1992) have pointed out that 'in reality, adaptive behaviour is rarely used as a criterion by researchers and in the diagnosis process by clinicians' (p. 150). The writers of the AAMR (1992) definition have gone to great length to demonstrate solutions to these difficulties.

The other popular definition of learning disability is categorical, has many similarities with Grossman's (1983) definition, and comes from the American Psychiatric Association's (1987) DSM-III-R Manual where learning disability is considered a developmental disorder whose essential features are: 'Significantly subaverage general intellectual functioning, accompanied by significant deficits or impairments in adaptive functioning, with onset before the age of eighteen' (p. 28). The DSM-III-R Manual also lists the following categories of 'mental retardation' which reflect the degree of intellectual impairment as measured by individually administered IQ tests:

1. Mild: 50–55 to approximately 70

2. Moderate: 35–40 to 50–55

3. Severe: 20–25 to 36–40

4. Profound: below 20 or 25.

LEVEL OF SUPPORT AS A BASIS FOR CLASSIFICATION

It is worth noting that the AAMR (1992) has radically moved away from such categories as those shown above in favour of defining four levels or intensities of support that the individual diagnosed as having a learning disability will *need*. These are: intermittent, limited, extensive, pervasive. Intermittent support may be required at specific stages in the life cycle, usually of short duration but may be of high or low intensity when provided. Limited support is also time limited but not of an intermittent nature, is consistent over time as exemplified by the support that might be required for employment training. Extensive support is delivered regularly in some environments and is not time limited; an example might be the daily support that a child with a learning disability needs from an education support worker for inclusion in an ordinary school. Pervasive support is constant and of high intensity delivered in all environments associated with the person. It may be life sustaining and is more intrusive and costlier than extensive or limited support (AAMR, 1992). Defining systems of support does not necessarily mean that a concept like 'severe intellectual disability' is meaningless, for 'individuals who have the most severe handicaps are those who require extraordinary supports and opportunities in order to allow them to gain a wide range of skill' (Evans, 1991, p. 39). The implication of this for the legal context is that it will not be sufficient simply to assess the person's intelligence and assign him or her to a category based on an IQ score. It will take time to establish how the law will ensure that providers give support at the level identified and to ensure that the level of support identified is appropriate for the individual concerned. It could be argued that providers would have a vested interest in providing the less expensive intermittent or limited level of support rather than the expensive pervasive level of support. The law will also have to ensure that the person who assesses the level of support required is independent of those who will have the duty to provide such support.

ASSESSMENT AND DIAGNOSIS OF LEARNING DISABILITY

Two important criteria concerning the valid diagnosis of learning disability are intellectual functioning and the level of adaptive skills. The assessment of intellectual functioning, although not without critique, continues to be one of the main criteria for the legal, educational and medical designation of a person as having a learning disability. In fact it can be argued that the repeated criticism of IQ tests in the decade of 1965–75 led the AAMR to include limitations in adaptive functioning in the 1983 definition of learning disability. The concern here will be about good practice that serves to limit the errors that are inherent in the assessment of intellectual functioning and adaptive skills, as well as current understanding of these two concepts.

ASSESSMENT OF INTELLECTUAL FUNCTIONING

Intellectual functioning must be assessed with valid, reliable, standardised and individually administered intelligence tests. Such tests should be administered by a psychologist with experience of people who have learning disability and who has been trained to a high standard in both the administration and the interpretation of IQ tests. The tests must also be administered in circumstances that allow the person being tested to perform maximally.

The measure has to be standardised to the individual's social, cultural, ethnic and linguistic background and ought to take into account any motor or sensory limitations that are likely to interfere with the person's performance. In circumstances where such standard measures are not available, the need for accurate and sensitive clinical judgement based on experience is critical. Cultural and linguistic diversity can seriously influence the accuracy of measurements of intellectual functioning. Both the sociocultural background of the individual and his or her main language must be considered in the selection and administration of assessment tools and in the interpretations of the results (Reschley, 1990). Attention has also been drawn to the need for assessors to be cautious about excessive reliance only on intelligence tests when making diagnostic decisions in such circumstances (Reschley and Ward, 1991).

The accurate assessment of intellectual functioning for individuals who experience sensory, motor or communicative limitations is especially difficult (Meacham et al., 1987). Non-verbal test instruments may be required by individuals with hearing impairments; those with visual impairments will have to rely on assessment materials that exclude the use of object manipulation. Individuals with motor disabilities will experience considerable problems with performance measures of intelligence and may need additional support in order to indicate their responses to test items. Some individuals may not have learnt how to behave in test situations (Browder and Snell, 1988) and this might lead to inaccurate conclusions about their levels of functioning.

Other factors that can contribute to inaccurate assessment of a person's intellectual functioning or level of adaptive skills include tiredness, low tolerance of frustration, low test motivation, non-compliance, drowsiness due to medication, anxiety and lack of understanding of instructions (Evans, 1991; Pollingue, 1987; Schuler and Perez, 1991). Inadequate assessments have implications for legal contexts in the sense that such assessments often constitute tests of the individual's capacity. Assessments made on one occasion may be relied upon, improperly, for many years to come. Accurate assessment is also the basis for defining the person's eligibility to assistance and services. The law could have a role in defining the expertise and competencies of those who undertake such assessments.

ASSESSMENT OF ADAPTIVE SKILLS

Adaptive behaviour refers to a range of personal skills which assists the individual to meet the demands of his or her social environment and relates to what the person actually does in practical every-day situations. Limitations of adaptive skills in one area are often compensated for by skills in other areas. Evans (1991) describes adaptive behaviour as 'the skills that will help an individual fit into a social niche, and the ability to change one's behaviour to suit the demands of a situation' (p. 34). Thus behaviour that is adaptive in a segregated community may not be as adaptive in more open community settings. A series of research studies by Robert Bruininks and his colleagues has demonstrated that adaptive behaviour corresponds to two basic concepts: personal independence and social responsibility (Bruininks and McGrew, 1987; Bruininks, Thurlow and Gilman, 1987; McGrew and Bruininks, 1989).

Adaptive skills are difficult to classify as they relate to a large range of behaviours and competencies, and are difficult to measure accurately as they occur in many situations, with some behaviours being very specific to particular situations.

The present AAMR (1992) definition of learning disability goes some way towards dealing with the problems inherent in the measurement of adaptive behaviour, and the confusion that exists about the concept (Foster-Gaitskell and Pratt, 1989), because it identifies the specific adaptive areas and the skills associated with each area. The requirement of skill limitation in at least two of ten identified areas to reflect generalised disability will also prove useful. It is hoped that the future will see greater use made of adaptive skills, in both the diagnosis of learning disability and in research, that will result from the development of appropriate instruments. Apart from its theoretically central position in the definition and diagnosis of learning disability, proper measurement of adaptive skill also provides the basis for designing the interventions, support and services that the person with a learning disability will need for continued growth and development.

> The purpose of measurement is not to establish normalcy but rather to determine what areas need special help, special training, special intrusion possibly leading even to denial of certain specific rights for a prescribed period of time (with the understanding that those rights will be restored, whether or not the habilitation program has been a success). (Leyland, 1991, p. 212)

Behaviours judged by others to be maladaptive and considered inappropriate, undesirable or challenging require careful consideration. Such behaviours in persons with severe disabilities have been shown to be adaptations to the environment, and in some instances are responses to lack of communicative function (Durand and Crimmins, 1988; Durand and Kishi, 1987; Evans and Scotti, 1989).

Most assessments of adaptive skills rely on information provided by third parties, such as parents, teachers, residential service workers and other providers of services, who are judged to be familiar with the person being assessed. Clearly direct observation of the person's adaptive behaviours or the person's self-report would be preferable but it is not always possible, either because of the person's communicative and cognitive abilities or because of time and cost. Care should be taken in the identification and selection of the people who provide information about an individual's adaptive behaviour. They should have observed and interacted with him or her for not less than three months. The use of more than one rater is likely to increase the validity of the results. Whenever possible it is desirable to include direct observation in the assessment of adaptive skills and to use more than one instrument to measure all the relevant domains of adaptive behaviour.

The assessment of intellectual functioning and level of adaptive skills has not always served the interests of people with severe disabilities (Evans, 1991). Functional assessment is an attempt to provide an alternative approach that does not focus emphasis on people's deficits nor result in negative labelling of people with severe learning disabilities. Gaylord-Ross and Browder (1991) have identified the main characteristics of functional assessment as focusing on practical, independent living skills, with an emphasis on an ecological approach to the understanding of the person's functioning in his or her environment, and a concern with the process of learning in order to suggest interventions that may be successful and which are continually monitored to evaluate treatment progress. The implication for the legal context is that the diagnosis of learning disability should be based on both the assessment of intellectual functioning and of adaptive skills, both of which could change over time. The diagnosis may have to be reviewed regularly for the person to be provided with appropriate support and safeguards.

ASSESSMENT OF MENTAL HEALTH

Assessment of psychological functioning and behaviour is also likely to uncover the significant minority of individuals with learning disability who may also need mental health services. Parsons, May and Menolascino (1984) have demonstrated that, in the USA, 20–35 per cent. of all non-institutionalised people with learning disability are diagnosed as having both a mental illness and a learning disability. This significant minority of people has needs for appropriate support and services.

The assessment of mental illness in persons with learning disabilities is especially difficult because of a range of factors which include lack of research, misunderstanding of what constitutes mental illness in people who also have learning disabilities, inconsistent diagnostic techniques, confusion about definition, and inappropriate classification in the past. Consider the following as an example of these problems: Warren, Holroyd and Folstein (1989) describe how a number of individuals with Down's syndrome, aged under 35 years of age, were mistakenly diagnosed as having Alzheimer's disease after they showed signs of loss of previously acquired adaptive skills. However, when the symptoms were correctly identified as those associated with depression, they all responded favourably to treatment with antidepressant medications. This is also an instance where the concurrent presence of a learning disability and symptoms of mental illness serve to decrease the diagnostic impact of the mental disorder. This is referred to as diagnostic 'overshadowing' (Reiss, Levitan and Szyszko, 1982; Reiss and Szyszko, 1983). There are concerns that adding the diagnosis of mental illness to a person who is also diagnosed as having a learning disability may be unnecessary and does not serve his or her best interest (Evans, 1991; Szymanski and Grossman, 1984).

A comprehensive range of information from multidisciplinary sources needs to be used to ascertain accurate assessment of mental illness in persons with learning disabilities. The AAMR (1992) suggest the following as possible sources of information: (a) personal interviews; (b) behavioural observations; (c) self-report and interviews with staff; (d) psychometric evaluations including social skills, personality, and maladaptive behaviour; (e) medical evaluations. An implication for the legal context is in ensuring that due care is taken in the assessment of mental illness in persons with learning disabilities. When such illnesses are undiagnosed the person's right to appropriate service and support is likely to be infringed. Inappropriate diagnosis and treatment of mental illness in a person with learning disability may also lead to unnecessary restrictions and infringement of his or her rights.

TREATMENTS AND SUPPORT

An essential element of the support system, habilitation and treatment programme for an individual with a learning disability is the environment in which the person lives, learns and works. The environment can either facilitate or inhibit the person's independence, productivity, community integration, exercise of citizenship rights and general well-being. Schalock and Kiernan (1990) have identified three essential characteristics of environments that promote growth and development: the providing of opportunities, fostering well-being, and promoting stability.

Providing opportunities to people with learning disabilities is one of the most important tasks that face supporters of people with learning disabilities. Much remains to be done to ensure that all people with learning disabilities have opportunities to be included in valued (positive) education provisions, live in non-segregated homes, are engaged in work and participate in integrated leisure and recreation activities. It is through such opportunities that people will have the chance to make friends and develop relationships, to find increased life satisfaction, to exercise choice and control. People with learning disabilities have been largely denied many opportunities because we have gone to great lengths to create all sorts of reasons why we think that they are unlikely to benefit from such opportunities. The lesson of contemporary approaches and research is that people with learning disabilities have taught us that they can and do make use of increased opportunities (Perske, 1988; Schalock, 1990; Smull and Bellamy, 1991). The main implication for the legal practice is that, in countries where specific anti-discrimination laws exist, there is a need to ensure advocacy of the rights of people with learning disabilities in order to encourage the exercise of these rights and to discourage their infringement. In countries, such as the UK, where there are no specific anti-discrimination laws concerning people with learning disabilities, there is a need for psychologists to add their voices to the many who are currently campaigning for such laws.

Well-being and stability are related to the physical, material, social and cognitive aspects of the environment (AAMR, 1992). The main focii are with health, wellness and personal safety, reduction of stress, material comfort and financial security, community presence, use of leisure and recreation facilities, social support and friendship, interesting, rewarding and worthwhile work and the development of personal competence (Blunden, 1988; O'Brien, 1987; Schalock and Kiernan, 1990).

In addition to providing individuals with learning disabilities with environments that are designed to facilitate personal growth and development, and which attend to their health and wellness needs, there are instances where some individuals have additional needs for support to enhance their intellectual functioning and adaptive skills. Others may also need support with psychological and emotional well-being. There is a growing interest in providing psychotherapy to people with learning disability; however, applied behaviour analysis continues to be the basis for most effective interventions to support people with learning disability to gain mastery over various aspects of their behaviours.

BEHAVIOURAL TREATMENT

Griffiths, Quinsey and Hingsburger (1989) refer to the need for establishing philosophical principles to direct the practices of a behavioural management programme. The following is an adaptation of the principles they describe:

1. Individuals with learning disability can live in the community but they need appropriate support and services to do so.

2. People with learning disability have the right to receive or to refuse interventions to change their 'problem' behaviour.

3. Effective intervention is based on the development of environments that support change and prevent future problems.

4. Behavioural support must transfer from professionals to the person's natural environments, from specialised services to community-based services, from treatment sessions to the person's daily routine.

5. 'Ethical behavior practices include an emphasis on providing positive approaches to behavior change, teaching new skills or increasing skills currently in the client's repertoire, ensuring that the consequences of a situation occur both naturally and normally, implementing the least intrusive approach to client routine, and interactions. Behavior programmes must promote respect for client rights and dignity.' (Griffiths, Quinsey and Hingsburger, 1989, p. 6).

Contemporary applied behaviour analysis began with two related events in 1968. The *Journal of Applied Behavior Analysis* began publication and in that inaugural issue, Baer, Wolf, and Risley produced their seminal article 'Some current dimensions of applied behavior analysis'.

They identified seven key elements of applied behaviour analysis: 'Obviously, the study must be *applied, behavioral, and analytic*, in addition, it should be technological, conceptually systematic, and effective, and it should display some generality' (p. 92). In this instance 'applied' refers to behaviours that are socially significant and important to the person the intervention is aimed at. They identified three criteria of a behavioural focus. First, the identified behaviour must be in need of improvement. Second, the behaviour must be operationally defined and measurable; resorting to the measurement of a non-behavioural substitute would invalidate the study. Third, observed changes in behaviour must be attributed to the variables that were manipulated in the study. This also relates to the analytic element referred to above. 'Technological' refers to the accurate and precise description and identification of all the procedures used in the study. A study is 'conceptually systematic' when it describes the procedures for behaviour change in terms of the relevant basic behavioural principles from which they originate. To be judged 'effective', applied behaviour analysis must produce results that are clinically and socially significant. 'Generality' is concerned with the behaviour being long-lasting, appearing in a range of environments and having positive effects on other behaviours. Interventions which can meet these exacting criteria are more likely to be of use to people with learning disabilities. Unfortunately many so-called behavioural interventions are carried out by workers who may not have the competencies to initiate programmes of treatment which meet such exacting standards.

There is considerable documented evidence to demonstrate the effectiveness of applied behaviour analysis in the support of people with learning disabilities (Carr, 1991; Remington, 1991; Whitaker, 1993). Applied behaviour analysis uses a range of procedures such as ecological interventions, and positive programming which makes use of methods that are described as non-aversive.

However, there are also many instances where so-called aversive methods are used. There is also considerable debate among professionals and advocates about the desirability and legitimacy of using aversive methods and pain to change the behaviour of persons with severe learning disabilities (La Vigna and Donnellan, 1986; Meyer and Evans, 1989; O'Brien, 1991).

There is also a need to consider the appropriateness of behavioural intervention, and a suggested decision-making model (Evans and Meyer, 1985; Gaylord-Ross, 1980) includes the following sequence:

i.   Is the behaviour serious enough to warrant behavioural intervention?

ii. Are there alterative biomedical or pharmacological explanations about the possible causes of the behaviour?

iii. Gather quantitative baseline data about the behaviour.

iv. Conduct a functional analysis of the behaviour.

v.   Generate hypotheses about the behaviour, its antecedent and consequence.

vi. Is an ecological intervention indicated? (Ecological interventions are aimed at using the method of applied behaviour analysis, involving service providers, service users and managerial procedures to create service systems that support learning and behaviour change.)

vii. Is an intervention based on the use of positive reinforcement, used to increase the frequency of a behaviour, indicated?

viii. Is antecedent control indicated?

SOME LEGAL IMPLICATIONS

We accept that in a complex society it is necessary to protect citizens in a number of different ways; for example we protect our basic human rights, safeguard our personal safety, protect against undue interferences in our private lives, protect against discrimination. People who have learning disabilities may not be so fortunate; in the past legislation was often concerned with protecting the community rather than safeguarding the rights of citizens with learning disabilities. People with learning disabilities are still vulnerable to having their rights abrogated and to other forms of exploitation (Wolfensberger, 1991; Wolfensberger and Zauha, 1972).

Being labelled as a person with a learning disability can have life defining consequences, such as involuntary sterilisation, for the person. The law has an important role to play in safeguarding the interest of the person at risk of being labelled, at the point of assessment and at diagnosis. Since the skills and judgement of the assessor are so important, appropriate qualification and experience ought to be essential requirements. For individuals who are at risk of being diagnosed as having both a learning difficulty and a mental illness there must be safeguards against inappropriate diagnosis.

Protective measures for people with learning disabilities should be guided by the following principles:

1. People's rights should be safeguarded without overprotection which can deny citizenship rights and keep the person dependent at the expense of his or her personal growth and development.

2. Sensible risk taking is an essential element of personal development and should not be denied to individuals.

3. Protective measures can act to separate individuals from their natural network of community support provided by families and friends by creating excessive reliance on professionals. People with learning disabilities should not be forced to live away from their communities and natural support networks.

Definition of learning disability is the basis for identifying individuals not as an end in itself, but for conferring eligibility to support and appropriate services. However, such labels may also act contrary to the interests of the person, for example in England and Wales sexual relationships are unlawful for some individuals with learning disability according to the Sexual Offences Acts 1956 and 1967 (Gunn, 1988).

Some of the problems faced by people with learning disabilities are direct consequences of society's negative attitudes. Disability should not continue to be a basis for discrimination against any person, and people with learning disability would benefit from a specific antidiscrimination law. Such laws exist in countries such as the USA (Rehabilitation Act of 1973; Sales, Powell and Van Duizend, 1982).

People with learning disabilities constitute a vulnerable group who have to depend on human service agencies and other individuals for support; some even depend on others for life sustaining support and services. The legal duty of care should include the provision of living, learning and working environments that enhance the growth and development of an individual with learning disabilities. The concept of least restrictive alternative is useful in deciding the balance between independence and protection, and there may be a need for services and professionals to demonstrate appropriate decision-making when planning and delivering services and support to people. Services could be required to demonstrate that models for making least restrictive decisions are actively used. One area where this is clearly indicated is in behavioural programmes that rely on intrusive methods or on inflicting pain.

Service agencies should also ensure that workers have adequate education and competencies for the work they are required to do in supporting individuals with learning disabilities.

Contemporary models of services and support systems for individuals with learning disabilities are concerned with enabling people with the exercise of choice and self-determination which is associated with the growing role of self advocates, family, friends and supporters. Such roles will include seeking legal redress and acting as lobbyists. Psychologists too have a role here that is not often emphasised. Psychologists do not have to restrict their role to the assessment, diagnosis and treatment of learning disabilities. Psychologists can make common cause with advocates in campaigning for laws that protect, enhance and safeguard the rights of people with learning disabilities. Psychologists could ensure that the enabling powers of existing law are used on behalf of people with learning disabilities such as protecting the rights of vulnerable individuals who do not have the communication ability or the cognitive ability to provide or withhold consent to life-sustaining medical treatment.

REFERENCES

AAMR (1992). *Mental Retardation: Definition, Classification, and Systems of Support*. Washington: American Association on Mental Retardation.

American Psychiatric Association (1987). *Diagnostic and Statistical Manual of Mental Disorders* (3rd ed. revised DSM-17I-R). Washington: APA.

Baer, D.M., Wolf, M.M. and Risley, T. (1968). Some current dimensions of applied behavior analysis. *Journal of Applied Behavior Analysis*, **1**, 91–7.

Blunden, R. (1988). Program features of quality services. In M.P. Janiki, M.M. Krauss and M. Seltzer (Eds), *Community Residences for Persons with Developmental Disabilities: Here to Stay*. Baltimore: Paul H. Brookes, pp. 117–22.

Browder, D.M. and Snell, M.E. (1988). Assessment of individuals with severe handicaps. In E.S. Shapiro and T.R. Kratchowill (Eds), *Behavioral Assessment in Schools: Conceptual Foundations and Practice Applications*. New York: Guilford Press, pp. 121–60.

Bruininks, R. and McGrew, K. (1987). *Exploring the Structure of Adaptive Behavior*. Minneapolis: University of Minnesota Press.

Bruininks, R., Thurlow, M. and Gilman, C.J. (1987). Adaptive behavior and mental retardation. *Journal of Special Education*, **21**, 69–88.

Carr, J. (1991). Recent advances in work with people with learning difficulties. *Behavioural Psychotherapy*, **19**, 109–120.

Dockrell, J. and McShane, J. (1992). *Children's Learning Difficulties: A Cognitive Approach*. Oxford: Blackwell.

Durand, V.M. and Crimmins, D.B. (1988). Identifying the variables maintaining self-injurious behavior. *Journal of Autism and Developmental Disorders*, **18**, 99–117.

Durand, V.M. and Kishi, G. (1987). Reducing severe behavior problems among persons with dual sensory impairments: an evaluation of a technical assistance model. *Journal of the Association for Persons with Severe Handicaps*, **12**, 210.

Evans, I.M. (1991). Testing and diagnosis: a review and evaluation. In L.H. Meyer, C.A. Peck and L. Brown (Eds), *Critical Issues in the Lives of People with Severe Disabilities*. Baltimore: Paul H. Brookes, pp. 25–44.

Evans, I.M. and Meyer, L.H. (1985). *An Educative Approach to Behavior Problems: A Practical Decision Model for Interventions with Severely Handicapped Learners*. Baltimore: Paul H. Brookes.

Evans, I.M. and Scotti, J.R. (1989). Defining meaningful outcomes for persons with profound disabilities. In F. Brown and D. Lehr (Eds), *Persons with Profound Disabilities: Issues and Practices*. Baltimore: Paul H. Brookes, pp. 83–107.

Foster–Gaitskell, D. and Pratt, C. (1989). Comparison of parent and teacher ratings of adaptive behavior of children with mental retardation. *American Journal of Mental Retardation*, **94**, 177–81.

Gaylord-Ross, R.J. (1980). A decision model for the treatment of aberrant behavior in applied settings. In W. Sailor, B. Wilcox and L. Brown (Eds), *Methods of Instruction for Severely Handicapped Students*. Baltimore: Paul H. Brookes, pp. 135–58.

Gaylord-Ross, R. and Browder, D. (1991). Functional assessment: dynamic and domain properties. In L.H. Meyer, C.A. Peck and L. Brown (Eds), *Critical Issues in the Lives of People with Severe Disabilities*. Baltimore: Paul H. Brookes, pp. 45–66.

Griffiths, D.M., Quinsey, V.L. and Hingsburger, D. (1989). *Changing Inappropriate Sexual Behavior: A Community Based Approach for Persons with Developmental Disabilities*. Baltimore: Paul H. Brookes.

Grossman, H.J. (Ed.) (1983). *Classification in Mental Retardation*. Washington: AAMD.

Gunn, M.J. (1988). The law and mental handicap. In A. Leighton (Ed.), *Mental Handicap in the Community*. Cambridge: Woodhead-Faulkner.

Hooper, S.R. and Willis, W.G. (1989). *Learning Disability Subtyping: Neuropsychological Foundations, Conceptual Models, and Issues in Clinical Differentiation*. New York: Springer-Verlag.

LaVigna, G.W. and Donnellan, A.M. (1986). *Alternatives to Punishment: Solving Behavior Problems with Nonaversive Strategies*. New York: Irvington.

Leyland, H. (1991). Adaptive behavior scales. In J.L. Matson and J.A. Mulick (Eds), *Handbook of Mental Retardation*. New York: Pergamon, pp. 221.

McGrew, K. and Bruininks, R. (1989). The factor structure of adaptive behavior. *School Psychology Review*, **18**, 64–81.

Meacham, F.R., Kline, M M., Stoval, J.A. and Sands, D.I. (1987). Adaptive behavior and low incidence handicaps: hearing and visual impairments. *Journal of Special Education*, **21**, 183–96.

Mental Health Act 1983. In The Public General Acts and General Synod Means, 1983, pp. 343–482.

Meyer, L.H. and Evans, I.N. (1989). *Nonaversive Iintervention for Behavior Problems*. Baltimore: Paul H. Brookes.

O'Brien, J. (1987). A guide to personal futures planning. In G.T. Bellamy and B. Wilcox (Eds), *A Comprehensive Guide to the Activities Catalog an Alternative Curriculum for Youth and Adults with Severe Disabilities*. Baltimore: Paul H. Brookes, pp. 176–89.

O'Brien, J. (1991). Against pain as a tool in professional work on people with severe disabilities. *Disability, Handicap and Society*, **6**, 81–90.

Parsons, J.A., May, J.G. and Menolascino, F.J. (1984). The nature and incidence of mental illness in mentally retarded individuals. In F.J. Menolascino and J.A. Stark (Eds), *Handbook of Mental Illness in the Mentally Retarded*. New York: Plenum, pp. 3–44.

Perske, R. (1988). *Circle of Friends*. Nashville: Abingdon Press.

Pollingue, A. (1987). Adaptive behavior and low incidence handicaps: use of adaptive behavior instruments for persons with physical handicaps. *Journal of Special Education*, **21**, 117–25.

Reiss, S., Levitan, G.W. and Szyszko, J. (1982). Emotional disturbances and mental retardation: diagnostic overshadowing. *American Journal of Mental Deficiency*, **86**, 16–20.

Reiss, S. and Szyszko, J. (1983). Diagnostic overshadowing and professional experience with mentally retarded persons. *American Journal of Mental Deficiency*, **87**, 396–402.

Remington, B. (Ed.) (1991). *The Challenge of Severe Mental Handicap*. Chichester: John Wiley.

Reschley, D.J. (1990). Adaptive behavior. In A. Thomas and J. Grimes (Eds), *Best Practices in School Psychology*. Washington: National Association of School Psychologists, pp. 29–42.

Reschley, D.J. and Ward, S.M. (1991). Use of adaptive behavior and overrepresentation of black students in programs for students with mental retardation. *American Journal on Mental Retardation*, **96**, 257–68.

Sales, B.D., Powell, D.M., Van Duizend, R. and associates (1982). *Disabled Persons and the Law: State Legislative Issues*. New York: Plenum Press.

Schalock, R.L. (Ed.) (1990). *Quality of Life: Perspectives and Issues*. Washington: AAMR.

Schalock, R.L. and Kiernan, W.E. (1990). *Habilitation Planning for Adults with Developmental Disabilities*. New York: Springer-Verlag.

Schuler, A.L. and Perez, L. (1991). Assessment: current concerns and future directions. In L. H. Meyer, C.A. Peck and L. Brown (Eds), *Critical Issues in the Lives of People with Severe Disabilities*. Baltimore: Paul H. Brookes, pp. 101–6.

Smull, M.W. and Bellamy, G.T. (1991). Community services for adult with disabilities: policy challenges in the emerging support paradigm. In L.H. Meyer, C.A. Peck and L. Brown (Eds), *Critical Issues in the Lives of People with Severe Disabilities*. Baltimore: Paul H. Brookes, pp. 527–36.

Szymanski, L. and Grossman, H. (1984). Dual implications of 'dual diagnosis'. *Mental Retardation*, **22**, 155–6.

Warren, A.C., Holroyd, S. and Folstein, M.F. (1989). Major depression in Down's syndrome. *British Journal of Psychiatry*, **155**, 202–5.

Whitaker, S. (1993). The reduction of aggression in people with learning difficulties: a review of psychological methods. *British Journal of Clinical Psychology*, **32**, 1–37.

Wolfensberger, W. (1991). *A Brief Introduction to Social Role Valorization as a High Order Concept for Structuring Human Services*. Syracuse, NY: Training Institute for Human Service Planning, Leadership and Change Agentry (Syracuse University).

Wolfensberger, W. and Zauha, H. (Eds) (1972). *Citizen Advocacy and Protective Services for the Impaired and Handicapped*. NIMR Canada.

Zigler, E. and Hodapp, R.M. (1986). *Understanding Mental Retardation*. New York: Cambridge University Press.

Part 3

Investigations: Seeking, Obtaining, Interpreting and Assessing Information

Evidence: Legal Perspective

John Jackson
Queen's University of Belfast

[A] legal system will do almost anything, tolerate almost anything, before it will admit the need for reform in the system of proof and trial. (Langbein, 1978, p. 19)

INTRODUCTION

One persistent theme of psychological literature on legal processes is that there has existed a credibility gap between psychologists and lawyers whereby the claims of the former to be able to make positive contributions which have relevance for legal processes are disputed by the latter (Clifford, 1979). This may be seen as an example of the general suspicion in which lawyers and scientists have regarded each other, no doubt because of the fundamentally different purposes of science and law. But the suspicion seems to have been particularly acute in the case of psychologists and lawyers. The reluctance of lawyers to accept the findings of psychologists goes back to the very early days of applied psychology. Much of the original hostility was directed at the unsophisticated and inappropriate techniques used by psychologists. Although experimental psychologists were quick to realise the potential relevance of discoveries about perception and memory to the issue of witness reliability (Munsterburg, 1908), the techniques recommended for testing the credibility of witnesses soon came under critical scrutiny by lawyers (Greer, 1971). For example, one of the leading evidence scholars of the early twentieth century, J.H. Wigmore, complained about the absence of exact and precise experimental methods of ascertaining and measuring the testimonial certitude of witnesses (Wigmore, 1909). Since then psychologists have refined their theories and methodology and there has been a much greater realisation that research has to be conducted less in the laboratory and more in the legal processes themselves (Lloyd-Bostock and Clifford, 1979). Psychologists have also broadened their focus away from the courtroom and looked at the process of eliciting and evaluating information from witnesses before court

Handbook of Psychology in Legal Contexts
Edited by R. Bull and D. Carson. © 1995 John Wiley & Sons Ltd

(Lloyd-Bostock, 1988, chs 1 and 2). Particular attention has been paid to the use of identity parades and to the techniques used to interview witnesses and suspects and this has helped to generate an awareness amongst lawyers of the dangers of identification evidence and confession evidence (Lloyd-Bostock and Clifford, 1979; Gudjonsson, 1992). Yet there continues to be resistance to the idea that psychological research can be sufficiently tailored to the needs of the legal system to provide the basis for change.

Some of this resistance continues to be directed at the assumptions psychologists employ in studying legal processes. One criticism is that psychological research takes insufficient account of the context of legal processes (King, 1986). Many findings reflect universal truths about human behaviour regardless of the cultural, geographical or temporary context in which the participants operate. There is also a view that research findings lack utility for the courts because they point to general flaws in certain kinds of testimony or certain kinds of methods of eliciting testimony which do not relate sufficiently to the reliability of a particular piece of evidence or a particular witness (Stone, 1984). This suggests that there might be greater willingness to accept the evidence of forensic psychologists who are able to assist in the evaluation of particular evidence but here too there has been a reluctance to relax the rules of evidence to allow greater use of psychological and psychiatric testimony. This attitude is well captured in the comment made by Lawton L.J. in *R. v Turner* that 'psychiatry has not yet become a satisfactory substitute for the common sense of juries' ([1975] 1 All E.R. 70, 75).

The resistance to change could be seen as the inevitable reaction of professionals determined to cling on to their traditional practices. But there would also seem to be a genuine belief that processes of legal proof express moral and political as well as epistemological values which cannot be impugned by any amount of scientific research (Bankowski, 1981, 1988). On this view if the validity of legal rules and procedures are independent of external scientific criteria, legal methods of gathering and evaluating evidence should also be independent of scientific scrutiny. To examine these claims we need to look at the context in which legal fact-finding takes place and at the assumptions underlying what some have called 'law's truth' (Nelken, 1994).

THE CONTEXT OF LITIGATION

Although most of the contentious issues in modern day litigation involve issues of fact, the primary purpose of litigation is not to resolve issues of fact but to contribute to the peaceful resolution of disputes and grievances (Eckhoff, 1965; Hart and McNaughton, 1959). Disputes do not have to be settled by resort to litigation and indeed many are settled by a variety of other means including negotiation, mediation and arbitration. The mediator helps the parties resolve their differences for themselves, while the arbitrator is chosen by the parties to reach a resolution for them. In either case the aim is not so much to look back at what has happened as to look forward to find a solution that will be acceptable to both sides. Even when parties take each other to court to have the dispute settled on the basis of existing rules or principles of law, and where it is then important to look back to see what happened in detail so that the rules can be applied, it is recognised that the main aim is not the enforcement of the rules as the resolution of the dispute. Most cases do not in fact go to trial but are settled through pretrial negotiation and sometimes through mediation or conciliation. Even where litigation centres around specific allegations of wrong-doing such as the commission of criminal offences, and where enforcement of the law is considered important, most cases, certainly in the Anglo-American world, are resolved by pleas of guilty made by the defendants concerned. The effect of this resort to settlement rather than to trial is that the outcome of cases may not correspond with what is prescribed by substantive law. 'The plaintiff accepts less than he claimed as his due; the accused pleads guilty to a lesser charge; instead of winner takes all, the risk of losing is distributed ...' (Twining, 1985, p. 94).

All this means that fact-finding is not conducted in a spirit of scientific inquiry. Once it is decided to pursue a claim or a charge lawyers and investigators must secure evidence pursuant to it and this involves a process of moulding the facts and the legal rules into a legal case (Morison and Leith, 1992). The process of case construction may begin by examining which claim or charge best suits the possible explanations of the facts, but because of the pressures that there can be to act, a specific claim or charge may be made before a systematic investigation of the facts has been completed and the process will then require construction of the evidence to justify the claim or charge advanced (McConville, Sanders and Leng, 1991). Throughout this process lawyers will be given the chance to form some view of the strength of the opposing claims through discovery procedures and will have to make judgements about what compromises to make in negotiation. The parties therefore prepare for trial, but at the same time they seek steps to achieve an acceptable outcome without going to trial because of the expense, the trauma and the risk of losing everything that a trial may involve.

If the case ends up being contested in court, then an attempt is made to prove those facts material to the claim or charge which are put in issue. But the trial cannot be viewed as a pure exercise of fact-finding. First of all, in the Anglo-American tradition at least the concern is not with the truth of all the material facts, but only with those facts which are contested and which are specifically identified for the tribunal of fact (Derham, 1963). Secondly, there are occasions when for reasons of policy or convenience the law may give artificial weight to certain inferences or presumptions and take judicial notice of facts that may be too difficult to prove. Thirdly, the advocates and decision-makers must constantly relate the facts to the relevant legal standards, a process that may call for different processes of reasoning than those involved in the ascertainment of past events (Damaska, 1975; Tillers, 1988). A distinction has been made between the 'brute' facts of the empirical world and the 'institutional' facts of the legal world (McCormick, 1974). Fourthly, the judgment delivered at the end of the trial prescribes what consequences are to follow for the parties. The judgment is therefore prescriptive and not merely descriptive. It follows that the parties must have sufficient confidence in the trial process to entrust the resolution of the case to it. Since in criminal cases the courts have the power to impose grave penalties on individuals convicted of criminal offences there also has to be sufficient public confidence in the impartiality and fairness of the trial procedures.

Given the heavy responsibility that trials bear in producing a judgment that is to be regarded as final, it is not surprising that they have not always depended on the fallible exercise of reaching conclusions of fact based on past events. In early centuries most of Europe was dominated by Germanic modes of proof which were based on the assumption that truth was revealed by an omniscient god. Germanic and Anglo-Saxon trials therefore prescribed certain authorised methods of proof and the accused who was able to pass through the appropriate form of proof—battle, compurgation or ordeal—was acquitted. Trials only gradually came to be associated with fact-finding. Under Roman-canon procedure, which succeeded the old Germanic system of proof in most of continental Europe, judges were appointed to hear the parties and in the Anglo-Saxon world local people were entrusted with swearing an account of the facts. As time progressed judges and juries were entrusted with the task of estimating for themselves the probative value of the evidence and this coincided with a general belief in the ability of factfinders to weigh evidence on their own, what has been called the principle of universal cognitive competence (Cohen, 1983).

Today much is made of the differences between so-called adversarial and inquisitorial modes of proof. Under the inquisitorial mode judges have the task of inquiring into the facts and are much less dependent on what the parties choose to present by way of evidence. In the adversarial mode, on the other hand, the parties themselves present the evidence before an impartial judge or jury. The former mode is often said to be more committed to truth-finding. Indeed, throughout this century adversarial procedures have been subjected to a barrage of criticism on the ground that they do not take truth-finding seriously enough. Although some lawyers have joined in the criticism (e.g. Frank, 1949), psychologists have been foremost among the critics (Kassin and Wrightsman, 1985). Thus the adversarial system has been depicted as a world of make-believe where relevant evidence may not be presented, counter evidence may not be made known and contradictions are unresolved (Marshall, 1966). But instead of comparing the capacity of adversarial and inquisitorial systems to find the truth, it is better to view both adversarial and inquisitorial systems as two different truth-certifying procedures which have been developed to take account of societal conceptions of how best to settle disputes and enforce the law (Damaska, 1986).

So, for example, the adversarial process is justified not merely as a method of fact-finding but as expressing a conception of the appropriate role of government in the resolution of disputes (Allen and Kuhns, 1989). In the Anglo-American world the government's function is considered to be primarily facilitative. There is an obligation on government to provide a forum for the impartial resolution of disputes, but that is all. Where law enforcement is considered particularly important, there is a need for the government to provide the resources for effective fact-finding mechanisms but this impetus towards greater governmental involvement is contained by an ideology of mistrust of state power and a reluctance to allow the state too large a role in the resolution of the case. Hence the need in criminal cases to erect high evidentiary barriers against conviction by requiring those entrusted with the investigation of crime to prove guilt where it is contested to a high standard of proof before a decision-making body which is viewed as completely independent of government (Damaska, 1973). The trial is not, therefore, an active truth-finding inquiry conducted by state officials (that is what is supposed to precede the trial) but a contest between the prosecution which seeks to prove its case beyond reasonable doubt and the defence which seeks to raise a reasonable doubt about the case. This conception of the trial brings with it other constraints such as the inability of the prosecution to require the defendant to enter the witness box and give his or her account of events. The defendant's right of silence, which also extends to pre-trial inquiries, imposes evidential restraints on the whole forensic process but it is justified in part by the need to impose an appropriate balance between governmental power and the rights of the accused. Certain rules of evidence have also been developed to protect the accused from undue state interference. There was for a long time a rule whereby a confession could not be admitted as evidence unless it was voluntary in the sense that it had not been obtained by threats or promises on the part of those in authority. Although the rationale for this rule was in part attributable to the fear that a confession obtained by these means may not be reliable, the rule was also attributable to the privilege against self-incrimination whereby defendants could not be compelled to incriminate themselves. More controversial rules have developed in the United States where evidence is excluded under constitutional provisions designed to regulate improper conduct by law enforcement officials no matter how reliable the evidence excluded thereby may be.

Apart from rules regulating state power, there are other values within the adversarial system which may compete with truth-finding. One value is that the parties involved should have some control over the process which finally makes decisions binding on them. It has been argued, for example, that there are certain process values independent of outcome to which parties are entitled, such as a right to be present during the proceedings, a right to be legally represented to enable their arguments to be put before the court and a right to confront and cross-examine witnesses on the opposing side (Summers, 1974). If a defendant risks losing liberty on conviction, for example, it may be argued that respect for his or her dignity requires the right to be heard and a right to confront accusers. These values explain the great attachment that is given in adversarial systems to the orality of testimony. A number of rules of evidence appear to encourage the primacy of direct oral testimony in trials. One of the most important is the hearsay rule which prohibits witnesses reporting the statements of others if they are adduced for the purpose of proving the truth of facts contained in them. This means that witnesses who have directly perceived the events in issue must come to court themselves to give evidence of what they saw and heard. Although the oral methods of examination and cross-examination have been defended as truth-finding mechanisms (Wigmore, 1940), there has recently been considerable scepticism about the effectiveness of these techniques for determining the truth, particularly where vulnerable witnesses such as children are involved (Spencer and Flin, 1993). Much effort has been put into devising alternative methods of eliciting children's evidence. Examples include the use of testimony by video-link to the courtroom and even the use of preliminary hearings at which the child would be interviewed by a specially trained child examiner (McEwan, 1992, ch. 4). Whatever the merit of these alternatives as methods of truth-finding, they are regarded with suspicion by legal traditionalists on the ground that they fail to meet the process concerns of defendants such as the need to confront accusers and to cross-examine them on their testimony.

Finally, another value expressed by legal procedures is that hearings are open to the public and indeed on occasions participated in by members of the public. The need for openness and publicity again emphasises the fear that closed hearings may easily be manipulated by state officials, but it also reflects the concern that the public must have confidence not only in the decision-makers but also in the procedures that produce the judgments at the end of the day. Sometimes the need for a public hearing extends beyond the trial process of adjudicating on particular claims or charges made into the realm of investigation. When a matter of concern arises within an area of state responsibility, such as the death of a person in police custody or an allegation of child abuse is made in a children's home, there is often insufficient confidence in officials to investigate these matters impartially, and if necessary to take the necessary action to prosecute wrong-doers. Mechanisms must then exist for ensuring that public investigations are carried out. Coroners sit with juries, for example, in cases where people have died in police custody and public inquiries are announced when an official cover up is suspected. Sometimes a potential conflict between truth-finding and public accountability can occur here. Public inquiries are sometimes resisted on the ground that the fear of publicity may discourage persons with relevant information from coming forward. Ultimately, however, the need to allay public concern must take priority over the need for legal procedures to adopt the most effective truth-finding mechanisms.

THE RULES OF EVIDENCE

Enough has been said to show that the legal process of litigation must take account of a whole range of considerations other than truth-finding if it is to achieve its aims of providing peaceful settlement of disputes and inspiring public confidence and trust in the judgments that emerge. At the same time few doubt that truth-finding has an important place in this process as confidence is undermined when judgments and settlements are seen to diverge from what is thought to have occurred. Within modern legal evidence scholarship, indeed, there has been a strong belief in the importance of rectitude of outcome or accuracy of decision-making which can be traced back to the writings of Jeremy Bentham who believed that decisions must conform with the law for it is by the law that citizens regulate their hopes and fears (Twining, 1985).

Twining (1990, ch. 3) has argued that nearly all specialised Anglo-American literature about evidence has its roots in English post-Enlightenment thought. This assumes a correspondence theory of truth, that events and states of affairs occur and have an existence independently of human observation and that true statements are statements which correspond with these facts. Present knowledge about past facts is possible but because it is based on incomplete knowledge establishing the truth about the past is typically a matter of probabilities. The characteristic mode of reasoning is inductive by which one starts with basic data and moves by way of inductive generalisation towards a possible conclusion. Although Twining has claimed that these assumptions represent a particular view of rationality with its roots in the English empirical writings of Bacon, Locke and Mill, it has been argued that the rationalist tradition appears to be based on a view of rationality common to Western civilisation (Galligan, 1988). From the central tenets of the rationalist tradition, Twining went on to postulate a rationalist model of adjudication as an ideal type which both fits a rationalist theory of evidence and represents a widely shared view heavily inspired by Bentham. According to this model, the direct end of adjective law is rectitude of decision making, although other values have to be taken into account in any overall evaluation of a particular system such as speed, cheapness, procedural fairness, humaneness, public confidence and the avoidance of vexation to participants. Rectitude of decision-making is then arrived at through the correct application of valid, substantive laws and through accurate determination of the facts material to previously specified allegations expressed in categories defined in advance by law (facts-in-issue) proved to specified standards of probability on the basis of evidence which is relevant and reliable and presented to a supposedly competent and impartial decision-maker.

This model of adjudication is prescriptive and we have seen that adversary procedures in particular have been criticised on the ground that they are insufficiently committed to truth-finding. At the same time a number of rules of evidence appear to reflect the central tenets of the rationalist tradition. Rule 401 of the Federal Rules of Evidence in the United States, for example, defines relevance as evidence which has some 'tendency to make the existence of any fact that is of consequence to the action more probable or less probable than it would be without the evidence'. It has been pointed out that this rule requires the application of the principles of inductive logic to persuade a judge that the evidence under consideration, alone or in combination with other evidence, supports an inference that increases or decreases the likelihood that a fact which is of consequence in the litigation is true (Anderson and Twining, 1991). Rule 402 then requires judges to admit relevant evidence unless there is a rule of exclusion; and rule 403 then articulates reasons for exclusion such as where the probative value of the evidence is outweighed by the danger of unfair prejudice, confusion of the issues, or misleading the jury, or by considerations of undue delay, waste of time or needless presentation of cumulative evidence. Although these rules on relevance are not articulated so clearly in English law, it is clear that judges in England and elsewhere in the common law world are guided by similar principles (Law Commission, 1993). If these rules require the application of inductive logic in order to weigh the probative value of the evidence, other rules may be seen as giving effect to the need for the courts to hear the primary data on which to draw inferences by the inductive method of proof. These assume that it is possible to make a distinction between evidence, the reports of events by witnesses who have directly perceived them, and inferences that are to be drawn by the triers of fact on the basis of induction from evidence (Loevinger, 1958). The opinion rule, for example, requires witnesses to state facts not opinions—facts being taken to mean what is directly perceived by sense experience. The hearsay rule prevents witnesses reporting the statements of others which go to the truth of facts contained in them because these witnesses do not have direct immediate knowledge of these events. Exceptions are made in the case of specialist knowledge where experts may state opinions on matters of expertise outside the knowledge of triers of fact and may draw on recognised knowledge within the field of expertise to reach opinions. Even here, however, care is taken to prevent experts from invading the province of the tribunal of fact, and further rules, such as the ultimate issue rule, have been developed to prevent this (Jackson, 1984).

In recent years there has increasingly been a move away from rules of evidence in favour of the principle of free proof under which triers of fact should be permitted to evaluate all evidence that is sufficiently relevant without the need for rigid exclusionary rules mandating the exclusion of entire categories of evidence. Bentham originally argued that rectitude of outcome was best achieved by a natural system of proof rather than by a technical system of proof. A distinction is sometimes made between rules designed to achieve rectitude of outcome and rules that are designed to protect values other than proof. Rules of the latter kind include some of the rules mentioned in the previous section which are designed to protect defendants against the police. It was rules of the former kind that were the main target of Bentham's antinomian thesis. But this thesis can be taken too far. For no matter how highly a system of adjudication values rectitude of decision-making, it is impossible to have a system of adjudication without some rules regulating proof. We have seen that in adjudication a decision must be reached on the issues in dispute one way or another. Adjudicators cannot conclude that they are not satisfied that the defendant is guilty but they are equally not satisfied that he or she is not guilty. Scientific inquiries, by contrast, can go on perpetually and the conclusions reached may be perpetually revised. As a consequence of the imperative to reach a decision, rules are needed to determine how the facts in issue are to be proved and when they are to be considered proved.

The adversary system usually places the burden of proof on the party claiming that the facts in issue occurred. The consequence of imposing burdens of proof is that if the burden is not met, the result is not a state of limbo in which no decision will be made but the affirmation of the status quo, the defendant will be declared not guilty or not liable (McCormick, 1978). Then there is the need for standards of decision to determine when the facts will be considered proved. It follows from the imperative to reach a decision that it may not be possible to prove the facts in issue to any degree of certainty and that the decision will then have to made in conditions of uncertainty. The rationalist tradition assumes, as we have seen, that knowledge is a matter of probability and not certainty and this is particularly the case in the kind of institutionalised and time-bound setting in which litigation is conducted. In addition to rules determining who wins and who loses in the event of the facts in issue being proved or not, there is therefore a need for rules to determine what standard of proof is necessary to enable the facts in issue to be considered proved or not. The standard required must be a degree of probability but it need not be the same degree for all kinds of litigation and it should take account of the magnitude of the harm that will be caused if a decision is mistaken. What is required here is an essentially political and moral judgement concerning the extent to which the various parties should be exposed to risks of error.

Standards of proof are conventionally different in civil and criminal cases. Since civil litigation has been traditionally viewed as a dispute involving private parties, it has been considered wrong to favour one party over another and the standard has thus been guided by the principle that the risk of errors should be allocated as evenly as possible between the parties. This has meant that parties advancing a claim have merely to prove the facts in issue instantiating the claim to a preponderance of evidence, a standard usually defined as 'more probable than not' (*Miller v Ministry of Pensions* [1947] 2 All E.R. 372). (If the parties were put in a position of complete equivalence then stalemate could occur where the probabilities were considered equal as between the truth or falsity of the facts in issue, and the purpose of adjudication to declare a winner or a loser could not be achieved.)

In criminal cases, on the other hand, it is considered preferable to allocate the risk of error in favour of the defendant because the risk of a person being wrongly convicted is considered much graver than the risk of a person being wrongly acquitted. The prosecution must therefore bear the burden of proving guilt beyond reasonable doubt, although not beyond all doubt as this might make it impossible to convict anyone. The need to skew decisions in a certain direction may also justify the kind of 'technical' rules of proof that Bentham so disapproved of. If the risk of error is to be allocated equally between the parties then it may be argued that each party must bear the risk of evidence being improperly evaluated against them. But if particular weight is to be given to the need to protect innocent defendants, then evidence which runs the risk of increasing this risk when it is evaluated may be excluded. So, for example, there have been rules restricting the admission of evidence of the previous bad character of defendants. Apart from rules of exclusion, corroboration rules requiring that certain kinds of dubious evidence be corroborated before they are acted upon may also be justified on the ground that they are a safeguard against undue weight being placed upon them.

FACTUAL REASONING IN LAW

Even adjudication systems that put a high premium on accuracy therefore need to have rules of evidence to reflect the particular truth-finding concerns of adjudication. But there remains the question whether the methods of factual reasoning in law differ from those in other disciplines. We have seen that most mainstream evidence scholarship has assumed that the principles of inductive logic apply in legal fact-finding. Schum (1986) has argued that the essential inferential processes of discovery, proof and deliberation present in the inferential contexts of medicine and science are also present in legal procedures although they may be played out in a more ordered sequence by actors with different roles such as investigators, advocates and fact-finders. He argues, for example, that abductive reasoning which involves the kind of creative reasoning involved in generating new hypotheses from factual data is commonly important in the discovery stage of fact investigation (see also Binder and Bergman, 1984; Tillers and Schum, 1991). Inductive reasoning, on the other hand, becomes important for advocates when there is a need to structure arguments based upon the data.

In recent years, however, a debate has opened up as to the applicability of conventional probability theory to legal processes (Lempert, 1986). The controversy was sparked off by a celebrated Californian case in which an erroneous attempt was made to use statistical reasoning to resolve problems of evidence that arose in the case (*People v Collins*, 68 Cal. 2d 319, 438 P.2d 33 (1968)). This prompted certain commentators to argue that the mistake in this case was not the attempt to use statistical reasoning but the failure to apply conventional probability theory, in particular Bayes' theorem, to do so (Finkelstein and Fairley, 1970). The use of Bayes' theorem in legal processes has been opposed, however, on a number of grounds. First of all, there is the view that although the theorem may be applied in legal contexts, it is dangerous to do so for a number of reasons, primarily because lay triers may become confused and give undue weight to the statistical data over the other unquantifiable data (Tribe, 1971). A more fundamental challenge has been made by Cohen (1977) who questioned the applicability of conventional probability theory to trial disputes. Cohen relied on a number of paradoxes to show that Bayesian probability is inconsistent with the rules of proof in legal trials. One of these is what he calls the gatecrasher paradox according to which 1000 people attended a rodeo of whom only 499 have paid admission and the rest were trespassers. If the rodeo owner sues all the 1000 who attended and introduces no other evidence other than the fact that only 499 people paid, the probability in each case that the defendant was a gatecrasher would be above 0.5, yet our intuition tells us that the owner would not recover from anyone. If we assume that the preponderance of the evidence standard means a probability of more than 0.5, this suggests that Bayes' theorem yields results that are inconsistent with the results that should be reached. Cohen developed his own theory of inductive probability and argued that most arguments about probabilities in forensic contexts fitted his theory better than any theory of mathematical probability.

Although hypothetical cases such as these have generated much heat, it is important not to exaggerate the extent of the disagreement between Bayesian and non-Bayesian theorists. Few deny that mathematical calculations have a place in the law. Cases such as the rodeo example also appear unconvincing to practising lawyers because of the decontextualised way in which they have been presented (Twining, 1990, pp. 362–3). Although statistical evidence is increasingly becoming more important in legal cases, for example, such evidence rarely constitutes the only evidence available. The intuition that naked statistical evidence should not form the foundation of legal verdicts would appear to be well founded but it may be based on moral rather than epistemic reasons. A case such as that of the rodeo, for example, should arguably not be allowed to go to the jury because the law's concern for the particular merits of the case means that individuals should be judged according to their particular qualities and circumstances and a decision against the defendant would be analogous to corporate punishment (Zuckerman, 1986). But much may depend on strength of the statistical evidence. Suppose, for example, there were 999 gatecrashers out of 1000 possible defendants. It may be thought better to leave such a case to the jury to make its own judgement about the significance of the statistical evidence (Friedman, 1986). Nevertheless, the example shows that moral considerations not only underlie the rules of evidence but may also influence the way the evidence is viewed.

FUTURE DIRECTIONS

Although the context in which legal fact finding is conducted is quite different from fact-finding in less institutionalised settings, this is not to say that other disciplines have nothing to contribute to legal fact finding. The courts are increasingly having to rely on the expertise of other disciplines to provide useful knowledge about evidence in particular cases. Although they are still reluctant to accept psychological evidence on the behaviour of 'normal' people, for example, it is gradually being realised that psychologists have much to offer in this regard. A recent decision of the English Court of Appeal recognises the relevance of psychological evidence of a defendant's likely mental state at the time of a police interview (*R. v. Silcott, Braithwaite and Raghip, The Times*, 9 December 1991). The courts are entitled to be satisfied that the techniques used to arrive at the conclusions have general acceptance in the relevant field of expertise. The Frye test in the United States has recently been held to have been superseded by Rule 702 of the Federal Rules of Evidence and it has been held that this requires the court to be satisfied that any scientific knowledge adduced establishes a standard of evidentiary reliability before it is admitted and a valid scientific connection to the inquiry (*Daubert v. Merrell Dow Pharmaceuticals* 113 S.Ct 2786 (1993)). It may be debated whether judges have the intellectual capacity to make these rulings and there is a continual concern as to whether judges and lay triers can evaluate scientific testimony. More could no doubt be done to improve the presentation of expert evidence (Oddie Committee, 1991), but it is difficult to see the removal of scientific issues to a tribunal of experts being accepted in present Anglo-American procedures, although the idea of science courts has been mooted in the United States. One difficulty is that it may not be easy to hive off the scientific questions from other factual and legal questions. Another problem is that even when the scientific questions are determined by scientists they are being determined within a forensic setting which requires that a decision is reached. This means that scientists must be trusted to apply the relevant decision standards in situations of uncertainty.

In so far as fact-finding in legal contexts does involve the gathering and evaluation of factual information, experts in other disciples are also able to question whether legal procedures and rules are effective in facilitating fact-finding. It can be claimed, for example, that certain rules make assumptions that are quite inconsistent with modern conceptions of fact-finding. The idea, for example, that individuals are the passive recorder of events and that these records do not fundamentally change as they are described, although they may fade from memory after time, displays an outmoded view of the way in which perception and memory are now regarded (Lloyd-Bostock, 1988). Yet the rules of evidence proceed, as we have seen, on the basis that witnesses must recount only what they have seen, often many months after the events occurred, and on the basis that a distinction can be made between direct perceptions and inferences. Witnesses may refresh their memories from written records made at the time but these records are not usually admitted as evidence and are merely seen as an aid with which to refresh memory rather than as the actual foundation of the evidence. This suggests that the courts' reliance on oral evidence long after the events in question may be misplaced and that there needs to be greater focus on the conditions in which witnesses and defendants first tell their stories (Jackson, 1988).

When other disciplines question the effectiveness of legal fact-finding procedures, however, due regard must be had to how any changes might affect the whole legal fact-finding process and the values inherent in it. Even here, though, other disciplines have some role to play. Earlier we saw that the right to cross-examination can be defended as an expression of defence participation. But although defence participation may be an important process value, the concept of process control does not imply that the parties must have control over the testimony of witnesses. There is a useful body of research emerging on what participants regard as fair process and from this it would seem that control over questioning is not universally recognised as an essential feature of procedural fairness (Lind and Tyler, 1988). Moreover, the destructive effect of cross-examination on witnesses of all kinds calls into question the extent to which it inspires a sense of fair process amongst those subjected to it (Jackson, 1991; Rock, 1993).

Ultimately, the appropriate balance in legal procedures between lay, judicial and expert participation and the appropriate boundaries between the domain of science and law are not matters that can be resolved by lawyers and scientists alone. We have seen that the efficacy of legal procedures depends on the degree of public acceptance and confidence that there is in them. Apart from the question of efficacy, we have seen that legal procedures are based on moral and political considerations of what are appropriate methods of dispute resolution and law enforcement. This means that decisions concerning the appropriate balance between truth-finding and other values, the appropriate standards of decision to be applied in truth-finding and the way in which legal rules and procedures should be structured to reflect these values and standards are matters that require to be decided by society as a whole. To decide otherwise would be to acknowledge that lawyers and scientists have some moral and political superiority which they have not. Where, therefore, arguments arise between lawyers and psychologists on the appropriateness of legal procedures, it would seem that these need to be aired before the wider public before they can be resolved.

REFERENCES

Allen, R.J. and Kuhns, R.B. (1989). *An Analytical Approach to Evidence*. Boston: Little Brown.
Anderson, T. and Twining, W.L. (1991). *Analysis of Evidence*. London: Weidenfeld.

Bankowski, Z. (1981). The value of truth: fact-scepticism revisited. *Legal Studies*, **1**, 257.

Bankowski, Z. (1988). The jury and reality. In M. Findlay and P. Duff (Eds), *The Jury Under Attack*. London: Butterworths.

Binder, D. and Bergman, P. (1984). *Fact Investigation: From Hypothesis to Proof*. St Paul: West.

Clifford, B. (1979). Eyewitness testimony: the bridging of a credibility gap. In D. Farrington, K. Hawkins and S. Lloyd-Bostock (Eds), *Psychology, Law and Legal Processes*. London: Macmillan.

Cohen, L.J. (1977). *The Probable and the Provable*. Oxford: Clarendon.

Cohen, L.J. (1983). Freedom of proof. In W. Twining (Ed.), *Facts in Law*. Wiesbaden: Verlag.

Damaska, M. (1973). Evidentiary barriers to conviction and two models of criminal procedure. *U. Pa. Law Review*, **121**.

Damaska, M. (1975). Presentation of evidence and fact-finding precision. *U. Pa. Law Review*, **123** 1083.

Damaska, M. (1986). *The Faces of Justice and State Authority*. New Haven: Yale.

Derham, D. (1963). Truth and the common law. *U. Malaya Law Review*, **5**, 338

Eckhoff, T. (1965). Impartiality, separation of powers, judicial independence. *Scand. Stud. Law*, **9**.

Finkelstein, M.O. and Fairley, W.B. (1970). A Bayesian approach to identification evidence. *Harvard Law Review*, **83**, 489.

Frank, J. (1949). *Courts on Trial*. New York: Princeton University Press.

Friedman, R.D. (1986). Generalised inferences, individual merits, and jury discretion. *B.U. Law Review*, **66**, 509.

Galligan, D.J. (1988). More scepticism about scepticism. *OJLS*, **8**, 249.

Greer, D.S. (1971). Anything but the truth? The reliability of testimony in criminal trials. *British Journal of Criminology*, **11**, 131.

Gudjonnson, G. (1992). *The Psychology of Interrogations, Confessions and Testimony*. Chichester: John Wiley.

Hart, H.M. and McNaughton, J.T. (1959). Some aspects of evidence and inference in the law. In D. Lerner (Ed.), *Evidence and Inference*. Free Press.

Jackson, J.D. (1984). The ultimate issue rule: one rule too many. *Criminal Law Review*, **75**.

Jackson, J.D. (1988). Two methods of proof in criminal procedure. *M. Law Review*, **51**, 549.

Jackson, J.D. (1991). Law's truth, lay truth and lawyers' truth: the representation of evidence in adversary trials. *Law and Critique*, **3**, 29.

Kassin, S.M. and Wrightsman, L.S. (Eds) (1985). *The Psychology of Evidence and Trial Procedure*. Beverly Hills: Sage.

King, M. (1986). *Psychology In and Out of Court*. Oxford: Pergamon.

Langbein, J.H. (1978). Torture and plea bargaining. *University of Chicago Law Review*, **46**, 3.

Law Commission (1993). *The Hearsay Rule in Civil Proceedings*. London: HMSO.

Lempert, R. (1986). The new evidence scholarship: analyzing the process of proof. *B.U. Law Review*, **66**, 439.

Lind, E. and Tyler, T. (1988). *The Social Psychology of Procedural Justice*. New York: Plenum.

Lloyd-Bostock, S. (1988). *Law in Practice*. London: Routledge.

Lloyd-Bostock, S. and Clifford, B.R. (1979). *Evaluating Witness Evidence.* Chichester: Wiley.

Loevinger, L. (1958). Facts, evidence and legal proof. *Western Reserve Law Review*, **9**, 154.

McConville, M., Sanders, A. and Leng, R. (1991). *The Case for the Prosecution*, London: Routledge.

McCormick. N. (1974). *Law as Institutional Fact. LQR*, **90**, 102.

McCormick, N. (1978). *Legal Reasoning and Legal Theory*. Oxford: Clarendon.

McEwan, J. (1992). *Evidence and the Adversarial Process*. Oxford: Blackwell.

Marshall, J. (1966). *Law and Psychology in Conflict*. Garden City: Anchor/Doubleday.

Morison, J. and Leith, P. (1992). *The Barrister's World*. Milton Keynes: Open University Press.

Munsterburg, H. (1908). *On the Witness Stand*. New York: Clark Boardman.

Nelken, D. (1994). *The Truth about Law's Truth*. London: Pluto.

Oddie Committee (1991). *Science and the Administration of Justice*. London: Justice.

Rock, P. (1993). *The Social World of an English Crown Court*. Oxford: Clarendon.

Schum, D.A. (1986). Probability and the processes of discovery, proof and choice. *B.U. Law Review*, **66**, 825.

Spencer, J. and Flin, R. (1993). *The Evidence of Children*. London: Blackstone.

Stone, M. (1984). *Proof of Fact in Criminal Trials*. Edinburgh: Clark.

Summers, R.S. (1974). Evaluating and improving legal processes: a plea for 'process values'. *Cornell Law Review*, **60**, 1.

Tillers, P. (1988). The value of evidence in law. *NILQ*, **39**, 167.

Tillers, P. and Schum, D.A. (1991). A theory of preliminary fact investigation. *University of California Davis Law Review*, **24**, 931.

Tribe, L.H. (1971). Trial by mathematics: precision and ritual in the legal process. *Harvard Law Review*, **84**, 1329.

Twining, W.L. (1985). *Theories of Evidence: Bentham and Wigmore*. London: Weidenfeld.

Twining, W.L. (1990). *Rethinking Evidence*. Oxford: Blackwell.

Wigmore, J.H. (1909). Professor Munsterburg and the psychology of evidence. *Illinois Law Review*, **3**, 399.

Wigmore, J.H. (1940). *Evidence in Trials at Common Law* (3rd edn). Boston: Little Brown.

Zuckerman, A.A.S. (1986). Law, fact or justice? *B.U. Law Review*, **66**, 487.

Chapter 3.2

Evidence: Psychological Perspective

Graham M. Davies
University of Leicester

Almost since its inception, the science of psychology has enjoyed a contentious relationship with the laws of evidence. According to Bartol and Bartol (1987), the first psychologist permitted to testify in a criminal court was a German, Albert von Shrenck-Notzing, who appeared for the defence in a murder trial in Munich in 1896. His testimony centred upon the contaminating effects of pretrial publicity. Witnesses, he argued, would be unable to distinguish what they had seen originally from what they had read subsequently, a viewpoint entirely consistent with modern concepts of post-event misinformation effects (Loftus, 1979). For the first, but certainly not the last time, the court disregarded his testimony and found the suspect guilty.

This review will attempt to draw out some of the general issues surrounding psychology's relationship to witness evidence. First, the different methods which psychologists employ to gather information concerning the reliability of eye-witnesses will be described and illustrated. Second, the perspective offered by psychological research will be contrasted with those of the legal system and the laws of evidence. Third, the continuing debate over the role which psychologists can play as expert witnesses in eye-witness cases will be considered. Lastly, some suggestions are offered as to how psychological research and researchers can operate more effectively in assisting the law courts in reaching sound judgments in cases involving eye-witness evidence.

METHODOLOGICAL APPROACHES

How much weight may we place on the word of an eye-witness? This question provoked a flurry of research from European psychologists around the turn of the century. Binet (1900) investigated the ability of schoolchildren to report freely and answer questions on pictures they had observed. Binet varied the style of questioning to include both leading and suggestive types and was among the first to note how these had an inevitable impact upon the amount and accuracy of information secured. Stern (1910) carried out similar studies with adults and concluded that 'error free recollection is not the rule but the exception—and even the oath is no protection against deceptions of memory' (p. 327). Munsterberg (1908) popularised these findings for American readers and accused lawyers of ignoring what psychology had to offer and being 'completely satisfied with the most haphazard methods of common prejudice and ignorance' (p. 44). Such criticisms from an upstart science brought forth a magisterial rebuke from Wigmore (1909), the noted American legal scholar, who decried the ignorance of law and legal procedure betrayed by some researchers and an over-readiness to generalise from limited research findings gathered in unrealistic settings. Wigmore was careful only to attack the relevance of existing knowledge and did not preclude psychology playing an important role in the future. He looked forward to a 'friendly and energetic alliance of psychology and law, in the noble cause of justice' (p. 432).

Is that friendly alliance any closer to reality? From the mid 1970s we have seen a resurgence of interest among psychologists in the behaviour of eye-witnesses. Such research has employed at least five different approaches in an effort to gain reliable evidence, as detailed below.

Laboratory Studies

Laboratory studies offer many advantages to the researcher, principally precision, control and replicability. However, the dangers emphasised by Wigmore of too ready extrapolation from laboratory findings to the witness in the real world, are still alive. One example of this concerns studies of face recognition. A series of slides of unfamiliar faces are shown in sequence to an audience of subjects who must later select them from a sequence containing both the original and some new faces. This technique has been employed to explore the impact of such issues as gender, age and racial origin on recognition ability and has led to significant advances in the understanding of how the brain processes faces (for an accessible review see Bruce, 1988).

Other researchers, however, have sought on occasion to use these findings as a basis for predicting the behaviour of witnesses to crime (Goldstein, 1977; Loftus, 1979), a dubious extrapolation given the differences between the laboratory and real world (Wells, 1993). One finding which underlies the need for caution concerns rates of misidentification or 'false alarms' which are much lower in laboratory studies than in more realistic crime enactments (Lindsay and Harvie, 1988) while correct recognition rates are appreciably higher in laboratory settings (Shapiro and Penrod, 1986).

The reason for these discrepancies is not that the mental processes occurring in a 'real' situation are necessarily different from those in the laboratory, rather that their impact is overlaid with other factors. These include the degree of emotional arousal of witnesses at the time of the crime (Christianson and Hubinette, 1993) and their motivation to select a suspect on any police identification test (Köhnken and Maass, 1985). In order to explore the influence of such variables it is necessary to forsake the austere surroundings of the laboratory for the more uncertain world of the staged incident.

Incident Studies

Incident studies are still regularly employed in modern research, using a variety of events from the most innocuous (a student interrupts a class to ask directions—Shepherd, Ellis and Davies, 1982) through to the violent and dramatic (a visiting speaker, introduced as a Mafiosi, is 'assassinated' in a crowded lecture theatre—Timm, 1981). In all instances the unsuspecting audiences will be asked to recall the events observed. The aim of such studies is to capture something of the disruptive and unexpected nature of crime. However, in encompassing these emotions, some loss of experimental control is almost inevitable. Witness subjects will see the event from different distances and varying durations; some witnesses will look away or be unsighted. Above all, save in a minority of studies, witnesses will be passive bystanders not active participants. While some real witnesses are bystanders, many will be victims of crime.

One problem common to both the traditional laboratory and incident studies is the representativeness of the subjects, who will generally be student volunteers. Clearly it is important to obtain data from a broad cross-section of the public before generalising findings to the population as a whole (O'Rourke et al., 1989). Thus, there has recently been a growth in field study methodology.

Field Studies

In these kinds of eye-witness studies, rather than the subject coming to the experiment, the experiment is taken to the subjects in their everyday surroundings.

An example of a field study is an unpublished experiment conducted by the author into cross-racial recognition. A White confederate visited small stores run by White and Asian shopkeepers to ask directions to a local landmark. Subsequently, an experimenter visited the shops and asked the shopkeeper to try to identify the confederate from an array of faces which did or did not contain a photograph of the confederate. Contrary to much laboratory research, Asian shopkeepers performed no worse than their White counterparts at identifying the White customer. Such a result may suggest that the familiarity induced by day-to-day interaction with members of another race may reduce or even eliminate the 'own race' superiority effect (Lindsay and Wells, 1983).

Ideally, all factors uncovered in laboratory or incident studies and thought to influence witness reports should be explored in field settings before psychologists advise the courts on their likely impact on actual witnesses. However, for all their realism, field studies have their problems, quite apart from the time and logistical effort involved in running them. Clearly, there are ethical constraints on what can be inflicted on members of the public: no physical assaults in the interests of science! For this reason, psychologists interested in crime are increasingly drawn to two other sources of information on the eye-witness: archival analysis and case studies.

Archival Analysis

In archival analysis, actual police files—including those on murders, robberies and assaults—are systematically examined in order to yield data on the quality and completeness of eye-witness reports. By appropriate partioning of cases it is then possible to look systematically at such factors as gender, race or witness role on the one hand and the nature of the incident on the other.

For instance, Farrington and Lambert (1993) used police records in order to compare the descriptions offered by victims and other witnesses to assault with the actual appearance of the offenders when they were identified and convicted. While sex, ethnicity and distinguishing facial characteristics were generally accurate, information on hair colour, age, height and build showed much lower agreement with actual appearance.

Archive data represent an underutilised and powerful source of information for psychologists concerned with eye-witness behaviour. However, even archive studies have their limitations. For many statements there will be no way of establishing the accuracy of the events described or the appearance of the suspect because the crime was never solved. Even when a photograph of a convicted person is available, the accuracy of many crime details cannot be checked. Moreover, the sheer variability of individual crimes makes it difficult to establish much beyond gross effects. More fine-grain analysis channels attention to individual case studies.

Case Studies

The Canadian psychologist John Yuille has argued forcefully for the importance of case histories as a source of information on witness behaviour (Yuille, 1993). A study by Yuille and Cutshall (1986) involved follow-up interviews on a group of witnesses who some four to five months previously had been caught up in a shooting incident following an armed robbery. While the researchers reported the same superiority of recall of actions over appearance details as had been found in experimental studies, they were struck by the general accuracy of witness reports relative to the known facts, which stayed remarkably high despite the extended delay.

Yuille has argued that conventional experiments underestimate the capacity of real witnesses, a view that has remained controversial. Analyses of other crimes of violence involving multiple witnesses have not always yielded such high levels of overall accuracy and the errors and confusions typical of laboratory studies have occurred (Davies, 1992). The sheer variability in crime, criminals and witnesses suggest the need for many more case studies before half a century's research on the eye-witness can be seriously challenged.

In short, psychologists have a range of methods for studying eye-witness behaviour. All make different compromises between realism on the one hand and experimental control on the other.

Each has its virtues and deficiencies and no one method is likely to be an unequivocal source of reliable information for the court. Thus, the most reliable guide to witness behaviour is likely to emerge by pooling the results from research which has used a variety of methodologies and looking for communality of findings. Such an approach has been widely advocated among legal psychologists and is termed convergent validity (Davies, 1992; Ellsworth, 1991; Yuille, 1993).

THE VALUE OF PSYCHOLOGICAL RESEARCH TO THE COURT

While psychologists have never been slow to claim the relevance of their research to the courtroom, it is important not to minimise the differences in thinking and approach between experimental psychology and the law (Aubert, 1963). As has been noted, psychologists derive their knowledge from an evolving literature embracing different methodologies: there is no one 'ultimate experiment' which can provide the last word for the court (Roesch et al., 1991). The law develops by drawing upon precedents derived from legal judgments and looks to psychology to provide 'facts' to buttress such authoratative rulings (Haney, 1980). As Monahan and Walker (1988) have argued, the social sciences by their nature are ill-equipped to provide such 'facts'. Rather the law should look upon policy-oriented psychological research as something closer to a judicial opinion: a state of the art statement, which is refined and developed in the light of increasing knowledge.

Psychologists differ from lawyers also in the way in which they conceptualise causes and effects in behaviour. An illustration of this confusion concerns the concepts of 'proof' and 'causation'. To the psychologist, proving a link between two events is essentially a statistical exercise, where degree of certainty is defined by varying confidence levels (.05, .01, .001, etc.). To the lawyer, proof has a technical meaning which refers to the level of certainty which will be acceptable to the court to prove the prosecution case. Level of proof varies between the civil (on the balance of probabilities) and the criminal (beyond reasonable doubt) courts. In criminal cases there are also restrictions as to what constitutes admissible evidence from the point of view of proving guilt: evidence as to character and pathology, of the kind generated by psychologists administering tests and questionnaires would not constitute proof in the narrower legal sense of the term.

Similarly, psychologists think of behaviour as being multiply determined; a range of factors will operate concomitantly to produce a given outcome. In law, however, 'causation' has a much narrower meaning: a given event B is caused by A and it is up to the prosecutor to demonstrate that B would not have happened but for the presence of A (the 'but for' rule, see Hart and Honoré, 1985). Technical vocabulary is always a barrier to collaboration between professionals, but when the two use the same terms in rather differing ways then this can frequently lead to misunderstanding.

Moreover, as Haney (1980) has argued, the focus of the enterprise differs in law and psychology. Law, he argues, is primarily idiographic in nature, concerned with the outcome of a given case. Empirical psychology, on the other hand, is nomothetic, attempting to derive general principles which encompass myriad individual instances but do not necessarily predict the outcome of a single case. Statements by psychologists, tend to be conditional ('The most likely outcome in these circumstances would be ...') which is at variance with the law's preference for fixed dichotomies and absolute statements.

The probabilistic nature of empirical psychology's findings has led some legal commentators to go so far as to argue that it has nothing to contribute to the jury's evaluation of witness evidence at trial (King, 1986; Stone, 1984). However, this view has not been accepted by the courts or many legal commentators in the United States, Britain or mainland Europe.

The acceptance of expert evidence on the vagaries of eye-witness testimony by the courts is probably most prevalent in the United States; by 1988, some 450 trials in 25 States had admitted evidence on this point (Brigham, 1988). Such evidence is generally given as part of the defence case: Kassin, Ellsworth and Smith (1989) report a figure of 87 per cent for defence-based evidence compared to only 13 per cent for the prosecution. The expert will summarise the research literature on the impact of 'estimator' and 'system' variables (Wells, 1978): that is the likely impact on accuracy of the conditions of the original observation and the procedures used by the police in collecting witness evidence, respectively.

In the *United States v. Ameral* (488 F2d 1148, 1973), four criteria were established for the admissibility of such expert evidence. These were (i) that the person tendering evidence should be a recognised expert, (ii) that such testimony should go beyond the common knowledge of the average juror, (iii) following the then prevailing criteria set by *Frye v. United States* (293 Fed.

1013 D.C. Cir., 1923) the evidence should conform to an explanatory theory which enjoys general acceptance, and (iv) that the evidence should be more probative than prejudicial in its likely impact upon the jury. The second and third criteria have provoked much continuing debate in the United States (see *Daubert et al. v. Merrell Dow Pharmaceuticals, Inc.* 113 s.ct. 2786, 1993).

As regard the common knowledge criterion, Loftus (1986) in her memoirs of ten years as an expert witness in this area has recalled how frequently her evidence was ruled inadmissible on these grounds; as one judgment notes 'everyone knows these things' (Loftus, 1986, p. 245). Psychologists have subsequently devoted a considerable amount of time to refuting such claims by demonstrating the widespread ignorance of the general public of many of the factors which have a demonstrable impact upon eye-witness behaviour under experimental conditions. Techniques have included providing scenarios involving witness behaviour to prospective jurors and inviting them to select the statement most likely to accord with research findings. In these circumstances members of the public show a grasp of some issues (cross-racial recognition, biased parades) but poor understanding of others (confidence and accuracy, weapon focus) (Deffenbacher and Loftus, 1982). Ignorance extends to professionals such as police officers (Yarmey, 1986) and attorneys (Brigham and Wolfskiel, 1983). Such studies do not address whether jurors appreciate the scale of impact of various factors: the 'calibration' issue (Wells, 1986). When the public have been asked to estimate the impact of a factor, such as identifying a suspect from a different race to one's own, accuracy of prediction is generally poor (Brigham and Bothwell, 1983). Studies clearly demonstrate a poor grasp of research findings by the public at large, though the question remains as to whether the results of research are representative and reliable (Elliot, 1993).

This latter point forms the focus of much of the debate which has surrounded the third of the *Ameral* criteria: whether the research findings enjoy general acceptance. In 1983 two experienced experimental psychologists, McCloskey and Egeth, provided a critique of the prevailing theory and data of eye-witness research. They pointed to its traditional reliance on laboratory experimentation and the sometimes inconsistent findings both in terms of size and outcome for many of the factors upon which psychologists were then testifying. Echoing the criticisms of some lawyers (Stone, 1984), they concluded that there were so few relevant and reliable findings in the eye-witness literature that it was better that psychologists stay silent than run the risk of misleading the jury.

McCloskey and Egeth's critique caused a furore in the scientific press. The leading journal in the area, *Law and Human Behaviour*, devoted a double issue to statements on the debate (1986, 10, No. 1/2). Loftus (1983) argued that the inconsistencies on particular findings ignored the consensus on a range of mundane issues which frequently came up in court and that the dangers of remaining silent outweighed the possibility of occasionally misleading jurors, a view shared by Wells (1986). In retrospect, the turmoil stirred up by McCloskey and Egeth can be seen to have had a generally positive impact on the quality and relevance of research in the field. There are today far more archive and field studies conducted on eye-witness research, though arguments continue as to whether the proportion is still not high enough (Wells, 1993; Yuille, 1993). Issues which the two critics highlighted as under-researched have received far more attention. Sometimes, as in study of the weapon focus, the results have provided convergent validity justifying expert testimony (Steblay, 1992). Sometimes, as in the case of 'unconscious transference' results have proved equivocal, supporting at least some of the strictures of McCloskey and Egeth (Read et al., 1990). Overall, however, there now appears to be a wider consensus over accepted findings in eye-witness research of the kind demanded by the courts.

Kassin, Ellsworth and Smith (1989) surveyed some 63 international authorities on eye-witness behaviour and found an impressive consensus among them as to the impact of such factors as the importance of parade fairness, the impact of leading questions, cross-racial identifications, and bias in estimates of time duration. While the issues stirred by McCloskey and Egeth are far from dead (Egeth, 1993) expert testimony in US courts on eye-witness behaviour is now widely accepted. In 1983 in *State v. Chapple* (135 Ariz. 281, 660 P.2d 1208, 1983) the Arizona Supreme Court overturned a guilty verdict on the grounds that an expert had not been permitted to testify on the variables likely to influence eye-witness behaviour, a finding which was also followed by the Washington Court of Appeals in *State v. Moon* (45 Wash. App. 692, 726 P.2d 1263, 1986). It appears that, 80 years after Munsterberg, the expert witness on eye-witness behaviour has finally arrived.

What of the role of the psychologist in Europe? In Germany and Scandinavia, psychologists are not restricted as in the United States to rehearsing research findings in front of the jury. Rather, suitably qualified psychologists may actually have the opportunity to restage crimes with the actual witnesses involved in order to test the veracity of their statements. One such exponent, Trankell (1972), has described how, when faced with conflicting testimony about a car journey the whole circumstances were re-enacted and the ambiguity of witness statements resolved. Such an approach is perhaps only possible within an inquisitorial system of justice, but it is one which, at a stroke, resolves many issues as to the relevance of psychologists' testimony. Interestingly, the impact of such specific testimony on jury decision making appears to be little different to that of the more general testimony typical of the United States (Maass, Brigham and West, 1985).

In Britain, the position of psychologists wishing to give evidence on evidential issues is governed by a series of judgments upholding the view (explicitly rejected by the US courts) that matters of witness reliability were within the province of the jury (Sheldon and Macleod, 1991). However, this view was severely qualified by the Devlin Report (1976). This had examined the issue of mistaken identification highlighted by a number of miscarriages of justice.

Devlin advised that 'Research should be directed to establishing ways in which the insights of psychology can be brought to bear on the conduct of identification parades and the practice of the courts' (Devlin, 1976, p. 149). Devlin did not recommend that psychologists should appear as expert witnesses which he felt was premature (Devlin, 1982). Rather, the judge should direct the jury as to the dangers of convicting on the basis of eye-witness identification alone. Devlin's recommendations are codified in the *Turnbull* judgments which require judges in their summing up explicitly to consider the circumstances surrounding a witness identification and to relate each aspect to the evidence tendered (Shepherd, Ellis and Davies, 1982). Deviation from this procedure has led to cases being overturned on appeal (e.g. *R. v. McNeill*, 1/2/90 Court of Appeal, unreported). With one or two exceptions (J. Boon, R. Bull personal communication) the role of the psychologist in Britain is solely one of providing reports, typically for the defence, and advising on lines of questioning: 'a second in the corner' rather than a contestant.

CONCLUSIONS

It is evident that after an uncertain beginning, psychologists are now having a significant impact on the way the courts treat witness evidence. Clearly, this process is most advanced in the United States but has some way to go in the United Kingdom. However, the recent Royal Commission on Criminal Justice (Runciman, 1993) called for a greater opportunity for experts to give testimony at trial in a manner which could educate the court and the jury. It is also evident that the impact of psychology and law has been by no means one way. Debates on the relevance and reliability of research findings have led psychologists to employ far more forensically relevant scenarios for experimentation (Wells, 1986) and to turn to underutilised sources such as archive material and case histories (Davies, 1992). Despite the objections of some academics, it seems likely that lawyers, particularly for the defence, will turn increasingly to psychologists as a source of insight and information in eye-witness cases.

Such a move brings with it some dangers as well as advantages. The most pressing is probably the question of misleading or damaging testimony. McCloskey and Egeth (1983) drew attention to the dangers of psychologically qualified witnesses inducing a general scepticism in jurors rather than sensitising them to dubious testimony. Accusations of such a process at work have been made in regard to the testimony sometimes offered by psychologists which undermined the evidence of children in sexual abuse trials (Spencer, 1992), though its impact can be neutralised by rival experts putting the other view (Goodman, 1993).

Two safeguards may serve to reduce the risk of renegade experts misleading the courts. The first is the application and rigorous enforcement of codes of practice and registration to ensure that the courts only hear well-qualified experts. In the United Kingdom, psychologists who have demonstrated research prowess in the field of psychology applied to law and have undergone a period of practical supervised training may qualify for the title of Chartered Forensic Psychologist. The Charter scheme was organised at the request of the Privy Council, an official government body which oversees the conduct of the Universities and the professions. It is supervised by the professional body representing psychologists in the United Kingdom, the British Psychological Society and its Division of Criminological and Legal Psychology. Chartered psychologists who testify on matters which lie outside their area of expertise leave themselves open to professional investigation and loss of chartered status. Such a process of internal policing provides perhaps the best guarantee of quality of evidence, though until the Charter scheme is more widely known, there will continue to be incidents where the courts are vulnerable to charlatanism masquerading as expertise.

The second safeguard is one which already exists in many countries employing the inquisitorial system of justice but could usefully be extended to Britain and the United States which share the adversarial system (Spencer, 1992). This is for psychologists to be appointed as *amicus curiae* or 'friends of the court': to appear not for one side or the other but in an educational role, dispassionately examining the evidence. Roesch et al. (1991) have described how the American Psychology-Law Society has prepared a series of briefs on a range of issues in the evidential area. Such briefs strive for consensus among research authorities in a bid to give juries a balanced and informative viewpoint of the research. A similar plea for psychologists to join a register of court-appointed experts has been made by Spencer (1992) who has observed the system at work in France. Such a call, however, is unlikely to be wholly successful in a court system dominated by the adversarial stance. Even the 1993 Royal Commission Report rejected the introduction of the 'court expert' on the grounds that it might curtail the rigorous examination of evidence. Until such dispassionate expertise is more widely accepted, any psychologists venturing to give their views in court are likely to find themselves as much a victim of the adversarial process as any other witness.

REFERENCES

Aubert, V. (1963). The structure of legal thinking. In J. Andenaes (Ed.), *Legal Essays: A Tribute to Fride Castberg on the Occasion of his 70th Birthday*. Boston: Universitetsforlaget, pp. 41–63.

Bartol, C.R. and Bartol. A.M. (1987). History of forensic psychology. In I.B. Weiner and A.K. Hess (Eds), *Handbook of Forensic Psychology*. Chichester: Wiley, pp. 3–21.

Binet, A. (1900). *La Suggestibilité*. Paris: Schleicher.

Brigham, J.C. (1988). Disputed eyewitness identifications: can experts help? *The Champion*, **8**, 5, 10–18.

Brigham, J. and Bothwell (1983). The ability of prospective jurors to estimate the accuracy of eyewitness identification. *Law and Human Behaviour*, **7**, 19–30.

Brigham, J.C. and Wolfskiel, M.P. (1983). Opinions of attorneys and law enforcement personnel on the accuracy of eyewitness identifications. *Law and Human Behavior*, **6**, 15–29.

Bruce, V. (1988). *Recognising Faces*. Hove: Erlbaum.

Christianson, S.-A. and Hubinette, B. (1993). Hands up! A study of witnesses emotional reactions and memories associated with bank robberies. *Applied Cognitive Psychology*, **7**, 365–80.

Davies, G.M. (1992). Influencing public policy in eyewitnessing: problems and possibilities. In F. Lösel, D. Bender and T. Bliesener (Eds), *Psychology and Law: International Perspectives*. Berlin: de Gruyter, pp. 265–74.

Deffenbacher, K.A. and Loftus, E.F. (1982). Do jurors share a common understanding concerning eyewitness behaviour? *Law and Human Behavior*, **6**, 15–29.

Devlin, Lord (1976). *Report to the Secretary of State for the Home Department of the Departmental Committee on Evidence of Identification in Criminal Cases*. London: HMSO.

Devlin, Lord (1982). Foreword. In J. Shepherd, H.D. Ellis and G.M. Davies, *Identification Evidence: A Psychological Evaluation*. Aberdeen University Press, Aberdeen.

Egeth, H.E. (1993). What do we know about eyewitness identification? *American Psychologist*, **48**, 577–80.

Elliot, R. (1993). Expert testimony about eyewitness identification: a critique. *Law and Human Behavior*, **17**, 423–37.

Ellsworth, P.C. (1991). To tell what we know or wait for Godot? *Law and Human Behavior*, **15**, 77–90.

Farrington, D.P. and Lambert, S. (1993). Predictive violence and burglary offenders from victim, witness and offense data. Paper presented to the First NISCALE workshop on criminality and law enforcement, The Hague, Netherlands.

Goldstein, A.G. (1977). The fallibility of the eyewitness. In B.D. Sales (Ed.), *Psychology in the Legal Process*. New York: Spectrum, pp. 223–47.

Goodman, J. (1993). Evaluating psychological expertise on questions of social fact. *Law and Human Behavior*, **17**, 249–55.

Haney, C. (1980). Psychology and legal change: on the limits of factual jurisprudence. *Law and Human Behavior*, **4**, 147–99.

Hart, H.L.A. and Honeré, T. (1985). *Causation in the Law* (2nd edn). Oxford: Clarendon Press.

Kassin, S.M., Ellsworth, P.C. and Smith, V.L. (1989). The 'general acceptance' of psychological research on eyewitness testimony. *American Psychologist*, **44**, 1089–98.

King, M. (1986). *Psychology in and out of Court*. Oxford: Pergamon Press.

Köhnken, G. and Maass, A. (1985). Realism, reactance and instructional bias in eyewitness identification. In F.L. Denmark (Ed.), *Social/Ecological Psychology and the Psychology of Women*. Amsterdam: North Holland, pp. 141–63.

Lindsay, R.C.L. and Harvie, V.L. (1988). Hits, false alarms, correct and mistaken identifications: the effect of method of data collection on facial memory. In M. Gruneburg, P. Morris and R. Sykes (Eds), *Practical Aspects of Memory: Current*

Research and Issues. Chichester: John Wiley, pp. 47–52.

Lindsey, R.C.L. and Wells, G.L. (1983). What do we really know about the cross-race identification effect? In S.M.A. Lloyd-Bostock and B. R. Clifford (Eds), *Evaluating Witness Evidence*. Chichester: John Wiley, pp. 219–33.

Loftus, E.F. (1979). *Eyewitness Testimony*. Cambridge, MA: Harvard University Press.

Loftus, E.F. (1983). Silence is not golden. *American Psychologist*, **65**, 9–15.

Loftus, E.F. (1986). Ten years in the life of an expert witness. *Law and Human Behavior*, **10**, 241–63.

Maass, A., Brigham, J. and West, S.G. (1985). Testifying on eyewitness reliability. Expert advice is not always persuasive. *Journal of Applied Social Psychology*, **15**, 207–29.

McCloskey, M. and Egeth, H. (1983). Eyewitness identification: what can a psychologist tell a jury? *American Psychologist*, **38**, 550–63.

Monahan, J. and Walker, L. (1988). Social science in law: a new paradigm. *American Psychologist*, **43**, 465–72.

Munsterberg, H. (1908). *On the Witness Stand: Essays on Psychology and Crime*. New York: McClure.

O'Rourke, T.E., Penrod, S.D., Cutler, B.L. and Stuve, T.E. (1989). The external validity of eyewitness identification research: generalising across subject populations. *Law and Human Behavior*, **13**, 385–95.

Read, J.D., Tollestrup, P., Hammersley, R., McFadzen, E. and Christensen, A. (1990). The unconscious transfer effect: are innocent bystanders ever misidentified? *Applied Cognitive Psychology*, **4**, 3–31.

Roesch, R., Golding, S.L., Hans, V.P. and Repucci, N.D. (1991). Social science and the courts: the role of *amicus curiae* briefs. *Law and Human Behavior*, **15**, 1–11.

Runciman, Lord (1993). *Report of the Royal Commission on Criminal Justice*. London: HMSO.

Shapiro, P.N. and Penrod, S. (1986). Meta-analysis of facial identification studies. *Psychological Bulletin*, **100**, 139–56.

Sheldon, D.H. and Macleod, M.D. (1991). From normative to positive data: expert psychological evidence re-examined. *Criminal Law Review*, November, 797–864.

Shepherd, J., Ellis, H.D. and Davies, G.M. (1982). *Identification Evidence: A Psychological Evaluation*. Aberdeen: Aberdeen University Press.

Spencer, J. (1992). Court experts and expert witnesses. In R.W. Rideout and B.A. Hopple (Eds), *Current Legal Problems 1992*. Oxford: Oxford University Press, pp. 213–36.

Steblay, N.M. (1992). A meta-analytic review of the weapon focus effect. *Law and Human Behavior*, **16**, 413–24.

Stern, L.W. (1910). Abstracts of lectures on the psychology of testimony. *American Journal of Psychology*, **21**, 273–82.

Stone, M. (1984). *Proof of Fact in Criminal Trials*. Edinburgh: W. Green.

Timm, H.W. (1981). The effect of forensic hypnosis techniques on eyewitness recall and recognition. *Journal of Police Science and Administration*, **9**, 188–94.

Trankell, A. (1972). *Reliability of Evidence*. Stockholm: Beckmans.

Wells, G.L. (1978). System and estimator variables. *Journal of Personality and Social Psychology*, **36**, 1546–57.

Wells, G.L. (1986). Expert psychological testimony: empirical and conceptual analysis of effects. *Law and Human Behavior*, **10**, 83–95.

Wells, G.L. (1993). What do we know about eyewitness identification? *American Psychologist*, **48**, 553–71.

Wigmore, J.H. (1909). Professor Munsterberg and the psychology of testimony: being the trial of Cokestone v. Munsterberg. *Illinois Law Review*, **3**, 399–445.

Yarmey, A.D. (1986). Perceived expertness and credibility of police officers as eyewitnesses. *Canadian Police Journal*, **10**, 31–52.

Yuille, J.C. (1993). We must study forensic eyewitnesses to know about them. *American Psychologist*, **48**, 572–3.

Yuille, J.C. and Cutshall, J.L. (1986). A case study of eyewitness memory for a crime. *Journal of Applied Psychology*, **71**, 291–301.

Chapter 3.3

Assessing the Accuracy of Eye-witness Identifications

Brian L. Cutler
Florida International University
and
Steven D. Penrod
University of Minnesota

Several legal scholars, beginning with Borchard (1932), have studied the causes of mistaken conviction in over 1000 criminal cases (see Brandon and Davies, 1973; Frank and Frank, 1957; Huff, Rattner and Sagarin, 1986). These studies clearly suggest that the single leading cause of false convictions is mistaken eye-witness identifications of defendants. While such archival evidence is indeed compelling, it speaks only to the fact that mistaken eye-witness identifications occur and not to the frequency, likelihood or manner of mistaken identification. The cases reviewed by Borchard and the others are unique in that there was some basis for confidently concluding that the identifications were mistaken. Unfortunately, there is no way to know how representative those cases are, and hence there is no way to estimate the likelihood that any given identification is mistaken. Using a somewhat different analytic strategy, this chapter addresses two primary questions concerning eye-witness identifications: how accurate are identifications, and how can we assess the accuracy of particular identifications?

Most of what is known about the psychology of eye-witness memory has been acquired through laboratory experiments. In laboratory experiments, crimes are simulated in various ways, and subjects' memories for the crimes are assessed. In some experiments (e.g. Cutler, Penrod and Martens, 1987) subjects view videotaped enactments of crimes. In others (e.g. Cutler and Fisher, 1990) thefts or other incidents are staged in classrooms in view of a large number of students, or thefts are staged for individual subjects who visit the laboratory believing they are there to participate in an unrelated experiment (e.g. Lindsay, Wells and Rumpel, 1981). In an unusually realistic laboratory experiment conducted by Hosch and Cooper (1982), the experimenters staged a theft of some subjects' watches, leading them to believe they were victims of an actual crime. Many of these experiments test the accuracy of identification performance by having eye-witnesses attempt identifications from identification parades/lineups (or photoarrays) in which the perpetrator is present or from which the perpetrator is absent. The purpose of using perpetrator-present lineups is to assess the ability of eye-witnesses correctly to identify crime perpetrators. The purpose of using perpetrator-absent lineups is to assess the extent to which eye-witnesses falsely identify lineup members as crime perpetrators. In other words, the perpetrator-present lineups resemble the situation in which the suspect is guilty, and the perpetrator-absent lineups resemble the situation in which the suspect is innocent.

Wells (1993) noted that across the many laboratory experiments on eye-witness identification, the rates of false identifications varied from nearly 0 per cent to nearly 100 per cent. The problem with generalising the accuracy rates from these experiments is that the crime simulations depart in many ways from actual crimes. Hence, even if we were to average the rates across experiments and find that false identification rates occur, say, 40 per cent of the time, we would want to question whether these levels of performance generalise to actual crimes involving eye-witness identification.

Perhaps the most relevant source of data pertaining to accuracy rates of actual eye-witness identifications emerges from field studies. Some researchers (Brigham et al., 1982; Krafka and Penrod, 1985; Platz and Hosch, 1988; Pigott, Brigham and Bothwell, 1990) have attempted to reap the benefits of laboratory procedures and realistic crime conditions by conducting well-controlled experiments in more realistic field settings. The primary purpose of this research, like laboratory experiments, is to estimate the effects of an isolated factor on identification accuracy. Two of the experiments (Brigham et al., 1982; Platz and Hosch, 1988) were primarily interested in the joint influence of witness and perpetrator race on identification accuracy. One (Krafka and Penrod, 1985) was primarily concerned the influence of procedures designed to improve the accuracy of eye-witness identifications. Pigott, Brigham and Bothwell's (1990) study examined the relation between accuracy of eye-witnesses' descriptions and identifications. Because these studies were conducted in more realistic settings, their identification accuracy rates might better enable us to estimate the accuracy rates in actual crimes, at least as compared to archival studies and laboratory experiments.

Brigham et al. (1982) conducted the first such experiment. Their procedure required two casually dressed males independently to enter, five minutes apart, a Tallahassee, Florida convenience store. Each engaged in an unusual (but safe) transaction with the convenience store clerk. One such 'customer' paid for a pack of cigarettes entirely with pennies, and either the customer or clerk would have to count them out (70 to 90 pennies). That customer would then ask for directions to a local airport, bus station, hospital or shopping mall. The other 'customer' carried a product to the counter as if he was going to purchase it, discovered that he did not have enough money, made for the door, found enough change, and returned to the counter to purchase the item. He then asked directions to one of the aforementioned locations. Each transaction lasted three to four minutes. Clerks were later asked to identify the customers from photoarrays. In their pilot work for this experiment, Brigham et al. tested the clerks 24 hours later and found that only 7.8 per cent were able correctly to identify the customers. (This accuracy rate was comparable to what one would find just from guessing.) They then modified the procedure to test for identification accuracy after only two hours. In all, 73 clerks then participated as eye-witnesses, each providing two identifications, one of each 'customer'. With the two-hour time delay, 50 out of 146 total identifications (34.2 per cent) were correct. Customer-absent photoarrays were not used in this experiment, so false-identification rates could not be estimated.

In Krafka and Penrod's (1985) experiment, a 'customer' entered convenience stores in Madison, Wisconsin and purchased a small item with a traveller's cheque. Either two or 24 hours later, an investigator, posing as a law intern, asked the clerks to identify the customer. Eighty-five clerks were shown either customer-present or customer-absent photoarrays. Here, the time delay (two versus 24 hours) did not significantly influence identification accuracy rates. When the customer was present in the photoarray, 41 per cent of the clerks correctly identified him. When the customer was absent from the photoarray, 34 per cent falsely identified another photograph as that of the customer.

Platz and Hosch (1988) used the same convenience store scenario as did Brigham et al. (1982) except that three accomplices entered the store rather than two. The convenience stores were in El Paso, Texas. The first two accomplices engaged the clerk in the same manner as in Brigham et al.'s experiment. The third attempted to pay for a purchase with a combination of dollars from the USA and pesos from Mexico. Upon being informed that the store did not accept pesos, the customer asked the clerk if the store carried a particular sports magazine. Identifications were tested using customer-present photoarrays two hours after the customers entered the stores. Each of 86 clerks attempted to identify all three customers. In all, 44.2 per cent of the identifications were correct. False identification-rate could not be assessed as customer-absent photoarrays were not used.

Apparently having exhausted all of the convenience stores in Tallahassee, Florida, Brigham and colleagues (Pigott, Brigham and Bothwell, 1990) turned to the use of local banks for their next field study. In each scenario, one of two accomplices entered a bank through its main entrance, walked to the centre island and pretended to fill out a deposit slip. The accomplice then approached a teller and attempted to cash a cheque. The cheque was a 'crudely altered United States Postal Service money order' in which the amount of $10 was altered to \$110. All tellers refused to cash the money order. Each time the accomplice argued with the teller, claiming that the alteration was made by post office personnel. After repeated refusals from the clerk, the accomplice became irate, took the money order and hurried out of the bank. The interaction lasted approximately 90 seconds. Four to five hours later an experimenter, posing as a law officer, showed the teller an accomplice-present or accomplice-absent photoarray. In all, 47 bank tellers participated as eye-witnesses. Among tellers shown a customer-present photoarray, 47.8 per cent made a correct identification. Among tellers shown a customer-absent photoarray, 37.5 per cent made a false identification. (Interestingly, 70 per cent of the bank tellers reported that they had received training for eye-witness situations.)

Cumulating across the above studies, data were gathered from 291 mock eye-witnesses in 536 separate identification tests. The correct identification-rates in these experiments were 34.2 per cent (Brigham et al., 1982), 41 per cent (Krafka and Penrod, 1985), 44.2 per cent (Platz and Hosch, 1988) and 47.8 per cent (Pigott, Brigham and Bothwell, 1990). The unweighted average is 41.8 per cent. False identifications were assessed in two of the studies. The rates were 34 per cent (Krafka and Penrod, 1985) and 37.5 per cent (Pigott, Brigham and Bothwell, 1990). The unweighted average is 35.8 per cent. What we learn from these experiments is that identifications of persons seen briefly, in non-stressful conditions, and attempted after brief delays, are frequently inaccurate. Based on the theory that customer-present photoarrays resemble the situation in which the suspect is guilty and customer-absent photoarrays represent the situation in which the suspect is innocent, only two out of five guilty persons were correctly identified and one out of three innocent persons was falsely identified. Although the scenarios used in these four studies do not resemble the events in some crimes such as armed robbery, rape or murder, they do resemble a great many other eye-witness situations. Eye-witnesses do not always experience violent or heinous crimes. Often, eye-witnesses are asked to identify persons whom they did not know were perpetrators at the time an interaction occurred.

The results from these four field experiments are also consistent with the findings of Shapiro and Penrod's (1986) meta-analysis of the results from nearly 1000 experimental conditions reported in 128 laboratory and field experiments examining facial recognition performance. They reported overall unweighted hit rates of 68 per cent and false alarm rates of 22 per cent across laboratory and field studies. However, they also note that there are systematic differences in eye-witness performance between laboratory and field experiments (with 75 per cent of the variance in performance explained by factors such as those considered below). Field experiments produced hit rates 16 per cent lower than laboratory experiments and false alarm rates more than 13 per cent higher than laboratory studies.

In sum, data from laboratory experiments and field studies complement the archival studies, which demonstrate that mistaken identifications have, on numerous occasions, led to miscarriages of justice. The laboratory experiments demonstrate that combinations of factors can produce eye-witness identification accuracy-rates that span the range of possibilities: from nearly 0 per cent accuracy to nearly 100 per cent accurate. And field studies demonstrate that, in some realistic crime-like situations, eye-witness identifications are often inaccurate.

But what accounts for these inaccuracies? Many psychologists have argued that a variety of factors systematically and predictably influence identification accuracy and that these factors can be used to evaluate the accuracy of particular identifications. Cutler and Penrod (in press) discuss the importance of seven classes of eye-witness variables:

i.   stable characteristics of eye-witnesses (e.g. gender, personality)

ii.   malleable characteristics of eye-witnesses (e.g. whether the eye-witness was intoxicated at the crime or identification)

iii. eye-witness testimony (e.g. the diagnosticity of other testimony given by the eye-witness, such as confidence in the accuracy of identification)

iv. stable target (perpetrator) characteristics (e.g. gender, attractiveness)

v.   malleable target characteristics (e.g. disguises worn by the perpetrator)

vi. eye-witness environment (e.g. lighting conditions, exposure duration)

vii. post-event factors (e.g. the amount of time between the crime and identification and what occurs during that time).

Below we summarise the findings in each class of factors. For details on the specific factors and research addressing them, see Cutler and Penrod (in press) and Shapiro and Penrod (1986).

Stable characteristics of eye-witnesses generally are not particularly useful predictors of identification accuracy. Sex of eye-witness, various forms of intelligence, and personality characteristics are only weakly, if at all, related to the tendency to make correct or false identifications. Age appears to be a more important predictor, with children and the elderly sometimes performing more poorly than other adults. Self-reports of face recognition skills are weakly related to actual recognition skills, meaning that not much faith should be put in people's claims that they never forget a face.

Malleable characteristics of eye-witnesses produce mixed results in the research literature. Whether or not the witness, while viewing the crime, expects to have to make an identification seems to matter little. However, the manner in which a witness processes a perpetrator's facial characteristics does matter. Witnesses who make superficial judgements about the perpetrator's facial features (e.g. 'he has a big nose') at the time of the crime, as compared to those who make more deep, impressionistic judgements (e.g. 'he looked like a my brother'), perform less accurately on identification tests. Some professions, such as bank tellers, undergo 'training' for witnessing. Research has not found training to be effective. Some studies have shown that intoxicated eye-witnesses perform more poorly on identification tests than do sober eye-witnesses.

Aspects of eye-witness testimony are poor indicators of identification accuracy. A large body of studies has demonstrated that accuracy, completeness, and congruence of prior descriptions of the perpetrator are weakly related to identification accuracy. Memory for details is inversely (though weakly) related to identification accuracy. Consistency of testimony (of crime details and person descriptions) is unrelated to identification accuracy. And confidence in ability to identify a perpetrator is unrelated to accuracy, but confidence in having made a correct identification is modestly associated with identification accuracy.

Stable target characteristics, such as sex and attractiveness, seem to have little bearing on eye-witness identification accuracy. The one characteristic in this class that does seem to matter is target distinctiveness. Distinctive targets are more accurately identified than less distinctive targets.

Malleable target characteristics are important predictors of identification accuracy. Changes in facial appearance and disguises worn by perpetrators produce significant decrements in identification accuracy. These factors are important not only because of their reliable effect on identification accuracy but because disguises and facial transformations are common in crimes involving eye-witnesses.

The eye-witnessing environment is also an important class of predictors. The extent of time for which the eye-witness views the target at the time of the crime is positively associated with identification accuracy. The presence of a weapon can create a 'weapon focus' effect. Witnesses tend to focus their attention more on the weapon and less on the perpetrator's facial and physical characteristics. The reduced attention to the perpetrator's facial characteristics makes accurate identification less likely. Witnesses have more difficulty recognising perpetrators of a different race than of their own race. Another potentially important factor is the amount of stress experienced by the eye-witness at the time of the crime. Crimes vary greatly in the amount of violence and induced stress. The research tends to support the conclusion that extreme stress reduces identification accuracy.

Post-event factors are important for evaluating eye-witness identification accuracy. Identifications that take place long after a crime are less likely to be accurate than those taking place shortly after a crime. Mugshot searches have the potential to influence identification accuracy in that persons identified in mugshots are more likely to be later identified (correctly or incorrectly) from a lineup. In such cases it is not clear whether the lineup identification is based on the mugshot identification or on memory for the crime. More generally, a number of possible sources of line-up bias, reviewed in more detail below, can influence witness performance.

Psychological research over the past few decades has cast considerable light on the processes governing eye-witness memory and on the specific factors that do and do not influence eye-witness identification accuracy. These findings can be used by police investigators to gauge the accuracy of witness descriptions, by attorneys to evaluate witness testimony in building their cases, and by judges and juries to determine the credibility of eye-witness testimony (Lindsay, Lea and Fulford, 1991; Wells, 1993; Cutler and Penrod, in press).

THE SUGGESTIBILITY OF IDENTIFICATION TESTS

This section focuses on the influence of factors associated with identification tests which are under the control of the criminal justice system. Specifically, we review four factors affecting the suggestibility of identification tests.

Lineup Instruction Bias

Instructions given to an eye-witness prior to an identification test can vary in their degree of suggestiveness. Suggestive instructions may convey to the eye-witness the impression that the perpetrator is, in fact, in the photoarray or lineup, and thereby enhance the likelihood that the eye-witness will make an identification. How can instructions convey this message? The following experiments examine this question empirically.

Malpass and Devine (1981) staged an act of vandalism during a lecture. Students attempted to identify the vandal from one of two live lineups within the following three days. Half of the subjects attempted to identify the vandal from a lineup in which he appeared (vandal-present lineup). The remainder attempted to identify him from a lineup in which he was replaced with a look-alike (vandal-absent lineup). The latter conditions simulates to some extent the situation in which an innocent suspect is placed in a lineup. Half of the subjects in each condition were given the following biased instructions (p. 484): 'We believe that the person ... is present in the lineup. Look carefully at each of the five individuals in the lineup. Which of these is the person you saw ...?' The form on which these subjects were to indicate their decisions contained the numbers 1 through 5 (for subjects to circle their choices) but no option for rejecting the lineup. The remainder were given the following unbiased instruction: 'The person ... may be one of the five individuals in the lineup. It is also possible that he is not in the lineup. Look carefully at each of the five individuals in the lineup. If the person you saw ... is not in the lineup, circle 0. If the person is present in the lineup, circle the number of his position.'

Among subjects who viewed a vandal-present lineup, 100 per cent of those who received biased instructions made a positive identification, 75 per cent of whom correctly identified the vandal. Within this same lineup condition, 83 per cent who received unbiased instructions made a positive identification, all of whom were correct. (These accuracy rates did not differ significantly.) Among subjects who viewed a vandal-absent lineup, 78 per cent of those who received biased instructions made a positive identification. Of course, all of them were incorrect. In contrast, only 33 per cent of those who received unbiased instructions made a false identification from the vandal-absent lineup. Thus, significantly more false identifications were obtained with biased instructions than with neutral instructions.

Our research (e.g. Cutler, Penrod and Martens, 1987) has also demonstrated that biased instructions lead to an increase in false identifications, even when the biased instructions were much more subtle than those used by Malpass and Devine (1981). An experiment by Paley and Geiselman (1989) provides additional evidence that biased instructions influence identification performance even when subjects are given the option of providing no response (i.e. 'don't know').

Maas and Köhnken (1989) challenged the generalisability of the research on lineup instruction bias. They argued that the suggestibility effect may result because eye-witnesses in these experiments know that they are taking part in a simulation and no real consequences follow from their judgements. Eye-witnesses to actual crimes might exert more caution and be less influenced by suggestive instructions. They conducted two experiments in an effort to test this hypothesis using students from a German university. Their experiments differed from the research reviewed above in two important respects: (1) some subjects did not know they were participating in a crime simulation and therefore believed the crime and the identifications to be real; and (2) during the lineup test, all subjects were given the option of giving no decision by indicating 'I don't know'.

In the first experiment, students witnessed a staged dispute between a professor and a student. One week later the subjects attempted to identify the perpetrator from a perpetrator-absent lineup. Half of the subjects were informed, just before the identification test, that the event and identification test were simulated but that, for the purposes of the research, they should be behave like actual eye-witnesses. The remainder were not so informed and were led to believe that the event and identification were real and important.

Half of the subjects in each belief condition were given 'biased' lineup instructions. They were told (p. 365): 'There are indications that one of these persons is the perpetrator. Please, try to recognise this person.' They were also given a response sheet containing those instructions and a space to write the number of the lineup member. Three additional options appeared on the response sheet. One stated: 'If you are absolutely sure that the culprit is not here, please mark here.' Two other responses allowed eye-witnesses to indicate: 'I don't know which of the persons is the perpetrator/I cannot remember the perpetrator' or 'The perpetrator is not present.'

The remainder were given 'unbiased' lineup instructions. They were told: 'Please check whether you can recognise any of these persons as the one that you observed last week.' These instructions appeared in writing on the response form together with the three response alternatives (the number of the lineup member believed to be the thief; don't know/can't remember; the thief is not present in the lineup). The statement 'If you are absolutely sure that the perpetrator is not present, please mark here' did not appear.

Eye-witnesses who were not informed that the event and lineup test were simulated and who received biased instructions were significantly more likely to use the 'don't know/can't remember' option than all other groups combined (50 per cent versus 25.8 per cent). False identification rates did not differ significantly. Maas and Köhnken concluded that the biased instructions may have made subjects more cautious if they believed that they were participating in an actual investigation.

In their second experiment, Maas and Köhnken replicated the Malpass and Devine (1981) experiment described above with one major change. As in their first experiment, half of the subjects were informed, prior to the identification test, that the event was simulated for the purposes of an experiment. The remainder were not so informed and were led to believe that the event and identification test were real. Instructions produced a significantly larger effect on identification performance among subjects who were informed that the event was simulated. Among them, 88.2 per cent who received biased instructions made a false identification, as compared to 33.3 per cent of those who received unbiased instructions. Among subjects who believed the event and identification test to be real, 62.5 per cent of the those who received biased instructions and 46.7 per cent who received unbiased instructions made false identifications; this difference was not statistically significant.

Maas and Köhnken concluded:

> Taken together, the present findings suggest that the instructional bias effect observed in previous experiments is limited to subjects who are fully aware that they are participating in an experiment. The fact that neither study provides evidence for a reliable increase of false [identifications] as a function of biased

instructions, suggests that eye-witnesses are better than their reputation. (Maas and Köhnken, 1989, p. 369)

Unfortunately, this conclusion is suspect, particularly because the difference in suggestiveness of the tested instructions is smaller than in the other experiments reviewed above. All subjects were explicitly given the option of indicating that the perpetrator was not in the lineup. That less suggestive instructions have no effect on identification performance does not threaten the conclusion that more suggestive instructions do enhance the likelihood of false identifications.

Maas and Köhnken's second experiment provides more convincing evidence that the effect of suggestive instructions is larger in staged crimes than in real crimes. Nevertheless, their results do not indicate that the effect is absent in real crimes. Although the difference in false identifications was not statistically significant (62.5 per cent versus 46.7 per cent), the lack of statistical significance is likely due to the low statistical power associated with the small sample size employed in the study (see Cutler and Penrod, in press).

In conclusion there is convincing evidence that suggestive identification instructions influence eye-witness performance. The research shows that suggestive instructions substantially increase the likelihood of false identifications. Furthermore, the results from Kassin, Ellsworth and Smith's (1989) survey of eye-witness experts indicates that experts are in substantial agreement that biased instructions have a deleterious effect on eye-witness performance. Although Maas and Köhnken's research suggests that the laboratory research may overestimate the influence of suggestive instructions, further research is needed to test this conjecture more conclusively.

Foil Bias

Lineups and photoarrays usually contain several 'look-alikes' in addition to the suspect. Wells (1993) recommends that each identification test contain only one suspect and several persons known to be innocent. The known innocents are referred to as 'foils'. The purpose of including foils in addition to the suspect is so that the eye-witness cannot merely identify the suspect by deduction (i.e. this is the person the police suspect, therefore he/she must be the perpetrator) but must instead rely on memory. By our definition, an identification test that permits an eye-witness to identify a suspect by deduction rather than by memory is suggestive.

Under what circumstances does the use of foils in an identification test reduce the suggestiveness of identification tests? The effectiveness of foils depends on the relation between the eye-witness' memory for the perpetrator and the physical characteristics of the suspect and foils. The eye-witness' description of the perpetrator, given at the time of the crime, is the best available index of memory for the perpetrator. Foils that do not resemble the eye-witness's memory for the perpetrator can be rejected easily (even by a non-witness who simply reads a good description given by an actual witness) and hence they do not serve the purpose of protecting the defendant from identification by deduction. Foils that do resemble the eye-witness' memory for the perpetrator have the desirable effect of making deduction difficult and forcing the eye-witness to rely on his or her memory for the perpetrator.

Wells (1993) proposed several criteria for minimising foil bias in identification tests. Foils should match the eye-witness' description of the perpetrator but vary on features not mentioned in the eye-witness' description. By following this procedure, according to Wells, foils would offer sufficient protection against identification by deduction, thus reducing suggestion in identification tests. At the same time Wells warns against attempting to find foils that resemble the suspect as closely as possible (a strategy that, if followed to its logical conclusion, would lead to a lineup of clones). Such lineups may protect the suspect from identification by deduction, but they also make it overly difficult to identify the suspect. Experiments that vary the physical similarity between the foils and suspect support Wells' proscription (see Wells, 1993).

Clothing Bias

Lindsay, Wallbridge and Drennan (1987) note that police typically ask eye-witnesses to describe the perpetrator's appearance, including the clothing worn while committing the crime. Sometimes, they note, suspects appear in identification tests wearing the same (or similar) clothing as that worn during the crime. To what extent do the clothes influence identification performance?

Subjects in three experiments conducted by Lindsay, Wallbridge and Drennan witnessed a staged theft of a relatively inexpensive object, described the appearance and attire of the perpetrator, and attempted to identify him from six-person, thief-present or thief-absent photoarrays. In all three experiments three photoarray conditions were tested: (1) the 'usual' condition in which each person whose picture appeared in the photoarray dressed differently and none wore clothing similar to that of the perpetrator; (2) the 'biased' condition in which only the suspect (the thief in the thief-present condition and the replacement in the thief-absent condition) wore clothing identical to that worn by the perpetrator during the crime (the foils wore clothing identical to that worn in the 'usual' condition); and (3) the 'dressed alike' condition in which all lineup members—including the perpetrator—were dressed alike (in clothing identical to that worn by the perpetrator during the crime). Naturally, the suspects and foils were the same people across photoarray conditions—only their clothing changed.

In summarising the results, Lindsay, Wallbridge and Drennan combined the data from the three experiments for a powerful test of the influence of clothing condition. Thus, the analysis included data from 392 subjects. Across all thief-present conditions, clothing produced a trivial and non-significant effect on identification performance. The overall rates of correct identification were 70 per cent, 65 per cent and 69 per cent for the biased, usual and dressed alike conditions, respectively. The respective rates of false identifications in these conditions were 38 per cent, 21 per cent and 10 per cent, which differed significantly.

Presentation Bias

The final aspect of bias pertains to the manner in which the suspects and foils are presented to the eye-witness in an identification test. The typical procedure is 'simultaneous' presentation, in which the suspect and foils are presented simultaneously and the eye-witness decides which, if any, is the suspect. Clifford and Bull (1978) and Lindsay and Wells (1985) reasoned that this typical procedure is suggestive because it encourages eye-witnesses to choose the best alternative (a 'relative judgement strategy') rather than determining whether each alternative is or is not the perpetrator (an 'absolute judgement strategy'). To test this hypothesis, Lindsay and Wells conducted staged thefts in view of undergraduate subjects. Five minutes after the staged theft, subjects were asked to identify the thief from a photoarray containing six persons. Half of the subjects were shown all six photographs simultaneously, as in traditional identification procedures. The remainder were shown the six photographs using a sequential presentation procedure. Subjects were instructed that they would view a series of photographs, one at a time. As each was presented, they were to indicate whether or not the photograph was of the thief. They were told that they could see each photograph only once. Although the sequentially presented photoarray, like the simultaneously presented one, contained six photographs, the experimenter held a stack of 12, deliberately misleading subjects to believe they would see all 12. The purpose behind this deception was to minimise any increased tendency to make a choice as the subject sees the experimenter exhausting the photographs. In addition, half of the subjects in each presentation condition viewed thief-present photoarrays and the other half viewed thief-absent photoarrays.

Among subjects shown the thief-present photoarrays, presentation style did not significantly influence identification performance: 58 per cent of subjects shown simultaneous presentation and 50 per cent of subjects shown sequential presentation correctly identified the thief. In contrast, among subjects shown thief-absent photoarrays, presentation style significantly influenced identification performance. Of those who experienced simultaneous presentation, 43 per cent made a false identification. Among those who experienced sequential presentation, only 17 per cent made a false identification. Sequential presentation substantially reduced false identification-rate, thus making identification tests less suggestive.

The effect of presentation bias on false identifications was demonstrated in two additional experiments conducted in our research laboratory (Cutler and Penrod, 1988). Lindsay, Lea and Fulford (1991) conducted three experiments to further clarify how various aspects of sequential presentation influence identification performance. Their three experiments demonstrated that the beneficial effects of sequential presentation were reduced if subjects were given a second chance after exhausting the photoarrays (particularly if the second chance uses simultaneous presentation) and if subjects were made aware of the number of photographs to be shown. A series of five experiments by Lindsay et al. (1991) found that sequential presentation reduced the independent and joint influences of foil bias, clothing bias and instruction bias on false identifications. Parker and Ryan (1993) found that sequential presentation had a comparably beneficial effect on identifications by children and adults.

In summary, the research on identification procedures converges on the conclusion that instruction, foil, clothing and presentation biases influence the suggestibility of identification procedures. The effects of these biases should be taken into consideration in forming standard practices for identification tests.

EFFECTIVENESS OF LEGAL SAFEGUARDS AGAINST ERRONEOUS CONVICTION RESULTING FROM MISTAKEN IDENTIFICATION

The fallibility of eye-witness identification has been acknowledged by social science and legal scholars (see earlier discussion) as well as by the US courts (see Wells, 1993). That false identifications occur is not necessarily a problem for the criminal justice system, for it is not the eye-witness who convicts a criminal defendant, it is the judge or jury. In recognition of the pitfalls of eye-witness identification testimony, US courts have designed procedures to serve as safeguards against erroneous conviction resulting from mistaken identification. These safeguards include: presence of counsel at post-indictment corporeal lineups, voir dire (the jury selection process), cross-examination of eye-witnesses, expert psychological testimony on the factors that influence eye-witness memory and judges' instructions pertaining to how the jury should evaluate eye-witness memory (some other countries have somewhat similar safeguards). This section briefly reviews research on the effectiveness of these safeguards. See Cutler and Penrod (in press) for an extended analysis.

Presence of Counsel and Cross-Examination as Safeguards

Criminal defendants in the US have the right to counsel at corporeal lineups conducted after indictment. This right does not extend to photoarrays or any identification tests conducted prior to indictment. The purposes of granting the right to counsel at lineups include: (1) to prevent the use of suggestive identification procedures, (2) to advise the defendants of their rights and obligations, and (3) to observe and record any suggestive identification procedures that are used. Observations can be used to support a motion to suppress the identification evidence or to attempt to discredit the identification evidence through cross-examination at trial. (In criminal cases defendants have the right to cross-examine witnesses who testify against them.) Cross-examination presumably serves as a safeguard by providing counsel with the opportunity to elicit testimony that casts doubt on the accuracy of the identi-fication, such as information concerning suggestive procedures used during a lineup test. The presence of counsel and cross-examination safeguards are discussed jointly because they rest on the same set of behavioural assumptions.

First is the 'attorney sensitivity' assumption, i.e. that attorneys recognise suggestive identification procedures when they encounter them. An effective attorney must know how to evaluate identification tests and must know what testimony to elicit from eye-witnesses during cross-examination.

The second assumption concerns 'judge sensitivity.' This assumption is relevant to the 'presence of counsel safeguard' for the following reason. An attorney who believes that suggestive identification procedures rendered an identification equivocal will make this argument in a motion to suppress the identification evidence. This motion would contain a description of the procedures believed by the attorney to be suggestive. The trial judge will rule on this motion. Thus, the 'presence of counsel safeguard' assumes that judges, like attorneys, can accurately discriminate between procedures that differ in level of suggestiveness (though the process of advocacy can obviously lead to different interpretations of the same evidence concerning level of suggestibility). The judge sensitivity assumption is relevant to the cross-examination assumption in that judges determine whether questions asked by attorneys during cross-examination are probative or relevant. If a judge determines that a question (for example, about how a lineup test was conducted) is not relevant the judge can order it withdrawn.

Third is the 'jury sensitivity' assumption. During a jury trial, an attorney might possibly expose suggestive identification procedures through examination and cross-examination of the eye-witness and of the officer in charge of conducting the identification test. But if jurors are not capable of accurately judging the suggestibility of identification tests, the elicited testimony will not have its intended effect, and the utility of the presence of counsel and cross-examination safeguards will be equivocal.

The three assumptions concerning attorney, judge and jury sensitivity are testable using psychological research methods. The only existing research pertaining to attorney sensitivity consists of surveys designed to assess attorney knowledge about factors that influence the accuracy of eye-witness identification (Rahaim and Brodsky, 1982; Brigham and Wolfskeil, 1983). Brigham and Wolfskeil obtained completed surveys from 89 public defenders, 69 state prosecutors and 77 private defence attorneys throughout Florida. Among the issues addressed in the survey was the attorneys' knowledge of the factors that influence eye-witness identification accuracy. Although the attorneys varied widely in their estimates of the accuracy of identifications, they generally perceived own-race identifications to be more accurate than other-race identifications and indicated that sex and education level of the witness did not impact on identification accuracy. When asked to list ten factors that do influence identification accuracy, their lists tended to include factors which emerge as predictors in the psychological literature as well (e.g., lighting, exposure duration, opportunity to view the witness). Rahaim and Brodsky (1982) reached similar conclusions based on their survey of 42 attorneys. Although the findings from these studies tend to support the attorney sensitivity assumption, the deficiencies in the studies make any conclusion premature. First, neither of the studies examined factors affecting suggestibility. Second, the survey methodology does not permit an assessment of what attorneys actually observe in identification tests.

While we know of no research assessing judge sensitivity, it is known that judges' instructions pertaining to eye-witness memory contain statements that are not supported by the psychological research (see below).

Considerably more research has examined juror sensitivity. Surveys of prospective jurors on three continents converge on the conclusion that they are insensitive to many of the factors that influence eye-witness memory (e.g. Deffenbacher and Loftus, 1982; Noon and Hollin, 1987; McConkey and Roche, 1989). Unfortunately, like the surveys of attorneys, none of the studies asks questions about the suggestibility factors discussed above. However, the results of these survey studies are complemented by several trial simulation experiments showing that mock-jurors' judgements do not vary predictably with eye-witness evidence (e.g. Cutler, Penrod and Stuve, 1988; Cutler, Penrod and Dexter, 1990), and that mock-jurors are unable effectively to discriminate between accurate and inaccurate eye-witnesses (e.g. Lindsay, Wells and Rumpel, 1981; Lindsay, Wells and O'Connor, 1989). These studies do not address the attorney sensitivity issue, but their trial presentations do presume that attorneys are sensitive and can, at least to a limited extent, identify relevant eye-witness factors (the studies manipulated the evidence presented to the mock jurors *and* used attorney cross-examination and arguments to underscore the state of the evidence). Of course, given the insensitivity of jurors to the manipulated evidence and arguments by counsel, one might argue that attorney (and judge) sensitivity are irrelevant, at least as far as juror decision-making is concerned.

In conclusion, the data addressing attorney and judge sensitivity are not particularly informative. The findings regarding juror sensitivity, in contrast, clearly reveal shortcomings in jurors' abilities to evaluate identification evidence which probably include suggestive identification procedures (Cutler, Penrod and Dexter, 1990). Given that both the presence of counsel and cross-examination safeguards require jury sensitivity, there is substantial reason to question the effectiveness of these safeguards.

Voir Dire as a Safeguard

Courts in the USA permit attorneys much more latitude in jury selection (voir dire) than do criminal court procedures world-wide. The principle is that attorneys can identify and exclude from service prospective jurors who are unable or unwilling to set aside their biases and to judge the case on the evidence and the law. In trials in which eye-witness testimony figures prominently, this means that jurors must be willing and able to scrutinise identification evidence. For voir dire to be effective, then, attorneys, through questioning by the attorneys and/or judge, must be able to identify prospective jurors who are unwilling or unable to scrutinise eye-witness identification evidence. How effective is this safeguard?

Two sources of research evidence are relevant. First, as demonstrated above, prospective jurors are generally insensitive to the factors that influence eye-witness identification accuracy. Thus, their ability to scrutinise the testimony is questionable. Second, a recent dissertation by Narby (1993) found that jurors' attitudes toward eye-witnesses, which presumably index their willingness to scrutinise identification evidence, were unreliably associated with their inclinations to convict in simulated trials centring on eye-witness identification. Narby's findings suggest that even with a reliable instrument for assessing willingness to scrutinise eye-witness evidence, attorneys will have difficulty in identifying biased jurors during voir dire. In fact, US federal courts and many state courts (e.g. Massachusetts, California) perform the most perfunctory voir dire and do not permit attorneys to ask questions about jurors' attitudes. Indeed, judges in these courts are not obligated to permit attorneys to ask any questions during voir dire. In short, it is unlikely that attorneys could, under the best of circumstances, identify more or less sensitive jurors. Thus, we conclude that voir dire does not serve as an effective safeguard against erroneous conviction in eye-witness trials.

Judges' Instructions as a Safeguard

Some courts have turned to the use of judges' instructions to educate the jury about how to evaluate eye-witness testimony, most notably *US v. Telfaire* (469, F.2d 552 (D.C.Cir.1972)). The *Telfaire* instruction focus the jury's attention on thirteen witnessing and identification factors, including the strength of the identification (which we take to mean the witness' confidence), the circumstances under which the identification was made, and the length of time between the crime and identification. Two important deficiencies in the *Telfaire* instruction are as follows. First, the instructions seem to include witness confidence as a predictor of identification accuracy. As noted above, witness confidence is not a strong predictor of accuracy. Second, many factors which are known to influence identification performance, such as the identification bias factors discussed earlier are not mentioned in the *Telfaire* instruction. Thus, the content of the instruction is flawed.

Do the *Telfaire* instructions have their intended effect on jury judgements? Several experiments (Greene, 1988; Katzev and Wishart, 1985; Cutler, Dexter and Penrod, 1990; Zemba and Geiselman, 1993) converge on the conclusion that judges' instructions about eye-witness testimony in general, and the *Telfaire* instructions in particular, have weak or undesirable affects on the judgements of mock-jurors. Thus, the effectiveness of judges' instructions as a safeguard remains questionable. Whether the ineffectiveness of judges' instructions is due to lack of judge sensitivity (which might result in inappropriate instruction content), jury sensitivity or some combination of these factors has yet to be determined.

Expert Psychological Testimony as a Safeguard

Expert psychological testimony about eye-witness memory typically involves a general description about how memory processes work and a discussion of the relevant factors that influence eye-witness identification accuracy. Unlike the presence of counsel, cross-examination, and voir dire safeguards, the expert psychological testimony safeguard does not assume jury sensitivity. In contrast, it assumes jury insensitivity. Unlike judges' instructions, expert psychological testimony is informed by the empirical research on factors affecting the accuracy of eye-witness identification. Thus, its potential to educate the jury is greater than that of judges' instructions. Even holding content constant there are reasons to believe that expert testimony has a more beneficial effect on jurors' judgements than does judges' instructions (see Cutler, Dexter and Penrod, 1990).

But does expert psychological testimony serve as an effective safeguard? For expert testimony to be effective, it must serve to enhance juror sensitivity.

Several experiments have examined the influence on jurors' decisions of expert psychological testimony on eye-witness memory. These experiments tend to find that expert testimony, presented on the behalf of the defence, results in reduced belief in the eye-witnesses (who testify against the defendant) and fewer convictions (Hosch, Beck and McIntyre, 1980; Loftus, 1980; Wells, Lindsay and Tousignant, 1980; Maas, Brigham and West, 1985; Fox and Walters, 1986). Based on this research it is not clear whether this reduced belief is due to improved juror sensitivity, to enhanced scepticism toward eye-witnesses (a potentially undesirable effect: see Cutler and Penrod, in press), or to both.

We have directly tested whether expert testimony enhances juror sensitivity (Cutler, Dexter and Penrod, 1989). Subjects were 538 undergraduates and 96 experienced jurors who viewed a simulated trial of a defendant charged with the armed robbery of a bank. By systematically varying the witnessing and identification conditions (known to influence identification accuracy) through the testimony of the eye-witness who identified the defendant as the robber, the confidence of the eye-witness in the accuracy of her identification (known to be a weak predictor of identification accuracy) and the presence of expert psychological testimony on eye-witness memory, we were able to test whether the expert testimony enhanced juror sensitivity. The findings showed that it did. Mock-jurors exposed to expert psychological testimony relied significantly more heavily on witnessing and identification conditions and less heavily on witness confidence in evaluating the accuracy of the eye-witness's identification than did mock-jurors not exposed to expert testimony. In short, the evidence indicates that expert testimony serves to increase juror sensitivity, whereas voir dire, attorney cross-examination and judges' instructions do not.

CONCLUSIONS

Of the primary legal safeguards designed to protect defendants against mistaken identification, most appear to be ineffective: cross-examination, voir dire and judges' instructions all fail to develop the sensitivity to trial evidence that is essential to discriminating judgements by jurors. On the other hand, expert psychological testimony is much more promising, but its use in criminal cases is negligible in the USA and even more limited elsewhere. Perhaps research such as that presented here will enhance the likelihood that expert psychological testimony will be used in future cases.

Even if generally admissible, expert psychological testimony is likely to remain rare because of its expense and inconvenience. More attention should perhaps be paid to making more common safeguards, such as cross-examination and judges' instructions more effective, or to devising new ones. Both approaches necessarily depend on educating members of the legal system about the psychological processes underlying eye-witness memory.

REFERENCES

Borchard, E.M. (1932). *Convicting the Innocent: Errors of Criminal Justice*. New Haven: Yale.
Brandon, R. and Davies, C. (1973). *Wrongful Imprisonment*. London: Allen & Unwin.

Brigham, J.C., Maas, A., Snyder, L.D. and Spaulding, K. (1982). Accuracy of eye-witness identifications in a field setting. *Journal of Personality and Social Psychology*, **42**, 673–81.

Brigham, J.C. and Wolfskeil, M.P. (1983). Opinions of attorneys and law enforcement personnel on the accuracy of eye-witness identification. *Law and Human Behavior*, **7**, 337–49.

Clifford, B. and Bull, R. (1978). *The Psychology of Person Identification*. London: Routledge.

Cutler, B.L., Dexter, H.R. and Penrod, S.D. (1990). Nonadversarial methods for improving juror sensitivity to eye-witness evidence. *Journal of Applied Social Psychology*, **20**, 1197–207.

Cutler, B.L., Dexter, H.R. and Penrod, S.D. (1989). Expert testimony and jury decision making: an empirical analysis. *Behavioral Sciences and the Law*, **7**, 215–25.

Cutler, B.L. and Fisher, R.P. (1990). Live lineups, videotaped lineups, and photoarrays. *Forensic Reports*, **3**, 439–48.

Cutler, B.L. and Penrod, S.D. (1988). Improving the reliability of eye-witness identification: Lineup construction and presentation. *Journal of Applied Psychology*, **73**, 281–90.

Cutler, B.L. and Penrod, S.D. (in press). *The Effectiveness of Legal Safeguards Against Erroneous Conviction Resulting from Mistaken Eye-witness Identification*. New York: Cambridge University Press.

Cutler, B.L., Penrod, S.D. and Dexter, H.R. (1990). Juror sensitivity to eye-witness identification evidence. *Law and Human Behavior*, **14**, 185–91.

Cutler, B.L., Penrod, S.D. and Martens, T.K. (1987). The reliability of eye-witness identifications: the role of system and estimator variables. *Law and Human Behavior*, **11**, 223–58.

Cutler, B.L., Penrod, S.D. and Stuve, T.E. (1988). Juror decision making in eye witness identification cases. *Law and Human Behavior*, **12**, 41–55.

Deffenbacher, K.A. and Loftus, E.F. (1982). Do jurors share a common understanding concerning eye-witness behavior? *Law and Human Behavior*, **6**, 15–30.

Fox, S.G. and Walters, H.A. (1986). The impact of general versus specific expert testimony and eye-witness confidence upon mock juror judgment. *Law and Human Behavior*, **10**, 215–28.

Frank, J. and Frank, B. (1957). *Not Guilty*. London: Gallancz.

Greene, E. (1988). Judge's instruction on eye-witness testimony: evaluation and revision. *Journal of Applied Social Psychology*, **18**, 252–76.

Hosch, H.M., Beck, E.L. and McIntyre, P. (1980). Influence of expert testimony regarding eye-witness accuracy on jury decisions. *Law and Human Behavior*, **4**, 287–96.

Hosch, H.M. and Cooper, S.D. (1982). Victimization as a determinant of eye-witness accuracy. *Journal of Applied Psychology*, **67**, 649–52.

Huff, R., Rattner, A. and Sagarin, E. (1986). Guilty until proven innocent. *Crime and Delinquency*, **32**, 518–44.

Kassin, S.M., Ellsworth, P.C. and Smith, V.L. (1989). The 'general acceptance' of psychological research on eye-witness testimony: a survey of the experts. *American Psychologist*, **44**, 1089–98.

Katzev, R.D. and Wishart, S.S. (1985). The impact of judicial commentary concerning eye-witness identifications on jury decision making. *The Journal of Criminal Law and Criminology*, **76**, 733–45.

Krafka, C. and Penrod, S. (1985). Reinstatement of context in a field experiment on eye-witness identification. *Journal of Personality and Social Psychology*, **49**, 1, 58–69.

Lindsay, R.C.L. and Wells, G.L. (1985). Improving eye-witness identifications from lineups: Simultaneous versus sequential lineup presentation. *Journal of Applied Psychology*, **70**, 556–64.

Lindsay, R.C.L., Lea, J.A. and Fulford, J.A. (1991). Sequential lineup presentation: technique matters. *Journal of Applied Psychology*, **76**, 741–5.

Lindsay, R.C.L., Wallbridge, H. and Drennan, D. (1987). Do the clothes make the man? An exploration of the effect of lineup attire on eye-witness identification accuracy. *Canadian Journal of Behavioural Science*, **19**, 463–78.

Lindsay, R.C.L., Wells, G.L. and O'Connor, F.J. (1989). Mock juror belief of accurate and inaccurate eye-witnesses: a replication and extension. *Law and Human Behavior*, **13**, 333–9.

Lindsay, R.C.L., Wells, G.L. and Rumpel, C.M. (1981). Can people detect eye-witness identification accuracy within and across situations? *Journal of Applied Psychology*, **66**, 79–89.

Lindsay, R.C.L., Lea, J.A., Nosworthy, G.J., Fulford, J.A., Hector, J., LeVan, V. and Seabrook, C. (1991). Biased lineups: sequential presentation reduces the problem. *Journal of Applied Psychology*, **76**, 796–802.

Loftus, E.F. (1980). Impact of expert psychological testimony on the unreliability of eye-witness identification. *Journal of Applied Psychology*, **65**, 915.

Maas, A. and Köhnken, G. (1989). Eye-witness identification: simulating the 'weapon effect'. *Law and Human Behavior*, **13**, 397–409.

Maas, A., Brigham, J.C. and West, S.G. (1985). Testifying on eye-witness reliability: expert advice is not always persuasive. *Journal of Applied Social Psychology*, **15**, 207–29.

Malpass, R.S. and Devine, P.G. (1981). Eye-witness Identification: lineup instructions and the absence of the offender. *Journal of Applied Psychology*, **66**, 482–9.

McConkey, K.M. and Roche, S.M. (1989). Knowledge of eye-witness memory. *Australian Psychologist*, **24**, 377–84.

Narby, D.J. (1993). Effectiveness of voir dire as a safeguard against erroneous conviction resulting from mistaken eye-witness identification. Unpublished doctoral dissertation, Florida International University, Miami, FL.

Noon, E. and Hollin, C.R. (1987). Lay knowledge of eye-witness behaviour: a British survey. *Applied Cognitive Psychology*, **1**, 143–53.

Paley, B. and Geiselman, R.E. (1989). The effects of alternative photospread instructions on suspect identification performance. *American Journal of Forensic Psychology*, **7**, 3–13.

Parker, J.F. and Ryan, V. (1993). An attempt to reduce guessing behavior in children's and adults' eye-witness identifications. *Law and Human Behavior*, **17**, 11–26.

Pigott, M.A., Brigham, J.C. and Bothwell, R.K. (1990). A field study of the relationship between quality of eye-witnesses' descriptions and identification accuracy. *Journal of Police Science and Administration*, **17**, 84–8.

Platz, S.J. and Hosch, H.M. (1988). Cross racial/ethnic eye-witness identification: a field study. *Journal of Applied Social Psychology*, **18**, 972–84.

Rahaim, G.L. and Brodsky, S.L. (1982). Empirical evidence versus common sense: juror and lawyer knowledge of eye-witness accuracy. *Law and Psychology Review*, **7**, 1–15.

Shapiro, P. and Penrod, S. (1986). A meta-analysis of facial identification studies. *Psychological Bulletin*, **100**, 139–56.

US v. Telfaire, 469, F.2d 552 (D.C. Cir. 1972).

Wells, G.L. (1993). What do we know about eye-witness identification? *American Psychologist*, **48**, 553–71.

Wells, G.L., Lindsay, R.C.L. and Tousignant, J.P. (1980). Effects of expert psychological advice on human performance in judging the validity of eye-witness testimony. *Law and Human Behavior*, **4**, 275–85.

Zemba, D.J. and Geiselman, R.E. (1993). Eye-witness identification instructions to the jury: help or hindrance in the decision making process? Unpublished manuscript, UCLA, Los Angeles, CA.

Chapter 3.4

Interviewing Adults

Günter Köhnken
Institut für Psychologie, Kiel University

INTERVIEWING: AN INTRODUCTION

The interview is one of the most frequently used methods of obtaining information from people. It is indispensable whenever the relevant information cannot be observed directly and when the data cannot be collected by means of psychological (psychometric) tests or questionnaires. This is the case, for example, when a victim or witness of a crime is required to give a description of the incident. For the police, in particular, interviewing is one of the major tools of investigation. Research in Germany has shown, for example, that police officers spend 70–80 per cent of their total working time interviewing witnesses, victims and suspects (Herren, 1976). Collecting as many facts as possible is of primary importance for criminal investigations. Fisher and Geiselman (1992) cite a comprehensive study of criminal investigation processes by the Rand Corporation where it was found that the principal determinant of whether or not a case is solved is the completeness and accuracy of the eye-witnesses' account. The investigation of accidents is often impossible without interviewing eye-witnesses. Furthermore, it may be necessary for an expert witness to interview a child and his or her parents in order to provide information for the court regarding custody and access in a divorce case. If the mental status of a perpetrator is questionable (e.g. because of mental illness) a thorough history-taking interview is normally conducted in order to examine his or her social development and the present state of social and intellectual maturity. An interview may also be conducted as a central part of a court's assessment of the competence of a young child witness.

In all these cases it is essential to adjust the process of collecting information to the particular individual as well as to the particular case—a task which cannot be solved by standardised psychometric tests or questionnaires. The interview, however, has the advantage of being an appropriate tool in a wide variety of circumstances. It is this flexibility that has led to the popularity of the interview as a method of gathering information. Furthermore, an interviewer has the opportunity to obtain a large *variety* of important information which may go far beyond the content of a statement. It is, for example, possible to observe and evaluate the interviewee's non-verbal and speech behaviour (Scherer and Ekman, 1982; Mahl, 1987) and relate this information to the content. Sometimes discrepancies may occur between the content of a statement and the accompanying behaviour (e.g. an interviewee reports a supposedly very distressing event but does so with a relaxed voice and a trace of a smile). Such discrepancies, which would be impossible to notice using a questionnaire, often carry more important information than the content or the behaviour alone.

The aims of interviews can be divided into two categories: first, interviews are conducted to evaluate present moods, attitudes, opinions, and/or to establish rapport with the interviewee. In all these cases retrieval of information from the interviewee's memory is only of minor importance.

Secondly, the subject may be questioned about past events or experiences which he or she has to retrieve from memory. This is almost always the case when victims or witnesses of a crime or parties in compensation claims are questioned as part of the legal proceedings. This chapter focuses on interviews that aim to retrieve information from memory, i.e. on investigative interviews.

AN INFORMATION PROCESSING APPROACH TO INTERVIEWING

While the advantages of an interview over other assessment techniques such as psychometric tests or questionnaires are rarely disputed, there has been frequent criticism about the comparatively poor reliability or accuracy of interview data (for overviews see Linehan, 1977; Haynes, 1978; Turkat, 1986). Indeed, many studies have shown that different interviewers may generate different information, that this information is more often than not incomplete and that it is not always in accordance with the facts. The reasons for this less than satisfying state of affairs lie in the complex nature of an interview. Conducting an interview is a highly complex process which makes great demands on the interviewer. He or she constantly has to be aware of the overall interview strategy and adhere to general rules and guidelines for interviewing. The wording of questions has to be adapted to the intellectual capacity of the interviewee. At the same time the interviewer has to process the flow of verbal information, store it in memory, take notes and decide upon follow-up questions. In addition to this the non-verbal and speech behaviour of both the interviewee and the interviewer has to be monitored and evaluated. This complexity may at times be beyond the information processing capacity of an interviewer with the consequence that unsystematic questioning, loss or distortion of information or biasing occurs.

However, abandoning the interview altogether, because of these potential problems, would be the wrong conclusion. It is simply too important and no other assessment technique can serve as a fully adequate alternative. The all important question, therefore, is: Is it possible to improve the completeness and reliability of interview data and, if so, what can be done in practice to achieve this? In order to answer these questions it is helpful to conceive the interview as a complex information processing task on the side of the interviewee as well as the interviewer, to identify and locate potential sources of unreliability and incompleteness and then to look for measures to counter any distorting influences. Figure 3.4.1 gives an overview of this process and shows the various stages of information processing.

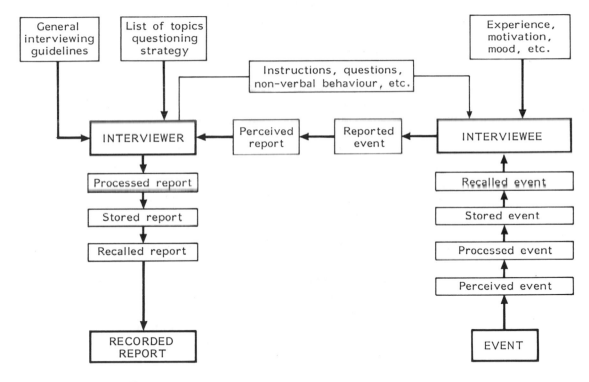

Figure 3.4.1

The ultimate goal of an investigative interview is the production of a report which covers all the relevant details of the event in question and which does not contain any incorrect or fabricated details. In this ideal case we would have a perfectly complete and accurate report. In the real world, however, a report is neither complete nor perfectly accurate. Even thoroughly trained interviewers may extract no more than 15– 20 per cent of the total possible relevant information from child interviewees (Milne et al., 1994; Wark et al.,

1994). (On average, after delays of up to three weeks some 80– 85 per cent of this information nevertheless is correct (Köhnken et al., 1994)).

Figure 3.4.1 shows where information may be lost and where incorrect or fabricated details (i.e. details that are mentioned by the interviewee but were not present in the original event) may creep in. The interviewee who experiences an event is unlikely to perceive and encode all available information. The information processing will be influenced by his or her general knowledge about this type of event. Such generic knowledge is called a cognitive schema (Bartlett, 1932; Alba and Hasher, 1983; Graesser and Nakamura, 1982; Pedzek et al., 1989). Cognitive schemata, social expectations and current motivation guide perception and may filter out more or less large amounts of detail. Details that do not fit the schema, or information that is incongruent with social expectations, or do not meet the motivational state, are more likely to be filtered out (Hastie, Park and Weber, 1984). A witness who is threatened by a criminal will probably not study the perpetrator's facial features but instead look for ways to escape the threat. On the other hand details that are part of the schema, but were not present in the event, may be 'filled in' and later recalled as having been perceived (Bower, Black and Turner, 1979; Holst and Pedzek, 1992). Furthermore, situational circumstances such as the presence of a weapon may narrow the focus of attention on to it and thus reduce the perceived information (Maass and Köhnken, 1989). In a similar vein, what is processed and eventually stored in memory also depends on a number of factors. In addition to cognitive schemata, which guide the storage of information in memory, high stress or even panic may severely disturb the information processing and often result in incomplete and/or distorted recollections (Deffenbacher, 1983).

Hence, when a person enters an interview he or she comes with only a limited amount of information about the event in memory (for overviews of research on eye-witness perception and memory see Clifford and Bull, 1978; Loftus, 1979; Wells and Loftus, 1984; Ross, Read and Toglia, 1994). It is important to keep this in mind when we look at the sometimes low completeness of interview data. Loss of information is not always the interviewer's fault. No interview technique, however sophisticated, will be able to recover information that has never been stored in memory.

What has been encoded and stored in memory has to be recalled during the course of the interview. Here lies another possible source of incompleteness. Rarely is an interviewee able to retrieve all potentially available details from memory. Some information may be lost due to forgetting while other details are difficult or even impossible to access without specific aids (Tulving and Thomson, 1973; Tulving, 1983). Furthermore, even details that have been successfully recalled to mind are not always overtly reported. The interviewee may suppress available information because he or she assumes it to be unimportant or because it is too embarrassing to be reported (Fisher and

Geiselman, 1992). Furthermore, as Fisher and Geiselman point out, an event is represented simultaneously at several different levels of precision, ranging from the very general to the very detailed (see also Fisher and Chandler, 1984, 1991). Which level the interviewee selects for reporting depends, among other things, on his or her immediate or past experiences with interviews, assumed communication rules and assumptions about the interviewer's knowledge. For example, an interviewee who expects the interviewer to know what a blood donation event consists of may decide that merely mentioning that a blood donation took place may be sufficient and may therefore not bother to describe it with many details. This would be an economic strategy in everyday communication but may be inappropriate in an investigative interview because it results in incomplete information.

What is reported depends not only on the interviewee's internal state, but to a large degree also on the interviewer's instructions, questions and general behaviour. It is important to keep in mind that the interview is a learning situation. This is particularly the case if the interviewee has no, or only very little, previous experience with interviews in general or with this type of interview in particular. In such a situation any interviewer behaviour (instructions, questions, interruptions, reinforcements, non-verbal behaviour) will not only have an immediate effect (e.g. on an answer), the interviewee will also learn from this behaviour what is expected and will try to adjust his or her behaviour according to these expectations. Interrupting a lengthy answer, for example, will stop this answer immediately *and* will make lengthy and detailed answers less likely in the further course of the interview. (The interviewee has learned that the interviewer expects short answers.)

Finally, what has passed all these various 'filters' described above has to be put into words and reported verbally to the interviewer. At this stage limited linguistic abilities or a restricted vocabulary may add to the various filtering processes (e.g. Leibowitz and Guzi, 1990). Interviewees with learning disabilities, for example, often have a limited vocabulary. This may make it difficult or even impossible for them to describe verbally certain aspects of the event in detail.

On the side of the interviewer the information processing passes through very similar stages. What the interviewee communicates verbally and non-verbally has to be perceived and encoded by the interviewer. Here, again, selective attention and schema guided information processing act as first filters. The interviewer holds certain hypotheses about the event in question and probably has a schema about this type of event. Information that is consistent with the schema receives preferential treatment while inconsistent details may be distorted to fit the schema or even filtered out completely (Schank and Abelson, 1977; Taylor and Crocker, 1981). (Other researchers have argued that schema inconsistent information is recalled better than is consistent information after a short delay, but more likely to be forgotten after longer delays (Smith and

Graesser, 1981).) Furthermore, the multitude of tasks—e.g. being aware of the general interviewing guidelines, the specific interviewing strategy, the list of topics to be investigated, the processing of verbal and non-verbal information, planning of the next questions and so on—put high demands on the interviewer. Since to any human being there is only a limited amount of cognitive resources available at any one time, the quality of the interview may deteriorate (e.g. important topics may be left out, questions may be inappropriate) and/or there will be incomplete perception and encoding of the available information (Kahneman, 1973; Navon and Gopher, 1979).

The encoded information is then stored in the interviewer's memory and later recalled to produce a written protocol. Apart from ordinary forgetting, further filters may affect the interviewer's storage and retrieval. Among other factors, schema guided processing, social perception, and a tendency to confirm existing hypotheses may determine what is stored and later retrieved. Finally, the interviewer's written report is subject to further loss of information. Kintsch and van Dijk (1978) have described a number of factors that may lead to reductions and a compression of information. Köhnken, Thürer and Zoberbier (1994) found that even a report that is written by the interviewer immediately after completion of the interview contains only about two-thirds of the information reported by the interviewee.

What can be done to improve the quality of interview data? The previous discussion of interviewing from an information processing perspective has identified four major areas of potential loss or distortion of information: the perception and encoding of an event by the interviewee, the retrieval of the encoded information from memory, the reporting of the recalled information, and the processing of the reported information by the interviewer. Obviously, any information that has not been perceived and encoded by the interviewee can never be recovered later during an interview. However, the completeness and accuracy of interview data can be enhanced by appropriate measures in the remaining three of these areas: (1) since one of the main sources of loss of information on the side of the interviewer is cognitive overload, everything that reduces this load should improve his/her information processing capacity; (2) the interviewee's retrieval of information from memory may be enhanced by means of specific mnemonic techniques; (3) the interviewer may help the interviewee, through supportive instructions, questions and non-verbal behaviour, to communicate as much of the retrieved material as possible.

INTERVIEWING ADULTS: GUIDELINES AND RECOMMENDATIONS

In the following sections several procedures and strategies will be discussed that may help to improve interview data. This discussion will be limited to recommendations and guidelines for interviewing *adults* whose intellectual capacity is somewhere within a normal range. Although most of the general guidelines also apply to interviewing children and people with learning difficulties, any *specific* requirements of these groups will not be covered here. Interviewing children will be discussed in detail in the next chapter (chapter 3.5), and the interviewing of people with communication disability in the chapter after that (chapter 3.6).

REDUCING THE COGNITIVE LOAD OF THE INTERVIEWER

Interviewing is a highly complex process that puts high demands on the interviewer. Since only limited cognitive resources are available at any one time every cognitive effort that is invested in conducting the interview will reduce that available for processing the information that is produced by the interviewee. Hence, the following general rule can be stated: *any procedure or technique that reduces the cognitive load on the interviewer increases the likelihood that more information will be processed by the interviewer*. Three measures are of particular importance here.

First, research has shown that controlled processing (i.e. acts that require a high degree of conscious attention), as opposed to automatic processing, requires more cognitive resources (Schneider and Shiffrin, 1977; Shiffrin and Schneider, 1977). An initially controlled process becomes automatic through extensive practice. Hence, thorough interviewer training together with extensive practice sessions will speed up the transition from controlled to automatic (i.e. less resource demanding) processing. When an interviewer has achieved a level of experience and expertise that allows him or her to conduct an interview without constantly paying conscious attention to general interviewing guidelines and appropriate behaviours, cognitive resources will be freed. These resources are then available for the processing of information produced by the interviewee.

Secondly, taking notes during the interview generally requires a high degree of conscious attention. The more complete the notes have to be the more attention (cognitive resource) is required. It is, therefore, highly recommended to audio or video record the interview and transcribe or otherwise evaluate the recording *after* completion of the interview. Only short notes in the form of keywords should be taken, which help to structure the further course of the interview. This will greatly reduce the cognitive demand during the interview and improve the perception and encoding of relevant information.

Thirdly, the amount of to-be-processed information is greater the less knowledge the interviewer already has about the event in question and about the interviewee. The interviewer should, therefore, collect as much information as possible about the event and the interviewee prior to the interview. Based on this information the interview should be carefully planned in advance. The interviewer could, for instance, compile a list of relevant topics that should be addressed in the interview, try to be familiar with possible linguistic idiosyncrasies, etc. All this will contribute to the reduction of the to-be-processed information and free cognitive capacity for those tasks which can be processed only during the interview.

HELPING INTERVIEWEES TO RETRIEVE MORE INFORMATION

A major task of the interviewer is to help the interviewee to recall as much information as possible from memory. Devising systematic attempts to improve recall is a rather recent development in interview research. It was not until 1981 that a first successful approach to enhance interviewees' memory reports was published. In an attempt to improve eye-witness performance Malpass and Devine described a procedure which they called the 'guided memory technique' (Malpass and Devine, 1981; Malpass, 1994).

This technique used the reinstatement of the original context of the event to enhance recall. Witnesses were reminded of many elements of the event (i.e. whether they attended it with someone, where they sat, where in the room the event took place, and where various actors in the event were positioned). They were asked to visualise many of these things. Interviewers asked, for example: 'Try to visualise the person. Can you picture him standing there? Try to picture his appearance. Was he a pleasant looking person? Did he look honest?' (Malpass and Devine, 1981, pp. 345–6). In the subsequent recognition test 60 per cent of those receiving the guided memory interview made correct identifications, while only 40 per cent of the witnesses not receiving this style of interview made correct identifications.

As just described, the guided memory technique was used by Malpass and Devine to enhance face recognition. A few years later, in 1984, two American Psychologists, Ed Geiselman and Ron Fisher, developed and evaluated a set of retrieval techniques designed to improve spoken, verbal recall (Geiselman et al., 1984). It was an attempt to help police officers obtain a more complete and accurate report from a witness. They called the procedure 'cognitive interview'. It is based upon well-known psychological principles of memory storage and retrieval of information, primarily on Tulving and Thomson's (1973) encoding specificity hypothesis (for a discussion of theoretical issues in the cognitive interview technique see Bekerian and Dennett, 1993).

The original version of the cognitive interview consists of four basic memory aids or mnemonic strategies.

First, interviewees are instructed mentally to reconstruct the context of the witnessed event, to form an image or impression of the environmental aspects of the scene, to remember their emotional feelings and their thoughts which existed at the time of the event.

The second strategy is to encourage interviewees to report everything they remember without any editing (often interviewees don't know exactly what information has investigative value), even if they think the details are not important or they cannot remember a particular aspect of the event completely. Furthermore, the recall of partial details may lead to the subsequent recall of additional relevant information (Geiselman, 1988).

The third component is to ask interviewees to recall the event in a variety of temporal orders or to make retrieval attempts from different starting points, for example from the most memorable element. Interviewees usually feel they have to start at the beginning of the story (and interviewers tend to ask them to). However, the cognitive interview procedure encourages additional focused and more extensive retrieval by asking interviewees to recall in a variety of orders, for example, from the end (i.e. backwards), from the middle, or from the most memorable element of the event.

Finally, the interviewees are encouraged to recall the event from different physical locations, just as if they were viewing it with the eyes of another person who was present.

Several studies have demonstrated the effectiveness of the original version of the cognitive interview (e.g. Geiselman et al., 1984; Geiselman et al., 1985, 1986; Geiselman et al., 1986). These results have been replicated in other laboratories (e.g. Aschermann, Mantwill and Köhnken, 1991; Newlands and MacLeod, 1992; Perry and Chapman, 1992). Across all studies which involved the original version of the cognitive interview, 25– 35 per cent more correct information was generated without producing any more incorrect details.

The original version of the cognitive interview focused primarily on witnesses' *retrieval of information* rather than their *verbally reporting* of information to the interviewer. Some of the early studies did not even use a face-to-face interview. Instead, the interviewees simply received a description of the retrieval aids, together with the instructions to use these aids, and then wrote down their recall. However, when the mnemonic aids were applied in real face-to-face settings it soon became clear that, in order to achieve the best effects, they had to be embedded in a comprehensive model of interviewing (including an overall structure for the interview, supportive interviewer behaviour, tactics of communication and questioning strategies). Based on a thorough analysis of real police interviews (Fisher, Geiselman and Raymond, 1987) Fisher, Geiselman, Raymond, Jurkevich and Warhaftig (1987) revised the original version and developed what is now known as the 'enhanced cognitive interview'.

THE ENHANCED COGNITIVE INTERVIEW

The most detailed description of the enhanced version of the cognitive interview is given in a book by Fisher and Geiselman (1992). The following overview is based on this description.

The Role of the Interviewer

Interviews are often viewed incorrectly as a situation where an active interviewer asks a series of questions to a more or less passive interviewee, whose only task it is to answer these questions and wait for the next question. The interviewer is the one who is in control of the situation. This is not the case for the cognitive interview. Here the role of the interviewer is that of a facilitator: he or she facilitates retrieval and helps the interviewee to recall information from memory.

Helping the interviewee to recall information from memory requires the interviewer to pass over control to the interviewee. This means, for example, that the interviewer should not ask a series of predetermined questions in a predetermined order that merely suits the interviewer's needs. Instead, the sequence in which the questions are asked is guided by the retrieval process of the interviewee. This requires some degree of flexibility from the interviewer. Furthermore, a good cognitive interviewer is not one who asks many questions. It is generally a much better strategy to stimulate the interviewee to talk uninterruptedly and only ask follow-up questions when necessary, for example, if some important aspect was omitted, or more information on an aspect is sought.

Supportive Interviewer Behaviour

Appropriate non-verbal behaviour during the interview is just as important for a successful interview as are the verbal instructions. Particularly with regard to the facilitation of recalled information the interviewer should create a relaxed atmosphere to support and reinforce the interviewee's communication. This requires, among other things, the interviewer to sit in a relaxed manner and to avoid any hectic movements and speech. According to the 'principle of synchrony' (Matarazzo and Wiens, 1985) the interviewer's behaviour will affect the interviewee's behaviour and general mood. Furthermore, the interviewer is encouraged to express friendliness and support (verbally and non-verbally), to express attention and interest (e.g. by frequent eye-contact, nodding) but to avoid any qualitative feedback ('good', 'this is really disgusting', etc.). Most important, however, is the principle never to interrupt the interviewee and to allow for pauses, even if they are long. This will stimulate the interviewee to continue the reporting and produce lengthy and detailed answers.

General structure of the Enhanced Cognitive Interview

The fact that a high degree of flexibility is required from the interviewer does not mean that a cognitive interview is completely unstructured. To the contrary, it is important to follow certain steps which are part of an overall structure. It is within these steps that the interviewer should follow the interviewee's retrieval process instead of imposing a predetermined sequence of topics. The enhanced cognitive interview comprises eleven phases:

Phase 1: Greeting and personalising the interview. Before the interview begins the interviewer should introduce himself or herself by name and greet the interviewee by name. Furthermore, during the course of the interview the interviewee should be referred to by name frequently.

Phase 2: Establishing rapport. Before the interviewee is asked about the event it is very important to create a relaxing atmosphere and to make him or her feel secure and confident. A good way to achieve this is to ask some questions which can be answered positively and therefore create a positive mood (e.g. referring to favourite music, films, hobbies). Building rapport is difficult if not impossible with a 'mechanical' sequence of questions. Instead, it requires a meaningful interaction with the interviewee. It may be helpful for the interviewer to begin to talk about him or herself. This openness could serve as a model to demonstrate what is required from the interviewee (self-disclosure; see Archer, 1979; Cozby, 1973). If the interviewee is tense or nervous it will be important to continue to build rapport until he or she is fairly relaxed.

Phase 3: Explaining the purpose of the interview. The interviewee may not know exactly why he or she is being interviewed. However, unless it is clear what the purpose of the interview is it will be difficult to obtain the required information. It is therefore important to direct the interviewee's attention to the event in question and to indicate explicitly the need for detailed information. Furthermore, the interviewee should be encouraged to describe everything that comes to mind as soon as he or she thinks of it. This includes details which may seem trivial or repetitious. However, the interviewee should be reminded not to guess or to fabricate.

Phase 4: Context reinstatement. Recall can be increased by recreating the event's original context at the time of the interview. The context of the original event can be recreated by explicitly requesting the interviewee to think about the context and by asking specific questions that require him or her to think about it (for example, '... Try to visualise the room ... What kind of furniture was there? ... What were you thinking when you entered the room? ... Did you smell anything? ...'). The interviewee must be given enough time to recreate the context. The questions should be asked slowly and deliberately with pauses.

Phase 5: Initiating a free report. When the interviewee has successfully recreated the event context he or she is asked to describe in narrative style his or her general recollections of the event. It is essential not to interrupt the interviewee during this narration or to ask specific questions. One goal of this narrative phase is to develop a strategy for the questioning part of the interview. It may be helpful to take brief notes and to record topics that should be followed up in the questioning part.

The interviewee may pause sometimes in the middle of the free report, even if he or she has more information to convey. This time may be required by the interviewee to find the appropriate words or phrases or to search through memory. It is, therefore, important to allow for pauses, even if they are long. Even if the interviewer has the impression that the interviewee has finished the narration he or she should not immediately begin to ask questions. Instead, the interviewee should first be encouraged to try to remember more.

Phase 6: The questioning part of the interview. Before asking any questions it may be helpful to repeat once again that the interviewee should describe everything that comes to mind as soon as he or she thinks of it but not to fabricate. It may also be helpful to remind him or her that this can be a difficult task that requires intense concentration.

Phase 7: Asking interviewee-compatible questions. Questioning in the cognitive interview does not mean asking a series of predetermined questions. Instead, the sequence of questions has to be adjusted according to the interviewee's retrieval process. This is what is meant by 'compatible questioning'. When an interviewee is asked a question about a certain element of the event, he or she will often activate a mental picture of that element and 'read out' the requested information. If the next question refers to a different picture the first picture has to be abandoned and the interviewee dredges up a different picture. Each act of drawing up a new picture code into consciousness interrupts the memory search and requires some mental effort. The interviewer should, therefore, present the questions in an order that minimises the number of times the interviewee must activate a mental picture. Only after an activated picture is exhausted of its contents should the interviewer ask questions about a different picture. The questioning part of the enhanced cognitive interview consists of a sequence of two steps: activating a picture, and probing it.

Activating a specific mental picture—this begins by recreating the psychological and environmental context. The context here is very specific in that it refers to a particular moment in the event. This specific context reinstatement is based on the interviewee's description in the previous free report.

Probing the picture—after the interviewee has activated the mental picture the interviewer begins to ask questions relating to this picture. This questioning should always begin with an open-ended question together with an explicit request to provide elaborate detail. After the interviewee has given a narrative answer to the first open-ended question progressively more specific questions related to this picture may be asked. If a question cannot be answered it is usually not helpful to repeat the same question in an identical form. Instead the interviewer should try to reword the question.

The sequence of pictures does not necessarily have to follow the temporal sequence of the event. It may sometimes be helpful to begin with the part of the event that was remembered best in the initial free report.

Phase 8: Recall from different perspectives. The recall of details may be improved if the interviewee describes the event from different perspectives. He or she could be instructed to take the position of another person who was present and describe what this person might have seen. The interviewer should, however, point out that this does not mean to infer what might have happened. The 'change perspective' technique is an aid to facilitate retrieval from the *interviewee's* memory, rather than to add speculation.

Phase 9: Recall in reverse order. Events are usually described in the order in which they occurred. It is, therefore, likely that the interviewee's first description followed the natural temporal order. The completeness and accuracy of the report may be enhanced if the interviewee now describes the events in a different order, for example, in backward order. He or she may begin with the last event, or some other prominent event in the sequence, and describe what happened just before that event, then what happened just before that, and so on. This phase helps people recall unusual aspects of an event which do not fit with their schemata, scripts or expectancies about this type of event (in general).

Phase 10: Summary. Particularly after a long interview it may be helpful if the interviewer summarises what has been reported by the interviewee in his or her own words (i.e. the interviewee's). This can be a safeguard against potential misunderstandings. It may also help to activate additional retrieval paths, resulting in additional details that could not be recalled previously.

Phase 11: Closure. In terminating the interview the interviewer should attempt to reduce any tensions and/or emotions that may have been activated through the interview and to leave a positive last impression. At the very least the interviewer should thank the interviewee for her or his co-operation and effort. A proper closure is particularly important if the event in question has been distressing and the interviewee is now upset or emotionally tense. If this is the case the interviewer should gradually switch to neutral topics and talk about these things for a while until the tensions are reduced.

EMPIRICAL EVALUATION OF THE COGNITIVE INTERVIEW

Since the first publication of the cognitive interview in 1984 a growing number of empirical studies have examined the effects of this new interview technique on the recall of correct and incorrect information. While some are field studies using real police interviews (Fisher, Geiselman and Amador, 1989; George, 1991) most are laboratory experiments. A recent meta-analysis (Köhnken et al., 1994) lists 32 experimental comparisons from 25 empirical reports representing a total of 1237 subjects. Of these reports, 12 were published manuscripts, 8 conference papers, one research report and 4 unpublished theses or dissertations.

In these experiments participants usually saw a film or witnessed a staged event, sometimes without knowing that they later would have to recall what they had seen. After a time delay, which usually varied between one hour and two weeks, they were interviewed using either the cognitive interview or a standard interview procedure. The standard interview typically involved untrained interviewers who were instructed to use the questioning procedures that they would normally use. In more recent studies, however, the standard interviewers received a training of similar length and quality as the cognitive interviewers, save for the cognitive interview techniques (e.g. Mantwill, Köhnken and Aschermann, 1995; Milne et al., 1994; Wark et al., 1994). In some early experiments and in the Aschermann, Mantwill and Köhnken (1991) study, interviewees gave written answers on a questionnaire. In further experiments, however, real face-to-face interviews were conducted. These interviews were tape-recorded and later transcribed. Finally, the number of correct and incorrect details were counted from these transcripts and compared. Some studies scored separately any confabulated details (i.e. details that were mentioned by the interviewee but were not present in the event).

The analysed set of studies covers a wide range of interviewees (children, adults, people with learning difficulties, students, members of the general public), interviewers (police officers, students, psychologists, members of the general public, people without any previous experience in interviewing) and to-be-remembered material (real crimes, staged robberies, violent and non-violent video films).

After correcting for homogeneity (Hedges and Olkin, 1985) the overall effect size for correct recall (i.e. the difference between recall of correct details in a cognitive interview and a standard interview) across all studies was $d = 0.86$ in favour of the cognitive interview. This effect is highly significant and indicates that substantially more correct details are recalled in a Cognitive Interview than in a standard interview. (The parameter d is an indicator of the size of an effect or of the amount of difference between the experimental conditions. Higher values of d indicate larger differences between, in this case, a standard interview and a Cognitive Interview. According to a rule of thumb suggested by Cohen (1977) ds of 0.80 and above can be conceived as large effects. Indeed, compared to other meta-analyses of psychological experiments a d of 0.86 is exceptionally large). However, in contrast to the early studies on the cognitive interview that showed no increase in incorrect details, the effect on the recall of incorrect details was also significant, although substantially smaller ($d = 0.30$). Therefore, the notion that the cognitive interview does *not* lead to an increase in the reporting of incorrect details can no longer be maintained.

In terms of percentage increase the cognitive interview produces on average 36 per cent more correct details than a standard interview while the incorrect details increase by 17.5 per cent. This does not mean that for every two more correct details one gets one more incorrect detail because the bases of these percentages have to be taken into account. If we assume that a standard interview produces 100 details of which 85 are correct then a cognitive interview would result in 115.6 correct (85 plus 36 per cent) and 17.6 (15 plus 17.5 per cent) incorrect details. The overall accuracy (i.e. the proportion of correct details relative to the total number of details) does not suffer. On average, across all 32 studies that were analysed, 82 per cent of all reported details were correct in the standard interviews compared to 84 per cent correct in cognitive interviews.

It is perhaps surprising that the enhanced cognitive interview does not seem to result in larger increase in correct recall than did the original cognitive interview. Some early studies using the original version reported large increases in correct recall with no increase in errors. Compared to these results the increase in correct details found with the enhanced version seems disappointing, particularly if the significant increase in errors is taken into account. However, it should be kept in mind that the research methodology has greatly improved and almost all of the more recent studies that examined the effects of the enhanced cognitive interview used more stringent control strategies (e.g. interviewers in the standard interview condition received an interview training that was comparable in quality and length with the cognitive interview training—save for the special cognitive interview techniques— while early studies used untrained standard interviewers).

To summarise, the cognitive interview is an innovative new technology that can substantially enhance the interviewee's recall of correct details. Although incorrect details increase as well, this effect is much smaller and the accuracy rates are virtually identical in both types of interview.

Taken together, the techniques described above provide a chance to improve the completeness and accuracy of interview data. Recent research has thus demonstrated how to conduct such interviews properly. There is therefore little excuse for interviews in legal contexts to be conducted inappropriately. Clearly, the better the interview is conducted (i.e. the more information that is collected and the more accurate this information is) the higher are the chances that a case can be solved. Apart from that, a good interview may also provide the information which is necessary to assess the reliability of a witness.

REFERENCES

Alba, J.W. and Hasher, L. (1983). Is memory schematic? *Psychological Bulletin,* **93**, 203–31.

Archer, R.L. (1979). Role of personality and the social situation. In G.J. Chelune (Ed.), *Self-disclosure*. San Francisco: Jossey-Bass.

Aschermann, E., Mantwill, M. and Köhnken, G. (1991). An independent replication of the cognitive interview. *Applied Cognitive Psychology*, **5**, 489–95.

Bartlett, F.C. (1932). *Remembering: A Study in Experimental Social Psychology*, Cambridge: Cambridge University Press.

Bekerian, D.A. and Dennett, J.L. (1993). The cognitive interview technique: reviving the issues. *Applied Cognitive Psychology,* **7**, 275–97.

Bower, G.H., Black, J.B. and Turner, T.J. (1979). Scripts in memory for texts. *Cognitive Psychology,* **11**, 177–220.

Clifford, B. and Bull, R. (1978). *The Psychology of Person Identification*. London: Routledge.

Cohen, J. (1977). *Statistical and Analysis for the Behavioural Sciences*. New York: Academic Press.

Cozby, P.C. (1973). Self-disclosure: a literature review. *Psychological Bulletin,* **79**, 73–91.

Deffenbacher, K.A. (1983). The influence of arousal on reliability of testimony. In S.M.A. Lloyd-Bostock and B.R. Clifford (Eds), *Evaluating Witness Evidence: Recent Psychological Research and New Perspectives*. Chichester: John Wiley.

Fisher, R.P. and Chandler, C.C. (1984). Dissociations between temporally-cued and theme-cued recall. *Bulletin of the Psychonomic Society,* **22**, 203–10.

Fisher, R.P. and Chandler, C.C. (1991). Independence between recalling interevent relations and specific events. *Journal of Experimental Psychology: Learning, Memory and Cognition,* **17**, 722–33.

Fisher, R.P. and Geiselman, R.E. (1992). *Memory-enhancing Techniques for Investigative Interviewing*. Springfield: Charles C. Thomas.

Fisher, R.P., Geiselman, R.E. and Amador, M. (1989). Field test of the cognitive interview: enhancing the recollection of actual victims and witnesses of crime. *Journal of Applied Psychology,* **74**, 722–7.

Fisher, R.P., Geiselman, R.E. and Raymond, D.S. (1987). Critical analysis of police interviewing techniques. *Journal of Police Science and Administration,* **15**, 177–85.

Fisher, R.P., Geiselman, R.E., Raymond, D.S., Jurkevich, L.M. and Warhaftig, M.L. (1987). Enhancing eye-witness memory: refining the cognitive interview. *Journal of Police Science and Administration,* **15**, 291–7.

Geiselman, R.E. (1988). Improving eyewitness memory through mental reinstatement of context. In G. Davies and D. Thomson (Eds), *Memory in Context: Context in Memory*. Chichester: John Wiley, pp. 245–65.

Geiselman, R.E., Fisher, R.P., Cohen, G., Holland, H. and Surtes, L. (1986). Eye-witness responses to leading and misleading questions under the cognitive interview. *Journal of Police Science and Administration*, **14**, 31–9.

Geiselman, R.E., Fisher, R.P., Firstenberg, I., Hutton, L.A., Sullivan, S., Avetissian, I. and Prosk, A. (1984). Enhancement of eye-witness memory: an empirical evaluation of the cognitive interview. *Journal of Police Science and Administration*, **12**, 74–80.

Geiselman, R.E., Fisher, R.P., MacKinnon, D.P. and Holland, H.L. (1985). Enhancement of eye-witness memory with the cognitive interview. *American Journal of Psychology*, **99**, 385–401.

Geiselman, R.E., Fisher, R.P., MacKinnon, D.P. and Holland, H.L. (1986). Eye-witness memory enhancement in the police interview: cognitive retrieval mnemonics versus hypnosis. *Journal of Applied Psychology*, **70**, 401–12.

George, R. (1991). A field and experimental evaluation of three methods of interviewing witnesses and victims of crime. Unpublished Master's thesis, Polytechnic of East London.

Graesser, A.C. and Nakamura, G.V. (1982). The impact of a schema on comprehension and memory. In G.H. Bower (Ed.), *The Psychology of Learning and Motivation,* vol. 16. New York: Academic Press.

Hastie, R., Park, B. and Weber, R. (1984). Social memory. In R.S. Wyer and T.K. Srull (Eds), *Handbook of Social Cognition*, vol. 2. Hillsdale, NJ: Erlbaum, pp. 151–212.

Haynes, S.N. (1978). *Principles of Behavioural Assessment*. New York: Academic Press.

Hedges, L.V. and Olkin, I. (1985). *Statistical Methods for Meta-analysis*. New York: Academic Press.

Herren, R. (1976). Das Vernchmungsprotokoll (the interview protocol). *Kriminalistik*, **7**, 313–7.

Holst, V.F. and Pedzek, K. (1992). Scripts for typical crimes and their effects on memory for eye-witness testimony. *Applied Cognitive Psychology*, **6**, 573–87.

Kahneman, D. (1973). *Attention and Effort*. Englewood-Cliffs: Prentice-Hall.

Kessler, B.H. (1988). Daten aus dem Interview. In R.S. Jäger (Ed.), *Psychologische Diagnostik*. Munich: Psychologie Verlags Union.

Kintsch, W. and van Dijk, T.A. (1978). Toward a model of text comprehension and production. *Psychological Review*, **85**, 363–94.

Köhnken, G., Thürer, C. and Zoberbier, D. (1994). The cognitive interview: are the interviewers' memories enhanced, too? *Applied Cognitive Psychology*, **8**, 13–24.

Köhnken, G., Milne, R., Memon, A. and Bull, R. (1994). Recall in cognitive interviews and standard interviews: a meta-analysis. Paper presented at the Conference of the American Psychology-Law Society, Santa Fe.

Leibowitz, H.W. and Guzi, L. (1990). Can the accuracy of eye-witness testimony be improved by the use of non-verbal techniques? Paper presented at the Conference of the American Psychology-Law Society, Williamsburg.

Linehan, M.M. (1977). Issues in behavioural interviewing. In J.D. Cone and R.P. Hawkins (Eds), *Behavioural Assessment*. New York: Bruner-Mazel.

Loftus, E.F. (1979). *Eye-witness Testimony*. London: Harvard University Press.

Maass, A. and Köhnken, G. (1989). Eye-witness identification: simulating the 'weapon effect'. *Law and Human Behavior*, **13**, 397–408.

Mahl, G.F. (1987). *Explorations in Nonverbal and Vocal Behaviour*. Hillsdale, NJ: Erlbaum.

Malpass, R.S. (1994). Enhancing eye-witness memory. In S.L. Sporer, R.S. Malpass and G. Köhnken (Eds), *The Psychology of Eye-witness Identification: New Evidence and Practical Guidelines*. Hillsdale, NJ: Erlbaum.

Malpass, R.S. and Devine, P.G. (1981). Guided memory in eye-witness identification. *Journal of Applied Psychology*, **66**, 343–50.

Mantwill, M., Köhnken, G. and Aschermann, E. (1995). Effects of the cognitive interview on the recall of familiar and unfamiliar events. *Journal of Applied Psychology*, February.

Matarazzo, J.D. and Wiens, A.N. (1985). *The Interview: Research on its Anatomy and Structure*. Chicago: Aldine.

Milne, R., Bull, R., Köhnken, G. and Memon, A. (1994). The cognitive interview and suggestibility. Paper presented at the European Congress of Psychology and Law, Barcelona.

Navon, D. and Gopher, D. (1979). On the economy of the human information processing system. *Psychological Review*, **86**, 214–55.

Newlands, P. and MacLeod, M.D. (1992). Continuing the cognitive interview. Poster presented at the European Conference of Psychology and Law, Oxford.

Pedzek, K., Whetstone, T., Reynolds, K., Askari, N. and Dougherty, T. (1989). Memory for real-world scenes: the role of consistency with schematic expectation. *Journal of Experimental Psychology: Learning, Memory and Cognition*, **15**, 587–95.

Perry, D.J. and Chapman, A.J. (1992). Applying the cognitive interview procedure to road accident witnesses. Paper presented at the Conference of the British Psychological Society, Blackpool.

Ross, D.F., Read, J.D. and Toglia, M.P. (1994). *Adult Eye-witness Testimony. Current Trends and Developments*. New York: Cambridge University Press.

Schank, R.C. and Abelson, R.P. (1977). *Scripts, Plans, Goals and Understanding*. Hillsdale, NJ: Erlbaum.

Scherer, K.R. and Ekman, P. (1982). *Handbook of Methods in Nonverbal Behaviour Research*. Cambridge: Cambridge University Press.

Schmidt, L.R. and Kessler, B.H. (1976). *Anamnese*. Weinheim: Beltz.

Schneider, W. and Shiffrin, R.M. (1977). Controlled and automatic human informartion processing: I. Detection, search, and attending. *Psychological Review*, **84**, 1–66.

Shiffrin, R.M. and Schneider, W. (1977). Controlled and automatic human information processing: II. Perceptual learning, automatic attending, and a general theory. *Psychological Review*, **84**, 127–89.

Smith, D.A. and Graesser, A.C. (1981). Memory for actions in scripted activities as a function of typicality, retention interval, and retrieval task. *Memory and Cognition*, **9**, 550–9.

Taylor, S.E. and Crocker, J. (1981). Schematic basis of social information processing. In E.T. Higgins, C.P. Herman and M.P. Zanna (Eds), *Social Cognition: The Ontario Symposium*, vol. 1. Hillsdale, NJ: Erlbaum, pp. 89–134.

Tulving, E. (1983). *Elements of Episodic Memory*. Oxford: Clarendon Press.

Tulving, E. and Thomson, D.M. (1973). Encoding specificity and retrieval processes in episodic memory. *Psychological Review*, 80, 353–70.

Turkat, I.D. (1986). The behavioural interview. In A.R. Ciminero, K.S. Calhoun and H.E. Adams (Eds), *Handbook of Behavioural Assessment*. New York: John Wiley.

Wark, L., Memon, A., Holley, A., Köhnken, G. and Bull, R. (1994). Children's memory for a magic's show. Paper presented at the European Congress of Psychology and Law, Barcelona.

Wells, G.L. and Loftus, E.F. (1984). *Eye-witness Testimony: Psychological Perspectives*. Cambridge: Cambridge University Press.

Chapter 3.5

Interviewing Children in Legal Contexts

Ray Bull
University of Portsmouth

Obtaining testimony from children poses many problems in legal contexts. For example:

> A couple accused of subjecting their two daughters to sexual abuse and cruelty were cleared yesterday after the elder child was unable to continue giving evidence. Judge Gerald Butler QC ordered the jury at Southwark Crown Court, South London to return verdicts of not guilty to cruelty, indecent assault and gross indecency charges against the parents. Peter Clarke, prosecuting, said the police investigation began after teachers at the elder girl's school noticed she was pulling her hair out. 'She pulled almost all of her hair out of her body even her pubic hair.' He said the girl, now aged 13, would screech, and shout words like 'bosoms', and touch female staff on their breasts and buttocks. He said she was subjected to 'unspeakable' abuse. She had made a statement to police alleging in detail how her father repeatedly abused her and forced her to watch him in 'bizarre' sex acts with his wife. During the 38 minutes she gave evidence on Wednesday, the girl was in a room linked to the court by closed circuit television. Det. Con. Timms said afterwards that letting children give evidence through closed circuit television was not enough. 'Too many cases of this kind are halted because children cannot bring themselves to tell the full story.' It had to be made easier for them to give evidence. He called for legislation to allow video recordings of children's first interviews at police stations to be used as evidence. (*The Guardian*, 22 June 1990).

In England and Wales the Criminal Justice Act 1988 permits children to testify in criminal trials via the 'live video link' from another room in the court building. Also the statutory ban on convicting on the uncorroborated of unsworn children was abolished, and with it the duty to warn the jury of the danger of accepting the evidence of a child.

Until recently the English criminal courts' requirement that witnesses be competent was interpreted as making it impossible to hear evidence from a child under six years of age. However, in 1991, the Court of Appeal ruled (*R. v. Z.*, [1990] 3 W.L.R. 113) that a child of any age could give evidence provided that the judge deemed her or him sufficiently able to recount what happened and to understand the duty of speaking the truth (Spencer and Flin, 1993). The Criminal Justice Act 1991 attempts to abolish the competency requirement altogether, save as it applies to all witnesses, but questioning the child must be conducted in such a way as to permit the court to conclude that the child has sufficiently recalled what happened (Bull and Spencer, 1992).

Legislation permitting video recordings of prior interviews to be allowed as child witnesses' evidence-in-chief in criminal trials was introduced in England and Wales in the Criminal Justice Act 1991. The Act permits a video recorded interview conducted by a police officer, social worker (or indeed anyone) to be shown to the jury as evidence-in-chief *if* the interview with the child was deemed by the judge to have been conducted appropriately.

This innovative legislation has resulted in an even greater emphasis on the quality of interviews conducted with child witnesses/victims. Much publicity has surrounded the reliability of interviews conducted with children especially those whom it is thought may have been sexually abused, and questions have been raised about the way some interviews have been conducted (see, for example, Lord Clyde's 1992 report of his inquiry into the removal of children from their homes in Orkney, Scotland). In the *Independent* newspaper (28 October, 1992) it was stated that 'A Scottish Office spokesman said it was widely accepted that this was a difficult area. "What we don't know about interviewing children would fill books" he said.'

The Criminal Justice Act 1991 allows the judge to order that the child not be examined-in-chief on any matter, which in the opinion of the court, has been adequately dealt with in the video-recorded interview. In this way the recording can take the place of the child's evidence-in-chief *if* the interview is deemed worthwhile by the court. Cross-examination (and any re-examination) is conducted live (often using a video link—see Noon and Davies (1993) for more on the live video link, and Flin et al. (1993) for more on the examination of child witnesses in criminal trials).

THE MEMORANDUM OF GOOD PRACTICE

Video recordings of such interviews allow the skills of the interviewer to be scrutinised. In order to obtain worthwhile evidence from children in a reliable way that can stand up to such scrutiny the Home Office (the relevant Government department) felt in 1991 that many interviewers (whether police, social workers, lawyers, or others) would welcome a document designed to assist them. In partnership with the Department of Health the Home Office published in the summer of 1992 the 'Memorandum of Good Practice on Video

Recorded Interviews with Child Witnesses for Criminal Proceedings'. The Home Office made considerable effort to try to ensure that the Memorandum was as useful as possible. Together with Di Birch (Professor of Law at Nottingham University) I was asked by the Home Office to produce by July 1991 a working draft memorandum. This initial draft was then revised by the Home Office, particularly with regard to its organisation. The Home Office set up a Policy Steering Group which consisted of a representative from each of a large number of relevant bodies (including those representing members of legal professions). This group helped the Home Office produce revisions to the document, and the final version was published by Her Majesty's Stationery Office in August 1992.

The 'Memorandum of Good Practice' covers a large range of issues. It was based not only on consensual professional opinion but also on published scientific research on the topic. It contains advice on the legal conditions about which a criminal court may wish to be satisfied before admitting a video recording, and on the legal rules to be observed in producing evidentially acceptable recordings. It gives guidance on what to do prior to an interview with a child witness including when and where to conduct the video recording, and on the planning of the interview. Some guidance is also offered on the equipment to be used. The main part of the Memorandum gives guidance on how to conduct the actual interview. Four main phases are recommended, to be conducted in the order of (i) rapport, (ii) free narrative account, (iii) questioning, and (iv) closing the interview. Much detailed guidance is given on what to do in each of these phases. Fuller discussion of the psychological research which informed the contents of the Memorandum is available in Bull (1992, 1994a, 1994b).

Psychologists' research in the last ten years has confirmed that children (even the very young) are usually able to give a worthwhile report of what happened to them *if* they are interviewed appropriately (see Davies, Stevenson-Robb and Flin, 1986; Hedderman, 1987; Myers, 1987; Faller, 1990; Fivush and Hudson, 1990; Saywitz, Goodman and Myers, 1990; Murray and Gough, 1991; Vizard, 1991; Spencer and Flin, 1993). However, inappropriate interviewing, especially that with a suggestive (King and Yuille, 1989; Baxter, 1990; Doris, 1991; Ceci et al., 1992; Toglia, Ross and Ceci, 1992), pressurising or leading style, can bias the child's report (White, 1990).

Research has been conducted in which children witness complex events either live or via a video recording. This has found that, when asked simply to describe what happened in their own words, children most often produce reliable accounts. That is, the vast majority of what most of them say in these (often ingenious) studies is an accurate account of what happened, but rarely is a full account given by anyone (Irish Law Reform Commission, 1990; Oates, 1990; Spencer et al., 1990; Perry and Wrightsman, 1991; Dent and Flin, 1992). However, young children usually report less than do older children or adults

(List, 1986; Flin et al., 1992). Therefore, especially with younger children, some form of questioning is often needed. However, such questioning should not affect the child's own account which should be requested before any questioning occurs.

In 1990 Sue White argued that 'Until relatively recently, suspected victims of child sexual abuse did not receive much special consideration with reference to how they should be interviewed' (p. 368). She suggested that 'Techniques for interviewing these young children have been based on practical experiences and are only now beginning to receive any research attention' (p. 369). She pointed out that 'While a number of authors have made detailed suggestions of how best to interact with a child suspected of being a victim of sexual abuse ... interviewers have been forced to discover clinical techniques which work best in their particular situation' (p. 369). She believes that 'The first goal in investigatory interviewing must be the gathering of data which are as true as possible a representation of the child's experiences and which are not subject to charges of being contaminated' (p. 370).

A considerable amount of psychological research has recently been conducted concerning the possible contamination (usually by adults, wittingly or unwittingly) of children's evidence (e.g. Ceci and Bruck, 1993; Goodman and Bottoms, 1993).

In 1988 a well respected British child psychiatrist experienced at interviewing children who may have been abused (David Jones) made the sensible recommendation (Jones and McQuiston, 1988) of dividing interviews with such children into four phases which can be described as: (i) rapport, (ii) free narrative, (iii) questioning, (iv) closure. In 1991 another very experienced psychiatrist (Eileen Vizard) made a similar recommendation, as did Hoorwitz in his 1992 book on interviewing children who may have been sexually abused.

The Memorandum of Good Practice on interviewing child witnesses recommends that normally interviews should be planned to pass through such phases which firstly provide the child with the opportunity to describe in his or her own words what happened, and then to proceed from general and open questions to specific and closed types of questions. Yuille et al. (1993) have similarly recommended that in order to obtain as full a statement as possible from the child that is uncontaminated by the interviewer, a 'step-wise' procedure be adopted. This 'step-wise' procedure was developed in Germany over a number of decades (see Undeutsch, 1982; Steller and Köhnken, 1989) by psychologists with substantial experience of interviewing children who may have been sexually abused. It was developed in order to obtain an appropriate statement from the child which could then be analysed (that is, the statement) to determine whether it demonstrated the criteria thought to be associated with genuinely experienced events (see Köhnken, 1990; Steller and Boychuk, 1992).

In July 1992 John Yuille presented at a seminar held in London, England some preliminary findings from his Canadian field study designed to evaluate the effects of training interviewers in the 'step-wise' approach. In British Columbia a joint training programme for police, social workers and prosecutors was set up. All the participants received several days' training in 'step-wise' interviewing. With the permission of the 'real life' witnesses interviewed before and after these interviewers had received the training, the tape recordings of nearly two hundred interviews with children were passed to researchers for evaluation. The research team developed a rating technique concerning the effectiveness of the interviews. Interviews were classified as 'useless' firstly if no conclusion could be drawn about whether the child had been abused, and secondly if the interviewer conducted a poor interview. Yuille reported that whereas 35 per cent of the pre-training interviews were classified as 'useless' (and this is a large percentage), only 14 per cent of the post-training interviews were classified as 'useless'. This is an important finding. In addition, of the 156 people who received the interview training only one made a negative remark about it. Most described it as easy to follow.

The phased or 'step-wise' approach may well be relatively easy to follow, and it should therefore prevent interviewers making the errors of the past. However, it is not necessarily that helpful in assisting a child witness who is having difficulty remembering. Some innovative ways of assisting children who wish to recall are now being developed.

INNOVATIVE WAYS OF INTERVIEWING CHILD WITNESSES

Recently there has been an increase, from a very low base in research on innovative methods of assisting children's recollection. These were not included in the Memorandum of Good Practice. One major reason for this was that there did not exist enough research-based information regarding their use in interviews relevant to criminal proceedings to determine the effectiveness of such procedures, for example the use of: (i) play materials to prompt a child who has as yet said nothing about abuse, or (ii) 'reconstructive' techniques in which the child is given scale models of houses, settings, people, or (iii) context reinstatement, for example as in the cognitive interview (Memon and Bull, 1991; Memon et al., 1993, 1994), or (iv) preparatory interviewing procedures (e.g. Warren, Hulse-Trotter and Tubbs, 1991; Saywitz and Snyder, 1993).

Use of Props

Mel Pipe's research in New Zealand (Pipe, Gee and Wilson, 1993) and work in Germany by Dahmen-Zimmer and Loohs (1992) suggest that props/toys may sometimes assist children to give valid accounts in an evidentially sound way. This contrasts with the claim by Raskin and Esplin (1991) that 'puppets, drawings, good touch/bad touch games, and toys are generally unnecessary and should be avoided whenever possible' (p. 270). Clearly such procedures can be used inappropriately, but much more research is necessary to develop adequate procedures. Raskin and Esplin have claimed that 'They frequently distract the child from the task of providing a complete and accurate description, and they can be suggestive, provoke fantasy and lack a scientific basis' (p. 270). Researchers urgently need to develop scientifically based recommendations for the use of props, toys and dolls based on proper research. (For a critical review of the use of dolls see Skinner and Berry, 1993.)

STATEMENT VALIDITY ANALYSIS

Research on the detection of deception has shown that there is no such thing as 'lie behaviour' (i.e. behaviour that is a consistent, accurate guide to honesty or deception) even though surveys of police officers' views on this have found them to be believe that 'lie behaviours' do exist (Bull, 1989). Further, people's ability successfully to discriminate between truthful and deceptive statements has been found by research to be only slightly better than chance level (Köhnken, 1990).

A technique, introduced in Germany, to discriminate truthful and fabricated statements from children involved in sexual abuse cases, is called 'statement validity analysis' (SVA). It involves the analysis of a statement (i.e. what the child has said) according to a set of 19 reality criteria which describe certain qualities of its content. The underlying theory states that a child witness will not be able to fabricate a statement with these qualities. Hence, if these qualities are found in a statement it is likely to be based on genuine personal experience (Köhnken, 1990).

A number of studies (e.g. Anson, Golding and Gully, 1993) have examined the effectiveness of SVA, and such research suggests that this procedure has quite good reliability and validity. The use of SVA rests very much on obtaining from the child an account uncontaminated by inappropriate interviewing. In fact, the German guidance of how best to obtain an account from a child suitable for 'statement validity analysis' informed my writing for the Home Office of the first working draft of the Memorandum of Good Practice.

THE 'COGNITIVE INTERVIEW'

In 1993 a booklet entitled *Investigative Interviewing* was given to every police officer in England and Wales. One of the few interviewing procedures recommended in this booklet was called the 'cognitive approach'. This approach is based on a procedure devised by American psychologists which has repeatedly been found in research in the USA, Germany and the UK to lead adult witnesses to remember more of what happened (Memon and Köhnken, 1992). In the last few years researchers have begun to test the usefulness of this 'cognitive interview' (CI) approach with children (Saywitz, Geiselman and Bornstein, 1992). This research is finding that some of the 'cognitive interview' instructions found useful by adults may need modification for use by children, especially young ones (Memon et al., 1993, 1994). Our own research is employing versions of the procedure we think suitable for children. Using this modified procedure we have found in separate studies that the CI helps children accurately recall over 20 per cent more information (Memon, Wark et al., 1994; Milne et al., 1994; Wark et al., 1994).

We are also investigating (i) the extent to which the procedures used in this 'cognitive interview' (e.g. asking the witnesses to reinstate in their minds the physical and psychological contexts of their initial witnessing of the event) reduce the undesirable effects upon children of misleading or suggestive questioning, and (ii) the usefulness of the CI with people (adults and children) who have 'learning disability' (what used to be described as mental handicap).

VISUAL AND AUDITORY FEEDBACK

The visual part of this new procedure (developed by Poole, 1992) consists of a green felt board on which are the outlines of a child's head and an adult's head. The aim of the felt board is to help young children realise that 'big', full answers are required. Research suggests that young children assume that all adults already know everything (Menig-Peterson, 1975; McGurk and Glachan, 1988; Fielding and Conroy, 1992) and therefore children often fail to realise what is required of them in investigatory interviews. White felt triangles are placed in the outline of the child's head. When the interview commences, the interviewer explains that the child knows lots about the event (represented by the triangles in the child's head) whereas the interviewer knows nothing about the event (hence the empty adult's head). The interviewer asks the child to give an account of the event, and as the child begins to do so the interviewer transfers triangles from the child's head to the adult's head. Preliminary research using this procedure suggests that it enhances the amount young children report of an event (Poole, 1992).

Preliminary research by Poole (1992) similarly suggests that the amount young children report of an event can be increased by playing back to them an audio-taped recording of their initial account of the event. Children undergoing this procedure may well remember more new information about the event (when asked, in a second recall attempt, to report anything they missed out from their first recall attempt) than those children merely asked to 'try to remember more' in a second recall attempt without hearing the audio-taped (or possibly video-taped) recording of their first recall. At Portsmouth we are conducting further research on the usefulness of such visual and auditory feedback.

SUGGESTIVE QUESTIONS

There is no doubt, as Dent (1986) noted, that children (like adults) are influenced by leading questions. Some research has examined the effect of preparing children for these. Warren, Hulse-Trotter and Tubbs (1991) told seven-year-old and twelve-year-old children (and adults) a story (twice) and then asked them questions about it. Some of these questions were purposely misleading. After answering the questions the children (and adults) were told that 'they had not performed very well' (p. 278), and the questions were asked again. Warren, Hulse-Trotter and Tubbs were interested in finding out (i) whether the misleading questions would influence the children's responses, (ii) whether the children would change their response to a question when it was posed a second time, and (iii) the effects of warning some of the children that the questions would be 'tricky' while telling them 'to be sure that their answers reflected only what they "really remembered" about the story' (p.278).

The researchers found that the younger children recalled less of the story and were more likely to acquiesce to suggestive leading questions than were the older children or the adults. The children also changed, upon second questioning, more of their answers (even to non-leading questions). These findings sit well with previous research with children (Bull, 1994b). Warren, Hulse-Trotter and Tubbs' innovative warning procedure was found to produce a significant reduction in the effect of the misleading questions, even for the younger children.

Saywitz, Moan and Lamphear (1991) conducted a somewhat similar study in which seven-year-old children witnessed a live event. Two weeks later half of the children received training to resist the effects of misleading questions and the other half (the control group) instead received motivating instructions to do their best. They were then asked questions about the event. Those in the former group made fewer errors in response to misleading questions, this suggesting that their training was beneficial. However, those children in the control group responded *more* correctly to 'non-leading' and to 'correctly leading' questions. Thus more work is needed on how best to assist child witnesses to resist inappropriate, misleading questions while responding correctly to more appropriate questions.

In 1990 Saywitz, Snyder and Lamphear made an initial attempt to train young children to be able to recall more of a staged, live event. They considered this to be important because of the well replicated finding that young children typically recall less than do older children or adults (though what they recall is no less accurate). Not only would child witnesses' increased recall be of benefit to justice systems, it might also lead to feelings of confidence and empowerment in children who may have been abused.

Saywitz, Snyder and Lamphear pointed out that while there exists a literature on the positive effects of preparing children for medical procedures very little empirical research exists on how to assist child witnesses to recall more of events. Their training was based on research studies relating to children's use of retrieval strategies which suggest that the use of 'external cues, categorisation and metamemory when accompanied by a rationale for their use, aid children's retrieval' (p. 5). It was also 'based on schema theories that describe how children represent events in memory' (p. 5). The training was based on Schneider and Pressley's (1989) model of 'a good memory strategy user' in which the application of appropriate memorial strategies initially requires considerable effort but with practice becomes more habitual and automatic. Saywitz, Snyder and Lamphear also trained the children to use external visual cues (e.g. schematic drawings representing 'who was there', 'what happened', 'where did it happen') to remind them to report an amount of detail (demonstrated by the trainer) for categories of information that would be useful in a criminal investigation (e.g. the setting, participants, conversations, affective states, actions and consequences). Those children who received these two types of training (i.e. memorial strategies, and use of visual cues) also received practice in putting both into effect.

Saywitz, Snyder and Lamphear compared the recall of children trained in this way with (i) a group who received instructions to be as complete as possible but which received no training, and (ii) a control group which received no such instructions nor training. The trained group correctly recalled significantly more information than did the other two groups (which did not differ from each other). However, they also produced significantly more incorrect recall. Further analysis found that the trained group's higher *in*correct recall was occasioned solely by the use of the visual cues. Nevertheless, a minority of the visual cues (e.g. that cueing recall of conversations) did aid correct recall. From this study we can conclude that more research is needed on the use of the kind of visual cues employed by Saywitz. Snyder and Lamphear. Indeed, these researchers noted 'the value of developing preparation techniques that are empirically tested and whose unintended side effects have been eliminated through revision and retesting' (p. 17). They pointed out that there is a need for continuing research on preparation techniques that are appropriate for various sorts of children, and that are easily implemented by relevant professionals.

CONCLUSION

This chapter has provided a brief overview of some of the contributions psychologists have made and are making relevant to the interviewing of children for legal purposes. Such interviews are often extremely difficult to conduct well.

REFERENCES

Anson, D., Golding, S. and Gully, K. (1993). Child sexual abuse allegations: reliability of criteria-based content analysis. *Law and Human Behaviour*, **17**, 331–41.

Baxter, J.S. (1990). The suggestibility of child witnesses: a review. *Applied Cognitive Psychology*, **4**, 393–407.

Bull, R. (1989). Can training enhance the detection of deception? In J. Yuille (Ed.), *Credibility Assessment*. Deventer: Kluwer.

Bull, R. (1992). Obtaining expertly: the reliability of interviews with child witnesses. *Expert*, **1**, 5–12.

Bull, R. (1994a). Innovative techniques for the questioning of child witnesses especially those who are young and those with learning difficulty. In M. Zaragoza (Ed.), *Memory, Suggestibility and Eye-witness Testimony in Children and Adults*. Newbury Park, CA: Sage.

Bull, R. (1994b). Good practice for video recorded interviews with child witnesses for use in criminal proceedings. In G. Davies, S. Lloyd-Bostock, M. McMurran and C. Wilson (Eds), *Law and Psychology*. Amsterdam: de Gruyter.

Bull, R. and Spencer, J. (1992). England's changes in child witness laws, procedures and a code of good practice. *Violence Update*, **3**, 3.

Ceci, S. and Bruck, M. (1993). The suggestibility of the child witness: a historical review and synthesis. *Psychological Bulletin*, **113**, 403–39.

Ceci, S.J., De Simone, M., Putnick, M.E. and Nightingale, N.N. (1992). The suggestibility of children's recollections. In D. Cicchetti and S. Toth (Eds), *Child Abuse, Child Development, and Social Policy*. Norwood, NJ: Ablex.

Clyde, J. (1992). *The Report of the Inquiry into the Removal of Children from Orkney in February 1991*. Edinburgh: HMSO.

Dahmen-Zimmer, K. and Loohs, S. (1992). Is there truth in the eye of the beholder? Paper presented at the Third European Law and Psychology Conference, Oxford.

Davies, G., Stephenson-Robb, Y. and Flin, R. (1986). The reliability of children's testimony. *International Legal Practitioner*, **11**, 95–103.

Dent, H. (1986). An experimental study of the effectiveness of different techniques of questioning mentally handicapped child witnesses. *British Journal of Clinical Psychology*, **25**, 12–17.

Dent, H. and Flin, R. (1992). *Children as Witnesses*. Chichester: Wiley.

Doris, J. (1991). *The Suggestibility of Children's Recollections: Implications for Eye-witness Testimony*. Washington, DC: American Psychological Association.

Faller, K.C. (1990). Types of questions for children alleged to have been sexually abused. *The Advisor: American Professional Society on the Abuse of Children*, **3**, 3–5.

Fielding, N. and Conroy, S. (1992). Interviewing child victims: police and social work investigations of child sexual abuse. *Sociology*, **26**, 103–24.

Fivush, R. and Hudson, J. (1990). *Knowing and Remembering in Young Children*. New York: Cambridge University Press.

Flin, R., Boon, J., Knox, A. and Bull, R. (1992). The effect of a five month delay on children's and adult's eye-witness memory. *British Journal of Psychology*, **83**, 323–36.

Flin, R., Bull, R., Boon, J. and Knox, A. (1993). Child witnesses in Scottish criminal trials. *International Review of Victimology*, **2**, 309–29.

Goodman, G. and Bottoms, B. (1993). *Child Victims, Child Witnesses: Understanding and Improving Testimony*. New York: Guilford.

Hedderman, C. (1987). Children's evidence: the need for corroboration. Research and Planning Unit, Paper 41. London: Home Office.

Hoorwitz, A. (1992). *The Clinical Detective*. New York: Norton.

Irish Law Reform Commission (1990). Report on child sexual abuse. Dublin: Law Reform Commission.

Jones, D.P.H. and McQuiston, M.G. (1988). *Interviewing the Sexually Abused Child*. London: Gaskell.

King, M.A. and Yuille, J.C. (1989). Suggestibility and the child witness. In S. Ceci, D. Ross and M. Toglia (Eds), *Child Witnesses*. New York: Springer-Verlag.

Köhnken, G. (1990). The evaluation of statement credibility: social judgement and expert diagnostic approaches. In J. Spencer, G. Nicholson, R. Flin and R. Bull (Eds), *Children's in Legal Proceedings: An International Perspective*. Cambridge: Faculty of Law.

List, J. (1986). Age and schematic differences in the reliability of eye-witness testimony. *Developmental Psychology*, **22**, 50–7.

McGurk, H. and Glachan, M. (1988). Children's conversation with adults. *Children and Society*, **2**, 20–34.

Memon, A. and Bull, R. (1991). The cognitive interview: its origins, empirical support, evaluation and practical implications. *Journal of Community and Applied Social Psychology*, **1**, 291–307.

Memon, A. and Köhnken, G. (1992). Helping witnesses to remember more: the cognitive interview. *Expert Evidence*, **1**, 39–48.

Memon, A., Cronin, O., Eaves, R. and Bull, R. (1993). The cognitive interview and child witnesses. In N. Clark and G. Stephenson (Eds), *Children, Evidence and Procedure*. Leicester: British Psychological Society.

Memon, A., Cronin, O., Eaves, R. and Bull, R. (1994). An empirical test of the mnemonic components of the cognitive interview. In G. Davies, S. Lloyd-Bostock, M. McMurran and C. Wilson (Eds), *Law and Psychology*. Amsterdam: de Gruyter.

Memon, A., Wark, L., Köhnken, G. and Bull, R. (1994). The performance of witnesses and interviewers using a structured or cognitive interview. Paper presented at the Biennial Convention of the American Psychology-Law Society, Santa Fe.

Menig-Peterson, C. (1975). The modification of communicative behaviour in preschool-aged children as a function of the listener's perspective. *Child Development*, **46**, 1015–18.

Milne, R., Bull, R., Köhnken, G. and Memon, A. (1994). The cognitive interview and suggestibility. Paper presented at the Fourth Biennial Conference of the European Psychology Law Association, Barcelona.

Murray, K. and Gough, D. (Eds) (1991). *Intervening in Child Sexual Abuse*. Edinburgh: Scottish Academic Press.

Myers, J. (1987). *Child Witness Law and Practice*. New York: Wiley.

Noon, E. and Davies, G. (1993). Child witnesses and the 'livelink'. *Expert*, **2**, 11–12.

Oates, R.K. (1990). Children as witnesses. *The Australian Law Journal*, **64**, 129–34.

Perry, N. and Wrightsman, L. (1991). *The Child Witness: Legal Issues and Dilemmas*. Newbury Park, CA: Sage.

Pipe, M-E., Gee, S. and Wilson, J. (1993). Cues, props and context: do they facilitate children's event reports? In G. Goodman and B. Bottoms (Eds), *Understanding and Improving Children's Testimony: Developmental, Clinical and Legal Issues*. New York: Guilford.

Poole, D.A. (1992). Eliciting information from children with nonsuggestive visual and auditory feedback. Paper presented at the NATO Advanced Studies Institute: The

Child Witness in Context, Tuscany, Italy.

Raskin, D. and Esplin, P. (1991). Statement validity assessment: interview procedures and context analysis of children's statements of sexual abuse. *Behavioural Assessment*, **13**, 265–91.

Saywitz, K., Geiselman, R. and Bornstein, G. (1992). Effects of cognitive interviewing and practice on children's recall performance. *Journal of Applied Psychology*, **77**, 744–56.

Saywitz, K., Moan, S. and Lamphear, V. (1991). The effect of preparation on children's resistance to misleading questions. Paper presented at the Annual Conference of the American Psychological Association on Child Development, San Francisco.

Saywitz, K.J. and Snyder, L. (1993). Improving children's testimony with preparation. In G. Goodman and B. Bottoms (Eds), *Child Victims, Child Witnesses: Understanding and Improving Testimony*. New York: Guilford Publications.

Saywitz, K.J., Goodman, G.S. and Myers, J. (1990). Can children provide accurate eye-witness reports? *Violence Update*, September, 3–11.

Saywitz, K., Snyder, L. and Lamphear, V. (1990). Preparing child witnesses: the efficiency of memory training strategy. Paper presented at the Annual Convention of the American Psychological Association, Boston.

Schneider, W. and Pressley, M. (1989). Memory development between 2 and 20. New York: Springer-Verlag.

Skinner, L.J. and Berry, K.K. (1993). Anatomically detailed dolls and the evaluation of child sexual abuse allegations: psychometric considerations. *Law and Human Behaviour*, **17**, 399–421.

Spencer, J. and Flin, R. (1993). *The Evidence of Children: The Law and the Psychology*. London: Blackstone.

Spencer, J., Nicholson, G., Flin, R. and Bull, R. (1990). *Children's Evidence in Legal Proceedings: An International Perspective*. Cambridge: Faculty of Law.

Steller, M. and Boychuck, T. (1992). Children as witnesses in sexual abuse cases. In H. Dent and R. Flin (Eds), *Children as Witnesses*. Chichester: Wiley.

Steller, M. and Köhnken, G. (1989). Criteria-based statement analysis. In D. Raskin (Ed.), *Psychological Methods in Criminal Investigation and Evidence*. New York: Springer.

Toglia, M., Ross, D. and Ceci, S. (1992). The suggestibility of children's memory. In M. Howe, C. Brainerd and V. Reyna (Eds), *The Development of Long-term Retention*. New York: Springer-Verlag.

Undeutsch, V. (1982). Statement reality analysis. In A. Trankell (Ed.), *Reconstructing the Past*. Deventer: Kluwer.

Vizard, E. (1991). Interviewing children suspected of being sexually abused: a review of theory and practice. In C.R. Hollin and K. Howells (Eds), *Clinical Approaches to Sex Offenders and their Victims*. Chichester: Wiley.

Wark, L., Memon, A., Holley, A., Köhnken, G. and Bull, R. (1994). Children's memory for a magic show. Paper presented at the Fourth Biennial Conference at the European Psychology Law Association, Barcelona.

Warren, A., Hulse-Trotter, K. and Tubbs, E. (1991). Inducing resistance to suggestibility in children. *Law and Human Behaviour*, **15**, 273–85.

White, S. (1990). The investigatory interview with suspected victims of child sexual abuse. In A. La Greca (Ed.), *Through the Eyes of a Child*. Boston: Allyn and Bacon.

Yuille, J., Hunter, R., Joffe, R. and Zaparniuk, J. (1993). Interviewing children in sexual abuse cases. In G. Goodman and B. Bottoms (Eds), *Child Victims, Child Witnesses: Understanding and Improving Testimony*. New York: Guilford.

Interviewing People with Communicative Disabilities

Ray Bull
University of Portsmouth

In this chapter 'communicative disabilities' includes both people whose intelligence is within the normal range but who may have, for example, speech or hearing impediments, and people with learning disability, who could be described as having lower intelligence (i.e. what used to be termed 'mental handicap'). As in any interview, the onus is on the interviewer to attempt to make his or her instructions or questions comprehensible to the interviewee, as well as to assist the interviewee to communicate with the interviewer. Just as some questioners of young child witnesses in court can accommodate in this way to the needs of such interviewees (e.g. see Flin et al., 1993), so interviewers have a duty to do so when the interviewee has a communicative disability. By doing this such interviewees may indicate their competency.

A number of people have argued that people with communicative disabilities may be more at risk of abuse (e.g. Endicott, 1992; Turk and Brown, 1992; Westcott, 1991). People with communicative disabilities are also probably over-represented in the population of those people detained at police stations to be interviewed because they are suspected of having committed a crime (Gudjonsson et al., 1993).

Thus it seems that people with disabilities are often victims of, witnesses to, and suspected of various crimes. Society has a responsibility to investigate such matters. As Coles (1990) pointed out, 'investigating cases of sexual abuse of persons with disabilities is extremely difficult' (p. 35) yet 'disabled persons have the right to be protected, and they have the right to live a life free of sexual abuse' (p. 43).

In England and Wales the Codes of Practice for the police to follow when investigating crime have been promulgated and updated under the Police and

Criminal Evidence Act 1984 (PACE). These emphasise the need for special care when police officers interview suspects who are 'mentally handicapped' or 'mentally ill'. However, as pointed out by Irving and McKenzie (1993), police 'training does not help the student to identify those who are "at risk"' (p. 88). They report one senior police instructor as saying that 'To be quite truthful, even though I've been teaching this stuff since before PACE came out, I don't know the difference between mental handicap and mental illness' (p. 89). They called for more positive advice and training on this topic, especially since, with a government endorsed policy of community care, more people with communication disabilities now live in the general community rather than within institutions.

LITTLE RESEARCH ON THIS TOPIC

Disabled people have the right, wherever possible, to be involved in decision-making processes which concern them. In 1981 Sigelman et al. noted that 'Recent emphasis on the rights of handicapped persons and legislation requiring their involvement in decisions affecting them have heightened interest in giving mentally retarded persons opportunities to speak for themselves' (p. 348). However, Sigelman et al. pointed out that very little prior research had been conducted on how best to interview people with communication disability. They noted, for example that 'there has been virtually no attention given to establishing the reliability and validity of answers given by mentally retarded persons' (p. 348). They stated that their own previous 'research program designed to assess the reliability and validity of answers given by mentally retarded children and adults in interviews leaves no doubt about the ruinous effects of acquiescence' (p. 348), by which they meant 'yeasaying in response to yes–no questions' (p. 348). They further stated that 'Not only were rates of acquiescence alarmingly high, but acquiescence was negatively correlated with IQ' (p. 348), and that 'mentally retarded people may be especially likely to give biased answers that are influenced by question structure and wording' (p. 348).

A BOOKLET FOR PROCURATORS FISCAL

Partly because so little published guidance existed on how best to interview witnesses with learning disability the Crown Office in Scotland (which has responsibility for criminal prosecutions) invited two psychologists (Bull and Cullen, 1992, 1993) to write a booklet giving guidance to Procurators Fiscal (i.e. prosecuting lawyers) on the interviewing of witnesses with learning disability. In this booklet we first provided information on 'what is learning disability', and then, prior to giving guidance on how to conduct such interviews, we covered a number of other topics of relevance.

For example, we pointed out to the Procurators Fiscal (who often interview prosecution witnesses in advance of the trial) that witnesses with learning disability are much more likely to be able to provide information about what happened to them if they are interviewed in situations with which they are happy and familiar. A novel location, such as the Fiscal's office or a courtroom, would probably have more deleterious effect on them than it would on other witnesses. In addition, we noted that information gained from a witness in one situation may not be equally forthcoming in an entirely different setting, such as a crowded courtroom. We pointed out the well-researched psychological principle behind this, the technical name for which is 'stimulus control'. Behaviour which is produced reliably in one setting is more likely to be reproduced in that or similar settings. As the characteristics of the setting change, so behaviour is likely to change. Therefore, we recommended to Fiscals that if a witness with learning disability was able to provide, in a setting familiar to him or her, information about what they had witnessed (as victim or bystander) it could be very worthwhile to familiarise such a witness with courts and their procedures before the witness was called to give evidence. No published investigation of the effectiveness of this seems to exist, though such procedures have been found to be useful for child witnesses (Dent and Flin, 1992; Spencer and Flin, 1993).

We also pointed out that:

> Many witnesses do not at all appreciate that they will not only be asked to give their evidence-in-chief, but will also be required to be cross-examined. Such witnesses do not appreciate that (and why) they will be questioned by two (or more) different people in court. It is essential that it be explained to mentally handicapped witnesses (in language appropriate to them) that they will probably be questioned in court by more than one person, and that some of the questions will be difficult or tricky. It should be explained to such witnesses that (i) the people questioning them in court really do not already know what took place, and (ii) why they will probably be questioned by a least two people. The role of the judge, jury, etc. should be briefly explained. It should also be explained to the witness that the accused will be present (and why). (Bull and Cullen, 1992, p. 11)

ANALYSIS OF POLICE INTERVIEWS

The quality of a statement obtained from an interviewee with communicative disability will often depend crucially on the skill of the interviewer. Although very little research has been conducted on the interviewing of such witnesses it may well be that enhanced interviewing skills may prove useful. In 1988 Cahill et al. undertook a study in London in which they were present at 100 police interviews of mentally vulnerable witnesses or suspects in serious crimes. They found the police to be quite open about their lack of training on this topic and they concluded that hazardous questions frequently occurred and that they were avoidable. These hazardous questions included leading questions, and the interviewer upgrading the interviewee's previous incomplete or unclear answers by putting these into his or her own words and then asking the interviewee if these (words) were correct. They pointed out that many police interviewers did not understand that a mentally handicapped person's criterion of what is satisfactorily accurate may be different from others, and that some mentally handicapped people may be willing to answer a question with 'yes' when this is unwarranted by their memory of an event.

The Irish Law Reform Commission's 1990 report on sexual offences against mentally handicapped people made the point that crucial issues surrounded the competence of such people to give evidence (that is to give an intelligible account of events, to appreciate the duty to tell the truth, to understand the difference between truth and falsehood, and to consent to sexual relations). The Commission's report emphasised that it was the mentally handicapped witness' provision of an intelligible account that should be the deciding factor in assessing competence. Thus the quality of the questioning of such a person becomes a paramount consideration.

CONFESSIONS

False confessions do nobody any good. Work on the psychology of confessions (Gudjonsson, 1992) suggests that the extent to which a person may be compliant during interrogation is sometimes (but by no means always) higher if the person is of below average intelligence. Gudjonsson (1989) found that people who in real life criminal proceedings had made confessions which were subsequently retracted had high levels of compliance on his questionnaire. This body of research suggested that there may be a relationship (though complex) between below average intelligence and the extent to which people sometimes come to accept the messages communicated to them by questioning.

It has also been found (Singh and Gudjonsson, 1984; Gudjonsson, 1991) that individuals' opinions of their own competence and intelligence are related to their suggestibility. Thus, if some people with communicative disability have a low opinion of their own competence (or if this is communicated to them) they may be more influenced by inappropriate, suggestive questioning. Similarly, Gudjonsson and Lister (1984) found that people who perceived themselves as lacking competence and control during the interview, and who judged the interviewer as being strong and powerful, showed more interrogative suggestibility. Thus to avoid false confessions interviewers should (i) strive to reduce the power/control difference that vulnerable interviewees may perceive between them and the interviewer, and/or (ii) try to avoid appearing to know what happened.

HAZARDS TO AVOID

Few people have conducted studies directly concerned with the interviewing of people with learning disability in legal contexts. One of these, Bryan Tully (see Cahill et al., 1988), has provided a list of hazards to avoid in such interviews including:

1. the witness acquiescing to leading questions which contain a suggestion as to the answer being sought

2. undue pressure leading the witness to confabulate (i.e. fill in parts of the event which were not witnessed)

3. repeated questioning on a particular point causing witnesses to guess or to deviate from their initial response (which repeated questioning leads them to assume was not the 'right' answer)

4. the interviewer prematurely 'upgrading' ambiguous or poorly expressed use of language by the witness

5. the interviewer offering compromise descriptions to a witness having difficulty in finding his/her own words, e.g. 'If the jacket wasn't dark or light, would you say it was a sort of tan colour?'

6. the interviewer offering limited alternatives to the witness, e.g. 'Did the men carry knives or clubs?'

7. the witness giving a string of 'don't knows' and then being offered a 'gift' guess so as not to leave the interviewer with nothing

8. ignoring a belated fragment of information from the witness which fails to fit with the interviewer's assumption of what happened

9. the interviewer misunderstanding what the witness means

10. the interviewer failing to check, using appropriate means, that he or she has understood the witness.

'YES–NO' QUESTIONS

As noted in the previous chapter on the interviewing of children, much recent experimental research has found that children are more likely to reply 'yes' to questions which only allow 'yes' or 'no' answers. Therefore, many guidelines for the interviewers of child witnesses (e.g. the 1992 Memorandum of Good Practice) recommend using such questions only as a last resort. Sigelman et al. (1981) posed the crucial question of 'If there is reason to avoid yes–no questions ... how then *can* one obtain valid answers from mentally retarded persons?' (p. 348). The aim of their 1981 study was to evaluate 'either-or questions as an alternative to yes–no questions in interviewing mentally retarded persons' (p. 348). They asked both children and adults with low IQ scores questions about their daily lives (the answers to which could be checked for accuracy). They compared the accuracy of the answers to yes–no questions with those to either-or questions. Sometimes questions were asked which if both were answered 'yes' would indicate inconsistency in the accuracy of responding (e.g. 'Are you usually happy?'; followed later by 'Are you usually sad?').

Sigelman et al. found that consistency of response was higher for the oppositely worded either-or questions (e.g. 'Are you usually happy or sad?' followed later by 'Are you usually sad or happy?') than for opposing yes–no questions (as explained at the end of the previous paragraph). They found that an average of 43.9 per cent of the respondents contradicted themselves by responding 'yes' to both of the oppositely worded yes–no questions. In comparison only 13 per cent of the adult respondents contradicted themselves by twice choosing the second alternative in response to oppositely worded either-or questions and only 2 per cent did so by choosing twice the first option. When the respondents' answers were checked for accuracy, if the correct answer to a 'yes–no' question was 'no', such responses occurred much less often than (i) correct 'yes' answers to 'yes–no' questions, and (ii) the correct answers to 'either–or' questions.

Sigelman et al. also examined the extra usefulness of replacing verbal either-or questions with pictorial either-or questions. They found that more interviewees answered the pictorial questions (89 per cent) than the verbal questions (72 per cent), that such answers were more consistent with each other than those to verbal questions, and that such answers were correct slightly more often. In particular, 'the picture questions yielded no sign of response bias' (p. 355).

Sigelman et al. concluded by pointing out that 'The present study is limited by small samples and by the restriction of test questions to a few, highly subjective topic areas ... conclusion ... need to be replicated ... the use of pictures in interviewing mentally retarded persons warrants further evaluation' (p. 355).

Much more recently Geoffrey Fisher (1990), when reporting on his considerable experience of interviewing children with learning disability, pointed out that the preliminary findings in the early 1980s by Sigelman and colleagues sat well with his experience. Also he recommended that 'interviewing retarded children follows essentially the same format as that for children with normal intelligence' (p. 98).

INTERVIEWING TECHNIQUES

In 1986 Dent conducted a study on the usefulness of some interviewing techniques for children with learning disability. She noted that few prior studies existed on this topic, and she pointed out that:

> Since children of normal intelligence have been found to be vulnerable to suggestion and other influences, it was considered important to discover whether recall from mentally handicapped children would be even more adversely affected. Research in the field of memory in the mentally handicapped (Glidden and Mar, 1978) has produced results indicating that there is a problem with retrieval of items from a memory store, since this was only found to be efficient when external cues were provided. Loftus (1975) has shown that the particular wording of questions can affect the later recall of an incident from subjects of normal intelligence. If mentally handicapped persons are more dependent on external cues, greater care must be taken not to influence their recall by careless interviewing techniques. (Dent, 1986, p. 13)

Dent noted that 'The problem is that of a cleft stick. On the one hand mentally handicapped persons are in need of prompts to access their memory, on the other hand their recall may be adversely influenced by the nature of the prompts used' (p. 14).

She examined the effects on children with learning disability (mean IQ = 62) of (i) free recall, (ii) general questions, and (iii) specific questions about a staged incident at their special school. The general questions were of the form 'What did the man look like?', and the specific questions of the form 'What colour was the man's hair?' Dent found that those children asked specific questions produced the most information, followed by those asked general questions, with those asked for free recall producing the least information. However, information produced in response to specific questions was the least accurate with more than 30 per cent of it being incorrect. The information provided in free recall was more accurate (around 20 per cent of it being incorrect), and that produced in response to general questions was the most accurate (with only 10 per cent of it being inaccurate). Dent argued that her findings lead to the recommendation that 'General, open-ended questions would appear to be optimal for use with mildly mentally handicapped children' (p. 17).

Perlman et al. (1994) also found, like Dent (1986), that 'short-answer questions' (i.e. similar to Dent's 'specific questions'), even non-leading ones, occasioned less correct responding from developmentally handicapped (DH) adults 'within the mild to borderline range of intellectual impairment' (p. 174). Their study looked at the effects of different question formats on adults' reports of an observed film. They found that:

> In general, on the less structured recall tasks (free recall and very general questions), control participants on average provided more than twice the number

of correct pieces of information provided by DH participants. However, the two groups did not differ significantly in the amount of incorrect information provided, and irrelevant information was rarely mentioned by either group. The two groups also showed little difference in terms of the percentage of correct information reported. For both groups, over 80 per cent of the information recalled using these unstructured formats was correct. This result suggests that although DH individuals do not provide as much information as control participants on unstructured recall tasks, the information provided by both groups tends to be quite accurate. (Perlman et al., 1984, p. 184)

Perlman et al. also examined the effects of short-answer leading questions (both those leading towards the correct answer, and those leading towards an incorrect answer). These only had a deleterious effect on the DH adults when they led the respondent towards an incorrect answer. However, when this question format led the respondents towards the correct answer no difference in performance was found between the DH group and the control group. Perlman et al. concluded that:

> Pragmatically, the study suggests some of the lines of questioning that may be used to obtain accurate information from the DH, such as free recall combined with specific questions, and some types of questions that should be avoided, such as short-answer questions (especially misleading ones) and leading statement questions. (Perlman et al., 1994)

They also noted that their DH participants seemed to have a 'desire to conform to the perceived wishes of an authority figure' (p. 185), that is the questioner. They seemed more willing than the control group to go along with the (misleading) suggestions included in some of the questions, even though their behaviour indicated to Perlman et al. that they realised something was wrong with such questions.

SUGGESTIBILITY

Dent (1986) raised the question of suggestibility in children who have learning disability. The very extensive review by Ceci and Bruck (1993) on the suggestibility of child witnesses says little on this particular topic (as does Doris, 1991), because so little is known. Gudjonsson's (1992) seminal overview of the role of suggestibility in adults, and Clare and Gudjonsson's (1994) paper on the implications for police questioning of the interrogative suggestibility and acquiescence of adults with learning disability, clearly indicate that such factors are very relevant to testimony. Gudjonsson (1992) has developed reliable methods of quantifying these factors in adults, but we should note Baxter's (1990) point that robust individual differences between children in suggestibility may not exist. Suggestibility is likely to be the result of factors relating to the interviewee, the questioning, environment, and the interviewer's behaviour.

ADVICE TO WITNESSES

Research by Saywitz, Moan and Lamphear (1991) has found that seven-year-old children's resistance to (mis)leading questions can be enhanced by telling them about the acquiescence effects of leading/misleading questions, that some questions may be tricky ones and others too difficult for the witness, that saying 'I don't know' is permissible, and why these strategies should aid their remembering. Other researchers have also found that appropriate warnings (e.g. telling the witness that some questions may inadvertently suggest the required answer or may be about matters the witness cannot recall) reduce the misleading effects some questions can have, especially for those who usually are more likely to acquiesce to leading questions. Therefore, this might be beneficial to witnesses with communicative disability.

THE 'COGNITIVE INTERVIEW'

One aspect of interviewer behaviour that has been found to increase the amount that people who were mentally retarded (Brown and Geiselman, 1990) could remember of an event is the use of the 'cognitive interview' (see chapter 3.4 by Köhnken for a description). Use of this interviewing procedure led to 32 per cent more correct information being recalled. However, the number of confabulations also increased with the use of this technique and so further research is necessary on refining it for use with witnesses who have learning disability.

RECENT LEGISLATION

In December 1992 Endicott's Technical Report to the Canadian Department of Justice was published. This report was concerned with the impact of Bill C-15 on persons with communication disabilities. His study 'addresses the amendments enacted in January, 1988 by Bill C-15 to the Criminal Code of Canada and the Canada Evidence Act'. The innovations brought in by this legislation included the possible use of videotaped interviews with witnesses and provision for witnesses (including adults with communication disabilities) to testify live but out of sight of the accused. In addition, it removed the requirement that witnesses (including adults) must first demonstrate that they are capable of being sworn or making a solemn affirmation. Endicott (1992) noted that 'This has opened the door to persons with communication disabilities, and resulted in a significant number of cases being prosecuted that would not have gone to court in the past because the key witnesses could not or would not have been permitted to testify' (p. iv).

Endicott pointed out that the topic of communication disability is not well understood by society:

> In the guise of ensuring the protection of persons with handicaps, but frequently more for the sake of the convenience and security of other persons, the law has traditionally concentrated on ways to establish formally the things that a person with a disability *cannot* do. All too often a person's perceived inability to do *some* things is translated by legal processes into a finding of inability to do *anything*. The law has not demonstrated much capacity to find ways in which the person's special needs can be accommodated so that he or she can participate in ordinary human activities, including the activity of doing justice in society.
>
> Bill C-15 was in part a recognition by Parliament that, when a citizen has special communication needs, the law's first response should no longer be to impose special restrictions and exclusions, but to seek to understand just what those special needs are and how they can be accommodated. (Endicott, 1992, p. 5)

The study conducted by Endicott included interviews 'with twenty well-informed experts from different parts of Canada, including judges, lawyers, police, and victim/witness support workers. They were selected because they were known to have particular skills in ensuring that complainants with communication disabilities were able to participate appropriately in the cases in which they were involved' (p. 111). He reported that these people emphasised how much we still have to learn about enabling such witnesses to give evidence, including how lawyers, police, etc. can make themselves understood by people with communication disabilities.

Endicott noted that 'The essential barriers and gaps in accommodating the special needs of witnesses with communication disabilities are a function of the lack of adequate training of sufficient numbers of personnel for such highly specialised work' (p. 55), and that 'In particular, if someone usually doesn't say anything without being prompted and being asked leading questions, then that person as a victim/complainant will not make a good witness unless someone has some skills in getting her to articulate experiences without specific prompts' (p. 59). Clearly, what is required is more research on the skills needed by those who interview people with communication disabilities.

THE NEED FOR MORE RESEARCH

Fisher (1990) suggested that the interviewing of child witnesses who have a learning disability should follow the same format as for other children. For these latter children I support (Bull, 1992, 1994b) the phased approach as outlined in the 1992 Memorandum of Good Practice. However, as Westcott (1992) has pointed out, in the Memorandum the real problems facing children with disabilities are not acknowledged. The reason is that so little has been published (let alone evaluated) on this topic. Sadly, psychological research (though it presently can give interviewers useful guidance on what *not* to do) has, at present, little to say on what special techniques will help, in a reliable and valid way, those who interview people who have communicative disability.

In 1993 the UK National Society for the Prevention of Cruelty to Children (NSPCC) published a booklet by Marchant and Page on the topic of child protection work with children with multiple disabilities. These authors are among the most experienced interviewers of such children. They pointed out that 'In our experience with multiply disabled children the principles involved in assessing indicators of abuse did not differ from that in use in child protection work, although their application was sometimes adapted to the needs of the children' (p. 7). They noted that among such children spontaneous disclosures of abuse are likely to be rare, and even when such a child tries to tell adults they may not be able to understand the child.

Marchant and Page give advice, based on their experience of tailoring interviews to the needs of child witnesses with communicative disability. Some of their interviews were conducted with the possibility of subsequent criminal and/or disciplinary proceedings. They provide a useful commentary on the extent to which the guidance provided in the 1992 Memorandum of Good Practice (especially its phased approach) is of use when interviewing child witnesses with communicative disability. By and large Marchant and Page seem to agree with the phased approach. However, they correctly point out that in the free narrative phase few children with communicative disability are likely to provide much information. Similarly, they note that open-ended questions may prove to be of little use in many such cases, and that the proportion of closed questions may need to rise in line with the severity of a child's communicative disability. Furthermore, the use of communication props (including dolls) may need to be more prevalent and more substantial with children with communicative disability (see Bull, 1994a), as should the avoidance of multiple questions within a single utterance of the interviewer. Marchant and Page also made the interesting suggestion that those children who, because of their communicative disability, are used to being asked 'yes–no' questions in their daily lives may be *less* likely to suffer from biasing effects of such questions than are other children. However, the research study by Sigelman et al. (1981) seems not to support this contention. (Marchant and Page do not cite Sigelman's study.)

Proper planning and extensive preparation was highlighted by Marchant and Page as being very important for such interviews. They provided (e.g. on pages 28 and 29) useful guidelines based on their experience of how to conduct these interviews, guidance which does seem to have helped these special children to communicate what had happened to them, and which has some similarity with that provided in the Memorandum of Good Practice. Sensible as these guidelines are, they do not preclude the need for more controlled research and evaluation on this topic.

CONCLUSION

Perlman et al. (1994) noted that 'Historically, the developmentally handicapped (DH), like young children, have been regarded as unreliable witnesses because it is believed that their memory systems are inherently defective' (p. 171). They noted that:

> The urgent need for research into the veracity of such perceptions about the witness capacity of the DH cannot be underestimated, given that this population is grossly over-represented in reported cases of sexual abuse. Perhaps the most important factor affecting vulnerability of the DH to abuse is that perpetrators perceive them to be less able to report the abuse ... It is important to determine whether and under what circumstances DH individuals can be considered reliable witnesses. (Perlman et al., 1994, p. 172)

Society has a right to expect psychologists and professionals from legal contexts to work together on this urgent topic. Difficult research is the most challenging, yet the most rewarding.

REFERENCES

Baxter, J. (1990). The suggestibility of child witnesses: a review. *Applied Cognitive Psychology*, **4**, 393–407.

Brown, C. and Geiselman, R. (1990). Eye-witness testimony of mentally retarded: effect of the cognitive interview. *Journal of Police and Criminal Psychology*, **6**, 14–22.

Bull, R. (1992). Obtaining evidence expertly: the reliability of interviews with child witnesses. *Expert Evidence*, **1**, 512.

Bull, R. (1994a). Innovative techniques for the questioning of child witnesses especially those who are young and those with learning disability. In M. Zaragoza (Ed.), *Memory and Suggestibility in Child Witnesses*. New York: Hemisphere.

Bull, R. (1994b). Good practice for video recorded interviews with child witnesses for use in criminal proceedings. In G. Davies, S. Lloyd-Bostock, M. McMurran and C. Wilson (Eds), *Law and Psychology*. Amsterdam: de Gruyter.

Bull, R. and Cullen, C. (1992). Witnesses who may have mental handicaps. Document prepared for The Crown Office, Edinburgh.

Bull, R. and Cullen, C. (1993). Interviewing the mentally handicapped. *Policing*, **9**, 88–100.

Cahill, D., Grebler, G., Baker, A. and Tully, B. (1988). Vulnerable testimony: police interviewing of mentally handicapped and mentally disordered people in connection with serious crime. Private paper.

Ceci, S. and Bruck, M. (1993). The suggestibility of the child witness: a historical review and synthesis. *Psychological Bulletin*, **113**, 403–439.

Clare, I. and Gudjonsson, G. (1994). Interrogative suggestibility, confabulations, and acquiescence in people with mild learning disabilities (mental handicap): implications for reliability during police interrogations. *British Journal of Clinical Psychology*, **32**, 295–301.

Coles, W. (1990). Sexual abuse of persons with disabilities: a law enforcement perspective. *Developmental Disabilities Bulletin*, **18**, 35–43.

Dent, H. (1986). An experimental study of the effectiveness of different techniques of questioning mentally handicapped child witnesses. *British Journal of Clinical Psychology*, **25**, 13–17.

Dent, H. and Flin, R. (1992). *Children as Witnesses*. Chichester: Wiley.

Doris, J. (1991). *The Suggestibility of Children's Recollections: Implications for Eye-witness Testimony*. Washington, DC: American Psychological Association.

Endicott, O. (1992). *Technical Report: The Impact of Bill C-15 on Persons with Communication Disabilities*. Ottawa: Research and Development Directorate, Department of Justice.

Fisher, G. (1990). Interviewing mentally retarded children. In P. Barker (Ed.), *Clinical Interviews with Children and Adolescents*. New York: Norton.

Flin, R., Bull, R., Boon, J. and Knox, A. (1993). Child witnesses in Scottish criminal trials. *International Review of Victimology*, **2**, 309–29.

Glidden, L. and Mar, H. (1978). Availability and accessibility of information in the semantic memory of retarded and non-retarded adolescents. *Journal of Experimental Child Psychology*, **25**, 33–40.

Gudjonsson, G. (1989). Compliance in an interrogative situation: a new scale. *Personality and Individual Differences*, **10**, 535–40.

Gudjonsson, G. (1991). Suggestibility and compliance among alleged false confessors and resisters in criminal trials. *Medicine, Science, and the Law*, **31**, 147–51.

Gudjonsson, G. (1992). *The Psychology of Interrogations, Confessions and Testimony*. Chichester: John Wiley.

Gudjonsson, G. and Lister, S. (1984). Interrogative suggestibility and its relationship with self esteem and self control. *Journal of the Forensic Science Society*, **24**, 99–110.

Gudjonsson, G., Clare, I., Rutter, S. and Pearce, J. (1993). Persons at risk during interviews in police custody: the identification of vulnerabilities. *Research Study Number 12 for The Royal Commission On Criminal Justice*. London: HMSO.

Irish Law Reform Commission (1990). *Report on Child Sexual Abuse*. Dublin: Law Reform Commission.

Irving, B. and McKenzie, I. (1993). A brief review of relevant police training. In *Research Study Number 21 for The Royal Commission On Criminal Justice*. London: HMSO.

Loftus, E. (1975). Leading questions and the eye witness report. *Cognitive Psychology*, **7**, 560–72.

Marchant, R. and Page, M. (1993). *Bridging the Gap: Child Protection Work with Children with Multiple Disabilities*. London: NSPCC.

Memorandum of Good Practice for Video Recorded Interviews with Child Witnesses for Criminal Proceedings (1992). London: HMSO.

Perlman, N., Ericson, K., Esses, V. and Isaacs, B. (1994). The developmentally handicapped witness: competency as a function of question format. *Law and Human Behaviour*, **18**, 171–87.

Saywitz, K., Moan, S. and Lamphear, V. (1991). The effect of preparation on children's resistance to misleading questions. Paper presented at the Annual Conference of the American Psychological Association on Child Development, San Francisco.

Sigelman, C., Budd, E., Spanhel, C. and Sehoenrock, C. (1981). When in doubt say yes: acquiescence in interviews with mentally retarded persons. *Mental Retardation*, **19**, 53–8.

Singh, K. and Gudjonsson, G. (1984). Interrogative suggestibility, delayed memory and self concept. *Personality and Individual Differences,* **5**, 203–09.

Spencer, J. and Flin, R. (1993). *The Evidence of Children.* London: Blackstone.

Turk, V. and Brown, H. (1992). Sexual abuse and adults with learning disabilities. *Mental Handicap,* **20**, 56–8.

Westcott, H. (1991). *Institutional Abuse of Children—From Research to Policy: A Review.* London: NSPCC.

Westcott, H. (1992). The disabled child witness. Paper presented at the NATO Advanced Studies Institute on The Child Witness in Context, Italy.

Chapter 3.7

Earwitness and Evidence Obtained by Other Senses

A. Daniel Yarmey
University of Guelph

The following fictional anecdote introduces most of the significant issues to be reviewed in this chapter:

> A 24-year-old white single woman, living alone, had just gone to bed. The only light in the otherwise dark bedroom was a faint amount of illumination from the outside hallway. Not quite asleep the woman heard footsteps outside her door. She then saw the silhouette of a person walking up to her bedside. A man jumped on to the bed and put his hand over her mouth. Pressing the edge of a knife against her throat he said, 'Don't scream or you'll get hurt. I have a knife.' The man continued to talk to her while she was forced to kiss him and perform various sex acts. The man then dressed, took some money from her purse and left.
>
> Approximately 30 minutes later the victim described the perpetrator to the police as: six feet tall; 190 lb; muscular build; moustache but no beard; short, curly hair; rough, calloused hands; about 25 years old. His clothing consisted of jeans with a large belt, long-sleeved shirt, and high cut cowboy boots. She remembered the smell of whisky and cigarettes on his breath. She told the police that it was too dark to see his face or any distinguishing marks, but she noticed that he had a peculiar shuffle in his walk. His voice was described as quiet, deep, nasal, with a slow rate of speech, and a slight Spanish accent. She claimed that she would positively remember his voice until the day she died because 'it was burned into her memory forever'. One week later, the victim was taken to the police station and given a six-person tape-recorded voice lineup. Within seconds of hearing the fourth voice on the tape, she identified with absolute certainty the man she believed sexually assaulted and robbed her.

How valid is this type of identification evidence? The victim's description in this fictional case did not include detailed visual information of the perpetrator's face, but did contain other types of information involving odour, touch, gait, body build characteristics, and especially voice identification

Handbook of Psychology in Legal Contexts
Edited by R. Bull and D. Carson. © 1995 John Wiley & Sons Ltd

evidence. Obscene phone calls, ransom demands, hooded robberies, sexual assaults and muggings done in darkness often yield identification evidence that leads to arrests and court convictions. Should the trier of fact trust speaker descriptions and other identification evidence made in poor observation conditions? Are speaker identifications similar to visual identifications, and are they susceptible to error through faulty police procedures? The answers to these questions is that some witnesses can be relatively accurate in both their descriptions and identifications, and some police procedures in gathering voice and other sensory evidence can bias witnesses testimony. Similar to eye-witness memory, the reliability of evidence for voice identification and other sensory information depends upon several personal, situational, and procedural factors. Sometimes this evidence is reliable, sometimes it is not.

This chapter will focus mainly on voice identification evidence but some attention will be given to memory for gait, odour and touch. The review of voice identification evidence is restricted to experimental investigations of voice recognition by nonexpert listeners under controlled laboratory conditions and less controlled field situations (see also, Bull and Clifford, 1984; Clifford, 1983; Deffenbacher et al., 1989; Hammersley and Read, 1993). The literature on voice recognition by machine, commonly called spectrographic voice identification or 'voiceprint' analysis (Bull, 1981), and analyses of prepared speech samples by expert linguists or phoneticians (Hollien, 1990), will not be reviewed.

THE LINDBERGH KIDNAPPING

Although voice identification evidence has been accepted by English courts since 1660 in the case of William Hulet (Hollien, Bennett and Gelfer, 1983), the most celebrated case involving voice identification evidence was the baby Lindbergh kidnapping case. Col. Lindbergh's positive identification of the suspect's voice, almost three years after hearing it, contributed to the guilty verdict in *United States v. Hauptmann* ([1935] Atlantic Report, 180, 809–829). Partly because of the controversy Lindbergh's identification aroused, and the general issue of the validity of voice recognition, McGehee (1937) investigated the accuracy of voice identification for unfamiliar voices after varying intervals of time. Accuracy of speaker identification declined from 83 per cent correct performance after one and two-day retention intervals to 13 per cent at five months. McGehee (1937) also found that recognition accuracy declined for any single voice if several voices were heard initially, and men generally were superior to women in speaker recognition. Although these early findings are historically important, their validity is questionable because of the faulty research design employed (Thompson, 1985). However, as we will see, contemporary research is consistent with some of McGehee's early work. It also must be emphasised that reporting absolute percentage scores, as indicated above, should not be interpreted as ultimate 'truths'. Variations in absolute percentage values between studies are common in psychology. What is most critical are whether or not the differences among experimental conditions and among similar research investigations are consistant and meaningful.

FAMILIAR VOICES

One of the myths still held by many laypersons and officials in the criminal justice system is the belief that eye-witness memory, including voice recognition, is merely common knowledge (Yarmey, 1994; Yarmey and Jones, 1983). Because of everyday experiences with family members, friends, and fellow workers the belief exists that memory for speakers' voices is valid. Just how good memory for familiar voices actually is has not been extensively examined. Anecdotal evidence, however, is available as seen in the following example: 'While driving to work in San Francisco, Doug Friday, 33, heard a women tell a radio phone-in audience that she had taken a lover because her husband neglected her. Recognising the voice of the speaker as his wife, Joanna, Doug filed for divorce' (*Toronto Star*, 15 August 1982). Recognition of familiar voices often depends upon our expectations, the situational context, and the closed set of familiar people likely to be encountered in particular settings. False positive identifications can occur, however, when a familiar person is expected, such as, expecting a telephone call from a friend but someone else calls.

Experimental investigations on recognition memory for familiar voices has received minimal attention. Bartholomeus (1973) used a five-month familiarisation period and investigated the ability of four-year old and five-year-old children and their teachers to say aloud the names of fellow classmates and teachers after hearing their two-sentence-long tape-recorded speech samples; 56 per cent of the children and 68 percent of the adults were accurate. Required to match each of the familiar voices with photographs of the speakers, 58 per cent of the children and 81 per cent of the adults were accurate. As might be expected, when messages were distorted by playing the voice tapes backwards, accuracy in naming the speakers declined to 41 per cent for children and 63 per cent for the adults. These results show that familiar voices are recognised better than chance expectations, but are not perfectly identified even for adults. Furthermore, speaker identification is not merely a matter of identifying acoustic properties of a voice, the meaningfulness or context of statements facilitates voice identification. Bartholomeus (1973) also found that some familiar speakers were easily identified in any condition, and others were consistently misidentified. Also, some children were as accurate as were the adults at voice identification.

Ladefoged (1981) tested the accuracy of ten highly skilled, experienced, phoneticians in identifying the voices of very familiar fellow laboratory workers. Recordings were made of 11 of the 25 people actively involved in the group. The only two black members of the laboratory group were not included in the test. Instead, a black male, who was relatively unfamiliar to most members of the group, was the twelfth target stimulus. Nine of the ten participants correctly identified all 11 members of the laboratory. Three of the ten listeners knew the black speaker and correctly identified him. Two of the remaining listeners stated they could not recognise this speaker. However, five of the expert phoneticians falsely identified the black speaker as one of the two blacks who worked in the Phonetics lab.

Goldstein and Chance (1985) tested the ability of 20 fraternity members to recognise the voices of nine very familiar 'brothers' (including room-mates and other fellow residents of the fraternity) in contrast to 11 other unfamiliar men. The participants' task was to recognise whether or not the speakers belonged to the fraternity. Tape recordings were made of speakers uttering seven short messages in sequence, each being separated by 5–8 seconds of silence. Only 60 per cent of the listeners were able to recognise all nine familiar voices by the end of the seventh and final speech sample. Listeners' responses to the 11 foil (unfamiliar) voices were relatively poor. Only one listener correctly identified 9 of the 11 foils by the end of the test as non-members of the fraternity. After hearing seven voice samples from each speaker, six of the eleven foils still could not be distinguished from members of the fraternity.

Voice recognitions for familiar voices chosen from a relatively large set of known speakers are not automatic and are prone to false identifications. Although it may be meaningless for the police to conduct a photo lineup for familiar persons, the above results suggest that it may be worthwhile to conduct a voice lineup for familiar speakers. Most voice identification issues of concern to the court, of course, are for voices of strangers. Over a decade ago, this writer stated that long-term speaker identification for unfamiliar voices must be treated with the utmost caution (Saslove and Yarmey, 1980). As the discussion below will show, more recent evidence reinforces this conclusion.

ACQUIRING VOICE INFORMATION

The better the opportunity to observe a perpetrator the greater the probability of accuracy of identification (*Neil v. Biggers*, [1972] 409 U.S. 188).Witnesses who are prepared to listen to a suspect's voice and intentionally attempt to remember voice characteristics are superior in identification performance to witnesses not prepared to attend to and remember the speaker's voice (Saslove and Yarmey, 1980). Although voice recognition is possible even with speech samples as short as two seconds (Bull and Clifford, 1984), an extended opportunity to listen to the voice of a perpetrator facilitates identification (Goldstein and Chance, 1985; Hammersley and Read, 1985). Yarmey and Matthys (1992) found that accuracy of identification (hits) in a suspect-present lineup improved from the two shortest voice samples of 18 seconds' and 36 seconds' duration to longer voice samples of two minutes' and six minutes' duration. However, the false alarm rate also reliably increased with longer durations. The false alarm rates were consistently high with suspect-absent lineups. These results were confirmed in a field study of telephone voice identification (Yarmey, 1991a). It is possible that the increase in false alarms with longer voice samples may have been the result of the operation of an availability heuristic. That is, witnesses may have felt that given the long period of time they listened to a speaker's voice, they should know the voice and, as a consequence, were more willing to make an identification response.

Another factor which may be important in the acquisition of voice information is whether or not the suspect's voice is heard repeatedly. Goldstein and Chance (1985) found that speaker identification after a two-week retention interval was superior for a target's voice heard for 20 seconds over each of three consecutive days, in contrast to hearing the whole voice-sample for 60 seconds in one session. These results were partially supported by Yarmey and Matthys (1992). Listeners were superior in identification with two distributed exposures to a suspect's voice separated by a five-minute interval than when given the voice in one massed trial. However, hearing the suspect's voice for three distributed trials did not improve performance over that found in hearing the whole voice sample.

Errors in acquisition are especially likely to occur when the event is complex and violent in nature. The more voices originally heard, the poorer the recognition scores (Goldstein and Chance, 1985; Legge, Grosmann and Pieper, 1984). Violence can create high levels of stress in a witness which may distract attention and encoding of speaker characteristics. Unfortunately, very little systematic research has been conducted on the influence of violence on voice recognition. Nevertheless, police officers in Alberta, Canada, drawing from their experiences in several real-world crimes, feel confident that speaker identification is highly reliable in violent crimes of rape and armed robbery (Mayor, 1985). Relying upon a flashbulb theory of memory explanation (Brown and Kulik, 1977), Mayor claims that witnesses' memory for voice characteristics in these type of crimes are 'burned' into the memory bank. Clearly, it may be beyond the capabilities of experimental psychologists using the kind of violence utilised in research to simulate real-world traumatic conditions (Kunzel, 1990). Acknowledging this limitation, Yarmey and Pauley (1993) examined the effects of weapon focus and abusive language on speaker identification in a simulated violent crime.

Participants viewed a 30-second video taped recording of a masked perpetrator holding either a gun or a rolled up newspaper and, speaking in an abusive or polite manner, order a woman to hand over her wallet and take off her clothes. One day later subjects were given two voice lineups, a suspect-present lineup and a suspect-absent lineup. No significant differences were found in either hits or false identifications in the suspect-present lineup. However, participants in the weapon condition, in contrast to the newspaper condition, made significantly more false negative responses (misses) (41 versus 21 per cent, respectively). The only significant difference in the suspect-absent lineup pertained to the analysis of correct rejection scores. Subjects who observed the newspaper-carrying-polite-perpetrator were reliably more accurate in rejecting the suspect-absent lineup (50 per cent correct) than subjects who observed the newspaper-carrying-abusive-perpetrator (20 per cent), the weapon-carrying-abusive-perpetrator (29 per cent), or the weapon-carrying-polite-perpetrator (11 per cent). It appears that violent language and weapon focus does not influence accuracy of performance or false identifications in voice lineups, but does allow guilty suspects more easily to escape detection.

The effects of voice disguise also influence earwitness memory (Reich and Duke, 1979). Even altering the tone of the perpetrator's voice between the original observational situation (angry, hostile voice) and the identification test (normal conversational tone) significantly decreases accuracy of performance (Saslove and Yarmey, 1980; Clifford and Denot, 1982). Similarly, hearing a perpetrator whispering, even for a relatively long period of time (eight minutes), and then tested two days later with a lineup of speakers using normal conversational tones substantially lowers performance (Orchard, 1993). Voice disguise, such as a whisper, probably reduces identification accuracy because it allows the most salient vocal characteristics to be concealed (Clifford, 1983).

In addition to event factors, witness factors such as age, sex, and race also influence speaker identification. Recognition accuracy has been found to increase from age 6 to age 10, where it approaches adult accuracy rates. However, for some reason, performance declined between the ages of 10 and 14 (Mann, Diamond and Carey, 1979). In a naturalistic field study involving a trip to the dentist, children actively conversed with the target speaker for five minutes and were tested 24- to 48-hours later (Peters, 1987). No significant differences in voice recognition accuracy were found among children ranging between three years of age and eight years of age. Because performance generally was so poor, Peters concluded that if these results are replicated 'accepting earwitness testimony (under similar circumstances) of young children should be seriously questioned' (p. 134).

Age-related differences in voice-recognition accuracy have also been found between young and older adults with individuals between the ages of 21 and 40 being superior to those over 40 years of age (Bull and Clifford, 1984). Earwitness identification has not been examined in elderly populations. Hearing loss is common with advanced age, especially for high frequency sounds. The perception of speech is adversely affected with ageing especially when listening occurs with background noise, or with distortions caused from poor acoustics or an amplification system (Yarmey, 1995). It would be expected that age declines would be found in healthy individuals on some speaker identification tasks such as accuracy measures, but not confidence–accuracy correlations (Adams-Price, 1988).

McGehee (1937) found that men were superior to women in identifying female speakers, but no sex differences were found for the identification of males speakers. More recently, Thompson (1985) failed to find any significant differences between men and women in speaker identification from a voice lineup after a one-week retention interval. Although male voices were more easily identified than female voices, a wide range in identifiability for voices of both sexes was found.

The effect of accents (or race) on voice identification has received only limited attention by researchers using forensically relevant research designs. Thompson (1987) found that monolingual English-speaking subjects were most likely to be accurate in identifying bilingual targets' voices when they spoke English, followed by speaking in English with a strong Spanish accent, and poorest when speaking in Spanish. These findings have been supported in four separate experiments by Goggin et al. (1991). The effects of accents or language familiarity do influence speaker identification.

RETAINING AND RETRIEVING VOICE INFORMATION

Research indicates little decrement in voice identification over a 24-hour period (Saslove and Yarmey, 1980); however, some studies show that retention intervals longer than 24-hours have a significant negative effect on identification (Clifford, Rathborn and Bull, 1981; Hammersley and Read, 1985). Delays of one, two and three weeks in testing produced decrements in identification performance to 50 per cent, 43 per cent and 9 per cent correct, respectively (Clifford, Rathborn and Bull, 1981). Yarmey and Matthys (1992) found that accuracy of identification of voices did not differ over a one-week interval; however, the false alarm rate increased over the interval. It should be noted that forgetting over time depends upon the extent of original learning; some voices because of their distinctiveness may be more easily learned and less effected by delay in testing.

WITNESS CONFIDENCE

Bull and Clifford (1984) report that their research in general has yielded significant within-subject relationships between witness confidence and earwitness accuracy, however, the sizes of these correlations were not stated. My own research which has focused on between-subject correlations of witness accuracy and witness confidence has yielded mixed results: no reliable correlation (Yarmey, 1986); a small but significant correlation of .26 (Saslove and Yarmey, 1980); a significant correlation of .36 with a target-absent lineup but no correlation with a target-present lineup (Yarmey, 1991a); a significant negative correlation of $-.24$ with a short 18-second voice-sample, no correlation with a 36-second voice-sample, a significant positive correlation of .18 for a two-minute voice sample, and a significant positive correlation of .17 for a six-minute voice sample (Yarmey and Matthys, 1992). These results suggest that across large numbers of witnesses (between-subjects) witness confidence is a weak but sometimes statistically significant predictor of earwitness performance. However, individual persons who are good at identifying a stranger's voice in one situation (within-subjects) may also be good in identifying a voice in another situation.

DESCRIBING SUSPECTS

Yarmey (1991b) found that listeners were consistent (reliable) over a one-week interval in their rated descriptions of pitch, expressive style, enunciation, inflection, and age for 'non-distinctive' voices. In contrast, rated descriptions for pace of speech, tempo variation, tremor, pauses, and nasality differed significantly over a one-week retention period. For highly distinctive voices, subjects reliably recalled all of the above features except pace of speech over a one-week interval.

How accurate are people in estimating a perpetrator's physical characteristics on the basis of hearing his or her voice alone? With the exception of estimations of sex of speaker (Lass, Hughes and Bower, 1976), estimations of age, height and weight have yielded wide inter-judge variations and should not be considered valid (e.g. Gunter and Manning, 1982; Kunzel, 1989; Yarmey, 1992). Also, claims that reliable judgements of speakers' personalities can be made from voice alone in forensic situations are confounded with stereotypes. Stereotypes about which voice best fits which type of criminal may be an extra-legal factor which can influence juror decision-making (Yarmey, 1993).

IDENTIFICATIONS FROM LINEUPS AND SHOWUPS

Memory, including memory for a perpetrator's voice, is a reconstruction rather than an exact copy of the original perceptual trace. The recommendations for constructions of 'fair' visual lineups also apply to voice lineups (Brigham, Ready and Spier, 1990). Furthermore, police procedures in the construction of voice lineups can be biased or suggestive (Yarmey, 1994). Speaker identifications from voice lineups are significantly inferior to person identifications from visual lineups (Yarmey, 1986).

The inherent dangers of suggestibility in visual lineups are well documented (e.g. Wells and Loftus, 1984; Yarmey, 1990). Similarly, the presentation of a single suspect (i.e. a show-up) is not recommended because of the high possibility of presumed suggestibility (Brooks, 1983; *Stovall v. Denno*, [1967] 388 U.S. 293, 302; Wagenaar and Veefkind, 1992). A recently completed field experiment (Yarmey, Yarmey and Yarmey, 1994) comparing identification accuracy from a six-person tape recorded voice lineup with that of a single-person voice showup, revealed that showups produced significantly more mistaken identifications of 'innocent suspects' than lineups (see also, Gonzalez, Ellsworth and Pembroke, 1993).

Finally, what impact does earwitness evidence have on jurors? Van Wallendael et al. (1992) in an experiment using undergraduate students as mock jurors found significantly more guilty verdicts when an earwitness testified than when only circumstantial evidence was presented. Delay in identification (same day, 7 days later, or 14 days later) had no effect on juror verdicts. Jurors were positively influenced by witness's confidence, and were influenced more by female witnesses than by males.

RECOGNITION BY GAIT

Cutting and Kozlowski (1977) demonstrated that viewers seeing only reflected lights mounted on body joints which are prominent during the act of walking recognised their friends solely on the basis of their gait. These perceptions were independent of familiarity cues such as clothing and hairstyle. Confidence and accuracy of recognition were positively correlated. Further studies by Cutting and his colleagues demonstrated that observers are able to recognise the sex of strangers by their walk at a rate significantly better than chance (Kozlowski and Cutting, 1977—63 per cent correct versus chance of 50 per cent; Barclay, Cutting and Kozlowski, 1978—67 per cent correct). Whether or not these findings would generalise to forensic situations involving eye-witness memory for strangers needs to be determined.

RECOGNITION BY TOUCH AND ODOUR

Individuals can use information derived from one sensory modality, such as touch, to make equivalence judgements about information from a second, such as sight (Jones, 1981). Unfortunately, these types of judgements have been investigated only with traditional laboratory procedures, and the results should not be generalised to forensic situations. There is no scientific basis at this time to state that a victim's estimation of a perpetrator's body build, height, weight, and so on, based on touch alone (during an assault) would be equivalent to, or even approximate, estimations of these characteristics by sight, or by voice.

The results of laboratory investigations of odour memory (Schab, 1991), also need to be tested in forensically relevant situations before their findings can be generalised. In brief, studies of odour memory indicate that recognition of a single ambient odour is highly susceptible to 'false alarms'. That is, presenting a similar but different odour at test from the one originally learned produces a high number of errors (Cann and Ross, 1989). In a study of 200 subjects with reportedly normal olfaction, naming of four very common odours (e.g. coffee) was correct on only 40–50 per cent of single-trial, free odour identifications (Sumner, 1962). Accuracy scores of 40–50 per cent in this type of test are a robust finding (Schab, 1991). Odours appear to be inherently confusable, difficult to name, and different subjects often generate different names for the same odourants (Engen, 1982).

SUMMARY

Psycho-legal researchers have done little or no forensically related research on recognition of strangers by their gait, touch, or odour. The generalisability of findings from traditional laboratory studies on these subject areas to legal decision-making is unwarranted at this time. In contrast, research on voice identification has yielded valid and consistent findings from American, British, Canadian, and German laboratories using different age groups of participants, research methodologies, and research designs. These results are based upon laboratory studies employing realistic videotaped crime scenarios as well as mock simulations of crimes and live-event methodology. Although this body of knowledge is still limited in scope, the results are meaningful and trustworthy, and can contribute to legal deliberations.

High levels of accuracy of voice identification are possible, especially under ideal conditions, that is, when the listener was paying high attention to a perpetrator's voice and expecting to remember it, when the listener was calm and heard a relatively long speech sample, and when the voice was highly distinctive. However, many crimes occur in poor observation conditions and witnesses' performance can be affected by a variety of disrupting factors. For example, voice identification is substantially disrupted by deliberate disguise and changes in voice qualities, foreign accents, lengthy retention periods, and complex situations involving several speakers. Even relatively long speech samples can increase the likelihood of false identifications. The way in which a suspect's voice is presented for identification also influences performance, for example, the use of one-person voice show-ups, or 'unfair' voice lineups. Even a familiar voice heard out of context may be mistakenly identified as a stranger's voice. Similarly, a briefly heard stranger's voice may be misidentified as familiar because of witness' expectations or situational cues. Finally, earwitness confidence is not a reliable predictor of identification accuracy of a briefly heard stranger's voice.

It is recommended that prosecutions based solely upon voice identification evidence not proceed under most circumstances. If voice identification evidence is used, it should be employed only with utmost caution, that is, when opportunities to listen were very good, the witness intentionally was prepared to remember the perpetrator's voice, and proper identification test procedures were followed.

REFERENCES

Adams-Price, C.E. (1988, October). Eye-witness memory and aging: accuracy and confidence in the identification of characters in crime scenes. Paper presented at the annual meeting of the Gerontological Society of America, San Francisco.

Barclay, C.D. Cutting, J.E. and Kozlowski, L.T. (1978). Temporal and spatial factors in gait perception that influence gender recognition. *Perception and Psychophysics*, **23**, 145–52.

Bartholomeus, B. (1973). Voice identification by nursery school children. *Canadian Journal of Psychology*, **27**, 464–72.

Brigham, J.C., Ready, D.J. and Spier, S.A. (1990). Standards for evaluating the fairness of photograph lineups. *Basic and Applied Social Psychology*, **11**, 149–63.

Brooks, N. (1983). Police guidelines: pretrial eyewitness identification procedures. Minister of Supply and Services Canada, Ottawa.

Brown, R. and Kulik, J. (1977). Flashbulb memories. *Cognition*, **5**, 73–99.

Bull, R. (1981). Voice identification by man and machine: a review of research. In S. Lloyd-Bostock (Ed.), *Psychology in Legal Contexts: Applications and Limitations*. London: Macmillan, pp. 28–42.

Bull, R. and Clifford, B.R. (1984). Earwitness voice recognition accuracy. In G.L. Wells and E.F. Loftus (Eds), *Eyewitness Testimony: Psychological Perspectives*. New York: Cambridge University Press, pp. 92–123.

Cann, A. and Ross, D.A. (1989). Olfactory stimuli as context cues in human memory. *American Journal of Psychology*, **102**, 91–102.

Clifford, B.R. (1983). Memory for voices: the feasibility and quality of earwitness evidence. In S.M.A. Lloyd-Bostock and B.R. Clifford (Eds), *Evaluating Witness Evidence*. Chichester: John Wiley, pp. 189–218.

Clifford, B.R. and Denot, H. (1982). Visual and verbal testimony and identification under conditions of stress. Unpublished manuscript, North East London Polytechnic, London, England.

Clifford, B.R. Rathborn, H. and Bull, R. (1981). The effects of delay on voice recognition accuracy. *Law and Human Behavior*, **5**, 201–8.

Cutting, J. and Kozlowski, L.T. (1977). Recognizing friends by their walk: gait perception without familiarity cues. *Bulletin of the Psychonomic Society*, **9**, 353–6.

Deffenbacher, K.A., Cross, J.F., Handkins, R.E., Chance, J.E., Goldstein, A.G., Hammersley, R. and Read, J.D. (1989). Relevance of voice identification research to criteria for evaluating reliability of an identification. *Journal of Psychology*, **123**, 109–19.

Engen, T. (1982). *The Perception of Odors*. New York: Academic Press.

Goggin, J.P., Thompson, C.P., Strube, G. and Simental, L.R. (1991). The role of language familiarity in voice identification. *Memory and Cognition*, **19**, 448–58.

Goldstein, A.G. and Chance, J.E. (1985, May). Voice recognition: the effects of faces, temporal distribution of 'practice,' and social distance. Paper presented at the Midwestern Psychology Association meeting. Chicago, Illinois.

Gonzalez, R., Ellsworth, P.C. and Pembroke, M. (1993). Response biases in lineups and showups. *Journal of Personality and Social Psychology*, **64**, 525–37.

Gunter, C. and Manning, W. (1982). Listener estimations of speaker height and weight in unfiltered and filtered conditions. *Journal of Phonetics*, **10**, 251–7.

Hammersley, R. and Read, J.D. (1985). The effect of participation in a conversation on recognition and identification of the speakers' voices. *Law and Human Behavior*, **9**, 71–81.

Hammersley, R. and Read, J.D. (1993). Voice identification by humans and computers. In S.L. Sporer, R.S. Malpass and G. Köhnken (Eds), *Suspect Identification: Psychological Knowledge, Problems and Perspectives*. Hillsdale, NJ: Lawrence Erlbaum.

Hollien, H.F. (1990). *The Acoustics of Crime: the New Science of Forensic Phonetics*. New York: Plenum.

Hollien, H., Bennett, G. and Gelfer, M.P. (1983). Criminal identification comparison: aural versus visual identifications resulting from a simulated crime. *Journal of Forensic Sciences*, **28**, 208–21.

Jones, B. (1981). The developmental significance of cross-modal matching. In R.D. Walk and H.L. Pick, Jr (Eds), *Intersensory Perception and Sensory Integration*. New York: Plenum, pp. 109–36.

Kozlowski, L.T. and Cutting, J.E. (1977). Recognizing the sex of walkers from a dynamic point-light display. *Perception and Psychophysics*, **21**, 575–80.

Kunzel, H.J. (1989). How well does average fundamental frequency correlate with speaker height and weight? *Phonetica*, **46**, 117–25.

Kunzel, H.J. (1990). Phonetische Untersuchungen zur Spechererkennung durch Linguistisch Naive Personen. Stuttgart: Franz Steiner Verlag.

Ladefoged, P. (1981, April). Expectation affects identification by listening. Paper presented at the 94th meeting of the Acoustical Society of America, New York.

Lass, N.J., Hughes, K.R. and Bowyer, M.D. (1976). Speaker sex identification from voiced, whispered and filtered isolated vowels. *Journal of the Acoustical Society of America*, **59**, 675–8.

Legge, G.E., Grosmann, C. and Pieper, C.M. (1984). Learning unfamiliar voices. *Journal of Experimental Psychology: Learning, Memory, and Cognition*, **10**, 298–303.

Mann, V., Diamond, R. and Carey, S. (1979). Development of voice recognition: parallels with face recognition. *Journal of Experimental Child Psychology*, **27**, 153–65.

Mayor, D. (1985). Subjective voice identification. *Royal Canadian Mounted Police Gazette*, **47**, 6–10.

McGehee, F. (1937). The reliability of the identification of the human voice. *Journal of General Psychology*, **17**, 249–71.

Orchard, T.L. (1993). Factors affecting voice identification accuracy. Unpublished Master's thesis, University of Guelph, Guelph, Ontario, Canada.

Peters, D.P. (1987). The impact of naturally occurring stress on children's memory. In S.J. Ceci, M.P. Toglia and D.F. Ross (Eds), *Children's Eyewitness Memory*. New York: Springer-Verlag, pp. 122–41.

Reich, A. and Duke, J. (1979). Effects of selected vocal disguises upon speaker identification by listening. *Journal of the Acoustical Society of America*, **66**, 1023–8.

Saslove, H. and Yarmey, A.D. (1980). Long-term auditory memory: speaker identification. *Journal of Applied Psychology*, **65**, 111–6.

Schab, F.R. (1991). Odor memory: taking stock. *Psychological Bulletin*, **109**, 242–51.

Sumner, D. (1962). On testing the sense of smell. *Lancet*, ii, 895–7.

Thompson, C.P. (1985). Voice identification: speaker identifiability and a correction of the record regarding sex effects. *Human Learning*, **4**, 19–27.

Thompson, C.P. (1987). A language effect in voice identification. *Applied Cognitive Psychology*, **1**, 121–31.

Van Wallendael, L.R., Surace, A., Brown, M. and Hall, D. (1992, November). 'Earwitness' voice recognition: accuracy and impact on jurors. Paper presented at the meetings of the Psychonomic Society, St. Louis, Missouri.

Wagenaar, W.A. and Veefkind, N. (1992). Comparison of one-person and many-person lineups: a warning against unsafe practices. In F. Lösel, D. Bender, and T. Bliesener (Eds), *Psychology and Law: International Perspectives*. Berlin: de Gruyter, pp. 275–85.

Wells, G.L. and Loftus, E.F. (Eds) (1984). *Eye-witness Testimony: Psychological Perspectives*. New York: Cambridge University Press.

Yarmey, A.D. (1986). Verbal, visual, and voice identification of a rape suspect under different levels of illumination. *Journal of Applied Psychology*, **71**, 363–70.

Yarmey, A.D. (1990). *Understanding Police and Police Work: Psychosocial Issues*. New York: New York University Press.

Yarmey, A.D. (1991a). Voice identification over the telephone. *Journal of Applied Social Psychology*, **21**, 1868–76.

Yarmey, A.D. (1991b). Descriptions of distinctive and non-distinctive voices over time. *Journal of the Forensic Science Society*, **31**, 421–8.

Yarmey, A.D. (1992). The effects of dyadic discussion on earwitness recall. *Basic and Applied Social Psychology*, **13**, 251–63.

Yarmey, A.D. (1993). Stereotypes and recognition memory for faces and voices of good guys and bad guys. *Applied Cognitive Psychology*, **7**, 419–31.

Yarmey, A.D. (1994). Earwitness evidence: memory for a perpetrator's voice. In D.F. Ross, J.D. Read and M.P. Toglia (Eds), *Adult Eyewitness Memory: Current Trends and Developments*. New York: Cambridge University Press.

Yarmey, A.D. (1995). The elderly witness. In S.L. Sporer, R.S. Malpass and G. Köhnken (Eds), *Suspect Identification: Psychological Knowledge, Problems and Perspectives*. Hillsdale, NJ: Lawrence Erlbaum.

Yarmey, A.D. and Jones, H.P.T. (1983). Is the psychology of eye-witness identification a matter of common sense? In S. Lloyd-Bostock and B.R. Clifford (Eds), *Evaluating Witness Evidence: Recent Psychological Research and New Perspectives*. New York: John Wiley, pp. 13–40.

Yarmey, A.D. and Matthys, E. (1992). Voice identification of an abductor. *Applied Cognitive Psychology*, **6**, 367–77.

Yarmey, A.D. and Pauley, T. (1993). The effects of weapon focus and perceived violence on voice identification. Unpublished manuscript, University of Guelph, Guelph, Ontario, Canada.

Yarmey, A.D., Yarmey, A.L. and Yarmey, M.J. (1994). Face and voice identifications in showups and lineups. *Applied Cognitive Psychology*, **8**, 453–64.

Part 4

Criminal Responsibility and Proceedings

Chapter 4.1

Criminal Responsibility

David Carson
University of Southampton

You are about to visit another country, for the first time. You know very little about it. Would you inquire about that country's laws, before you visited? Are you, in particular, anxious about what that country's criminal law involves, how it might vary from the law of your own country? If you propose driving on that country's roads you will, certainly, wish to know more: which side of the road do they drive on, what are their speed limits, must you wear safety belts, what is their rule at roundabouts, if they have them? But, otherwise, you are unlikely either to need or to want to know much more. You are unlikely to have been contemplating killing anyone there. So you may think that you have no need to know about their homicide law. But you might be negligent and kill someone with your car. Would that constitute manslaughter, or a similar offence? What constitutes 'theft' in that country; when is it a crime not to go to someone's assistance? You may be much more interested in learning about that country's norms and customs than their law; more interested in gaining a 'flavour' of that country and avoiding social embarrassment.

Simply, there is such a degree of correspondence in the criminal laws of different countries that, generally, we can visit and behave in other legal systems without needing special training or experience. Common ideas and expectations are generally sufficient. Signs, such as speed limits, should meet any special needs. At one level this ought to be surprising, given the extent to which the criminal law of each legal system is an area of specialist knowledge and study. But it should not be surprising given how little non-lawyers know about the criminal law of their own country, let alone other countries. Non-lawyers negotiate the law quite satisfactorily in most instances. Indeed it is frequently declared, to general approval, that ignorance of the law is no defence to the commission of a crime. However this negotiation of the law is achieved —for example, the core ideas might be thought to be somehow 'natural' or 'common sense' interpretations of community values or they may be learnt, well or poorly, through socialisation—we manage quite well in distinguishing what is criminal. If there is a lack of correspondence, between our expectations of and the reality of the law, we seem to overestimate, rather than under-estimate, what is criminal; for example, many in the UK wrongly believe that it is a crime to discriminate on grounds of race or ethnic origin.

Nevertheless, substantially because of the need to draw explicit lines to distinguish proscribed behaviour, criminal law has become a highly specialised body of knowledge. It is the detail which varies between countries. Would you commit a crime, in your country, by flashing your car's headlights to warn oncoming drivers of the presence of police officers? Indeed some of that detail can surprise through being counter-intuitive or unexpected; who commits the crime, the person who voluntarily accepts a duty to help a stranger injured by the side of the road (but who helps in a reckless manner), or the person who could help but walks by on the other side of the road (*Stone and Dobinson*, [1977] Q.B. 354)? This chapter aims, by describing and explaining some key concepts in the criminal law, to indicate the potential for further contributions from psychology and psychologists. For consistency it will highlight concepts in UK law although there will be considerable similarity with other legal systems' law, especially that of other common law countries.

CRIMINAL STAGES

Criminal procedure separates two key stages, the finding of guilt or innocence and, if guilt, then the imposition of a penalty. However, the two stages are not as separate as theory might suggest. The nature and seriousness of the crime alleged will provide a starting point for the form and degree of any punishment. Plea-bargaining, such as where the defendant contests a particular allegation or charge but offers to plead guilty to a lesser offence, takes place in many legal systems. It can occur as a formal procedure after the charges have been finalised, or prosecutors can take into account the greater likelihood of a guilty plea, and thereby considerable financial savings, when framing the charges. But pleas in mitigation and the submission of reports to inform the sentencing decision take place after, and depend upon, a finding or plea of guilt. Psychologists' contributions are not limited to the sentencing stage (e.g. Fitzmaurice and Pease, 1986). They are demonstrating a growing contribution to the investigation stage, such as through improvements in interviewing techniques (e.g. Fisher and Geiselman, 1992; Gudjonsson, 1992; Bull, 1994) and offender profiling (Canter, 1994). There is also a contribution to be made with regard to the substantive rules of the criminal law (see Working Party, 1993).

As a heuristic, a crime may be seen as comprising four key ingredients; (i) the proscribed act or consequence (known as the *actus reus* in common law systems), (ii) the accompanying proscribed 'mental attitude' (the *mens rea*), (iii) causation, that is the defendant's acts must be shown to have caused (in a legal sense) the proscribed consequences, and (iv) the absence of a recognised defence which is applicable to that crime. However, each 'ingredient' is not analytically distinct and each is not required for all crimes. Take the example of 'voluntariness'.

Voluntariness

A key distinction between most lawyers and psychologists is the extent to which lawyers believe that people have 'free will' whether to commit a criminal act, and the extent to which psychologists believe that people are 'determined' into behaving in particular ways, including criminal behaviour, whether through social background, learned responses or heredity. If a person's behaviour is not 'voluntary' then, the law agrees, the actor commits no crime. But what is the nature of this 'voluntariness', is it a denial of the *mens rea*, the *actus reus*, causation, or does its absence constitute a defence? Examples involving duress and automatism highlight the issues, including the moral and practical.

Alan terrifies Bill that, unless Bill stabs Clem, Alan will kill Bill. This is a case of duress, in legal terms. Bill's mind is 'overborne' with fear for his own life. If, as a result, Bill stabs Clem then Bill will have a defence, of duress, provided first that a reasonable person with Bill's relevant characteristics would also have so acted in fear and, second, that Clem does not die. Duress is a defence (in England and Wales) to crimes other than murder, attempted murder and treason (*Howe*, [1987] 1 All E.R. 771; *Gotts*, [1992] 1 All E.R. 832). Duress is not a defence to murder as it would not be possible to 'regard a law as either "just" or "humane" which withdraws the protection of the criminal law from the innocent victim and casts the cloak of its protection on the coward and the poltroon in the name of a "concession to human frailty"' (Lord Hailsham, *Howe*, [1987] 1 All E.R. 771, 779-780).

Note that duress provides a *defence*. There was a crime but the presence of duress provides an 'excuse'. Note that there is no suggestion that the defendant's acts, Bill's in the above example, were involuntary. Bill had a choice: stab another or be killed himself. If Bill stabs Clem then it will be a voluntary, even if pressurised, act. Bill will, also, only have a defence of duress if his conduct measures up to that of a relatively objective standard, that is whether a sober person of reasonable firmness with the same relevant characteristics, would have acted similarly. The 'voluntariness' of such an act may be doubted. But that is the way in which the law uses the term. For lawyers the behaviour, act or not act, evidences a choice which demonstrates 'voluntariness' (see, generally, Ashworth, 1991; Smith and Hogan, 1992). Psychologists are unlikely to adopt such a dichotomous categorisation of 'voluntary' versus 'involuntary'.

You are driving your car. Without any fault on your part your brakes fail causing an accident. That was involuntary (*Burns v. Bidder*, [1967] 2 Q.B.

227). You are driving your car when a swarm of bees flies in through your open window. You are terrified, drive erratically, and cause an accident. Would your erratic driving be voluntary? Not according to *Hill v. Baxter* ([1958] 1 Q.B. 554). You would be regarded as not having control over your body, you would be like an automaton. You would have a defence of automatism. You would not even be guilty of a 'strict liability' or 'absolute' offences, where there is no requirement to prove any *mens rea*. Because your acts are involuntary you could be said not to be 'driving', not to be performing the *actus reus* of the crime. Thus involuntariness can, at least in respect of different crimes, be analysed as a defence, as an absence of *actus reus* and as denying *mens rea*; because involuntary it was not intentional.

However, in some common law countries, the cause of the automatism is important. If the automatism is the consequence of a 'disease of the mind' the defendant will have to plead 'insane' automatism or choose to plead guilty. The expression 'disease of the mind' comes from the *McNaghten Rules* ((1843) 10 Cl & Fin 200). They provide the legal test of insanity for several common law countries and have been highly influential in others, including the USA. The expression has caused considerable difficulties. In recent years, in England and Wales, defendants who have injured others during a psychomotor epileptic seizure (*Sullivan* [1984] A.C. 156), whilst 'sleep-walking' (*Burgess*, [1991] 2 Q.B. 92, but see the different approach in Canada in *Parks* ((1993) 95 DLR 27)) and while in a diabetic coma, (*Hennessy*, [1989] 2 All E.R. 9) have all been required to plead insane, rather than non-insane, automatism. Their automatism arose from an internal rather than an external factor such as a blow to the head. A finding of automatism leads to complete acquittal whereas a finding of insanity, or insane automatism, leads to an acquittal but has regularly led, particularly in the past, to detention, although in hospital rather than prison.

Whether the automatism, the absence of voluntary control over your body, derives from a 'disease of the mind' or otherwise, the law imposes a dichotomous structure upon the issue. If the defendant falls within the category then he or she has a defence (lacks *actus reus* or *mens rea*). An inquiry is not conducted into how overpowering the event was or how involuntary the response. Bill, who has been threatened with his life, may be able to think, perhaps not in a very analytical or calculating manner, about his dilemma: stab Bill or risk Alan carrying out his threat to kill him. Indeed, if it was suggested that Bill was capable of such a 'rational' exercise doubt would be raised about whether his mind was really 'overborne'.

Lawyers have a very particular conception of human self-control. Psychologists might be expected to see the issues in terms of degree and scale. However, throughout the criminal law, conceptual analysis is overlaid with beliefs about moral responsibility and anxieties about how people might behave if the law was different. It is assumed that, if duress is a defence to murder, then people will take advantage of that 'concession to human frailty'. The likelihood that the person put in the unenviable position will know that rule, think about it and be able to reason about it, is not taken into account. Psychologists might identify cases where people respond to danger, such as a threat of death, in an automatic or relatively reflex manner without time for articulated (even if just to self) reasoning. Yet those people have no defence of duress if they should actually kill, rather than just injure.

The voluntariness examples also demonstrate the interrelationship between the key components of criminal liability; the act, causation, the 'mental element' and defences. Voluntariness has variously been analysed as a feature of each element. It is not just a feature of *mens rea*. Finally, the examples demonstrate that legal notions of involuntariness take no account of determinist theories of human behaviour.

MENS REA—MODELS FOR JUSTIFYING BLAME

It is very difficult to find an accurate alternative expression to explain the requirement of *mens rea*. It includes, but is not limited to, 'criminal intent' or 'state of mind'. Some crimes can be committed if there is negligence, carelessness or similar. But those are not descriptions of states of mind, except in the negative sense that they may include lack of care, absence of attention, being unaware. They describe a quality of behaviour rather than a state of mind. But they are still *mens rea* concepts. Criminal responsibility and punishment are considered justified, in such cases, because the individuals *ought* to have been aware of their behaviour, ought to have been behaving to a higher standard. Indeed with strict liability offences, where there is no requirement of *mens rea* at all (other than voluntariness), there is no need to prove carelessness or similar, just that the act was committed and/or the consequence caused.

Mens rea concepts and expressions which refer to qualities of behaviour are regularly described as 'objective'. The alternative is a 'subjective' *mens rea* where the defendant has, as a base-line minimum, an awareness of a key feature of the *actus reus*, for example is aware of the possibility of an injury to the person or damage to property. Many issues, concerned with the ethics and the efficacy of punishment, relate back to this dichotomous distinction. Is it appropriate to regard someone as criminally responsible if he or she was unaware of, for example, any danger, risk or illegality? Some justify imposing criminal responsibility because the individual ought to have been aware of a risk or standard of conduct. That person's low standards deserve punishment. Punishing him or her might also encourage others to improve their standards, although that assumes, substantially falsely, that people hear about and learn from court proceedings that they are not directly involved in.

Judges also have pragmatic concerns. How are they and juries accurately to distinguish between those who actually were unaware and those who, using the distinction to their own benefit, falsely claim to have been unaware? Indeed anxiety has been expressed that people who 'close their minds' to a danger would escape liability (e.g. *Parker*, [1977] 1 W.L.R. 600). That the argument involves a contradiction—in order to close your mind to a topic you have to be aware of the topic you are ignoring—is often overlooked. The judge's concern is a kind of anti-social behaviour rather than analytical category.

A further issue, likely to be more alive in the minds of psychologists, is whether punishing people for 'objective' crimes is likely to be effective. Amongst the traditional goals of punishment are rehabilitation and prevention. How likely are people to learn, particularly from punishments which are delayed in time-consuming legal procedures, where the grounds for blaming them are that they had not been thinking? The issue is particularly acute where the particular defendant could not have known that his or her standards or knowledge base were deficient. In *Elliott v. C* ([1983] 2 All E.R. 1005) a cold, tired and hungry 14-year-old girl with a learning disability, entered someone else's garden shed late at night and, in order to warm herself, poured white spirit on the floor, lit a match and set fire to it. She endangered herself as well as damaged the shed. The court found that the danger was not obvious to her, indeed that she was unaware of it. However, she was found guilty of recklessly causing criminal damage because it would have been obvious to other, objectively reasonable people who, by definition, would not have had a learning disability. (See also *Stephenson* ([1979] Q.B. 695) where a man experiencing schizophrenia set fire to a haystack, in which he was sheltering, to keep himself warm, and *Reid* ([1992] 1 W.L.R. 793) where there are comments which might lead to these and similar decisions being reversed for the future.)

What is to be gained by imposing criminal responsibility in cases where the defendant was unaware of, including the risk of, wrong-doing? If punishment is to 'teach people a lesson', a model with which psychologists could help develop the law and practice, then the wrong people were prosecuted in those cases. 'Psychological treatment is the social analogue of remedial education' (Working Party, 1993, p. 15). Would it not be more appropriate to consider the 'criminality' of those who could and should have taught the girl with learning difficulties about the dangers of fire? 'I submit that the apparent ineffectiveness of the criminal law may be due to the fact that we do not operate the system simply as a teaching technology, but as a way to make people suffer' (Crombag, 1984, p. 64). If the justification for 'objective' *mens rea* is that people must be pushed into achieving a certain minimum standard of behaviour then the law ought, explicitly, to adopt an educational framework and model, where psychologists could clearly assist.

Mens Rea—A Question of Degree

Substantially, a criminal lawyer's job is to analyse a defendant's behaviour, its consequences and the defendant's attitudes towards the behaviour at the time, to see whether it fits into the categories that have been enunciated for the crimes alleged. One classic, and regularly utilised *mens rea* concept, is 'intention'. It is, for example, a requirement of the crime of murder. Again it is difficult to find adequate synonyms. Having decided that you are going to kill a particular person, you drive to his house to carry out the deed. On the way someone steps in front of your car. You cannot stop in time. You knock him down. You step out and discover, to your delight, that it is the person you had decided to kill and that he has died. You did not intend *that* act. You are not guilty.

It is useful to distinguish between the act (e.g. stabbing), and the consequence (e.g. death). It is also useful to notice an implicit balancing operation being undertaken between 'internal' mental states and their 'external' referents. Intention (internal) connotes knowledge of such consequences as death (external) and a willingness, if not a decision, to bring them about with the chosen behaviour. You wish (motive) to make an omelette. So you pick an egg, you aim and hit it with a knife. That was intentional. You are being provoked and, suddenly, you lose your temper and lash out at the person who was taunting you. That was, also, an intentional act. An 'instantaneous' act can be intentional. The degree of planning does not affect the *nature* of the crime; a meticulously planned theft and a spur-of-the-moment theft are both crimes, although the punishments may be different. The question is: 'Intention to do what (consequences)?', rather than: 'How intentional?' The deliberate, powerfully motivated and meticulously planned murder, the angry fatal fight, the 'snap' where a sudden—and immediately retracted—desire for another's death is achieved, are all equally intentional and fit the same crime. Qualitatively different degrees of *mens rea*, within each conceptual category, may lead to different punishments. They do not affect guilt; they may affect sentence.

Different kinds and degrees of culpability can be encapsulated by *mens rea* concepts, for example 'intention' contrasted with 'negligence'. These analytical categories may appear specific but are actually remarkably broad. Balancing the application of *mens rea* concepts with flexibility in sentencing is not enough. Psychologists, it is argued below, could assist lawyers to elaborate schemes which assess degrees of culpability. That could then be reflected in the statement of *mens rea* concepts. The psychological work, for example on decision-making, descriptive and normative, could provide a framework here. However, it must be recognised that there will be a continuing anxiety about the interrelationship between *what* the *mens rea* is that has to be proved and *how* it can be proved.

Mens Rea—**Proof**

Previously, at least in England and Wales, people were presumed, whether they actually did or not, to intend the 'natural and probable consequences' of their acts (*D.P.P. v. Smith*, [1961] A.C. 290). Certain consequences were regarded as intrinsically linked to particular acts. The natural and probable consequences of stabbing someone are, it would almost certainly be decided, that grievous bodily harm would be caused, that firing a gun in a theatre would cause a panic. The rule of law to this effect has been abolished (Criminal Justice Act 1967, s. 8) but it remains legitimate for judges and juries to utilise it as a decision aid.

In attempting to make sense of other people's behaviour juries must be expected to take advantage of insights from their own experience: 'What would I, or most people, have been thinking if I, or they, stabbed someone like that?' Even though the test that the jury must apply may be subjective—for example, did *the* defendant intend?—the method of proof is objective in that it involves such considerations as the probability that the defendant actually did not intend 'the natural and probable consequences' of his or her acts. The 'common sense' observation that 'the facts speak for themselves', for example that a stab was intentional, is very powerful. It is very difficult to counter. Psychologists, however, may be able to help lawyers explain, to judges and juries, how someone could hold an unusual belief against the tide of probability. Unfortunately the current rules of evidence, which prohibit an expert witness giving evidence on an 'ultimate issue' (such as whether a defendant had the *mens rea*), means that such a contribution would need to be given indirectly—for example, by advising the defence lawyers about the kinds of arguments to develop.

Problems have occurred where a defendant knows the consequences of his or her acts but does not wish them to occur. Does that person intend the consequences? In *Hyam v. D.P.P.* ([1975] A.C. 55) the defendant's motive was to frighten someone into moving away from the area. She poured petrol into a house and set fire to it. A child was killed in the ensuing blaze. Some of the judges involved treated certain degrees of knowledge (internal) of certain degrees of likelihood of the consequences (external) as sufficient to justify a conviction for murder. One judge, in the House of Lords, decided that it was murder if the Defendant intended (internal) to expose the victims to the serious risk (external) of death or serious harm. Another specified that knowledge (internal) that death or harm was a highly probable (external) consequence, was enough. And a third stated that knowledge that the consequences were probable would be enough. No attempt was made to explain what those probabilities would represent in statistical terms.

Mens Rea—Balancing Cognitive States with Likely Degrees Consequences

Note the implicit balancing of what have been termed, here, 'internal' and 'external' factors. 'Intention' (internal) is a narrow and relatively specific concept but it is coupled with 'serious risk' (external) which encompasses a relatively broad degree of probability. 'Knowledge' (internal) is a broader, or more encompassing, word than 'intention' but 'highly probable' (external) is narrower, and more specific, than 'serious risk'. The *Hyam* decision was severely criticised and has been, effectively, reversed (*Hancock and Shankland* [1986] A.C. 455; *Nedrick*, [1986] 3 All E.R. 1). In the process notions of the 'moral certainty' of (external) consequences were developed (Lord Bridge in *Maloney* [1985] A.C. 905) which seem designed to defy any form of statistical analysis!

Similar exercises in 'balancing' kinds of mental state with probabilities of harm occurring can be seen in relation to other *mens rea* categories. It occurs with 'recklessness', which has caused judges considerable problems (Law Commission, 1994). Here the dispute involves such pairings as actual awareness (internal) of specific risks (external), such as of physical harm, and being unaware (internal) of obvious risks (external) of physical harm. Perhaps psychologists could develop this kind of a model. If scales, with several intervals, of both the 'internal' cognitive states and the associated 'external' type of harm and its likelihood, could be developed then more explicit ways of both analysing and assessing culpability might be declared. At the very least, such a framework could help people to assess the blameworthiness of their, and other people's, conduct.

There is a problem because lawyers are seeking to draw out and distinguish conceptually explicit categories from culpability which is, in fact, a relative concept. We can recognise different concepts—for example, that 'knowledge' differs from 'awareness' and 'intention'. But, whilst the core meaning of one word is different from the others, their penumbra meanings shade into each other. The Law Commission, for England and Wales (1994), recognising the problems in creating explicit categories and concepts, has proposed a general formula, for the law of manslaughter, which leaves a good deal of judgement to the jury. This, they believe, is both inevitable and right. However, it is submitted, psychologists could help lawyers to develop any such broad formula into a system for scaling and balancing cognitive states against degrees and forms of outcomes.

Mens Rea—**Quality of Decision-making**

The problem of imposing categorical boundaries on relative concepts is particularly clear when 'recklessness' is applied to decision-making. In one sense almost every act can be analysed and assessed in terms of the quality of the decision-making. The careless driver and the drunken thug might both be analysed in terms of their decision-making. But the frame would be rather forced; such people will often not have used a self-consciously rational decision-making system. A decision-making conceptual framework is much more appropriate for such cases as the doctor choosing whether to operate in a particular manner, the company directors deciding whether to put an unsafe (a relative concept) but cheap product on the market.

The law's focus is primarily on the (internal) cognitive form, awareness or unawareness, with secondary concern for what that awareness (external) was focused, or should have been focused, upon. For lawyers the key question is: 'Should the decision-maker have to be aware of the risk?' The degree of risk is variously described: sometimes 'serious', 'some', 'obvious'. What those words mean is most unclear; for example, do they refer to the likelihood of the harm, the degree of the harm, or to an amalgam of both? It is as if 'recklessness' and 'dangerousness' are characteristics of the individual, rather than features of the individual's interaction with external events. It is submitted that if more attention were paid to the nature and degree of the (external) risk, which the defendant was or should have been thinking about, then we might be able to make more progress.

In *Prentice* ([1993] 3 W.L.R. 927), some doctors were accused of manslaughter because they caused death through gross negligence. The Court of Appeal declined to provide an exclusive definition of 'gross negligence' but declared that:

> proof of any of the following states of mind in the defendant might properly lead a jury to make a finding of gross negligence:
>
> (a) indifference to an obvious risk of injury to health;
>
> (b) actual foresight of the risk coupled with the determination nevertheless to run it;
>
> (c) an appreciation of the risk coupled with the intention to avoid it but also coupled with such a high degree of negligence in the attempted avoidance as the jury considered justified the conviction;
>
> (d) inattention or failure to advert to a serious risk which went beyond 'mere inadvertence' in respect of an obvious and important matter which the defendant's duty demanded he should address. (Lord Taylor, C.J., p. 937)

Note that the degree of risk is qualified in (a) and (d). It is effectively qualified in (c) also. But note that there is no qualification of 'risk' in example (b). That test was clearly designed to be subjective. According to that test foresight or awareness before the event, of the risk being run, is sufficient to justify criminal liability if the risked consequence occurs. Whilst driving in the country you come upon a blind corner. The thought that there might be an obstruction around the corner crosses your mind. However, you decide to take the risk. In the event you run into and kill a sheep. You are blameworthy because you foresaw but ignored the risk. But some risks, such as surgical interventions, car journeys, even trying people for crimes, have to be justifiable. Some risks are worth it. The risk in (b) needs to be qualified.

Some argue that the courts are only referring to 'unjustified' risks; that their references to 'risks' should be read as 'unjustified risks'. One of the leading textbooks, (Smith and Hogan, 1992) states: 'Whether it is justifiable to take a risk depends on the social value of the activity involved relative to the probability and the gravity of the harm that might be caused. ... It is impossible to say in general terms that recklessness requires any particular degree of probability of the occurrence of the harm in question' (p. 60). But if people are to be discouraged from committing acts, that may later be described as reckless, particularly if an educational model or potential is recognised, then some indication of degrees of probability and how that can be balanced with the social utility, or otherwise, of the activity need to be articulated.

But recklessness needs to be understood as also referring to the quality of decision-making. It is not just what was decided but *how* it was decided. The manner in which, or procedure by which, a decision was taken could be investigated. For example, not seeking relevant information before making a decision, which the defendant appreciates needs to be taken into consideration, could be regarded as reckless. It could also refer to the decision's contents. For example, the way in which the decision-maker rated the various possible consequences might have been valued inappropriately. For example, the likelihoods of, and the valuation of, the outcomes might be confused. The likelihood or chance of someone being killed might, correctly, have been rated as 'seriously' as the likelihood of damage to some property. However, the seriousness, in terms of value, of those two different outcomes ought to be rated differently. Thoroughly inappropriate assessments of likelihood might be made. Such analyses could provide a means of assessing recklessness.

DEFENCES

What if someone makes a mistake when assessing a risk, or 'thinking through' a decision. Should he or she be regarded as reckless or culpable? A man wrongly thinks that a woman is consenting to sexual intercourse with him. Is he guilty of rape? Not in the law of England and Wales if he believes she consented? The *mens rea* of rape requires that the man knows that woman does not consent or is reckless as to her consent. The defence of mistake produces the same conclusion; if the man mistakenly believes that the woman consents then he does not have the *mens rea*. Understandably this rule is controversial. It is often argued that a man should be considered 'reckless' if his belief is objectively foolish. But should rape, particularly as it is such a serious offence, both in terms of the harm caused and the punishments available, be an exception to the generally accepted principle that the defendant should be aware of some degree of wrongdoing before being considered guilty?

Again, it is submitted, we might make progress by examining the decision-making process both as an aid to determining what the defendant was aware of and as a means of assessing culpability. Indeed, it could be particularly valuable with such an offence as rape which is primarily, contrary to the violent stranger stereotype, an offence concerning the abuse of power by people already known to the victim. That a particular man, for example, fails to take into consideration his greater power, as manifested (*inter alia*) through physical strength, wealth, status, age, could be used to question the genuineness of his professed ignorance of the woman's lack of consent. The law could focus on *mens rea* as a decision-making *process* rather than as conceptual categories of cognitive product.

No matter how ridiculous and unreasonable the mistaken belief in the woman's consent, the defendant has a defence. Of course, in practice, the jury will regularly use the ridiculous quality of the belief as an aid to deciding that it was not actually believed. In that way the subjectivist principle remains sacrosanct. Understandably, anxious judges remind juries that it must be an 'honest belief' or 'genuine belief' (e.g. *Beckford v. R.* [1988] AC 130) without noticing the impossibility of a dishonestly, or non-genuinely held belief. The criminal law ought to be encouraging people to think about relationships, consequences, likelihoods. Men, for example, contemplating intercourse with a woman, must decide whether they think she is consenting. In making this decision they must consider a number of factors. It is not inappropriate for the law to provide a framework, or basic checklist, of key factors to be considered. In making a decision defendants will undergo a reasoning process, not just reach conclusions. That process may still lead to erroneous conclusions but, surely, it is appropriate to examine the quality of that process against the individual's own standards.

As has been indicated, a mistake is a defence to criminal liability whether it was a reasonable mistake to make or not. But not when the mistake was due to intoxication (*Woods*, (1981) 74 Cr App Rep 312; Smith and Hogan, 1992). Policy considerations intrude (*O'Grady*, [1987] Q.B. 995). But when is a mistake due to intoxication? The problem is, once again, one of imposing categorical distinctions upon relative concepts. Taking alcohol usually has a disinhibiting effect. Perhaps that contributes to a misunderstanding, say of a woman's consent, or another's apparent aggression. How drunk is drunk? More research is required; perhaps involving participant observation.

SUMMARY

This chapter has tried, through the medium of describing certain key areas of law, to highlight certain assumptions and methods of lawyers. Hopefully it has also indicated that there are areas of substantive law where psychologists' skills and interests in rating and structuring decision-making, could be of considerable value to the law.

REFERENCES

Ashworth, A. (1991). *Principles of Criminal Law*. Oxford: Clarendon.

Bull, R. (1994). Innovative techniques for the questioning of child witnesses especially those who are young and those with learning disabilities. In M. Zaragoza (Ed.), *Memory, Suggestibility and Eyewitness Testimony in Children*. Newbury Park, CA: Sage.

Canter, D. (1994). *Criminal Shadows*. London: HarperCollins.

Crombag, H. (1984). Some psychological observations on *mens rea*. In D.J. Müller, D.E. Blackman and A.J. Chapman (Eds), *Psychology and Law*. Chichester: John Wiley.

Fisher, R.P. and Geiselman, R.E. (1992). *Memory-enhancing Techniques for Investigative Interviewing: The Cognitive Interview*. Springfield, IL: Thomas.

Fitzmaurice, C. and Pease, K. (1986). *The Psychology of Judicial Sentencing*. Manchester: Manchester University Press.

Gudjonsson, G. (1992). *The Psychology of Interrogations, Confessions and Testimony*. Chichester: John Wiley.

Law Commission (1994). *Involuntary Manslaughter: A Consultation Paper*. London: HMSO. (Law Commission consultation paper no. 135.)

Smith, J.C. and Hogan, B. (1992). *Criminal Law* (7th edn). London: Butterworth.

Working Party (Convenor: Berry, M.) (1993). *Psychology and Antisocial Behaviour*. Leicester: British Psychological Society.

The Psychology of Crime: Influences and Constraints on Offending

David P. Farrington
Cambridge University

INTRODUCTION

While lawyers assume that people have free will and are responsible for their freely-chosen actions, psychologists argue that human behaviour is influenced and constrained by individual and environmental factors. The aim of this chapter is to review psychological research and theories on factors promoting and inhibiting criminal behaviour. I will begin by reviewing the natural history of offending, and then outline some key findings on individual difference factors (intelligence, personality and impulsivity), and on family, peer, school, and situational influences on offending. I will then review key elements of psychological theories about the development of offending and antisocial behaviour, focusing especially on energising, directing and inhibiting factors, and on decision-making in criminal opportunities. For a review of more sociological research on demographic, socio-economic, neighbourhood, community and society features that influence offending see, for example, Farrington (1993b, d).

PSYCHOLOGY AND CRIME

The distinctive contributions of psychologists to research and theories on offending follow from their commitment to the scientific study of human behaviour (Farrington, 1984, 1991c). Lawyers are less interested in the scientific method, with its emphasis on quantitative data, falsifiable theories, controlled experiments, systematic observation, valid and reliable measures, replications of empirical results, and so on. Lawyers have different standards

Handbook of Psychology in Legal Contexts
Edited by R. Bull and D. Carson. © 1995 John Wiley & Sons Ltd

of proof from psychologists, and prefer legal concepts such as 'beyond reasonable doubt' rather than the exact probabilities that psychologists prefer.

Psychologists view offending as a type of behaviour, similar in many respects to other types of antisocial or deviant behaviour. Hence, the theories, methods, and knowledge of other types of antisocial behaviour can be applied to the study of crime. Their focus is on the types of offences that dominate the official criminal statistics in Western countries, principally theft, burglary, robbery, violence, vandalism and drug abuse. Most research has concentrated on offending by males, since this is generally more frequent and serious than offending by females (Farrington, 1987).

Psychologists are interested in the causes of offending. They believe that, like other types of behaviour, criminal behaviour results from the interaction between a person (with a certain degree of criminal potential or antisocial tendency) and the environment (which provides criminal opportunities). Some people will be consistently more likely to commit offences than others (in various environments), and conversely the same person will be more likely to commit offences in some environments than in others. Hence, human behaviour is, to a considerable degree, consistent and predictable. A major problem in psychological theories is to explain the development of individual differences in criminal potential. It is often assumed that offences and other types of antisocial acts are behavioural manifestations of an underlying theoretical construct such as 'antisocial personality'.

In order to understand the causes of offending, it is important to study developmental processes such as onset, persistence, escalation, and desistance. However, it is also important not to restrict this study narrowly to offending, which is part of a much wider phenomenon of childhood and adult antisocial behaviour. Psychological theories often aim to explain more general antisocial behaviour, not just offending. An underlying antisocial tendency may lead to offending in some circumstances and to other types of antisocial acts in other circumstances, forcing attention to interactive effects of influencing factors. In particular, there will be different antisocial manifestations at different ages from birth to adulthood. For example, the antisocial child may be troublesome and disruptive in school, the antisocial teenager may steal cars and burgle houses, and the antisocial adult male may beat up his wife and neglect his children. The variation in antisocial behaviour with age is one of the key issues that any theory needs to explain.

In comparison with sociologists, psychologists emphasise the importance of individual difference factors, and especially the consistency within individuals of antisocial tendency across situations and its continuity over time. In general, the antisocial child tends to become the antisocial teenager and the antisocial adult, just as the antisocial adult then tends to produce another antisocial child. The relative ordering of any cohort of people on antisocial tendency is significantly consistent over time (Farrington, 1991a). Psychologists also argue that officially convicted offenders are significantly different from non-offenders in numerous respects —before, during, and after their offending careers. Similarly, psychologists argue that the most frequent and serious offenders according to self-reports are significantly different from the remainder of the population in numerous respects.

Psychologists have made many contributions to the understanding of criminal behaviour, and it is possible to mention only a small number of these, without a great deal of detail, in this paper. Blackburn (1993), Hollin (1989) and Wilson and Herrnstein (1985), among others, have provided more extensive reviews. I will refer especially to knowledge gained in the Cambridge Study in Delinquent Development, which is a prospective longitudinal survey of over 400 London males from age 8 to age 32 (Farrington and West, 1990). However, similar results have been obtained in similar studies elsewhere in England (Kolvin et al., 1988; Kolvin et al., 1990), in the United States (McCord, 1979; Robins, 1979), in the Scandinavian countries (Wikstrom, 1987; Pulkkinen, 1988), and in New Zealand (Moffitt and Silva, 1988a).

NATURAL HISTORY OF OFFENDING

Developmental research shows that the prevalence of most types of offending increases with age to a peak in the teenage years, and then decreases in the twenties and thirties. This pattern is seen in cross-sectional and longitudinal research with both self-reports and official records of offending. For example, in our London longitudinal survey of over 400 males, the prevalence of convictions increased to a peak at age 17 and then declined (Farrington, 1990a). Self-reports showed that burglary, shop-lifting, theft of and from vehicles, and vandalism all decreased from the teens to the twenties, but the same pattern was not seen for theft from work, fraud, or drug abuse (Farrington, 1989).

While the absolute prevalence of offending varies with age, there is also considerable continuity in offending over time. In the London longitudinal survey, nearly three-quarters of those convicted as juveniles (age 10–16) were reconvicted between ages 17 and 24, and nearly half of the juvenile offenders were reconvicted between ages 25 and 32 (Farrington, 1992a). An early age of onset of offending predicted a long criminal career. The males first convicted at the earliest ages (10–13) tended to commit large numbers of offences at high rates over long time periods. Furthermore, this continuity over time did not merely reflect continuity in police reaction to crime (e.g. in detecting previously known offenders). Farrington (1989) showed that, for ten specified offences, the significant continuity between offending in one age range and offending in a later age range held for both self-reports and official convictions.

INFLUENCES ON OFFENDING

The focus of much psychological research has been to identify risk factors or predictors of offending. Loeber and Dishion (1983) and Loeber and Stouthamer-Loeber (1987) extensively reviewed these predictors for males. They concluded that poor parental child-management techniques, offending by parents and siblings, low intelligence and educational attainment, and separations from parents were all important predictors. All of these factors will be reviewed here.

Intelligence and Cognitive Factors

Longitudinal (and indeed cross-sectional) surveys have consistently demonstrated that children with low intelligence are disproportionally likely to become offenders. In the London longitudinal survey, West and Farrington (1973) found that one-third of the boys scoring 90 or less on a non-verbal intelligence test (Raven's Progressive Matrices) at age eight to ten were convicted as juveniles, twice as many as among the remainder. Low non-verbal intelligence was highly correlated with low verbal intelligence (vocabulary, word comprehension, verbal reasoning) and with low school attainment, and all of these measures predicted juvenile convictions to much the same extent.

Low non-verbal intelligence was especially characteristic of the juvenile recidivists (who had an average IQ of 89) and those first convicted at the earliest ages (10–13). Furthermore, low non-verbal intelligence predicted juvenile self-reported offending to almost exactly the same degree as it predicted juvenile convictions, suggesting that the link between low intelligence and delinquency was not caused by the less intelligent boys having a greater probability of being caught. Also, measures of intelligence predicted measures of offending independently of other variables such as low family income and large family size. Similar results have been obtained in other projects (Wilson and Herrnstein, 1985; Moffitt and Silva, 1988a; Lynam, Moffitt and Stouthamer-Loeber, 1993).

Low intelligence may lead to delinquency through the intervening factor of school failure, as Hirschi and Hindelang (1977) suggested. However, a more plausible explanatory factor underlying the link between intelligence and offending is probably the ability to manipulate abstract concepts. People who are poor at this tend to do badly in intelligence tests such as the Progressive Matrices and in school attainment, and they also tend to commit offences, mainly because of their poor ability to foresee the consequences of their offending and to appreciate the feelings of victims (i.e. their low empathy). Certain family backgrounds are less conducive than others to the development of abstract reasoning. For example, lower class, poorer parents tend to live for the present and to have little thought for the future, and tend to talk in terms of the concrete rather than the abstract, as Cohen (1955) pointed out many years ago. A lack of concern for the future is also linked to the concept of impulsivity, which will be discussed in the next section.

Modern psychological research studies not just intelligence but also detailed patterns of cognitive and neuropsychological deficit. For example, in a New Zealand longitudinal study of over 1000 children from birth to age 15, Moffitt and Silva (1988b) found that self-reported offending was related to verbal, memory and visual-motor integration deficits, independently of low social class and family adversity. Neuropsychological research might lead to important advances in knowledge about the link between brain functioning and delinquency. For example, the 'executive functions' of the brain, located in the frontal lobes, include sustaining attention and concentration, abstract reasoning and concept formation, anticipation and planning, self-monitoring of behaviour, and inhibition of inappropriate or impulsive behaviour (Moffitt, 1990). Deficits in these executive functions are conducive to low measured intelligence and to offending. Moffitt and Henry (1989) found deficits in these executive functions especially for delinquents who were both antisocial and hyperactive.

The importance of abstract reasoning and thinking is also emphasised in other psychological theories of offending, for example in the moral development theory of Kohlberg (1976). According to Kohlberg, people progress through different stages of moral development as they get older: from the pre-conventional stage (where they are hedonistic and only obey the law because of fear of punishment) to the conventional stage (where they obey the law because it is the law) to the post-conventional stage (where they obey the law if it coincides with higher moral principles such as justice, fairness and respect for individual rights). The pre-conventional stage corresponds to rather concrete thinking, whereas abstract thinking is required to progress to the post-conventional stage. Clearly, advances in moral reasoning are related to advances in intelligence, and there is a good deal of evidence that offenders show lower levels of moral reasoning than non-offenders (Nelson, Smith and Dodd, 1990; Smetana, 1990). Also, low levels of moral reasoning are related to low guilt feelings (Ruma and Mosher, 1967).

Personality and Impulsivity

Robins (1979) suggested that there is an 'antisocial personality' that arises in childhood and persists into adulthood, with numerous different behavioural manifestations, including offending, and this idea is embodied in the psychiatric (DSM-IV) diagnosis of antisocial personality disorder (American Psychiatric Association, 1994). The antisocial male adult generally fails to maintain close personal relationships with anyone else, performs poorly in his jobs, is involved in crime, fails to support himself and his dependents without outside aid, and tends to change his plans impulsively and to lose his temper in response to minor frustrations. As a child, he tended to be restless, impulsive, and lacking in guilt, performed badly in school, truanted, ran away from home, was cruel to animals or people, and committed delinquent acts.

Psychologists have carried out a great deal of research on the relationship between different personality factors and offending. However, the personality scales that correlate most reliably with offending (i.e. the psychopathic deviate scale of the Minnesota Multiphasic Personality Inventory and the socialisation scale of the California Psychological Inventory: see Tennenbaum, 1977) are probably measuring much the same antisocial personality construct that underlies offending itself. Hence, these personality constructs could not be regarded as possible causes of offending.

One of the best-known theories linking personality and offending was proposed by Eysenck (1977). He viewed offending as essentially rational behaviour, and assumed that a person's criminal tendency varied inversely with the strength of their conscience. The conscience was essentially a conditioned anxiety response that was built up in a process of classical conditioning. Eysenck concluded that offenders tended to be those who had not built up strong consciences, because they were constitutionally poor at building up conditioned responses. He also linked conditionability to his dimensional theory of personality, predicting that those who were high on extraversion (E), neuroticism (N) and psychoticism (P) would tend to have the weakest consciences and hence that they were the most likely to be offenders.

Farrington, Biron and LeBlanc (1982) reviewed studies relating Eysenck's personality dimensions to official and self-reported offending. They concluded that high N (but not E) was related to official offending, while high E (but not N) was related to self-reported offending. High P was related to both, but this could have been a tautological result, since many of the items on the P scale describe antisocial behaviour or were selected in the light of their ability to discriminate between prisoners and non-prisoners. In the London longitudinal survey, those high on both E and N tended to be juvenile self-reported offenders, adult convicted offenders and adult self-reported offenders, but not juvenile convicted offenders. Furthermore, these relationships held independently of other variables such as low family income, low intelligence, and poor parental child-rearing behaviour. However, when individual items of the personality questionnaire were studied, it was clear that the significant relationships were caused by the items measuring impulsivity (e.g. doing things quickly without stopping to think). Hence, it was concluded that the major contribution of research inspired by the Eysenck theory was to identify the correlation between impulsivity and offending.

Psychologists have demonstrated a clear link between the constellation of personality factors variously termed 'hyperactivity-impulsivity-attention deficit', or HIA (Taylor, 1986; Loeber, 1987) and offending. For example, in the London longitudinal survey, Farrington, Loeber and Van Kammen (1990) showed that hyperactivity at age eight to ten significantly predicted juvenile convictions independently of conduct problems at age eight to ten. Hence, it might be concluded that hyperactivity is not merely another measure of antisocial personality. Other studies have also concluded that hyperactivity and conduct disorder are different constructs (Blouin et al., 1989). Similar constructs to hyperactivity, such as sensation seeking, are also related to offending (White, Labouvie and Bates, 1985). In the London survey, the rating of 'daring' or risk-taking at age eight to ten by parents and peers significantly predicted convictions up to age 32 independently of all other variables (Farrington, 1990b, 1993a), and poor concentration or restlessness was the most important predictor of convictions for violence (Farrington, 1994).

Family Influences

Loeber and Stouthamer-Loeber (1986) completed an exhaustive review of family factors as correlates and predictors of juvenile conduct problems and delinquency. They found that poor parental supervision or monitoring, erratic or harsh parental discipline, marital disharmony, parental rejection of the child, and low parental involvement with the child (as well as antisocial parents and large family size) were all important predictors of offending. Utting, Bright and Henricson (1993) have provided the most recent extensive review of the literature on family influences on offending.

In the London longitudinal survey, West and Farrington (1973) found that harsh or erratic parental discipline, cruel, passive or neglecting parental attitude, poor supervision, and parental conflict, all measured at age eight, all predicted later juvenile convictions of boys. Similar results have been obtained in other surveys, for example by Wilson (1980) in Birmingham. Furthermore, poor parental child-rearing behaviour (a combination of discipline, attitude and conflict) and poor parental supervision both predicted juvenile self-reported as well as official offending (Farrington, 1979), and poor parental child-rearing behaviour predicted offending independently of other factors such as low family income and low intelligence. Poor parental child-rearing behaviour was related to early rather than later offending (Farrington, 1986), and was not characteristic of those first convicted as adults (West and Farrington, 1977).

Widom's (1989) follow-up study of abused children in Indianapolis showed that there was intergenerational transmission of violence. Children who were physically abused up to age 11 were significantly likely to become violent offenders later on in life. Similarly, harsh parental discipline and attitude at age eight significantly predicted later violent as opposed to non-violent offenders in the London survey (Farrington, 1978). However, more recent research showed that it was equally predictive of violent and frequent offending (Farrington, 1991b).

Psychologists have also shown that broken homes and early separations predict offending. In the Newcastle Thousand Family Study, Kolvin et al. (1988) reported that marital disruption (divorce or separation) up to a boy's age five predicted his later convictions up to age 33. Farrington (1992c) found that both permanent and temporary (more than one month) separations before age ten predicted convictions and self-reported delinquency, providing that they were not caused by death or hospitalisation, and similar results were obtained in the National Survey by Wadsworth (1979). However, homes broken at an early age (under age five) were not unusually criminogenic in the London survey. Separations predicted convictions up to age 32 independently of all other variables (Farrington, 1990b, 1993a).

Many studies show that large families predict delinquency (Fischer, 1984). In English research this was reported in the National Survey by Wadsworth (1979) and by the Newsons in their Nottingham study (Newson, Newson and Adams, 1993). In the London survey, if a boy had four or more siblings by his tenth birthday, this doubled his risk of being convicted as a juvenile (West and Farrington, 1973). Large family size predicted self-reported delinquency as well as convictions (Farrington, 1979), and adult as well as juvenile convictions (Farrington, 1992b). Large family size was the most important independent predictor of convictions up to age 32 in a logistic regression analysis (Farrington, 1993a). There are many possible reasons why a large number of siblings might increase the risk of offending. Generally, as the number of children in a family increases, the amount of parental attention that can be given to each child decreases. Also, as the number of children increases, the household will tend to become more overcrowded, possibly leading to increases in frustration, irritation and conflict.

Criminal, antisocial and alcoholic parents also tend to have criminal sons, as Robins (1979) found in St Louis. In the London longitudinal survey, the concentration of offending in a small number of families was remarkable. West and Farrington (1977) discovered that less than 5 per cent of the families were responsible for about half of the criminal convictions of all family members (fathers, mothers, sons and daughters). West and Farrington (1973) showed that having convicted mothers, fathers, and brothers by a boy's tenth birthday significantly predicted his own later convictions. Furthermore, convicted parents and delinquent siblings were related to self-reported as well as to official offending (Farrington, 1979). Unlike most early precursors, convicted parents were related less to offending of early onset (age 10–13) than to later offending (Farrington, 1986). Also, convicted parents predicted which juvenile offenders went on to become adult criminals and which recidivists at age 19 continued offending (West and Farrington, 1977), and they predicted convictions up to age 32 independently of all other variables (Farrington, 1990b, 1993a).

These results are concordant with the psychological theory that offending occurs when the normal social learning process, based on rewards and punishments from parents, is disrupted by erratic discipline, poor supervision, parental disharmony and unsuitable (antisocial or criminal) parental models (e.g. Trasler, 1962; see later). However, some part of the link between criminal parents and delinquent sons may reflect genetic influences (Mednick, Gabrielli and Hutchings, 1983).

Peer Influences

The reviews by Zimring (1981) and Reiss (1988) show that delinquent acts tend to be committed in small groups (of two or three people, usually) rather than alone. In the London longitudinal survey, most officially recorded juvenile and young adult offences were committed with others, but the incidence of co-offending declined steadily with age from age ten onwards. Burglary, robbery and theft from vehicles were particularly likely to involve co-offenders, who tended to be similar in age and sex to the study males and lived close to the boys' homes and to the locations of the offences. The study males were most likely to offend with brothers when they had brothers who were similar in age to them (Reiss and Farrington, 1991). In Ontario, Jones, Offord and Abrams (1980) discovered that male delinquents tended to have a preponderance of brothers, and proposed that there was male potentiation (and conversely female suppression) of antisocial behaviour. However, this was not found in the London survey.

The major problem of interpretation is whether young people are more likely to commit offences while they are in groups than while they are alone, or whether the high prevalence of co-offending merely reflects the fact that, whenever young people go out, they tend to go out in groups. Do peers tend to encourage and facilitate offending, or is it just that most kinds of activities out of the home (both delinquent and non-delinquent) tend to be committed in groups? Another possibility is that the commission of offences encourages association with other delinquents, perhaps because 'birds of a feather flock together' or because of the stigmatising and isolating effects of court appearances and institutionalisation. It is surprisingly difficult to decide among these various possibilities, although most researchers argue that peer influence is an important factor.

There is clearly a close relationship between the delinquent activities of a young male and those of his friends. Both in the USA (Hirschi, 1969) and in the UK (West and Farrington, 1973), it has been found that a boy's reports of his own offending are significantly correlated with his reports of his friends' delinquency. In the American National Youth Survey of Elliott, Huizinga and Ageton (1985), having delinquent peers was the best independent predictor of self-reported offending in a multivariate analysis.

In the London longitudinal survey, association with delinquent friends at age

14 was a significant independent predictor of convictions at the young adult ages (Farrington, 1986). Also, the recidivists at age 19 who ceased offending differed from those who persisted, in that the desisters were more likely to have stopped going round in a group of male friends. Furthermore, spontaneous comments by the youths indicated that withdrawal from the delinquent peer group was seen as an important influence on ceasing to offend (West and Farrington, 1977). Therefore, continuing to associate with delinquent friends may be a key factor in determining whether juvenile delinquents persist in offending as young adults or desist.

School Influences

It is clear that the prevalence of offending varies dramatically between different secondary schools, as Power et al. (1967) showed more than 20 years ago in London. However, what is far less clear is how much of this variation should be attributed to differences in school climates and practices, and how much to differences in the composition of the student body.

In the London longitudinal survey, Farrington (1972) investigated the effects of secondary schools on offending by following boys from their primary schools to their secondary schools. The best primary school predictor of juvenile offending in this study was the rating of troublesomeness at age 8–10 by peers and teachers, showing the continuity in antisocial behaviour. The secondary schools differed dramatically in their official offending rates, from one school with 21 court appearances per 100 boys per year to another where the corresponding figure was only 0.3. Moreover, going to a high delinquency-rate secondary school was a significant predictor of later convictions (Farrington, 1993a).

It was, however, very noticeable that the most troublesome boys tended to go to the high delinquency-rate schools, while the least troublesome boys tended to go to the low delinquency-rate schools. Furthermore, it was clear that most of the variation between schools in their delinquency rates could be explained by differences in their intakes of troublesome boys. The secondary schools themselves had only a very small effect on the boys' offending.

The most famous study of school effects on offending was also carried out in London, by Rutter et al. (1979). They studied 12 comprehensive schools, and again found big differences in official delinquency rates between them. High delinquency-rate schools tended to have high truancy rates, low ability pupils, and low social class parents. However, the differences between the schools in delinquency rates could not be entirely explained by differences in the social class and verbal reasoning scores of the pupils at intake (age 11). Therefore, they must have been caused by some aspect of the schools themselves or by other, unmeasured factors.

In trying to discover which aspects of schools might be encouraging or inhibiting offending, Rutter et al. (1979) developed a measure of 'school process' based on school structure, organisation and functioning. This was related to children's misbehaviour in school, academic achievement and truancy independently of intake factors. However, it was not significantly related to delinquency independently of intake factors. The main school factors that were associated with delinquency were a high amount of punishment and a low amount of praise given by teachers in class. Unfortunately, it is difficult to know whether much punishment and little praise are causes or consequences of antisocial school behaviour, which in turn is probably linked to offending outside school. Therefore, it is not clear what school factors are conducive to delinquency.

Situational Influences

While most psychologists have aimed to explain the development of offending people, some have tried to explain the occurrence of offending events. Offenders are predominantly versatile rather than specialised. The typical offender who commits violence, vandalism or drug abuse also tends to commit theft or burglary. For example, in the London longitudinal survey, Farrington (1991b) reported that 86 per cent of convicted violent offenders (43 out of 50) also had convictions for non-violent offences. Hence, in studying characteristics of offenders, it seems unnecessary to develop a different theory for each different type of offence. In contrast, in trying to explain why certain offences occur, the situations are so diverse and specific to particular crimes that it probably is necessary to have different explanations for different types of offences.

The most popular theory of offending events suggests that they occur in response to specific opportunities, when their expected benefits (e.g. stolen property, peer approval) outweigh their expected costs (e.g. legal punishment, parental disapproval). For example, Clarke and Cornish (1985) outlined a theory of residential burglary which included such influencing factors as whether a house was occupied, whether it looked affluent, whether there were bushes to hide behind, whether there were nosy neighbours, whether the house had a burglar alarm and whether it contained a dog. Clarke (1992) argued that crime could be prevented by such situational changes as target hardening (e.g. security devices in cars), access control (e.g. entry-phones in blocks of flats) and surveillance (e.g. closed circuit television cameras). Other rational choice theories will be reviewed later.

In the London longitudinal study, the most common reasons given for offending were rational ones, suggesting that most property crimes were committed because the offenders wanted the items stolen (Farrington, 1993c). The next most common reasons focused on seeking excitement or enjoyment or relieving boredom. In Montreal, LeBlanc and Frechette (1989) also reported that most offences (e.g. burglary, theft, drug trafficking) were motivated by the utilitarian need for material goods, while others (e.g. shop-lifting, vandalism, joy-riding) were predominantly committed for excitement.

In agreement with the idea of deterrence, a number of cross-sectional surveys have shown that low estimates of the risk of being caught were correlated with high rates of self-reported offending (Erickson, Gibbs and Jensen, 1977). Unfortunately, the direction of causal influence is not clear in cross-sectional research, since committing delinquent acts may lead to lower estimates of the probability of detection as well as the reverse. Farrington and Knight (1980) carried out a number of studies, using experimental, survey, and observational methods, that suggested that stealing involved risky decision-making. Hence, it is plausible to suggest that opportunities for delinquency, the immediate costs and benefits of delinquency, and the probabilities of these outcomes, all influence whether people offend in any situation.

EXPLAINING OFFENDING

Motives and Causes in Psychology and Law

In psychology, motivation refers to the energising of behaviour (e.g. Jones, 1955). A classic idea in psychology was that biological needs or physiological deficits such as hunger and thirst produced motivational drives to satisfy the needs or remedy the deficits, for example by searching for and obtaining food and water (e.g. Hull, 1943). Hence, a drive was an aroused state that motivated a person to seek to satisfy a need. Needs led to drives, which led to goal-oriented behaviour. These ideas were inspired by the biological concept of homeostasis, which specifies that an organism acts to maintain biological variables such as body temperature at a tolerably constant level. This concept can be seen clearly in the idea of an optimum level of arousal which a person acts to maintain (e.g. Hebb, 1955).

Motivational ideas in psychology soon became less biological (for a review, see Weiner, 1992). Social and psychological needs were identified, such as the need for approval from one's family and the need for status among one's peers. Externally as well as internally aroused drives were recognised; Hull (1951) distinguished the 'push' of the drive from the 'pull' of the incentive or goal object. Just as tempting food might arouse a hunger drive, provocative and insulting behaviour might arouse anger and an aggressive motivation. Consideration of anger and aggression, and indeed the arousal level, shows the close link between ideas of emotion and ideas of motivation.

One of the most fundamental motivational ideas in psychology is that people (and especially children) are naturally hedonistic and selfish, seeking pleasure and avoiding pain, and hence that children need to be trained to behave pro-socially rather than antisocially. Another classic idea is that people are motivated to maintain an optimum level of arousal; if their level falls below the optimum, they will try to increase it (e.g. by stimulation-seeking), while if it is above the optimum they will try to decrease it. As examples, people might try to decrease their feelings of anger by hitting out against someone who is provoking them, and might try to decrease their empathetic distress by helping a victim. A third fundamental idea is that people are essentially rational decision-makers, weighing the expected benefits of outcomes against their expected costs in deciding whether to commit any act. Also, ideas of reinforcement and learning are important, suggesting that people learn how to behave by experience, according to their past history of rewards and punishments.

Unlike psychology, the law is based on the idea of the conscious mind, free will, intended or motivated behaviour, and individual responsibility for actions (see e.g. Bentley, 1979). However, as in psychology, the utilitarian ideas of Bentham (1948) are still influential, suggesting that people are essentially rational, weighing the likely benefits of offending against the likely costs. It follows that offenders might be deterred by increasing the legal punishments to tip the scales against crime. An important question is how far people are responsible for their offending, or alternatively how far their behaviour is caused by forces beyond their control, whether internal (e.g. low intelligence) or external (e.g. poor parenting). As already noted, psychologists are more likely than lawyers to emphasise the importance of these internal and external forces.

The idea of criminal responsibility is important in the law, suggesting that people cannot intentionally commit offences unless they know that the acts are wrong and can foresee the likely consequences of their actions. Traditionally in English common law, the minimum age of criminal responsibility was set at ten, because of the assumption that children under age ten did not have the appropriate *mens rea* or guilty mind. There is some relevant psychological research on the development of the concept of intentional behaviour in children. For example, Piaget (1932) asked children to judge naughtiness in hypothetical stories and found that these judgements were mainly influenced by consequences under age nine but by intentions from age nine onwards. However, Keasey and Sales (1977) in American research concluded that judgements of naughtiness were mainly based on intentions even for children as young as five. Hence, children of five understood the concept of intended or goal-directed behaviour and therefore in principle could commit legally defined crimes and give motivational explanations for their behaviour. Judges typically take account of both intentions and consequences in setting legal punishments.

Energising and Directing Factors

In research in which males are asked to give motives or reasons for their offending, the most important motives are as follows (see e.g. Cusson, 1983):

1. Economic or utilitarian motives, to obtain goods or money.

2. To obtain excitement, fun, thrills, daring, risk-taking, to relieve boredom.

3. To achieve self-esteem, peer approval, admiration, status, or popularity.

4. To demonstrate masculinity, toughness and bravery.

5. To show off and gain attention.

6. To reduce tension caused by anger, frustration or anxiety (e.g. by hurting someone).

7. To gain revenge.

8. To gain pleasure or excitement by seeing someone suffer, frightening someone, exerting power over someone, or victimising someone who is more fortunate.

9. To gain pleasure (e.g. substance abuse).

10. Curiosity (e.g. substance abuse).

11. Sexual gratification.

The major problem of interpreting such proffered reasons is that people may not have much insight into their mental processes or may merely be giving justifications or excuses. More criminal people, because they are particularly poor at manipulating abstract concepts, may also be particularly lacking in introspective insight about the motivations underlying their behaviour. In addition, their memories may be faulty or biased, as many people's memories often are. Another problem is that people may be more aware of immediate influences such as their need for money or excitement and may be unaware of or forget longer-term influences such as poor parenting or school failure. Just as delinquents are more influenced by immediate gratification rather than long-delayed future consequences, they may also be more aware of immediate motivations rather than those attributable to events in the distant past. Psychologists emphasise the importance of validating verbal reports against actual behaviour (Farrington et al., 1980).

A key issue is why a particular type of behaviour is engaged in to achieve a particular type of goal arising from a motivational need. For example, why do people who need money choose to steal or burgle rather than to obtain money through legitimate work? Why do people who need excitement choose to shop-lift or damage property rather than to obtain excitement through legitimate means? Most of the needs and drives hypothesised to underlie offending could be satisfied in legitimate ways, and antisocial behaviour might be reduced if they could be channelled into legitimate outlets. These questions require a study of the directing of behaviour.

Most psychological theories of offending include motivational constructs. For example, the psychoanalytic theory of Freud included the id as the source of motivational (instinctual) energy, the ego as a structure for controlling and directing the release of this energy, and the superego as an inhibitory mechanism, containing the conscience and guilt feelings. (For a review of psychoanalytic theory as applied to crime, see Kline, 1987.) Many other psychological theories include energising, directing, and inhibiting mechanisms.

In explaining violence, Berkowitz (1962) distinguished between angry and instrumental aggression. He argued that frustration was an important motivator of angry aggression, while instrumental aggression was governed more by cost-benefit considerations. He also proposed that aggression may have some reinforcing value, since some people may learn to hurt merely for the pleasure of hurting. Megargee's (1982) key explanatory constructs for aggression included instigation (motivating factors), habit strength (learning processes), inhibition, and stimulus (situational) factors. He provided an extensive list of motivating factors, classified as instrumental or extrinsic and angry or intrinsic.

My own theory (Farrington, 1986, 1992b, 1993c) was designed primarily to explain property offending by males, but it can be extended to explain other types of offending (e.g. violence and drug use) and other types of antisocial acts. It explicitly distinguishes between energising, directing, inhibiting, and decision-making processes, and also distinguishes between influences on an underlying criminal potential (or antisocial tendency) and influences on the behavioural manifestation of that potential in offending. It also emphasises the need to distinguish between influences on the onset, persistence, and desistance of offending. Differences between individuals are assumed to be in degree rather than in kind; it is postulated that individuals can be ordered on a single dimension of antisocial tendency, and that their relative positions on this dimension tend to be consistent over time.

My theory proposes that the main long-term energising factors that ultimately lead to between-individual variations in antisocial tendency are desires for material goods, status among intimates, and excitement, while the main short-term energising factors are boredom, frustration, provocation, anger, and alcohol consumption. The desire for excitement may be greater among children from poorer families, perhaps because excitement is more highly valued by lower-class people than by middle-class ones, because poorer children think they lead more boring lives, or because poorer children are less able to postpone immediate gratification in favour of long-term goals (which could be linked to the emphasis in lower-class culture on the concrete and present as opposed to the abstract and future).

In the directing stage, these motivations produce antisocial tendency if socially disapproved methods of satisfying them are habitually chosen. The methods chosen depend on maturation and behavioural skills; for example, a five-year old would have difficulty stealing a car. Some individuals (e.g. children from poorer families) are less able to satisfy their desires for material goods, excitement and social status by legal or socially approved methods, and so tend to choose illegal or socially disapproved methods. The relative inability of poorer children to achieve goals by legitimate methods could be because they tend to fail in school (Cohen, 1955) and tend to have erratic, low status employment histories. School failure in turn may often be a consequence of the less stimulating intellectual environment that lower-class parents tend to provide for their children, and their lack of emphasis on abstract concepts (Trasler, 1965).

Inhibitory Factors in Theories

Many psychological theories of offending focus on factors inhibiting offending rather than on factors encouraging (energising and directing) it. Trasler (1962) developed one of the most explicitly stated social learning theories of offending. Like Eysenck (1977), he proposed that tendencies to offend were inhibited by a conditioned anxiety response that was built up in childhood. However, unlike Eysenck's emphasis on genetic or constitutional differences in conditionability, Trasler focused on differences in child-rearing techniques.

Trasler proposed that, if parents consistently punished disapproved behaviour by children, the pain and anxiety aroused by the punishment tended to become associated with the disapproved behaviour by a process of classical conditioning. The conditioned anxiety then tended to arise automatically when the person contemplated the disapproved behaviour and tended to prevent the behaviour occurring. If the person committed the disapproved act, the conditioned anxiety would be experienced subjectively as guilt. Children were unlikely to build up the link between disapproved behaviour and anxiety unless their parents supervised them closely, used punishment consistently, and ensured that punishment was made contingent on disapproved acts. Hence, poor supervision, erratic discipline and inconsistency between parents were all conducive to delinquency in children. It was also important for parents to explain to children why they were being punished, so that they could discriminate precisely the behaviour that was disapproved.

Trasler argued that middle-class parents were more likely to explain to children why they were being punished and were more likely to be concerned with long-term character-building and the inculcation of general moral principles. This was linked to the greater facility of middle-class parents with language and abstract concepts. In contrast, according to Trasler, lower-class parents supervised their children less closely and were more inconsistent in their use of discipline. Generally, middle-class parents used love-oriented discipline, relying on withdrawal of love as the main sanction, whereas lower-class parents used much more physical punishment, but less consistently. Trasler contended that lower-class children committed more crimes because lower-class parents used less effective methods of socialisation.

Many other inhibitory factors have been proposed in theories of offending. In Gottfredson and Hirschi's (1990) theory, the key inhibitory factor is the degree of self-control, which is supposed to depend on parental child-rearing methods rather than on any genetic or biological factors. The most popular internal inhibitory factor is the the conscience (usually defined in terms of consciously articulated moral principles rather than biological responses), while the most popular external inhibitory factor is the likelihood of negative consequences such as legal punishment or parental disapproval.

My theory postulates that antisocial tendencies can be inhibited by internalised beliefs and attitudes that have been built up in a social learning process as a result of a history of rewards and punishments. The belief that offending is wrong, or a strong conscience, tends to be built up if parents are in favour of legal norms, if they exercise close supervision over their children, and if they consistently punish socially disapproved behaviour using love-oriented discipline. In addition, a strong conscience might be fostered by a genetically or biologically high degree of fearfulness (Kagan, Reznick and Snidman, 1988) or high conditionability. Antisocial tendency might also be inhibited by empathy, which may develop as a result of parental warmth and loving relationships. The belief that offending is legitimate, and anti-establishment attitudes generally, tend to be built up if children have been exposed to attitudes and behaviour favouring offending (e.g. in a modelling process), especially by members of their family, by their friends, and in their communities.

Decision-making in Criminal Opportunities

As already noted, many psychological theories assume that the commission of offences involves a cost-benefit decision. For example, Wilson and Herrnstein's (1985) theory includes elements of impulsivity, social learning, and rational decision-making. They proposed that offences were committed in order to obtain either primary reinforcers such as sexual gratification or food, or secondary reinforcers such as money or status. Offending essentially involved a rational decision in which the expected benefits were weighed against the expected costs. People who gave relatively less weight to future consequences (e.g. legal punishment) as opposed to more immediate ones (e.g. loot) were more likely to offend. Wilson and Herrnstein also included equity ideas in their theory, suggesting that people who thought they were the victims of inequity (receiving lower benefits than their efforts or worth deserved) might commit offences in order to restore their subjective equity.

Historically, the most important cost-benefit theory in psychology has been the subjectively expected utility or SEU theory (Edwards, 1961). This suggests that people will choose behaviour in order to maximise their SEU, defined as the product of the subjective probability and utility (subjective value or attractiveness) of an outcome. For example, a person might decide to commit a crime if the SEU of the crime exceeded the SEU of each alternative course of action (Farrington and Knight, 1980). In calculating the SEU of a crime, the person might compare the subjective probability and utility of getting away with it (e.g. loot, peer approval) with the subjective probability and disutility of getting caught by the police (e.g. legal punishment, parental disapproval).

My theory includes a decision-making stage, which specifies that whether a person with a certain degree of antisocial tendency commits an antisocial act in a given situation depends on opportunities, costs and benefits, and on the subjective probabilities of the different outcomes. The costs and benefits include immediate situational factors such as the material goods that can be stolen and the likelihood and consequences of being caught by the police, as perceived by the individual. They also include social factors such as likely disapproval by parents or spouses, and encouragement or reinforcement from peers. In general, people make rational decisions. They choose to commit antisocial acts if the net benefits (expected benefits minus expected costs) of these acts exceed the net benefits of alternative acts. However, more impulsive people are less likely to consider the possible consequences of their actions, especially consequences that are likely to be long delayed. Impulsive people give relatively more weight to immediate rather than longer-term outcomes, and hence are more likely to commit antisocial acts.

The consequences of offending feed back to antisocial tendency and to the cost-benefit calculation in a learning process. If the consequences include official labelling, stigmatisation, and isolation with other offenders, this may make it more difficult for offenders to achieve their goals legally, and hence it may lead to an increase in antisocial tendency. If the consequences of crime are reinforcing (e.g. gaining material goods or peer approval) or punishing (e.g. legal sanctions or parental disapproval), this may affect the person's future subjective estimation of costs, benefits and probabilities.

Offending may increase to a peak between ages 14 and 20 because boys (especially lower-class school failures) have especially high desires for excitement, material goods and social status between these ages, little chance of achieving their desires legally, and little to lose (since legal penalties are lenient and their intimates—male peers—often approve of offending). In contrast, after age 20, desires become attenuated or more realistic, there is more possibility of achieving these more limited goals legally, internal inhibitions may be greater, and the costs of offending are greater (since legal penalties are harsher and their intimates—wives or girlfriends—disapprove of offending).

CONCLUSIONS

Psychologists argue that there are many influences and constraints on criminal behaviour. Individual factors such as low intelligence, poor school attainment, a poor ability to manipulate abstract concepts and high impulsivity all make offending more likely. Environmental factors such as poor parental supervision and discipline, broken homes, large families, criminal parents, delinquent friends and high delinquency-rate schools also increase the probability of offending. Some people are consistently more likely to offend than others (i.e. have higher criminal potential) over time and in different situations. Therefore, psychologists would argue that people do not have complete free will, or a completely unconstrained choice, in deciding whether to commit crimes.

While offending is not completely unconstrained, it is not completely determined either. Cusson (1983, p. 12) complained about the view of the delinquent as 'a monstrous puppet, tied hand and foot, and committed to the manipulations of an interminable series of bio-psycho-socio-cultural factors'. Instead, he argued that delinquents had some freedom to pursue goals and objectives in order to satisfy their perceived needs, although they were also constrained by factors over which they had little control, such as their heredity, childhood and environment. This seems a reasonable argument.

Psychological theories of offending typically include energising, directing, inhibiting and decision-making processes. The energising and directing processes, such as a need for money or excitement, are not entirely a person's individual responsibility, since they depend on upbringing and social circumstances. The same is true of the inhibiting processes, which depend on social learning, punishment, the degree of guilt or anxiety, and the strength of the conscience. However, psychology and law are in greatest agreement when discussing decision-making processes, which are under conscious control and which involve the weighing of expected costs (e.g. legal punishment) against expected benefits (e.g. loot).

To conclude, lawyers focus primarily on individual decision-making processes, but psychologists regard these as the final stage of a long chain of processes influencing offending. People faced with criminal opportunities differ greatly in their underlying criminal potential or prior probability of offending, and to that extent do not make completely free choices. In this chapter, I have tried to summarise psychological research and theories on the origins of these consistent individual differences in criminal potential, to make this knowledge accessible both to lawyers and to psychologists who appear in court as expert witnesses.

REFERENCES

American Psychiatric Association (1994). *Diagnostic and Statistical Manual of Mental Disorders* (4th edn). Washington, DC: APA.

Bentham, J. (1948). *An Introduction to the Principles of Morals and Legislation.* Oxford: Blackwell. (Original work published 1779.)

Bentley, D. (1979). The infant and the dream: psychology and the law. In D.P. Farrington, K. Hawkins and S.M. Lloyd-Bostock (Eds), *Psychology, Law, and Legal Processes.* London: Macmillan, pp. 35–43.

Berkowitz, L. (1962). *Aggression: A Social Psychological Analysis.* New York: McGraw-Hill.

Blackburn, R. (1993). *The Psychology of Criminal Conduct.* Chichester: John Wiley.

Blouin, A.G., Conners, C.K., Seidel, W.T. and Blouin, J. (1989). The independence of hyperactivity from conduct disorder: methodological considerations. *Canadian Journal of Psychiatry*, **34**, 279–82.

Clarke, R.V. (1992). Introduction. In R.V. Clarke (Ed.), *Situational Crime Prevention.* New York: Harrow and Heston, pp. 3–36.

Clarke, R.V. and Cornish, D.B. (1985). Modelling offenders' decisions: a framework for research and policy. In M. Tonry and N. Morris (Eds), *Crime and Justice*, vol. 6. Chicago: University of Chicago Press: pp. 147–85.

Cohen, A.K. (1955). *Delinquent Boys.* Glencoe, IL: Free Press.

Cusson, M. (1983). *Why Delinquency?* Toronto: University of Toronto Press.

Edwards, W. (1961). Behavioural decision theory. *Annual Review of Psychology*, **12**, 473–98.

Elliott, D.S., Huizinga, D. and Ageton, S.S. (1985). *Explaining Delinquency and Drug Use.* Beverly Hills, CA: Sage.

Erickson, M., Gibbs, J.P. and Jensen, G.F. (1977). The deterrence doctrine and the perceived certainty of legal punishment. *American Sociological Review*, **42**, 305–17.

Eysenck, H.J. (1977). *Crime and Personality* (3rd edn). London: Routledge & Kegan Paul.

Farrington, D.P. (1972). Delinquency begins at home. *New Society*, **21**, 495–7.

Farrington, D.P. (1978). The family backgrounds of aggressive youths. In L. Hersov, M. Berger and D. Shaffer (Eds), *Aggression and Antisocial Behaviour in Childhood and Adolescence.* Oxford: Pergamon, pp. 73–93.

Farrington, D.P. (1979). Environmental stress, delinquent behaviour, and convictions. In I.G. Sarason and C.D. Spielberger (Eds), *Stress and Anxiety*, vol. 6. Washington, DC: Hemisphere, pp. 93–107.

Farrington, D.P. (1984). Delinquent and criminal behaviour. In A. Gale and A.J. Chapman (Eds), *Psychology and Social Problems.* Chichester: John Wiley, pp. 55–77.

Farrington, D.P. (1986). Stepping stones to adult criminal careers. In D. Olweus, J. Block and M.R. Yarrow (Eds), *Development of Antisocial and Prosocial Behaviour.* New York: Academic Press, pp. 359–84.

Farrington, D.P. (1987). Epidemiology. In H.C. Quay (Ed.), *Handbook of Juvenile Delinquency.* New York: Wiley, pp. 33–61.

Farrington, D.P. (1989). Self-reported and official offending from adolescence to adulthood. In M.W. Klein (Ed.), *Cross-national Research in Self-reported Crime and Delinquency.* Dordrecht, Netherlands: Kluwer, pp. 399–423.

Farrington, D.P. (1990a). Age, period, cohort, and offending. In D.M. Gottfredson and R.V. Clarke (Eds), *Policy and Theory in Criminal Justice: Contributions in Honour of Leslie T. Wilkins*. Aldershot: Avebury, pp. 51–75.

Farrington, D.P. (1990b). Implications of criminal career research for the prevention of offending. *Journal of Adolescence*, **13**, 93–113.

Farrington, D.P. (1991a). Antisocial personality from childhood to adulthood. *The Psychologist*, **4**, 389–94.

Farrington, D.P. (1991b). Childhood aggression and adult violence: early precursors and later life outcomes. In D.J. Pepler and K.H. Rubin (Eds), *The Development and Treatment of Childhood Aggression*. Hillsdale, NJ: Erlbaum, pp. 5–29.

Farrington, D.P. (1991c). Psychological contributions to the explanation of offending. In M. McMurran and C. McDougall (Eds), *Proceedings of the First DCLP Annual Conference*, vol. 1. Leicester: British Psychological Society, pp. 7–19.

Farrington, D.P. (1992a). Criminal career research in the United Kingdom. *British Journal of Criminology*, **32**, 521–36.

Farrington, D.P. (1992b). Explaining the beginning, progress and ending of antisocial behaviour from birth to adulthood. In J. McCord (Ed.), *Facts, Frameworks and Forecasts: Advances in Criminological Theory*, vol. 3. New Brunswick, NJ: Transaction, pp. 253–86.

Farrington, D.P. (1992c). Juvenile delinquency. In J.C. Coleman (Ed.), *The School Years* (2nd edn). London: Routledge, pp. 123–63.

Farrington, D.P. (1993a). Childhood origins of teenage antisocial behaviour and adult social dysfunction. *Journal of the Royal Society of Medicine*, **86**, 13 7.

Farrington, D.P. (1993b). Have any individual, family or neighbourhood influences on offending been demonstrated conclusively? In D.P. Farrington, R.J. Sampson and P.O. Wikstrom (Eds), *Integrating Individual and Ecological Aspects of Crime*. Stockholm: National Council for Crime Prevention, pp. 3–37.

Farrington, D.P. (1993c). Motivations for conduct disorder and delinquency. *Development and Psychopathology*, **5**, 225–41.

Farrington, D.P. (1993d). The psycho-social milieu of the offender. In J. Gunn and P. Taylor (Eds), *Forensic Psychiatry: Clinical, Legal and Ethical Issues*. Oxford: Butterworth-Heinemann, pp. 252–85.

Farrington, D.P. (1994). Childhood, adolescent and adult features of violent males. In L.R. Huesmann (Ed.), *Aggressive Behaviour: Current Perspectives*. New York: Plenum, pp. 215–40.

Farrington, D.P. and Knight, B.J. (1980). Four studies of stealing as a risky decision. In P.D. Lipsitt and B.D. Sales (Eds), *New Directions in Psycholegal Research*. New York: Van Nostrand Reinhold, pp. 26–50.

Farrington, D.P. and West, D.J. (1990). The Cambridge study in delinquent development: a long-term follow-up of 411 London males. In H.J. Kerner and G. Kaiser (Eds), *Criminality: Personality, Behaviour, Life History*. Berlin: Springer-Verlag, pp. 115–38.

Farrington, D.P., Biron, L. and LeBlanc, M. (1982). Personality and delinquency in London and Montreal. In J. Gunn and D.P. Farrington (Eds), *Abnormal Offenders, Delinquency, and the Criminal Justice System*. Chichester: John Wiley, pp. 153–201.

Farrington, D.P., Loeber, R. and Van Kammen, W.B. (1990). Long-term criminal outcomes of hyperactivity-impulsivity-attention deficit and conduct problems in childhood. In L.N. Robins and M. Rutter (Eds), *Straight and Devious Pathways from Childhood to Adulthood*. Cambridge: Cambridge University Press, pp. 62–81.

Farrington, D.P., Knapp, W.S., Erickson, B.E. and Knight, B.J. (1980). Words and deeds in the study of stealing. *Journal of Adolescence*, **3**, 35–49.

Fischer, D.G. (1984). Family size and delinquency. *Perceptual and Motor Skills*, **58**, 527–34.

Gottfredson, M. and Hirschi, T. (1990). *A General Theory of Crime*. Stanford, California: Stanford University Press.

Hebb, D.O. (1955). Drives and the CNS (conceptual nervous system). *Psychological Review*, **62**, 243–54.

Hirschi, T. (1969). *Causes of Delinquency*. Berkeley, CA: University of California Press.

Hirschi, T. and Hindelang, M.J. (1977). Intelligence and delinquency: a revisionist review. *American Sociological Review*, **42**, 571–87.

Hollin, C.R. (1989). *Psychology and Crime*. London: Routledge.

Hull, C.L. (1943). *Principles of Behaviour*. New York: Appleton-Century-Crofts.

Hull, C.L. (1951). *Essentials of Behaviour*. New Haven, CT: Yale University Press.

Jones, M.B., Offord, D.R. and Abrams, N. (1980). Brothers, sisters and antisocial behaviour. *British Journal of Psychiatry*, **136**, 139–45.

Jones, M.R. (1955). Introduction. In M.R. Jones (Ed.), *Nebraska Symposium on Motivation*. Lincoln, Nebraska: University of Nebraska Press, pp. vii–ix.

Kagan, J., Reznick, J.S. and Snidman, N. (1988). Biological bases of childhood shyness. *Science*, **240**, 167–71.

Keasey, C.B. and Sales, B.D. (1977). An empirical investigation of young children's awareness and usage of intentionality in criminal situations. *Law and Human Behaviour*, **1**, 45–61.

Kline, P. (1987). Psychoanalysis and crime. In B.J. McGurk, D.M. Thornton and M. Williams (Eds), *Applying Psychology to Imprisonment*. London: HMSO, pp. 59–75.

Kohlberg, L. (1976). Moral stages and moralisation: the cognitive-developmental approach. In T. Lickona (Ed.), *Moral Development and Behaviour*. New York: Holt, Rinehart & Winston, pp. 31–53.

Kolvin, I., Miller, F.J.W., Fleeting, M. and Kolvin, P.A. (1988). Social and parenting factors affecting criminal-offence rates: findings from the Newcastle Thousand Family Study (1947–1980). *British Journal of Psychiatry*, **152**, 80–90.

Kolvin, I., Miller, F.J.W., Scott, D.M., Gatzanis, S.R.M. and Fleeting, M. (1990). *Continuities of Deprivation?* Aldershot: Avebury.

LeBlanc, M. and Frechette, M. (1989). *Male Criminal Activity from Childhood through Youth*. New York: Springer-Verlag.

Loeber, R. (1987). Behavioural precursors and accelerators of delinquency. In W. Buikhuisen and S.A. Mednick (Eds), *Explaining Criminal Behaviour*. Leiden, Netherlands: Brill, pp. 51–67.

Loeber, R. and Dishion, T. (1983). Early predictors of male delinquency: a review. *Psychological Bulletin*, **94**, 68–99.

Loeber, R. and Stouthamer-Loeber, M. (1986). Family factors as correlates and predictors of juvenile conduct problems and delinquency. In M. Tonry and N. Morris (Eds), *Crime and Justice*, vol. 7. Chicago: University of Chicago Press, pp. 29–149.

Loeber, R. and Stouthamer-Loeber, M. (1987). Prediction. In H.C. Quay (Ed.), *Handbook of Juvenile Delinquency*. New York: Wiley, pp. 325–82.

Lynam, D., Moffitt, T. and Stouthamer-Loeber, M. (1993). Explaining the relation between IQ and delinquency: class, race, test motivation, school failure or self-control? *Journal of Abnormal Psychology*, **102**, 187–96.

McCord, J. (1979). Some child-rearing antecedents of criminal behaviour in adult men. *Journal of Personality and Social Psychology*, **37**, 1477–86.

Mednick, S.A., Gabrielli, W.F. and Hutchings, B. (1983). Genetic influences on criminal behaviour: Evidence from an adoption cohort. In K.T. Van Dusen and S.A. Mednick (Eds), *Prospective Studies of Crime and Delinquency*. Boston: Kluwer-Nijhoff, pp. 39–56.

Megargee, E.I. (1982). Psychological determinants and correlates of criminal violence. In M.E. Wolfgang and N.A. Weiner (Eds), *Criminal Violence*. Beverly Hills, CA: Sage, pp. 81–170.

Moffitt, T.E. (1990). The neuropsychology of juvenile delinquency: a critical review. In M. Tonry and N. Morris (Eds), *Crime and Justice*, vol. 12. Chicago: University of Chicago Press, pp. 99–169.

Moffitt, T.E. and Henry, B. (1989). Neuropsychological assessment of executive functions in self-reported delinquents. *Development and Psychopathology*, **1**, 105–18.

Moffitt, T.E. and Silva, P.A. (1988a). IQ and delinquency: a direct test of the differential detection hypothesis. *Journal of Abnormal Psychology*, **97**, 330–3.

Moffitt, T.E. and Silva, P.A. (1988b). Neuropsychological deficit and self-reported delinquency in an unselected birth cohort. *Journal of the American Academy of Child and Adolescent Psychiatry*, **27**, 233–40.

Nelson, J.R., Smith, D.J. and Dodd, J. (1990). The moral reasoning of juvenile delinquents: a meta-analysis. *Journal of Abnormal Child Psychology*, **18**, 231–9.

Newson, J., Newson, E. and Adams, M. (1993). The social origins of delinquency. *Criminal Behaviour and Mental Health*, **3**, 19–29.

Piaget, J. (1932). *The Moral Judgement of the Child*. London: Kegan Paul.

Power, M.J., Alderson, M.R., Phillipson, C.M., Shoenberg, E. and Morris, J.N. (1967). Delinquent schools? *New Society*, **10**, 542–3.

Pulkkinen, L. (1988). Delinquent development: theoretical and empirical considerations. In M. Rutter (Ed.), *Studies of Psychosocial Risk*. Cambridge: Cambridge University Press, pp. 184–99.

Reiss, A.J. (1988). Co-offending and criminal careers. In M. Tonry and N. Morris (Eds), *Crime and Justice*, vol. 10. Chicago: University of Chicago Press, pp. 117–70.

Reiss, A.J. and Farrington, D.P. (1991). Advancing knowledge about co-offending: results from a prospective longitudinal survey of London males. *Journal of Criminal Law and Criminology*, **82**, 360–95.

Robins, L.N. (1979). Sturdy childhood predictors of adult outcomes: replications from longitudinal studies. In J.E. Barrett, R.M. Rose and G.L. Klerman (Eds), *Stress and Mental Disorder*. New York: Raven Press, pp. 219–35.

Ruma, E.H. and Mosher, D.L. (1967). Relationship between moral judgment and guilt in delinquent boys. *Journal of Abnormal Psychology*, **72**, 122–7.

Rutter, M., Maughan, B., Mortimore, P. and Ouston, J. (1979). *Fifteen Thousand Hours*. London: Open Books.

Smetana, J.G. (1990). Morality and conduct disorders. In M. Lewis and S.M. Miller (Eds), *Handbook of Developmental Psychopathology*. New York: Plenum, pp. 157–79.

Taylor, E.A. (1986). Childhood hyperactivity. *British Journal of Psychiatry*, **149**, 562–73.

Tennenbaum, D.J. (1977). Personality and criminality: a summary and implications of the literature. *Journal of Criminal Justice*, **5**, 225–35.

Trasler, G.B. (1962). *The Explanation of Criminality*. London: Routledge & Kegan Paul.

Trasler, G.B. (1965). Criminality and the socialisation process. *Advancement of Science*, **21**, 545–50.

Utting, D., Bright, J. and Henricson, C. (1993). *Crime and the Family*. London: Family Policy Studies Centre.

Wadsworth, M. (1979). *Roots of Delinquency*. London: Martin Robertson.

Weiner, B. (1992). *Human Motivation*. Newbury Park, CA: Sage.

West, D.J. and Farrington, D.P. (1973). *Who Becomes Delinquent?* London: Heinemann.

West, D.J. and Farrington, D.P. (1977). *The Delinquent Way of Life*. London: Heinemann.

White, H.R., Labouvie, E.W. and Bates, M.E. (1985). The relationship between sensation seeking and delinquency: a longitudinal analysis. *Journal of Research in Crime and Delinquency*, **22**, 197–211.

Widom, C.S. (1989). The cycle of violence. *Science*, **244**, 160–6.

Wikstrom, P.O. (1987). *Patterns of Crime in a Birth Cohort*. Stockholm: University of Stockholm Department of Sociology.

Wilson, H. (1980). Parental supervision: a neglected aspect of delinquency. *British Journal of Criminology*, **20**, 203–35.

Wilson, J.Q. and Herrnstein, R.J. (1985). *Crime and Human Nature*. New York: Simon & Schuster.

Zimring, F.E. (1981). Kids, groups and crime: some implications of a well-known secret. *Journal of Criminal Law and Criminology*, **72**, 867–85.

Chapter 4.3

Legal and Psychological Concepts of Mental Status

R. Glynn Owens
University of Wales

INTRODUCTION

In considering a crime it is necessary, in forming a judgement, to consider *actus reus, mens rea,* causation and defence. At first glance, these might appear relatively straightforward. *Actus reus* simply refers to the notion that the accused caused the particular act in question—the accused did, in fact, break into the house, take the car, or shoot the victim. Note that it is important that the act be performed voluntarily; if someone is killed as a result of a driver having an unpredictable heart attack, this would not normally constitute an *actus reus*.

It is not usually sufficient, however, to show that the defendant performed the act in question; most crimes will also require that the defendant was in a particular 'state of mind' at the time—the *mens rea*. It is important to note that some crimes (e.g. strict liability offences, such as parking in a prohibited place) may not involve *mens rea*, and others (e.g. manslaughter) may be satisfied by gross negligence or recklessness. Generally, however, *mens rea* will involve showing that the defendant intended to perform the *actus reus* or was prepared to take the risk. By implication, causing the *actus reus* accidentally will not indicate guilt outside of strict liability offences.

Even when both *actus reus* and *mens rea* requirements are satisfied, the defendant may still be found not guilty, or have the crime charged reduced as a result of a defence. Consequently, an individual who intentionally kills another may raise as a defence that this was done in self-defence or because provoked.

From a psychological perspective, it is interesting to look at each of these and

Handbook of Psychology in Legal Contexts
Edited by R. Bull and D. Carson. © 1995 John Wiley & Sons Ltd

consider why the law has felt it necessary to incorporate them into decisions regarding guilt and innocence. Taken to an extreme, it can be argued that a central role of the law is to maximise the likelihood that members of society will behave in a manner deemed acceptable, and to do so in a manner which is regarded as fair and just. The law, therefore, needs to be concerned with distinguishing acceptable and unacceptable behaviour and exerting appropriate controls (usually some form of punishment) in an equitable and effective manner. From this viewpoint, each of the elements of a crime—*actus reus*, *mens rea*, causation and defence—are of psychological interest. Examined closely, it might be argued that many of these concepts are less well defined than we might like to think, and that their logical foundation is suspect. One purpose of this chapter is to argue that the courts have a central role to play in deciding (in each case) what is 'reasonable' and that this role is given greater importance the more the weaknesses of other concepts are recognised.

ACTUS REUS

A crucial element of the *actus reus* is that the behaviour in question is voluntary. The purpose of this is to exclude behaviour which the individual 'could not help'. To take a trivial example, people who kick the doctor as a result of a test of the patellar reflex would not be guilty of battery—it is of the nature of the test that the foot will jerk forwards, and under these circumstances the behaviour is not 'wilful'. The same principle may apply in other circumstances. For example, the popular notion of an epileptic seizure involves the so-called 'grand mal' attack, with the individual falling to the floor, exhibiting jerky movements, etc. When, however, the focal centre of the epilepsy is in the temporal lobe of the brain, the effect of a seizure may be quite different, and the individual may simply perform some automatic act without being aware of doing so. Again, this would not constitute 'wilful' activity and the conditions for *actus reus* would not necessarily be satisfied; it might be possible for the defence to argue that the epilepsy constituted a 'disease of the mind' leading to 'insane automatism'.

Now consider a young person standing in the street shouting obscenities as people pass by. One might imagine such an individual to be a prime candidate for a charge of 'behaviour likely to cause a breach of the peace' or such like. It could be, however, that the individual suffers from a condition known as De Tourette's syndrome, amongst whose characteristics is this very behaviour of (involuntarily) shouting out obscenities. Presumably such an individual would not be considered to be guilty of any offence, since the behaviour was not 'wilful'. However, there is some evidence that, for some such patients at least, the therapeutic use of punishment can lead to a reduction in the frequency of the obscene utterances. If the individual is capable of holding in check the urge to shout obscenities once punishment is involved, is it appropriate to regard the behaviour as wilful?

Here we begin to see how the concept of what is 'reasonable' can be seen as central to judicial decision-making. If the court were to decide that the behaviour was indeed wilful, it might still be argued that, given the relatively trivial nature of the offence, the use of a punishment programme would be unreasonable. An alternative might be to go beyond the simple dichotomy of 'wilful/unwilful' to a continuum, of which these two represented the extremes. To do so, however, might involve a major upheaval of the legal system. For example, Eysenck (1964) has presented a theory of criminal behaviour which suggests that certain personality types, characterised by high levels of extraversion, neuroticism and psychoticism, might be predisposed to criminal behaviour. Moreover, he has argued that these personality characteristics are largely inherited, so that individuals can no more be held responsible for these than for the colour of their eyes or the size of their feet.

As it happens, Eysenck's theory of criminality has a number of difficulties, and is far from being generally accepted by psychologists. But this is not to say that this theory, or one like it, could not be true. How might the law respond? It is not possible to argue that the individual with a particular genetic make-up 'had no choice' but to become criminal, since many individuals of this type remain law-abiding (a similar observation has been made in the context of genetic abnormalities like the XYY syndrome—see, for example, Owens and Ashcroft, 1985). Clearly, if the 'wilfulness' of an act were seen on a continuum, one might wish to argue that an individual genetically predisposed to crime might be less responsible for his or her own behaviour than one not so predisposed.

One possibility might be to regard such a predisposition as a mitigating circumstance, with due allowance for this characteristic being made in the sentence. This could be problematic, however, if the theory implies that such individuals would need more, not less, punishment. That a theory may have such implications is far from implausible, and indeed Eysenck's theory argues exactly this; extroverts are seen as more difficult to 'condition' into pro-social behaviour, and thereby need more, not less, punishment. The law, therefore, has two conflicting objectives; to provide a just sentence, which would imply a lighter punishment for those less culpable, and to provide an effective sentence, which would imply a heavier punishment. The most obvious resolution of this conflict would presumably involve the courts deciding what balance between justice and rehabilitation was reasonable.

Thus, whichever way the courts decide to construe an act as 'wilful'—either a dichotomy or a continuum—the same end point is reached. Ultimately, the court has to decide what is 'reasonable'. This is not, of course, to say that issues of wilfulness should be ignored, or that the courts should continue as they have always done. Rather, it is to say that the court's final decision, as to what is reasonable under the circumstances, will need to take account of the extent to which individuals might be said to be in control of their own behaviour and to balance this against the needs of deterrence. The basic decision is still one of what is reasonable, but this now has to be reasonable in the light of what we know about the causes of crime and the extent to which we can hold an individual responsible.

MENS REA

Mens rea, the state of mind of the individual, is perhaps the element of crime which most obviously concerns psychology. A central notion here is that of intention. For a crime that requires proof of intention, it is critical to discover what the defendant's intentions were at the time of the offence. For example, I was once called in in defence of a man charged with shop-lifting. The man had been in a high street store with his small child when the child had suddenly run outside into the main street. The father pursued the child and found himself outside the store still holding the goods he had intended to purchase but had not paid for. He was apprehended by the store detective and charged with shop-lifting. In this instance, the *actus reus* was not in doubt—the defendant had appropriated property belonging to another (Theft Act 1967, s. 1). However, it was argued that he had no 'intention to permanently deprive' the rightful owner, and he was found not guilty. Other notions of particular relevance in considering *mens rea* are those of awareness (e.g. whether the individual knew that what (s)he doing was wrong and dangerous) and negligence (e.g. whether the individual acted without due consideration for others).

Motive and Intent

It should be noted that these *mens rea* concepts go beyond the notion of an act being wilful. For example, if a scaffolder throws his hammer to the ground, the throwing behaviour is certainly wilful. If, however, the hammer strikes someone on landing and causes death or injury, *mens rea* concepts will still need to be addressed. It will be important to determine whether the scaffolder intended to hit the victim with the hammer, or was just reckless in throwing it.

Unfortunately, none of the *mens rea* issues is open to independent observation. One cannot see other people's intention, awareness, recklessness; one can only infer them from other observations. Usually, an individual will be aware of his or her own state of mind, and sometimes it will be possible to determine such state of mind by direct questioning. The scaffolder in the above example may be asked: 'Did you intend to hit the victim with the hammer when you threw it?' Obviously there are problems here. The scaffolder may have had such an intention but deny it, given that an admission of guilt might lead to unpleasant consequences. Under such circumstances, it is necessary for the prosecution to submit further evidence to support the case that, despite the denial, the defendant did indeed intend to cause harm. From a psychological viewpoint, the prosecution needs to show that circumstances were such that it would be reasonable to infer that the defendant had intent. In practice, this may be extremely complicated. Taking the example of the scaffolder and the hammer, this would involve recognising the kinds of processes which might lead to an aggressive response. These might include showing that the victim had previously caused harm or distress to the defendant, or that the defendant stood to gain from injuring the victim, i.e. motive. Similarly, evidence against the alternative explanation—that the dropping of the hammer was accidental— may be submitted. For example, if the defendant was unable to give an innocent explanation of being in possession of a hammer at exactly the time the victim passed underneath, this might further support the notion of the behaviour being intended. In an ideal world, it would be possible to identify various 'markers' of deceit in the individual's behaviour; however, from the early attempts at 'lie detecting' through changes in skin conductivity to more recent behavioural attempts, such methods have had spectacular lack of success (for a review of relevant work see Druckman and Bjork, 1991).

Note that none of this demonstrates for certain that the defendant's behaviour was indeed with intent to cause harm. For example, an individual may be in a position to gain from injury or death of another, may have reason to wish that other harm, yet still fail to act on the implied motives. In particular, they may be inhibited by strong moral or religious feelings that it is wrong to do harm to others, or simply be too afraid of the possible consequences of being found out. If such an individual did (in the present example) then drop the hammer accidentally, it might be extremely difficult for the court to decide whether or not the behaviour was indeed intentional or not.

An interesting aside on this problem is offered by a traditional Freudian perspective on human behaviour. Throughout his writings, Freud maintained a strictly determinist view of psychology; whatever people did, he argued, they did for a reason. Since such reasons were not always apparent to the individual, Freud invented the notion of the unconscious as a repository for those motives etc. of which the individual was unaware. One implication of Freud's view, which he discussed at length in his *Psychopathology of Everyday Life* (an excellent summary of which can be found in Storr, 1989), was that there is no such thing as an accident; rather, the behaviours we call accidental reflect unconscious motivations. So, if an individual 'accidentally' dropped a hammer on another, a Freudian might explain this in terms of an unconscious wish to do that person some harm. The process would thus be something like: circumstances motivate the defendant to do harm to the victim, the defendant finds such a motive personally unacceptable and represses it. In consequence the motive remains in the unconscious, ready to find expression at a suitable opportunity. According to such a model no one's behaviour is truly accidental and everything we do reflects some motivation, either conscious or unconscious. Although such hard-line Freudianism is not generally accepted by psychologists, it is worth noting that similar arguments could be adduced from other determinist psychologies such as radical behaviourism (Skinner,

1969). Radical behaviourism applies a strictly materialist perspective to the whole of human behaviour; moreover it adopts a definition of behaviour which is considerably wider than the commonplace concept, subsuming 'behaviours' such as seeing, thinking, paying attention, and so on. Apart from possibly deciding that only conscious motives come within the scope of the courts, it is hard to imagine how the legal system might deal with such a viewpoint. Indeed, the acceptance of any wholly determinist model of human behaviour would present the legal system with so many other problems that this is unlikely to become an issue in the foreseeable future.

A particular problem with deciding issues of intent is that innocent individuals may, under certain circumstances, lay claim to having had guilty intentions. For example, an individual who accidentally injures another may later claim that an action was, in fact, intended to cause harm. To the casual observer, it may seem unlikely that anyone would behave in this way, with the almost inevitable punishment which would ensue. Why should anyone confess unless they really did have criminal intent? There are several possibilities here: (i) the individual mistakenly comes to believe that (s)he really did have some criminal intent at the time; (ii) the individual may realise that (s)he is not guilty but nevertheless make a deliberate decision to claim guilt; and (iii) the individual may make false confessions whilst her/his judgement is for some reason disturbed, later regretting having done so.

It is important to remember that individuals are not necessarily correct when assessing their own motivations. People may forget, or their interpretation of their motivation may be excessively influenced by others (e.g. police, counsel). Gudjonnson (1991, 1992) has shown that people of normal intellectual ability may nevertheless be highly suggestible; such suggestibility may occur through 'yield' (changing a viewpoint in the light of misleading information) or 'shift' (changing a viewpoint in response to interpersonal pressure). A recent study by Sharrock and Gudjonsson (1993) indicated very low correlations between IQ and both dimensions of suggestibility, and implied 'a sizeable proportion ... of those of normal [IQ] ... score abnormally high in suggestibility' (p. 174). This may be problematic where a court regards the testimony of an expert witness regarding suggestibility as inadmissible when the defendant shows no signs of mental impairment.

Similar problems occur when an individual chooses to confess falsely to guilty actions or intentions. Outside of romantic novels, confessing to protect others is probably rare, but individuals may falsely confess while their judgement is disturbed, later regretting having done so.

Several processes may be important here. First, it is important to remember that people are often very much more influenced by immediate consequences than ones which will occur at some indeterminate time in the future. An obvious example here is the way in which people continue to smoke despite the long-term dangers. An implication of this is that an individual who is being questioned by police officers, finding the whole business extremely distressing, may be at risk of agreeing to whatever the questioning officer suggests simply in order to be allowed to leave and go home; the fact that this is storing up trouble for the future is less significant than the immediate consequence of escape from the situation.

A second important factor is the effect of severe and sustained stress in behaviour. One of the first victims of continued stress may be the individual's psychological processes. Stressed individuals may have difficulty perceiving situations accurately, and the stress may produce severe impairment of judgement and decision-making ability. Moreover, the individual under stress may become particularly vulnerable to influence by others who are seen as strong and capable—partly because, recognising that their own judgement is impaired, the temptation to defer to the judgement of others may be heightened.

This was apparent in the aforementioned shop-lifting case, for the father, when questioned by the police, was separated from his child while a statement was taken. The father panicked, his overriding concern being to be reunited with his child, to extricate himself from the situation and to return home. He paid little attention to what was being said to him and simply agreed with whatever the interviewing officer said. At the time he was being questioned, and during the preparation of his statement, he was in no position to think clearly. For example, he showed no signs of considering the longer-term consequences of his actions, felt unable to cope with the situation and, as a result, was all too willing to concur with the suggestions of an authority figure. At the time, his concern was for his child and his main priority was to escape from the situation and have his child returned to him. Only later, at home, did he have the opportunity to calm down and realise the seriousness of his situation. Fortunately, it was possible to produce for the court a detailed account of the defendant's mental processes during the whole episode whereupon it was agreed that, under the circumstances, it might be considered reasonable to act as he did and as mentioned earlier, despite having agreed in interview that he had intended to steal the goods, he was found not guilty of theft.

As far as intent is concerned, therefore, a psychological perspective implies several issues. First, given that a guilty defendant may have excellent reasons for lying, it may be necessary to show at least the plausibility that certain intentions were present. It may, at this point, be necessary to draw a distinction between conscious and unconscious intent. Secondly, it is unfortunate that even when guilty intent is admitted, this cannot always be taken at face value, and the court needs to take account of possible suggestibility, where the individuals mistakenly believe themselves to have had guilty intent. In addition, the court will need to take account of the possibility that, for reasons of their own, defendants may admit to intentions they never believed themselves to have.

Awareness

In much the same way, other *mens rea* concepts may also prove problematic. The court might wish to consider aspects of the individuals' 'awareness' of their own behaviour: did they appreciate what they were doing? Awareness of one's own behaviour is, for most of us, a straightforward issue; doing something is synonymous with knowing that we are doing it. Indeed, a 'common sense' approach to human behaviour (often a tactic deployed by cognitive psychologists) suggests that our various actions are of necessity preceded by a thought process which directs such actions.

Unfortunately for such common-sense notions, however, it is quite apparent that behaviour need not always be associated with this kind of self-awareness. Behavioural psychologists now recognise that perceiving and attending are active, not passive processes, and can be considered actions or behaviours in their own right. Most of the time, this observation is of little significance, since we normally attend to and perceive our own behaviour. However, it does not necessarily follow that this will always be the case and, under some circumstances, this synchrony between the cognitive process and the overt behaviour may be disrupted. Interestingly, one of the earliest demonstrations of this within psychology is described in a paper co-authored by psychologist Richard Solomons and the author Gertrude Stein (1896). In this they describe Stein's numerous self-observations on her experience in developing automatic writing. At first, she remarks, when trying to write without conscious intervention, there was always some awareness of what she was writing. With practice, however, she found it possible first only to be aware of what she was writing when she did so, and eventually only to be aware after she had written. Thus, in the beginning, the thoughts came before the actions. Later, the two occurred simultaneously and eventually the actions preceded the behaviour. The implication of this is that a simple common-sense model of behaviour, in which every action is preceded by a thought, is inadequate to provide a complete account of psychological functioning. An individual may perform actions without being aware of doing so.

In a similar way the notion of 'objective recklessness' may be a difficult one for psychology. In principle, the notion that someone acted recklessly should be straightforward; they acted in such a way as to be relatively insensitive to the possible negative consequences of their actions. One might expect here that a rough criterion for recklessness might be the extent to which the individual fails to act in a rational manner and indeed it happens that a suitable 'gold standard' for rational decision-making already exists. When deciding on a course of action under conditions of uncertainty, it can be shown that (according to certain technical criteria) a rational approach to decision-making involves consideration of the probabilities associated with different events, the utilities associated with certain outcomes, and nothing else. Such a strategy for decision-making, known as a Subjective Expected Utility (SEU; Savage,

1954; Smith, 1988), has been extensively researched, with particular attention being paid to the numerous ways in which humans may fail to live up to the standards set by SEU. It turns out, however, that conformity to SEU standards is the exception, rather than the rule in human behaviour, and that human decision-making is routinely sub-optimal by comparison with SEU standards. Several different types of common error have been identified. For example, individuals may be inconsistent in their preferences, claiming to prefer A to B, B to C, and C to A. Perhaps most relevantly for the concept of recklessness, individuals may also make a number of errors in judging the probability of various events. Accordingly, an individual asked to estimate the probability of a hypothesis, can then be given various items of information, each of which supports the hypothesis. According to a rational SEU model, it is possible to calculate how much the individual's estimate of the probability should be revised in the light of these observations; a phenomenon termed 'conservatism' (nothing to do with politics) reflects the finding that people typically fail to revise their original probability estimate as much as (according to SEU) they should (Edwards, 1967). In practice, this could mean that an individual may decide upon a course of action believing that the probability of risk is low. For example, a sports instructor may believe that the risk of a gale developing when taking a group sailing is negligible. Conservatism suggests that if such an individual is then given further information suggesting the risk of gales, the original low estimate will not be revised as much as it should. The individual's probability estimate may change from 'no real risk' to 'a slight risk'. Similarly, the instructor may feel that there is no real danger because the emergency services will, as a last resort, be able to come to the rescue. On being told that one of the local lifeboats is out of action, the estimate of risk may still be disproportionately low. Such errors are, of course, part of our common experience, reflected in notions such as 'it couldn't happen to me'.

Estimates of danger or risk may also be inappropriate because of the way in which individuals make judgements of probability. A rational individual, for example, when asked to make a probability judgement about a risk, would do so in terms of the percentage of similar situations in which the risky event occurred. In practice, real individuals tend to estimate such probabilities in terms of their own experience; if they find it hard to think of examples, then a probability will be judged as low. This has been described as an 'availability' hypothesis about probability judgements, as the easier it is to retrieve an example from memory, the more likely the event will be judged to be (Tversky and Kahneman, 1973). Unfortunately, this can mean that probability estimates can be distorted because of the way in which memory is organised. Asked which are more common, words beginning with 'p' or words where 'r' is the third letter, it is tempting to opt for the former because, off-hand, it is easier to think of many such words; thinking of words in terms of their first letter is considerably easier than trying to think of words in terms of their third letter. For these, and other reasons, people's estimates of the probability of events may be hopelessly wild or inconsistent.

Again it can be argued here that the courts have a central role in deciding what might be considered reasonable. It would, presumably, be thought unreasonable to expect a human being to act at all times in a perfectly rational manner. However, with an awareness of the various ways in which human judgement can be influenced by external factors and, in particular, a recognition of the degree of impairment of judgement that can be involved, courts may well wish to consult experts to advise on what factors need to be considered and then to decide on whether, in the light of what is known about such factors in the case in question, a reasonable person would take the risks alleged.

DEFENCES

Even when there is no dispute regarding *actus reus* and *mens rea*, it is still open to the defendant to argue that the behaviour was not criminal by submitting some form of defence. There are, of course, many well-known defences. For example, an individual who kills another may be able to show that the act was performed in self-defence, and that the behaviour was therefore justifiable. Several defences are of interest from a psychological viewpoint. It is widely known that a defence may be on the grounds of insanity; that the defendant, at the time of the offence, suffered from a defect of reason, due to a disease of the mind, so that (s)he did not know the nature and quality of her/his acts, or, if (s)he did, (s)he did not know that they were wrong (McNaghten (1843) 10 Cl Fin. 200). Perhaps the most obvious kinds of 'defeat of reason' here are in terms of hallucinations or delusions on the part of the individual. An individual who believed that an auditory hallucination was a divine instruction to commit a crime might use this as a defence.

In general terms, the law here falls in an interesting middle ground between two extreme conceptualisations of what is meant by insanity. Traditional psychiatric classifications have followed what has come to be termed a 'medical model', ascribing the odd behaviour of the patient to some supposed illness. Psychological conceptualisations, by contrast, have for over 40 years raised objections to this kind of formulation (see, for example, Bandura, 1969), preferring instead to consider the odd behaviour in its own right. Arguably, it could be appropriate for a court to draw on elements of both of these, expecting medical expertise to decide whether the putative illness is indeed present, but then adopting a position much closer to a psychological one to determine how exactly this relates to the crime under consideration.

Space does not permit a detailed account of the ways in which psychological and medical models of bizarre behaviour may, at times, conflict with each other and at others be complementary. An example may, however, illustrate the general principle. Psychologists studying aggressive behaviour have long recognised that two basic processes may be involved (for a detailed account see Owens and Ashcroft, 1985). First, and perhaps most simply, an individual may show aggressive behaviour because such behaviour has a pay-off; if I knock someone unconscious and steal his/her wallet, it is probably easy to understand my actions. Such processes can be easily modelled in the laboratory, with animals rewarded for aggression showing high levels of such behaviour. Further, paralleling real-life experience, behaviour developed in this way may be suppressed by appropriate use of punishment.

A second process may also lead to aggressive behaviour. Individuals who are presented with inescapable unpleasant events may also act aggressively. Again, this can be shown in the laboratory; if two rats are placed in a cage and given an electric shock, they will react by fighting. In one form or another, these two processes, either acting to obtain reward or in response to an unpleasant event seem to be present in all examples of aggressive behaviour.

Knowledge of these processes may be invaluable when a defence of insanity is presented in cases of violence. To know that an individual suffers auditory hallucinations is not sufficient to explain his or her violent behaviour. Consideration of the nature of the hallucinations may, however, show a link to the processes described above. Possible examples include: hallucinations which say that the victim is an enemy of society, and that attacking people will be applauded; hallucinations which persuade the offender that to assault the person is not wrong, and therefore that punishment (either by society or self-punishment through guilt) will not occur; hallucinations which say that the victim is doing unpleasant things directed at the offender. Given that an individual has come to acquire such beliefs as a result of, say, an episode of paranoid schizophrenia, then a legal defence of insanity would be reasonable. However, it should be remembered that the person who suffers one or other kind of mental disturbance is also, at times, capable of all the other psychological processes which underlie the behaviour of individuals who are not disturbed. An individual may suffer a schizophrenic attack involving hallucinations which suggest it is necessary to go out and take lots of fresh air. If such an individual, while out, sees and acts upon an opportunity to attack and rob a passer-by, this is incidental to the hallucinations and the response of the courts may be no different than to any other individual acting similarly. Thus, an understanding of normal psychological processes may be essential in determining whether or not an abnormal mental state may or may not be implicated in a particular criminal episode. Again, from the court's point of view, the need is to determine whether or not it is reasonable to expect that someone with beliefs like those of the hallucinating defendant should have acted in the way (s)he did. A similar psychological contribution may be made with respect to other defences. For example, 'defences' of lack of *mens rea* might be made for those with learning disabilities, dementing older people etc. Once again, it would be important to avoid assuming that because the disability and the crime co-exist, that the latter is caused by the former. Rather, it is important to understand the process to determine whether the behaviour might be reasonable. For example, a dementing older person may have difficulty remembering recent events but no problem remembering the distant past. Recognition of the specific nature of these memory difficulties might be relevant if the person is accused of taking something: is it reasonable to expect them to remember that the object does not belong to them? A defence of intoxication would be relevant only to the extent that it could be shown that the impairments produced by intoxication had an influence on the criminal behaviour in question. Drugs like marijuana, for example, usually appear to reduce the likelihood of aggressive behaviour, and it would not be obvious that the use of marijuana could be used as a defence in a violent offence (although it should be noted that the effects of all drugs on behaviour are complex, and would require a more thorough analysis of each individual case before a final decision was made). In legal terms, the question would be, basically, whether the drugs or alcohol meant that the defendant could not have 'intended' the act *and* that 'intention' is the only *mens rea* for that crime.

SUMMARY AND CONCLUSIONS

In a brief account like this it is not possible to do more than give a flavour of how an understanding of psychological concepts might cast light on some aspects of legal process. To the extent that the *actus reus* implies wilfulness on the part of the individual, it is necessary to consider to what extent one might consider degrees of wilfulness and how these might be dealt with by the courts, particularly when (as with Eysenck's theory) this may imply a conflict between efficacy and justice. It is probably fair to say, though, that it is with respect to *mens rea* concepts that psychological notions have the most obvious relevance. Indeed, we have seen that a strictly Freudian perspective would have it that there are no 'accidents' and would imply the need to seek out unconscious motives. Although such hard-line Freudianism has few adherents among scientific psychologists, similar issues might arise from other wholly deterministic approaches.

The determination of intent is, of course, central to decisions regarding guilt, and courts have the dual problem of dealing with those who dishonestly deny their guilty intentions and, less obviously, lay claim to guilty intentions which they never had. The latter may reflect suggestibility on the part of the individual or the way that individual responds to potentially stressful situations like a police interview. It is important to note that people are not always aware of the reasons for their own behaviour, or even terribly aware of the behaviour itself (anyone who drives the same road to work every day will be aware of the sensation of having driven 'automatically', remembering little of the journey by the end). Similarly, the concept of recklessness implies a degree of judgement which may need to be considered in the light of the prevailing circumstances and the kinds of reasoning about which humans are notoriously bad. Few, if any, individuals make decisions entirely rationally. With respect to *mens rea*, as with the *actus reus*, a central role is for the court to decide on what is reasonable given what is known about the circumstances of the offence and the kinds of psychological processes operating. Then the court may solve the problem before it by applying the standard of proof. Almost always (an exception being the insanity defence), if the court decides that a reasonable doubt remains about the defendant's guilt, then they must acquit.

Lastly with regard to defences, as in *actus reus* and *mens rea*, there is much to be gained from an understanding of psychological processes. In particular, understanding the normal psychological processes which might lead to particular behaviours can clarify such issues as the extent to which these can be seen to be a function of abnormal processes like hallucinations, delusions, etc. Once again, it is for the courts to decide, in the light of what is known about such processes, whether it was reasonable for the person to behave in such a way. However, there is a problem in that expert evidence is usually excluded on 'normal' behaviour in many countries.

There are, thus, several ways forward in exploiting psychological knowledge for the furthering of justice. Already courts are making use of psychologists as expert witnesses, preparing reports and giving testimony with respect to the psychological processes relevant in particular cases. In addition, the legal system could make increasing use of psychological expertise, both in framing particular Acts and in laying down rules for police procedure. For example, the current Police and Criminal Evidence Act 1984 makes no explicit recognition of possible variation in suggestibility of suspects of normal intelligence, yet research suggests that some individuals may need some degree of protection. Finally, the legal system might well direct a great deal of psychological research, indicating those areas where it feels clarification is still needed. Examples might include the specific effects of stress and anxiety on judgement, the precise factors which lead to automatic behaviour, the ways in which presentation of information influences decision-making and the way in which witnesses' (including children's') accounts are influenced by cross-examination in court. Often much of the information required will already be available in different contexts; others may open up new areas for collaborative research involving teams of lawyers and psychologists.

REFERENCES

Bandura, A. (1969). *Principles of Behaviour Modification*. New York: Holt, Reinhart & Winston.

Druckman, D. and Bjork, R.A. (Eds) (1991). *In the Mind's Eye: Enhancing Human Performance*. Washington DC: National Academy Press.

Edwards, W. (1967). *Decision Making: Selected Readings*. Harmondsworth: Penguin.

Eysenck, H.J. (1964). *Crime and Personality*. London: Routledge.

Gudjonsson, G.H. (1991). Suggestibility and compliance among alleged false confessors. *Medicine, Science and the Law*, **31**, 147–51.

Gudjonsson, G.H. (1992). *The Psychology of Interrogations, Confessions and Testimony*. Chichester: John Wiley.

Owens, R.G. and Ashcroft, J.B. (1985). *Violence: A Guide for the Caring Professions*. Beckenham: Croom Helm.

Savage, L.J. (1954). *The Foundations of Statistics*. New York: John Wiley.

Sharrock, R. and Gudjonsson, G.H. (1993). Intelligence, previous convictions and interrogative suggestibility: a path analysis of alleged false-confession cases. *British Journal of Clinical Psychology*, **32,** 169–75.

Skinner, B.F. (1969). *Contingencies of Reinforcement: A Theoretical Analysis*. New York: Appleton Century Crofts.

Smith, J.Q. (1988). *Decision Analysis: A Bayesian Approach*. London: Chapman & Hall.

Solomons, R. and Stein, G. (1896). Normal motor automatism. *Psychological Review*.

Storr, A. (1989). *Freud*. Oxford: Oxford University Press.

Tversky, A. and Kahneman, D. (1973). Availability: a heuristic for judging frequency and probability. *Cognitive Psychology*, **5**, 207–32.

Chapter 4.4

Does the Unequal Application of Legal Defences Reflect Sexism in the Law?

Hedy Red Dexter
University of Northern Colorado

Under scrutiny in this chapter is the even-handedness (or not) with which the criminal law allows defences: that is, are there occasions when sexism contaminates decision-making in legal contexts? For example, why is it that the victim's provocation appears to provide a defence, or lessen the seriousness with which the crime is treated, when women provoke (e.g. when a woman's behaviour is alleged to have contributed to her rape), but it does not seem to apply in the same way when crimes of passion are provoked by men (e.g. when a woman, after a period of abuse, kills her male abuser otherwise than in the midst of her abuse)? My task is to discuss how psychology informs the law regarding legal defences. The task is complicated because psychology and the law, as separate social institutions with different motives, disagree fundamentally about the nature of human behaviour.

Psychology, like all of the sciences, seeks to describe, explain, predict, and control behaviour. Its methods are empirical. The law, not compelled by scientific methodologies, seeks to uphold principles of order and justice in service of society. The law is concerned with ascribing and re-enforcing responsibility. To do this, the law also presumes a knowledge of human behaviour, but its methods are intuitive rather than scientific. Psychology and the law both presume knowledge of human behaviour but their respective explanations are, philosophically, at odds.

As always when dealing with abstract constructs, one must define one's terms which, as symbols, do not correspond directly with reality. The criminal law defines certain defences, for example, but their legal definition is already an interpretation. Contrary to popular belief, laws do not constitute *objective* truth, which is why we have appellate courts, whose job it is to *interpret* the law. To complicate matters, jurors, in service of the law and society, interpret and apply the terminology of defences in subjective ways; this is what social institutions and ordinary people everywhere do. In order to discuss, then, how psychology informs the law regarding issues of mitigation I must set the discussion in its proper philosophical context.

Because psychology assumes that behaviour is determined it looks for cause and effect linkages in the natural world including human nature. Determinism, as a philosophical doctrine, rules out human agency or free will as the cause of human action. Instead it claims that humans respond reliably to situational stimuli in predictable ways. Whether one invokes biological or environmental determinism, psychology, agreeing with Skinner (1971), assumes that free will is a myth. This flies in the face of the law's assumption that humans freely choose to misbehave. The law must assume this in order to justify holding individuals accountable and punishable by society which is seeking to maintain illusions of control (Shaver, 1985). However, in trying to decide whether behaviour is determined or free one must examine the motives that underpin particular assumptions. In the case of the law, it is more threatening to assume that people do bad deeds because they could not do otherwise than to assume that people make specific behavioural choices. Seeking to locate causality in the environment or the individual, respectively, such irreconcilable philosophical differences often preclude productive dialogue between psychologists and legal policy makers (Hart, 1968).

Much of this disagreement is captured by a social psychological principle, the fundamental attribution error. Otherwise rational information processors make this error when they over-implicate dispositional factors in the production of outcomes (Ross, 1977). To the degree that observers underestimate the influence of situational constraints, the locus of crime-related misbehaviour, for example, is thought to reside within the individual actor. Ordinary people are sometimes quick to excuse criminal offenders who have been provoked by their victims but fail to factor in criminogenic influences (such as socioeconomic or biological conditions) when making determinations of blame. Not surprisingly, individuals, and the law, are better served by blaming and removing deviant individuals—both the provocateur and the offender—than by blaming a dysfunctional society, which is not so easily got rid of; or, worse still, by blaming human biology, as that would mean that behaviour, ultimately, is not directly under individual human control.

Humans are philosophically biased towards perceiving actors as causal agents of harm, unless, of course, one happens to be the actor. Ordinary people need to feel in control of their outcomes and of their world. They, like the law, assume that individuals, as agents of good and bad, are alone responsible for their good and bad outcomes. If one assumes that individuals freely choose to act badly, meaning that responsibility justifiably is attributed to them, then removing the guilty agents restores order to the community and with it the coveted illusion of control. Based on this line of reasoning, one can say that the law, in so far as it assumes behaviour is free, falls prey to the fundamental attribution error. Because this psychological concept directly bears on defences, both in terms of how they are defined by the law and how they are interpreted and applied by jurors, I will come back to it again in this discussion.

There is, however, a sense in which psychology and law share a common goal. Psychology, in so far as it reliably predicts, seeks to control human behaviour because society feels more comfortable with steady states than it does with change (Parsons, 1937). By rewarding and extinguishing appropriate and inappropriate behaviours, respectively, society, informed by psychology, ensures maintenance of its status quo. Similarly the law, by imposing sanctions against antisocial behaviour, reassures a society made uncomfortable by threats to its status quo (Kelley, 1967). If control over outcomes is what humans desire, and if the law, ideally, implements as legal policy that which psychology discovers to be truth about human nature, it should follow, then, that psychology and law would engage in productive reciprocity. Put another way, psychological discovery should translate into legal policy. This, however, is not always the case.

Returning to the questions originally posed, contributors to the psycholegal literature on legal defences come from a different forensic perspective. Be they practitioners or researchers of law, medicine, psychiatry, or psychology, each seeks to inform legal proceedings. Some do that by presenting research findings, others by describing, based on clinical experience, the causes and behavioural implications of mental disorders. The published literature comes in a variety of formats, each appropriate to its respective forensic task. Broken down into roughly three categories, the extant research comprises (i) philosophical treatises, (ii) experimental studies which invoke attribution theory as an explanatory framework and (iii) reports from clinicians which delineate the criminogenic factors implicated in mitigation and which form the basis of testimony proffered by expert practitioners in the courts. I would argue that psychology informs the law best not by behaviourally defining legal constructs, like insanity, or psychopathological constructs, like multiple personality disorder, but by revealing how causality, responsibility, and blame are construed in the minds of ordinary people, people who, as the triers of fact, make decisions based on their interpretations of abstract psychological and legal terms.

Miethe (1984) empirically examined the interpretive mechanism by which mock jurors balance legal responsibility between the victim and the offender in a homicide. In addition to victim provocation, empirical findings suggest that harm suffered by an offender during commission of a crime reduces both legal responsibility and penalty attributed to an offender (e.g. Shaw and McMartin, 1975). People in Miethe's (1984) study were asked to apportion legal responsibility to both the victim and the offender where (a) degree of physical victim provocation and (b) harm suffered by the offender were manipulated. Findings suggest that victim provocation is positively correlated with victim responsibility and inversely correlated with offender culpability. Apparently, people subtract from offender culpability and penalty the degree to which the victim provokes the offence. They reason that had the offender not been provoked the offence may not have occurred. Harm suffered by the offender, however, did not significantly influence Miethe's mock jurors' judgements though Shaw and McMartin (1975) found that it did. This was based on their subjects' belief that the harm suffered by the offender, while doing the deed, is partial punishment for it.

Although victim provocation influenced attributions of culpability and penalty, it accounts for surprisingly little of the variance in mock juror judgements (Miethe, 1984). Referring to Shaver (1975), Miethe suggests that lay people tend to attribute *moral* accountability to criminal offenders disproportionately based on crime severity. They fail to factor in situational contingencies which is why victim provocation, despite its salience, lacks explanatory power. This is an example of the fundamental attribution error. Alternatively, Miethe (1984) suggests that differential interpretations between and within victim provocation conditions explain why it accounts for little of the variance in legal responsibility attributed to the offender. He goes on to say that abstract legal constructs do not mean the same thing to all people, a finding which clearly has implications for jury decision-making.

Critics of the psycholegal research charge that experimental studies lack realism (unlike jurors, experimental subjects do not make important decisions about other people's lives) and that the findings cannot be generalised because the subjects themselves (i.e. college undergraduates) are unrepresentative of people generally, let alone of legal personnel. (Berkowitz and Donnerstein, 1982, disagree.) Responding to the critics, Howe (1991) compared perceptions of *mens rea* (the proscribed state of mind specified for each crime) and of mitigation in samples of students and judges. Invoking Shaver's (1985) 'levels of responsibility' analysis, Howe (1991) looked at how mitigation, intention, and outcome damage are combined in a unitary evaluation and at the relative weight assigned to each component. Pointing out that, like ordinary people, legal theory distinguishes between justification and excuse as different classes of mitigation (e.g. Austin, 1957; Greenawalt, 1986), Howe hypothesises that perceived justification (which is continuous rather than dichotomous) probably depends more on degree of outcome damage than on intentionality. Importantly, Howe points out that the evaluative strategies utilised by ordinary people depend less on legal definition and prescription than on cognitive psychological description (Anderson, 1981, 1983a, b).

Extending the blame schema, Sebba (1980) found that, among student subjects, intention and outcome damage both factor into perceptions of mitigation (as justification) additively rather than interactively. The problem of how perceivers integrate elements of mitigation, intention, and outcome damage into a net evaluative judgement was considered by Howe (1991), also within Anderson's information integration and functional measurement theory (Anderson, 1981, 1983a, b). In three experiments, two levels each of the three evaluative elements (i.e. mitigation, intent, outcome damage) were factorially crossed for two different criminal scenarios (self-defence under provocation and altruistic defence of another). Like Sebba (1980), Howe (1991) found that informational elements combine additively, irrespective of crime scenario, but only for student subjects. Differences between real-life judges' and students' evaluative strategies centred on the use of mitigation information such that the judges integrated information interactively (i.e. simple interaction effects between mitigation and both outcomes damage and type of case) rather than additively, presumably reflecting their greater experience and concern. Interpretations of mitigation, because they are more variable, may complicate the otherwise straightforward additive evaluations of offender culpability in the intent–damage paradigm.

As have the other experimental studies in this review, Alicke (1990) analyses the effects of incapacitating conditions that sometimes mitigate legal sanction within an attributional framework. Subjects were asked to attribute blame for a variety of criminal offences where the following incapacitating conditions existed: altered state of consciousness (intentional or unintentional); emotional stress; disadvantageous socialisation; chronic thought disorder; and failure of impulse control. The greatest and least mitigators of blame were chronic thought disorder and intentionally altered state of consciousness, respectively. Influencing these results, however, were perceptions of the seriousness of the offence, the degree of anger it aroused, and the actor's personal stake in the outcome. The relationship between anger and mitigation, in the case of disordered reasoning, may be especially relevant in judgements concerning the insanity defence. Alicke (1990) found that for heinous or bizarre crimes, where the perceiver's anger interacts with mitigation, the existence of a chronic thought disorder did not reduce attributions of blame. It may be that precisely those crimes where the most anger is engendered are the most indicative of disordered reasoning, but because ordinary people, whose moral sensibilities are offended, resort to moral versus legal accountability, they blame more when, legally, they should blame less: 'Thus there may exist the greatest tendency to avoid exculpation in precisely those cases that warrant it from the perspective of the *mens rea* criterion of legal responsibility' (Alicke, 1990, p. 663).

Previous research suggests that legal responsibility may be mitigated where control over one's behaviour is limited by obstacles residing either within the individual or within the environment (Fincham and Schultz, 1981; Fincham, 1985; Fincham and Roberts, 1985). These issues bear directly on controversial problems in jurisprudence dealing with questions of personal control.

Classified in law as capacity constraints, defences of infancy, automatism, intoxication, insanity, diminished responsibility, and more recently a variety of syndromes such as battered wife syndrome, policeman's syndrome, love–fear syndrome, chronic brain syndrome, holocaust syndrome, and post-traumatic stress syndrome (Low, Jeffries and Bonnie, 1986) support the excuse that a person could not help her or himself. Failure to control one's impulses is variously attributed to organic or psychogenic dysfunctions, but may also be attributable to temporary alterations of consciousness, emotional stress, and lack of impulse control. That blame attributions were mitigated least of all by dysfunctional socialisation (in fact, socialisation was perceived as irrelevant to judgements of blame) demonstrates, yet again, the power of the fundamental attribution error, that is, the underestimated influence of environmental constraints on an actor's behaviour. Bred into our collective psyches is the belief that we control all of our outcomes (Rotter, 1966), so that limits to personal control are unacceptable excuses. Evidence of this is the increased blame attributed to offenders as a result of incapacitating conditions. In his discussion, Alicke suggests that because we are expected to overcome emotional stress and to control our impulses as a matter of everyday living, these excuses are not grounds for mitigation in the minds of ordinary people. Chronic thought disorders, on the other hand, are relatively rare and as such do not pose a pervasive threat to social order. And, like most of the others, Alicke pays requisite lip service to the ungeneralisability of findings sampled from college undergraduates. That subjects in psychology experiments (i.e. ordinary people) attribute greater blame where dysfunctional socialisation is implicated whereas the law, paradoxically, claims that bad socialisation is probably the most reasonable ground for mitigation (e.g. insanity or diminished capacity) points, yet again, to the fundamental philosophic incompatibility between the law's and psychology's assumptions about human behaviour.

Yet to be addressed is the most pressing question. Can victim provocation mitigate blame attributed to an offender? Importantly, whether or not the offender did the deed is not at issue. The issue is whether the victim did something to instigate or otherwise influence the offender's actions. In the general case, determinations of guilt are based unidimensionally on whether or not the offender was the causal agent of harm. But where victims provoke the actions that harm them they contribute to the offence by making it more likely. Here decisions are not made unidimensionally; they are made by subtracting victim responsibility—because she or he could have prevented by not provoking—from offender responsibility in the ordinary causal sense. The law states that victim provocation mitigates a charge if it is 'of a nature calculated to inflame the passions of the ordinarily reasonable man' (Perkins, 1946, p. 413) and that 'if the retaliatory act is not in excess of the provocative act, then legal grounds for mitigation are established' (see Perkins, 1946). [In England and Wales the test is whether, on a charge of murder, 'there is evidence on which the jury can find that the person charged was provoked (whether by things done or by things said or by both together) to lose his self-control, the question whether the provocation was enough to make a reasonable man do as he did shall be left to be determined by the jury' (s. 3, Homicide Act 1957).] Though the law sets down basic guidelines, decisions about defences are made subjectively by ordinary people. Moreover, given these legal definitions, one might cynically ask whether or not a defence applies in cases where battered women kill. As we will see, rape victims are blamed for actions taken against them; whereas, men murdered by women they have battered are seldom blamed for actions they have provoked.

What of the research which investigates the effects of victim provocation on lay persons' perceptions of culpability? For example, Scroggs (1976) demonstrated that the rapist of a *provocatively* dressed female would receive a lighter sentence. In this study, and, indeed, in the few psychological studies that examine the factors implicated in defences, researchers explain the subjects' behaviour in terms of attribution theory. Smith et al. (1976) found that personal characteristics (e.g. Catholic nun, social worker, topless dancer) significantly influenced subjects' willingness to infer that a rape victim behaved irresponsibly thereby diminishing the legal responsibility attributed to the rapist. Such results are not surprising given that rape mythology is greatly endorsed in Western culture (e.g. MacKinnon, 1989; Tong, 1984).

From where do misogynous assumptions underlying rape law originate? The scene of woman as a lying temptress is Chapter One of Western religion: 'had it not been for Eve's sexual charms, Adam would have never eaten of the forbidden fruit' (Tong, 1984, p. 100). In the story of the Fall, woman fares badly. Not only is she condemned to pain, suffering, and submission (to man) but in the Eden myth, God—when he brings forth life (Eve from Adam's rib) without woman's assistance—expropriates woman's life force, the one creative activity that is uniquely hers. Interpreted by Kate Millet (1970), the Eden myth is a story about how humans invented sexual intercourse. Sex is blamed for the loss of Eden which should, but cannot, implicate man and still blame the world's suffering on woman. Instead, as the story goes, woman *tempted* man and for that she is to blame. If seduction is the problem, why hold Eve primarily responsible? She didn't initiate. Eve is seduced by the serpent/phallus, but Eve is convicted for Adam's participation in sex. We have here the story of the proprietary father/God punishing his disobedient daughter for her sexuality. Woman's nature, then, robs the world of innocence and introduces sin. Hereafter, woman/sex/sin constitutes the paradigmatic pattern of patriarchal thought. The Eden story explains both the effect (loss of innocence) and the cause (woman) of human suffering.

From this account, some interesting questions, relevant to contemporary rape laws, arise. First, why was not Adam's failure to resist Eve at issue? He consented, obviously, but little was made of it not by God and not by a male tradition built on a sanctified male supremacy (God gave man dominion over earth and its creatures, including woman). Second, why is it that Adam and Eve are not punished equally harshly. Why does Adam's punishment seem reduced as a function of Eve's culpability? And why emphasise Eve's role, not Adam's? They both did the deed. But, just as it goes in a rape trial, the victim and the offender are judged along a single continuum; that is, to the degree that the woman is held responsible because she 'asked for it', the rapist is excused. Unlike a rape trial, however, where society (jurors) blames the victim (woman) for not resisting, the ostensible victim (man) in the Eden fiasco is not blamed although, clearly, he failed to resist. And what of the serpent's role? He tempted Eve just as Eve tempted Adam, yet Eve (woman) bears the brunt of God's wrath which she must in order to justify a male-dominated social order. If anyone doubts the sturdiness of rape mythology in Western culture just listen to the opinions and explanations proffered by jurists, attorneys, jurors during a rape trial (e.g. Burt and Albin, 1981; MacKinnon, 1989).

Misogynous images of woman pervade rules of evidence and criminal procedure in rape cases. For example, the law, reflecting society, assumes that rape victims lie. Why else do rape laws protect men against false accusation? Tong (1984, p. 101) quoted John H. Wigmore, an influential historical figure in American law, who, in 1934, wrote:

> Modern psychiatrists have amply studied the behaviour of errant young girls and women coming before the court in all sorts of cases. Their psychic complexes are multifarious, distorted by bad social environment, partly by temporary psychological or emotional conditions. One form taken by these complexes is that of contriving false charges of sexual offences by men. The unchaste (let us call it) mentality finds incidental but direct expression in the narration of imaginary sex incidents of which the narrator is the heroine or the victim. On the surface the narration is straight-forward and convincing. The real victim, however, too often in such cases is the innocent man; for the respect and sympathy naturally felt by any tribunal for a wronged female helps to give easy credit to such a plausible tale. (Wigmore, 1934, cited in Tong, 1984, p. 101)

Prior to the 1980s (only now just about to be removed in England and Wales!), many statutes required cautionary instructions to warn jurors of the dubious nature of rape complaints (see Tong, 1984, p. 105): 'A charge such as that made against the defendant in this case, is one which is easily made and, once made, difficult to defend against, even if the person accused is innocent. Therefore, the law requires that you examine the testimony of the female person named in the information with caution.' And from the Model Penal Code (see Estrich, 1986):

> [O]ften the woman's attitude may be deeply ambivalent. She may not want intercourse, may fear it, or may desire it but feel compelled to say 'no.' Her confusion at the time of the act may later resolve into non-consent. ... The deceptively simple notion of consent may obscure a tangled mesh of psychological complexity, ambiguous communications, and unconscious restructuring of the event by the participants. (Estrich, 1986)

The criminal justice system's preoccupation with false accusations in the case of rape is unfounded. Research on false complaints fails to support the notion that charges of rape are more likely to be false than charges of other violent crimes (Brownmiller, 1975). Indeed, in Borchard's (1933) *Convicting the Innocent*, the single most common cause of mistaken conviction was erroneous eye-witness identifications, and not fabrication of testimony.

The law, again, reflecting society, assumes that because women tempt men they deserve what they get. Witness the differentially harsh punishments meted out to Adam and Eve in the Eden story. In rape-trial terms this means that if men interpret a woman's clothes, her verbal and non-verbal behaviour, her drinking and dancing, and her presence in a bar or in his apartment as desire for sex, then, according to the law, he is not to blame for doing what he believes she wanted—she is. And why is it that, unlike other criminal trials where the burden of proof is on the state to show guilt beyond a reasonable doubt, in a rape trial the burden is on the rape victim to show her innocence?

Asking whether or not the rape victim consented to sex—the central issue in most rape trials—is asking the wrong question. That rape defences presume provocation and consent, begs, rather than asks the question. Asking, instead, whether consent is ever a choice that women really have and whether rape happens because men believe that women provoke it are the better questions. Answering them means unpacking these terms, showing how androcentric bias mystifies power relations (over women), justifies sacrifice (of women), and induces passivity (in women). Translated into rape-trial terms, this means that women get screwed not only by the rapist but by courts of law where women are hard pressed to prove that their claims of rape are not really just consensual sex. After all, everyday pornography (e.g. commercial advertising, rock videos) teaches us that there is no rape; there are only women wanting real men to take them by force (MacKinnon, 1989). From books, movies, and conversations among ordinary people we learn that women who dress provocatively, who go home with strangers or acquaintances, who drink or take drugs, who allow themselves to be wined and dined, are asking for sex. Or, maybe she did not want it, but she deserved it. In social psychological terms, woman becomes victim of the fundamental attribution error: if she had sex, it's because she wanted to (similarly, in cases of wife battering, jurors often reason that if a woman doesn't leave, it's because she wanted to stay).

And what of the other question raised, namely homicide in self-defence; that is, when is the use of deadly force justified? Increasingly, forensic psychologists are called upon by the courts to testify on post-traumatic stress disorder (PTSD) as regards exculpatory, diminished, or mitigated criminal responsibility. Often raised as a legal defence in criminal cases, PTSD includes among its classes of victims those who were exposed to (a) consummated, attempted, and threatened violent crimes, (b) child and spouse abuse, (c) auto accidents involving severe injury, (d) civilian catastrophes, and (e) war and associated activities (Hall and Hall, 1987; Higgins, 1991). Problems arise because PTSD regardless of which cause, comprises a range of symptomatic behaviours and, because not all sufferers exhibit the full range or even a consistent subset thereof, some practitioners and legal personnel doubt its clinical legitimacy (e.g. Higgins, 1991). Nevertheless, PTSD, has been used successfully to defend sentences in crimes such as manslaughter, drug dealing, and assault with intent to murder (Davidson, 1988).

While they constitute the majority, legal defences built on PTSD are not limited to violent crimes committed by Vietnam combat veterans. Battered-woman syndrome, as another possible consequence of trauma, has been raised, though largely unsuccessfully, to justify homicide committed in self-defence. Because assumptions underlying legal policy discriminate against women, PTSD as legal justification for self-defence is fraught with problems when battered women kill. When deconstructed, self-defence, which is based on the 'reasonable man' criterion, reveals its inherent prejudice against women. For example, to meet the criterion for self-defence she, who seeks to justify homicide, first, cannot have countered her aggressor's attacks with more force than his. But what of the physical strength inequalities or the fact that women, because they are socialised differently, are disinclined toward aggressive behaviour? Second, she, in order to avoid retaliating with deadly force, has the duty to retreat—except from one's castle—stipulates the law. Clearly, battered women would retreat from the home if there was somewhere else to go. [In England and Wales, and perhaps other countries, the duty to retreat has been withdrawn, in recent years, and while the force used ought not to be excessive, a defence of mistake may be available to the defendant who miscalculated the amount of force necessary to defend her or himself.] Third, and most controversial, there must be imminent danger, otherwise killing in self-defence is not justified. But in the case of battered women who kill, requiring imminent danger ignores the circumstances leading to the use of deadly force. Moreover, if she waits for direct confrontation, physical strength inequalities will surely work to her disadvantage. With a mind toward reform, Ewing (1990) suggests that self-defence, logically, can be raised not only when one's physical body is threatened but when one's psychological stability is at risk. Restating the terms of the 'reasonable man' criterion, Ewing makes the use of deadly force in self-defence against psychological destruction reasonable grounds for actions taken by battered women who kill.

As with rape, the law, reflecting society, makes certain assumptions about the nature of women. For example, and this comes up often in the prosecution's arguments, women are thought to be masochists who are sexually stimulated by rough treatment. Or, when she is thought to have provoked the battering, she is the shrew who needs to be tamed or the nag who needs to be silenced. The liberal state is reticent to intervene in the private domain, believing, as does society, that the family is a peaceful retreat from a violent world where the king of the castle manages his own affairs and where, short of grievous injury, the law expects women to honour the marriage contract (Tong, 1984). Implicit in the liberal state's practice of non-intervention is the belief that husbands are within their rights to rape or batter their wives, a belief that is reflected in the attitudes of the police to calls from battered wives (e.g. Tong, 1984; MacKinnon, 1989); though some police forces are now making special efforts to adopt a policy of intervention (e.g. the London Metropolitan Police).

Unlike the case of rape, where victim provocation often mitigates legal responsibility attributed to the rapist, when battered women kill, victim provocation does not reduce their culpability. Women are held fully responsible despite the fact that, as ordinary people reason in the case of rape, were the victim not to have provoked, the offence would likely not have occurred.

To whatever degree PTSD is implicated in homicide committed by battered women, forensic specialists are as yet uncertain but, despite the uncertainty, experts like Lenore Walker testify often in the USA as to its special circumstances. Also, concerned with the criminal law's prejudicial treatment of battered women who kill, Ewing (1990) reports that of 100 cases he researched, all were charged with murder, manslaughter, or some form of criminal homicide. Of the 100, 85 went to trial claiming self-defence; 63 of these were convicted and imprisoned, 12 receiving life sentences. Even when raised successfully, murder in self-defence is excused—rather than justified—as temporary insanity, the penalty for which is involuntary commitment to a mental institution, Some would argue that deadly force—it was either her or him—is justified, that, in the case of woman-battering, intentional killing is a logical act for the woman. At the insistence of certain feminist groups (e.g. Tong, 1984), legal scholars are looking at inequities in legal policy with a mind toward rewriting the 'reasonable man' criterion making PTSD-induced violent crime as excusable for women as it is for men. If forensic psychologists agree that PTSD constitutes mitigation in sentencing or grounds for a new trial, and if they agree further that battered-woman syndrome belongs within the DSM III-R category of post-traumatic stress disorders, then evidence of it should carry the same weight whether the defendant is a Vietnam veteran re-experiencing general adaptation behaviours or a battered woman who kills in self-defence.

In conclusion, then, is there value to discussion along these lines for practising attorneys? A review of the issues raised herein, reveals (a) that contrary to popular opinion, the law does not contain objective truth, that the law is applied as it is differently interpreted by legal personnel and by ordinary people; (b) that psychology and the law, as separate social institutions, make fundamentally different assumptions about human behaviour, differences which often preclude fruitful dialogue between them; and (c) that as regards provocation, mitigation, and responsibility raised in legal defences, women are victimised by the misogynous assumptions reflected in sexist legal policy. Knowledge of these issues probably will not impact the practice of law in definitive ways but I would argue that knowledge, as consciousness raising, as promoting empathy for those whom the law systematically disadvantages, is valuable. Estrich (1986) argues—and I agree—that the law could influence —rather than merely reflect—society by breaking with traditional views and by setting an example for law-abiding, freedom-desiring citizens to follow.

REFERENCES

Alicke, M.D. (1990). Incapacitating conditions and alteration of blame. *Journal of Social Behavior and Personality*, **5**, 651–64.

Anderson, N.H. (1981). *Foundations of Information Integration Theory*. New York: Academic Press.

Anderson, N.H. (1983a). Schemas in person cognition. (Technical Report Chip 118.) San Diego, CA: Center for Human Information Processing. University of California San Diego.

Anderson, N.H. (1983b). Psychodynamics of everyday life: blaming and avoiding blame. (Technical Report Chip 120.) San Diego, CA: Center for Human Information Processing, University of California San Diego.

Austin, J.L. (1957). A plea for excuses. *Proceedings of the Aristotelian Society*, **57**, 1–30.

Berkowitz, L. and Donnerstein, E. (1982). External validity is more than skin deep: some answers to criticisms of laboratory experiments. *American Psychologist*, **37**, 245–57.

Borchard, D. (1933). *Convicting the Innocent*. New York: Academic Press.

Brownmiller, S. (1975). *Against Our Will: Men, Women and Rape*. New York: Bantam.

Burt, M.R. and Albin, R.S. (1981). Rape myths, rape definitions, and probability of conviction. *Journal of Applied Social Psychology*, **11**, 212–30.

Davidson, M.J. (1988). Post-traumatic stress disorder: a controversial defense for veterans of a controversial war. *William and Mary Law Review*, **29**, 415–17.

Estrich, D. (1986). *Women in Law*. Ithaca, NY: Cornell University Press.

Ewing, P. (1990). Psychological self-defense: a proposed justification for battered women who kill. *Law and Human Behavior*, **14**, 579–94.

Fincham, F.D. (1985). Outcome valence and situational constraints in the responsibility attributions of children and adults. *Social Cognition*, **3**, 218–33.

Fincham, F.D. and Roberts, C. (1985). Intervening causation and the mitigation of responsibility for harm doing: the role of limited mental capacities. *Journal of Experimental Social Psychology*, **21**, 178–94.

Fincham, F.D. and Schultz, T.R. (1981). Intervening causation and the mitigation of responsibility for harm. *British Journal of Social Psychology*, **21**, 113–20.

Greenawalt, K. (1986). The perplexing borders of justification and excuse. *Columbia Law Review*, **84**, 8, 1897–927.

Hall, H.V. and Hall, F.L. (1987). Post-traumatic stress disorder as a legal defense in criminal trials. *American Journal of Forensic Psychology*, **5**, 453.

Hart, H.L.A. (1968). *Punishment and Responsibility*. New York: Oxford University Press.

Higgins, S.A. (1991). Post-traumatic stress disorder and its role in the defense of Vietnam veterans. *Law and Psychology Review*, **15**, 259–76.

Howe, E.S. (1991). Integration of mitigation, intention, and outcome damage information, by students and circuit court judges. *Journal of Applied Social Psychology*, **21**, 875–95.

Kelley, H.H. (1967). Attribution theory in social psychology. In D. Levine (Ed.), *Nebraska Symposium on Motivation 1967*. Lincoln, NE: University of Nebraska Press, pp. 192–238.

Low, P.W., Jeffries, J.C. Jr. and Bonnie, R.J. (1986, 2nd edn). *Criminal Law: Cases and Materials*. Mineola, New York: The Foundation Press.

MacKinnon, C. (1989). *Toward a Feminist Theory of the State*. Cambridge, MA: Harvard University Press.

Miethe, T.D. (1984). The impact of victim provocation on judgments of legal responsibility: an experimental assessment. *Journal of Criminal Justice*, **12**, 407–14.

Millett, K. (1970). *Sexual Politics*. Garden City: Doubleday.

Parsons, T. (1937). *The Structure of Social Action*. New York: McGraw Hill.

Perkins, R. (1946). The law of homicide. *Journal of Criminal Law and Criminology*, **36**, 412–26.

Ross, L.D. (1977). The intuitive psychologist and his shortcomings: distortions in the attribution process. In L. Berkowitz (Ed.), *Advances in Experimental Social Psychology*, vol. 10. New York: Academic Press, pp. 173–220.

Rotter, J.B. (1966). Generalized expectancies for internal versus external locus of control of reinforcement *Psychological Monographs*, **80**, 1–28.

Scroggs, J.R. (1976). Penalties for a rape as a function of victim provocativeness, damages, and resistance. *Journal of Applied Social Psychology*, **6**, 4, 360–8.

Sebba, L. (1980). Is mens rea a component of perceived offense seriousness? *The Journal of Criminal Law and Criminology*, **71**, 124–35.

Shaver, K.G. (1975). *An introduction to attribution processes*. Cambridge, MA: Winthrop.

Shaver, K.G. (1985). *The Attribution of Blame: Causality, Responsibility, and Blameworthiness*. New York: Springer-Verlag.

Shaw, M.E. and McMartin, J.A. (1975). Perpetrator or victim: Effect of who suffers in an automobile accident on judgemental strictness. *Social Behavior and Personality*, **3**, 1, 5–12.

Skinner, B.F. (1971). *Beyond Freedom and Dignity*. New York: Knopf.

Smith, R.E., Keating, J.P., Hester, R.K. and Mitchell, H.E. (1976). Role and justice considerations in the attribution of responsibility to a rape victim. *Journal of Research in Personality*, **10**, 346–57.

Tong, R. (1984). *Women, Sex, and the Law*. Savage, MD: Rowman & Littlefield.

Wigmore, J. (1934). *Evidence*. Boston: Little, Brown.

Chapter 4.5

Psychology of Offender Profiling

David Canter
University of Liverpool

ORIGINS

The term 'offender profiling' was first regularly used by members of the FBI's Behavioral Science Unit to describe the process of drawing inferences about a suspect's characteristics from the details of his or her actions in a crime. Concerned mainly with rape and homicide (Hazelwood and Burgess, 1987; Ressler, Burgess and Douglas, 1988), they demonstrated that it was possible to draw general conclusions about the life style, criminal history and residential location of a person who had committed a number of crimes, from careful examination of where, when and how those crimes had been committed.

Although the inference processes on which the FBI agents drew were illuminated by interviews they themselves had conducted with a few dozen convicted offenders, and by their own experiences of investigating many crimes, their processes of inference derivation were broadly *deductive*, being based upon common sense as might be the basis of judicial decisions. In the tradition of the detective novel, and other less fictional accounts of the solving of crimes, the processes that the FBI agents used focused on the clues derived directly from the crime scene. They drew upon general principles, drawn from everyday experience, to deduce the implications that the internal logic of a crime might have. So, for example, a well-organised and planned crime would be hypothesised to be perpetrated by an individual who typically was well organised and planned in general (Ressler et al., 1988).

Subsequently, a number of studies—the majority of which have been conducted by the Investigative Psychology Research Group at the University of Surrey (now at the University of Liverpool)—have been able to demonstrate that the valuable insights of FBI agents can be developed by using the *inductive* processes of science. By considering empirical results from the study of the actions of a large number of criminals it has been possible to propose both theories and methodologies that elaborate the relationships between an offender's actions and his or her characteristics.

Two interrelated issues need to be distinguished here. One is the common procedure of inferring general characteristics about a person from particulars of his or her behaviour. The second issue has its roots more clearly in the traditions of scientific psychology. This is the possibility of building psychological theories that will show how and why variations in criminal behaviour occur.

The first meaning for 'offender profiling' with its origins in everyday experience, described the process whereby experienced investigators, and other people with direct knowledge of criminal activities, could give advice to detectives. As such, this procedure has roots that can be traced at least to biblical times. It is, therefore, not surprising that from the earliest years of criminal investigations, there have been attempts to draw upon similar ideas in order to give assistance to the conduct of enquiries. The senior medical officer at the time of the Jack the Ripper enquiry in 1888, provided suggestions about the characteristics of the offender in an attempt to help the police locate the killer (Rumbelow, 1988). Earlier in the nineteenth century the novelist Edgar Allan Poe had given guidance, with a similar lack of success, to police investigations in the United States. Much of what is called 'profiling' today still has its roots in this application of 'common sense'.

In what follows, I will focus on the second meaning that is developing for 'offender profiling', dealing with the psychological issues involved.

CONSTRAINTS

There are constraints on both the information available to the police during an investigation and also on the type of information on which they can act. The constraints on the information available about the crime relate to the fact that only an account of what has happened, who the victim is, where it took place and when, is available to investigators. There is hardly ever any direct observation by the investigator, or the possibility of direct contact with the offender during the commission of the crime. This is very different from most areas of psychology, where the person of focal interest is available for close, direct observation and detailed questioning. If there is a victim who survives a crime, then that victim may be able to give the details of what occurred. But even in this case, it is unlikely that the victim can give any reliable information about the internal, cognitive processes of the perpetrator during the criminal acts. So the predictor variables are limited to those that are external to the offender.

The criteria variables (i.e. important features of the offender) are also restricted, because the information on which the police can act is limited to what is available to them in the investigative process. Details of a person's criminal history, as well as descriptions of age and appearance, occupational characteristics and domestic circumstances are all potentially available to investigating officers for any particular suspect. However, personality characteristics, detailed measures of intelligence, attitudes and fantasies are all more difficult for investigating officers to uncover. Similarly, in relation to giving guidance as to where detectives should look to find possible suspects, information about residential location, or recreational activities, for example, are more likely to be of immediate value than the issues with which psychologists are more conventionally concerned, such as locus of control or sexual predilections.

THE CANONICAL EQUATIONS

The methodological difficulties and the need for theory in this area can be illustrated by consideration of the inferential problem at the heart of profiling as a Canonical Correlation (see Tabachnick and Fidell, 1983). Such a procedure has the objective of analysing 'the relationships between two sets of variables' (p. 146). In other words, it is an attempt to derive multiple regression equations that have a number of criterion variables as well as a number of predictor variables.

On one side of this equation are variables derived from information about the offence which would be available to investigators. On the other side, there are the characteristics of the offender that are most useful in facilitating the police enquiry. So, if $A_{1...n}$ represents n actions of the offender (including, for example, time, place and victim selection) and $C_{1...m}$ represents m characteristics of the offender, then the empirical question is to establish the values of the weightings ($F_{1...n}$ and $K_{1...m}$) in an equation of the following form:

$$F_1 A_1 + ... + F_n A_n = K_1 C_1 + ... K_m C_m$$

If such canonical equations could be established for any subset of crimes then they would provide a powerful basis for police investigations, as well as raising some fascinating psychological questions about criminal behaviour.

The first step in producing such equations is to demonstrate that there are reliable relationships between A(ction)s and C(haracteristic)s, even at the one-to-one level. Indeed, the whole possibility of an empirically based approach to offender profiling depends upon the presence of these relationships.

A Study of the Relationship of Sexual Actions in Assaults and Offenders' Offence History

A number of studies conducted at the University of Surrey do show that this *a priori* assumption can be supported fairly readily. For example, in an unpublished study of 60 serial rapists that I carried out with Rupert Heritage, we classified the first offence of each offender in terms of the presence or absence of four sexual aspects of the assault that had a frequency that was neither very high, nor very low in the sample: i.e. (i) insistence by the offender that the victim masturbate him, (ii) oral ejaculation by the offender, (iii) aggression by the offender during the sexual activity, and (iv) aggression after it. These four A(ction) variables were each independently correlated with two variables created on the basis of whether or not the offender had a criminal record for, first, indecent exposure, and secondly indecent assault. A further two C(haracteristic)s variables were created to indicate the frequency of indecency convictions, thirdly, as a juvenile and fourthly as an adult. Each of the four A variables was then correlated with each of the four C variables.

Using conventional indicators of statistical significance, 15 out of the 16 values would be considered significant, providing definite evidence that the occurrence of certain actions during a sexual assault are more likely to be made by a man with a criminal history for indecency than not. But such results also raise many questions. For example, in this instance frequency of juvenile convictions for indecency has the highest correlation with the sexual actions, but without extensive examination of a variety of other possible C variables and the relationships they have to each other it is difficult to tell how reliable such a correlation is likely to be with other samples. This correlation may drop considerably if the sample had a lower age range, for it may just be an artefact of the age of the offenders.

An Example of the Relationships between Rapists' Behaviour and Offender Characteristics

Carrying out a further study on the same sample of 60 rapes, a number of characteristics beyond the criminal history of the offenders were considered; these were correlated with a range of distinct offence behaviours, such as wearing gloves, binding the victim, and so on. The association coefficients in this case were not as high as for the previous analysis but the majority would pass conventional criteria for statistical significance. However, the problem that these results illustrate is that there are no uniquely strong relationships between a given A variable and a given C variable. This means that there will be a mixture of correlations within the A variables and within the C variables that will contaminate any initial attempts to establish specific relationships between these two groups of variables.

These results, thus lend some support to the possibility of establishing empirical links between the A and the C variables of the canonical correlation, for one type of crime at least. Other unpublished studies have indicated similar possibilities for burglary (Barker, 1989), workplace crime (Robertson, 1993) and child abuse (Corstorphine, 1993; Kirby, 1993). But in no case are there simple relationships between one A variable and one C variable. The central problems of canonical equations thus emerge. A variety of combinations of A weightings can just as validly give rise to a variety of combinations of C weightings. There is not one, but many possible relationships within any data set linking the As to the Cs. In concrete terms this could mean for instance that one pattern of behaviour could indicate a young man with little criminal history or just as readily an older man with a lot of criminal experience.

A second problem was identified by Tabachnick and Fidell (1983). This is the sensitivity of the solution in the A set of variables to the inclusion of variables in the C set. Minor variations in the variance or the inclusion of particular variables in the A set may radically change the weightings in the C set. So, for example, leaving out of the calculations an action because a witness or victim was not sure about it, could produce different proposals about the offender than if that action were included.

THE OFFENDER CONSISTENCY HYPOTHESIS

One hypothesis central to profiling is that the way an offender carries out a crime on one occasion will have some characteristic similarities to the way he or she carries out crimes on other occasions. If the inherent variations between contexts, for any aspect of human behaviour, is greater than the variations between people then it is unlikely that clear differences between individuals will be found for those behaviours. This hypothesis is applicable to the situation in which a person has committed only one crime. Even in that case a 'profile' has to be based upon the assumption that the criminal is exhibiting characteristics that are typical of that person, not of the situation in which the crime was committed.

An Examination of the Linking of Three Rapes to one Offender

This can be illustrated by an exploratory study of 17 serial rapists carried out by Hammond (1990). For each rapist three rapes were selected, representing attacks that occurred in the early, middle and late stages of their series. For each rape 16 actions were identified to cover the range of actions that occurred in the rapes. Treating the actions as all or nothing occurrences within the whole sample the probability profile for each rape was drawn up. This consisted of the expected frequency of each action for each profile of actions, derived from the frequency of each action and the frequency of each profile. Joint probability calculations were then performed for each of the 51 (3 x 17) offences by comparing their actual dichotomous profiles with the expected frequency profile. This gave an index, presented as a probability, of the specificity of the three offences for each of the 17 individuals.

The results demonstrated that in fewer than 15 per cent of the cases the probability was so low as to indicate, wrongly, that the offence was not committed by the offender convicted of it. Eleven out of the 17 rapists (65 per cent) had all their offences correctly attributed to them, showing consistency across all three offences. It is also interesting to note that in this small, exploratory study the first and third offences seemed to be more accurately identified than the middle offence. Indeed, none of the third offences were assigned a probability below 0.72.

A small study such as this, that inevitably assumes all the convictions were 'safe', cannot be taken as evidence for offender consistency, but it does serve to show that such consistency can be demonstrated by the application of conventional probability theory to a mathematical profile of criminal actions. Such procedures could be developed both as analytic tools to help establish the conditions under which consistency did occur and even have the potential for contributing directly to criminal investigations.

An Illustration of the Comparison of a Target Offence with the Action Profiles of Other Offenders

Offender consistency has two components; the degree of variation within one offender's actions and the range of variation across a number of offenders. Although these two questions are distinguished by apparently small changes in emphasis there are potentially large differences in their implications. The actions that may be characteristic of a person across a series of offences may be quite different from those actions that help to discriminate him or her from other possible offenders in a large pool.

This can be illustrated by a study examining the actions of one rapist in relation to 45 others. This man was known to have committed 73 offences of many kinds, but for the purposes of this illustration his first known rape was examined. For this comparison ten aspects of rape were identified (drawing on the model of Canter and Heritage, 1989). Each of the 45 known rapists was assigned a characteristic profile by determining their modal behaviour across all the rapes for which they were convicted. The first rape of the target offender was then correlated with all the modal profiles of the 45 rapists, using the ten actions as the basis for the correlation.

Only 14 offenders produced correlations greater than 0.00, and only one, the target, obtained a perfect correlation. Furthermore, only two others came close in their similarity coefficients. These results illustrate that target offences can be linked to the characteristic patterns of their perpetrators, but much larger samples would be necessary to demonstrate the generality of these findings.

The Home Range Hypothesis

One set of actions of particular significance to police investigations are those that relate to the distance that an offender travels from home in order to commit the crime. The offender consistency hypothesis would lead to the proposal that there will be some structure, (identifiable pattern) to the locations at which an offender chooses to commit crimes. A number of studies have given general support to this proposition (reviewed in Brantingham and Brantingham, 1981; Evans and Herbert, 1989).

Recent studies (Canter and Larkin, 1993) have developed this proposition to show that there are reasonably precise relationships between the distances that rapists travel between their crimes (an A variable) and the distance they are travelling from home (a C variable). Barker (1989) has also shown similar relationships for burglars. The distances that rapists travel also appears to relate to other aspects of their offence, such as whether it is committed indoors or outdoors. Therefore by combining the purely geographical information with other aspects of the offence it has been possible to produce a data base search procedure that could narrow the area of likely residence of a known offender, on average, to less than a 3 km radius (Canter and Gregory, 1994). Whatever the eventual practical benefits of these studies their theoretical import is further to support the general proposition that the way an offender commits crimes is characteristic of that individual and distinguishable from the offence 'style' of other offenders committing similar crimes.

THE OFFENCE SPECIFICITY HYPOTHESIS

If there is the possibility that an offender will reveal some consistency in any particular crime there is the further question about how much of a criminal specialist he or she is. Much of the criminology literature suggests that especially younger offenders are quite eclectic in their forms of crime, to the extent that individuals who have committed one type of crime are likely to have committed crimes of other types. Thus even establishing distinct groups of offenders on the basis of their types of crime may prove problematic.

A Study of the Specialisms of Juvenile Delinquents

The whole enterprise of deriving characteristics of offenders that could be reliable enough to be of utility in police investigation would be under serious threat if, as some argue, offenders are typically versatile in the types of offence that they commit. If (a) opportunity and particular circumstances are seen to determine the particular crime that is committed, and (b) social processes and aspects of individual learning give rise to a preparedness on the part of anybody to carry out a criminal act, but (c) which particular act is carried out is as much due to chance and circumstance as to the propensities of the criminal, then no criminal could be distinguished from another. Such a perspective would argue that really any criminal could commit one of a great variety of different types of offence and, therefore, it would not be possible to infer anything about the person from his or her particular crime.

Another argument, that is probably more relevant in relation to violent and obviously emotional crime, is the one that assumes these crimes are committed in states of impulsive, unplanned action. For these crimes it is postulated that people react in such an unstructured way that no aspect of their characteristics is likely to be revealed, other than possibly their characteristic impulsivity. For instance the location chosen will be a haphazard one that bears no relationship to other aspects of the individual's life. Similarly, their victims may be regarded as of no particular significance. The contrasting argument may be thought of as the *modus operandi* argument. The view that a criminal's actions are unique to that individual and therefore patterns and trends that allow the groupings of individuals are very unlikely. Any theory that is a basis for offender profiling will need to fit somewhere between the idiosyncratic perspective that is typical of *modus operandi* arguments and the generalist perspective that might be drawn from some criminological theories.

APPROACHES TO THEORY

The challenge is to establish the themes that will help to identify and explain the links between crime-based consistencies and characteristics of the offender.

Cause or Relationship

Conceptually there are number of different roles that a theory can play in helping to link the A and the C variables. One is to explain how it is that the C variables are the cause of the A variables. A different theoretical perspective would be to look for some common third set of intervening variables that was produced by the C variables to cause the A variables. Yet a third possibility is that some third set of variables was the cause of both the A and the C variables. A variety of theoretical perspectives that reveal greater or lesser clarity on possible relationships between A and C are available.

Psychodynamic Typologies

Psychodynamic theories see the differences not so much in the crimes as in the internal emotional dynamics of the criminal, as reflected, for example, in the often quoted, rape typology of Groth and Birnbaum (1979), with its distinctions between offenders who are acting out their anger and those who are acting out desires for power. By their very nature, these theories are specific to particular types of crime. These tend to be crimes of violence and especially sexual crimes. There appear to be no attempts to apply similar psycho-dynamic consideration to, say, burglary or fraud.

What this approach usually gives rise to is the proposal of a few broad types. In effect, a small number of simple equations that link the A and C variables are proposed. Each of these equations is shaped by a trend common to the A and the C variables; the need for power, anger, control and so on. These trends may be explained in term of displacement of anger from other targets, or the feeling of lack of power and the consequent compensatory search to obtain it illegally. Stephenson (1992) has reviewed such displacement compensation theories as general explanations of criminal behaviour and found little evidence for them. Such theories are the basis of the FBI typologies of rape and murder.

Personality Differences

An approach that emerges more directly from experimental psychology is the proposal that the A and the C variables will share underlying personality characteristics. Research conducted to explore this thesis has tended to focus on simple A variables; the crime for which a person has been convicted. Such studies compare people who have committed different crimes so, for example, robbers are compared with rapists, or burglars with child abusers. The comparison process of such studies need not have this artificial, quasi-experimental design to it, but people who have this type of hypothesis do tend to think in terms of some particular cause that has led a person to become involved in burglary or buggery and so there is a tendency to set the studies up as if a comparison of some direct causal influence were being examined.

Perhaps the most direct illustration of such an exploration is the work of Eysenck (1977), who argued that there are personality differences between different types of criminal. By comparing groups of people convicted of one particular offence on personality measurements, conclusions are drawn about the personality differences between different offenders.

The evidence for the variety of crimes in which any given individual is involved, throws some very real doubt on the possibility of explaining or predicting criminal characteristics from the particular type of crime that he or she carried out. Furthermore, any examination of the legal definition of crimes will demonstrate that there is some arbitrariness in terms of what the actual actions are that characterise a particular crime.

Despite these difficulties, however, it does seem unlikely that a person's personality is not reflected in some way in how he or she commits crimes. A person's intelligence or extroversion would be expected to have some bearing on what and how a criminal offends. The problem is identifying those 'real world' A and C variables that do have direct links to personality characteristics.

Career Routes

A rather different approach to distinguishing between offenders can be drawn from general, criminology theory. Here the idea is that a person starts off in his or her life of crime, much as the junior office worker may start off in a large organisation. A variety of opportunities are presented and a variety of experiences are gained. Through this process, the individual learns that he or she is particularly successful or particularly attracted to certain types of activities and so a form of specialism evolves. In this framework, people become muggers, burglars or rapists as their criminal career unfolds.

There is certainly broad evidence in support of this career conceptualisation. The criminological literature shows that when aggregates of crimes are examined, serious violent crimes are typically committed by offenders who are older than those involved in minor theft. Cohort studies (notably Farrington, 1986) have also indicated the variations in crimes that cohorts are involved in at different ages. However, for such an approach to be of direct value to profiling a number of detailed studies of individuals would be necessary in order to establish just what number and variety of career routes could be found through the criminal jungle.

This perspective offers two possible forms of elaboration of the canonical correlation by adding a temporal dimension. The most complex temporal elaboration is to propose that a matrix of equations would be necessary, in essence one equation for each stage in the criminal career. This would be a daunting research task requiring considerable resources and large data sets. A simpler framework deals with the C variables as aspects of the stage a criminal is at, i.e. other personal criminal experiences.

Socio-economic Sub-groups

A more strongly socially oriented theory of offender differences would draw attention to the sub-groups from which they are likely to come. A detailed proposal of how 'social profiles' could be drawn up for sexual mass murderers was presented by Leyton in 1983. He argued that the general social characteristics of sexual mass murderers were known, citing matters such as family breakdown and socio-economic status. Here, then, the link between the A and the C variables is postulated because they are both hypothesised to be the reflections of the same social processes of anomie and social breakdown. This perspective has potential for development if the social characteristics of sub-groups of offenders could be established. The difficulty is likely to be that most criminals are drawn from similar socio-economic circumstances so that discriminating between them in terms of these characteristics could prove very challenging. However, current studies (e.g. Robertson, 1993) do suggest that in certain types of crime, notably workplace crime and fraud, there may be quite strong differences in the types and styles of crime in relation to social sub-groups.

Interpersonal Narratives

A further theoretical perspective (Canter, 1994) is emerging which attempts to build links between the strengths of all the approaches outlined above. This approach sees any crime as an interpersonal transaction that involves characteristic ways of dealing with other people. It leads to hypotheses both about the range of crimes in which an individual will be involved and his or her characteristic ways of committing those crimes. Furthermore, it leads to hypotheses about consistencies between forms of criminal activity and other aspects of a criminal's life.

In essence, it is argued that although there will be some generality of criminal activity, common across a range of offenders who have committed similar types of crime, there will none the less be a sub-set, or repertoire, of criminal activity that an individual will tend to operate within. This will be reflected both in the types of crime committed, as well as the repertoire of actions engaged in for any particular type of crime. The origin of these interpersonal themes is hypothesised to have routes in the learning of styles of interpersonal interaction. Drawing on general theories in social psychology, it can be proposed that styles of transactions will essentially be directed against other people as objects to be abused, or as vehicles that provide an opportunity for some type of interpersonal exploitation.

Two sets of hypotheses can be derived from this conceptualisation. One set of hypotheses relates to the existence of sub-sets of interrelated activities. These may be classes of crimes which offenders tend to commit, or classes of behaviour that tend to be committed within a crime. An important point here is that individuals are expected to have overlapping sets of repertoires that will have characteristic themes associated with them. It is not expected that every person will fit distinctly into one type of offender or another.

The second set of hypotheses relates to predictions about the correlations between the themes that an offender exhibits and other characteristics that he or she might have. At the most elementary level this is an hypothesis about the characteristic style of criminal transaction. So, for example, a person who goes to some trouble to control his victim during the committal of a sexual offence, binding and gagging her, for example, would be hypothesised to be someone who has thought through the exploitation of others in order to avoid capture while escaping with a criminal act. Such a person, therefore, would be hypothesised as having a range of criminal history, including the committing of offences that are not necessarily of a sexual nature.

The study by Canter and Heritage (1989) shows one approach that can help develop the narrative perspective into a set of more precise, testable hypotheses. By content analysing the actions that occurred in 63 rapes they were able to identify 57 distinct actions. A subsequent analysis of the co-occurrence of these actions demonstrated that while there were a number of actions that were common to the great majority of sexual assaults there were also interpretable trends that characterised sub-sets of the less frequent actions. These trends were interpreted in terms of the interpersonal focus of the assault: (a) the victim as an object of no concern to the offender, (b) the victim as a target to be aggressively controlled, (c) the victim as a sexual object, (d) the victim as a source for criminal activity, and (e) the victim as a person with whom a pseudo-relationship is desired. Heritage (1992) has been able to indicate that there may be important differences between the characteristics of these sub-groups, especially in terms of their previous criminal history and relationships with women.

CONCLUSIONS

The general experience of providing 'profiles' of offenders for police investigations has been drawn upon to formulate reasonably precise research questions. It has been shown that even the elementary models that underlie these questions have an inherent complexity to them, readily encapsulated in canonical equations. The demands on theory which these complexities generate are further extended by an awareness of the practical constraints under which any theory must be applied.

It has been proposed that central to all theory building in this area is the need to demonstrate consistencies within the actions of offenders and identifiable differences between them. Examples have been presented from a range of exploratory studies to show that there are indeed likely to be differences between offenders that are based upon consistencies in the actions of individual criminals. However, it is unlikely that rigid typologies of offenders will be empirically supported; rather, there will be thematic trends to their actions that will be characteristic of both their target offence and other aspects of their personal history and life style.

Two points that emerge repeatedly from a number of studies help to give more shape to these general findings. The first is that the consistencies in a criminal's action broadly relate to whether his or her crimes involve some form of psycho-social, interpersonal contact or whether they may be described as psychologically distant exploitations of other people. The second is that the best predictor of later crime behaviour is indeed earlier criminal activity.

Taken together these two points put into high relief the central problem of recidivism; that it is rooted in psychologically entrenched ways of dealing with others. But they also point out the importance of going beyond general explanation of why people continue to offend and the need to explain why they continue to offend in a particular way.

REFERENCES

Barker, M. (1989). Criminal activity and home range: a study of the spatial offence patterns of burglars. Unpublished Master's dissertation, University of Surrey.

Brantingham, P.J. and Brantingham, P.L. (Eds) (1981). *Environmental Criminology*. Beverley Hills, CA: Sage.

Canter, D. (1994). *Criminal Shadows*. London: HarperCollins.

Canter, D. and Gregory, A. (1994). Identifying the residential locations of rapists. *Journal of Forensic Science Society*, **34**, 169–75.

Canter, D. and Heritage, R. (1989). A multivariate model of sexual offence behaviour. *Journal of Forensic Psychiatry*, **1**, 185–212.

Canter, D. and Larkin, P. (1993). The environmental range of serial rapists. *Journal of Environmental Psychology*, **13**, 63–9.

Corstorphine, E. (1993). A comparison of sexual and physical abusers of children. Unpublished Master's dissertation, University of Surrey.

Evans, D.J. and Herbert, D.T. (1989). *The Geography of Crime*. London: Routledge.

Eysenck, H. (1977). *Crime and Personality*. London: Paladin.

Farrington, D. (1986). Stepping stones to adult criminal careers. In D.Olweus, J.Block and M. Radke-Yarrow (Eds), *Development of Antisocial and Prosocial Behaviour*. London: Academic Press.

Groth, N. and Birnbaum, H. (1979). *Men who Rape: The Psychology of the Offender*. New York: Plenum.

Hammond, S. (1990). Statistical approaches to crime linking. University of Surrey: Internal Report.

Hazelwood, R.R. and Burgess, A. (Eds) (1987). *Practical Aspects of Rape Investigation: A Multidisciplinary Approach*. Amsterdam: Elsevier.

Heritage, R. (1992). Facets of sexual assault: first steps in investigative classifications. Unpublished M.Phil. dissertation, University of Surrey.

Kirby, S. (1993). *The Child Molester: Separating Myth from Reality*. Unpublished PhD dissertation, University of Surrey.

Leyton, E. (1983). A social profile of sexual mass murderers. In T. Fleming and L.A. Visano (Eds), *Deviant Designations*. London: Butterworth.

Ressler, R.K., Burgess, A.W. and Douglas, J.E. (1988). *Sexual Homicide: Patterns and Motives*. Lexington, MA: Lexington.

Robertson, A.R.T. (1993). A psychological perspective on blue-collar workplace crime. Unpublished Master's dissertation, University of Surrey.

Rumbelow, D. (1988). *The Complete Jack the Ripper*. London: Penguin .

Stephenson, G.M. (1992). *The Psychology of Criminal Justice*. Oxford: Blackwell.

Tabachnick, B.G. and Fidell, L.S. (1983). Using Multivariate Statistics. London: Harper & Row.

Chapter 4.6

Violence

Ronald Blackburn
University of Liverpool

INTRODUCTION

Legal attempts to regulate violent behaviour are universal. Not only do violent crimes attract the most severe penalties, the possibility of future violence by an individual influences civil and criminal justice decisions on many issues, such as bail, child custody, parole, or the involuntary commitment of the mentally ill. In sentencing offenders convicted of serious violence, English courts are required to consider aggravating or mitigating factors, but psychologists are most likely to be involved when questions of mental disorder arise. Of the four classes of specific disorder recognised in the Mental Health Act 1983 (mental illness, mental impairment, severe mental impairment, and psychopathic disorder), psychopathic disorder is particularly implicated in violence, being defined as 'a persistent disorder or disability of mind ... which results in abnormally aggressive or seriously irresponsible conduct on the part of the person concerned'.

Clinicians have criticised this legal concept because of its circularity and lack of concordance with clinical concepts of psychopathic personality or personality disorder. However, psychologists may be called on to identify the causes of an offender's aggression, and where psychopathic disorder is agreed by psychiatrists, the court requires evidence of treatability before imposing a hospital order. This generally entails consideration of psychological treatment. Psychologists may also treat violent offenders in prison, or on probation, and may be required to give evidence about the dangerousness of detained mentally disordered offenders to Mental Health Review Tribunals.

The prediction of dangerous behaviour is considered in Chapter 7.2 of this volume. This chapter discusses psychological theories and research relevant to an understanding of violent crime, the focus being on crimes against the person. A more detailed account of these issues can be found in several recent

Handbook of Psychology in Legal Contexts
Edited by R. Bull and D. Carson. © 1995 John Wiley & Sons Ltd

texts (Berkowitz, 1993; Blackburn, 1993a; Thompson and Cowen, 1993).

CONCEPTS AND DEFINITIONS

Violence is part of the wider phenomenon of aggression, but everyday use of these terms is imprecise and value-laden. Portrayals of 'violence' in the news media, for example, often include behaviours as diverse as vandalism, joy-riding, or youngsters jeering at the police. Vigorous competition in sport or forceful argument are also sometimes described as 'aggressive'. However, vigorous or destructive actions are carried out for many reasons. Psychologists now agree that to cover a unitary set of phenomena, the term aggression should be limited to behaviour in which the intended goal is harm or injury of another living being who is motivated to avoid it (Zillmann, 1979; Berkowitz, 1993). This definition covers psychological as well as physical injury. It also distinguishes malevolent injury from benevolently intended injury, such as surgical intervention, and from injury infliction which is accidental or is sought masochistically by the victim.

Violence is the forceful and intended infliction of physical injury on an unwilling victim. This includes injurious actions legitimised by social norms, such as those resulting from self-defence or disciplinary punishment. Although these are not usually labelled as violence or aggression, this reflects the influence of moral judgements of what is justified on everyday use of these terms. Such behaviour, however, frequently constitutes *counter-aggression*, and support from social norms contributes significantly to the level of violence in a society.

Aggression, then, may entail physical attack, verbal abuse, or passive obstruction, and its consequences range from loss of life to psychological hurt. To subsume such varying phenomena under a single heading implies a common function. However, *angry aggression*, in which harm to the victim reduces an unpleasant emotional state, is generally distinguished from *instrumental aggression*, in which harm or injury facilitates the attainment of non-aggressive goals. Criminologists similarly distinguish expressive from instrumental violence. As the distinction implies, *anger*, which is an emotional state with physiological, cognitive, and expressive components, can occur independently of aggression. Although anger arousal makes aggressive behaviour more likely, aggression is not a necessary outcome of anger, nor is all aggression accompanied by a state of anger.

Aggression and anger are also distinguished from *hostility*, which denotes negative evaluations or attitudes of resentment, mistrust, or hate. Negative attitudes do not necessarily lead to attempts to injure, nor need aggression entail hatred of the victim. One further distinction is that between an aggressive act and aggressiveness as a disposition or trait. A trait of aggressiveness implies a tendency or readiness to act with aggression under certain conditions, but not all offenders who have engaged in a violent crime have a pronounced aggressive disposition.

Criminal Violence

Criminal violence is the illegal use of force, and includes criminal homicide, assault, robbery, rape, and other sexual assaults. Robbery represents instrumental aggression, but most unplanned or impulsive violence is probably mediated by anger. Crimes such as arson, criminal damage, dangerous driving, and violations of industrial safety legislation, may also entail serious personal injury, but do not generally qualify as violent, unless intentional harm of a person is involved.

Rates of violence vary widely between countries. Rates of homicide and rape are some seven times greater in the United States than in Britain, while homicide rates in Mexico are double those of the United States, suggesting the influence of sociocultural factors. Violent crimes amount to some 7 per cent of offences recorded by the police in England and Wales, and about 9 per cent of males and 4 per cent of females before the courts are convicted of crimes against the person. Although recorded violence has increased along with crime generally during the past three decades, serious (life-endangering) violence has increased at a lower rate than less serious violence. An exception is rape, which has increased almost six-fold since the 1960s. Recent increases partly reflect changes in police procedures for dealing with rape victims in 1985, which have encouraged more victims to come forward. Nevertheless, much violence does not come to the attention of the police.

Whether violence in the family has increased is uncertain, but child and wife abuse have become an acknowledged social problem during the last two decades and it has been increasingly accepted that assaults on family members merit criminal justice intervention. Family violence nevertheless remains tolerated within society. For example, in American surveys, over 90 per cent of parents report inflicting physical pain on their children during disciplinary encounters. The National Survey of Family Violence in the United States in 1985 (Straus and Gelles, 1988) found that 16.1 per cent of couples had experienced an incident of violence, while 6.3 per cent had experienced severe violence, such as kicking, punching, or using a knife or gun, during the previous year. Severe violence had been directed by husbands to 3.4 per cent of wives, by wives to 4.8 per cent of husbands, and by 53 per cent of children towards a sibling. These figures cannot be readily extrapolated to other countries, but violent behaviour is clearly common, and family violence is a major source of criminal violence. For example, a fifth of all homicides in the United States and more than a third in Britain are family murders.

Demographic characteristics of violent crime are similar to those of crime more generally. Rates are higher in urban areas and poorer parts of towns and cities, and known offenders are more likely to be male, young, and from lower socioeconomic groups. Sexual aggression and domestic violence, however, are less clearly related to social status.

Studies show consistently that over two-thirds of violent crimes are perpetrated by less than a fifth of offenders, who tend to be the most recidivist. However, 'specialisation' in violence is rare, and a majority of offenders convicted of violence have records of non-violent offending. On the other hand, evidence seems to favour specialisation among sexual aggressors. Hall and Proctor (1987), for example, found that among 'sexual psychopaths' released from an American state hospital, prior arrests for sex offences against adults predicted later offences of a similar kind, while arrests for child offences predicted later child offences. They also found that previous sex offences against adults predicted later non-sexual offences, including violence, but this was not so for previous offences against children. Other research also suggests that rapists have a propensity to offend more generally.

Detailed analyses of violent crime have been mainly confined to homicide and assault. In a classic study, Wolfgang (1958) examined 588 homicides committed in Philadelphia between 1948 and 1952. Two-thirds of the crimes occurred between 8.00 p.m. on Friday and 8.00 p.m. Sunday, and both offenders and victims were most likely to be black, male, and aged under 30. Victims and offenders were acquainted or related in 59 per cent of male killings, and 84 per cent of female deaths, and where men killed and were killed more often outside the home, women were most commonly killed in the home, 41 per cent of them by their partner. In contrast, only 11 per cent of male victims were killed by their wives. While stabbing was the most frequent method of killing, a third of offences involved shooting, and recorded antecedents were vague altercations, domestic quarrels, jealousy, or arguments over money. Less than 3 per cent of offenders were declared insane, but 4 per cent committed suicide following the homicide.

Similar patterns have been reported in other studies. However, a British study of homicide by Gibson (1975) found that the racial element was less apparent (although this is now changing), and fewer homicides involved shootings or robbery-murders, while a greater proportion of victims were females or males who were acquainted. Also, about 30 per cent of murderers in England are regularly judged to be mentally disordered, and until the 1960s, some 30 per cent of killers in Britain committed suicide. This figure has in more recent years fallen to about 8 per cent.

Most homicides are 'crimes of passion' involving an interaction between acquaintances, and data obtained by Block (1977) in Chicago suggest that many are assaults which go further than intended, the outcome depending on the victim–offender interaction and the weapon used. However, serious assaults are demographically and spatially similar to homicide. Robbery is more commonly directed to male strangers 'on the streets'. It is again a large city crime, offenders being mainly young males, and most offences are either planned robbery of those in charge of money as part of their employment, or unplanned and opportunistic acts, such as handbag snatching or mugging in public places. Although weapons may be used to threaten compliance, most robberies do not result in injury to the victim. Nevertheless, the psychological consequences of assault may be considerable. For example, Kilpatrick et al. (1985) found that among American females reporting some form of physical or sexual assault, 19 per cent of those who had experienced rape, and 12 per cent of victims of attempted robbery reported suicide attempts, compared with 2 per cent of non-victimised women.

THEORIES OF AGGRESSION

The extensive research on aggression has been guided by a variety of theories, which differ in their emphasis on unlearned or learned components, affective or cognitive processes, and internal or external determinants. The major competing assumptions are represented by biological, psychodynamic, social learning, and social psychological perspectives.

Biological Perspectives

In comparison with other species, humans have a greater capacity for learning different ways of achieving the same injurious goals. However, like any co-ordinated activity, physical aggression is dependent on inborn structural properties of brain and musculature. Biologial approaches propose that this co-ordination is under the control of innate and specific neurochemical systems, and emphasise similarities between humans and other animals.

From studies of lower vertebrates, Lorenz (1966) proposed that there is a 'universal instinct' of aggression which functions to ensure population control, selection of the strongest animals for reproduction, brood defence, and social organisation. Instinct relates to a spontaneously generated energy source in the nervous system which discharges through fixed action patterns in response to specific releasing stimuli. The theory postulates that human behaviour is governed by a constant need to discharge aggressive energy.

Moyer (1981) also assumes phylogenetic continuity, and draws on studies of the effects of electrical brain stimulation and surgical lesions in animals and in patients with organic pathology. He suggests that there are 'organised neural circuits' in the brain which are sensitised by hormones and blood constituents, and which when fired in the presence of a relevant target, produce integrated attacking behaviour. Human learning can influence the selection of targets and the inhibition of behaviour, but feelings of hostility will be experienced, whether or not aggressive behaviour occurs. Mark and Ervin (1970) similarly propose that there are centres in the limbic lobes of the brain which control aggressive behaviour, and that these are damaged in a substantial proportion of violent people.

Psychodynamic Perspectives

Psychoanalysts generally assume an aggressive instinct or drive. Interest centres on how aggressive drive is accommodated within the hypothesised psychic structures of id, ego, and superego, and how it comes to be channelled and controlled in the course of individual development.

Freud initially saw aggression as a reaction to frustration and pain. He later proposed a death instinct (Thanatos), a tendency to self-destruction which is diverted by the self-preserving libidinal instinct (Eros) to the external world. Many psychoanalysts accept the idea of an instinct of aggression, but reject the notion of a death instinct. Manifestations of aggressive instinct are held to include the rage reaction to frustration, which mobilises the organism for combat, but aggressive drive is also subject to the same developmental processes as the libido. It is therefore manifest in biting (oral sadism) or faeces retention (anal sadism). Through fixation these reactions may be transformed into aggressive character traits. Aggression may be provoked by external events, but instinctual aggressive impulses are constantly generated, and may erupt as irrational violence in pathological characters lacking superego control. However, aggressive energy may also be displaced to other targets, and aggressive tension purged through substitute expression, or catharsis.

Ego psychologists propose that the destructive aims of aggression become modified by displacement or sublimation, while through neutralisation, constructive energy is supplied to the ego, enabling it to fulfill self-assertive and adaptive functions. Superego development permits the internalisation of aggressive energy in the form of guilt. Instinctual energy is nevertheless still generated and may conflict with the demands of the libido, the superego, or reality. Continuous sublimation or neutralisation is therefore held to be necessary for healthy functioning.

Social Learning and Cognitive Perspectives

While accepting the possibility of primitive connections between threatening events and motor responses, learning theorists reject the concept of an aggressive instinct. Some theorists argue for a specific reactive drive of anger aroused by aversive experiences (Berkowitz, 1993), but others question this. Learning theorists hold that aggression is acquired and maintained by rewarding or reinforcing contingencies. An aggressive response which successfully attains a desired reward, such as material goods, status, or approval, is likely to be strengthened and repeated (positive reinforcement), as is one which removes an aversion or threat (negative reinforcement). These apply to instrumental and angry aggression, respectively. Aggression followed by immediate punishment is less likely to be repeated. Social learning theorists, however, emphasise that much learning takes place in a social context through observing the behaviour of others, or modelling.

Learning theories evolved from studies of conditioning processes in animals. While recent theorists such as Berkowitz allow a role for cognition, social cognitive approaches place greater emphasis on cognitive mediators of appraisal and attribution. Frustration and punishment, for example, are less likely to provoke aggression if the recipient perceives them as justified. This clearly entails normative judgements and cognitive appraisals about the intent of a frustrator. Similarly, physiological arousal energises aggressive behaviour, but only when it is attributed to frustration or provocation. When people are provoked to anger, further arousal from extraneous sources, such as noise or heat, may be mis-attributed and intensify aggression (Zillmann, 1979).

The most comprehensive social cognitive theory of aggression is that of Bandura (1983). He sees aggression as originating in modelling and reinforcement, through which people develop expectations about the likely outcomes of different behaviours in meeting their goals. These, however, include consequences for the self, and behaviour is adjusted to meet personal and social standards through self-regulatory processes of self-reward and punishment. Standards may nevertheless be overridden or neutralised by cognitive distortions such as blaming or dehumanising the victim.

Bandura rejects the notion of a specific aggressive drive, and proposes that both aversive experiences and positive incentives produce a general increase in emotional arousal. This motivates whatever relevant responses are strongest in the behavioural repertoire. In coping with aversive experiences, aggression is only one of several possible strategies, which might include avoidance or constructive problem-solving, depending on the individual's skills. Antisocial aggression may therefore reflect the failure to learn non-aggressive solutions to conflict situations.

Bandura gives no special attention to anger, but this is a current focus of interest for several cognitive theorists (Novaco and Welsh, 1989). Anger is not itself pathological, but the frequent and intense experience of anger impairs social functioning. However, aggression is only one way of alleviating anger. Cognitive mediators of anger are not fully agreed, some arguing that it depends on the cognitive label applied to a state of arousal, others that a state of emotional arousal is determined by cognitive appraisal of the personal significance of an event. Beck (1976), for example, sees anger as resulting from the appraisal of an 'unwarranted violation' of one's personal domain. Others note the dependence of anger on specific causal attributions of whether a provoking event is intentional, malevolent, foreseeable and unjustified.

Social Psychological Perspectives

Social learning approaches focus on the process of learning. Some social psychologists argue that aggression has to be understood in terms of the social context and meaning of an aggressive act to the aggressor. Toch (1969), for example, saw threats to masculine self-image and self-image promotion as significant in violent encounters between police and delinquents. Felson (1978) similarly proposes that aggression is a means of 'impression management', which restores a person's threatened identity.

A popular sociological theory proposes a 'subculture of violence' in urban ghettos (Wolfgang and Ferracutti, 1967). This is held to comprise a 'machismo' pattern of attitudes favouring honour, status, and masculinity, which dictates that violence is appropriate when these are threatened. This is claimed to be pervasive among young male and lower social class groups, but the hypothesis has not been well supported by research. Some sociologists argue that it is the dominant culture in Western society which maintains norms of violence.

Cultural factors have also been implicated in sexual aggression. Feminists have argued that rape is encouraged by prevailing norms of power relationships between men and women, which tacitly legitimise the keeping of women in a subordinate role. The prevalence of rape myths is held to be a manifestation of this.

ISSUES IN THE EXPLANATION OF AGGRESSION

There are four critical questions in understanding aggressive behaviour: (1) how does it originate? (2) how is it provoked or instigated? (3) how is it regulated or controlled? (4) how is it maintained over time?

Origins of Aggression

The concept of an aggressive instinct in humans has not generally been accepted by behavioural scientists, and biological theorists such as Lorenz have been criticised for anthropomorphic extrapolation and lack of attention to human symbolic capacities. Research has failed to uncover evidence to support the hydraulic model of a reservoir of energy, even in lower animals, or to support the idea of human brain systems exclusively concerned with aggression (Valenstein, 1976). While organic damage to the brain can sometimes produce heightened irritability and aggressiveness, this appears to reflect non-specific disorganisation rather than interference with specific brain centres. The psychodynamic instinct model is subject to the same criticisms. The proposal that many constructive activities are a manifestation of transformed destructive energy also allows virtually any activity to be construed as aggressive, and is hence not susceptible to a scientific test. However, the psychodynamic view that disruptions in early development are a source of later aggression now has general support.

Instinct theories do not differentiate between angry and instrumental aggression. Since the latter is mainly confined to humans, and serves non-aggressive purposes, its origins must be sought in cultural evolution and individual development. Biological theories may be more applicable to angry aggression. Reis (1974) categorised animal aggression as affective or predatory. Predatory aggression involves food-seeking behaviour which is largely controlled by innate mechanisms, and is species-specific. Affective or defensive aggression, which is characterised by arousal of the autonomic system, has more obvious human parallels, and most current theories of emotion recognise innate components of physiological arousal and expression in human anger. Anger, however, is a reaction to events, and not the result of spontaneously generated instinctual energy.

There is evidence from twin studies that aggressiveness is influenced by genetic factors, but this probably reflects the inheritance of non-specific factors, such as activity level or emotional reactivity. Some infants, for example, appear to create more opportunities for aversive exchanges with care-takers or siblings, and hence more readily learn aggressive solutions to conflict.

The learning theory view that aggression originates primarily in family modelling and reinforcement is currently the most influential. Longitudinal studies show that family histories of aggressive children and delinquents are characterised by higher rates of parental deviance, marital conflict, parental indifference and lack of supervision, and violent adults frequently report a history of witnessing violence and experiencing abuse in childhood. Detailed studies of interactions between antisocial children and their mothers also demonstrate how aggression can be acquired through inconsistent parental discipline. However, family variables provide only a partial account of later violence, and there is evidence that the violence of adolescents is significantly influenced by delinquent peers. This may reflect both the transmission of beliefs about the acceptability of violence and the reinforcement of aggression by the peer group.

Instigation and Provocation of Aggression

Dollard et al. (1939) drew on early Freudian theory in formulating the frustration–aggression hypothesis, which asserted that all aggression is a consequence of frustration in the form of thwarting of goal-directed activity. Frustration instigates a motive to injure the source of frustration, but if punishment is anticipated, the response is inhibited unless displaced to an alternative target.

Although influential, the original theory has not been widely accepted, since frustration instigates responses other than aggression, and aggression is equally provoked by insult or attack, threats to self-esteem or pain. Berkowitz (1993) has long defended a modified theory, arguing that there are elements of frustration in such antecedents. He currently argues that the frustration–aggression relation is a special case of a more general relation between aversive stimulation and aggression, and that negative affect is the source of angry aggression. This is aroused when events are perceived as unpleasant and activate memory networks which then prime anger-related thoughts.

Social cognitive theorists, however, propose that it is not merely the perception of unpleasantness which provokes angry aggression, but the appraisal of an event as threatening and unjustified. Perceived inequity, for example, is often significant in group violence. There is also evidence that aggressive boys have an attributional bias to perceive malevolent intent on the part of their peers. This emphasises the need to consider violent acts from the perspective of the aggressor. What may appear to an observer to be 'unprovoked' aggression is often the result of the aggressor's distorted appraisals or mis-attributions.

Attempts to identify regularities in the sequence of events leading to a violent crime suggest that many assaults may be victim-precipitated, in that the victim was the first to resort to violence (Wolfgang, 1958). While some see this as 'blaming the victim', it is consistent with the view that aggression involves impression management, and analyses of event sequences in reports of homicide and assault indicate that reciprocal retaliation is a significant factor. Retaliation may be either an attempt to save face or a strategic form of self protection. A violent outcome may thus be more the result of events causing a conflict to escalate than the characteristics or initial goals of the participants.

Environmental changes affecting biological, psychological, or social functioning may be experienced as aversive or frustrating, and there is a relationship between human aggression and environmental factors such as noise levels and climate. For example, field studies show that hotter regions, and hotter years, seasons, months, and days are associated with increased rates of murder, rape, assault, riot, and wife-beating (Anderson, 1989). While the effects may be partly mediated by changes in social contact and opportunities for aggression, the evidence is consistent with effects at the individual level, such as increased negative affect, or mis-attribution of arousal, although environmental stressors are probably not themselves sufficient to provoke aggression.

Regulation of Aggression

Psychodynamic theorists argue that violent individuals lack internalised controls in the form of superego development, and early learning theorists also stressed that restraints against harmful behaviour depended on the acquisition of emotional inhibitors such as anxiety, guilt, empathy, and tolerance for frustration. These emotional attributes are often deficient in violent offenders. However, where traditional approaches focus on affective experiences, current theories emphasise the role of cognitive factors which mediate these experiences, and which may be involved in both the inhibition and facilitation of aggression.

Intellectual deficits appear to play a role in violence. Neuropsychological studies suggest that reduced left hemispheric lateralisation may be particularly characteristic of delinquents showing psychopathic traits and a history of violence, and this may reflect a relative inability to modulate control by means of inner speech. Several studies also indicate an association of aggression with low intelligence, although this seems most significant in the early development of aggression.

Deficient social skills also characterise many aggressive offenders. It has been assumed that sex offenders lack heterosocial skills, but the evidence suggests that this applies mainly to child molesters. In conflict situations, it appears to be negotiation skills which are important, consistent with the social cognitive view that the use of aggression is more likely when alternative coping skills are lacking. Cognitive problem-solving skills have been investigated in aggressive boys, who have been found to generate fewer solutions to interpersonal problem situations, and also produce more aggressive and less effective solutions. Evidence from violent offenders is limited, but Slaby and Guerra (1988) found that in comparison with unaggressive schoolboys, violent delinquents and aggressive schoolboys showed more problem-solving deficits. They also endorsed more positive and neutralising beliefs about the consequences of aggression, such as self-esteem enhancement, and minimal suffering to the victim.

Both psychodynamic and learning theories regard anticipation of punishment as a significant inhibitor of aggression, and failure to consider consequences is likely to be one effect of limited problem-solving skills. This may also occur at high levels of arousal, for example when anger is intense. Alcohol and drugs may have a similar effect. Alcohol is generally regarded as a disinhibitor of aggression, and several studies find that high percentages of violent offenders and their victims have been drinking at the time of the offence. However, the effects of alcohol are influenced by expectations and situational factors, and there is no simple relation between aggression and alcohol ingestion.

Maintenance of Aggression

Although there have been debates about the consistency of personality traits, the stability of aggressiveness as a personality characteristic is now established. Olweus (1979) reviewed studies of the stability of aggression in males measured by a variety of methods, and found a high correlation between initial assessments and those obtained from six months to 21 years later. In the Cambridge study on delinquent development, Farrington (1989) found that almost a quarter of boys rated as highly aggressive by teachers at age 12 to 14 subsequently had a conviction for violence, compared with 7 per cent of less aggressive boys, and the former accounted for 60 per cent of the violent offenders. However, since only some aggressive children go on to exhibit violence in adulthood, continuity must be regarded as relative.

The learning of aggression as a solution to conflict situations under early adverse family conditions is not sufficient to explain the perpetuation of an aggressive style of interaction across the life course, since learning theory predicts that unreinforced behaviour extinguishes. Several theorists now account for continuity in terms of expectancy confirmation processes. Expectations function as rules about future stimulus and response outcomes, and once established as relatively general rules, they may override the objective contingencies, and become self-fulfilling prophecies. For example, a hostile person expects others to be hostile, and behaves in ways which elicit the expected reaction. Opportunities for changing expectancies and learning alternative ways of coping are therefore minimised.

Mothers who abuse their children show deficiencies in their anger control and parenting skills, and are likely to report having experienced abuse themselves. There is a common belief in a cycle of violence, in which abused children reproduce aggression towards their own children and others. However, many abusers do not have a history of being abused, and less than a third of abused children are likely to become abusers themselves. From a review of child abuse and later criminal violence, Widom (1989) concluded that the majority of abused children do not become violent offenders.

PERSONALITY AND PSYCHOPATHOLOGY IN VIOLENT OFFENDERS

Since situational factors and a person's temporary state clearly contribute to violent incidents, involvement in a single act of violence is not a reliable index of a violent disposition, and violent acts may be perpetrated by people who are not habitually aggressive. Personality variables are not in themselves sufficient to account for a violent act, but hostile attitudes or low self-esteem may bias people to perceive malevolent intent. An aggressive disposition and limited cognitive and social skills make aggressive resolutions of conflict more likely.

Only a minority of violent offenders exhibits serious mental illness, but personality disorder is generally believed to be a significant contributor. Carney (1976) described violent offenders as unable to trust because of role-playing deficits, unable to feel as manifest in acting out to defend against pain, unable to fantasise as shown in impulsivity and lack of empathy, and unable to learn as shown by failure to generalise from experience. This represents the traditional psychodynamic concept of psychopathic personality. The association of aggression with psychopathy is supported by Hare (1993), who has found that most prisoners meeting research criteria of psychopathy have a history of violent crimes, and are more likely to be aggressive in prison.

Violent offenders, however, are not homogeneous in personality. Megargee (1966) proposed that some violent offenders are over-controlled. He argued that under-controlled offenders, who are likely to be identified as psychopaths, have weak inhibitions against aggression, and respond aggressively with some regularity. Over-controlled offenders, in contrast, have strong inhibitions, and aggress only when instigation (anger arousal) is sufficiently intense to overcome inhibitions. They are expected to attack others rarely, but with extreme intensity, and to be found among those who have been extremely assaultive or homicidal. Megargee found support for this hypothesis among boys with a record of extreme assault, who were more controlled, unaggressive, and conventional than moderately assaultive and non-violent delinquents.

Further support comes from studies of mentally disordered offenders, but there is evidence for two over-controlled types (Blackburn, 1986). One denies angry or hostile tendencies, and describe themselves as sociable, non-anxious, and conforming. This comes closest to Megargee's original concept. The second group describes strong anger experiences, social avoidance, and poor self-esteem, and is more likely to display social skill deficits. However, two under-controlled groups are also apparent, which are identified as primary and secondary psychopaths. Both show strong impulsive and aggressive tendencies, but the former is less anxious, more socially assertive, and higher in self-esteem. The same four types have been identified among murderers and assaultive male prisoners. They also represent the most prominent personality patterns among violent mentally disordered offenders more generally.

In terms of the categories recognised in the English and Welsh Mental Health Act, then, personality deviation or disorder may contribute to violence among the mentally ill as well as among those in the psychopathic disorder category. Nevertheless, while the Act does not require demonstration of a causal link between mental illness and an offence for a hospital order to be made, mental illness is likely to be a direct factor in many cases.

The extent to which there is a general relation between violence and mental disorder has been disputed. Social scientists have argued that any links are coincidental, but clinicians have maintained that systematic links exist at the individual level. Evidence now favours the latter view, and schizophrenia in particular has been shown to increase the risk of violence (Monahan, 1992). While most schizophrenics do not become violent, a significant minority does, especially those experiencing active psychotic symptoms of a delusional nature. The presence of learning difficulties (mental handicap) also appears to elevate the risk, and some recent studies further implicate post-traumatic stress disorder. Evidence regarding violence in other disorders is equivocal.

It must be emphasised that none of the major categories of psychiatric disorder is strongly associated with a risk of violence, and violent behaviour by the mentally ill accounts for only a small part of violent crime overall. The presence of symptoms of disorder is also rarely sufficient to explain an act of violence, and must be seen in terms of an interaction with personal, social, and situational factors associated with aggression more generally.

TREATMENT INTERVENTIONS

Hospital orders for offenders in the categories of psychopathic disorder and mental impairment require justification in terms of treatability in England and Wales. The legal criterion is that treatment should 'alleviate or prevent deterioration of his condition'. Clinical judgements of treatability have been shown to be unreliable, and few differences have been found between offenders judged treatable and those regarded as untreatable. One problem is uncertainty in specifying treatment goals, which requires a theory of mediators of aggression. Another is the failure to distinguish the prediction of treatment outcome from the assessment of amenability to treatment as a constellation of personal and social factors. The former depends on evidence of the efficacy of available treatment techniques. The latter calls for assessment of several factors, including prior history of treatment response, motivation, and availability of appropriate resources. Without these conceptual distinctions, the reliability of treatability decisions will remain low.

Improvements in judging treatability are particularly hampered by the lack of firm evidence about the effectiveness of treatment methods with aggressive offenders. The argument that 'nothing works' in rehabilitating offenders generally has been effectively challenged by recent analyses of the existing literature and the introduction of new treatment techniques based on social cognitive theories. There are, however, few adequate studies of treatment efficacy with violent or psychopathic populations.

Many clinicians maintain that psychopaths are untreatable. This belief rests more on anecdote than empirical evidence, and recent reviewers conclude that despite the large number of reports on the treatment of psychopaths, too few meet basic methodological requirements to merit any firm conclusions (Blackburn, 1993b; Dolan and Coid, 1993). Persisting problems are the vague use of the term 'psychopath', and lack of attention to the heterogeneity of populations identified as psychopathic or violent. It is unlikely, for example, that a single treatment approach will have the same impact on the behaviour of over-controlled individuals and those who use aggression instrumentally.

Several approaches have none the less been tried, and some have achieved at least short-term changes in deviant behaviour. Pharmacological interventions are not a prominent treatment of choice, but temporary control of violence has been observed in a few instances with drugs such as lithium or amphetamine derivatives. Since evidence for specific brain mechanisms controlling aggression has not been forthcoming, any effects seem attributable to non-specific calming, and these are limited to the duration of drug administration.

A more common choice is group psychotherapy. The goal is typically to achieve insight into early developmental traumas and their effect on current relationships, but it is doubtful whether this alone will reduce offending or improve coping skills. Some limited successes have been reported, but systematic outcome studies are rare.

It is often claimed that the therapeutic community has the most to offer violent offenders with personality disorders. Therapeutic communities are democratic regimes engaging residents in a living and learning environment which encourages open exploration of feelings and relationships. Full implementation of this philosophy in secure institutions is not easy to achieve, but in Britain one prison and a few small units operate along these lines. Much has been written about therapeutic communities, but only limited outcome research has been carried out. This has found psychological changes, but little effect on criminal behaviour. Since therapeutic communities encourage a therapeutic climate, there is some enthusiasm for their wider application. However, there is no firm evidence that they are superior to other modalities in modifying violence.

Cognitive-behavioural therapies aim to eliminate maladaptive coping styles and to promote more constructive coping skills. The use of procedures to enhance social skills, self-control techniques, interpersonal problem solving, anger management, moral reasoning, and realistic cognitive appraisals has accelerated in penal contexts in recent years, and some significant effects on the recidivism of delinquents have been found. Applications with aggressive offenders, however, have been limited. On theoretical grounds, anger management would seem to hold promise in helping violent people. This approach targets cognitive appraisals, self-control, and the development of coping skills, and its effectiveness in reducing disruptive behaviour has been demonstrated with married couples, child-abusing parents, and institutionalised young offenders. Whether it can achieve long-term reduction of violent tendencies remains to be demonstrated.

Recommendations about treatability must therefore currently reflect more an act of faith than an empirically based claim. Nevertheless, some aggressive offenders are changed by exposure to treatment, and not all become recidivists. It is therefore appropriate to counter the therapeutic nihilism of 'nothing works' with the more realistic argument that we do not yet know what works with violent offenders.

REFERENCES

Anderson, C.A. (1989). Temperature and aggression: ubiquitous effects of heat on occurrence of human violence. *Psychological Bulletin*, **106**, 74–96.

Bandura, A. (1983). Psychological mechanisms of aggression. In R.G. Geen and E.I. Donnerstein (Eds), *Aggression: Theoretical and Experimental Reviews*, Vol. One. New York: Academic Press, pp. 41–69.

Beck, A.T. (1976). *Cognitive Therapy and the Emotional Disorders*. New York:

International Universities Press.

Berkowitz, L. (1993). *Aggression: Its Causes, Consequences, and Control*. New York: McGraw-Hill.

Blackburn, R. (1986). Patterns of personality deviation among violent offenders: replication and extension of an empirical taxonomy. *British Journal of Criminology*, **26**, 254–69.

Blackburn, R. (1993a). *The Psychology of Criminal Conduct*. Chichester: John Wiley.

Blackburn, R. (1993b). Clinical programmes with psychopaths. In K. Howells and C.R. Hollin (Eds), *Clinical Approaches to the Mentally Disordered Offender*. Chichester: John Wiley, pp. 179–208.

Block, R. (1977). *Violent Crime*. Lexington, MA: Lexington Books.

Carney, F.L. (1976). Treatment of the aggressive patient. In D.J. Madden and J.R. Lion (Eds), *Rage, Hate, Assault and Other Forms of Violence*. New York: Spectrum, pp. 153–74.

Dolan, B. and Coid, J. (1993). *Psychopathic and Antisocial Personality Disorders. Treatment and Research Issues*. London: Gaskell.

Dollard, J., Miller, N., Doob, L., Mowrer, O.H. and Sears, R.R. (1939). *Frustration and Aggression*. New Haven, CT: Yale University Press.

Farrington, D.P. (1989). Early predictors of adolescent aggression and adult violence, *Violence and Victims*, **4**, 79–100.

Felson R.B. (1978). Aggression as impression management. *Social Psychology*, **41**, 205–13.

Gibson, E. (1975). *Homicide in England and Wales 1967–1971*. London: HMSO.

Hall, G.C.N. and Proctor, W.C. (1987). Criminological predictors of recidivism in a sexual offender population. *Journal of Consulting and Clinical Psychology*, **55**, 111–12.

Hare, R.D. (1993). Psychopathy and crime: a review. In K. Howells and C.R. Hollin (Eds), *Clinical Approaches to the Mentally Disordered Offender*. Chichester: John Wiley, pp. 179–208.

Kilpatrick, D.G., Best, C.L., Veronen, L.J., Amick, A.E., Villeponteaux, L.A. and Ruff, G.A. (1985). Mental health correlates of criminal victimisation: a random community survey. *Journal of Consulting and Clinical Psychology*, **53**, 866–73.

Lorenz, K. (1966). *On Aggression*. London: Methuen.

Mark, V.H. and Ervin, F.R. (1970). *Violence and the Brain*. New York: Harper & Row.

Megargee, E.I. (1966). Under-controlled and over-controlled personality types in extreme antisocial aggression. *Psychological Monographs*, **80**, Whole No. 611.

Monahan, J. (1992). Mental disorder and violent behavior: perceptions and evidence. *American Psychologist*, **47**, 511–21.

Moyer, K. (1981). Biological substrates of aggression: implications for control. In P.F. Brain and D. Benton (Eds), *The Biology of Aggression*. Alphen aan der Rijn: Sijthoff and Noordhoff, pp. 15–32.

Novaco, R.W. and Welsh, W.N. (1989). Anger disturbances: cognitive mediation and clinical prescriptions. In K. Howells and C.R. Hollin (Eds), *Clinical Approaches to Violence*. Chichester: John Wiley, pp. 40–60.

Olweus, D. (1979). Stability of aggressive reaction patterns in males: a review. *Psychological Bulletin*, **86**, 852–75.

Reis, D.J. (1974). Central neurotransmitters in aggression. *Research Publications of the Association for Research in Nervous and Mental Diseases*, **52**, 119–48.

Slaby, R.G. and Guerra, N.G. (1988). Cognitive mediators of aggression in adolescent offenders: 1. Assessment. *Developmental Psychology*, **24**, 580–8.

Straus, M.A. and Gelles, R.J. (1988). How violent are American families? Estimates from the National Family Violence Resurvey and other studies. In G.T. Hotaling, D. Finkelhor, J.T. Kirkpatrick and M.A. Straus (Eds), *Family Abuse and its Consequences: New Directions in Research*. Beverly Hills, CA: Sage, pp. 14–36.

Thompson, C. and Cowen, P. (1993). *Violence: Basic and Clinical Science*. Oxford: Butterworth-Heinemann.

Toch, H. (1969). *Violent Men*. Harmondsworth: Penguin.

Valenstein, E.S. (1976). Brain stimulation and the origin of violent behavior. In W.L. Smith and A. Kling (Eds), *Issues in Brain/ Behavior Control*. New York: Spectrum, pp. 101–24.

Widom, C.S. (1989). The cycle of violence. *Science*, **244**, 160–6.

Wolfgang, M.E. (1958). *Patterns in Criminal Homicide*. Philadelphia: University of Pennsylvania Press.

Wolfgang, M.E. and Ferracutti, F. (1967). *The Subculture of Violence*. London: Tavistock.

Zillmann, D. (1979). *Hostility and Aggression*. Hillsdale, NJ: Erlbaum.

Weighing the Pound of Flesh: the Psychology of Punishment

Bill Hebenton
Manchester University
and
Ken Pease
University of Huddersfield

INTRODUCTION

Some 50 years ago, one commentator opined that 'an English criminal trial, properly conducted is one of the best products of our law, provided you walk out of court before the sentence is given' (Jackson, 1940, p. 184). Criminologist Don Gottfredson in 1975 wrote of judicial decisions that it would be difficult to find other contexts affecting the liberty, the future and the lives of large numbers of people in which decisions are made with so little knowledge of the way in which they are made. Andrew Ashworth (1992, p. 310) notes: 'Relatively little is known about the thought processes of the judiciary; researchers have been at kept at bay.' Part of the problem has been the attitude of the senior judiciary to research, revealed in Ashworth's undisputed account of his Crown Court study which was halted at the behest of the Lord Chief Justice. Ashworth restates Lord Lane's reasoning:

> Research into the attitudes, beliefs and reasoning of judges was not the way to obtain an accurate picture: sentencing was an art and not a science, and the further judges were pressed to articulate their reasons the less realistic the exercise would become ... In his view the available textbooks give a fairly clear account of the factors which judges take into account in sentencing, and he could not think of any aspects of judicial sentencing upon which research might prove helpful. (Ashworth et al., 1984, p. 64)

These assertions, veering from regarding sentencing as an ineffable mystery to a process characterised by strong formalism, fail to convince.

Fitzmaurice and Pease observe:

> We either have to believe that judges are superhuman and that our understanding is satisfactory (in the same way that God's superiority makes him ineffable and consequently makes theology necessarily imperfect), or alternatively that judges share the cognitive frailties of other people, in which case research into the principles of sentencing must be put on a sounder footing, or based less on judicial accounts. Given judicial power, and given the opacity of the mental processes underpinning sentence, the practice of judicial sentencing demands scrutiny from all concerned citizens, not least the professional psychologist. (Fitzmaurice and Pease, 1986, p. 5)

THE LEGAL PERSPECTIVE (AS INTERPRETED BY TWO CYNICAL PSYCHOLOGISTS)

Munro (1992) defines the judicial function as that of finding the facts and applying relevant law. When sentencing, judges are engaged in a different exercise. A contemporary judge, Sir Thomas Bingham, contends that:

> An issue falls within a judge's discretion if, being governed by no rule of law, its resolution depends on the individual judge's assessment (within such boundaries as have been laid down) of what it is fair and just to do in the particular case. He has no discretion in making his findings of fact. He has no discretion in his rulings on the law. But when, having made any necessary finding of fact and any necessary ruling of law, he has to choose between different courses of action, orders, penalties or remedies, he then exercises a discretion ... the imposition of criminal penalties [is a] pre-eminently discretionary field. (Bingham, 1990, p. 27)

The two most frequently cited justifications for punishment are retributivism, and (following Walker's (1972) terminology), crime reductivism (for a detailed examination, see Lacey, 1988). Retributivism justifies punishment on the ground that it is deserved by the offender. The future is irrelevant to the retributive sentencer. Reductivism is 'consequentialist', in the sense that it looks to preventive consequences of sentences; if punishment is inflicted, it is claimed, the incidence of crime will be less whether by deterrence (of the offender or the observing public), reform or incapacitation. There are several other possible justifications for punishment, including reparation, reintegrative shaming (Braithwaite, 1989) and communication with the offender (Duff, 1986). Duff introduces his argument by reference to the general practice of suspending a capital sentence if a convicted person becomes insane *after* being found guilty. None of the conventional justifications of punishment will explain that.

The aspiration to change people by punishment through rehabilitation and special deterrence now lies at the margins of penal purpose, at least in western Europe and North America. This is less attributable to negative research evidence than to policy fashion. The aspiration to assuage the public by punishing an offender (general deterrence) is somewhat less peripheral, as is the wish physically to prevent further offending (incapacitation). However, the central sentencing purpose of the moment appears to be retribution (see Von Hirsch and Ashworth, 1992). This is defended by arguments of principle in the wake of clearly oppressive sentencing motivated by benevolence (see Moore, 1992).

According to Thomas (1979), in his definitive legal work on sentencing, the judge first decides whether the sentence should emphasise the seriousness of the offence or the rehabilitation of the offender, i.e. whether a 'tariff sentence' or an 'individualised measure' should be imposed. If 'tariffing' is appropriate, the judge's task is to fix sentence length proportional to the culpability of the offender: this depends on the seriousness of the circumstances of the offence and usually, any factors by way of mitigation. If the individualised measure is appropriate, the court has to select the sentence most likely to maximise the offender's chance of rehabilitation. Characterising the sentencing process as involving the prior choice between tariff and individualised sentence modes has presentational advantages. It precludes criticism about sentence inconsistency, since individualised sentences *cannot* be inconsistent with tariff sentences, being informed by different principles. Wilkins (1983) discusses a case cited by Thomas (1979) in which an appellant was sentenced to five years' imprisonment, while his co-defendant with a worse record received a probation order. An appeal was dismissed on the grounds that each sentence was appropriate 'along different lines'. Since the range of application of the two sentencing modes is unspecified, different sentences in the same circumstances and the same sentence in different circumstances can be justified by different sentencing principles. There is a Catch-22 quality in this. Joseph Heller's Catch-22 referred to flying bombers: nobody sane wished to fly on bombing raids; one could be excused flying on the grounds of insanity, but applying to be excused flying was proof of sanity, so you had to fly. If sentences seem disparate, they are justifiable on different principles. Applying different principles means that sentences cannot be disparate. 'Disparate' sentences may be evidence of the application of different principles and so cannot be disparate.

There are difficulties with such received wisdom. Judges deny that they sentence as they 'should'. The previously cited Crown Court study by Ashworth et al. (1984) shows that judges perceived the sentencing task as involving *both* scaling seriousness and matching individualised measures to offenders in the *same* case. A judge cited by Fitzmaurice (1981) describes the process as involving 'the mental mixer of sentencing'. The resulting semi-lottery can be disguised by intellectual sleight of hand in the discussion of sentencing principles.

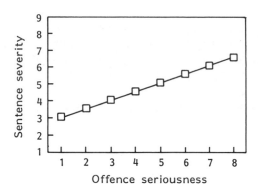

Figure 4.7.1   Retributive scaling 1

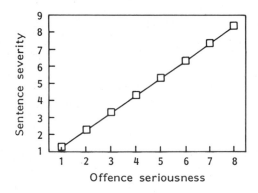

Figure 4.7.2   Retributive scaling 2

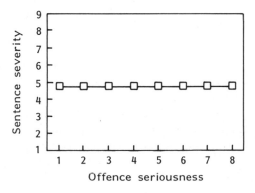

Figure 4.7.3   Retributive scaling 3

THE PSYCHOLOGIST'S VIEW

In conventional psychology textbooks, punishment is dealt with alongside other issues of reinforcement in shaping behaviour. In the clinical context, for punishment to stand a chance of being effective it should be close in time to the behaviour to be shaped and contingent/dependent upon it. Such understandings of punishment are largely irrelevant to the legal context, other than indirectly as the substance of treatment programmes to which offenders may on rare occasions be referred. Punishment via sentencing is neither close in time to the action being punished nor reliably contingent upon it. How could it be when only 3 per cent of offences result in a conviction (Barclay, 1993, p. 3)?

Before the lawyer reading this decides there is nothing in sentencing for the psychologist to explain, let him or her consider the simple matter of the units in which sentences are expressed. Lengths of prison sentences are typically 3, 6, 9, 12, 18, 24, 36, 48 months and upwards. Five-month sentences are virtually never imposed, and the gaps between the sentences which are imposed get bigger and bigger. In the list above (which corresponds to sentencing practice over a century; see Galton 1895; Sampson and Pease, 1977; Moxon, 1988) the gaps are first three months, then six months, then 12 months. It is as though having rejected a particular sentence length as too lenient, the next step up must conform to a rule (a multiple of three) and be a minimum proportional increase on the sentence rejected as too lenient. While the scale for prison sentences is in terms of units of three, six and 12 months, the scale for fines is decimal (£10, £20, £50, and so on). Concentrating on what a year's imprisonment actually means in terms of intervening events, or by expressing sentences in unfamiliar units like days or weeks, is likely to have the effect of reducing the sentence deemed appropriate (Sampson and Pease, 1977). There is thus a lot of hidden psychology even in the choice of sentencing numbers.

Assuming a retributive framework, the relationship between crime and punishment can be depicted as Figure 4.7.1, wherein a perception of crime is translated into a punishment response. The area under the line can be considered as the level of punitiveness of an individual or system, whereas the slope of the line can be considered to reflect the differentiation of punishment response across offences. A similar level of punitiveness can be achieved by a system which differentiates strongly by offence seriousness (Figure 4.7.2) and a system which does not differentiate at all by offence seriousness (Figure 4.7.3). The process operates differently in different countries. Polvi and Pease (1990) show that in Canada the effect of parole is to reduce sentence differentials (i.e. reduce the slope) whereas in England and Wales the opposite is true. This brief excursion is intended merely to establish that punishment calibration (slope) and punitiveness (area under the line) are linked but separate aspects of the punishment process, and that the relationships can be described in simple scaling terms. Self-evident as it is, this way of proceeding invites the central questions. If you think one offence is 50 per cent more serious than another, should the fine, prison term or whatever, be 50 per cent higher, less than 50 per cent higher, or more? Should doubling the weight of a drug haul double the appropriate sentence? Figures 4.7.1 to 4.7.3 offer a conceptual handle on issues of punishment. However, they must be considered in relation to the principles and polemics of sentencing.

The variable on the horizontal axis in the figures may change according to the principle in use. That variable is crime seriousness if the principle is retributive, assuming that more serious offenders deserve more severe punishment. For most crime reductive sentencing, the variable is also offence seriousness. If deterrence of the public from offending is the central purpose, then offence seriousness should co-vary with sentence severity, if the wish to reduce serious crimes is greater than the wish to reduce trivial offences. The same would be true if deterrence of the offender were the primary consideration, or if incapacitation were the main concern *and* the offender were presumed to be consistent in the seriousness of his or her nature of offending. The major exception to this would be reform, wherein sentence extent and intensity should co-vary with personality damage. Although true in principle, in practice it matters little. This is because personality damage is inferred from offence seriousness (he or she must be damaged to do something like that).

To summarise, the characterisation of punishment in the legal context as the scaling of offence seriousness against sentence severity has three important things going for it; it is conceptually simple; it is extremely heuristic; and it reflects currently preferred sentencing principles.

INSIDE THE MENTAL MIXER

What happens inside the 'mental mixer of sentencing'? To restate, we are here considering differentiation among cases, not the general level of sentencing imposed (punitiveness). There are two ways to approach the issue, the analytic and the synthetic. In the analytic approach, there is an attempt to tease out the range of factors which bear upon sentence. In the synthetic approach, the only issue of concern is the translation of case seriousness into sentence severity. The two approaches will be dealt with in turn.

The discretion exercised by the judge in an individual case can, following Ashworth (1992), be seen as influenced by four broad groupings of factors: demographic features of sentencers; views on crime and punishment; views on the principles of sentencing; views of the facts of the case. The 1984 Crown Court study by Ashworth et al. found that most judges interviewed rejected the idea of ranking the various dispositions in order of severity in favour of a notion of matching sentence and offender in each particular case. On weighting aggravating and mitigating factors, Corbett (1987) in her experimental study using a simulated sentencing exercise with magistrates, found that, at least in the reasons they gave, different sentencers tended to place different values on the same factors.

In relation to 'views on the facts of the case' it is undoubtedly true that facts of individual cases differ; however, it is also clear that facts do not determine cases, rather it is the selection, classification and combination of these facts that is crucial. The knee-jerk response of judges and magistrates that each case is treated on its merits is meaningless unless there is agreement on which merit is to be judged, and which variables should be deemed irrelevant to merit. Moxon (1988) in his study of Crown Court cases showed the importance of some factors over others, with some factors co-varying less across cases. More generally, in selecting case factors, for example in robbery, one could argue that the general significance of factors such as degree of organisation, violence and value of theft is well settled. However, this is not always so, particularly where an individual case, rather than a class of cases, is being examined. There are factors that may weigh heavily in the final decision in the minds of some judges and yet whose significance is an open issue among others (see, for example, Lovegrove, 1989, pp. 15-16). The problem of combining is probably the most intractable. Ashworth in classic understatement refers to the 'awkward issue of balancing' required (Ashworth, 1992, p. 138). Any aggregation of the type required involves two elements. First, there are weighting factors. Second, there are 'rules' governing the combination of individual assessments. In other words, is the overall assessment achieved by adding or subtracting the effects of aggravating or mitigating case factors, allowing for their relative weights, or is it for certain circumstances the presence of a single factor which may enhance the effect of another? Thomas, in his legal description, is of the opinion that 'the weight of a combination of mitigating factors will usually be greater than the sum of their individual values considered separately, as the presence of one factor will enhance the significance of another' (Thomas, 1979, p. 194). Why this should be so is anyone's guess. In dealing with rape, for example (see Harvey and Pease (1987a), and more generally below), aggregating aggravating factors results in each one having a lesser individual impact. Clearly, much psychological research is consistent with the view that as decisions increase in complexity the less people are able to allow accurately for the combined effects of contributing factors (see for example, Pitz and Sachs, 1984).

The alternative approach to sentencing regulation was termed synthetic. In this approach (assuming sentencing which is at bottom retributive) only three things are necessary: rough agreement on the scaling of offence seriousness among judges, rough agreement on the relative severity of available sanctions, and agreement on the translation of the first into the second. There is no attempt to tease out the factors which contribute to the assessment. Discrepancy on these is important only if it leads to a difference on the translation of case facts into sentence.

There is substantial agreement in judging the relative seriousness of offences (see Pease, 1988). The scaling of penalties is much more problematic (Perry and Pease, 1992). If a synthetic approach is adopted, a sample of cases would be assessed by a set of judges, and line height and slope would be determined. Judges could then be classified (this judge has an unusually steep slope, that has a high line, and so on) and trained into conformity. Thereafter many simple ways are available of monitoring judicial performance. Note that judicial independence is quite uncompromised by ensuring a common slope and area under the line in Figure 4.7.1.

Making the Link

Although the scaling approach is not in favour, the sentencing philosophy under which its use is most compelling is so. Under the Criminal Justice Act 1991 s. 2, the quantum of the sentence must be commensurate with the 'seriousness of the offence'. Proportionality (just dessert) is made the primary rationale of sentencing. The 1991 Act also incorporates assumptions about how people scale punishments. The three-tiered scale of sentence severity involves custody, community sentences, and monetary fines. Perry and Pease (1992) conclude that particular problems are posed for the Act in respect of judging non-custodial sentences and in respect of commensurability within the three tiers. Put brutally, such empirical research as has been done on sentence scaling shows no group of people who scale as they are required to do by the 1991 Act. The Act thus requires sentencers to translate offence seriousness into a sentencing scale with which few of them will agree. If they translate according to the Act, some of those they deem guilty of more serious offences will receive less serious sentences in their view than others whom the same judges deem guilty of less serious offences. It seems that the resurgence of strict retributive sentencing has taken place without the provision of the relevant scaling research and infrastructure which would allow it to make sense. This is also true of the other major British attempt of recent years to regulate sentencing discretion, the 'guideline judgment'.

Guideline Judgments

Internationally, there have been many attempts to 'structure' judicial discretion. Typically, they involve presumptive sentences, based upon offence seriousness (and often prior criminal record). They incorporate a requirement to give reasons for departure from the presumptive range. Much ingenuity has gone into this, for example in the appropriate use of non-custodial sentences (see Von Hirsch, Wasik and Greene, 1992; Von Hirsch, 1993). The reader is referred to Wasik and Pease (1987), Tonry (1987) and Von Hirsch, Knapp and Tonry (1987) for general reviews of the impacts and problems of sentencing reform of this kind.

In England and Wales, guidelines have been promulgated for magistrates, which are frankly inadequate in failing to limit the range within which sentences may vary. For more serious cases a judiciary-led approach to specifying the proportionality link has come in the shape of the guideline judgment. These are promulgated when an appeal is used as the platform for offering general guidance for sentencing an offence type, the aggravating and mitigating features to be considered, and an appropriate 'starting point' or several different starting points for sentence consideration. Judgments are devised by the Court of Appeal sitting with five judges, instead of the usual three, chaired by the Lord Chief Justice. It is difficult to overstate the importance of guideline judgments, both in their attempt to constrain judicial caprice and in their reflection of the thinking of the highest sentencing authorities. To date, in excess of a dozen guideline judgments have been handed down, covering offences as diverse as manslaughter (diminished responsibility), counterfeiting, production of amphetamine, and rape (Ashworth, 1992).

Harvey and Pease (1987a) argued that if the goal of retributive sentencing is just desserts or proportionality between culpability and sentence: 'Retributive justice requires one to go further and specify the nature of the proportionality link.' (Harvey and Pease, 1987a, p. 96). They take guideline judgments as an attempt by the judiciary to specify such a link. Three judgments are examined by Harvey and Pease in their study: *Aramah* ((1983) 4 Cr.App.R.(S) 407) relating to drug offending, *Barrick* ((1985) 7 Cr.App.R.(S) 142) relating to theft by an employee, and *Boswell* ((1984) 6 Cr.App.R.(S) 257) relating to reckless driving. All were cases where culpability could be measured by use of a direct proxy—for example, weight of drugs imported. Using these proxy measures, with length of custody as the other variable measured, Harvey and Pease unravel the proportionality link(s) underpinning the three cases. They found that while 'the guideline judgments yield plots which are similar in the very general sense that the worse the offence the longer the sentence, the way in which sentence and offence covary is fundamentally different in different guideline judgments.' (p. 101). In the *Aramah* judgment, importation of even a small amount of a class-A drug attracted a heavy sentence, but doubling or tripling the amount did not double or triple sentence. For class-B drugs, the opposite was true, in that a doubling or tripling of drug amount more than doubled or tripled sentence length.

Sentencing Rape: *Billam*

In what follows we present the results of a case study of one guideline judgment, *R. v. Billam and Others* ((1986) 8 Cr.App.R.(S) 48) dealing with rape (see Ranyard, Hebenton and Pease (1994) for a fuller account). The most contentious post-*Billam* rape sentence to date came on 2 February 1987, at the Old Bailey, imposed on those convicted of the rape of a young woman at a vicarage in Ealing, London. Media concern suggested that the sentences were too 'lenient', with calls for the resignation of the judge, Mr Justice Leonard.

Harvey and Pease (1987b) argue that the judge had applied the current guidance scrupulously. Analysis of the internal logic, and the use made of the *Billam* judgment, seems long overdue. Home Office evidence suggests that rape is one of the offences for which sentence levels have increased over the period from the early 1970s (see Lloyd and Walmsley, 1989). Can the *Billam* judgment have contributed to that change?

Sentencing Rapists

The central points of *Billam* are summarised as Table 4.7.1. A primary division is made into five classes of rape. In the least culpable, in wholly exceptional circumstances, an immediate custodial sentence can be avoided. In the second, a 'basic' single rape has a starting point sentence of five years. In the third, attended by one or more of the first-order aggravating factors listed, a starting point of eight years is recommended. In the fourth, 'a campaign of rape', the suggested starting point is 15 years. Where a rapist is deemed likely to remain a danger indefinitely, a life sentence is appropriate. The discount for a guilty plea is appropriately larger than customary in rape cases. The starting point is to be adjusted into a settled sentence by other factors. Considerations deemed relevant and irrelevant by the *Billam* judgment are summarised in Table 4.7.2.

Anchoring, Adjustment, and *Billam*

Specifying a starting point and adjusting from it is known as anchoring and adjustment (see Tversky and Kahneman, 1974). It is one cognitive 'heuristic' available to reduce complex judgements of quantities, and it is a defensible variant of the analytic approach to sentencing criticised earlier. Payne, Bettman and Johnson (1992) note that anchoring and adjustment has been investigated in a wide range of domains. Suppose you need to estimate the value of a second-hand car you wish to buy. An appropriate anchor might be the price of a new car of the same model. From this starting point you would adjust downwards to take account of, for example, depreciation over time. Typically, you might use your general knowledge of the depreciation rates of second-hand cars for this. Anchoring and adjustment works quite well, although it has been shown to lead to judgemental biases. Inappropriate anchors might be selected or insufficient adjustment made (leading you to overvalue the second-hand car in the above example).

'Anchoring and adjustment' can be evaluated on two criteria. Does the strategy make unrealistic demands on the cognitive capacities of its users? Is its application likely to lead to improvements in the consistency of sentencing? On *Billam* the anchoring stage appears to reflect well on the above criteria. The cognitive demands of the 'task' are not onerous: the judge is recommended to classify a new case into one of only five categories. The adjustment stage appears more problematic. There are a number of difficulties with the *Billam* use of adjustment. The number of variables according to which adjustment is

Table 4.7.1 Types of rape offence ordered by seriousness, defining criteria and recommended starting points proposed in the Billam Guideline Judgment

Type of offence	Criteria	Starting point for immediate custodial sentence
Wholly exceptional circumstances	Rape in the legal sense, but not in ordinary understanding	Note an immediate custodial sentence
Single rape, no aggravating circumstances	Adult offender, contested case	5 years
Single rape, with first-order aggravating circumstances	Plus one or more of the following: two or more men acting together; broke into victim's home; in a position of responsibility towards victim; victim abducted	8 years
Multiple rape	Campaign of rape, more than ordinary danger	15 years
(Multiple*) rape perverted or with psychopathic tendencies	Likely to ramin a danger for an indefinite time	Life

* The guideline judgment does not explicitly state that a life sentence is reserved for *multiple* rape with these characteristics, but this seems to be intended.

Table 4.7.2 Checklist of aggravating, mitigating and irrelevant factors for the adjustment of sentence length listed in the Billam Guideline Judgment

Type of factor	Factors
Aggravating factors	• additional violence • weapon used (for wounding or threat) • repeated rape • careful planning • previous convictions • further sexual indignities or perversions • very old or very young victim • serious mental or physical effect on victim
Mitigating factors	• guilty plea • victim behaved in a manner calculated to lead the defendant to believe she would consent • defendant's previous good character*
Irrelevant factors	• victim acted imprudently and exposed herself to danger • victim's previous sexual experience

* Only a minor mitigating factor

made is large. The cognitive demands are high—a total of 13 aggravating, mitigating or irrelevant factors must be considered. The cognitive load can be reduced somewhat by decomposing the task into three components: (1) identify, and then isolate and ignore *irrelevant* factors; (2) identify *second-order aggravating* factors and adjust upwards; (3) identify *mitigating* factors and adjust downwards. Even so, there are eight second-order aggravating factors to consider.

The second problem is that the first-order factors specifying anchors in the central range have no cumulative effect. In principle, a rape committed by men acting together should have the same starting point as a rape committed by men acting together, entering the victim's home as trespassers, and abducting her. Where all of these three first-order factors apply, there is no way of using two of them to increase sentence length. This offends against any sensible scaling of seriousness. The third and crucial problem is that the range within which adjustments may occur is not specified. It has been suggested to us that judges may envisage anchors or 'starting points' as sentencing brackets, with the lower limit of that bracket being the starting point, and the range being upwards from there to the bottom of the next bracket. This would make a nonsense of the 'starting point' and range of adjustment. The adjustment should not be such as to make the sentence imposed equivalent to that yielded as a starting point for one of the other classes of offence. For example, aggravation of a 'single rape, no first-order aggravating circumstances' by second-order aggravating circumstances should never yield a sentence of eight years or more. If this did happen, it would mean that the selection of first-order factors was wrong, or that the whole exercise was misconceived. A single rape by two or more men acting together (a first-order aggravator) would yield a starting point for sentence of eight years. A single rape by a man acting alone but with previous convictions for rape (a second-order aggravator) would have a starting point of five years, but sentence would be adjusted upwards on the basis of the aggravating factor. If the sentence imposed in such a case were to be eight years or more, this calls into question the status of men acting in concert as a first-order aggravating factor, and/or previous convictions for rape as merely a second-order aggravator. If the record is that important, why is it not a first-order aggravation? If offending with others is so unimportant, why is it a first order aggravation? In short, if the anchoring and adjustment process is to make sense in this context, the anchoring points must be sufficiently distant that no amount of adjustment takes the decision-maker to another anchoring point. Some second-order aggravating factors seem inherently difficult to judge, especially the effect of the rape on the victim or the 'harm' caused (but see Von Hirsch and Jareborg (1991) for the development of an estimating measure in this area). In summary, attempts to apply the adjustment stage are predicted to lead to inconsistencies of judgement.

Analysis of Cases

Our analysis was based upon twelve post-*Billam* cases where a sentence for rape was appealed. Cases were chosen at random from cases reported in Thomas (1992). We analysed:

Clarke (1990) 12 Cr.App.R.(S) 10
Daley (1986) 8 Cr.App.R.(S) 429
Davids (1991) 13 Cr.App.R.(S) 468
Faulkner (1987) 9 Cr.App.R.(S) 321
Gearing (1987) 9 Cr.App.R.(S) 465
Gibson (1987) 9 Cr.App.R.(S) 30
Hawkins (1989) 11 Cr.App.R.(S) 429
Jepson (Attorney-General's Reference No. 8 of 1991) (1992) 13 Cr.App.R.(S) 360
Malcolm (1987) 9 Cr.App.R.(S) 487
Maskell (1991) 12 Cr.App.R.(S) 638
Rowe (1989) 11 Cr.App.R.(S) 342
Williams (1987) 9 Cr.App.R.(S) 491

Table 4.7.3 shows the distribution of the selected cases across Thomas' classification of recent decisions. Our cases covered all categories with the exception of 'previous conviction for rape'.

Table 4.7.3   The twelve cases categorised by Thomas' classification of recent decisions on the offence of rape

Categories	Cases
Rape with abduction or false imprisonment	*Malcolm*
Rape by burglars	*Gearing, Hawkins*
Rape by person in position of authority or trust	*Jepson*
Rape by men acting in concert	*Davids and others*
Campaigns of rape	*Gibson*
Rape without situational aggravating factors	*Daley, Clarke*
Rape by husband or previous sexual partner	*Maskell*
Attempted rape	*Williams*
Rape accompanies by grave violence	*Rowe*
Rape of young child	*Faulkner*

The analysis of the cases took the following form:

a.   *Billam* as described in Tables 4.7.1 and 4.7.2

b.   Appeal Court summary of original facts of case

c.   Examination of application of *Billam*.
     i. starting point (anchor)
     ii. adjustment for second-order aggravating factor(s)
     iii. adjustment for mitigating factor(s).

This approach shows how the Court of Appeal revises sentence according to the *Billam* judgment on the basis of its own description of the salient factors in the case. The disadvantage is that the frequency of adherence to *Billam* in uncontentious cases is not determined.

In important ways the Court of Appeal does not impose the levels implicit in *Billam*, which is strong evidence that anchoring and adjustment in the form exemplified by *Billam*, is not an adequate basis for regulating sentence disparity. The 12 cases highlighted a number of shortcomings. Adjustments for second-order factors were particularly problematic. In *Hawkins* ((1989) 11 Cr.App.R.(S) 429) we were faced with the effect of second-order aggravators in *doubling* the pre-discount sentence length. Such a massive 'correction' by second-order aggravators nullifies any meaning which two-tier guidance might have. The view that the Court looked at the package as a whole and 'magnitude estimated' seriousness is strengthened by the reference as an aggravator to the attempted buggery of the *daughter* when the offence which effectively determined sentence length had nothing to do with her. Behaviour to the daughter (away from the mother) was being used as an aggravator of the rape of the mother. Furthermore, there appeared to be widespread confusion over separation of first and second-order factors. In *Jepson* (*(Attorney-General's Reference No.8 of 1991)* (1992) 13 Cr.App.R.(S) 360) the Court appears not to have made this crucial distinction. It takes the starting point as eight years, whereas following *Billam* it should have been eight years adjusted upwards for the second-order aggravating factors of 'degree of planning' and 'age'. There are also instances where even the anchor point on *Billam* does not appear to have been adopted.

An important matter is the effect of rape on its victims. *Roberts and Roberts* ((1982) 4 Cr.App.R.(S) 8) stated that rape was aggravated where 'the victim sustains serious injury (whether that is mental or physical)'. In *Billam* this definition was narrowed to where 'the effect upon the victim, whether physical or mental, is of *special seriousness*' (emphasis added). There was wide variation in use of this as an aggravator. While almost all cases described the plight of the victim, only *Gearing* ((1987) 9 Cr.App.R.(S) 465) referred to the definition in the *Billam* guideline judgment. It is unclear how and in what ways this 'factor' mediated the adjustment of sentence length. In *Gibson* ((1987) 9

Cr.App.R.(S) 30) there is extensive description of the horrors suffered with a reduction of three years on appeal. *Rowe* ((1989) 11 Cr.App.R.(S) 342) used this factor to justify a very long sentence where *no* first order factor was present. 'Effect on the victim' clearly merits further examination.

Our study questions the value of current guideline judgments. They do not 'calibrate' by specifying the range of normal variation around the guideline. With proportionality as the primary rationale for sentencing under the Criminal Justice Act 1991 there is a duty to take account of *both* aggravating and mitigating factors, as they relate to the seriousness of the offence (see Ashworth, 1992, p. 137). It has been pointed out to us that *Billam* may not comply with the 1991 Act, which requires the sentencer to take account of aggravating and mitigating factors which impinge on seriousness, and allows the sentencer to take account of mitigating (but not aggravating) factors which are in his or her view relevant, for example a guilty plea or clean record. While previous experimental research (e.g. Corbett, 1987) has found sentencing disparities resulting from trying to balance aggravating and mitigating factors, the above study of a sample of Court of Appeal cases has revealed how the application of a particular sentencing 'heuristic' of anchor and adjustment can lead to problems at both stages.

Of the many lessons which this detailed analysis of the *Billam* judgment teaches, perhaps the most significant is the impression that judges convert offence seriousness into sentence length and justify the conversion by selective references to *Billam*.

THE FUTURE OF PUNISHMENT

It may be that the fashion for retribution will pass. If so, the role of the the psychologist will change. The most plausible mode of change on the basis of current developments will concern an improved understanding of criminal careers. Crime reductive sentencing based upon an understanding of the probability of further offending by an individual offender is a prospect for the middle term. Already it is possible to predict an individual offender's likely rate of reconviction (see Nuttall et al., 1977; Ward, 1988). In the future, this may be refined to clarify an individual's residual career length at the point of sentence and the likely offences which remain to be committed. The analysis of criminal careers affords the possibility of much more effective crime-reductive sentencing (see for example Blumstein et al., 1986). The debate has so far centred upon selective incapacitation, whereby the most active offenders receive lengthy sentences. In ten years it may be possible to offer sentencers the prospect of sentencing which does reduce the rate of crime. In this eventuality, it will be interesting to see whether the retributive tradition will continue to occupy the moral ground—or indeed whether the judiciary will notice.

REFERENCES

Ashworth, A. (1992). *Sentencing and Criminal Justice*. London: Weidenfeld & Nicholson.

Ashworth, A., Genders, E., Mansfield, G., Peay, J. and Player, E. (1984). Sentencing in the Crown Court: report of an exploratory study. Oxford: Centre for Criminological Research Occasional Paper No. 10.

Barclay G.C. (Ed.) (1993). *A Digest of Information on the Criminal Justice System*. London: Home Office.

Bingham, T. (1990). The discretion of the judge. *Denning Law Journal*, 25–30.

Blumstein, A., Cohen, J., Roth, J.A. and Visher, C.A. (Eds) (1986). *Criminal Careers and Career Criminals*, 2 vols. Washington: National Academy Press.

Braithwaite, J. (1989). *Crime, Shame and Reintegration*. Cambridge: Cambridge University Press.

Corbett, C. (1987). Magistrates' and court clerks' sentencing behaviour: an experimental study. In D. Pennington and S. Lloyd-Bostock (Eds), *The Psychology of Sentencing*. Oxford: Centre for Socio-Legal Studies, University of Oxford.

Duff, R.A. (1986). *Trials and Punishments*. Cambridge: Cambridge University Press.

Fitzmaurice, C. (1981). On measuring distaste in years: a psychophysical study of the length of prison sentences. M.A. (Econ) thesis, University of Manchester.

Fitzmaurice, C. and Pease, K. (1986). *The Psychology of Judicial Sentencing*. Manchester: Manchester University Press.

Galton, F. (1895). Terms of imprisonment. *Nature*, **52**, 174–6.

Gottfredson, D.M. (1975). Diagnosis, classification and prediction. In D.M. Gottfredson (Ed.), *Decision-Making in the Criminal Justice System*. Rockville: NIMH.

Harvey, L. and Pease, K. (1987a). Guideline judgments and proportionality in sentencing. *Criminal Law Review*, February, 96–104.

Harvey, L. and Pease, K. (1987b). Sentencing rapists. *Lynx*, June, 3–4.

Jackson, R.M. (1940). *The Machinery of Justice in England*. Cambridge University Press.

Lacey, N. (1988). *State Punishment*. London: Routledge.

Lloyd, C. and Walmsley, R. (1989). *Changes in Rape Offences and Sentencing*. Home Office Research Study No. 105. London: HMSO.

Lovegrove, A. (1989). *Judicial Decision Making, Sentencing Policy and Numerical Guidance*. London: Springer-Verlag.

Moore, M. (1992). The moral worth of retribution. In A. Von Hirsch and A. Ashworth (Eds), *Principled Sentencing*. Edinburgh: Edinburgh University Press.

Moxon, D. (1988). *Sentencing Practice in the Crown Court*. Home Office Research Study 103. London: HMSO.

Munro, C. (1992). Judicial independence and judicial functions. In C. Munro and M. Wasik (Eds), *Sentencing, Judicial Discretion and Training*. London: Sweet & Maxwell.

Nuttall C.P., Barnard, E., Fowles, A.J., Frost, A., Hammond, W.H., Mayhew, P., Pease, K., Tarling, R. and Weatheritt, M. (1977). *Parole in England and Wales*. Home Office Research Study 38. London: HMSO.

Payne, J.W., Bettman, J. and Johnson, E. (1992). Behavioral decision research: a constructive processing perspective. *Annual Review of Psychology*, **43**, 87–131.

Pease, K. (1988). Judgements of offence seriousness: evidence from the 1984 British Crime Survey Research and Planning Unit. Paper 44. London: Home Office.

Perry, C. and Pease, K. (1992). The 1991 Criminal Justice Act and the scaling of sentence severity. *Justice of the Peace*, July, **18**, 452–4.

Pitz, G. and Sachs, N. (1984). Judgment and decision: theory and application. *Annual Review of Psychology*, **35**, 139–63.

Polvi, N. and Pease, K. (1990). Parole and its problems: a Canadian–English comparison. *Howard Journal of Criminal Justice*, **30**, 218–30.

Ranyard, R., Hebenton, B. and Pease, K. (1994). An analysis of a guideline judgment as applied to the offence of rape. *Howard Journal of Criminal Justice*, **33**, 3, 203–17.

Sampson, M. and Pease, K. (1977). Doing time and marking time. *Howard Journal*, **16**, 59–64.

Thomas, D.A. (1979). *Principles of Sentencing*. London: Heinemann.

Thomas D.A. (1992). *Current Sentencing Practice Recent Decisions*. London: Sweet & Maxwell.

Tonry, M. (1987). *Sentencing Reform Impacts*. Washington, DC: National Institute of Justice.

Tversky, A. and Kahneman, D. (1974). Judgement under uncertainty: heuristics and biases. *Science*, **185**, 1124–31.

Von Hirsch, A. (1993). *Censure and Sanctions*. Oxford: Clarendon Press.

Von Hirsch, A. and Ashworth, A. (Eds) (1992). *Principled Sentencing*. Edinburgh: Edinburgh University Press.

Von Hirsch, A. and Jareborg, N. (1991). Gauging criminal harm: a living-standard analysis. *Oxford Journal of Legal Studies*, **11**.

Von Hirsch A., Knapp, K.A. and Tonry, M. (1987). *The Sentencing Commission and its Guidelines*. Boston, MA: Northeastern Universities Press.

Von Hirsch, A., Wasik, M. and Greene, J. (1992). Scaling community punishments. In A. Von Hirsch and A. Ashworth (Eds), *Principled Sentencing*. Edinburgh: Edinburgh University Press.

Walker, N. (1972). *Sentencing in a Rational Society*. Harmondsworth: Penguin.

Ward, D. (1988). *The Validity of the Reconviction Prediction Score*. Home Office Research Study 94. London: HMSO.

Wasik, M. and Pease, K. (Eds) (1987). *Sentencing Reform*. Manchester: Manchester University Press.

Wilkins, L.T. (1983). *Consumerist Criminology*. London: Heinemann.

Part 5

Civil Proceedings

Civil Proceedings: Legal Frameworks for Psychology's Contributions

David Carson
University of Southampton

One of the most basic of legal distinctions is that drawn between civil and criminal law, between civil and criminal proceedings. But it is not a clear distinction. The criminal law, it may be argued, punishes while the civil law compensates. However, in some legal systems, criminals can be required to 'compensate' their victims. Those who have been successfully sued, in civil proceedings, can occasionally be ordered to pay 'punitive' compensation. Compensation orders made by civil courts regularly exceed fines imposed by criminal courts. Failure to pay a debt is usually a civil matter but not, for example, where it concerns failure to pay a television licence fee or certain kinds of taxes in the UK. Different buildings, judges, officials and procedures might be expected between civil and criminal proceedings, but there is considerable overlap. Indeed, in the UK, there has been continuing concern that magistrates, primarily viewed as judges of criminal disputes, also have an extensive jurisdiction in relation to matrimonial and child care issues, which are civil law issues. Social attitudes, such as willingness to use the civil law, may be influenced by distaste for criminal associations arising from the courts involved. If legal remedies are to be effective, particularly in preference to self-help, then lawyers need to seek and learn more about people's knowledge and opinion about the law (e.g. see Podgorecki et al., 1973). The work of Tyler (1992, and further sources cited therein) on litigants' attitudes is an exemplar.

WHAT DISTINGUISHES 'CIVIL' FROM 'CRIMINAL'?

Widely shared understandings and perceptions lead to most disputes quickly being categorised as either civil or criminal, as a matter for the police or not.

Handbook of Psychology in Legal Contexts
Edited by R. Bull and D. Carson. © 1995 John Wiley & Sons Ltd

But some areas of disagreement remain. For example, in several countries there have been ambivalent attitudes about treating 'matrimonial violence' as a crime. Many civil wrongs, particularly against people but also against property, are also crimes. The doctor can be sued for negligence; he or she can also be prosecuted for manslaughter if the patient dies and there was 'gross' negligence (*Prentice,* [1993] 3 W.L.R. 927). Instead of treating criminal and civil law as separate categories it would be more appropriate to regard criminal law as just at one end of a continuum which includes civil wrongs. The dichotomising of civil and criminal law may 'make sense' in terms of the history of separate trial procedures. But it does not similarly 'make sense' that such dichotomies should follow through into research and teaching. Each violent act is not pre-ordained to be treated as a crime or a civil wrong. Psychological research should be prepared to concentrate upon the phenomenon rather than the legal system's response to and management of it.

A great deal has been invested in the 'reality' of a distinction between civil and criminal law. It is convenient to be able to distinguish and declare other people as being criminal, as being distinctively different from we 'law-abiding' people. Should some or all motoring offences be reclassified as civil wrongs rather than as crimes? People who drive too fast, who have momentary lapses of attention, who have not checked the state of their tyres recently, are not 'real criminals', it may be argued. They would never commit a 'real crime'. They would be more supportive of the police, would be more willing to become witnesses and give evidence against 'real' criminals, if their motoring and similar offences were not portrayed as crimes. There is an implicit balancing operation which runs throughout the legal system. Do we have the appropriate balances?

The criminal law tends to involve base-line standards; the same basic rule, thou shalt not steal, applies to everyone. (However this is not to deny variation in practice; office workers' thefts from their employers (stationery, phone calls) and other forms of 'white collar' crime are regarded and enforced in a different way from factory workers' thefts from their employers.) The civil law permits greater flexibility and individualisation. For example, the law of negligence encourages the development of professional standards of practice. The law of contract may be seen as permitting individuals to write their own laws, within a broad framework, with the state being called upon to enforce those laws, if necessary, when a breach occurs.

Are civil laws more effective than criminal laws in ensuring the maintenance of standards? This is a very important issue in such areas as industrial safety where, for example, UK law and practice has been criticised for too much reliance upon persuasion and informal approaches. It would help if we knew more about the extent to which our perception of laws, their forms and symbols, influenced our behaviour in terms of obeying the law and supporting its enforcement (see generally Cotterrell, 1984).

STANDARD OF PROOF

Hitting a person is, in Anglo-American law, a civil wrong or tort. It is also a crime. Whether it will be treated as a crime or a tort (and in the UK a claim for compensation from the Criminal Injuries Compensation Board), will depend upon a number of factors, including the degree of harm caused, the ability to identify and prove the culprit culpable, perceived degrees of maliciousness of the act and the dangerousness of perpetrator. Depending upon the type of proceedings chosen a different degree of proof will be required. In criminal proceedings the general rule is that the prosecution must prove the defendant guilty beyond reasonable doubt. In a civil case the person bringing the case, the plaintiff, must prove that his or her case is, on a balance of probabilities, more credible than the other party's (also known as a 'defendant'). However, this standard has been varied in recent years, with some judges suggesting, in civil proceedings, that the seriousness of the allegations must be taken into account: the more serious the consequences, the higher the standard of proof.

This difference in proof requirements is likely to prove increasingly important for developments in psychology and law. First, research may tease out what judges and jurors understand, or should understand, by probability and such concepts as 'reasonable doubt'. Second it is directly relevant to services for some psychologists' clients. In some countries the victim of a crime is entitled to sue and receive compensation, even if the defendant has been found not guilty of the crime. For example, adult victims of childhood sexual abuse may sue, provided they are within certain time limits, even though a prosecution is likely to fail. (Contrast the approach of Canadian and British courts, *Gray v. Reeves*, (1992) 89 DLR (4th) 315 with *Stubbings v. Webb and another*, [1993] 1 All ER 322.) Concern about a witness' memory, and the possibility that it has been falsified during therapy, may contribute to a not guilty finding. The evidence may not justify a criminal conviction, beyond reasonable doubt. But that same evidence may be sufficient to produce a civil law finding, on the balance of probabilities, against a defendant. Particularly because of the effects of such a finding, some would argue that the right to sue, for what is 'really' an allegation of a crime, should be withdrawn. Psychologists must expect increasingly to be drawn into court to advise about the potential for interviews and therapy to distort memory (Loftus and Rosenwald, 1993). Interviewers and therapists would be well advised to develop good practice guidelines, plus ways of proving that they followed them, if they wish to avoid having their conclusions doubted by courts. A court might indicate that it was not satisfied by a therapist's evidence that, for example, childhood abuse took place. That 'official' doubt, even if consequent upon the rules about burden of proof, could cause the client, once again, to experience all the problems of self-doubt. Guidelines could avoid some problems.

Civil proceedings may also be preferred because of concerns about a witness' credibility. A judge's or jury's doubts over a victim's or witness' credibility might prevent a criminal conviction but be insufficient to disturb the balance of probabilities. Turk and Brown (1992) suggest that, in the UK at least, whilst a large number of people with learning disabilities are sexually assaulted relatively few prosecutions are brought. This is largely because of problems of proof. The assumed unreliability of people with learning disabilities, and other vulnerable witnesses, particularly within the context of an adversarial trial system with vigorous cross-examination, is very likely to lead to findings that there are reasonable doubts. The prosecution cannot lead expert evidence to show a witness to be credible; that is a matter for the judge and jury to decide (*Robinson*, (1993) *New Law Journal* 1643). Such victims may prefer to sue for compensation where they need to prove their case only on the balance of the probabilities. While they will not be able to see the defendant imprisoned they will increase the likelihood of a vindicating verdict while retaining greater control over the process.

Similar considerations apply when the dilemma is whether parents accused of abusing their children should be proceeded against in the courts. If proceedings are taken then the child may suffer further in the court proceedings and therapy may be delayed in case defence lawyers might argue that it has interfered with the evidence. Civil proceedings may have the advantage of a different standard of proof but the child's evidence still has to be investigated, and cross-examination may be very distressing (Spencer and Flin, 1993; Brennan, 1993).

It is understandable that psychologists and lawyers should spend time trying to improve the system for children. But, perhaps, we should be paying more attention to prevention. For example, it might be possible, on an analogy with alcoholism, for people to be told about danger signs of predisposition towards child abuse. Then people who are anxious about their attitudes or behaviour towards children might be encouraged to seek assistance from well-publicised, but nevertheless confidential services, offered to those prepared and willing to co-operate. Such a scheme could mean that abusers are not prosecuted for so long as they do not repeat their abuse. However, the child would not be made to feel responsible for breaking up the family, for drastic reductions in household income, for a parent being gaoled, etc., but would have a measure of protection against repetition of the abuse. Unattractive as it may appear, allowing the perpetrators of crimes against children to go unprosecuted, such a scheme could, in practice, be both more preventive and in children's interests. Children's interests are supposed to be paramount in UK law (Children Act 1989). Too often the principal goals, such as prevention of occurrence and repetition, get lost within legal frameworks and approaches. Here is an area where co-operation between lawyers, psychologists and others is urgently required.

PROTECTING PERSONALITY

The civil law protects a range of interests, in personality and property. While stated in different terms there are similar provisions in continental European legal systems. For example in Germany the Civil Code, in §823, provides, in translation (Markesinis, 1990) that: 'A person who wilfully or negligently injures the life, body, health, freedom, property, or other right of another contrary to law is bound to compensate him for any damages arising therefrom.' Similar interests are protected in Anglo-American law but through a variety of separately stated provisions. While the laws of trespass have given way, in terms of frequency of use, to the law of negligence, they remain very significant particularly for articulating base-line standards or principles. The law of negligence is substantially about maintaining and developing standards, be they of drivers, surgeons, psychologists or solicitors. The laws of trespass restate more basic principles. Assault and battery, particular species of trespass, prohibit the threatening of immediate, or the actual infliction, of violence to the person, without some lawful authority. The surgeon commits battery unless he or she has authority, usually the patient's consent. The surgeon may have performed the operation in an exemplary fashion but, unless there is legal authority, it is a battery. Few may wish to sue when they have been competently treated but they are nevertheless entitled to sue if the treatment was non-consensual or otherwise unauthorised. Trespass laws protect our right to say 'No' and to prevent others acting in our 'best interests', without authority. The police suspect detained without authority has been falsely imprisoned for we may not be restricted in our movements without authority. Note the negative manner in which these rights are stated; they are not a right to go or to do but rights not to be detained or to be impeded.

The strictness of these rules has created practical problems. Strictly neither a police officer, nor anyone else, is entitled to place a hand on another person without authority. In recent years the UK courts have ameliorated the strictness of the rule. In *Collins v. Wilcock* ([1984] 1 W.L.R. 1172) for example, when a police officer touched a man, in order to get his attention, the man hit the officer and claimed he was acting to stop the police officer trespassing upon him. It was decided that the police officer's acts were not sufficient to constitute a trespass. Hospitals are not entitled to prevent patients leaving their wards unless they have authority to do so. Otherwise it would be false imprisonment. This poses dilemmas for those caring for confused patients who may wander from their ward and be injured. It creates tensions with service philosophies.

The dichotomous nature of the law is evident with trespass law; either there is legal authority or there is not. Trespass law reminds those who wish to intervene that they must have authority to do so. In doing so it emphasises the core legal concept of consent, about which psychologists and psychological research have much to offer. Developments in therapeutic jurisprudence, with its emphasis upon inter-disciplinary approaches and pragmatic but yet principled outcomes, may help us to tackle these problems. It argues that, subject to the protection of basic civil liberties, law and legal procedures ought to promote therapeutic outcomes (see, for example, Wexler, 1990; Wexler and

Winick, 1991). For example it may be possible to develop the role of contracts. Patients who are involved in, who consent to, and are consulted about their treatment are more likely to co-operate with and benefit from it (Winick, 1991).

Reputation

Interests in maintaining a reputation are protected through such laws as defamation and confidentiality. In Germany §824 of the Civil Code provides, in part: 'A person who maintains or publishes, contrary to the truth, a statement calculated to endanger the credit of another, or injure his earnings or prospects in any other manner, must compensate the other for any damage arising therefrom, even if he does not know of its untruth, provided he ought to know' (Markesinis, 1990). In English and Welsh law a false statement of fact, about a living person, which leads to that person losing reputation in the eyes of responsible people, constitutes defamation. Certain otherwise defamatory statements can be justified. For example, false statements made in good faith and only to people who have an interest in hearing of them, for example a doctor learning about one of his or her patients from a nurse, have qualified privilege.

How should people be compensated for being defamed? The principles governing compensation for personal injury are relatively clear. They may result in it being 'cheaper' to kill someone, than to cause him or her serious long-term disability, but the objective of trying to place the individual back in the position he or she would have been in, as far as money can, provides a clear focus. Could psychology help to articulate the consequences, say to self-image and social status, that defamatory statements can cause? Such assistance is needed both so that we may better appreciate the significance of injuries to our self-respect and social perception, but also because defamation awards (usually made by juries rather than judges in England and Wales) have been notoriously variable.

A false statement of fact about an individual, leading to loss of reputation, is liable to be defamatory. This has not developed into a remedy for discriminatory behaviour. Discrimination, whether based upon ethic origin, gender, age, disability or other, is fed by false information and, among many other things, damages reputation and self-esteem. Statute, rather than common law, has had to be developed. Hartnett (1984), a psychologist, has stressed:

> that psychologists have it in their power to contribute enormously towards ameliorating many of the problems which confront both the letter and the spirit of equal opportunities legislation. Inherent in this problem are forms of behaviour which are core topics in the discipline of psychology: for example, prejudice; stereotyping; change; allocation of roles, status and esteem; conflict and altruism; expectations; perceptions; cognitions; achievement; personal abilities and attributes; socialisation; and the reinforcement of behaviour. (Hartnett, 1984, pp. 24–5)

McCrudden (1981), a lawyer, doubted whether UK courts will make use of social scientific insights or learning. More imaginative ways of employing psychological evidence may be necessary. Tomkins and Pfeifer (1992), writing about the USA where the courts have clearly been more willing to consider social scientific evidence concerning discrimination, note the problem of giving evidence about small effects. There may be a discernible variation in the treatment of different people but how are courts to be convinced that it was due to the differences, for example gender or ethnic origin. They recommend moving away from statistical effects to adopting a broader educative role, 'to make sure that although they may not be able to see it, taste it, hear it, touch it, or smell it does not mean that it is not there' (p. 403). This might best be achieved by concentrating upon the effects of discrimination, articulating the direct and indirect effects it has upon reputation, self-esteem and more broadly.

Trust and confidentiality are essential to many professional relationships. Generally the law supports such relationships, but it also recognises that there can be conflicting obligations. For example, a client may indicate that he or she is an imminent danger to another person. What should the professional do? In the USA the controversial *Tarasoff v. Regents of the University of California*, (17 Cal. 3d 425, 1976) decision requires clinicians to warn those at risk. Exceptions to the duty of confidence are recognised in England and Wales although a *Tarasoff* duty has not, at least yet, been recognised.

Certain relationships, for example that between a prisoner and a psychologist, cannot be confidential. The psychologist's duty is to the prison service rather than the prisoner. Thus the prisoner may withhold information for fear that it would adversely affect the psychologist's opinion and recommendation. It is noteworthy then that while the law recognises, values and protects confidential relationships, little distinction appears to be drawn in practice between expert evidence that is based upon such a relationship and that which is not. The empirical question, although it would be difficult to test, is whether the existence of a duty of confidence affects the amount and value of what people reveal about themselves. Is there a qualitative and quantitative difference with non-confidential relationships? Policy implications include such questions as whether prison psychologists, and others in a comparable situation, should be allowed to create confidential relationships whereby they could inform courts of their conclusions—for example, that a prisoner is or is not dangerous—and yet not be required to divulge the reasons for their conclusions. It may be more important that someone is in close, confidential if necessary, contact with an individual than that a court is informed of the reasoning processes.

There is no separate, distinct, law of privacy in the UK although such a law has been developed, upon English case-law, in the USA. However, even there the potential for psychological insights into the consequences of invasions of privacy has not been developed to any significant extent (Small and Weiner, 1992). In the UK other laws have to be relied upon to encourage privacy. For example, the law of trespass to land can be used to sue snoopers who go on to private land. The European Convention on Human Rights promises to protect certain privacy rights. However, such proceedings are slow. And a key problem is that anyone wishing a remedy for a breach of confidence has to reveal that confidence during the litigation process. The law's interest in compensation, rather than prevention, is evident in this context.

NEGLIGENCE

Negligence is a ubiquitous concept which, with its emphasis upon balancing interests and appeals to reasonableness, insinuates its way into many areas of law. It is particularly important for its role in enforcing standards of conduct. In doing this it, almost entirely, reflects and reinforces existing and developing professional standards. However, this is insufficiently appreciated. A consequence is that reactive, rather than proactive, strategies have been developed. For example, risk management has tended to become associated with learning from past errors, rather than developing strategies for preventing errors, old or new, in the future (e.g. Brooten and Chapman, 1987; Snowden, 1993).

Psychologists' involvement with the law of negligence has tended to focus upon questions of compensation for personal injuries and, indirectly, its influence upon their professional practice. Weiner and Small (1992) have argued for a much broader involvement, but towards greater understanding of what happens in legal proceedings rather than possible amendment of the concepts and tests involved. Reform might be more successful through adoption of a therapeutic jurisprudence approach. For example Schuman (1992) has argued that the standard of care, in the law of negligence, should favour rather than penalise those who have sought assistance with such psychological problems as stress.

Considerable confusion is caused by the word 'negligence' being used both as an adjective or adverb, to describe the quality of certain conduct, and as a noun to describe a legal concept which depends upon a number of interacting tests. One test that negligence law adopts, in order to limit its application, is the concept of duty of care. There can only be liability if the person harmed, the plaintiff, was owed a duty of care by the perpetrator. The limits of this liability are sometimes determined by applying a 'reasonable foresight' test. While sub-tests, such as the proximity between the parties, suggest that the test is descriptive of capacity to foresee, the requirement of 'reasonableness' involves the application of someone's standards. Psychologists have a great deal to offer in describing what individuals do and could contemplate and predict but the test is made moral rather than scientific by the requirement of 'reasonable'.

Duties of care can also exist where the harm could be caused through an omission, through failure to act. It is relatively easy to ascribe harm to acts of commission, say giving erroneous advice. It is more difficult to trace harm to an omission, say a failure to give some advice, or a failure to do something. If the plaintiff does not know all that should have happened then he or she is unlikely to know that something was missed out. Any resulting harm may be attributed to fate. Weiner and Small (1992) suggest that the ability to 'think like a lawyer' primarily involves having more detailed 'scripts' with which to classify acts as lawful or unlawful. Thus there may be an educational role for psychologists in helping lawyers to think about causal chains and helping lay people to appreciate how omissions or failures to act may have been instrumental in causing the loss or other harm about which they are concerned.

The UK courts acknowledge that they interpret 'public policy' and use that to justify the imposition or exclusion of duty relationships. They have, for example, declared that educational psychologists in England and Wales do not owe an enforceable statutory duty of care to the parents of the children they assess, with regard to whether there are learning difficulties which call for special intervention, but there might be a duty of care in the law of negligence (*E. A Minor v. Dorset County Council,* [1994] 3 W.L.R. 853). They have also decided that police officers do not owe a duty of care to the public (*Hill v. Chief Constable of West Yorkshire*, [1988] 2 W.L.R. 1049) or to individuals whom they know are at risk from particular individuals (*Osman v. Ferguson*, [1993] 4 All E.R. 344).

Once a duty of care is established then the associated standard of care needs to be ascertained and applied. This is usually stated in terms of whether a responsible body of co-professionals would have acted or decided similarly. Thus it is primarily a factual question which depends upon professional standards. Expert witnesses can be called upon to state what is acceptable conduct. In this way the profession concerned can exercise considerable influence over the content of the standards. The test is not what a majority would have done. That would prevent new and improved standards developing. Nor does the test require the highest standards. Provided that a responsible body of co-professionals would have done the same thing the standard of care has not been breached. Thus groups of professionals can, pro-actively, develop statements of standards. These may be informally recognised by the courts, particularly if they gain recognition through publication and similar. In this way, for example, risk-taking assessments and procedures may gain some recognition (Carson, 1992). However, it should be noted that judges reserve, but rarely exercise, the right to declare that particular standards are too low.

The judges' reasons for deciding that the British police do not owe a duty of care to the public, or specific individuals at risk, are closely related to their understanding of how the police operate.

> The manner of conduct of such an investigation must necessarily involve a variety of decisions to be made on matters of policy and discretion, for example

as to which particular line of inquiry is most advantageously to be pursued and what is the most advantageous way to deploy the available resources. (*Hill v. Chief Constable of West Yorkshire*, [1988] 2 W.L.R. 1049, Lord Keith at p. 1056.)

But that does not isolate any qualitative difference between decision-making by the police and by other people, for example clinicians, who are regularly sued. The police would not breach the standard of care just because they did not pursue, whether with or without the benefit of hindsight, the most advantageous techniques. The best approach is not required. The question would be whether the particular police officers adopted investigative and other techniques which other responsible police officers would have adopted in those circumstances. Particularly as the 'intuitive' and experiential approach to policing gives way to more scientific approaches (for example Canter, 1994), the immunity of police officers to negligence actions is analytically indefensible. Psychologists might wish to investigate whether particular goals of police services—for example, ensuring the use of high quality investigative interviews—is actually assisted by the police not being liable to negligence actions. Is there something distinctively different about decision-making by police officers? Better arguments could be developed about the inefficiency of the negligence compensation scheme, the proportion of the money involved going in fees and administration in comparison with that going in compensation. But those arguments equally apply elsewhere.

A negligent act may be sufficient to justify disciplinary proceedings by a professional body or employer. But the law of negligence also requires proof that the breach of standard caused losses of a kind which the law compensates. And those losses must be of a kind that are reasonably foreseeable. Psychologists certainly have a role in advising courts about the nature and extent of the injuries that the plaintiffs experienced. However, their role in relation to questions of causation appears more limited. The causal concepts, in this context, have more to do with attribution of responsibility than strict assessment of cause. 'Unfortunately, the attribution of causality and responsibility studied in social psychology does not fit in well with the causality discussed in the law of torts' (Weiner and Small, 1992, p. 440)

Many accidents, for example on a road, will have multiple causes, from the driver's skills, through safety design and condition of the vehicle to state of the road and weather. However, in practice, only a few will be seized upon for litigation. Economic realities, such as whether the defendant is covered by insurance and can thus meet compensation awards, cannot be ignored.

FAULT OR NO-FAULT?

The negligence scheme depends upon fault, upon blameworthy behaviour. A number of countries, such as New Zealand, have introduced no-fault schemes where, with exceptions and variations, those injured obtain compensation whether or not they are able to identify and prove someone else was at fault. This targets the money more efficiently, but thinly, to a broader class of people. However, some argue that a fault-based scheme is necessary or desirable to maintain standards. If people realise, the argument runs, that they will not be accused of negligence then their standards will drop. Psychological insights on accident causation and prevention would both inform this debate and, possibly, encourage lawyers to think about possible managerial liability for inadequate approaches to safety issues. Lawyers should, for example, pay close attention to such work as that of Reason (1990) on psychological factors influencing the occurrence of accidents. Doing so might lead to more emphasis upon how the potential for accidents, which is pervasive, is managed not just by front-line employees but also their managers and trainers.

The greatest potential for psychological insights within a negligence law framework is, it is submitted, in the development of 'managerial negligence'. Present law and practice concentrates upon individual negligence although the ever greater interdependence of people makes this increasingly inappropriate. Once it has proved possible to identify a negligent employee, or other insured person, then compensation flows. There is no need to look beyond the atomised individual. However, there can be cases where there is no negligent individual, but there is a negligently designed service (*Bull v. Devon Area Health Authority* [1993] 4 Med L.R. 117), or where there is a negligent individual but it is more appropriate to concentrate upon the negligence of the supervisors or system designers (see speech of Browne-Wilkinson, V-C, in *Wilsher v. Essex Area Health Authority*, [1986] 3 All E.R. 801 from 832, although the decision was reversed on other grounds).

Psychological and other research is being adopted and adapted by management scientists and incorporated into management courses (for example Cooke and Slack, 1991; Russo and Schoemaker, 1989). Some of these ideas might be developed. For example, it would be poor, possibly negligent, practice to set up a system of decision-making which did not provide for feedback of information from which the decision-makers could learn. Just as decision-makers need libraries to keep up to date with developments in their specialist area so do they need quality data on the success or otherwise of their decision-making. Personnel policies are a common feature of modern employment practices, manufacturing and services. Should any less attention be paid to developing similar policies and procedures to assist people to perform their decision-making tasks? Are managers expecting people to make decisions which require the manipulation, at the same time, of more pieces of information than they can manage? If so, they are flying in the face of psychological research findings.

Contract

By making a valid contract the parties effectively make law because they can call upon the machinery of the state to enforce it. However, agreements must satisfy specific legal tests if they are to constitute enforceable contracts. One requirement concerns the capacity of the parties to make the contract. Capacity might be impaired by mental disorder, the effects of drugs, a learning disability. Clearly psychology has much to offer here. However, this is minimised where, as in the UK, capacity is not the sole criterion. Even if a contracting party is incapable of understanding, such a contract cannot be avoided if the other party is unaware of that incapacity. While incapacity may be evident in some cases it will not be in many more, especially with the increasingly effective integration of people with disabilities into the community.

Contracts are based upon agreement. This may appear to invite tests of mental operations but the problems are more prosaic in practice. Agreement can be inferred from behaviour; the mute exchange of newspaper and price money is a contract. Only a very small proportion of contracts need to be in writing. What did the parties agree? Did they agree that the newspaper would have all the pages for that issue, the same as last week, that the regular cartoonist would not be on holiday? The law provides inferential rules to help fill out what the parties 'agreed'.

To be a contract, in common law systems and outside certain very special circumstances, each party to the contract must give, even if it is only a promise to give, the other party something of value. This is called 'consideration'. The relative values of these 'reciprocal gifts' is not directly relevant. Contract law emphasises the right of the parties to make their own bargains. Other requirements stress that only the parties to the contract can enforce it. These requirements create problems for many service providers in the UK.

If a psychologist is employed, say by a hospital, a prison service, an education authority, to provide services for the clients or customers of his or her employer, then contract law does not govern the relationship between the psychologist and the client or patient. Patients pay taxes. Some of those find their way to the national health service. Psychologists employed in the public sector provide a service because a client is assessed as having a need. Psychologists, whether in the private, voluntary or public sectors, have a contract with their employers. They and the employer can specify special rules and procedures in that contract. But there is only a contract between client and psychologist when the latter is directly employed by the client, not through an intermediary such as an insurance company.

'Contracts' are often developed between psychologists (and other service providers) and their clients. These have many advantages and are likely to encourage clients to comply with the treatment or other arrangements. The parties may have agreed upon consequences if a breach of the agreement occurs. There is nothing improper in that. But that agreement cannot be enforced in law. The psychologist may not be entitled, for example in terms of negligence law, to refuse to provide a service for a client just because the latter breached a 'treatment contract'.

The development of community care, at least in the UK, has involved case managers placing contracts for an agency to meet the client's needs. Unless the client contributes towards this, as 'consideration' rather than as the result of a means test, he or she cannot rely upon contractual remedies. The client is not a party to the contract between the case manager and the provider. However, if the case manager gave the client a voucher, which could be redeemed by one of a number of approved services, then the client would have something of value that could constitute consideration when exchanged with one of those services. Now the client would be able to use contractual remedies. Mental health laws, both in the USA (e.g. Petrila, 1992) and the UK (Health Committee, 1993) have paid too little attention to the economic organisation of services, for example assumption of institutional rather than community care. Laws based more upon the principles of contract may be appropriate.

There are, of course, many more requirements of a valid contract. There are also several ways in which a contract can be invalidated. One area—and one in which psychologists may be able to extend the insights developed in other contexts—concerns undue influence. If fraud is used to induce a contract, it can be invalidated. Indeed, a crime may have been committed. But the contract may not be so much the product of fraud as an imbalance in the power relationship between the parties, for example between a client and a clinical psychologist. The courts have invalidated a number of contracts where there has been too great an imbalance and no counter-vailing independent advice. More could be done to develop notions and tests of 'psychological dependence'.

CONCLUSION

This chapter has sought to provide an overview, perhaps dangerously brief, of key areas of civil law where psychology already has or may develop a role. This area of the law regulates both the manner in which psychologists carry our their work and some of the tests to which they work. It has been suggested that there is a wider role than is currently undertaken but that this involves adopting educational roles and new approaches, for example towards demonstrating forms of managerial negligence.

REFERENCES

Brennan, M. (1993). A question of language: your quick and easy guide to verbal assault and battery. In W. Stainton Rogers and M. Worrel (Eds), *Investigative Interviewing with Children*. Milton Keynes: Open University Press.

Brooten, K.E. and Chapman, S. (1987). *Malpractice: A Guide to Avoidance and Treatment*. Orlando: Grune & Stratton.

Canter, D. (1994). *Criminal Shadows*. London: HarperCollins.

Carson, D. (1992). Presenting risk opinions. *Inside Psychology*, **1**, 1, 3–7.

Cooke, S. and Slack, N. (1991). *Making Management Decisions* (2nd edn). Hemel Hempstead: Prentice Hall.

Cotterrell, R.B.M. (1984). *The Sociology of Law: An Introduction*. London: Butterworth.

Hartnett, O.M. (1984). Sex discrimination legislation and psychology. In D.J. Müller, D.E. Blackman and A.J. Chapman (Eds), *Psychology and Law*. Chichester: John Wiley.

Health Committee (1993). *Community Supervision Orders*. London: HMSO. (Fifth report of the House of Commons Select Committee on Health, 1992–93 session.)

Loftus, E.F. and Rosenwald, L.A. (1993). Buried memories, shattered lives. *American Bar Association Journal*, **79**, 70–3.

Markesinis, B.S. (1990). *The German Law of Torts: A Comparative Introduction* (2nd edn). Oxford: Clarendon.

McCrudden, C. (1981). Anti-discrimination legislation and the role of the social sciences. In S. Lloyd-Bostock (Ed.), *Law and Psychology*. Oxford: Centre for Socio-Legal Studies.

Petrila, J. (1992). Redefining mental health law. *Law and Human Behavior*, **16**, 1, 89–106.

Podgorecki, A., Kaupen, W., Van Houtte, J., Vinke, P. and Kutchinsky, B. (1973). *Knowledge and Opinion about Law*. London: Martin Robertson.

Reason, J. (1990). *Human Error*. Cambridge: Cambridge University Press.

Russo, J.E. and Schoemaker, P.J.H. (1989). *Confident Decision-making; How to Make the Right Decision Every Time*. London: Piatkus.

Schuman, D.W. (1992). Therapeutic jurisprudence and tort liability: a limited subjective standard of care. *Southern Methodist University Law Review*, **46,** 2, 409–32.

Small, M.A. and Weiner, R.L. (1992). Rethinking privacy torts: a view toward a psycholegal perspective. In D.K. Kagehiro and W.S. Laufer (Eds), *Handbook of Psychology and Law*. New York: Springer-Verlag.

Snowden, P. (1993). Taking risks. *Journal of Forensic Psychiatry*, **4**, 2, 198–200.

Spencer, J. and Flin, R. (1993). *The Evidence of Children: The Law and the Psychology* (2nd edn). London: Blackstone.

Tomkins, A.J. and Pfeifer, J.A. (1992). Modern social-scientific theories and data concerning discrimination: implications for using social scientific evidence in the courts. In D.K. Kagehiro and W.S. Laufer (Eds), *Handbook of Psychology and Law*. New York: Springer-Verlag.

Turk, V. and Brown, H. (1992). Sexual abuse and adults with learning disabilities: preliminary communication of survey results. *Mental Handicap*, **20**, 2, 56–8.

Tyler, T.R. (1992). The psychological consequences of judicial procedures: implications for civil commitment hearings. *Southern Methodist University Law Review*, **46**, 2, 433–45.

Weiner, R.L. and Small, M.A. (1992). Social cognition and tort law: the roles of basic science and social engineering. In D.K. Kagehiro and W.S. Laufer (Eds), *Handbook of Psychology and Law*. New York: Springer-Verlag.

Wexler, D.B. (Ed.) (1990). *Therapeutic Jurisprudence: The Law as a Therapeutic Agent*. Durham, NC: Carolina Academic Press.

Wexler, D.B. and Winick, B.J. (1991). *Essays in Therapeutic Jurisprudence*. Durham, NC: Carolina Academic Press.

Winick, B.J. (1991). Harnessing the power of the bet: wagering with the government as a mechanism for social and individual change. In Wexler, D.B. and Winick, B.J., *Essays in Therapeutic Jurisprudence*. Durham, NC: Carolina Academic Press.

Compensation for Brain Injury

Neil Brooks
Case Management Services, Edinburgh

INTRODUCTION

The psychologist who ventures into personal injuries litigation must have a thorough grasp of the relevant literature, substantial experience in the assessment and management of such conditions, capacity to write clearly, and ability to communicate under pressure. This chapter aims to guide the psychologist in this field.

BRAIN INJURY

This chapter will concentrate on the most common cause of acute brain injury; that is, trauma. Other conditions are important, including damage resulting from medical negligence, and the ingestion of toxic substances (for further information see O'Doerr and Carlin, 1991). However, different causes of acute brain injury have consistent consequences, and severe injury is used as a basic model (for reading on minor injury see Binder, 1986, 1990; Beers, 1992).

The psychologist examining a patient with traumatic brain injury (TBI) must be able to measure the severity of deficits, and relate these to the severity of brain damage. This demands a knowledge of the pathophysiology of TBI and the different ways of measuring its severity. This cannot be left to a physician or surgeon, who will know little about psychological consequences and less about assessing those consequences.

As far as pathophysiology is concerned, TBI may be an open (penetrating) or, more commonly, a closed (blunt) injury. In the latter, the brain is shaken violently as the moving head is rapidly decelerated, or the stationary or slowly

Handbook of Psychology in Legal Contexts
Edited by R. Bull and D. Carson. © 1995 John Wiley & Sons Ltd

moving head is rapidly accelerated. The brain swirls violently (Genarelli et al., 1982), and nerve fibres (axons) are stretched and torn, hence the commonly used term for this form of injury: diffuse axonal injury (DAI). The greater the acceleration/deceleration, the greater the damage (Adams et al., 1982, 1985, 1991; Gade et al., 1990). In addition to primary damage to nerves, secondary effects may be set in motion including bleeding inside the skull and brain, brain swelling, and infection (see Gade et al., 1990; for a more complete discussion see Miller, Pentland and Berrol, 1990).

In penetrating TBI the damage depends in part on the velocity of the missile. A high velocity rifle bullet is likely to cause massive and fatal damage, whereas a lower velocity small calibre bullet may cause only a small focal wound. Lesions in penetrating TBI are likely to be focal, and classic DAI is not common, although there are non-focal effects such as haematoma and swelling. In blunt TBI the damage is diffuse, or multi-focal (Wilson et al., 1992) with the precise distribution of damage depending on chance factors such as the angle of the head at the time of the injury. However, there are consistent sites of damage in blunt TBI, most particularly frontal and temporal cortex.

There are three main ways of measuring severity: the patient's conscious level; the evidence of brain imaging; the patient's neurological status and the need for clinical, particularly surgical intervention.

Conscious Level

After a severe blunt TBI the patient is immediately unconscious. As consciousness recovers, the patient is confused, and as confusion clears it then becomes obvious that the patient had been amnesic for a period in which he or she showed apparently normal behaviour. Two common indices of conscious state are the initial depth or total duration of coma, and the duration of post traumatic amnesia (PTA—the period between the injury and regaining continuous day-to-day memory). Coma is measured on the Glasgow Coma Scale (GCS; Teasdale and Jennett, 1974) in which the patient is scored on the ability to open eyes, move, and make a verbal response, giving a minimum score of 3 (very deep coma) and a maximum of 15 (full consciousness). A GCS of 13–15 indicates a mild injury, 9–12 indicates moderate injury, and 8 or below indicates severe injury.

A PTA of less than an hour denotes a mild injury, 1–24 hours is moderate, and up to 7 days is severe (Russell, 1932). PTA over 7 days is very severe, and over 4 weeks is extremely severe (Jennett, 1990). PTA is usually measured by clinical questioning, although other methods are available. Clinically, PTA is estimated by identifying when the patient's continuous day-to-day memory returned, neglecting any early 'islands' of memory. The examiner tries to identify what the patient remembers of the incident and its immediate consequences (i.e. examinations carried out, transfers within hospital units, etc.). This is a crude procedure, but this is of little consequence, as very fine distinctions in PTA (for example 13 or 14 days) are of no practical consequence.

Brain Imaging

The most widely used method of brain imaging is the CT (Computed Tomography) scan, supplying an X-ray of slices of the brain. The more recently developed MRI (magnetic resonance imaging) has greatly improved resolution compared with CT. Both methods identify structural complications such as haematoma, other space occupying lesions, brain swelling, and (using MRI) contusions. The more severe the brain damage and the deeper the coma, the more likely the patient is to show abnormalities on imaging (Wiedmann et al 1989), which relate to outcome (Wilson et al., 1989; Levin et al., 1990; Newton et al., 1992).

Neurological Status and the Need for Intervention

The more severe the brain damage, the more likely the patient is to have neurological signs such as weakness or spasticity, and to need surgical or other intervention. The patient who did not lose consciousness immediately and whose PTA was minutes would be thought to have a minor injury. If the patient then deteriorated due to intracranial haematoma, and developed hemiparesis and aphasia, the injury would be considered serious as indicated by the complication (haematoma), the neurological status (hemiparesis and aphasia), and the need for intervention (evacuation of the haematoma).

With increasing severity of TBI there is an increasing likelihood that the patient will show neurological signs, but the relationship is not symmetrical. Neurological signs indicate damage to the brain, but the absence of such signs need not indicate an undamaged brain. Patients may have serious problems of cognition and behaviour yet show no neurological signs.

MEASURING OUTCOME

Brain damage causes physical, cognitive, and emotional problems (disabilities), and these may cause family distress, social isolation, and failure to return to work (handicaps). Many patients recover well from physical difficulties (McKinlay et al., 1981), but cognitive difficulties are the rule, and include difficulties in memory, speed and efficiency of thinking, problem-solving and planning, and attention. Most patients with a severe injury will have some difficulties in these areas (Brooks, 1989, 1990a). Memory difficulties will be found in almost all patients with a PTA of two weeks or more (Paniak, Shore and Rourke, 1989; Dikmen et al., 1990; Levin et al., 1990). The main problem is in new learning, although deficits in storage and retrieval can be prominent (Ruff et al., 1991). Severity of brain damage is a good predictor of severity of cognitive deficit although its efficiency as a predictor reduces over time (Dikmen et al., 1990) as factors other than injury severity (pre-trauma cognitive status, clinical management, recovery environment, etc.) become important.

Attentional deficits are common (Van Zomeren and Saan, 1990). The fundamental problem is in mental slowness when attention has to be divided so that choice reaction time, decision making and response selection are slow (Ponsford and Kinsela, 1992). Disturbances in thinking, planning, and problem-solving are very common resulting in part from damage to frontal lobe structures, so patients are poor in many aspects of cognition having a deficiency in the intention to learn, and the effective deployment of cognitive strategies (Matison and Levin, 1990).

Language deficits are common but subtle, so that the patient has difficulties in rapid and effective word finding, and in sticking to the point and is rigid, concrete, and tangential, with a slow verbal output. Gross difficulties in perception of the kind found after a stroke (neglect, visual disorientation, etc.) are not common, except very early after injury. However, patients with TBI will have difficulty in any kind of constructional or perceptual task which requires planning, error checking, and speed—characteristics found in many mental tests.

Emotional/behavioural deficits are very common and are extremely handicapping. They are particularly prominent in mood (depression and anxiety), emotional control (anger, irritability, emotional lability), and difficulties in recognising the nature and severity of behaviour change (Brooks et al., 1987; Lezak, 1987; Prigatano, Altman and O'Brien, 1990; O'Carroll, Woodrow and Maroun, 1991). Patients may be crude, abusive, and violent towards family members and others.

Depression and anxiety are also common, (Fedoroff et al., 1992; Jorge et al., 1993) with symptomatology being found in at least 60 per cent of severe TBI patients within five years of injury (Brooks et al., 1987). It is difficult to know the true incidence of problems here as most of the figures in the literature are based on symptomatic reporting by the patient which underestimates the problem (Prigatano, Altman and O'Brien, 1990; Melamed, Groswasser and Stern, 1992). Furthermore, few researchers use well validated scales of affective status which allow 'caseness' cut-offs (caseness being a level of distress above which treatment would normally be thought to be warranted), and even fewer (see Fedoroff et al., 1992; for exceptions see Jorge et al., 1993) attempt formal psychiatric diagnoses using conventionally recognised schemes such as that based on the Diagnostic and Statistical Manual of Mental Disorders (DSM-III-R).

The physical, cognitive, and emotional/behavioural disabilities have significant handicapping social, family, and vocational/educational consequences. For medico-legal purposes, it is the last area that is of great significance, having enormous financial implications in terms of compensation for loss of future earnings. As far as family consequences are concerned, family members report very high levels of distress or 'subjective burden'. These levels frequently rise during the first five years after injury as family members begin to appreciate the full consequences of the injury. The levels of burden are not trivial; around 25 per cent of relatives have caseness levels of anxiety or depression (Brooks, 1990b), and there is a high risk of divorce or separation.

TBI impairs the ability to work. Before injury around 80 per cent of patients are working, whereas after injury the figure drops to around 30 per cent (Brooks et al., 1987; Jacobs, 1988; Wilkinson, Fisher and Bromfield, 1989; McMordie, Barker and Pauolo, 1990; Ruff et al., 1993). These figures may be improved for patients in specialised neuro-rehabilitation programmes (Wehman et al., 1989, 1990), but few patients have access to such programmes. The predictors of failure to return to work are similar to those of family distress, involving emotion/behavioural problems which in turn relate to severity of injury (McMordie, Barker and Pauolo, 1990; Ruff et al., 1993). Patients who have continuing problems in anger control, and socially inappropriate behaviour, are much less likely to return to work (Brooks et al., 1987), as are those with significant deficits in memory, attention, or communication.

ASSESSING THE PATIENT

The psychologist may be instructed by either side in civil litigation. The side is irrelevant. The psychologist should apply the same process, same care, and same diligence no matter who gave the instruction. The assessment must be appropriate, comprehensive, professionally and ethically defensible, and consistent with current information concerning clinical practice and the theoretical basis of that practice. The purpose of the examination is to identify the injured person's cognitive and behavioural strengths and weaknesses, and to construct a formulation to explain these. The examiner should identify the functional consequences of these strengths and weaknesses, and the need for rehabilitation and further management. The examination can be sub-divided as follows:

1. Records review
2. Patient interview
3. Mental status examination
4. Cognitive examination
5. Assessment of emotional state
6. Interview with a relative
7. Interviews with others (employers, workmates, teachers, etc.).

Records Review

Before obtaining records, the patient's written permission must be obtained, or the permission of lawyers acting for the patient. This stage of the examination sets the context for the rest of the examination (severity of injury, complications, etc.). The examiner should obtain initial accident and emergency (A & E) notes; neurosurgical notes or other acute notes. Follow-up clinic notes and the general practitioner's (GP) records for the situation in the two years or so before the injury and since the injury are also very useful. The initial A & E notes should give information about severity of injury, particularly GCS score. The neurosurgical notes give information about the severity, extent, and nature of brain damage (contusions, haematomas, etc.), with further information coming from neuroradiology reports. Armed with this information, the psychologist should be building hypotheses about patterns of deficit long before the patient is examined.

A perusal of GP records can be revealing. It is not uncommon for a patient to report no problems before injury, yet for his or her GP records to show many attendances for 'nerves' pre-trauma. It is far better to find out about a significant pre-traumatic medical/psychiatric history before a court appearance rather than in court under cross-examination.

Patient Interview

The interview is a source of information (the patient's view of the current situation, duration of post-traumatic amnesia, etc.), which may be flawed because of the patient's cognitive deficits, inability to recognise deficits, or (less commonly) the intention to deceive. The interview is an opportunity for observing many facets of cognition (rate, speed, and efficiency of thinking, memory, comprehension, word finding, ability to stick to the point, etc.), emotion (smiling or laughing inappropriately, frustration tolerance, emotional lability), and behaviour (socially inappropriate comments, inability to take turns in conversation, etc.). During this part of the examination, the psychologist simply tries to elicit the history from the patient, in order to identify current problems, their evolution over time, the patient's understanding of any problems, social, environmental, or other factors that may have a significant impact on cognitive performance, and pre-traumatic features including medical history, and vocational and marital status.

The interview begins by encouraging the patient to tell the story of the injury and its consequences, although most will have no memory of this early period. Duration of PTA should be assessed by finding out when the patient regained ongoing day to day memory, and the examiner should consider its consistency with other indices of severity such as GCS score. The examiner should record problems reported spontaneously by the patient, and then should go through a checklist designed to elicit other physical, cognitive and emotional/

behavioural problems. In the physical domain, the examiner should briefly record physical problems reported by the patient, or observed by the psychologist. In the cognitive domain the examiner should record spontaneously reported or elicited difficulties in memory, attention, problem solving, language, or visuo-spatial function. It is useful to distinguish between the speed and efficiency of cognitive processes, and patients may report that they can do the things they did before, but at lower speed, or with more effort. In the emotional/behavioural domain the examiner should again separate spontaneously reported, and elicited changes in mood, emotional control etc. For all symptoms it is useful to record them in terms of severity (none, some, moderate/severe) or frequency (never, once a week, once a day).

The examiner should enquire about the patient's pre-traumatic medical situation, paying particular attention to previous accidents or injuries, previous claims for compensation, and any pre-existing or current medical condition that may affect cognitive performance or emotional presentation. It is important to ask about pre-traumatic problems with 'nerves', and any pre-traumatic emotional difficulties such as depression, agoraphobia etc. In addition the patient's alcohol consumption before and after trauma should be recorded. The patient's educational and vocational history should be taken in detail, starting with the age at leaving school and the nature of any certificates taken, then moving on to a sequential account of jobs, looking for the highest level of employment reached, and the pattern of that employment (rapid job changing, consistent career track).

Mental Status Examination

A full cognitive examination is necessary to construct a detailed profile of a patient's strengths and weaknesses, but often the patient is not able to tolerate such an examination, or time is limited. In this situation, a brief mental status screen can be performed, the basic requirements of which are outlined in Brooks (1990a).

Cognitive (Neuropsychological) Examination

The neuropsychological examination is a detailed appraisal of many areas of cognition. There is much debate about what function should be assessed and how. There is an American preference for large test batteries, and a British preference for a more flexible approach offering the chance to explore specific deficits. Each approach has its pros and cons (for a full discussion see Ziskin and Faust, 1988a, b, c). The large battery ensures a comprehensive examination, but may be unwieldy, and its components may age as research leads to changes in thinking and practice. The flexible approach enables an examination to be tailored to a specific patient, but can be challenged by the sharp cross-examiner by distorting its nature ('so basically doctor you just make it up as you go on'—Ziskin and Faust, 1988c). A compromise is to ensure that a basic battery is well chosen to cover all the relevant areas (for further details see Brooks, 1990a) with the option of exploring specific individual problems in more detail. Such a basic battery should include measures of pre and post-traumatic intellectual function, memory, thinking, planning and foresight, concentration/attention, perceptual motor function, scholastic attainment (not always necessary), and emotional/behavioural status.

The various tests used will generate quantitative scores, and these are often standardised. That means that the test has been administered to large numbers of people (either those with or without traumatic brain injury), and the examiner can then compare an individual's score with that of age peers. This is valuable in constructing profiles of abilities, but a word of caution is necessary. All scores need to be interpreted clinically in the light of the patient's injury, and pre and post-traumatic situation. The fact that a patient has an 'average' score on a particular test may either be of no consequence at all or, if that patient had a history of post-graduate education before the injury, an average score may indicate a substantial cognitive decline.

Assessment of Emotional State

Many patients report emotional symptomatology, and the examiner should ask routinely about disturbances in emotion and behaviour, and should be able to identify and distinguish problems in mood and anxiety, and conditions such as major depression/dysthymia, agoraphobia, and other anxiety disorders. Measures such as the Structured Clinical Interview for DSM-III-R (SCID; Spitzer, Williams and Gibbon, 1987) or Munich Diagnostic Check Lists (Hiller, Zaudig and Mombour, 1990) can be used here. These take the examiner step by step through a clinical interview to diagnose mental disorder.

Emotional symptomatology should be measured. There are many question-naires available, but one which is particularly useful is the General Health Questionnaire and in particular the 28-question version (GHQ28; Goldberg and Williams, 1988). This allows a caseness threshold but the conventional threshold of 4/5 on the GHQ28 is too low for brain injured patients, generating large numbers of false positives (people who are diagnosed on the scale as being at caseness levels, yet who clinically are below such a level). A more appropriate cut-off score is around 11 or 12, to allow for the somatic and cognitive symptoms associated with brain injury. The GHQ28 gives a measure of overall distress, but more specific measures such as the Beck Depression (Beck et al., 1979) or Anxiety Inventory (Beck et al., 1988), or Hospital Anxiety and Depression Scale (Zigmond and Snaith, 1983) are required for quantifying the levels of specific symptoms such as anxiety and depression.

Clinical Interview with a Relative

Often a patient with a severe TBI will under-estimate the extent of emotional and cognitive disturbances, so it is crucial to try to interview someone who knows the patient well, particularly a close relative. If an interview is not possible, the examiner should prepare a simple questionnaire for a relative or other person to complete.

Interviews with Others

The purpose of these interviews is to find out whether or not the informant has seen any change in the patient since the injury, and to identify its nature and severity. Such informants are often quite neutral in terms of the medico-legal process, and can supply unbiased corroboration.

TREATMENT AND REHABILITATION

The psychological examination takes place in an office or at the bedside, but the results of the examination must be interpreted in terms of the day-to-day consequences of any deficits found. The lawyer reading the report will be particularly interested in three aspects—the need for further treatment or rehabilitation (and availability and costs); the likelihood of return to work; and the likelihood that the patient will be able to care for him or herself (with or without additional help).

As far as rehabilitation is concerned, there is now excellent evidence that specialist rehabilitation is clinically effective, and also cost-effective, by reducing disability and the consequent need for care and attendance (for a review see Brooks, 1991). Deficits in memory and in planning can be reduced by effective rehabilitation. The earlier the rehabilitation starts, the better, but gains can be made even many years after injury. So, patients who present with continuing cognitive difficulties may need specialist rehabilitation, and the psychologist should signal this in the report, giving an estimation of its nature (inpatient/out-patient; private/public), availability, and likely effectiveness, duration and cost.

As already discussed, failure to return to work is a particular problem after TBI, and the predictors of such failure are now well known. The psychologist should ensure that the vocational consequences of cognitive and emotional deficits are signalled, and the management of those consequences should be outlined (generic rehabilitation, specialist vocational rehabilitation, etc.).

The very severely injured patient will not be able to live independently. Problems that prevent independent living include very physical or severe cognitive deficits, making the patient unable to plan a day or to anticipate and react to danger (e.g. in the kitchen) or exploitation. The report should comment on the patient's ability to care for him or herself and should attempt an estimate of how much care and assistance the patient needs, what level that should be (friend, nurse, etc.), what regime of care is necessary, and for how long (lifelong, some years, etc.). Further specialist examination will usually be needed to identify a precise schedule and cost of prolonged care.

PREPARING THE REPORT

The better the report, the less likely it is that the writer will have to attend Court. A report that is comprehensive, logical, and accurate, is hard to challenge and may simply be agreed by both sides in the litigation. This section of the chapter will consider what background information a report should contain, and will then consider the different sections of the report.

Background—The Examiner

The writer of the report wants to be taken seriously as an expert whose views should be listened to with respect. The best way to ensure this is to write a good report. In addition, the examiner may like to prepare for the instructing lawyer a brief statement (one side of paper) of qualifications—in effect a minor curriculum vitae. In the event that the case comes to court, then the instructing lawyer (and in Britain and the Commonwealth the barrister) will want a more complete account and this can be given at that time.

The Structure of the Report

The report should have numbered pages. It should begin with a title indicating the nature of the report: 'Neuropsychological Report on ...', 'Psychological Report on ...', 'Needs Report on ....'; and incorporate the patient's name, date of birth, and address. This information should be incorporated as a running header or footer, appearing on every page.

The first section of the report should set out the background to the examination indicating where, when, for how long, and why the patient was seen: 'This person was seen for three hours on ... at the ... clinic at the request of ..., who are acting for the defenders in an action raised by ...; The examination was carried out in order to identify any ...'. It is important to indicate how the examination was carried out (by interview, clinical examination, formal cognitive testing, questionnaire measures of emotional status, etc.), and to indicate what extra information was available to the examiner (medical notes, etc.).

The next section deals with the history. As this is usually taken at least in part from the patient, it may be combined with a further section into one heading reading 'History and clinical examination' or something similar. The history should describe the initial accident, the injuries suffered by the patient, evidence of severity (GCS, PTA, neurosurgical intervention, etc.), and the nature and duration of hospital stays. The report should then deal with the patient's early clinical state and the evolution to the current clinical state, identifying the range and severity of current symptoms. Noting that a symptom is absent can be as valuable as recording its presence.

Most patients with severe TBI will need a full cognitive evaluation, and this should be the topic of a further formal section. Some examiners incorporate an appendix giving a list of tests and scores (either single scores, or scores together with error ranges). Others incorporate such information into the body of the report, while others give little if any quantitative information. The latter approach is bad practice and is open to serious challenge in court. Test scores should be incorporated, but in such a way as to make them meaningful for the naive reader. For example, most non-specialist readers will have difficulty with the concept of standard deviation, but will understand centile scores, for example: 'On the Object Assembly Sub-Test he scored X which puts him at the fifth centile—as good as or better than only 5 per cent of his age peers.' The section should record what areas of cognition were examined, and how. For example, the report might read: 'General aspects of cognition were assessed by means of the National Adult Reading Test, and Sub-Tests from the Wechsler Adult Intelligence Scale—Revised. Memory was assessed by means of copy and recall of the Rey Complex Figure, Sub-Tests for the Wechsler Memory Scale—Revised, and ....' The section can then proceed by noting clinically obvious problems (slowness, word finding difficulties, etc.), and any identified on the mental status examination before describing the results of the formal cognitive examination. Finally in this section the overall pattern of performance should be described, noting any clinically or statistically significant highs and lows.

The next section records the results of questionnaire evaluations of emotional problems, commenting on the size and clinical and diagnostic significance of the scores. Following this it is useful to have a separate section dealing with interviews with, or information from, others such as a relative, before moving to the next section which is the relevant medical and social history. Information from the patient's general practitioner report can be incorporated here.

The next section is the Formulation, and it is the most important. Here the known severity of injury, cognitive and emotional complaints, cognitive test performance, questionnaire results, and views of significant others are all integrated. Any discrepancies must be signalled and discussed. In this section the examiner inevitably has to form clinical judgements, so the report should differentiate between facts, inferences from facts, and clinical judgements. When a judgement is given, the source of the judgement, and its strength should be signalled—'While this is a clinical judgement, it is consistent with known facts and is one that the examiner would be confident to defend'; 'This is a judgement based on only partial information, and as such is open to serious challenge.' The final heading should be a Summary or Conclusions.

Reports can be tested in court. The structure described above is designed in part to reduce the likelihood of a significant challenge to a report, but challenge will happen, and the psychologist should be prepared for it. Challenges to psychological testimony, are dealt with in great detail in the multi-volume work by Ziskin and Faust (1988a, b, c). This text (particularly volumes 2 and 3) gives very detailed information about potential challenges to psychological practice including a 59-page account of general challenges to psychological tests, a 48-page chapter challenging intellectual testing specifically, and an 83-page chapter devoted to challenging neuropsychological assessment. In addition, volume 1 contains detailed information about challenging the status, nature, training, and experience of psychologists (and psychiatrists), and volume 3 contains detailed reports and transcripts of personal injury trials, giving annotated accounts of cross-examination. These three volumes make for nervous reading but forewarned is forearmed.

MALINGERING AND FAKING

Whenever a patient is being examined in a medico-legal context, the possibility of malingering, faking, or outright lying must be considered. Miller (1961) believed that claimants frequently deceived examiners and/or exaggerated symptomatology for personal gain. While his report had a major impact in the medico-legal world, the nature of the sample, the *ex cathedra* nature of the discussion, and the generalisation from a small number of individual cases make the work hard to take seriously, particularly so as more recent workers (Kelly, 1975; Guthkelch, 1980; McKinlay , Brooks and Bond, 1983) have failed to replicate Miller's results, and have shown that symptomatology in those who are claiming compensation is little different from those who are not. Certainly every examiner will have had experience of one or two litigants whose symptomatology is at the very least suspicious, but often they are remembered simply because they are unusual.

In the case of the severe TBI the greatest danger is not that the patient will intentionally 'fake bad', but that, by reason of lack of insight, will underestimate the magnitude of difficulties (McKinlay and Brooks, 1984; Prigatano, Altman and O'Brien, 1990; Melamed, Grossvasser and Stern, 1992). However, within the literature and within clinical practice there is an understandable concern that because the clinical examination of personal injury cases rests partly upon the report of the patient and partly upon scores on psychological tests, then the possibility of faking is ever present (Heaton et al., 1978; Pankratz, 1988; Bernard, 1990; Binder, 1990, 1992; Franzen, Inverson and McCracken, 1990; Guilmette and Giuliano, 1991; Pankratz and Erickson, 1990). The experienced examiner will look for a variety of sources of evidence including unusual patterns of performance, inconsistency between the known severity of injury and current severity of deficit, evasiveness on the part of the patient, and improvement in score when challenged.

CONCLUSIONS

Most personal injury cases settle out of court. When this does not happen it is because there are issues that cannot be agreed on the basis of evidence collected by the two sides in the litigation. The better the psychologist's examination, and the clearer the report, the less likely it is that the report will be challenged in court. Getting the examination and report right first time is better that having to justify them in court.

REFERENCES

Adams, J.H., Doyle, D., Graham, D.I., Lawrence, A.E. and McLellan, D.R. (1985). Microscopic diffuse axonal injury in cases of head injury. *Medicine Science and Law*, **25**, 265–9.

Adams, J.H., Graham, D.I., Genarelli, T. and Maxwell, W.L. (1991). Diffuse axonal injury in non-missile head injury. *Journal of Neurology, Neurosurgery and Psychiatry*, **54**, 481–3.

Adams, J.H., Graham, D.I., Murray, L.S. and Scott, G. (1982). Diffuse axonal injury due to non-missile head injury in humans: an analysis of 45 cases. *Annals of Neurology*, **12**, 557–63.

American Psychiatric Association (1982). *Diagnostic and Statistical Manual of Mental Disorders (Third Edition—Revised)*. Washington DC: American Psychiatric Association.

Beck, A.T., Rush, A.J., Shaw, B.F. and Emergy, G. (1979). *Cognitive Therapy of Depression*. New York: Guilford Press.

Beck, A.T., Epstein, N., Brown, G. and Steer, R.A. (1988). An inventory for measuring clinical anxiety: psychometric properties. *Journal of Consulting and Clinical Psychology*, **56**, 893–7.

Beers, S.R. (1992). Cognitive effects of mild head injury in children and adolescents. *Neuropsychology Review*, **3**, 281–320.

Bernard, L.C. (1990). Prospects for faking believable memory deficits on neuropsychological testing and the use of incentives in simulation research. *Journal of Clinical and Experimental Neuropsychology*, **12**, 715–28.

Binder, L.M. (1986). Persisting symptoms after mild head injury: a review of the postconcussive syndrome. *Journal of Clinical and Experimental Neuropsychology*, **8**, 323–46.

Binder, L.M. (1990). Malingering following minor head trauma. *The Clinical Neuropsychologist*, **4**, 25–36.

Binder, L.M. (1992). Forced-choice testing provides evidence of malingering. *Archives of Physical Medicine and Rehabilitation*, **73**, 377–80.

Brooks, N. (1989). Closed head trauma: assessing the common cognitive problems. In M. Lezak (Ed.), *Assessment of the Behavioural Consequences of Trauma*. New York: Liss, ch. 6.

Brooks, N. (1990a). Cognitive defects. In M. Rosenthal, E.R. Griffith, M.R. Bond and J.D. Miller (Eds), *Rehabilitation of the Adult and Child with Traumatic Brain Injury*. Philadelphia: Davis, pp. 163–78.

Brooks, N. (1990b). The head injured family. *Journal of Clinical and Experimental Neuropsychology*, **13**, 1–34.

Brooks, N. (1991). The effectiveness of post-acute rehabilitation. *Brain Injury*, **5**, 1–7.

Brooks, N., McKinlay, W., Symington, C., Beattie, A. and Campsie, L. (1987). Return to work within the first seven years of severe head injury. *Brain Injury*, **1**, 5–19.

Dikmen, S., Machamer, J., Temkin, N. and McLean, A. (1990). Neuropsychological recovery in patients with moderate to severe head injury: a two year follow up. *Journal of Clinical and Experimental Neuropsychology*, **12**, 507–19.

Fedoroff, J.P., Starkstein, S.E., Forrester, A.W., Geisler, F.H., Jorge, R.E., Arndt, S.V. and Robinson, R.G. (1992). Depression in patients with acute traumatic brain injury. *American Journal of Psychiatry*, **149**, 918–23.

Franzen, M.D., Inverson, G.L. and McCracken, L.M. (1990). The detection of malingering in neuropsychological assessment. *Neuropsychology Review*, **1**, 247–379.

Gade, G.F., Becker, D.P., Miller, J.D. and Dwan, P.S. (1990). Pathology and pathophysiology of head injury. In J.R. Youmans (Ed.), *Neurological Surgery: A Comprehensive Reference Guide to the Diagnosis and Management of Neurological Problems*. London: W.B. Saunders, pp. 1965–2016.

Genarelli, T.A., Thibault, L.E., Adams, J.H., Graham, D.I., Thompson, C.J. and Marcini, R.P. (1982). Diffuse axonal injury and traumatic coma in the primate. *Annals of Neurology*, **12**, 564–74.

Goldberg, D. and Williams, P. (1988). *A User's Guide to the General Health Questionnaire*. Windsor, Berks: NFER-Nelson.

Guilmette, T.J. and Giuliano, A.J. (1991). Taking the stand: issues and strategies in forensic neuropsychology. *The Clinical Neuropsychologist*, **5**, 192–219.

Guthkelch, A.N. (1980). Posttraumatic amnesia, post concussional symptoms and accident neurosis. *European Neurology*, **19**, 91–102.

Heaton, R.K., Smith, H.H., Lehman, R.A.W. and Vogt, A.T. (1978). Prospects for faking believable deficits on neuropsychological testing. *Journal of Consulting and Clinical Psychology*, **46**, 892–900.

Hiller, W., Zaudig, M. and Mombour, W. (1990). Development of diagnostic check lists for use in routine clinical care. *Archives of General Psychiatry*, **47**, 782–4.

Jacobs, H. (1988). The Los Angeles Head Injury Survey: procedures and initial findings. *Archives of Physical Medicine and Rehabilitation*, **69**, 425–30.

Jennett, B. (1990). Scale and scope of the problem. In M. Rosenthal, E.R. Griffith, M.R. Bond and J.D. Miller (Eds), *Rehabilitation of the Adult and Child with Traumatic Brain Injury* (2nd edn). Philadelphia: Davis, pp. 3–7.

Jorge, R.E., Robinson, R.G., Arndt, S.V., Starkstein, S.E., Forrester, A.W. and Geigler, F. (1993). Depression following traumatic brain injury: a 1 year longitudinal study. *Journal of Affective Disorders*, **27**, 233–43.

Kelly, R. (1975). The post-traumatic syndrome: an iatrogenic disease. *Forensic Science*, **6**, 17–24.

Levin, H.S., O'Donnell, V.M. and Grossman, R.C. (1979). The Galveston Orientation and Amnesia Test: a practical scale to measure cognition after head injury. *Journal of Nervous and Mental Disease*, **167**, 675–84.

Levin, H.S., Gary, H.E., Elsenberg, H.M. et al. (1990). Neurobehavioural outcome one year after severe head injury. *Journal of Neurosurgery*, **73**, 699–709.

Lezak, M. (1987). Brain damage is a family affair. *Journal of Clinical and Experimental Neuropsychology*, **10**, 111–21.

McKinlay, W.W. and Brooks, D.N. (1984). Methodological problems in assessing psychosocial recovery following severe head injury. *Journal of Clinical Neuropsychology*, **6**, 87–99.

McKinlay, W., Brooks, D.N. and Bond, M. (1983). Post-concussional symptoms, financial compensation and outcome of severe blunt head injury. *Journal of Neurology, Neurosurgery, and Psychiatry*, **46**, 1084–91.

McKinlay, W.W., Brooks, D.N., Bond M.R., Martinage, D.P. and Marshall, M.M. (1981). The short-term outcome of severe blunt head injury as reported by relatives of the injured person. *Journal of Neurology, Neurosurgery and Psychiatry*, **44**, 527–33.

McMordie, W.R., Barker, S.L. and Pauolo, T.M. (1990). Return to work (RTW) after head injury. *Brain Injury*, **4**, 57–69.

Matison, A.J. and Levin, H.S. (1990). Frontal lobe dysfunction following closed head injury. *Journal of Nervous and Mental Disease*, **178**, 282–91.

Melamed, S., Groswasser, Z. and Stern, M.J. (1992). Acceptance of disability, work involvement, and subjective rehabilitation status of traumatic brain injured (TBI) patients. *Brain Injury*, **6**, 233–44.

Miller, H. (1961). Accident neurosis. *British Medical Journal*, i, 991–8.

Miller, J.D., Pentland, B. and Berrol, S. (1990). *Pathophysiology of Head Injury, in Rehabilitation of the Adult and Child with Traumatic Brain Injury* (2nd edn) (Eds M. Rosenthal, E.R. Griffith, M.R. Bond and J.D. Miller). Philadelphia: Davis.

Newton, M.R., Greenwood, R.J., Britton, K.E., Charlesworth, M., Nimmon, C.C., Carroll, M.J. and Dolke, G. (1992). A study comparing SPECT with CT and MRI after closed head injury. *Journal of Neurology, Neurosurgery and Psychiatry*, **55**, 92–4.

O'Carroll, R.E., Woodrow, J. and Maroun, F. (1991). Psychosexual and psychosocial sequelae of closed head injury. *Brain Injury*, **5**, 303–14.

O'Doerr, H.O. and Carlin, A.S. (1991). *Forensic Neuropsychology: Legal and Scientific Bases*. New York: Guilford Press.

Paniak, C.E., Shore, D.C. and Rourke, B.P. (1989). Recovery of memory after severe closed head injury: dissociations in recovery of memory parameters and predictions of outcome. *Journal of Clinical and Experimental Neuropsychology*, **11**, 631–844.

Pankratz, L. (1988). Malingering on intellectual and neuropsychological measures. In R. Rogers (Ed.), *Clinical Assessment of Malingering and Deception*. New York: Guilford Press, pp. 169–92.

Pankratz, L. and Erickson, R.C. (1990). Two views of malingering. *The Clinical Neuropsychologist*, **4**, 379–89.

Ponsford, J. and Kinsella, G. (1992). Attentional deficits following closed head injury. *Journal of Clinical and Experimental Neuropsychology*, **14**, 822–38.

Prigatano, G., Altman, I.M. and O'Brien, K.P. (1990). Behavioural limitations that traumatically-brain-injured patients tend to underestimate. *The Clinical Neuropsychologist*, **4**, 163–76.

Ruff, R.M., Marshall, L.F., Crough, J., Klauber, M.R., Levin, H.S., Barth, J., Kreutzer, J., Blunt, B.A., Foulkes, M.A., Eissenberg, H.M., Jane, J.A. and Marmarou, A. (1993). Prediction of outcome following severe head trauma: follow-up data from the traumatic coma data bank. *Brain Injury*, **7**, 101–11.

Ruff, R.M., Young, D., Gautille, T., Marshall, L.F., Barth, J. Jane J.A., Kreutzer J., Marmarou, A., Levin, H.S., Eisenberg, H.M. and Foulkes M.A. (1991). Verbal learning deficits following severe head injury: heterogeneity in recovery at 1 year. *Journal of Neurosurgery*, **75**, 550–8.

Russell, R. (1932). Cerebral involvement in head injury. *Brain*, **55**, 549–603.

Spitzer, R.L., Williams, J.B. and Gibbon, M. (1987). *Structured Clinical Interview for DSM-III-R (SCID)*. New York: Biometrics Research Department, New York State

Psychiatric Institute.

Teasdale, G. and Jennett, B. (1974). Assessment of coma and impaired consciousness: a practical scale. *Lancet*, **2**, 81–4.

Van Zomeren, A.H. and Saan, R. (1990). Effect of severe head injury on cognitive and social function. In R. Braakman (Ed.), *Handbook of Clinical Neurology*, Vol 13 (57): Head Injury. Elsevier, pp. 397–420.

Wehman, P.H., Kreutzer, J.S., West, M.D., Suerron, P.D., Zasler, N.D., Groah, C., Stonnington, H.H., Burns, C.T. and Sale P.R. (1990). Return to work for persons with traumatic brain injury: a supported employment approach. *Archives of Physical Medicine and Rehabilitation*, **71**, 1047–52.

Wehman, P., Kreutzer, J., West, M., Sherron, P., Diambra, J., Fry, R., Groah, C., Sale, P. and Killam, S. (1989). Employment outcome of persons following traumatic brain injury: pre-injury, post-injury, and supported employment. *Brain Injury*, e, 397–412.

Wiedmann, K.D., Wilson, J.T.L., Wyper, D., Hadley D.M., Teasdale, G.M. and Brooks, D.N. (1989). SPECT cerebral blood flow, MR imaging and neuropsychological findings in traumatic head injury. *Neuropsychology*, **3**, 267–81.

Wilkinson, S.M., Fisher, L.R. and Bromfield, P. (1989). Survey of severely head injured people in the Southampton Health District. *Clinical Rehabilitation*, **3**, 317–28.

Wilson, J.T.L., Wiedmann, K.D., Hadley, D.M. and Brooks, D.N. (1989). The relationship between visual memory function and lesions detected by magnetic resonance imaging after closed head injury. *Neuropsychology*, **3**, 255–66.

Wilson, J.T.L, Hadley, D.M., Wiedmann, K.D. and Teasdale, G.M. (1992). Intercorrelation of lesion detected by magnetic resonance imaging after closed head injury. *Brain Injury*, **6**, 391–400.

Zigmond, A.S. and Snaith, R.P. (1983). The Hospital Anxiety and Depression Scale. *Acta Psychiatrica Scandinavica*, **67**, 361–70.

Ziskin, J. and Faust, D. (1988a). *Coping with Psychiatric and Psychological Testimony; vol 1: Basic Information* (4th edn). California: Law and Psychology Press.

Ziskin J. and Faust, D. (1988b). *Coping with Psychiatric and Psychological Testimony; vol 2: Special Topics* (4th edn). California: Law and Psychology Press.

Ziskin, J. and Faust, D. (1988c). *Coping with Psychiatric and Psychological Testimony; vol 3: Practical Guidelines, Cross-Examination and Case Illustration* (4th edn). California: Law and Psychology Press.

Chapter 5.3

Compensation for Psychological Injury

Neil Brooks
Case Management Services, Edinburgh

HISTORY AND INTRODUCTION

Exposure to extreme traumatic events can cause distressing and enduring symptoms, which have no physical basis (Trimble 1981, 1985; Platt and Husband, 1986; Silverman, 1986; Mendelson, 1987; Kolb, 1988). This was recognised in the last century and although few doctors understood the nature of the symptoms, writers such as Pepys in the seventeenth century clearly described symptomatology that we now recognise as a characteristic response to trauma. Pepys described the progress of the Great Fire of London towards his home, and the terror as people were unable to protect their property or belongings. He 'developed dreams of the fire and falling down of houses'.

The sequelae of wars prompted medical interest in the effects of trauma, although there was a preference for an organic aetiology of emotional symptomatology; for example, damage to the spine or brain brought on by explosion. The rise of the railways meant a rise in accidents, and in the number of claimants for compensation. Herbert Page writing in 1891 (referred to in Trimble, 1981), surgeon to the London and North West Railway, noted: 'Most of the strange nervous symptoms so commonly seen after railway accidents were not due to physical injury by the spinal cord, but were the more or less immediate consequences of the profound mental emotion aroused by the unquestionably special features and incidents of every collision.'

The current consensus is that there is a characteristic psychological response to a disaster or similar event and in the American Psychiatric Association's Diagnostic and Statistical Manual, fourth edition (DSM-IV) a specific condition is identified (Posttraumatic Stress Disorder—PTSD) and is considered to be an anxiety disorder along with phobias, panic disorder, and

Handbook of Psychology in Legal Contexts
Edited by R. Bull and D. Carson. © 1995 John Wiley & Sons Ltd

the like. The clinical psychologist or psychiatrist in diagnosing PTSD should take care to use the DSM-IV criteria. While the criteria may still be a matter of clinical debate, they are very widely used, and allow consistency in diagnostic practice.

Increasingly, the survivors of compensatable events (e.g. collapse of structure, transportation disasters, terrorist events for which a failure of security can be partly blamed) are claiming compensation for the psychological harm suffered in such events. Those carrying out medico-legal examinations of such claimants need a detailed knowledge of the nature, natural history, and predictability of psychological response to disasters or similar 'negative life events'. This chapter will attempt to define best practice in the medico-legal examination of the claimant for compensation for psychological harm. Throughout the chapter, reference will be made to the relevant literature. The reader wanting a single source in this field can do no better than peruse the recent handbook edited by Wilson and Raphael (1993).

IS THERE A CHARACTERISTIC SYNDROME?

There is a highly characteristic syndrome found after exposure to many different traumatic events. It has been called Posttraumatic Stress Disorder (PTSD), and its central features are described in DSM-IV as follows:

a.   Experiencing a specific *event* or series of events.

b.   The person suffering has *persistent re-experiencing* of the event.

c.   The sufferer persistently *avoids* experiences or events.

d.   Arousal is persistently *increased*.

e.   The *duration* is more than one month.

f.   The disturbance causes clinically significant distress or impairment.

Experiencing an Event

The sufferer must have been exposed to a traumatic (specifically an 'extreme') event, 'extreme' being defined as 'life threatening' or similar. If the stressor is less extreme, then a different diagnosis such as 'adjustment disorder' may need to be used.

To make the diagnosis of PTSD both of the following should be present:

1. the person experienced, witnessed, or was confronted with an event or events that involved actual, or threatened death or serious injury, or a threat to the physical integrity of self or others

2. the person's response involved intense fear, helplessness, or horror.

Persistent Re-experiencing

The event can be re-experienced in a number of different ways. Very commonly, the sufferer has recollections, flashbacks or dreams of the event. The recollections are recurrent and intrusive. Some patients ruminate constantly about the event and its sequelae, and the ruminations can be triggered by an intrusive memory or flashback. The memories or flashbacks may appear out of the blue, or may be triggered by concrete or symbolic stimuli. The dreams are similarly recurrent and distressing. Occasionally, the sufferer experiences a dissociative state in which he or she relives part of the experience, and behaves as if he or she were actually re-experiencing the event. This is widely reported in military cases, particularly in Vietnam veterans, but is rare in civilian cases. A common form of re-experiencing happens when the sufferer is exposed to situations that bear a concrete (noises, smells, sights, etc.) or symbolic (anniversary of the event, reading about a similar event elsewhere) relationship to the original event.

Persistent Avoidance or Numbing

In addition to re-experiencing, the sufferer makes a deliberate attempt to avoid thinking about the trauma, and its associated feelings, and may actively avoid situations that provoke memories of the event. In some people, this avoidance is strong enough to present as an actual amnesia (psychogenic amnesia) for aspects of the traumatic event. The numbing, or reduced responsiveness to the outside world has been termed 'emotional anaesthesia'. It usually begins soon after the event, and the sufferer commonly reports feeling of estrangement, detachment, and inability to become engaged in previously enjoyable activities; and unable to feel emotions, particularly emotions associated with intimacy, tenderness and sexuality.

Persistent Feelings of Increased Arousal

In this context, 'arousal' refers to difficulty in sleep, and persistent hypervigilance. The sleep disturbance involves a problem in getting off to sleep, or remaining asleep. Many patients complain that their sleep is very light so that they are very easily wakened, and once awake, remain awake ruminating about the event and its consequences. Sleep may be punctuated by nightmares which wake the sufferer who then remains awake. The nightmares may involve the actual event, or may consist of symbolically related material (a patient who lost many workmates in a helicopter crash had persistent dreams that both his wife and daughter were drowning, and he had to save one or the other, but could not save both).

Sufferers may be hypervigilant, being constantly alert to the possibility of further danger, and show exaggerated startle responses. Hypervigilance is a protective mechanism in which the environment is closely attended to for signs of danger. Complaints of failure in memory or concentration are common, as are reports of greatly increased levels of irritability and aggression.

Duration of More Than One Month

If the above features lasted for less than one month, the diagnosis of PTSD would not be used. Instead, some other diagnosis such as 'adjustment disorder' may be used.

The Disturbance Causes Distress or Impairment

The distress should reach clinical significance, and impairments may be in social, occupational, or 'other important' areas of functioning.

COMORBIDITY

'Comorbidity' is a term indicating that certain psychological conditions are commonly found together rather than in isolation. This is particularly so for PTSD which is often not the only condition found in people who have been subjected to trauma. The US literature points to other diagnoses such as substance abuse, depression and personality disorder in PTSD sufferers. Certainly comorbidity was a marked feature in Lockerbie residents claiming compensation for psychological damage after the Lockerbie disaster in which a PanAm passenger jet was blown up by a terrorist bomb over Scotland (Brooks and McKinlay, 1992). In Lockerbie, PTSD was by far the commonest diagnosis, but there were substantial numbers of people with major depression, and with other anxiety disorders in addition to PTSD. The diagnoses were not independent, in that depression, or other anxiety disorders were never seen in the absence of PTSD. So, PTSD was very much the primary morbidity with depression and other anxiety conditions only seen in people who had PTSD. The primary response to a disaster is therefore anxiety (PTSD being one of the anxiety disorders).

Recent clinical experience has shown the importance of obsessive-compulsive disorder. In examinations of survivors of recent Scottish industrial and transportation disasters a striking feature has been the frequency of obsessive-compulsive disorder in addition to PTSD and depression. In a number of cases lengthy checking rituals developed around the concept of safety, so that before going to bed, all electric appliances, all gas appliances, all windows and so on have to be checked, and the checking can be repeated many times. Many other claimants had bought smoke alarms, and often they had bought fire extinguishers also.

EPIDEMIOLOGY?

The medico-legal examiner must have some idea about the base rate (normal rate of occurrence) of PTSD and related conditions in the community at large in order to make the most informed judgement about the causal link between a trauma and subsequent symptomatology. Unfortunately, while there have been many studies of PTSD in specific 'at risk' populations, such as victims of war, there is much less information on the community prevalence of PTSD. Helzer, Robins and McEvoy (1987) used the Diagnostic Interview Schedule to identify psychological disorder in a well characterised stratified urban US sample. The complete syndrome of PTSD was not common, with a lifetime prevalence of 5 males and 13 females per 1000. In males, the trauma was either combat or seeing someone else hurt or die. In females the most common event was physical attack (including rape). If a less stringent criterion was taken (any, or some, but not all of the DSM-III-R symptoms—DSM-III-R is the precursor to DSM-IV) prevalence was 15 per cent for men and 16 per cent for women. The main traumatic event for men was Vietnam combat, but for women it was seeing someone hurt or die. For male Vietnam veterans the most recent estimates are 11.1 per cent current prevalence and 49.3 per cent lifetime prevalence (Schlenger et al., 1992; Weiss et al., 1992). Comorbidity was high with PTSD victims having a raised risk of obsessive compulsive disorder, dysthymia, and manic-depressive disorder.

Breslau and Davis (1992) and Breslau et al. (1991) found a lifetime prevalence of exposure to traumatic events in an urban US population of 39.1 per cent, and in those exposed, the rate of PTSD was 23.6 per cent yielding a lifetime prevalence of 9.2 per cent. PTSD sufferers were at risk of other disorders, particularly major depression and alcohol abuse/dependence. Males, those with early conduct disorder, and those with less than college education were more at risk. Some of the PTSD sufferers were chronic (57 per cent) having symptoms for over a year. These were likely to be women (82 per cent), and had an increased risk of manic episodes and dysthymia. Also they were likely to have pre-existing anxiety or affective disorders, and to have a family history of anxiety, or antisocial behaviour, or early separation.

WHAT CAUSES PTSD?

The medico-legal examiner must be able to identify a causal link between a trauma and subsequent symptomatology. DSM-III-R makes confident statements about particular causes but with little supporting evidence. In DSM-IV PTSD is considered to be caused by a trauma or series of traumas or stressors.

The trauma may be experienced alone (e.g. rape or assault), or in company with others. The trauma can be a natural disaster (flood, earthquake); accidental disaster (car accident, plane crash, large fire, collapse of structure); or deliberately caused disaster (bombing, war, torture, concentration camp experience). An important point to bear in mind is that direct harm to oneself is not a necessary feature, and the medico-legal maze opened up by this possibility is obvious. Watching a loved one or another person being seriously injured, or even threatened with serious injury, i.e. 'confronted', can be a sufficient stressor. The worst case of PTSD seen by the writer was in a woman who watched news bulletins on TV showing her daughter and son-in-law's house (90 miles away) in flames with them and their children in it. There was no doubt that the event, watched on TV had caused the PTSD, but where should a line be drawn? Consider a relative watching the Hillsborough football crowd disaster on TV, subsequently finding out that their family member attending the match was unharmed, yet the TV watcher still presented with PTSD. What caused the PTSD in this case? If it is accepted that just watching unpleasant things on TV can cause PTSD, the civil courts will be flooded with claimants, and the TV companies would screen the blandest of material. Indeed the House of Lords recently excluded compensation from those suffering PTSD following exposure to the Hillsborough disaster only via TV (*Alcock v. Chief Constable of S. Yorkshire* [1991] 3 WLR 1057).

WHO IS MOST AT RISK?

The medico-legal examiner must know the major risk factors for PTSD and related conditions in order to make an informed judgement about the cause of symptomatology. This is a particularly important point as, with the same objective trauma, one person may present with a severe and persistent PTSD (Lyons, 1991), one with a transient minor disturbance, and one with complete normality. Obviously, to be at risk, the person must have been exposed to some traumatic event (Titchener and Kapp, 1976; Levy and Neumann, 1984; McCaughey, 1986). Yet there is huge individual variability in response to a trauma (McFarlane, 1988a, b; Gibbs, 1989; Breslau et al., 1991; Emery et al., 1991; Brooks and McKinlay, 1992), and it is important to try to identify some key predictors of severe and persistent clinical symptomatology. Possible predictors of who will present with a severe and persistent PTSD include:

- Demographic features such as age and gender.

- Nature and closeness of the involvement in a trauma.

- Nature and cognitive appraisal of the trauma.

- Pre-trauma variables.

- Coping strategies, the meaning of the event, and treatment given.

Demographic Features

The features most discussed here are age and gender. Prior to DSM-III-R there had been a tendency to assume that PTSD was essentially an adult disorder. This resulted from a misunderstanding of how distressed children show their distress. It is now well recognised that the disorder can occur at any age, including childhood and adolescence (Terr, 1979; Garmezy and Rutter, 1985; Lyons, 1987; Saigh, 1991). The elderly are a further specific group. In Lockerbie claimants there was no evidence that old age imposes particular additional risks (Brooks and McKinlay, 1992; Livingston et al., 1992) as far as PTSD was concerned, although elderly claimants did have higher questionnaire-measured levels of anxiety (Brooks and McKinlay, 1992). Indeed, in the literature there is a thread that suggests that the elderly may cope better than younger people. In general, age has little specific effect on the likelihood of PTSD, and neither do other demographic variables such as gender, race, marital status, employment status or lower educational level (Madakasura and O'Brien, 1987), although some of these variables (e.g. poor education) may predict a chronic condition (Breslau et al., 1991).

Nature of Involvement in a Disaster

Disaster workers have, until recently, been a neglected group. This is partly because they are thought to be unlikely to claim compensation for psychological harm suffered in the course of their duties, and partly because of a pervasive myth among disaster workers that cool professionalism insulates against distress. To some extent this is true, in that training can increase coping competence. However, denial of distress is a central part of the ethos of workers such as police officers and doctors, and both groups make extensive use of coping mechanisms such as grisly humour. There has been a recent interest in the reactions of disaster workers (Duckworth, 1986; Martin, McKean, and Veltkamp, 1986; Dyregov and Mitchell, 1992), with the following figures emerging for the incidence of PTSD:

- 15 per cent—Bradford police officers involved in the Bradford City fire

- 20 per cent—personnel involved in the recovery, repackaging, and identification of badly damaged bodies (Mt Erebus DC10 crash)

- 26 per cent—police officers exposed to the traumas of routine police work

- 14 per cent—various people involved in an apartment building collapse

- 17 per cent—various workers involved in a tornado

- 30 per cent—firefighters involved in a major Australian bush fire.

Nature of the Stressor

This is a centrally important issue for the medico-legal examiner. A knowledge that, for example, exposure to human remains, or loss of a family member or friend is a potent predictor of psychological symptomatology is of great value in understanding why an individual claimant presents with a specific pattern and severity of symptoms. Within any disaster there are certain features which appear to make the experience worse; for example, clear threat to life, more prolonged exposure, greater proximity (Nader et al., 1990), damage to one's own home (but see Brooks and McKinlay, 1992), loss of friends or family (Brooks and McKinlay, 1992), and exposure to human remains (McFarlane, 1988a, 1989; Brooks and McKinlay, 1992).

Pre-trauma Variables

Some of the clearest work here comes from McFarlane (1988a, b) concerning the effects of a massive bush fire on the firefighters who were themselves at risk as were their homes and families. McFarlane found cases of PTSD, but varying patterns of symptomatology over time. Not everyone who presented with PTSD symptoms initially went on to have a prolonged condition, and of those well shortly after the fire, not all remained well during and after the first year. When he tried to predict who would develop a chronic condition, he found that those with a chronic presentation were more likely to have had before the traumatic event a history of treatment of psychological disorder, a more neurotic personality, and more adverse life events. The 'chronic' cases were therefore already a vulnerable group by virtue of predisposition or experience.

For the medico-legal examiner, the implications of this are obvious. A detailed pre-trauma history must be taken, identifying any pre-trauma psychological symptoms. An examination of the general practitioner records can be very revealing, showing in some cases that the current symptoms are part of a long-standing problem, bearing no relationship to the trauma for which compensation is sought. In other cases there may be a long pre-trauma psychological history, yet in the period immediately preceding the trauma the claimant had been coping well in terms of vocational, social, and family life. Here there is obviously a pre-trauma vulnerability, yet without the trauma (or other negative life event) the claimant would have continued to live a normal life.

TREATMENT

The medico-legal examiner has a responsibility not only to identify the sequelae of an event and to relate these causally to the event, but also to specify the likely prognosis both with, and without treatment. To do this demands a knowledge of the range and effectiveness of the various different treatment approaches. There is a growing literature on treatment coming from a number of distinct sources. The Vietnam experience stimulated much work on the treatment of chronic and severe PTSD, using approaches ranging from discussion groups and self help on the one hand, to medication. (For examples, see the work of Van der Kolk, 1987; Faustman and White, 1989; Fesler, 1991; Davidson, 1992). Other treatments have involved behavioural (Schindler, 1980; Fairbank, DeGood and Jenkins, 1981; Keane and Kaloupek, 1982; McCaffrey and Fairbank, 1985; Saigh, 1986; Shapiro, 1989; McClusky et al., 1991), or cognitive-behavioural principles (Harvey et al., 1991; Kellner, Singh and Irigoyen-Rascon, 1991; Kellner et al., 1992). Psychotherapeutic approaches have been popular in the United States (Lindy et al., 1983; Horowitz, 1986; Benyakar et al., 1989; Brom and Kleber, 1989; Brom, Kleber and Defares, 1989; Kingsbury, 1992). For an excellent overview of different treatment approaches see McFarlane (1989).

The ideal treatment programme has the following elements, although not all would be necessary for all patients:

- Information giving.

- Counselling, support, and formal psychotherapy to deal with the existential challenge resulting from trauma.

- Pharmacology, particularly for agitation, depression and (most important of all) sleep impairment.

- Behavioural and cognitive-behavioural intervention for specific symptoms of PTSD and comorbid conditions.

EXAMINING THE CLAIMANT

The medico-legal examiner of the patient claiming compensation for psychological harm has to complete a number of tasks. The first is to identify the nature, proximity, and degree of exposure to a traumatic event or events, and to use this information together with a knowledge of the literature to evaluate the likely psychological consequences. Indeed, the examiner will be building diagnostic hypotheses about the claimant before he or she is actually examined, based on the known history of exposure. This is good practice provided that the examiner retains a constant open-minded approach, and is able to admit to error.

The second task facing the examiner is to identify the nature, range and severity of current symptomatology, paying particular attention to comorbidity. Diagnoses should be made using DSM-IV, although occasionally the patient will have significant symptoms but not of enough of them, or of insufficient severity to warrant a formal diagnosis. Here the examiner has two choices: the first is to record the diagnosis (e.g. PTSD), but describe it as 'in remission' (if previously, the claimant had a full syndrome); the second choice is to acknowledge that the patient's symptoms do not warrant a full diagnosis, but to highlight their clinical significance (perhaps preventing return to work) and their causal relationship to the trauma. Where suicide is a possibility this should be signalled, and the examiner should record in the report what action has been taken (referring to a further clinician, etc.).

The third task facing the examiner is to make a formulation by relating the current symptoms picture to the trauma, and to what is known about any pre-disaster psychological symptoms, and post-disaster experiences such as other stressors, or access to treatment.

The final task for the examiner is to come to some conclusion about the likely prognosis of any symptoms both with and without treatment, and to deal with the issue of possible increased psychological vulnerability in the future. The PTSD literature shows that pre-disaster unpleasant experiences are a predictor of post-disaster symptoms; so, the trauma for which the claimant is being examined is likely to raise vulnerability for the future, so that a further negative life event could trigger a significant resurgence of psychological symptoms.

The cornerstone of evaluation after trauma is DSM-IV. The DSM-IV criteria supply the core essential features that most clearly differentiate PTSD from other psychiatric conditions, but other phenomena are important also. Many patients with PTSD will also have disabling symptoms of anxiety and depression to a level that warrant separate additional diagnoses. Others may be abusing alcohol or other drugs, and this may supply the basis for a further additional diagnosis. The establishment of the PTSD diagnosis is not the end of the story—it is often just the beginning.

Lyons et al. (1988) propose an ideal model of evaluation of the patient with PTSD which is now being used in many research centres. It is laborious, labour intensive and expensive. Not all patients will need all parts of the evaluation, but it is nevertheless a useful model which includes:

- demographic information

- structured interview

- psychometric assessment

- interviewer ratings

- behavioural observation

- archival data

- collateral information.

Demographic Information

This forms the introductory part of any clinical interview, and serves not only to identify the patient, but also to give a context for the interview (age, marital status, medical, educational, social, occupational history, previous compensation claims). More detailed information about some of these features will be required, and this is detailed later in the discussion.

Structured Interview

No single interview schedule is the best, and many clinicians have constructed their own based on clinical experience, and the research literature. Any structured interview should ask about the pre-traumatic adjustment/coping of the patient, together with an account of childhood/adolescence (problems, pathology, etc.). Performance at work should be evaluated, and the previous medical history should be obtained (see more about this later).

The examiner should identify clearly and completely the nature and duration of the traumatic event suffered by the patient, and the nature, severity, and current status (continuing pain, impairment of mobility, disfigurement, etc.) of any physical injuries sustained in the trauma. As much factual information as possible should be obtained, including diagrams of workplaces, helicopters, oil rigs etc. if that is where the disaster happened. The examiner should obtain relevant medical records, and be alert to the possibility that there may be a significant head injury which could be the cause of some of the symptomatology (memory and concentration impairment, irritability, etc.).

The significance of other factors in the trauma should be assessed: did the person lose family or friends; did he or she lose property; was he or she exposed to human remains; was the person in control of the traumatic situation, or a passive victim; how has the person coped since the event?

The interviewer should then deal specifically with symptomatology. This section of the interview should be conducted by first listening to the patient's spontaneous complaints, only secondly going on to look for specific symptomatology of PTSD and related conditions if this has not emerged already. Not only should the specific PTSD symptoms be sought, but the interviewer should conduct a general mental examination looking for disorders of mood, thinking, perceiving and behaving. This part of the examination will also reveal the presence of any 'associated phenomena' such as depression, anxiety, and substance abuse. The severity and natural history of the symptomatology should be assessed, as should the presence of any triggers. If the patient has periods of subjective well being, it is important to find out what it is that triggers the end of these periods.

The interview may have been designed by an individual examiner, but there are also diagnostic schedules that are being used increasingly. Litz et al. (1992) review a number of schedules including SCID (Structured Clinical Interview for DSM-III-R; Spitzer and Williams, 1985), DIS (Diagnostic Interview Schedule; Robins et al., 1981), and Jackson Interview for Combat-Related PTSD (Keane et al., 1985). As discussed below, none is totally specific to PTSD, but the first two are particularly useful for ensuring that a full examination is carried out, missing no significant psychological symptoms.

Psychometric Assessment

There are as yet no tests specific for PTSD, although these are under development (see Eldridge, 1991; Litz et al., 1992), and the Revised Impact of Event Scale (Horowitz, Wilner and Alvarez, 1979) comes close to being such a test. There are a number of measures of general psychological well being, and of anxiety and depression, and some of these should routinely be used to identify the presence and severity of specific and associated PTSD symptoms. Examples include the General Health Questionnaire (GHQ28; Goldberg and Williams, 1991), and Hospital Anxiety and Depression Scale (Zigmond and Snaith, 1983). These are short, quick to administer, able to be self administered, and often very revealing.

Interviewer Ratings

This is a way of trying to scale the magnitude of the symptomatology. DSM-IV includes a section (Axis V) for assessing the global functioning of the patient, and Lyons et al. (1988) urge that each of the PTSD symptoms should be scored on a 1–5 scale with 1 representing absence of symptoms, and 5 the presence of a symptom to an extreme degree.

Behavioural Observation

This should be a routine part of any evaluation. The patient's behaviour should be observed closely. This will very often reveal depression, agitation, irritability etc. An unwillingness to discuss the trauma, or failure to keep appointments (very common) may indicate the avoidance of relevant situations that is a central feature of PTSD.

History

The medical, social, and educational history has already been referred to. The interviewer should ensure that specific records are obtained. Records from every medical specialist involved with the patient should be scrutinised, and records of promotions etc. at work should be obtained. The general practitioner's records can also be very revealing and these should always be sought, looking for psychological symptomatology in the years before the relevant trauma.

Collateral Information

It is not enough just to interview the patient. Significant others such as family members not directly involved in the trauma should also be interviewed. These can supply vital information about the patient's adjustment, and may reveal the full extent of problems such as aggression or obsessive-compulsive disorder which the patient may have been reluctant to disclose. The patient may be currently receiving treatment from other clinicians, in which case they should be informed about the examination, and asked for a report.

MALINGERING AND EXAGGERATION

Suspicions that the patient may be lying, telling only part of the truth, or magnifying symptoms have been a central issue in PTSD and its early variants (traumatic neurosis, etc.) for many years. A fundamental problem is that the diagnosis relies at least in part upon what the patient says (see Platt and Husband, 1986). It is very difficult to refute a claim of nightmares or persistent re-experiencing. This becomes a particular issue when the severity of the event is in dispute.

A further problem is what Platt and Husband refer to as 'role enactment' (learning what is expected) as the person undergoes the round of medico-legal investigations. As the same questions reappear, the patient may become expert in presenting a black and white picture rather than the more usual clinical grey. Furthermore, as the examination round continues, the patient may report more *post*-traumatic symptomatology, and less *pre*-trauma pathology (previous alcohol consumption, etc.). In effect, the claimant is in a conflict; if the claimant improves clinically, having less symptomatology, he or she will have less of the compensation that would be due because of the presence of symptoms. In fact, clinically, it seems rather rare that claimants opt for symptomatology and maximum compensation rather than for symptom removal (by appropriate treatment) and reduced compensation.

There is in fact, very little experimental work on the characteristics and detection of the malingerer. What there is up to 1981 was reviewed by Trimble

(1981), and later work was reviewed by Resnick (1988). Trimble notes that there are only two situations in which malingering can be diagnosed with certainty. The first is that in which the patient is caught out in *flagrante delicto*, and the second is when the patient confesses. Every clinician will have memories of each occurrence, but the main reason why they are remembered is because of their rarity. Much more common is the situation in which the patient behaves in a way which is inconsistent with the diagnosis or symptom pattern, but in a way which the lay person believes is actually consistent. Resnick, dealing mainly with Vietnam veterans proposed a checklist to evaluate whether faking is likely, although it is difficult to say how good the evidence is to support his views. He suggested that any one of the following could raise suspicion in the examiner's mind: poor work record, prior 'incapacitating' injuries, discrepant capacity for work and recreation, unvarying repetitive dreams (not uncommon in genuine people in the writer's experience), antisocial personality traits, over-idealised functioning before the trauma, evasiveness, and inconsistency in symptom presentation.

Resnick went on to propose a 'clinical decision model' to establish malingering of PTSD comprising the following criteria:

A: Understandable motive to malinger PTSD.

B: At least two of the following criteria: (a) irregular employment or job dissatisfaction; (b) prior claims for injuries; (c) capacity for recreation but not work; (d) no nightmares, or if present, exact repetitions of the trauma; (e) antisocial personality traits; (f) evasiveness or contradictions; (g) nonco-operativeness in the evaluation.

C: Confirmation of malingering by one of the following criteria: (a) admission of malingering; (b) psychometric evidence of malingering or strong corroborative evidence of dissimulation.

Simple faking of symptomatology for monetary gain should disappear shortly after financial settlement. There is not much evidence here, but what there is (Merskey and Woodforde, 1972; Tarsh and Royston, 1985) suggests strongly that this is not the case. In fact most patients who after injury were severely disabled remain the same after settlement.

CONCLUSIONS

After trauma, those exposed are at risk of psychological symptomatology. PTSD is the most frequent syndrome, but depression, other anxiety disorders, substance abuse and obsessive-compulsive disorder will all be found in concert with PTSD. The medico-legal examiner has to identify accurately symptomatology, diagnose it, relate it to the trauma, predict its course, and ensure that the claimant is not exaggerating or lying. This is a difficult task, and it demands a thorough knowledge of the literature, confident experience in the handling and diagnosis of post-traumatic symptomatology, a determination to identify not only current but also pre-trauma symptoms, and a knowledge of who is likely to benefit from which treatment and by how much.

REFERENCES

American Psychiatric Association (1987). *Diagnostic and Statistical Manual of Mental Disorders (Third Edition—Revised)*. Washington, DC: American Psychiatric Association.

American Psychiatric Association (1994). *Diagnostic and Statistical Manual of Mental Disorders (Fourth Edition)*. Washington, DC: American Psychiatric Association.

Benyakar, M., Kutz, I., Dasberg, H. and Stern, M.J. (1989). The collapse of structure: a structural approach to trauma. *Journal of Traumatic Stress*, **2**, 431–50.

Breslau, N. and Davis, G.C. (1992). Post-Traumatic Stress Disorder in an urban population of young adults: risk factors for chronicity. *Archives of General Psychiatry*, **149**, 671–5.

Breslau, N., Davis, G.C., Andreski, P. and Peterson, E. (1991). Traumatic events and Post-Traumatic Stress Disorder in an urban population. *Archives of General Psychiatry*, **48**, 216–22.

Brom, D. and Kleber, R.J. (1989). Prevention of Post-Traumatic Stress Disorders. *Journal of Traumatic Stress*, **2**, 335–51.

Brom, D., Kleber, R.J. and Defares, P.B. (1989). Brief psychotherapy for post-traumatic stress disorders. *Journal of Consulting and Clinical Psychology*, **57**, 607–12.

Brooks, N. and McKinlay, W. (1992). Mental health consequences of the Lockerbie disaster. *Journal of Traumatic Stress*, **5**, 527–44.

Davidson, J. (1992). Drug therapy for post-traumatic stress disorder. *British Journal of Psychiatry*, **160**, 309–14.

Duckworth, D.H. (1986). Psychological problems arising from disaster work. *Stress Medicine*, **2**, 315–23.

Dyregov, A. and Mitchell, J.T. (1992). Work with traumatised children— psychological effects and coping strategies. *Journal of Traumatic Stress*, **5**, 5–18.

Eldridge, G.D. (1991). Contextual issues in the assessment of post-traumatic stress disorder. *Journal of Traumatic Stress*, **4**, 7–23.

Emery, V.O., Emery, P.E., Shama, D.K., Quiana, N.A. and Jassani, A.K. (1991). Predisposing variables in PTSD patients. *Journal of Traumatic Stress*, **4**, 325–43.

Fairbank, J.A., DeGood, D.E. and Jenkins, C.W. (1981). Behavioral treatment of a persistent post-traumatic startle response. *Journal of Behaviour Therapy and Experimental Psychiatry*, **12**, 321–4.

Faustman, W.O. and White, P.A. (1989). Diagnostic and psychopharmacological treatment characteristics of 536 inpatients with Post-Traumatic Stress Disorder. *Journal of Nervous and Mental Disease*, **177**, 154–9.

Fesler, F.A. (1991). Valproate in combat-related Post-Traumatic Stress Disorder. *Journal of Clinical Psychiatry*, **52**, 361–4.

Garmezy, N. and Rutter, M. (1985). *Acute Reactions in Stress, in Child Psychiatry: Modern Approaches* (2nd edn) (Eds M. Rutter and L. Herzov). Oxford: Blackwell Scientific.

Gibbs, M.S. (1989). Factors in the victim that mediate between disaster and psychopathology: a review. *Journal of Traumatic Stress*, **2**, 489–514.

Goldberg, D. and Williams, P. (1991). *A Users Guide to the General Health Questionnaire*. Windsor, Berks: NFER-Nelson.

Harvey, J.H., Orbuch, T.L., Chwalisz, K.D. and Garwood, G. (1991). Coping with sexual assault: the roles of account-making and confiding. *Journal of Traumatic Stress*, **4**, 515–31.

Helzer, J.E., Robins, L.N. and McEvoy, L. (1987). Post-Traumatic Stress Disorder in the general population. *New England Journal of Medicine*, **317**, 1630–4.

Horowitz, M. (1986). *Stress Response Syndromes* (2nd edn). New York: Jason Aronson.

Horowitz, M., Wilner, N. and Alvarez, W. (1979). Impact of Events Scale: a measure of subjective stress. *Psychosomatic Medicine*, **41**, 209–18.

Keane, T.M. and Kaloupek, D.G. (1982). Imaginal flooding in the treatment of a Post-traumatic Stress Disorder. *Journal of Consulting and Clinical Psychology*, **50**, 138–40.

Keane, T.L., Fairbank, J.A., Caddell, J.M., Zimering, R.T. and Bender, M.E. (1985). A behavioural approach to assessing and treating post-traumatic stress disorder in Vietnam veterans. In C.R. Figley (Ed.), *Trauma and its Wake*. New York: Brunner/Mazel, pp. 257–94.

Kellner, R., Singh, G. and Irigoyen-Rascon, F. (1991). Rehearsal in the treatment of recurring nightmares in Post-Traumatic Stress Disorders and Panic Disorder: case histories. *Annals of Clinical Psychiatry*, **3**, 67–71.

Kellner, R., Niedhardt, K.N., Krakow, B. and Pathak, D. (1992). Changes in chronic nightmares after one session of desensitisation or rehearsal instructions. *American Journal of Psychiatry*, **149**, 659–63.

Kingsbury, S.J. (1992). Strategic psychotherapy for trauma: hypnosis and trauma in context. *Journal of Traumatic Stress*, **5**, 85–95.

Kolb, L.C. (1988). A critical survey of hypotheses regarding post traumatic stress disorders in light of recent research findings. *Journal of Traumatic Stress*, **1**, 291–305.

Levy, A. and Neumann, A. (1984). The role of suggestion in the treatment of combat reactions within a specific military installation during the war in Lebanon. *International Journal of Psychiatry and Related Sciences*, **21**, 85–91.

Lindy, J.D., Green, B.L., Grace, M. and Titchener, J. (1983). Psychotherapy with survivors of the Beverly Hills Supper Club fire. *American Journal of Psychotherapy*, 593–610.

Litz, B.T., Penk, W.E., Gerardi, R.J. and Keane, T.M. (1992). Assessment of post-traumatic stress disorder. In P.A. Saigh (Ed.), *Post-traumatic Stress Disorder: A Behavioural Approach to Assessment and Treatment*. Boston, MA: Allyn and Bacon, pp. 50–84.

Livingston, H.M., Livingston, M.G., Brooks, D.N. and McKinlay, W.W. (1992). Elderly survivors of the Lockerbie air disaster. *International Journal of Geriatric Psychiatry*, **7**, 725–9.

Lyons, J.A. (1991). Strategies for assessing the potential for positive adjustment following trauma. *Journal of Traumatic Stress*, **4**, 93–111.

Lyons, J.A., Gerardi, R.J., Wolfe, J. and Keane, T.M. (1988). Multiaxial assessment of PTSD: phenomenological, psychometric and psychophysiological considerations. *Journal of Traumatic Stress*, **1**, 373–94.

Lyons, U.J. (1987). Post traumatic stress disorder in children and adolescents: a review of the literature. *Developmental and Behavioral Paediatrics*, **8**, 349–56.

Madakasura, S. and O'Brien, K. (1987). Acute Post-Traumatic Stress Disorder in victims of natural disaster. *Journal of Nervous and Mental Disease*, **175**, 286–90.

Martin, C.A., McKean, H.E. and Veltkamp, L.J. (1986). Post traumatic stress disorder in police and working with victims: a pilot study. *Journal of Police Science and Administration*, **14**, 98–101.

McCaffrey, R.J. and Fairbank, J.A. (1985). Behavioural assessment and treatment of accident-related Post-traumatic Stress Disorder: two case studies. *Behaviour Therapy*, **16**, 406–16.

McCaughey, B.G. (1986). The psychological symptomatology of a US naval disaster. *Military Medicine*, **151**, 162–5.

McClusky, H.Y., Milby, J.B., Switzer, P.K., Williams, V. and Wooten, V. (1991). Efficacy of behavioural versus Triazolam treatment in persistent sleep-onset insomnia. *American Journal of Psychiatry*, **148**, 121–6.

McFarlane, A. (1988a). The longitudinal course of posttraumatic morbidity: the range of outcomes and their predictors. *Journal of Nervous and Mental Disease*, **176**, 30–9.

McFarlane, A. (1988b). Relationship between psychiatric impairment and a natural disaster: the role of distress. *Psychological Medicine*, **18**, 129–39.

McFarlane, A. (1989). The treatment of post traumatic stress disorder. *British Journal of Medical Psychology*, **62**, 81–90.

Mendelson, G. (1987). The concept of post traumatic stress disorder: a review. *International Journal of Law and Psychiatry*, **10**, 45–62.

Merskey, H. and Woodforde, J.M. (1972). Psychiatric sequelae of minor head injury. *Brain*, **95**, 521–8.

Nader, K., Pynoos, R., Fairbanks, L. and Frederick, C. (1990). Children's PTSD reactions one year after a sniper attack at their school. *American Journal of Psychiatry*, **147**, 1526–30.

Platt, J.J. and Husband, S.D. (1986). Post traumatic disorder in forensic practice. *American Journal of Forensic Psychology*, **4**, 29–56.

Resnick, P.J. (1988). Malingering of post-traumatic disorders. In R. Rogers (Ed.), *Clinical Assessment of Malingering and Deception*. New York: Guilford Press, pp. 84–103.

Robins, L.N., Helzer, J.E., Croughan, J. and Ratcliff, K. (1981). National Institute of Mental Health Diagnostic Interview Schedule. *Archives of General Psychiatry*, **38**, 381–9.

Saigh, P.A. (1986). In vitro flooding in the treatment of a 6-year-old boy's Post-traumatic Stress Disorder. *Behaviour Research and Therapy*, **24**, 685–8.

Saigh, P.A. (1991). The development of Post-Traumatic Stress Disorder following four different types of traumatization. *Behaviour Research and Therapy*, **29**, 213–16.

Schindler, F.E. (1980). Treatment by systematic desensitisation of a recurring nightmare of a real life trauma. *Journal of Behaviour Therapy and Experimental Psychiatry*, **11**, 533–54.

Schlenger, W.E., Kulka, R.A., Fairbank, J.A., Hough, R.L., Jordan, B.H., Marmar, C.R. and Weiss, D.S. (1992). The prevalence of post-traumatic stress disorder in the Vietnam generation: a multimethod multisource assessment of psychiatric disorder. *Journal of Traumatic Stress Studies*, **5**, 333–66.

Shapiro, F. (1989). Eye movement desensitisation: a new treatment for Post-Traumatic Stress Disorder. *Journal of Behaviour Therapy and Experimental Psychiatry,* **20**, 211–17.

Silverman, J.J. (1986). Post traumatic stress disorder. *Advance in Psychosomatic Medicine,* **16**, 115–40.

Spitzer, R.L. and Williams, J.B. (1985). Structured clinical interview for DSM-III. Unpublished manuscript, Biometrics Research Department, New York State Psychiatric Institute, New York.

Tarsh, M.J. and Royston, C. (1985). A follow-up study of accident neurosis. *British Journal of Psychiatry,* 18–25.

Terr, L.C. (1979). Children of Chowchilla: a study of psychic trauma. *Psychoanalytic Study of the Child,* **34**, 547–623.

Titchener, J. and Kapp, F.T. (1976). Family and character change at Buffalo Creek. *American Journal of Psychiatry,* **133**, 295–9.

Trimble, M. (1981). *Post Traumatic Neurosis: From Railway Spine To The Whiplash.* Chichester: John Wiley.

Trimble, M. (1985). Post Traumatic Stress Disorder—history of a concept. In C.R. Figley (Ed.), *Trauma and its Wake: The Study and Treatment of Post-traumatic Stress Disorder.* Brunner Mazel, pp. 5–14.

Van Der Kolk, B.A. (1987). The drug treatment of Post-Traumatic Stress Disorder. *Journal of Affective Disorders,* **13**, 203–13.

Weiss, D.S., Marmar, C.R., Schlenger, W.E., Fairbank, J.A., Jordon, B.H., Hough, R.L. and Kulka, R.A. (1992). The prevalence of lifetime and partial post-traumatic stress disorder in Vietnam theater veterans. *Journal of Traumatic Stress Studies,* **5**, 365–76.

Wilson, J.P. and Raphael, B. (1993). *International Handbook of Traumatic Stress Syndromes.* New York: Plenum.

Zigmond, A.S. and Snaith, R.P. (1983). The hospital anxiety and depression scale. *Acta Psychiatrica Scandinavica,* **67**, 361–70.

Chapter 5.4

Child Custody

Chrissie Verduyn
University Hospital of South Manchester
and
Helen Carlton Smith
Bolton General Hospital

INTRODUCTION

The contribution of child psychology to the understanding of children's development and needs has been considerable. This influence has been reflected in changes in law and, over recent years, in increasing requests for psychologists' expert evidence on the child's best interests. Psychology is not an exact science and its probabilistic and multifactorial explanations can appear unsatisfactory to legal professionals. A strength of psychologists, however, is their ability to identify and elucidate key issues while considering relative uncertainties of outcomes and weighting or prioritising these in order to identify the optimal course of action. In the field of complex decision-making this should be a very positive asset.

The question of who should care for a child and whom the child should see comes under the jurisdiction of the court in two areas. First, in divorce and separation proceedings parents, unable themselves to agree about the residence and contact arrangements in the best interests of the child, require the court's decision. Secondly, in cases of parental abuse or neglect, the courts, in many countries, may make an order regarding the child's future care.

Furthermore, in an increasing minority of cases, it appears that questions of abuse are raised within the context of separation or divorce (King and Trowell, 1992). In both of these areas the governing standard in many countries is 'the best interests of the child'. From the assessing clinician's perspective the issues of 'significant harm to the child' and parental competence, and questions regarding the optimal placement of the child in the immediate or extended family, frequently affect the nature of assessments.

In England and Wales, the Children Act 1989 has drawn together proceedings in each of these areas of civil law. The implications from a psychologist's perspective are identical in any legal system working from the child's interests. The legal system has increasingly addressed issues relating to its own impact on these interests. Under the Children Act 1989 the speed with which decisions are made is directly specified, reducing the effects of prolonged uncertainty and minimising the likelihood of decisions essentially being made because of the length of time a specific arrangement has been in place. Scope for the independent representation of children and parents introduces clarity but may, in some cases, add further to the proliferation of experts when all parties have sought an opinion.

There has been increasing understanding about the child's point of view and about the use of children as witnesses (Spencer and Flin, 1993). Both of these in many countries are now accorded more importance in law. The 'Memorandum of Good Practice' (Home Office and Department of Health, 1992) details requisite standards of interviewing techniques. Materials such as the Child Witness Pack (NSPCC, 1993) assist in preparing children for court.

The Welfare Checklist

The Children Act 1989 summarises the factors to which the English and Welsh Courts must have regard when considering whether to make an order. These are as follows [s.1(3)]:

(a) the ascertainable wishes and feelings of the child concerned (considered in the light of his age and understanding);
(b) his physical, emotional and educational needs;
(c) the likely effect on him of any change in his circumstances;
(d) his age, sex background and any characteristics of his which the court considers relevant;
(e) any harm which he has suffered or is at risk of suffering;
(f) how capable each of his parents, and any other person in relation to whom the court considers the question to be relevant, is of meeting his needs;
(g) the range of powers available to the court under the Act in the proceedings in question.

The Act emphasises partnership with parents when intervening on behalf of the child. Psychologists have experience of such on a day-to-day basis in their clinical work where developing working relationships with parents is frequently essential in effecting change.

The psychologist's view can be considered as an assessment of the child's present mental health and well-being, an opinion on the likely contributory factors from the past, a view to the future outcome and possible ameliorating influences. In all cases of assessment regarding child custody the decision involves identifying what is best for the future. In cases where child protection is involved there is inevitably a consideration of how the past has influenced the present and, as far as parental behaviour is concerned, the extent to which it predicts the future.

PSYCHOLOGY'S CONTRIBUTION TO THE LAW REGARDING CHILDREN'S WELFARE

The Consequences of Child Maltreatment

It is not within the scope of this chapter to consider fully the extensive psychological literature on child maltreatment. Rather the focus will be on dimensions of maltreatment of importance in considering children's needs and the characteristics of children's behaviour which may result from and hence indicate maltreatment.

Awareness of child maltreatment in the form of physical abuse inevitably drew attention to physical injury and bodily survival, to concepts such as 'frozen watchfulness' (Kempe et al., 1962) and to a lesser extent to the emotional trauma of painful events. With developments in knowledge about child sexual abuse there came increased understanding of the significance of emotional sequelae. The effects of chronically distorted relationships within families as well as the effects of specific events became better conceptualised. It is this framework which more recently has informed understanding and practice regarding the psychological consequences of emotional abuse and emotional and physical neglect.

Although some children survive emotionally, it has repeatedly been demonstrated that child maltreatment often has a substantial long-term impact on the psychological well-being of the individual. Briere (1993) described three stages of response to maltreatment— initial reaction to victimisation, accommodation to ongoing abuse, and long-term elaboration with secondary accommodation. Initial reactions include alterations in normal childhood development, distress and poor self-esteem. With continuing abuse, coping mechanisms develop which, although intended to increase safety or decrease pain during victimisation, may be self-destructive. These effects develop and consolidate over the longer term, being compounded by their distorting effects on normal development.

With child maltreatment there is a common theme of serious distortion of the parent–child relationship. There is a complex interaction between the parents' competence, the child's characteristics and vulnerabilities, wider family influences and their socio-economic context (Beslky, 1988).

There are sometimes effects which are specific to the form of maltreatment. Neglected children may show attachment disorders in the form of a lack of reserve with strangers and indiscriminate seeking of affection and approval from adults. Generalised developmental delays, particularly in areas of cognitive and social development in infants may also be present. These children often show an increase in behaviour problems, aggression and school problems.

Children who have been physically abused demonstrate a higher frequency of behaviour problems including non-compliance, temper tantrums, poor empathy and school-related difficulties (Lamphear, 1985). It is a consistent finding that abused children have a more negative self-concept and greater problems in social interaction than non-abused children. These difficulties are likely to continue to impair the child's emotional and social development in the long term as they often result in restriction of the child's experience.

Children who have been sexually abused may show behaviours resulting from their premature sexualisation such as seeking out sexual stimulation either from themselves or others. There are multiple emotional, cognitive and behavioural effects and these often persist (Finkelhor and Browne, 1985). Immediate effects may include re-enacting aspects of the abuse in play, inappropriate sexual behaviour, nightmares, and fearful or avoidant responses to stimuli associated with abuse. The long-term consequences of abuse are more severe the longer the period of time and the more extensive the abuse (particularly if penetration has occurred, Bagley and Ramsay, 1986).

There are considerable effects on self-esteem. Re-experiencing the abuse in the form of intrusive thoughts and flashbacks may continue for many years, including sexual preoccupations and sexually inappropriate behaviour with other children and adults. Severely abused girls tend to show passivity or engage in self-harming behaviour, whereas boys are more likely to be aggressive and hostile and are more likely to re-enact abuse (Bentovim, 1991a). The strategies used by the perpetrator to avoid discovery may include inducing guilt in the victim. This may be exacerbated by the family's response at disclosure. Belief by the carer of the child's statements and a supportive response appears to be a protective factor to the child in the longer term and increases the likelihood of full disclosure by the child to child protection authorities (Lawson and Chaffin, 1992). Frequently the emotional impact on the individual is amplified by the consequences of family breakdown.

Maltreatment commonly occurs in families in more than one of the defined areas of physical and sexual abuse and physical and emotional neglect (Lynch, 1988). Some children appear superficially unaffected but may later show signs of psychological difficulties. When indicators of behavioural and emotional disturbance are present, careful assessment is required to understand the possible process of development of the problem or difficulties, considering the extent to which these might involve non-abusive processes or temperamental or other characteristics of the child.

When children present with behavioural disturbances that might or might not be indicative of abusive experiences further understanding of their presentation is required. The training of clinical psychologists is underpinned by good theoretical knowledge of the processes involved in the development and maintenance of behaviour, including the extent to which it is likely to occur in specific contexts. Experienced clinicians are, therefore, skilled in the observation and interpretation of a child's experience and can comment on whether or not any account given is consistent with the child's behavioural presentation.

Effects of Parental Separation and Divorce

Separation and divorce of parents is a common experience of children in Western society. In the UK at least one in five children experience this before the age of 16 (OPCS, 1988). Of these a significant proportion will lose contact with one parent, usually their father. Up to a third are likely to experience the remarriage of one or both parents within two and a half years (Central Statistical Office, 1988). However, divorce should not be seen as a single event but part of a process which may have followed long-term marital discord. Parents may continue to suffer months or years of emotional disturbance, continuing discord with their ex-spouse, a change in standard of living, and further partnerships involving the challenge of step-parenting. For children there is likely to be a continuous process of change and adaptation as their parents make their own emotional adjustment. These factors need to be taken into account in considering children's problems following divorce (Sales, Manber and Rohman, 1992).

The major, large-scale controlled prospective studies of the effects of parental divorce on children show very similar results (Hetherington, Cox and Cox, 1982; Wallerstein and Kelly, 1980). In the period immediately following separation there is a marked increase in emotional and behavioural disturbance, with reactions varying according to age. Preschool children tend to regress behaviourally and show significant anxiety at times of separation from both parents. These features are often interpreted by parents as indicative of the child being upset by contact itself rather than as representing an emotional reaction to the parents' separation.

Children early in the school years may be depressed, preoccupied with the parent's departure and experience this as rejection. Conflicts of loyalty are common with boys, in particular, likely to be angry with their mothers whom they blame for the loss of their fathers. Children in early adolescence are more likely to perceive one parent as responsible and take sides, becoming intensely angry with one or both parents. Both of these older groups (i.e. children of school age) may be very aware of, and sensitive to, the parents possibly replacing the lost spouse and tend to show a decline in school performance. Parents in conflict with one another are likely to interpret any change in their child's behaviour as a sign of disturbance for which the other party is responsible.

Most children show good recovery within a few months from the intensity of the initial reactions but long-term follow up studies show, for some, continuing disturbance persisting up to ten years after the parental separation. In general, the older the children at the time of separation the more likely they are to show persisting difficulties.

With time there is a change in the types of difficulties experienced by children and in the behavioural manifestation. Boys have a tendency to be more seriously affected by parental divorce than are girls, a gender difference which persists into adulthood. Boys are more likely to manifest disturbance by antisocial behaviour; girls by exhibiting depressed or withdrawn behaviour. There is some evidence that children benefit from living with the same-sex parent although the data are insufficient to provide a basis for active promotion of this practice and are likely to be mediated by factors more complex than gender alone.

There is little research on the effects of remarriage and on the difficult task of raising another person's child. Remarriage often alleviates the economic and social problems created by divorce. The progress of children in step-families appears very similar to that in two natural parent families. However, problems may result from confusion in roles and relationships between step-parents and children, and lack of realistic expectations. Difficult parent–child relationships and sibling conflict are more common in step-families (Ferri, 1984).

Factors that have been shown to be consistently associated with children's satisfactory adjustment relate to the parents' management of the divorce process. Children are rarely informed about the possibility of separation and divorce, and parents appear to feel that the less said the better, but several research studies demonstrate that more open communication with the child is associated with good adjustment (De'Ath, 1989). Children want and need information to make sense of their situation and come to terms with change. They will inevitably be distressed and this should be acknowledged and supported. Also of importance is: (i) each parent supporting the other's relationship with the children, (ii) a continuing good relationship of the child with at least one parent, and (iii) satisfaction with residence and contact arrangements (Herbert, 1993).

The change in emphasis in law from concepts such as 'fitness to parent' to the 'child's best interest' is to be welcomed. The Children Act 1989 consolidated this by defining continuing parental responsibility by both parents as central, and emphasised the importance of negotiated agreements by the 'no order' rule. Many parents will require access to conciliation services to enable them to focus on their children's needs during the divorce period.

The extensive literature briefly described above demonstrates the complexity of the inter-relationship of variables related to children's post-divorce adjustment. Misapprehensions of the causes of children's disturbed behaviour may fuel parental conflict or mislead decision-making. Those involved in the legal process should receive continuing education about results of research to help them act preventatively and protect children's interests. Conciliation or mediation procedures typically involve many of the skills in uncovering underlying issues, managing conflict, and problem-solving used by psychological therapists (Scott and Emery, 1987).

Children's Responses to Uncertainty and Change

Throughout this chapter, emphasis has been placed on the importance of viewing issues related to child custody as involving a range of processes to which the child must adjust. The decision-making process inevitably involves delay, although the Children Act 1989 explicitly seeks to limit this. Uncertainty is inevitably a consequence in the short term at least. This places stress both on the adults and the children involved. A problem of assessment may involve separating out transitory reactions to uncertainty from more persistent emotional or behavioural disturbance. Information from adults who know the child well is essential in defining changes in children's behaviour in response to events. However, if adults are parties in legal proceedings the information they provide may need to be interpreted with caution. The adversarial nature of proceedings may promote differing interpretations (at best) or attempts to colour the picture (at worst) which may make assessment more difficult. Angry or distressed parents are more likely to misinterpret and misattribute behaviour problems in their children.

The response of the preschool child to change or disruption is generally one of regression to more infantile behaviours. This may include an increase in tantrums as well as behaviours such as clinginess which are more obviously emotional in origin. Older children will have greater understanding of legal processes, but their superficial sophistication may conceal considerable anxiety and irrational fears about likely outcomes. Stress-related behaviours in this age group include bed-wetting, sleep disturbance and impaired concentration on school work. The cognitive development of adolescents allows for an understanding of events similar to that of adults, but their emotional reactions are likely to impair behaviour based on reason alone. Acting out or antisocial behaviour may be a response, as may misery and withdrawal.

Children and adolescents with pre-existing emotional or behavioural problems are more vulnerable and are likely to show an exacerbation of difficulties. Stability of some aspects of the child's life and relationships, predictability and routine are protective factors. Open communication, considering the child's ability to understand, and thorough preparation for assessments, meetings and other events involved in legal procedures will also facilitate optimal coping.

Adoption

A sizeable psychological literature involving adoption arose from the 'genetics versus environment' debate in relation to the development of intelligence, of various personality traits and of problem behaviours. Theorists on processes of attachment and bonding have explored variables of more direct relevance to professionals concerned with placement of children in substitute care. However, generalisations from research are invariably limited in their applicability by changes in social policy which have increasingly promoted adoption for children of all ages, including those with special needs. Only very recently has research examined longer-term outcomes for these children.

It is widely accepted that children who cannot remain with their birth parents or cannot be returned to them because of the continuing risk of harm, are best placed (with only a few exceptions) in permanent alternative family care. Adoption has been seen as one way of promoting children's development by removal from an adverse environment and placing in families thought likely to advance their intellectual, social and emotional development.

There have been marked changes in adoption practice over the past 25 years, with a drop in the number of adoptions since 1968, an increase in adoption by step-parents, a general decline in the proportion of children adopted under two years of age and an increase for children aged ten years and over. Some authorities have emphasised the hazards of using adoption as the major method of permanency planning for children (King and Trowell, 1992). The Children Act 1989, with its emphasis on the natural family, should allow for a wider range of options than adoption of children without their parents' consent or complete loss of contact with their family of origin. Problems remain with finding families prepared to adopt on a more open basis. In England and Wales the Government's 1993 proposals for adoption practice include criteria for consideration of prospective adopters specifically in relation to age and race.

Studies of adoption outcome show that most adopted children are well within the normal range in behavioural and emotional adjustment, and in academic attainment. Only minor differences are shown between early adopted and 'control' children, and even older children can be successfully adopted (Hersov, 1990). However, adopted children constitute a heterogeneous group and for the minority, where significant psychological disorder develops, the full range of contributory factors should be assessed for each individual, as for any child. However, over-representation of adopted children among psychiatric clinic attenders has consistently been demonstrated (Hersov, 1990). For children and their adoptive families, where problems arise the psychological meaning of adoption and attendant expectations and attributions are often crucial in determining the survival of the family.

Professional workers in adoption have long regarded communication in the family about the child's adoptive status as crucial; both as an indicator of the parents' adjustment to their role and because it allows the child to accommodate to the knowledge over time and avoid the risks of attempted secrecy. Children's understanding of adoption develops with age (Brodzinsky, 1987). By six years of age most children differentiate meaningfully between birth and adoption and appreciate the permanence of adoptive relationships. This understanding develops further between eight and eleven years, although greater knowledge may give rise to anxiety about permanence. The vulnerability of this period is confirmed by identification of disturbance in some longitudinal studies (Lambert and Streather, 1980). In the teenage years, uncertainty diminishes and the legal process is recognised and understood. It has been found that adoptive parents often overestimate children's knowledge and assume unrealistically that this means that there is no continuing need for discussion. This aspect should be stressed in advice to parents as possibly preventing later problems (Hersov, 1990).

Many studies have shown that the likelihood of adoption disruption increases with age at adoption (Barth and Berry, 1988). Other features increasing risk are previous adoptive placement, existing problems with behaviour or relationships, and the presence of natural children of the adoptive parents of a similar age. There is a greater possibility of breakdown the longer the period of disrupted attachments and the larger the number of carers that the child has had. Sibling adoptive placements in homes with no other children seem to reduce risk. Contact, not necessarily face to face, with the child's family of origin is linked to better outcome but is often a problem for adoptive parents (Fratter et al., 1991). Children in disrupted placements are more likely to show high levels of antisocial behaviour and show less positive increases in parent–child relationship over time compared to children in successful placements (Barth et al., 1986).

The outcome in adoption results from complex factors involving child and adoptive parent characteristics and adoption practice variables. Research which informs current practice is limited, partly as a result of the rate of change of adoption practice and as a result of difficulties in longitudinal research. There is increasing understanding of problems with inter-country adoption (Tizard, 1991). Knowledge of this field is of great importance in balancing the risks of various types of placement for children in need.

THE PROCESS OF PSYCHOLOGICAL ASSESSMENT FOR COURT

The process of assessment is guided by the questions asked in relation to the child and family. In practice it is common for the request to be that a psychological assessment is undertaken, leaving the psychologist to apply guesswork regarding the lawyer's or court's reasons for this. It is not surprising that this hit-and-miss approach results in reports which are unhelpful to the key issues in a case. Equally, reports may be requested in the interests of comprehensive assessment when the child's psychological well-being is not at question or when other reports cover this area quite adequately. On occasions, particularly in divorce proceedings, it may be the psychologist's expert status rather than expertise which is being sought and many courts are, quite appropriately, resistant to this.

Good communication between lawyers and psychologists, which provides opportunity to discuss the details of cases prior to referral, can be effective in enabling psychological questions to be framed in a way that truly assists decision-making.

In the following section, the process of assessment is discussed in relation to a range of questions commonly asked. Frequently an assessment will involve addressing several of these.

What is the Child's Point of View?

The welfare checklist (Children Act 1989) defines the 'ascertainable wishes and feelings of the child' as first in the series of factors to be considered by the court, 'in the light of his age and understanding'. The latter variables are of vital importance, but because the decisions concerned inevitably are likely to be of considerable emotional significance, other factors need to be taken into account in assessment.

The age of the child is only a rough guide to his/her competence. Children may perceive the situation in ways different from the adults concerned, and hence their 'understanding' may require clarification. For instance, in contested divorce proceedings three children aged 12, 9 and 5 years were cared for by their mother, with their father seeking a residence order. The eldest child, a girl, expressed the clear wish to live with her father, the nine-year-old appeared to do so less firmly, and the youngest to live with her mother. The eldest child was seen as exerting a very strong influence on the wishes of the younger two. Over several sessions it became clear that the older girl correctly identified her father's failure to come to terms with the end of the marriage and hence, wanting to live with both parents, 'understood' that living with her father was most likely to effect reconciliation between the parents thus furthering her 'true' wish.

Assessing the child's understanding of the situation is a vital first step. Methods include interviewing, but observation, 'listening' through play, and other forms of non-verbal communication are important. Verbal report can be misleading —children may say what they guess adults want to hear, misunderstand questions or simply not know. The context of interview is important, particularly the presence or absence of significant adults. Children are likely to experience difficulty in answering questions that are not specific and are susceptible to being led (Spencer and Flin, 1993). If the child expresses specific wishes it is important to consider the stability of these over time and context, and to recognise that children may have difficulty in expressing ambivalence verbally. Adults must also be prepared to accept that children may not wish what is desired on their behalf.

What are the Child's Relationships Within the Family?

Where decisions regarding children's residence are to be made, questions commonly involve assessment of the quality of the child's relationships with parents, siblings and members of the extended family. Placements with siblings have been shown in a variety of contexts to protect against placement breakdown. Despite this, it is not unusual in practice to discover attitudes of professionals in favour of placing siblings apart, with an older child who has adopted a parental role being viewed as likely to benefit from separate placement. Increasingly grandparents or other members of the extended family are viewed as potential substitute carers where there is parenting breakdown. There is evidence that this is linked to better long-term outcome for the child (Rowe et al., 1984).

Questions regarding residence are commonly asked in terms of attachment. Assessment of the individual child in isolation can rarely provide sufficient information regarding quality of relationships. The child should also be observed with other family members and, particularly with younger children, details should be obtained from a range of adults regarding the child's behaviour.

Simplistic notions of attachment tend to prevail. It is only under very unusual circumstances that children have no attachment to their parents or other family members. They may remain attached and express a wish to live with severely abusive or neglectful parents. Attachment is not an all-or-none phenomenon and the quality of the attachment, particularly the child's sense of security within it, is an important factor in his or her future emotional adjustment. In older children the sense of an attachment may well survive despite years of separation from the parent or carer concerned, at times detrimentally affecting their ability to form other attachments.

In assessing quality of attachment the psychologist will observe or enquire about a range of behaviours and pay particular attention to the context in which they occur. These observations are likely to include the child's behaviour at times of meeting and separation, talk about the parents in their absence, proximity-seeking during contact visits, from whom the child seeks help, and behavioural indicators of emotional distress when away from parents. These accounts will be considered both in the light of the child's age and general level of adjustment and with regard to the context from which the information is obtained.

Presence of a specific attachment behaviour is significant but often its absence must be interpreted with caution. Children who do not rush to greet a parent on first sight after separation may be in effect signalling their anger at the parent's apparent rejection of them. Detachment can be a consequence of separation over a prolonged period and in the parent's presence over time the child may become increasingly responsive.

Psychologists discriminate between secure and insecure attachment. Clear signs of attachment to substitute carers do not necessarily imply any change in attachment to parents. Particularly when there is a familiar routine of contact, absence of distress at separation may indicate the child's sense of security in the parent. Securely attached children show much distress at separation from their parents but have the ability to form a new attachment after mourning. An insecurely attached child may show little response at separation and seem to attach to a new carer with ease. In the longer term patterns of behaviour from previous relationships are likely to recur including provoking aggression, sexualisation and inability to develop from the superficial to a more meaningful relationship.

The child's attachment to a parent is one facet of a complex interaction between parent and child in which the parent's role must be fully assessed. This is further considered below.

The interrelationships of siblings are complex. In families where parenting is inadequate or where the children have been a focus of marital discord the parents' behaviour and attitudes will have influenced the children's relationships. There may possibly be high levels of competition between siblings, scapegoating of one child or conversely development of mutually supportive pseudo parental relationships which exclude adults. An older child's care for a younger sibling may have provided a valuable source of self-esteem but then challenge the efforts of substitute carers. The presence of strong emotional bonds between siblings, whether positive or negative, cannot be ignored and avoidance of problems, by separation of the siblings, will not necessarily resolve the issues which may subsequently be reflected in other relationships.

The role of extended family members in the substitute care of children must inevitably pose problems in a wider sense because of potential conflicts of loyalty between family members. The Children Act emphasises the importance of the extended family, members of which can be invaluable particularly when there are good existing relationships or prior involvement in routines. In terms of assessment of children's relationships there are similar principles to those used to guide assessment of parents' relationships. Information will need to be sought regarding previous contact within the family and the specificity of contact to each child.

Has the Child Suffered Significant Harm?

The concept of 'harm' is defined in the Children Act, 1989 as 'ill-treatment of the impairment of health or development' (s. 31(9)). Ill-treatment includes physical, sexual or emotional abuse. Impairment of health or development must be 'compared with what could reasonably be expected of a similar child' (s. 31(10)). Whatever the nature of the harm, the court has to consider whether the harm is significant and whether the child is suffering harm currently or is likely to suffer it. The court has also to be satisfied that the harm is attributable to the care given, or likely to be given, to the child and that this care is different from 'what it would be reasonable to expect a parent to give'.

Significant harm includes major long-term effects on all aspects of the child's development and functioning—behavioural, social-emotional and cognitive as well as on physical development, growth and health. It is not only the stressful events of abuse that are harmful, but the family context in which they occur (Bentovim, 1991b).

Psychological assessment of the child (as we describe in Chapter 2.4) considers the child's current level of functioning in terms of cognitive skills and general development, behaviour, emotional life, family and group relationships, and educational attainments. Impairments, difficulties or problems presented in specific areas of function are identified. Information is gathered from parents, other carers, school staff and other professionals as appropriate. Observational and interview methods are used.

A formulation of the child's present psychological status is made which describes background factors, causal factors to any problem, and any features of the child's experience which may be contributing to maintenance of difficulties or problems. Background factors may include any special needs, illnesses, events or temperamental features which may have increased the child's vulnerability. In addition, an anticipated outcome and possible variables influencing this, such as specific intervention, will be outlined. The extent to which parental behaviour has contributed to the child's present functioning will be considered in the context of causal and/or maintaining factors in any problems or difficulties.

Are the Child's Parents 'Good Enough'?

Assessment of parents' capacities to bring up children is likely to be a feature of assessing significant harm to their child. The question must be addressed to a specific child or children. This is of particular importance if a child's level of special need is such that he or she requires a high level of skill in parenting. This may result, for instance, from chronic insecure attachments leading to challenging and active behaviour requiring positive control and consistency, or from intellectual impairment requiring high levels of stimulation and nurturance to promote 'normal' development.

Various checklists have been published identifying features of 'good enough' parenting; with key features including provision of adequate nurturance and care, security and safety, affection, stimulation and encouragement of learning, socialisation and self actualisation of children (Department of Health, 1988). The parents' own personal histories and childhood experiences in their families of origin will be considered in the assessment as likely to provide clues to the basis of strengths and weaknesses in parenting. There will be assessment of the quality of supports available to the parents, both from each other and within the extended family. The relationship of parents as partners in rearing the children will be considered—particularly in terms of shared understanding of the tasks involved, mutual support and general quality of relationship in terms of problem-solving, negotiation, conflict resolution and commitment.

The parents' understanding of the child's needs will be assessed, both in general terms and in relation to any specific problems that the child has experienced. Assessment of parent–child relationships is likely to include observation of their interactions. Responsiveness of the parent to the child, ability to control the child's behaviour, ability to play or provide stimulation for the child, and enjoyment of interactions are features of parental behaviour which are likely to be considered.

Is There Potential for Change to Improve Conditions for the Child Suffering Sigificant Harm?

This question involves consideration of three dimensions of the change process. Is an effective intervention known for the identified problem? Is this family likely to respond to the known intervention? Is any change likely to take place in the time period required for the child's normal development?

Intervention methods are generally based on individual problems identified rather than focusing specifically on maltreatment, although those factors most central to possible abuse are key areas for work. Any of the psychological approaches discussed in Chapter 2.4 may be applied in principle. Large-scale outcome studies of interventions with abusing families are prone to considerable methodological difficulty because of the problems in selection, in the diversity of such families, and in difficulties in assessing change. Several projects have used behavioural counselling focused on parenting skills. However, there are consistent problems in recruiting families, securing their co-operation, and preventing high levels of drop-out (Cohn and Daro, 1987).

Severe types of sexual abuse are consistently reported as resistant to treatment particularly when there is denial of the offence or of responsibility on the part of the perpetrator (Pithers et al., 1989).

Predictions about potential for change are very likely to rely on assessment of the individual family's response. Despite the fantasies of the lay public, psychologists are not able to work with unconscious processes such that change can occur without the active involvement of the individual concerned. Individuals are not infrequently referred through the legal process when there has been no acceptance by that individual of either a need for help or a need for change, nor acknowledgement of any responsibility for the current situation. These are essential prerequisites and almost invariably need to be present at the time of referral. It is extremely unlikely that attributions such as these will develop during the process of psychological assessment. While it is not essential that a parent describes a problem in similar terms to that used by the professionals involved, some acknowledgement of a problem and motivation of that individual to change is essential. Lack of acknowledgement can cause serious problems for children during contact in any future alternative family placement.

Further considerations include the previous attempts at change and their effectiveness. Possibly the present situation is different in a way that might facilitate change now. Openness and co-operation with professionals is also necessary. During the process of assessment tasks may be set to establish the level of understanding and commitment, to establish preliminary changes, and to obtain information on the potential of the parents to reflect on the content of a session prior to the next session. Another important variable in predicting change is the level of family organisation. Parents with minimal routines and structure to relationships are unlikely to be able to respond to advice or attend sessions with required consistency, however willing.

Ability to understand and comply with the processes of intervention may be impaired by generally low intellectual ability, personality variables such as a highly passive approach, mental illness or substance abuse. Any successful intervention which involves work with the child alone must have a supportive stable home environment as an essential pre-requisite.

PSYCHOLOGISTS' CONTRIBUTION TO THE DECISION-MAKING PROCESS

In simple terms, the outcome of psychological assessment will be an opinion on the child's present level of development and adjustment with a statement of the child's future needs. As part of the assessment the psychologist will have generated further evidence for the court's consideration in relation to the child's view, and information from parents and professionals involved with the child, as well as providing a developmental perspective and theoretical framework to the issues.

An opinion is likely to be provided on the likelihood of various custody/living arrangements meeting these needs, whether at present or in the future. Prediction involves risk. In almost all disputes involving child custody the decision-making process involves weighing-up the possible outcomes in the child's long-term interests and may include balancing short-term and long-term outcomes—for instance, the short-term effects of contact with father now and family disruption as a consequence against the long-term consequences of less contact with father. Pragmatic considerations are involved—for instance the likelihood of finding adopters who will accept continuing contact with the child's mother.

A further approach may involve the assessment process continuing through the monitoring and evaluation of a trial period of intervention—for instance supervised contact in divorce or family centre input for an abusing family. The factor of time may be of importance in balancing risks of intervention. Although the notion of critical periods in attachment has received much criticism (Herbert, Sluckin and Sluckin, 1983) this has related to its overspecificity in defining 'critical period'. Young children require stability of carers over time. Regular changes of carer are damaging to emotional development. Hence, failed attempts of rehabilitation may be abusive because the resultant delay in finding a long-term placement impairs the possibility of that child forming new attachments. There is evidence that a single breakdown of foster placement is sufficient to discriminate between unsuccessful and successful adjustment of children in care (Berridge and Cleaver, 1987). There is strong evidence that maintenance of contact has a protective value (Fratter et al., 1991). Increasingly in adoptive placements contact is being maintained with grandparents, siblings or the key family members.

PROFESSIONAL ISSUES

A number of issues arise for psychologists and lawyers as a result of increased requests for psychological opinions. First, there are too few psychologists working with children to meet the potential demand for assessments in England and Wales. Understanding of the requirements of assessments for court will require advanced training on the part of the psychologist. The emphasis in training should be on producing good-quality reports oriented to assist the courts in formulating appropriate questions, answers to which will promote decision-making in the child's best interests. Training in court craft is a secondary aspect, although clearly any anxiety-reducing strategy is likely to make the psychologist feel and possibly perform better. If the psychologist is to act on the child's behalf it is of considerable importance that his or her own professional standing is acceptable to the court. The psychologist may need to clarify the nature of his or her expertise such that the court can accept that this does not rely solely on the number of very similar cases he or she has previously assessed.

As the use of psychologists' opinions has increased the potential devaluation of others' expertise in matters relating to children becomes a risk. Health visitors, social workers and teachers are very familiar with the development and behaviour of normal children. It is therefore only rarely necessary to have a psychologist establish the satisfactory nature of a child's emotional and behavioural well-being. As with other expert witnesses, issues of conflicting opinions between psychologists instructed by different parties may arise. In issues concerned with child care and custody there is a case for using one, or at most two, experts, agreed on by all parties, and for psychologists to be formally instructed by the child's legal representative.

A further concern arising from the shortage of psychologists is the need to consider what future options a child may have for intervention. It may be useful for lawyers to consider using psychologists from neighbouring areas. If the child subsequently requires referral to the local child psychologist, this might not later be acceptable to parents when an opinion unfavourable to them had been previously expressed by that same individual.

REFERENCES

Bagley, C. and Ramsay, R. (1986). Disrupted childhood and vulnerability to sexual assault: long term sequelae with implications for counselling. *Social Work and Human Sexuality*, **4**, 33–48.

Barth, R.P. and Berry, M. (1988). *Adoption and Disruption Risks and Responses*. New York: Aldine de Gruyter.

Barth, R.P., Berry, M., Carson, M.I., Goodfield, R. and Feinberg, B. (1986). Contributions to disruption and dissolution of older-child adoptions. *Child Welfare*, **65**, 359–71.

Bentovim, A. (1991a). Clinical work with families in which sexual abuse has occurred. In C.R. Hollin and K. Howells (Eds), *Clinical Approaches to Sex Offenders and their Victims*. Chichester: John Wiley.

Bentovim, A. (1991b). Significant harm in context. In M. Adcock, R. White and A. Hollows (Eds), *Significant Harm*. Croydon: Significant Publications.

Berridge, D. and Cleaver, M. (1987). Research into fostering breakdown. *Adoption and Fostering*, **10**, 4–5.

Beslky, J. (1988). Child maltreatment and the emergent family system. In K. Browne, C Davies and P Stratton (Eds), *Early Prediction and Prevention of Child Abuse*. Chichester: John Wiley.

Briere, J.N. (1993). *Child Abuse Trauma*. London: Sage.

Brodzinsky, D.M. (1987). Adjustment to adoption: a psychological perspective. *Clinical Psychology Review*, **7**, 25–47.

Central Statistical Office (1988). *Social Trends No. 18*. London: HMSO.

Cohn, A. and Daro, D. (1987). Is treatment too late: what 10 years of evaluative research tells us! *Child Abuse and Neglect*, **11**, 433–42.

De'Ath, E. (1989). Families and children. In B. Kahan (Ed.), *Child Care Research, Policy and Practice*. London: Hodder & Stoughton.

Department of Health (1988). *Protecting Children, A Guide for Social Workers Undertaking a Comprehensive Assessment*. London: HMSO.

Ferri, D. (1984). *Stepchildren: A National Study*. London: NFER-Nelson.

Finkelhor, D. and Browne, A. (1985). The traumatic impact of child sexual abuse: a conceptualisation. *American Journal of Orthopsychiatry*, **55**, 530–41.

Fratter, J., Rowe, J., Sapsford, D. and Thoburn, J. (1991). *Permanent Family Placement—A Decade of Experience*. Batsford: British Agencies for Adoption and Fostering.

Herbert, M. (1993). *Working with Children and the Children Act*. Leicester: BPS Books.

Herbert, M., Sluckin, A. and Sluckin, N. (1983). *Maternal Bonding*. Oxford: Blackwell.

Hersov, L. (1990). Aspects of adoption. *Journal of Child Psychology and Psychiatry*, **31**, 493–510.

Hetherington, E.M., Cox, M. and Cox, R. (1982). Effects of divorce on parents and children. In Lamb M.E. (Ed.), *Non-traditional Families*. Hillside, NJ: Lawrence Erlbaum.

Home Office and Department of Health (1992). *Memorandum of Good Practice on Video Recorded Interviews with Child Witnesses for Criminal Proceedings*. London: HMSO.

Kempe, C.H., Silverman, F.N., Steele, B.F., Droegemuller, W. and Silver, H.K. (1962). The battered child syndrome. *Journal of the American Medical Association*, **181**, 17–24.

King, M. and Trowell, J. (1992). *Children's Welfare and the Law. The Limits of Legal Intervention*. London: Sage.

Lambert, L. and Streather, J. (1980). *Children in Changing Families: A Study of Adoption and Illegitimacy*. London: Macmillan.

Lamphear, V.S. (1985). The impact of maltreatment on children's psychological adjustment: a review of the research. *Child Abuse and Neglect*, **9**, 251–63.

Lawson, L. and Chaffin, M. (1992). False negatives in sexual abuse disclosure interviews. *Journal of Interpersonal Violence*, **7**, 532–42.

Lynch, M. (1988). The consequences of child abuse. In K. Browne, C. Davies and P. Stratton (Eds), *Early Prediction and Prevention of Child Abuse*. Chichester: John Wiley.

Office of Population Censuses and Surveys (1988). General household survey, 1987 OPCS.

Pithers, W., Beal, L., Armstrong, J. and Pretty, J. (1989). Identifying risk factors through clinical interviews and analysis of records. In Laws, R. (Ed.), *Relapse Prevention with Sex Offenders*. New York: Guilford.

NSPCC (1993). The child witness pack (obtainable from NSPCC, 67 Saffron Hill, London, EC1N 8RS), UK.

Rowe, J., Cain, H., Hundleby, M. and Keane, A. (1984). *Long Term Foster Care*. Batsford: British Agencies for Adoption and Fostering.

Sales, B., Manber, R. and Rohman, L. (1992). Social science research and child-custody decision making. *Applied and Preventative Psychology*, **1**, 23–40.

Scott, E.S. and Emery, R. (1987). Child custody dispute resolution: the adversarial system and divorce mediation. In Weithorn L.A. (Ed.), *Psychology and Child Custody Determinations*. Lincoln: University of Nebraska Press.

Spencer, J.R. and Flin, R. (1993). *The Evidence of Children* (2nd edn). London: Blackstone.

Tizard, B. (1991). Intercountry adoption: a view of the evidence. *Journal of Child Psychology and Psychiatry*, **32**, 743–56.

Wallerstein, J.S. and Kelly, J.B. (1980). *Surviving the Break-up: How Children and Parents Cope with Divorce*. London: Grant McIntyre.

Chapter 5.5

Dangerousness and Risk

Christopher D. Webster
Simon Fraser University
R.J. Menzies
Simon Fraser University
and
S.D. Hart
Simon Fraser University

Psychologists assess dangerousness and risk of violence as a matter of routine. Decisions about these two related constructs are rendered at several points in the mental health and criminal justice systems (see Shah, 1978; Monahan, 1981). There are different opinions as to whether psychologists and other mental health workers should attempt this task. Some would have it that, given the weight of the largely negative scientific evidence, psychologists and psychiatrists should have no place in the making of such predictions (e.g. Stone, 1985; Faust and Ziskin, 1988). Others think that, granted appropriate guidelines and safeguards (American Psychological Association, 1992), there is not only reason for them to execute this function (Greenland, 1985) but a positive obligation to be of help to society in this respect (Dietz, 1985; Grisso and Applebaum, 1992). In this chapter we take the pragmatic view that courts (Freeman, 1990), review boards (Hodgins, Webster and Paquet, 1991), and tribunals (Pickersgill, 1990) are not going to cease asking for psychological assessments of dangerousness and risk (see Webster, Harris et al., 1994, ch. 2), and that, this being the case, it is timely here to publish a new account of 'the prediction problem'. This task was attempted handsomely in 1981 by Monahan and has subsequently been revisited by Mulvey and Lidz (1984), Webster and Menzies (1987), Prins (1990), Otto (1992) and Steadman et al. (1993). Our aims are to present some current data which would be of interest to psychologists, lawyers, and colleagues in related disciplines and also, most importantly, to discuss how research in this area is now proceeding.

Handbook of Psychology in Legal Contexts
Edited by R. Bull and D. Carson. © 1995 John Wiley & Sons Ltd

THE LITERATURE

Monahan's 1981 book reviewed in considerable detail the studies published up to that time (see especially Table 3, p. 79). In the most general terms he concluded that, because the design of most studies left much to be desired and, because very few indeed had been based on clearly defined actuarial and clinical variables, the correlation between predictions and outcomes was discouragingly low. He drew attention to the fact that 'dangerousness' appeared to have been markedly overpredicted in American studies where large numbers of forensic patients had been released against psychiatric advice or as a result of court rulings (Kozol, Boucher and Garofalo, 1972; Steadman and Cocozza, 1974; Thornberry and Jacoby, 1979). This is usually referred to as the 'false positive' problem, meaning that, when tested, the dire consequences of positive predictions of violence tend not to be realised.

Monahan listed several ways in which error could probably be reduced (see especially pp. 145–61) and offered a list of variables which might have power as actuarial predictors. More specifically, he suggested previous violence, age, gender, race, socioeconomic status and employment stability, opiate or alcohol misuse (pp. 104–12). As well, he mentioned family, peer, and job environments, and the availability of victims, weapons, and alcohol (pp. 132–7). Of particular note was the fact that he listed mental disorder as a *non*-correlate of violence (pp. 112–18). Monahan contended in his book and in subsequent articles (1984, 1988) that a 'second generation' of research was needed, one which examined predictions over the short term and with careful attention to the definitions of predictor and outcome variables. More has been written recently on the methodological problems commonly found in this area of research (Mulvey and Lidz, 1993).

Monahan's advice has been followed over the last dozen years or more. Many studies have been published on the power of actuarial variables and the ability of clinicians to predict violence over the short term, usually days or weeks following emergency psychiatric assessment (e.g. Convit et al., 1988; Janofsky, Spears and Neubauer, 1988; Klassen and O'Connor, 1988a, b; McNiel and Binder, 1991; Steadman et al., 1994). There has also been a shift in thinking by Monahan (1992), who is now of the view that there probably are links between mental disorder and violence. This literature is not easy to summarise briefly, but it can be asserted that, collectively, these studies show the possibilities of making more accurate predictions than heretofore through concentration on defining predictors and observing behaviour closely over the short term. There is at least a suggestion that, through these methods, false positive error can be reduced in limited-term follow-up studies, though perhaps not to the full extent suggested by Otto in 1992 (see Hart, Webster and Menzies, 1993).

Rather than attempt here a full review of the literature on the prediction of dangerousness and the management of risk, we have preferred to discuss four studies in some detail. These four projects were selected for review on the basis of their recency and the fact that they cover fairly different populations using a variety of methodological innovations. Information extracted from the studies is then consolidated to propose, tentatively, a general approach to the assessment of risk and the prediction of dangerousness.

Study 1: McNiel, Binder and Greenfield (1988)

This paper deals with the prediction of violence over the short term. Patients were evaluated under emergency psychiatric conditions to determine whether or not they should be hospitalised involuntarily. The authors were interested in finding out the extent to which pre-admission violence in the community predicts violence in the hospital. They sought also to determine what background characteristics would best predict violence during the hospital stay.

Records were examined for 238 patients. All patients had been admitted for 72 hours on the basis of ascribed danger to others, danger to self, or grave disability (i.e. inability to care for themselves); 42 per cent were committed on the grounds that they were dangerous to others. From the records search it was possible to gain information about the extent of violence during the two weeks before committal. Three types of behaviour were coded: attacks on persons (22 per cent of patients in the study); a 'fear-inducing' category which combined attacks on objects, threats of attack to persons, and verbal attacks against others (27 per cent); and a third 'residual' category of no attacks or threats (51 per cent). Just as there were three levels of violence prior to admission, the authors measured three levels of violence in the hospital; 18 per cent engaged in attacks on other people, 40 per cent exhibited fear-inducing behaviour, and the balance, 42 per cent, showed no violence. As anticipated, there was a highly significant association between violence pre and post admission. This confirms what has long been known: namely that prior violence is a fairly strong predictor of future violence (see Monahan, 1981, pp. 104–5, 151). Also in accord with previous findings was the fact that, when prior violence was used as a predictor, a fair proportion of the total positive 'predictions' of violence were false (28 out of 116).

McNiel, Binder and Greenfield (1988) undertook a statistical search to determine what kinds of variables, other than prior violence already considered, might possess predictive power. Several variables were distinguished by their *lack* of connection to violence. These deserve mention and were as follows: social class, ethnic group, age, residence with the family as opposed to other arrangements, and substance abuse. This held true whether violence in the community or hospital was considered. Suicidal patients were less likely than their counterparts to be violent in either the hospital or the community. Single patients were more likely to induce fear; married patients were more apt to be actually assaultive. From this can be deduced the observation that many variables show consistent effects across community/ hospital situations. Yet, as the researchers make clear, situational effects are to be noted. They showed, for example, that in the community men were more apt than women to show fear-induction and actual attacks. But in the hospital the women were more assaultive than the men. Similarly, manic-depressive patients were especially prone to be assaultive in the hospital and, along with schizophrenics, were at elevated risk for assaultiveness in the community. Even though most of the predictor variables exerted negligible or weak connection to the outcome criteria, the authors reported some power when they were combined statistically. It is also of interest to note that results from such a statistical analysis are in rough accord with raw clinical judgement at time of assessment. The statistical approach yielded generally greater overall accuracy than the clinicians' judgements but the clinical method succeeded in identifying a relatively high proportion of patients who attacked or threatened others.

The McNiel, Binder and Greenfield article is important because, as is the case with the three other studies considered here, base rates of violence were higher than might have been expected according to research published before 1980 (see Monahan, 1981). As well, the project drives home the importance of prior violence as an important predictor variable. This reinforces the need to collect baseline violence data with considerable care and attention to detail. Finally, the study affirms the fact that simple, relatively easy-to-collect background data can reveal reliable statistical effects.

Study 2: Lidz, Mulvey and Gardner (1993)

Lidz, Mulvey and Gardner (1993) set out to determine how well clinicians could predict the post-release violence of patients first assessed in a university-based urban psychiatric emergency service. The patients were examined by two clinicians. Both clinicians were asked to predict potential violence to others over a six-month period. Independent opinions of the two clinicians were in general agreement. Scores from the two clinicians—a nurse-clinician or a junior resident (doctor) and the attending psychiatrist—were summed to yield a score ranging from 0 to 10. Patients scoring 3 or higher were predicted to be violent. A distinctive feature of this study was the use of a design according to which the patients were matched into two groups by age, race, gender and psychiatric admission status. There were 357 patients in a group predicted to be violent, with the same number in the contrast group. Another strong design point was the collection of outcome data from several sources. Too often past studies have relied on a single, often unverified, source that has not been checked against other kinds of information. In this study the authors gained data from patients themselves and from 'collaterals' (friends, relatives, employers, etc.). These data supplemented the conventional infor-mation obtained from police, hospital, and other such records. In this study violence meant laying hands on or threatening a person with a weapon.

There were two main findings of interest. First, the base-rate of violence was high (45 per cent), especially given the relatively short follow-up period. This confirms the finding of McNiel, Binder and Greenfield (1988) mentioned above (see also Monahan, 1981, pp. 59–62; Webster, Dickens and Addario, 1985, p. 25; and Quinsey who early on (1980) had pointed out that it may be a mistake to expect only rare occurrences of violence during follow-up). The Lidz, Mulvey and Gardner (1993) finding, due in part no doubt to the thoroughness of their outcome measures, suggests that the monitoring of violence is possible even when subjects are discharged to varied arrangements in the community. Another point of note with respect to levels of violence concerns diagnosis. The researchers found schizophrenic patients in both groups were significantly less violent than those with other diagnoses. They also found personality disordered patients in the predicted-violent group (but not the comparison group) to be reliably more violent than those with other diagnoses. This may be because past violence is a criterion for the diagnosis of some personality disorders.

A second finding by Lidz, Mulvey and Gardner was that clinicians were able to predict violent outcome at least to some extent. Their design, with the effects of race, age, and gender controlled by means of matching, allowed a seemingly simple direct test of clinical ability. Although it was clear that clinicians were able to predict violence at a level exceeding chance, the data are not wholly impressive. All of the predicted patients were, of course, expected to behave violently during follow-up; 53 per cent did so and the balance, 47 per cent, were not recorded as having acted violently. None of the comparison group were expected to show violence but 36 per cent did so, with 64 per cent apparently remaining peaceful. Of this result the researchers remarked that 'there is substantial room for improvement' (p. 1009). The finding is reminiscent of an earlier observation by Sepejak et al. (1983) where clinical judgement of violence potential was statistically significant without exerting a great deal of power. When clinicians in the Lidz, Mulvey and Gardner study predicted violence they were relatively correct in that those patients more than their matched counterparts committed serious violence. Yet the fact that clinicians were especially concerned about violence potential in some cases had no predictive value. As the authors put it, 'Clinical judgments were no more accurate when the level of concern about a patient judged dangerous was high than when it was low' (p. 1009). This would suggest that confidence in opinion does not mean that judgments are necessarily accurate.

Some might argue that clinicians exceeded chance in their predictions of violence due not to their clinical acumen in predicting 'dangerousness' but to their making use of available information concerning a key 'risk factor', namely prior history of violence. When this variable was controlled statistically, though, the clinicians still showed predictive power. The Lidz, Mulvey and Gardner study suggests, in the words of the authors, 'that clinical judgment has been undervalued in previous research' (p. 1010). While this may be true, it must be noted that the clinicians were apparently particularly inaccurate with respect to the women, who numbered about half the sample.

Mulvey is a member of a multi-site study sponsored by the McArthur Foundation. His work with Lidz was done in Pittsburgh. Data similar to those described above have also recently been combined and published by colleagues in Kansas City and Worcester in Massachusetts (Steadman et al., 1994). There was, in this preliminary report on the field trial, the same emphasis on outcome data being collected from community 'collaterals' as well as from self-report. There was also a similar, relatively-short, six-month follow-up period during which there were up to three contacts with discharged patients. As in the study by Lidz, Mulvey and Gardner, the base rate level of violence during follow-up was quite high, especially considering the short duration of the post-release period. Over a quarter (27 per cent) of the subjects themselves reported at least one violent incident. This figure rose to 34 per cent with the addition of data from the collaterals. The MacArthur project is distinguished by the attention devoted both to predictor variables, not described here because of space limitations, and outcome data (which in due course will be fleshed out with information from arrest and hospital records). This study project is clearly the biggest and most ambitious venture ever contemplated in this area and promises to provide data more definitive than those presently available.

Study 3: Menzies, Webster, McMain, Staley and Scaglione (1994)

In 1985 the authors reported on the reliability and predictive accuracy of an instrument called the Dangerous Behaviour Rating Scheme (DBRS; Menzies, Webster and Sepejak, 1985a). Patients were attending a brief assessment on psychiatric remand from the courts at the Metropolitan Toronto Forensic Service (METFORS). The main issue in these routine evaluations was fitness to stand trial. As part of the examination accused persons were rated according to the DBRS. This instrument consists of 22 defined items (Slomen et al., 1979). Items in the DBRS were similar to those proposed earlier by Megargee (1976) and consisted of passive aggressivity, hostility, anger, rage, emotionality, guilt, capacity for empathy, capacity for change, self-perception as dangerous, control over actions, tolerance, environmental stress, environmental support, dangerousness increased with alcohol, dangerousness increased with drugs, manipulative, accurate information and sufficient information. Ratings were made on a seven-point scale by two non-involved, specially trained coders and clinicians in the various disciplines. Two years post assessment these same prisoner-patients were followed using hospital, police, correctional and coroners' files. The 1985a report, which was based on data from the two coders only, concluded that although reasonable reliability could be demonstrated for the DBRS, its predictive ability was limited. The overall correlation between coders' composite DBRS scores and outcome was +0.34. Since perfect correspondence between prediction and outcome would be +1.00 and total absence of correspondence would be zero, it is evident that the obtained result was at the 'low end'. This seems especially the case given that the coders were party to background information which was itself likely to have had some predictive power. Certainly the authors warned against use of the instrument for routine clinical purposes (Menzies, Webster and Sepejak, 1985a, p. 54).

The recently reported research on the DBRS extended the earlier work in two main ways: first, the follow-up interval was lengthened from two to six years; second, data from the clinicians were analysed. A total of 162 subjects, mostly men, were tracked over the six-year period. Their behaviour was monitored in three main environments: hospital, prison and community. The main aim, as should be clear, was to determine further the strengths and weaknesses of the DBRS. Also considered were, general, global, predictions of violence.

With DBRS data from a pool of psychiatrists and also from specially trained lay raters, it was possible to find out if both types of evaluators employed the DBRS in the same manner. There was some correspondence between psychiatrists and raters but at the same time enough differences to suggest that the two groups used the DBRS scale in ways which were dissimilar. Concerning psychiatrists, some 70 per cent of the variance was accounted for in terms of four factors: anger presentation, controlled aggression, interpersonal irresponsibility, and impulsivity. The external coders also yielded four factors: interpersonal irresponsibility, anger presentation, controlled hostility, and social ineptitude.

As was also found in the McNiel, Binder and Greenfield (1988) and Lidz, Mulvey and Gardner (1993) studies summarised above, base rates for violence over the six-year follow-up period were relatively high. On average there were 2.8 violent incidents for each individual and the same number of threats of violence. The bulk of these violent transactions occurred in the community. When corrected for opportunity for violence, however, it became clear that, as reported in the 1985a report, most violence occurred in the hospitals. This, of course, may be due to the fact that violence in hospitals is especially apt to be registered officially. Recorded violence peaked at about three years and dropped gradually thereafter.

The DBRS performed, as expected, for the two trained coders at roughly the same level as was found in the earlier report (correlations of +0.24 at year 2 tailing off to +0.15 by year 6). In the hands of psychiatrists pooled together as a group it had no utility. Of this result the authors say: 'There would appear to be little justification, based on these findings, for inscribing such decisions into routine forensic practice or for establishing legal or clinical policies that rested on generic and unqualified predictions of dangerousness to others' (p. 18). This much said, the authors noted that, generally, the DBRS, limited as it may be in predictive power, did fare better than simple global predictions of danger to others in the future (assessed on a seven-point scale). It is also worth observing that, in this study, trained lay raters achieved more consistent positive effects than experienced clinicians from a variety of disciplines. These clinicians showed an almost uncanny knack for predicting global 'criminality' in the opposite direction. When criminal charges rather than violent incidents were taken as the criterion, the clinicians were singularly incapable of achieving correctness in prediction. Correlations for psychiatrists, psychologists, correctional officers, and the like were significant and of the order of –0.20 at the end of year 1.

The lay coders were, as has been said, the most effective predictors of violence in this study. Yet their ability to make such predictions was uneven across contexts. Their success was due largely to their ability to predict violence in the hospital (with correlations at peak of +0.35). Of this, the authors say: 'There is some irony, for example, in the discovery that it is lay coders, using psychometric instruments, who are best at assessing future behavior in clinical settings' (p. 20).

A final point to be taken from Menzies et al. is that individual clinicians varied widely in their predictive acumen. Some were characterised by an ability to produce consistently significant negative correlations with outcome (though of low magnitude) while others did achieve positive correlations (though, again of modest size). This finding is consistent with reports by the same authors using a different data set (see Sepejak et al., 1983). The implications of this finding, anticipated some time ago by Shah (1981), need careful consideration. It certainly means that clinicians who offer opinions in these matters should be at pains to document and analyse their own performances as a matter of routine. It is, in other words, incumbent upon them to be able to demonstrate their predictive acumen (see Webster, 1984).

Study 4: Harris, Rice and Quinsey (1993)

The researchers are in possession of a large data base spanning many years. Their cases are from the Oak Ridge Division of the Penetanguishene Mental Health Centre in Ontario, Canada. Oak Ridge is a maximum-security hospital for men, serving men detained as unfit to stand trial, those not criminally responsible by reason of mental disorder, and those sent for assessment on remand from the courts. The programmes of research and treatment have been described in numerous publications (e.g. Quinsey, 1981; Rice et al., 1990).

Of interest in the present context is a recent paper which aims to determine the power of a number of variables in 'predicting' violent outcome. This is a carefully constructed retrospective file study. Between 1965 and 1980 332 men were admitted to Oak Ridge for treatment. Most of these were matched with men admitted for brief assessment only (286 cases). Matching was on the basis of criminal charge, past violent and non-violent criminality, age, and time of occurrence of index offence. The men in this overall population had highly violent backgrounds. On average, the Oak Ridge sample was held for some five years before having opportunity to recidivate. As noted already, all data were extracted from the files. Separate research assistants coded outcome data. Sources for outcome were similar to those used by Menzies et al. (1994) discussed above. To be classified as a violent failure the individual had to have been charged with a new criminal offence against persons or have committed equivalent violent acts that resulted in return to hospital. Average time at risk was nearly seven years.

As in all of the studies discussed in this chapter, violence was high during follow up. A total of 191 (31 per cent) acted violently. Of especial interest in this report was the elucidation of variables which would predict violent failure. Discriminant analysis yielded 12 such variables. In order of importance these were: (1) Score on Hare's (1991) Psychopathy Checklist (PCL) (+0.34); (2) elementary school maladjustment (+0.31); (3) DSM-III personality disorder (+0.26); (4) age at time of index offence (−0.26); (5) separation from parents under age 16 (+0.25); (6) failure on prior conditional release (+0.24); (7) property offence history (+0.20); (8) never married (+0.18); (9) DSM-III diagnosis of schizophrenia (−0.17); (10) victim injury in the index offence (−0.16); (11) alcohol abuse history (+0.13); and (12), female victim in the index offence (−0.11). The correlation for all 618 subjects using the 12 variables against violent outcome was +0.46 (when variables were weighted to take their relative power into account and only slightly less when unweighted). Correlations were a little higher for treated (+0.53) rather than assessed patients (+0.45) and similar correlations between prediction and outcome were achieved when the sample was split randomly into two halves.

It bears note that Harris, Rice and Quinsey's overall correlations between prediction and outcome generally matched or exceeded those of Menzies et al. (1994) discussed above (see Menzies and Webster, in press). Recently Menzies et al. (1994), adopted 'best shot' statistical procedures similar to those of Harris, Rice and Quinsey (1993). They achieved multiple correlations of +0.43 for psychiatrists and +0.44 for independent lay coders. Included in their list were factors such as previous hospitalisation, country of origin, employment at the time of offence, age at time of assessment (which correlated negatively), violence in the history, factor scores from the DBRS and a global clinical prediction of dangerousness. Analyses showed that it was more the background variables that held the predictive power than the clinical judgements.

A possible criticism of the Harris, Rice and Quinsey (1993) study is that its strongest predictor proved to be the revised Psychopathy Checklist (PCL-R), (Hare, 1991) and that this instrument, though capable of being considered an 'actuarial' variable, relies heavily on clinical judgement. Most readers will know that the PCL-R consists of 20 items. These are rated on a three-point scale. Items centre around concepts like glibness, impulsiveness, remorselessness, grandiosity, promiscuity, irresponsibility, delinquency, and proneness to boredom. Usually they are rated by a clinician especially trained to do the task. The Harris, Rice and Quinsey study departed from tradition in that these ratings, like all others, were obtained from the clinical files. Their point would be that, whatever the intended purpose of the PCL-R, they were able to extract the pertinent information and code it. Throughout, they stress the fact that appreciable predictive accuracy can be achieved without recourse to 'live' clinical judgement and that, indeed, these actuarial scores may prove more robust than clinical opinion (something not hard to appreciate if the variability in clinical opinion found by Menzies et al. is any guide). As a *tour de force* demonstration the authors deleted five items from the 12-variable list. These were the ones like PCL-R, DSM-III diagnosis, and childhood variables where information is normally difficult to obtain. This reduced seven-item list applied to all 618 subjects yielded an overall correlation of +0.36. Though lower than that obtained with their full set of variables, it is still higher than most of those obtained by Menzies et al. (1994), using clinical judgement (with chance of including information of an actuarial nature). Harris, Rice and Quinsey reach the general conclusion that 'the data on the prediction of violence indicate that clinicians are insensitive to variations in the base rate of violent offending, show poor agreement among themselves, make the same judgments as laypersons, and are less accurate than actuarial models' (p. 332).

At this stage the reader needs perhaps to be reminded that all of the men in the Harris, Rice and Quinsey study had committed serious violent acts in the past. That is, the researchers had to find predictive variables over and above the one single variable, previous violence, repeatedly shown to be the most powerful in previous studies. Also to be remembered is the fact that only about half of their population had gone the full 'mental health route' with the other half being sent through the criminal justice system. This would seem to suggest that their scheme may have reasonably wide applicability to 'high risk' groups.

Implications for Future Research on Dangerousness and Risk

It has been recognised for some time that failure to take into account base-rates of violence can constitute a serious source of error in the prediction task (Monahan, 1981; Webster, Phillips and Stermac, 1985). There is, too, the related point that base-rates vary widely across different populations and under different assessment conditions (Monahan, 1981, p. 104). Unless base-rates continue to be established for defined groups—something that can be done only through longitudinal study— it is hard to see how predictive acumen can be properly evaluated.

That several recent studies, in a variety of contexts, have demonstrated higher-than-expected rates of outcome violence, suggests the importance of devoting effort to amassing and cross-checking data with care (see Monahan and Steadman, 1994b, pp. 9–10). Part of the 'false positive problem' may be due to researchers' inability to locate the essential outcome data. It is quite clear that outcome data should be collected from a variety of sources and converged statistically. Because prediction–outcome correlations normally shrink when studies are 'cross-validated,' that is, when predictive variables extracted from one study are tested against a new sample, it is very important that such verification exercises be conducted before results of the kind summarised above are accepted with too much alacrity. Readers should note that all four of the studies reviewed above, while by no means without merit, require much by way of replication, verification and validation. Results are more suggestive than substantive.

Just as it is vital to stress outcome data, so too is it necessary to be rigorous in obtaining clear histories of violent conduct (see Monahan, 1984). This variable has long been considered powerful (Gunn, 1990, p. 15); recent studies considered above endorse this basic observation. It seems perfectly apparent that attention to this variable, and ones related to it, can capitalise on the known links between past and future violent conduct. There is a gradual increase in understanding that whether the assessment and prediction tasks are approached from either a clinical or an actuarial position (Menzies, Webster and Hart, 1994), there requires to be rigorous effort toward information collection and review (see Prins, 1990, p. 19). Impressionistic and intuitively formed clinical opinion is no substitute for painstaking and disinterested analysis of file data.

Although special-to-purpose clinical assessment instruments remain largely unvalidated (e.g. Hall, 1984, 1987) or disappointing in predictive power (Menzies, Webster and Sepejak, 1985a, b), some commentators (Monahan and Steadman, 1994a) suggest that there are enough contemporary conceptual ideas to enable further refinements and encourage future positive results. This much said, it is apparent that to date the main published findings have stressed the importance of simple actuarial variables over complex clinical ones. Whether this is due to the fact that study designs tend to favour the former at the expense of latter is not known but, generally, it seems highly advisable to take actuarial considerations strongly into account (Dowie, 1990, p. 28).

The way forward in evaluating the dangerousness and risk constructs would seem to entail breaking the assessment task into components. Three general areas are important. The first has to do with historical or background factors. Such data can likely best be coded by historians or other assistants trained to gather and extract pertinent information in systematic and reliable ways. Very likely the variables important in one type of situation will be less important in another. A careful reading of Monahan (1981) together with the four studies mentioned above (and others like them: see Harris, Rice and Cormier, 1991; individual chapters in Monahan and Steadman, 1994a; and individual chapters in Hodgins, 1993) gives a wide range of possibilities.

The second general approach has to do with the face-to-face clinical assessment. Traditionally, this has been a main focus for clinicians as they prepare reports for court, parole boards, and the like. Ethical codes in fact *require* such examinations (see, for example American Psychological Association, 1992, 7.02). Yet the view of the present authors is that, while there may be some value in focusing attention on items like insight, attitude, symptoms, stability and treatability (Webster, Eaves et al., 1995), it may be in error to over-weight these and related variables.

The third general approach involves estimation of the power of 'risk variables'. As with historical and clinical variables, to be incorporated into routine assessment work these would require better definitions than are currently available. They could be organised around constructs such as discharge plan feasibility, access to victims, social support, possible compliance with medications and other possible interventions and procedures, and likely reactions to stress (Webster, Eaves et al., 1995). The important point is that clinicians and researchers together evolve item definitions and that there be agreed understanding about both predictor and outcome variables. At a certain point, too, it would seem wise to include former patients and prisoners in the conceptualisation of new research undertakings in this area (Erickson et al., 1973). There should be recognition that the latter day availability of enhanced computer technologies and data storage and analysis capabilities does not in itself ensure better outcomes. It has been thoroughly established that, at least in particular kinds of circumstances, there exist statistically significant, even if pragmatically equivocal, relationships between historical, clinical and risk factors and actual and threatened violence. In contention now is whether the sizes of correlations summarised in this chapter can be improved upon and the extent to which such correspondences ought, in terms of emerging policy and ethical fairness, ever to be used in helping decide individual cases.

REFERENCES

American Psychological Association (1992). *Ethical Principles of Psychologists and Code of Conduct.* Washington, DC: American Psychological Association.

Convit, A., Jaeger, J., Lin, S.P., Meisner, M. and Volavka, J. (1988). Predicting assaultiveness in psychiatric inpatients: a pilot study. *Hospital and Community Psychiatry*, **39**, 429–34.

Dietz, P.E. (1985). Hypothetical criteria for the prediction of individual criminality. In C.D. Webster, M.H. Ben-Aron and S.J. Hucker (Eds), *Dangerousness: Probability and Prediction, Psychiatry and Public Policy.* New York: Cambridge University Press, pp. 87–102.

Dowie, J. (1990). Clinical decision making: risk is a dangerous word and hubris is a sin. In D. Carson (Ed.), *Risk-taking in Mental Disorder; Analyses, Policies and Practical Suggestions.* Chichester: SLE Publications, pp 28–39.

Erickson, R.J., Crow, W.J., Zurcher, L.A. and Connett, A.V. (1973). *Paroled But Not*

Free: Ex-offenders Look at What They Need to Make it Outside. New York: Behavioral Publications.

Faust, D. and Ziskin, J. (1988). The expert witness in psychology and psychiatry. *Science*, **241**, 31–5.

Freeman, M. (1990). How might the Courts respond to alternative analyses of risk? In D. Carson (Ed.), *Risk-taking in Mental Disorder: Analyses, Policies and Practical Strategies.* Chichester: SLE Publications.

Greenland, C. (1985). Dangerousness, mental disorder, and politics. In C.D. Webster, M.H. Ben-Aron and S.J. Hucker (Eds), *Dangerousness: Probability and Prediction, Psychiatry and Public Policy.* New York: Cambridge University Press, pp. 25–40.

Grisso, T. and Appelbaum, P. (1992). Is it unethical to offer predictions of future violence. *Law and Human Behavior*, **16**, 621–33.

Gunn, J. (1990). Clinical approaches to the assessment of risk. In D. Carson (Ed.), *Risk-taking in Mental Disorder: Analyses, Policies and Practical Suggestions.* Chichester: SLE Publications, pp. 13–17.

Hall, H.V. (1984). Predicting dangerousness for the courts. *American Journal of Forensic Psychology*, **4**, 5–25.

Hall, H.V. (1987). *Violence Prediction. Guidelines for the Forensic Practitioner.* Springfield, IL: Charles C. Thomas.

Hare, R.D. (1991). *The Revised Psychopathy Checklist.* Toronto: Multi-Health Systems.

Harris, G.T.; Rice, M.E. and Cormier, C. (1991). Psychopathy and violent recidivism. *Law and Human Behavior*, **15**, 625–37.

Harris, G.T., Rice, M.E. and Quinsey, V.L. (1993). Violent recidivism of mentally disordered offenders: the development of a statistical prediction instrument. *Criminal Justice and Behavior*, **20**, 315–35.

Hart, S.D., Webster, C.D. and Menzies, R.J. (1993). A note on portraying the accuracy of violence predictions. *Law and Human Behavior*, **17**, 695–700.

Hodgins, S. (Ed.) (1993). *Crime and Mental Disorder.* Newbury Park, CA: Sage.

Hodgins, S., Webster, C.D. and Paquet, J. (1991). *Canadian Database: Patients Held on Lieutenant Governors' Warrants.* Ottawa: Department of Justice, Canada.

Janofsky, J.S., Spears, S. and Neubauer, D.N. (1988). Psychiatrists' accuracy in predicting violent behavior on an inpatient unit. *Hospital and Community Psychiatry*, **39**, 1090–4.

Klassen, D. and O'Connor, W.A. (1988a). Predicting violence in schizophrenic and non-schizophrenic patients: a prospective study. *Journal of Community Psychology*, **16**, 217–27.

Klassen, D., and O'Connor, W.A. (1988b). A prospective study of predictors of violence in adult male mental health admissions. *Law and Human Behavior*, **12**, 143–58.

Kozol, H., Boucher, R., and Garofalo, R. (1972). The diagnosis and treatment of dangerousness. *Crime and Delinquency*, **18**, 371–92.

Lidz, C.W., Mulvey, E.P. and Gardner, W. (1993). The accuracy of predictions of violence to others. *Journal of the American Medical Association*, **269**, 1007–11.

McNiel, D.E. and Binder, R.L. (1991). Clinical assessment of risk of violence among psychiatric inpatients. *American Journal of Psychiatry*, **148**, 1317–21.

McNiel, D., Binder, R. and Greenfield, T.K. (1988). Predictors of violence in civilly committed acute psychiatric patients. *American Journal of Psychiatry*, **145**, 965–70.

Megargee, E.I. (1976). The prediction of dangerous behavior. *Criminal Justice and Behavior*, **3**, 3–22.

Menzies, R.J. and Webster, C.D. (in press). The construction and validation of risk predictions in a six-year follow-up of forensic patients: a tridimensional analysis. *Journal of Consulting and Clinical Psychology*.

Menzies, R.J., Webster, C.D. and Hart, S.D. (1994). Observations on the rise of risk. Paper presented at the bi-annual meeting of the American Psychology-Law Society, Santa Fe, New Mexico.

Menzies, R.J., Webster, C.D. and Sepejak, D.S. (1985a). The dimensions of dangerousness: evaluating the accuracy of psychometric predictions of violence among forensic patients. *Law and Human Behavior*, **9**, 35–56.

Menzies, R.J., Webster, C.D. and Sepejak, D.S. (1985b). Hitting the forensic sound barrier: predictions of dangerousness in a pre-trial psychiatric clinic. In C.D. Webster, M.H. Ben-Aron and S.J. Hucker (Eds), *Dangerousness: Probability and Prediction, Psychiatry and Public Policy*. New York: Cambridge University Press, pp. 115–43.

Menzies, R.J., Webster, C.D., McMain, S., Staley, S. and Scaglione, R. (1994). The dimensions of dangerousness revisited: assessing forensic predictions about violence. *Law and Human Behavior*, **18**, 1–28.

Monahan, J. (1981). *The Clinical Prediction of Violent Behavior: An Assessment of Clinical Techniques*. Beverly Hills, CA: Sage.

Monahan, J. (1984). The prediction of violent behavior: toward a second generation of theory and policy. *American Journal of Psychiatry*, **141**, 10–15.

Monahan, J. (1988). Risk assessment of violence among the mentally disordered: generating useful knowledge. *International Journal of Law and Psychiatry*, **11**, 249–57.

Monahan, J. (1992). Mental disorder and violent behavior: perceptions and evidence. *American Psychologist*, **47**, 511–21.

Monahan, J. and Steadman, H.J. (Eds) (1994a) *Violence and Mental Disorder: Advances in Risk Assessment*. Chicago: University of Chicago Press.

Monahan, J. and Steadman, H.J. (1994b). Toward a rejuvenation of risk assessment research. In J. Monahan and H.J. Steadman (Eds), *Violence and Mental Disorder: Developments in Risk Assessment*. Chicago: University of Chicago Press, pp. 1–17.

Mulvey, E.P. and Lidz, C.W. (1984). Clinical considerations in the prediction of dangerousness in mental patients. *Clinical Psychology Review*, **4**, 379–401.

Mulvey, E.P. and Lidz, C.W. (1993). Measuring patient violence in dangerousness research. *Law and Human Behavior*, **17**, 277–88.

Otto, R.K. (1992). Prediction of dangerous behavior: a review and analysis of 'second-generation' research. *Forensic Reports*, **5**, 103–34.

Pickersgill, A. (1990). Balancing the public and private interests. In D. Carson (Ed.), *Risk-taking in Mental Disorder: Analyses, Policies and Strategies*. Chichester: SLE Publications.

Prins, H. (1990). Dangerousness: a review. In R. Bluglass and P. Bowden (Eds), *Principles and Practice of Forensic Psychiatry*. London: Churchill Livingstone.

Quinsey, V.L. (1980). The baserate problem and the prediction of dangerousness: a reappraisal. *Journal of Psychiatry and Law*, **8**, 329–40.

Quinsey, V.L. (1981). The long term management of the mentally disordered offender. In S.J. Hucker, C.D. Webster and M.H. Ben-Aron (Eds), *Mental Disorder and Criminal Responsibility*. Toronto: Butterworth, pp. 137–55.

Rice, M.E., Harris, G.T., Quinsey, V.L. and Cyr, M. (1990). Planning treatment programs in secure psychiatric facilities. In D.N. Weisstub (Ed.), *Law and Mental Health: International Perspectives*, vol. 5. New York: Pergamon, pp. 162–230.

Sepejak, D., Menzies, R.J., Webster, C.D. and Jensen, F.A.S. (1983). Clinical predictions of dangerousness: two-year follow-up of 408 pre-trial forensic cases. *Bulletin of the American Academy of Psychiatry and the Law*, **11**, 171–81.

Shah, S.A. (1978). Dangerousness: a paradigm for exploring some issues in law and psychology. *American Psychologist*, **33**, 224–38.

Shah, S.A. (1981). Dangerousness: conceptual, prediction and public policy issues. In J.R. Hays, T.K. Roberts, and K.S. Solway (Eds), *Violence and the Violent Individual*. New York: SP Medical and Scientific Books, pp. 151–78.

Slomen, D.J., Webster, C.D., Butler, B.T., Jensen, F.A.S., et al. (1979). The assessment of dangerous behaviour: two new scales. METFORS Working Paper No. 14. Toronto: Metropolitan Toronto Forensic Service.

Steadman, H.J. and Cocozza, J. (1974). *Careers of the Criminally Insane*. Lexington, MA: Lexington Books.

Steadman, H.J., Monahan, J., Robbins, P.C., Appelbaum, P., Grisso, T., Klassen, D., Mulvey, E. and Roth, L. (1993). From dangerousness to risk assessment: implications for appropriate research strategies. In S. Hodgins (Ed.), *Mental Disorder and Crime*. Newbury Park, CA: Sage, pp. 39–62.

Steadman, H.J., Monahan, J., Appelbaum, P.S., Grisso, T., Mulvey, E.P., Roth, L.H., Robbins, P.C. and Klassen, D. (1994). Designing a new generation of risk assessment research. In J. Monahan and H.J. Steadman (Eds), *Violence and Mental Disorder: Developments in Risk Assessment*. Chicago: University of Chicago Press, pp. 297–318.

Stone, A.A. (1985). The new legal standard of dangerousness: fair in theory, unfair in practice. In C.D. Webster, M.H. Ben-Aron and S.J. Hucker (Eds), *Dangerousness: Probability and Prediction, Psychiatry and Public Policy*. New York: Cambridge University Press, pp. 13–24.

Thornberry, T. and Jacoby, J. (1979). *The Criminally Insane: A Community Follow-up of Mentally Ill Offenders*. Chicago: University of Chicago Press.

Webster, C.D. (1984). On gaining acceptance: why the courts accept only reluctantly findings from experimental and social psychology. *International Journal of Law and Psychiatry*, **7**, 407–14.

Webster, C.D. and Menzies, R.J. (1987). The clinical prediction of dangerousness. In D.N. Weisstub (Ed.), *Law and Mental Health: International Perspectives*. New York: Pergamon Press, pp. 158–208.

Webster, C.D., Dickens, B.M. and Addario, S. (1985). *Constructing Dangerousness: Scientific, Legal and Policy Implications*. Toronto: University of Toronto Centre of Criminology.

Webster, C.D., Phillips, M. and Stermac, L. (1985). Persons held on Warrants of the Lieutenant Governor in Canada. *Canada's Mental Health*, **33**, 28–32.

Webster, C.D., Eaves, D., Douglas, K. and Wintrup, A. (1995). The HCR-20 Scheme: the assessment of dangerousness and risk. Vancouver: Mental Health, Law and Policy Institute, Simon Fraser University and Forensic Psychiatric Services Commission of British Columbia.

Webster, C.D., Harris, G.T., Rice, M.E., Cormier, C.A. and Quinsey, V.L. (1994). *The Violence Prediction Scheme: Assessing Dangerousness in High Risk Men*. Toronto: Centre of Criminology, University of Toronto.

Chapter 5.6

Anti-discrimination Legislation and its Impact on Occupational Psychology

Rajvinder Kandola
Pearn Kandola, Oxford

INTRODUCTION

This chapter examines the development of anti-discrimination and its effect on psychologists involved in employment-related issues such as recruitment, selection, promotion and test development.

Definitions are provided of the key concepts contained in the legislation, in particular direct discrimination and indirect discrimination. Case law is presented to demonstrate the ways in which these concepts have been interpreted by industrial tribunals and the courts.

Another significant development which is considered to be related to the application of anti-discrimination legislation is the increasing involvement of the equality commissions, (e.g. the Commission for Racial Equality in the United Kingdom, the Equal Opportunities Commission in the United States) in areas which have traditionally been the preserve of occupational psychologists. In particular, the commissions have turned their gaze slowly, determinedly and with increasing sophistication on the fair use of tests and other popular selection procedures such as interviews.

The impact and increasing influence of the European Union and its stated concern on the state of equality between men and women is also considered.

Handbook of Psychology in Legal Contexts
Edited by R. Bull and D. Carson. © 1995 John Wiley & Sons Ltd

THE IMPACT OF THE ANTI-DISCRIMINATION LEGISLATION

In the United Kingdom there has been some form of anti-discrimination legislation in place since 1965. The Race Relations Act 1965 made discrimination unlawful in public places. The Race Relations Act of 1968, the Sex Discrimination Act 1975 and the Race Relations Act 1976 gradually widened the scope of the original definition of discrimination to include issues of employment.

Direct Discrimination

The Sex Discrimination Act, section 1 states: 'a person discriminates against a woman in any circumstances relevant for the purposes of any provision of this act if, (a) on the grounds of her sex he treats her less favourably than he treats, or would treat, a man.' Similar provisions exist under the Race Relations Act 1976 and the Fair Employment (Northern Ireland) Act 1989.

In the early years of the legislation this was often interpreted as a man or a woman showing some degree of hostility towards a person of the opposite sex. However, over time the courts have broadened their understanding of what constitutes *direct* discrimination to such an extent that the issue of stereotyping has arisen under case law. In the case of *Horsey v. Dyfed County Council* ([1980] IRLR 395) the words 'on the grounds of sex, marital status or race', were ruled to cover cases where the reason for discrimination was the generalised assumption that people of a particular sex or marital status possess or lack certain characteristics.

Once the issue of stereotyping had been introduced into the law it obviously meant that the work of psychologists on this subject would be considered of interest by industrial tribunals. For example, in the celebrated 1993 case of Alison Halford, the Assistant Chief Constable of Merseyside Police, the issue of stereotyping was central to the case and a special paper on the subject was produced for the Equal Opportunity Commission by Dr Michael Pearn, an occupational psychologist. This paper reviewed the literature on stereotyping, showed the conditions under which stereotyping would most likely take place, and finally made an evaluation of the extent to which those conditions applied in this particular case. It surely must be the case that psychologists are the people best placed to provide this type of evidence.

Indirect Discrimination

Section 1 (1)(b) of the Sex Discrimination Act defines indirect discrimination as follows:

he applies to her a requirement or condition, which applies or would apply equally to a man, but—

i)   which is such that the proportion of women who can comply with it is considerably smaller than the proportion of men who can comply with it, and

ii) which he cannot show to be justifiable irrespective of the sex of the person to whom it is applied, and

iii) which is to her detriment because she cannot comply with it.

Similar provisions exist within the Race Relations Act 1976 and the Fair Employment (NI) Act 1989.

The section on indirect discrimination is an important one for psychologists involved in developing selection or promotion procedures. If the criteria that are established cannot be shown to be justified, and they have an adverse impact on one group or another, they could well be found to be indirectly discriminatory, and legal proceedings might ensue.

The issue of motive is not necessarily considered to be relevant when considering instances of indirect discrimination. In the case of *Perera v. the Civil Service Commission* ([1982] IRLR 147) it was felt that indirect discrimination was an entirely objective issue to resolve. Quite simply: was there a requirement or condition and was it more difficult for those of the applicant's ethnic group to meet such requirements? The issue was not one of trying to determine whether employers established a requirement in order to make it difficult for one ethnic group or other to be successful, but whether that requirement or condition had that effect.

However, being a far more complex concept to deal with, the issues relating to indirect discrimination are still being explored. The judgment made in the case of *Jones v. Chief Adjudication Officer* ([1990] IRLR 533) should help not only those involved in the legal profession, but psychologists involved in developing selection procedures:

> The 'demographic' argument is one way in which indirect discrimination can be established. Where one qualification is being challenged, the process takes the following shape:
>
> 1. Identify the criteria for selection.
> 2. Identify the relevant population comprising all those who satisfy the other criteria for selection.
> 3. Divide the relevant population into groups representing those who satisfy the criteria and those who do not.
> 4. Predict statistically what proportion of each group should consist of women.
> 5. Ascertain what are the actual male/female balances in the two groups.
> 6. Compare the actual with the predicted balances.
> 7. If women are found to be under-represented in the first group and over represented in the second, it is proved that the criteria is discriminatory.

As a set of guidelines to inform psychologists when developing procedures, these could form an important starting point when considering issues relating to indirect discrimination.

Indirect discrimination is of growing importance within the European Union and has also been considered by the European Court of Justice. As is stated in the report *Social Europe* (Commission for the European Community, 1992) 'the concept of indirect discrimination provides a tool with which to challenge the employment structures which perpetuate sex discrimination' (p. 38). Nevertheless, in the same report, it is stated that 'the concept of indirect discrimination is still not widely understood, let alone applied across the Community' (p. 38).

It is to be expected that as more people become aware of what indirect discrimination means the number of cases brought under these provisions will increase over time. Indeed, the European Union is committed, in its third action programme on equal opportunities for women, to increase awareness of this concept.

The issue of indirect discrimination is an extremely important one for psychologists working in the employment field. For example, if psychologists have developed new selection procedures for an organisation they have an obligation to show an objective justification for the criteria and the processes that have been developed. If this cannot be done and the selection outcomes reveal adverse impact then there could be a real danger of being found guilty of indirect discrimination.

THE ROLE OF THE EQUALITY COMMISSIONS

There are three commissions established by statute in the UK. They are the Commission for Racial Equality (CRE) which is concerned about racial equality within Great Britain, the Equal Opportunity Commission (EOC) which is concerned with sex equality, and the Fair Employment Commission (FEC) which operates in Northern Ireland.

There is little doubt that the Commissions have become far more sophisticated in addressing technical issues which have traditionally been the preserve of psychologists. This can be seen by examining their statements made on the subject of test use over the years.

For example, the CRE, in their *Code of Practice* (1984) stated under the heading of 'Selection Criteria and Tests' that 'in order to avoid direct or indirect discrimination, it is recommended that selection criteria and tests are examined to ensure that they are related to job requirements and are not unlawfully discriminatory' (p. 15).

They state: 'selection tests which contain irrelevant questions or exercises on matters which may be unfamiliar to racial minority applicants, should not be used (for example, general knowledge questions on matters more likely to be familiar to indigenous applicants)', and: 'selection tests should be checked to ensure that they are related to the job's requirements, i.e. an individual's test marking should measure ability to train for the job in question' (p. 16).

It could be argued that these statements are vague and consequently allow a lot of leeway to both test publishers and to test users in the way that tests can be used. However, it is quite evident that as the use of tests in occupational settings has grown, so has the interest and concern of both the CRE and EOC. To such an extent that both have carried out research specifically into test use within organisations and have detailed guidelines (Pearn, Kandola and Mottram, 1987; CRE, 1993).

Concerns are also expressed by Sir Michael Day, the chairman of the CRE (CRE, 1993) when presenting their research which had involved surveying test practice amongst large users of the tests. He states that 'current test practice falls short of the CRE's advice in many respects—only one-third of all the respondents were monitoring test results by ethnic origin, and in only 8 per cent of cases had validation—the process of checking the relevance of a test— been used in choosing test' (p. 5).

It is clear that the Commissions are going to maintain and pursue their interest in the use of such techniques in selecting, promoting and developing people within organisations. This view is supported by the increasing number of investigations, either formal or informal, that they are now carrying out on the use of tests within specific organisations. For example, a CRE investigation into the selection procedures, including interviews and tests, used at London Underground in a promotion exercise were published in a report, Lines of Progress (CRE, 1991). In it the CRE stated that this report 'draws attention to the use of psychological tests for job selection in a multi-racial labour market, and demonstrates that employers cannot assume that a generally reliable test will be equally reliable for a particular population or for a particular job. They must first check if the tests were designed for and tried out on a similarly diverse population and if the results had a racially discriminatory pattern' (p. 5). In this case, the tests were shown to have a statistically significant relationship with job performance, i.e. they were statistically valid. The Commission's view, however, is quite clear:

> Wherever possible, all test users must validate tests by trying them out on a similar group in terms of racial origin, gender and age ... we believe that the differences [in this case] in performance between the white and ethnic minority test candidates are unlikely to be wholly explained by differences in age, educational background, managerial training and experience. (CRE, 1991, p. 21)

There is little doubt that the codes of practice and other guidance produced by the Commissions will over time have an increasing impact on the work of psychologists working with employers.

THE IMPACT OF THE EUROPEAN UNION

Whatever individual governments in Western Europe may think about of anti-discrimination, they will be forced to maintain an interest because of the priority given to such issues, in particular to sex equality, by the European Union. Indeed, Article 119 of the Treaty of Rome guarantees equal pay for male and female workers. In 1973, very few member states had laws on equal treatment for men and women, but a series of directives have been introduced which has meant that member states have had to take action in this area. According to the EC Treaty Article 189 'a directive shall be binding, as to the results to be achieved, upon each member state to which it is addressed, but shall leave to the national authorities the choice of form and methods'. In other words, once a directive has been agreed, it has to be implemented within each member state. On the issue of equality, there have been five directives:

- Council Directive of 10 February 1975 (75/117/EEC) on the approximation of the laws of the Member States relating to the principle of equal pay for men and women (OJ L 45/19, 19.2.1975)

- Council Directive of 9 February 1976 (76/207/EEC) on the implementation of the principle of equal treatment for men and women as regards access to employment, vocational training and promotion and working conditions (OJ L 39/40, 14.2.1976)

- Council Directive of 19 December 1978 (79/7/EEC) on the progressive implementation of the principle of equal treatment for men and women in matters of social security (OJ L 6/24, 10.1.1979).

- Council Directive of 24 July 1986 (86/378/EEC) on the implementation of the principle of equal treatment in occupational social security schemes (OJ L 225, 12.8.1986, p.40).

- Council directive of 11 December 1986 on the application of the principle of equal treatment between men and women engaged in an activity, including agriculture, in a self-employed capacity, and on the protection of self-employed women during pregnancy and motherhood (OJ L 359/56, 19.12.1986).

In addition, the Community has adopted two action programmes on equal opportunities (1982–85 and 1986–90) which were designed to advance issues of equality within each of the member states. A third community action programme on equal opportunities for women and men started in 1991 and will continue until 1995. It has established three aims, of which the first is 'the implementation and development of the legislation' (Commission for the European Community, 1992). This will be done partly through monitoring the way the law is being applied in each member state, but also by increasing awareness of what the law states.

The Commission has also made it a priority to ensure that there are effective sanctions and penalties in place for those organisations which are found guilty of unlawful discrimination. The principle of appropriate sanctions and penalties was emphasised in the Court of Justice of the European Communities decision on *von Colson and Kamann v. Land Nord-Westphalian* (Case 14/83, 10 April 1984). The effects of such judgments can be seen within the UK where the limit for the level of awards, for sex and race discrimination cases has been removed.

COMPARISON WITH THE UNITED STATES

The pattern of legislation within the UK and Europe bears striking similarity with that in the United States. The Civil Rights Act 1964 outlawed employment practices that 'adversely affect' individuals because of their race, colour, religion, sex or national origin, these provisions being contained in Title VII of the Act, called Equal Employment Opportunity.

As originally framed the Act was intended to protect individual rights. However, with cases in the Supreme Court and the work of the Equal Employment Opportunity Commission (EOEC), the emphasis moved away from practices which had the intention to discriminate to those that had an adverse impact against protected groups (Hartigan and Wigdor, 1989). In Europe, this movement is indicated by the shift from direct discrimination exclusively to indirect discrimination. It can also be seen in the increasing involvement and sophistication of the bodies charged with ensuring fair practices in employment.

The most detailed guidance of this kind was produced by the EEOC, the Department of Labor, and the Office of Personnel Management entitled the *Uniform Guidelines on Employee Selection Procedures* (29 CFR Part 1607 [1985]). The level of detail it goes into, however, and the degree of validation evidence it calls for, has been criticised for laying down virtually impossible standards to meet without spending millions of dollars (Hartigan and Wigdor, 1989).

Several judgments made by the United States Supreme Court, particularly in the late 1980s, were felt by Congress to be going against the spirit embodied in the Act. This led to the Civil Rights Act of 1991. This reintroduced the notion of job-relatedness of selection procedures and that it is the employer that bears the burden of persuasion. However, if an employer can demonstrate business necessity for the process, it could still be discriminatory if the employer could have used alternative practices which would have led to less disparate impact, but refused to adopt them.

The 1991 Act also outlawed the use of 'race norming', i.e. the process of adjusting test score cut-offs on the basis of race, sex, religion, or national origin.

EMPLOYMENT OF PEOPLE WITH DISABILITIES

In England and Wales the Employment Department has published research on employment policies for people with disabilities (Lunt and Thornton 1993). The overall aim of the project was to conduct a review of the legislation relating to people with disabilities in the European Union, Australia, Canada, Sweden and the United States.

Overall the study concluded that there seemed to be a dichotomy between European Union member states' approach to the issue and that of other countries. European Union countries have a historical commitment to compulsory employment measures, such as stipulation of targets for the employment of people with disabilities. But an interesting and recent development is that of anti-discrimination legislation for people with disabilities. Such legislation has now been introduced at federal level in Australia, Canada and the USA. The non-European Union countries, furthermore, were more likely to have promoted the issue of employment of people with disabilities through policies such as contract compliance. (This is where the government or other public sector organisations would stipulate to all contractors that they must have equal opportunity measures for people with disabilities if they wish to work in that organisation.)

The Americans with Disabilities Act 1992 in Sec. 102(b)(6) makes specific references to issues of selection, and, as with the Civil Rights Act, the test is job-relatedness and business necessity. The definition of discrimination is taken further in Sec. 102(b)(7) where it is taken to mean:

> failing to select and administer tests concerning employment in the most effective manner to ensure that, when such test is administered to a job applicant or employee who has a disability that impairs sensory, manual, or speaking skills, such test results accurately reflect the skills aptitude, or whatever factor of such applicant or employee that such test purports to measure, rather than reflecting the impaired sensory, manual, or speaking skills of such employee or applicant (except where such skills are the factors that the test purports to measure).

The implications and ramifications of this legislation are still being explored but it will place a greater obligation to look as closely at the format and method of presentation of the test as well as the content.

There is increasing pressure from disability groups for similar anti-discrimination legislation for people with disabilities in Europe. However, at this stage neither individual governments nor the European Union appear to support such legislation.

THE ROLE OF PSYCHOLOGISTS

It is clear that the combination of legislation, subsequent case law and the increasing involvement and sophistication of various commissions will have an impact on psychologists working within the employment field. Furthermore, the costs of discriminating unlawfully are increasing. There is a growing obligation for psychologists to ensure that their work is able to withstand detailed scrutiny in industrial tribunals and other legal arena.

At a minimum, when developing new selection processes psychologists should be able to demonstrate the following:

- that a thorough job analysis has been conducted in order to establish the selection criteria. Wherever possible, the sample of people included within the analysis should have included women and ethnic minorities. If this was not possible then the criteria should be examined by someone knowledge-able about both selection and equal opportunity issues.

- the procedures to be developed should map onto the competencies identified from job analysis and there should be good point-to-point correspondence. Furthermore, the more closely the task to be performed in the selection process reflect the tasks to be carried out in the role, the fairer and more valid the procedure will be (Arvey and Faley, 1988; Robertson and Kandola, 1982).

- processes should be piloted using diverse samples. Where discrepancies in performance occur these should be examined in this stage and if necessary some re-piloting may be necessary. Feedback should be obtained from the sample about how they felt about the process. This could be valuable information about how the procedures should be presented.

- training needs to take place of the people who will be involved in the selection process. This should include skills elements demonstrating how the process needs to be operated but also elements on improving objectivity and reducing bias.

- monitoring needs to take place. At a minimum this should include gender and ethnic monitoring. If there are few ethnic minorities or women among the applicants then the attraction methods used should be reviewed to ensure that they are not indirectly discriminatory (e.g. by the use of word of mouth recruitment).

- review the processes on a regular basis and ensure that the competences used and consequently the processes themselves are still relevant.

There is one more action that psychologists must take, and that is to engage with the policy makers. Arnold (1991) provides the example of state legislators in the United States becoming involved in the issues of psychological testing and proposing to introduce legislation to restrict their use. He concludes that: 'If personnel psychologists expect to preserve and protect their rights to develop, administer, and interpret valid, reliable, and fair instruments, they must make it part of their professional commitment to educate and inform state legislators' (p. 282).

CONCLUSIONS

As the preceding discussion demonstrates, there are many legal issues which psychologists will be faced with regarding the anti-discrimination legislation.

The anti-discrimination legislation, the earliest of which was established nearly 30 years ago, has been evolving since it was first introduced. The concept of direct discrimination, for example, has become much more sophisticated, moving away from the early notions of hostility towards an individual or group towards one which incorporates stereotyping.

Indirect discrimination or disparate impact was a revolutionary concept when introduced as an interpretation of the Civil Rights Act 1964. This concept has clearly influenced European policy makers and is the aspect of the legislation which has the potential of having the greatest impact on the work of psychologists, even if it has not made much of an impression to date. However, the European Union, under its third action programme for women, has announced that increasing awareness of indirect discrimination is one of its priorities. It can be expected therefore that more cases involving indirect discrimination will be brought to tribunals and this will have a significant impact on psychologists particularly in their work in developing selection, promotion and appraisal systems.

Furthermore, the role of psychologists is coming under increasing scrutiny from the various equality commissions. The commissions have become increasingly knowledgeable and informed about selection procedures and tests. They are no longer willing to accept passively the professional judgements or the accepted wisdom provided by psychologists. As recent cases have demonstrated, they are reinterpreting the standards by which selection tests should be developed, validated and maintained. From views expressed in their reports it is no longer acceptable to them to have a test which is valid—it must also be demonstrated to be fair. This must undoubtedly have an impact on the way that psychologists carry out their work.

There are also other areas which could lead to pressures being placed on psychologists. Most significantly there is the impact of the European Union and the equality directives which have been passed previously and more of these can be expected in the future. Furthermore, different legislation exists across the European Union on issues such as disability and discrimination against lesbians and gay men. It may be expected that some uniformity on these issues may be attempted at some point in the future.

The legal context in which psychologists carried out their work is now changing, and changing quite dramatically. Psychologists need to be prepared and knowledgeable about what the legislation says and how it will impact upon their work. The starting point for this needs to be the courses, particularly post-graduate training courses, which occupational psychologists currently undergo.

Unless psychologists review the way psychology is taught and incorporate fully the issues of equality and legislation, they may not only be seen to be peripheral to the changes taking place within society, but also as an obstacle to them.

REFERENCES

Arnold, D.W. (1991). Potential legislative inroads into personnel psychology: appropriate reaction measures. *Journal of Business and Psychology*, **16**, 279–82.

Arvey, R.D. and Faley, R.H. (1988). *Fairness in Selecting Employees* (2nd edn). New York: Addison-Wesley.

Commission for the European Community (1992). *Social Europe: Equal Opportunities for Women and Men*. Luxembourg: Office for Official Publications for the European Communities.

CRE (Commission for Racial Equality) (1984). *Race Relations Code of Practice: For the Elimination of Racial Discrimination and the Provision of Equality of Opportunity in Employment*. London: HMSO.

CRE (Commission for Racial Equality) (1990). *Lines of Progress*. London: Commission for Racial Equality.

CRE (Commission for Racial Equality) (1993). *Towards Fair Selection: A Survey of Test Practice and Thirteen Case Studies*. London: Commission for Racial Equality.

Hartigan, J.A. and Wigdor, A.K. (1989). *Fairness in Employment Testing*. Washington, DC: National Academy Press.

Lunt, N. and Thornton, P. (1993). *Employment Policies for Disabled People: A Review of Legislation in Fifteen Countries* (Research series 16). Sheffield: Employment Department.

Pearn, M.A., Kandola, R.S. and Mottram, R.D. (1987). *Selection Tests and Sex Bias: The Impact of Selection Testing on the Employment Opportunities of Women and Men.* London: HMSO.

Robertson, I.T. and Kandola, R.S. (1982). Work sample tests: Validity, adverse impact and applicant reaction. *Journal of Occupational Psychologists*, **55**, 171–83.

Part 6

Trials and Decision-making

Adversarial and Inquisitorial Proceedings

Jenny McEwan
University of Keele

The classic description of the adversarial trial is Damaska's; the proceedings should be structured as a dispute between two sides, strictly, in a position of equality (Damaska, 1973). It is said that deep-rooted distrust of judges, based on fear of methods of inquiry in continental Europe, inspired in Britain a system of litigation deliberately designed to minimise the involvement of officials, leaving the conduct of the case as far as possible in the hands of the interested litigants or parties.

There are differing views as to the involvement in torture of continental European secular judicial proceedings, as opposed to those of the Holy Inquisition (Damaska, 1973; Munday, 1993), but that spectre caused the development of the adversarial model in England, thence to the rest of the British Isles, the United States of America and the Commonwealth. The judge's role is deliberately kept to a minimum, which is one of the key features of the adversarial trial. Damaska identifies other characteristics such as the jury, the principle of orality and the partisan role of the advocate. In continental European systems, on the other hand, judges may have a considerable role, frequently in an attempt to curb any excesses by the police. They may actively supervise the pretrial accumulation of evidence, although this is rare in practice. They play a major part in the preparation of evidence before the trial and the questioning of witnesses during it. The defendant in a criminal trial is questioned largely by the judge, so the advocate's role consists mainly of objecting to questions and asking supplementary questions. In contrast the 'Anglo-Saxon' system accords the central role to the litigant or to his or her advocate. He or she chooses those issues which are to form the subject matter of the case, selects witnesses and questions them at trial. Griffiths (1970) has called this the 'battle model' of trial, as opposed to the 'family model' which implies a basic trust in public officials, and common or reconcilable interests.

Handbook of Psychology in Legal Contexts
Edited by R. Bull and D. Carson. © 1995 John Wiley & Sons Ltd

In modern times the closest to the adversarial paradigm (Damaska, 1973) is the Anglo-Saxon criminal trial, at least in terms of orality, exclusionary rules, presence of a jury, passivity of the judge, and the element of surprise. But now that prosecutions are state funded and organised, major inequalities of resource detract from adversarial principles. The imbalance has been said to be corrected by the prosecution obligation to disclose material which may prove helpful to the defence. (In the UK see *R. v. McIlkenny,* [1992] 2 All ER 417.) The prosecution now has extremely strict duties to disclose not only material they intend to use, but material which has been discarded, just in case it could assist the defence. This is a departure from adversarial theory, which imposes on the parties the obligation to gather their own evidence. In the UK the Royal Commission on Criminal Justice recently recommended a further departure, that the defence should disclose the nature of their case in advance of the trial (Runciman, 1993). In his Note of Dissent, Zander argued that this undermined the vital corollary of the presumption of innocence, that the defence is under no obligation to assist the prosecution who have the entire burden of proof. Part of his case rests on the lesser resources commonly available to the defence; but the argument that the defendant should not have to do the prosecution's work for them is an essentially adversarial one. Lawyers in continental Europe argue that their systems also operate a presumption of innocence.

Pretrial procedures, which familiarise all parties with the issues and evidence, merely facilitate the thorough inquiry of both incriminatory and exculpatory matters. In England and Wales there has been increasing use of pretrial reviews to reduce the climatic or surprise element of criminal trials. The practice of holding informal hearings before the judge developed in about 1975, but any agreement is unenforceable at present (*Hutchinson*, (1986) 82 Cr App R 51). Some people attempted to persuade the Royal Commission that these reviews should be held in many more cases, more formally, and with binding consequences, but with little success. An inquiry into the practical problems which arise when scientific issues fall to be determined by courts, chaired by a judge, had concluded that pretrial review of scientific issues is at present too informal (Oddie, 1991).

Civil proceedings in England and Wales are closer to the adversarial paradigm in terms of the equality of the opponents, for although litigants are unequally resourced, the imbalance is likely to be randomly distributed amongst plaintiffs and defendants. Until recently the parties were supported by a reasonably comprehensive civil legal aid scheme. However, judges in civil cases have, for many years, relied much more heavily than is the custom in criminal trials, on written evidence. This effectively ignores inconveniences such as the hearsay rule. Procedural developments in some courts, involving total disclosure by both sides to each other and to the judge of their witness statements, and provision of skeleton arguments and written submissions, has reduced the length and significance of the oral hearings. Such practices bring civil trials much nearer to the European model (McEwan, 1992). There is no means at present of assessing the relative efficiency, in terms of cost or outcome, of the old style as opposed to 'lever-arch' litigation.

Non-adversarial proceedings in Britain include, arguably, care proceedings. These are inevitably concerned with the welfare of a child (*Humberside C.C. v. D.P.R.*, [1977] 3 All ER 964). A coroner's inquest also is a 'fact finding exercise and not a method of apportioning guilt'. It should be more like an 'inquisitorial process' demanding rules and procedures different from a standard criminal trial (*McKerr v. Armagh Coroner,* [1990] 1 All ER 865).

No country can be said to have a purely inquisitial system for criminal proceedings. It would probably be too elaborate for any nation to operate such a scheme for every crime committed on its territory. Even in France, usually held out as the closest to the inquisitorial paradigm, the vast majority of cases never go through *instruction*, which involves an investigation by the examining magistrate (Delmas-Marty, 1991). Instead most cases go straight before the *Tribunal Correctionel* for proceedings which have not inspired undiluted admiration (Monahan, 1991). Germany has no examining magistrate. The prosecutor is expected to exercise a degree of impartial supervision of the investigation. There is the traditional inquisitorial emphasis on dossier evidence (Leigh and Zedner, 1993). The systems in Scandinavia and The Netherlands also vary in structure, but all see it as the role of the police to investigate matters pertinent to the defence, at the instigation of the prosecutor, examining magistrate or defence lawyers (Leigh and Hall Williams, 1981). Shifting power from the police to the examining magistrate did not eliminate corruption problems in Italy, and so although their system is still mixed, it has been made far more adversarial since the enactment of the 1988 Code of Criminal Procedure. The trial proceeds on the basis of oral rather than dossier evidence (Amadio and Selvaggi, 1989; Pizzi and Marafioli, 1989).

MERITS OF THE TWO SYSTEMS

It is possible to regard the adversarial trial merely as a facility which allows the just settlement of a dispute. Parties are provided with a forum, a neutral referee and enforcement of any settlement or decision. This enables the resolution of differences without personal violence. Many critics refer sourly to the 'sporting' ethos (Frankel, 1975; Bennett and Feldman, 1981; McEwan, 1992). The Court of Appeal, in England and Wales, has historically perceived its role in criminal cases in terms redolent of a facilitative or 'sporting' theory of justice. It has emphasised that it was the parties' responsibility to advance their own cases as effectively as possible on the day. Appeals have largely concentrated on technical irregularity, a failure by the state to provide a proper forum, rather than upon the unreliability of the verdict. Fresh evidence has rarely been treated as grounds for appeal, unless it was unavailable to the parties at the time (*Parks*, (1962) 46 Cr App R 29; *Beal*, (1964) 48 Cr App R

342). The Royal Commission on Criminal Justice has argued, however, that a defendant should not have to suffer for the mismanagement of his case by his lawyers, although neither should the Crown Court trial be seen as 'nothing more than a practice run, which, in the event of a conviction, will leave them free to put an alternative defence to the Court of Appeal in whatever manner they please' (Runciman, 1993, p. 173).

The notoriety of recent miscarriage of justice appeals in England has forced a recognition that the public demands a commitment to discovery of the truth in criminal proceedings; hence the Royal Commission's recommendation that there be an independent body to investigate alleged miscarriages (Runciman, 1993, p. 180). This body would operate totally outside the adversarial structure.

Admirers of the adversarial tradition, rejecting the 'sporting' or 'facilitative' theories, claim that an adversarial model represents the best means for ascertainment of the truth. Two warring parties are highly motivated to search for self-serving evidence and to discredit the opposition. They offer the court two selective versions from which it may choose the likeliest, or it may decide that the truth lies somewhere between the two. Critics would reply that if it suits neither party to adduce all relevant evidence in a particular case, certain evidence will not be heard at all. Further criticisms centre upon the level of control advocates have over witnesses' testimony, the potential for theatrical 'tricks', and the impact of technical and procedural rules on the outcome (Frankel, 1975; Bennett and Feldman, 1981; McEwan, 1992). In continental European systems the parties are less able to control the direction of the inquiry. For example, the defendant is not allowed to shut down discussion of the whole of the case by pleading guilty, which in adversarial systems effectively denies the court any role in the determination of fact. In inquisitorial models it is for the tribunal to satisfy itself of the defendant's guilt.

Recently there have been suggestions that the introduction of more inquisitorial elements such as the examining magistrate into English criminal investigations would reduce the risk of miscarriages of justice. The Runciman Commission's research study (Leigh and Zedner, 1993) concluded that only a major restructuring of all relevant institutions could sustain such a change. The thorough paperwork characteristic of major continental European investigations would make the kind of mistakes which led to the notorious British miscarriages of justice unlikely only when there is genuine neutrality and active intervention by the examining magistrate. In most cases, pressure of case load renders the active participation of the French examining magistrate or the German prosecutor in the inquiry virtually impossible. Where it does occur, cases proceed extremely slowly. The investigation in France into the *Ekmund*, a ship apparently used for smuggling weapons for the IRA (Irish Republican Army), lasted over three years, building up enormous dossiers. Meanwhile, three of the suspects languished in prison. The trial itself lasted for three days. Judgment was given two months later. The Report of the Royal

Commission (Runciman, 1993) concludes that emulation of the French system, slow and affording few rights to suspects in custody, is not the way forward.

It seems from the work of Thibaut and Walker (1975; see also Lind, Kanfer and Earley, 1990) that the adversarial system is perceived to be fairer than the inquisitorial method by participants and observers of mock trials, whether or not those subjects came from an adversarial background. But the imbalance of resources between genuine litigants should be borne in mind. Experimenters are hard put to reproduce the practical problems faced by the real-life parties to adversarial proceedings. This research has been criticised further because, in the mock trials, the facts were not in dispute. Parties were seen in the inquisitorial model to be unable to govern choice of issue, which may have made it more likely that subjects would perceive it as unfair (Stephenson, 1992).

PRINCIPLE OF ORALITY

In theory an adversarial trial could proceed mainly on paper. But, if the parties are to test the strength of each other's witnesses, with the judge acting as umpire, then inevitably proceedings will become primarily dependent on oral evidence. In the Anglo-Saxon trial this has resulted in a formal and symmetrical structure in which the party with the right to begin calls those witnesses whose evidence supports his or her version of the facts, as part of the case in chief. Each witness presents this evidence in chief in the form of answers to questions from counsel. These must not be leading questions, that is, they must not suggest the answer or assume the existence of facts which have yet to be proved.

Judicial preference for spontaneity in evidence-in-chief has been a major problem for those attempting to use, in lieu of a child's evidence at trial, a videotaped interview in which he or she discloses abuse. It has led to the production in England and Wales of complicated models to guide the professional interviewers concerned. It directs them to achieve as much spontaneous disclosure as is possible (Memorandum, 1992). Yet young children may have difficulty in recall without some leading questions (Marin et al., 1979; Ceci, Ross and Toglia, 1987). Also, the apparent spontaneity of conventional evidence-in-chief is illusory. Witnesses may in fact refresh their memory from their own witness statements before going into court (*Richardson* (1971) 55 Cr App R 244) or even interrupt their testimony to look through them if having trouble remembering the facts, as long as they have not already read through them outside the court (*Da Silva* [1990] 1 W.L.R. 31). These witness statements themselves are often the product of leading questions and suggestions from the police officer who took them and who wove the replies into the required structure in his or her own language (Maguire and Norris, 1993).

After examination-in-chief a witness faces cross-examination from the other side, who may employ leading questions and attack his or her credibility on any basis. Although it is perceived by many lawyers as a vital forensic instrument which remorselessly exposes dishonesty and untrustworthiness, cross-examination is actually an inevitable product of the adversarial structure with its dependence on oral evidence and party control (McEwan, 1992). However, it provides cause for concern if cross-examination is used merely to frighten or humiliate, as with rape complainants or child witnesses (Temkin, 1987; Morgan, 1956). The right to cross-examine is assumed to be so important that it has led to resistance to proposals to modify the rule against hearsay evidence (McEwan, 1992) and to the campaign concerning children's evidence which led to the halfhearted reforms of the Criminal Justice Act 1991. The ability to replace a child witness's evidence-in-chief with a videotaped interview is countered by the requirement that in every case the child concerned must attend to court in order to submit to cross-examination. Barristers specialising in criminal law argued, very strongly, that a defendant who cannot cross-examine a child who makes accusations of abuse is severely and unfairly disadvantaged.

Are leading questions the best means of testing a witness's reliability? Psychologists have much to say on the subject of suggestion, although not in this context. The conditions for suggestibility set out by Gudjonsson and Clark (1986) may or may not exist, depending on the circumstances, in the courtroom setting. Whether a particular witness is highly suggestible is not a matter on which a court can hear expert evidence (*Silcott, Braithwaite and Raghip, The Times*, 9 December 1991; Gudjonsson, 1992). They cannot, properly, hear evidence about the credibility of witnesses generally, barring 'abnormality' (*Toohey v. M.P.C.*, [1965] 595).

To lawyers, the hesitancy and confusion that cross-examination may cause witnesses vindicates their faith in it. Loss of confidence by the witness will discourage the jury from relying on his or her evidence (Wells, Leippe and Ostrom; 1979; Wells, Lindsay and Ferguson, 1979; Wells, Ferguson and Lindsay, 1981; Lindsay, Wells and Rumpel, 1981; Daffenbacher and Loftus, 1986). But researchers can find no consistent relationship between a witness's perceived confidence and his or her reliability (Wells, Ferguson and Lindsay, 1981; Lindsay, Wells and Rumpel, 1981). The Royal Commission on Criminal Justice (for England and Wales) was sufficiently aware of the danger that indications of nervousness might be misconstrued, that they were cautious on the suggestion that videotaped interrogations of suspects be used as evidence in criminal trials (Runciman, 1993).

The hearsay rule not only places tremendous store on the discrediting power of cross-examination, but makes the assumption that magistrates and juries cannot be trusted to understand the inherent weaknesses of hearsay. This doubt may be unfounded (Park, Koverra and Penrod, 1992), according to research which, possibly misleadingly, used undergraduates as subjects. Other curious assumptions lie behind the common law exceptions to the hearsay rule such as that of *res gestae*. This rule provides that a hearsay statement may be admitted provided that it amounted to a spontaneous reaction to an event by a witness who is absent, whether or not it was exactly contemporaneous, provided that the events were 'so unusual or startling or dramatic as to dominate the thoughts of the victim so that his reaction was an instinctive reaction to that event, thus giving no real opportunity for reasoned reflection' (*Andrews* [1987] A.C. 281). Psychologists could usefully compare the legal assumption that such evidence is, because of the lack of opportunity to concoct, inherently more reliable than other kinds of hearsay, with the work done on arousal and reliability, and with the weapon effect studies (e.g. Clifford and Scott, 1978; Penrod, Loftus and Winkler, 1982; Yuille and Cutshall, 1986; Maas and Köhnken, 1989).

JURIES

Jury trial is not an essential element of adversarial procedure, although it is found most regularly within Anglo-Saxon systems. Damasaka (1973) argues that jury trial follows naturally from an adversarial structure. Continental systems have very varied approaches, some using panels of assessors or judges rather than juries, others variants on the jury. In France the judge now retires with the jury and participates in the determination of guilt. When this change was effected the conviction rates in French trials rose sharply, as they did when juries became involved in the sentencing decision, possibly because a jury is more reluctant to convict if it fears excessive punishment (Munday, 1993). In Anglo-Saxon systems there is increasing disquiet about the reliability of jury decisions (Baldwin and McConville, 1979; Roskill, 1986; Stephenson, 1992). Shadow juries sitting in on trials have come to decisions alarmingly inconsistent with the actual verdict (McCabe and Purves, 1974) and psychologists have sounded the alarm about group decision-making (James, 1982). But the alternatives to jury trial may be no more dependable (Carlen, 1976; McBarnett, 1983).

Psychological research into the operation of juries is hampered in some countries by the secrecy which surrounds actual deliberations, sometimes forcing reliance on simulations. One finding, which lawyers should perhaps bear in mind, is that gaps in the evidence before a jury appear to make comprehension and recall difficult if they hamper the construction of a narrative (Thorndyke, 1977; Hastie, Penrod and Pennington, 1983). Many of our exclusionary rules appear to be designed to destroy narrative flow, and so may make a decision unreliable for that reason alone.

EFFECT OF LIMITED RESOURCES

Oral proceedings are potentially time-consuming, and costly and disruptive of the lives of those required to attend. Courts therefore restrict the scope of the inquiry by various means including strictly limiting those issues which can be investigated in detail. This involves an artificially narrow conception of relevance. In *Blastland* ([1985] 2 All E.R. 1095), for example, the House of Lords decided that the accused may not suggest by means of circumstantial evidence that someone else committed the crime, because that is not directly relevant to the question of his or her own guilt.

Matters of only 'collateral' importance may not be pursued at the same length as those which are central (McEwan, 1992). Matters collateral include the credibility of witnesses and, apart from cases which form exceptions to the general rule, the discussion is strictly confined. The distinction here, between evidence related to guilt and evidence going only to credibility is probably spurious in logic (Zuckerman, 1989), and inevitably will confuse jurors, particularly when they have to deal with evidence of the defendant's previous criminality.

Evidence of criminal record is admissible on the issue of guilt, in British and similar legal systems, only where it satisfies the 'similar facts' principle; its probative value must outweigh its prejudicial effect (*Makin v. AG for New South Wales,* [1894] A.C. 57). The assumption is that jurors will attach too much weight to evidence which merely demonstrates the defendant's unsavoury character. The law on when charges can be tried together is partly governed by the 'similar facts' principle. Research by psychologists shows that trying separate charges together does indeed create a bias against the defendant so that he or she is more likely to be convicted (Horowitz, Bordens and Feldman, 1979; Tanford and Penrod, 1982; Bordens and Horowitz, 1983; Bordens and Horowitz, 1985). But the fundamental assumptions of the decisions on 'similar fact' have, so far, not been challenged. For example, judges' insistence on there being a similarity between the previous offences and the current charge (although this no longer needs to be a striking similarity, *R. v P.*, [1991] 3 W.L.R. 161) disregards the wealth of information about patterns of offending on which offender profiling is based.

Suppose, for example, that the defence in a rape case is that the complainant consented to intercourse, or that she has identified the wrong person. The defendant's previous convictions for sexual offences are admissible on this point only if there are common features linking them to the current charge. However, the true probative value may not depend upon there being a 'system' but, in some cases, upon the indication of a personality that is so abnormal that it is unlikely that in this particular instance the complainant is lying or mistaken. There is a wealth of literature on sadistic offenders which could assist courts to determine the true significance of previous criminal and antisocial tendencies (de River, 1956; Gebhard et al., 1965; Brittain, 1970; McCullock *et al.*, 1973; Walker and McCabe, 1973; Groth, 1978; Morneaux and Rockwell, 1980; Ressler, Burgess and Douglas, 1985; Bluglass, 1980; Ressler et al., 1986). The psychological debate on the comparative influence of trait over situation, in the case of abnormal personalities (Alker, 1972), would also clearly be of vital relevance here.

In most Anglo-Saxon jurisdictions legislation allows for the cross-examination of the accused on his or her criminal record if he or she attacks the character of prosecution witnesses or adduces evidence of his or her own good character. In this context, the convictions are relevant only to the credibility of the accused as a witness in his or her own defence. Studies of the effect on jurors of such evidential provisions found that, irrespective of guidance from the trial judge, previous convictions were more instrumental to effect convictions than affect perceptions of credibility (Hatton, Snortum and Oskamp, 1971; Doob and Kirschbaum, 1972; Wissler and Saks, 1985; Hans and Doob, 1975). These findings are questionable since all the evidence before the mock jurors was in documentary form; the jurors did not see the defendant giving evidence, but were required to adjudicate on his or her credibility. There is considerable scope here for more persuasive research on the use juries make of such information, and also for investigating the effect of different kinds of criminal record on juries' perceptions of defendant credibility (but see Cornish and Sealy, 1973). Lawyers are currently much exercised by the question whether the only previous convictions genuinely relevant to the defendant's credibility are those involving dishonesty (McEwan, 1992, p. 160). It should be noted, however, that other witnesses are regularly cross-examined on all their previous convictions in order to discredit them.

EXPERT EVIDENCE

Credibility is, in adversarial systems, an issue of only collateral importance. To the judicial mind, judging the veracity of others is an assessment jurors are accustomed to make in their daily lives. Their common sense and experience make them ideally suited to the task, which they should perform unaided. Experts have no business telling juries what to think, unless they have claim to superior judgement. On matters of credibility, such a claim exists only where the witness has a personality or has characteristics (such as being a child) which take the issue beyond the everyday experience of jurors. Mental abnormality, for example, is a field of knowledge where there can be genuine expertise. Thus such an expert may discuss the likely effect of that abnormality on the behaviour and testimony of persons suffering from it. The expert witness may not, however, state an opinion as to whether *that* witness is telling the truth (*Toohey* above). Whether or not such abnormality exists is for the court to say. Until recently, British judges were reluctant to admit expert evidence on the reliability of confessions where the defendant is 'normal', even though his or her personality might be vulnerable. In *Masih* ([1986] Crim L.R. 395) an IQ of 72 was treated as 'normal' by the Court of Appeal. It followed that the trial judge had been right to exclude expert evidence on the reliability of the defendant's confession. But in more recent cases (*Raghip* above) it has been held that the admissibility of expert evidence should not depend on where the accused's IQ might fall in relation to an arbitrary line, wherever placed: 'The expert evidence of a psychiatrist or a psychologist may properly be admitted if it is to the effect that a defendant is suffering from a condition not properly described as mental illness, but from a personality disorder so severe as properly to be categorised as mental disorder' (*Ward*, [1993] 2 ALL E.R. 577 per Glidewell LJ at 641).

Work on false confessions is now receiving considerable judicial attention and respect (Gudjonsson, 1992). It has influenced the Codes of Practice issued under the Police and Criminal Evidence Act 1984, in an effort to protect particularly vulnerable suspects at the police station. 'Appropriate adults' should attend the police interviews of all suspects with a mental illness or learning disability, or if there is any doubt about the suspect's mental capacity. Specialist and psychiatric social workers are increasingly called upon to act as 'appropriate adults' in such cases (Brown, Ellis and Larcombe, 1993). Research carried out for the Royal Commission chaired by Lord Runciman found that, although the police missed some cases of mental illness or learning disability, they were able to identify the most serious cases and take the necessary steps to ensure that they were properly represented (Gudjonsson et al., 1993).

Concern about the potential unreliability of confessions generally, reinforced by the finding that any questioning in a police station inspires chronic anxiety (Irving, 1980) has led to the proposal that in every criminal prosecution there should be independent evidence supporting a confession. Nevertheless the Royal Commission, while accepting that there is no apparent basis for the traditional legal assumption that a statement against the interests of the person making it is likely to be true, rejects the suggestion that there should be a blanket corroboration requirement for confessions. Few convictions are sustained on confession evidence alone, and only 5 per cent of convictions would probably have been acquittals had there been such a requirement (McConville, 1993). The problem of the unreliable confession should instead be dealt with by a warning from the judge of the risks attached to unsupported confessions. This leaves it open to the jury to convict on the strength of the confession alone. However, very vulnerable suspects are now regarded by the Court of Appeal as a special category that should be treated with caution. In *McKenzie* ([1992] N.L.J. 1162), the defendant's IQ was about 76 and he was found to be highly suggestible under pressure. He confessed, during questioning about another matter, to ten murders, some of which he could not have committed. There was no evidence apart from his confessions in relation to those for which he was tried. The convictions for murder were quashed on appeal. It was held that in cases where the defendant suffers from a significant degree of mental handicap and the confessions are unconvincing to the point where the jury could not properly convict upon them, the judge should withdraw the case from them at the end of the prosecution case, if there is no other evidence.

It should be noted that in *Ward* the Court of Appeal made it very clear that the admissibility of expert evidence on confession reliability was a very different matter from that of *mens rea* (intention). That is still entirely a jury issue. The distinction here rests on the supposed rule that where expert evidence is admissible, it should not be offered on the 'ultimate issue', that is the matter that the jury has to decide, such as whether the defendant intended the results of his or her actions (*Turner* [1975] Q.B. 834). But it is recognised that there are major departures from this rule. For example, psychiatrists are commonly allowed to give their opinions on the question of whether the defendant is legally insane, although that is actually a matter for the jury. Similarly, an expert witness would in a homicide case be allowed to suggest the probable cause of death, again technically usurping the function of the jury but in an area where the jury need assistance (*D.P.P. v. A and B.C. Chewing Gum* [1968] 1 Q.B. 159).

The double standards here are typical of the haphazard use of scientific evidence in courts. This may be because distrust of 'trick cyclists' (see Lawton L.J. in *Turner* above) motivates judges to confine psychiatric and psychological evidence within narrow limits. But more probably the explanation is a fear of the 'hired gun' expert witness adjusting his or her opinion in a quest for lucrative court work. Such an individual might be perceived to be the natural consequence of an adversarial system. Whether or not there are such witnesses operating, as is frequently claimed, in the courts of the United States, there has been no serious suggestion that this is so in the United Kingdom. The Royal Commission therefore saw no necessity for a system of statutory accreditation, but did recommend that professional bodies 'assist the court' by maintaining registers of members qualified to act as expert witnesses in particular fields (Runciman, 1993, p.161). But it may be that to ensure the financial security of experts is the best way to promote professional independence and integrity.

REFERENCES

Alker, H.A. (1972). Is personality situationally specific or intrapsychically consistent? *Journal of Personality*, **40**, 1–16.

Amadio, E. and Selvaggi, E. (1989). An accusatorial system in a civil law country: the 1988 Italian Code of Criminal Procedure. *Temple Law Review*, **62**, 1211.

Baldwin, J. and McConville, M. (1979). *Jury Trials*. Oxford: Clarendon.

Bennett, W.L. and Feldman, M. (1981). *Reconstructing Reality in the Courtroom*. London: Tavistock.

Bluglass, R. (1980). Indecent exposure in the West Midlands. In D.J. West (Ed.), *Sexual Offenders in the Criminal Justice System*. Cambridge: Cambridge Institute of Criminology.

Bordens, K.S. and Horowitz, I.A. (1983). Information processing in joined and severed trials. *Journal of Applied Social Psychology*, **13**, 351–70.

Bordens, K.S. and Horowitz, I.A. (1985). Joinder of offences: a review of the legal and psychological literature. *Law and Human Behaviour*, **9**, 4, 339–53.

Brittain, R.P. (1970). The sadistic murderer. *Medicine Science and the Law*, **10**, 202.

Brown, D., Ellis, T. and Larcombe, K. (1993). *Changing the Code; Police Detention under the Revised PACE Codes of Practice*, Home Office Research and Planning Unit. London: HMSO.

Carlen, P. (1976). *Magistrates Justice*. Oxford: Martin Robertson.

Ceci, S.J., Ross, D.F. and Toglia, M.P. (1987). Suggestibility of children's memory: psycho-legal implications. *Journal of Experimental Psychology: General*, **116**, 1, 38–49.

Clifford, B.R. and Scott, J. (1978). Individual and situational factors in eyewitness testimony. *Journal of Applied Psychology*, **63**, 3, 353–9.

Cornish, W.R. and Sealy, A.P. (1973). Juries and the rules of evidence. *Criminal Law Quarterly*, **16**, 208–23.

Daffenbacher, K.A. and Loftus, E.F. (1986). Do jurors share a common understanding concerning eyewitness behavior? *Law and Human Behavior*, **15**.

Damaska, M. (1973). Evidentiary barriers to conviction and two models of criminal procedure: a comparative study. *University of Pennsylvania Law Review*, 506.

Delmas, Marty (1991). Report of the Commission Justice Pénale et Droits de l'Homme, *La Mise en Etat des Affaire Pénale*. Paris: Documentation Francaise.

Doob, A.N. and Kirschbaum, H. (1972). Some empirical evidence on the effect of s.12 Canada Evidence Act upon an accused. *Criminal Law Quarterly*, **15**, 88–96.

Frankel, M.E. (1975). The search for truth: an umpireal view. *University of Pennsylvania Law Review*, 1031.

Gebhard, P.H., Gagnon, J.H., Pomeroy, W.B. and Christianson, C.V. (1965). *Sex Offenders*. London: Heineman.

Griffiths, J. (1970). Ideology in criminal procedure or a third 'model' of the criminal process. *Yale Law Journal*, **79**, 359.

Gudjonsson, G.H. (1992). *The Psychology of Interrogations, Confessions and Testimony*. Chichester: John Wiley.

Gudjonsson, G.H. and Clark, N.K. (1986). Suggestibility in police interrogation: a social psychological model. *Social Behaviour*, **4**, 189–93.

Gudjonsson, G.H., Clare, I., Rutter, S. and Pearse, J. (1993). *Persons at Risk During Iinterviews in Police Custody: The Identification of Vulnerabilities*. London: HMSO. (Royal Commission on Criminal Justice Research Study No. 12.)

Hans, V.P. and Doob, A.N. (1975). Section 12 Canada Evidence Act and the deliberations of simulated juries. *Criminal Law Quarterly*, **18**, 235–53.

Hastie, R., Penrod, S. and Pennington, N. (1983). *Inside the Jury*. Cambridge, MA: Harvard University Press.

Hatton, D.E., Snortum, J.R. and Oskamp, S. (1971). The effects of biasing information and dogmatism upon witness testimony. *Psychonomic Science*, **23**, 425–7.

Horowitz, I.A., Bordens, K.S. and Feldman, M.S. (1979). A comparison of verdicts obtained in severed and joined trials. *Journal of Applied Social Psychology*, **10**, 16–27.

Irving, B. (1980). *Police Interrogations; A Case Study of Current Practice*. Royal Commission on Criminal Procedure Research Study No. 2.

James, I.L. (1982). *Victims of Group-think*. Boston, MA: Houghton Mifflin.

Leigh, L.H. and Hall Williams, J.E. (1981). *The Management of the Prosecution Process in Denmark, Sweden and the Netherlands*. Leamington: James Hall.

Leigh, L.H. and Zedner, L. (1993). *A Report on the Administration of Criminal Justice in the Pretrial Phase in France and Germany*. London: HMSO. (Royal Commission on Criminal Justice Research Study No. 1.)

Lind, E.R., Kanfer, R. and Earley, P.C. (1990). Voice, control and procedural justice, instrumental and non-instrumental concerns in fairness judgments. *Journal of Personality and Social Psychology*, **59**, 952.

Lindsay, R.C., Wells, G.L. and Rumpel, C.M. (1981). Can people detect eyewitness identification accuracy within and between situations? *Journal of Applied Psychology*, **66**, 798–9.

Maas, G.M. and Köhnken, G. (1989). Eyewitness identification and the selection of distractors for lineups. *Law and Human Behavior*, **15**, 43–57.

McBarnett, D.J. (1983). *Conviction*. Oxford: Macmillan.

McCabe, S. and Purves, R. (1974). *The Shadow Jury at Work*. Oxford: Blackwell/ Oxford University Penal Research Unit.

McConville, M. (1993). *Corroboration and Confessions: The Impact of a Rule Requiring that No Conviction can be Sustained on the Basis of Confession Evidence Alone*. London: HMSO. (Royal Commission on Criminal Justice Research Study No. 13.)

McCullock, M.J, Snowden, P.R., Wood, P.J. and Mills, H.E. (1973). Sadistic fantasy, sadistic behaviour and offending. *British Journal of Psychiatry*, **143**, 20–9.

McEwan, J. (1992). *Evidence and the Adversarial Process: The Modern Law*. Oxford: Blackwell.

Maguire, M. and Norris, C. (1993). *The Conduct and Supervision of Criminal Investigations*. London: HMSO. (Royal Commission Research Study No. 5.)

Marin, B.V., Holmes, D.L., Guth, M. and Kovac, P. (1979). The potential of children as eye-witnesses. *Law and Human Behavior*, **3**, 295.

Memorandum of Good Practice on Video-recorded Interviews with Child Witnesses for Criminal Proceedings (1992). London: Home Office/Department of Health.

Monahan, J. (1991). Sanctioning injustice. *New Law Journal*, 679.

Morgan, E.M. (1956). *Some Problems of Proof Under the Anglo-American Systems of Litigation*. New York: University of North Carolina.

Morneaux, R.H. and Rockwell, R.R. (1980). *Sex, Motivation and the Criminal Offender*. Springfield, IL: Charles C. Thomas.

Munday, R. (1993). Jury trial, Continental style. *Legal Studies*, **13**, 204.

Oddie, C. (1991). *Science and the Administration of Justice*. London: Justice.

Park, R.C., Koverra, M.B. and Penrod, S.D. (1992). Jurors' perception of hearsay evidence. Paper presented at Third European Conference on Law and Psychology, Oxford.

Penrod, S.D., Loftus, E.R. and Winkler, J. (1982). The reliability of eyewitness testimony: a psychological perspective. In N.K. Kerr and R.M. Bray (Eds), *The Psychology of the Courtroom*. London: Academic Press.

Pizzi, W.T. and Marafioli, L. (1989). The new Italian code of criminal procedure: the difficulties of building an adversarial trial system on a civil law foundation. *Yale Journal of International Law*, **17**, Winter.

Ressler, R.K., Burgess, A.W. and Douglas, J.E. (1985). Rape and rape-murder: one offender and twelve victims. In A.W. Burgess (Ed.), *Rape and Sexual Assault*. New York: Garland.

Ressler, R.K., Burgess, A.W., Hertman, C.R., Douglas, J.E. and McCormack, A. (1986). Murderers who rape and mutilate. *Journal of Interpersonal Violence*, **1**, 3, 273–87.

de River, J.P. (1956). *The Sexual Criminal: A Psychoanalytical Study*. Springfield, IL: Charles C. Thomas.

Roskill, the Right Honourable the Lord Roskill, P.C. (1986). *Fraud Trials Committee Report*. London: HMSO.

Runciman (1993). *Report of the Royal Commission on Criminal Justice*, Cm 2263. London: HMSO.

Stephenson, G.M. (1992). *The Psychology of Criminal Justice*. Oxford: Blackwell.

Tanford, S. and Penrod, S. (1982). Biases in trials involving defendants charged with multiple offences. *Journal of Applied Social Psychology*, **12**, 453–80.

Temkin, J. (1987). *Rape and the Legal Process*. London: Sweet & Maxwell.

Thibaut, J.N. and Walker, L. (1975). *Procedural Justice and Psychological Analysis*. New York: John Wiley.

Thorndyke, P.W. (1977). Cognitive structure in comprehension and memory of narrative discourse. *Cognitive Psychology*, **9**, 77–110.

Walker, N. and McCabe, S. (1973). *Crime and Insanity in England Vol II*. Edinburgh: Edinburgh University Press.

Wells, G.L., Ferguson, T.J. and Lindsay, R.C. (1981). The tractability of eyewitness confidence and its implications for triers of fact. *Journal of Applied Psychology*, **66**, 688–96.

Wells, G.L., Leippe, M.R. and Ostrom, T.M. (1979). Guidelines for empirically assessing the fairness of a lineup. *Law and Human Behavior*, **3**, 283–93.

Wells, G.L., Lindsay, R.C. and Ferguson, T.J. (1979). Accuracy, confidence and juror perceptions in eyewitness identification. *Journal of Applied Psychology*, **66,** 798.

Wissler, R.L. and Saks, M.J. (1985). On the inefficacy of limiting instructions: when jurors use prior conviction evidence to decide guilt. *Law and Human Behaviour*, **9**, 1, 37–48.

Yuille, J.C. and Cutshall, J.L. (1986). A case study of eyewitness memory of a crime. *Journal of Applied Psychology*, **71**, 291.

Zuckerman, A. (1989). *Principles of Criminal Evidence*. Oxford: Oxford University Press.

Chapter 6.2

Judicial Decision-making: A Theoretical Perspective

John A. Michon
Netherlands Institute for the Study of Criminality and Law Enforcement
and
Francis J. Pakes
Netherlands Institute for the Study of Criminality and Law Enforcement

INTRODUCTION

Decision-making is a very common, yet rather ill-defined category of human action. For instance, it is involved in determining what clothes to buy, what to have for lunch, which partner to choose and in considering possible career moves. Rapid judgements are involved when someone tells us 'You are driving too fast' or when simple preferences such as 'I'll have coffee' are expressed. Complex decisions, often extending over a period of years may, for instance, concern the construction of a new airport or the election of a new president. For quite some time now psychologists have been studying the processes that underlie the making of such decisions, trivial and complex.

Experts in the field are regularly consulted by policy-makers looking for better and more efficient discussion and judgement methods that may help them to optimise the decision-making process. Optimal decision-making is obviously desirable in criminal law. Society demands that decisions be made in a manner that is 'rational' and free of individual preferences and biases. However, judicial decision-makers are only human; consequently psychological decision theory, which aims at modelling the peculiarities and fallacies of human decision-making, has a lot to offer to the criminal justice system. Conversely, judicial decision-making is an interesting area of research for decision theorists because of the complexity of the information that has to be decided upon and the impact of most judicial decisions for the individuals involved. This chapter sets out to describe where and how this cross-fertilisation between the criminal justice system and psychological decision theory is to be achieved.

Handbook of Psychology in Legal Contexts
Edited by R. Bull and D. Carson. © 1995 John Wiley & Sons Ltd

STRATEGIC, OPERATIONAL AND TACTICAL DECISIONS

Decisions can be studied from different perspectives, and at different levels of analysis. The hierarchical distinction between strategic, tactical and operational decisions, common in traffic research (Michon, 1971, 1985) is also applicable to judicial decisions. An example is the public prosecutor's decision of how to proceed in an attempted murder case. Imagine a situation in which a suspect is arrested and held in custody. A *strategic* decision will concern what to do at a highest level: whether or not to prosecute. *Tactical* decisions are related to the manner in which this strategic decision is implemented, such as the specific terms of the charge: for example, causing actual or grievous bodily harm? On what grounds can the suspect be kept in custody: to permit further investigations or to prevent further crimes? A string of *operational* decisions (the decisions that are lowest in the hierarchy) is to be made in order to carry out all the steps needed to implement decisions at the tactical and strategic level. These decisions concern the filling out of forms, reading files, talking to police officials for more information, and the like.

Strategic decisions provide conditions (or 'givens') for tactical decisions; subsequently tactical decisions play the same role for operational decisions. Strategic decisions are stronger and more comprehensive, they are related to principled choices and personal commitments. They represent the goals the actor ultimately wants to achieve. Tactical decisions require less intellectual effort and are more strongly related to a personal style according to which strategic decisions are actually carried out. Operational decisions are usually constrained by routines and regulations. They are more influenced by transient or random circumstances than are tactical decisions.

Although the distinction between strategic, tactical and operational decisions is relative, the notion that decisions are usually embedded in a hierarchical structure is an important one. Higher level decisions determine conditions and constraints for decisions that fit into the lower levels in the hierarchy.

NORMATIVE AND DESCRIPTIVE APPROACHES TO DECISION-MAKING

A distinction is often made in decision theory between normative and descriptive models of decision-making. Normative models describe optimal decision-making behaviour, whereby the method of decision-making will always lead to an optimal decision provided that neither capacity nor temporal limits exist. Typical normative decision methods are the maximin method: each decision should be in favour of the alternative with the highest utility value under the most unfavourable circumstances; or the minimal regret method, where regret is defined as the difference between the gain derived from the best possible outcome and the actual gain. Each decision should favour the alternative for which the regret is minimal (Coombs, Dawes and Tverski, 1970).

Descriptive models, on the other hand, describe how real-life decisions are actually made. These models bear a closer relation to everyday decision-making and its shortcomings. A basic assumption underlying these models is that real decision-makers are inherently imperfect. Their ability to gather relevant information is limited which makes them necessarily selective in their use of information. The strategies people actually use in order to achieve their goals are incorporated in descriptive models.

Normative and descriptive models are often, quite erroneously, thought of as inevitable contrasts, but in fact the two should be viewed as complementary. While the normative approach offers a strictly rational way of dealing with problems which is never seen in real life, the descriptive approach gives insight into the heuristics and strategies that decision-makers actually use. Looking at decision-making both ways enables us to tune decision-making procedures to the limitations and peculiarities of the decision-maker actually dealing with the problem. Descriptive research can help to specify the constraints to be taken into account when decision procedures are designed that are as practical, efficient and 'rational' as possible.

In the realm of criminal justice, the law offers decision-making procedures; it prescribes what to do in a given situation: for example, a person may be convicted only when guilt is proven beyond a reasonable doubt. In decision-theoretical terms, the law can be viewed as a normative model. By implication, it is also prescriptive to the extent that it prescribes how decisions are to be made: the alternatives are listed and the decision criteria (such as 'reasonable grounds', 'preponderance of the evidence', or 'beyond reasonable doubt') are stated as well. Furthermore it is assumed that all the information that is needed is indeed available and taken into account.

Psychology offers the descriptive side of the coin. It describes how decision-makers reach these judgements, how they assess likelihoods of certain outcomes and their utilities. It focuses on the strategies people actually use in order to overcome their limited mental resources and incomplete knowledge. In short, it aims to describe the cognitive processes involved in decision-making.

THE DECISION-MAKING PROCESS: PRINCIPAL STAGES AND COMPONENTS

In the decision-making process we distinguish several steps. The following description is by no means the only possible one. Several models exist, but most are consistent with the following description, based on that of Vlek and Michon (1980).

1. *Problem recognition.* The first step is that the decision-maker perceives that there is a problem—that is, a discrepancy between the actual state of affairs and the desired state. For example, an arrested person, suspected of burglary, is in a police cell. The desired state of affairs is that, ultimately, the suspect is punished if found guilty, or released if innocent, and the problem is how to achieve that desired state.

2. *Decision-making problem.* The recognised problem becomes a decision-making problem if the decision-maker must decide what should be done about the current situation and if the options will have to be considered within a limited time frame. Action is required regarding arrested suspects as they can only be kept in a police cell for a limited period of time.

3. *Identification of consequences.* Available options have consequences, which are typically uncertain. The public prosecutor may wish to bring the suspect to trial, yet cannot be certain that the suspect will be convicted. When convincing evidence is available he or she may decide to prosecute. If there is insufficient evidence the suspect has to be released within a given period. The prosecutor may want pre-trial custody or other restrictions to be imposed upon the suspect and may therefore put in such a request before the examining judge.

4. *Utility and likelihood assessment.* The implications of taking particular decisions need to be evaluated on their value or utility. It is, for instance, of little utility to a prosecutor if a suspect is acquitted. In that case, time and effort are said to have been 'wasted'. Such evaluations will frequently result in a simple rank-ordering of the consequences but in a good many cases it is also possible to weigh the differences in more quantitative terms that allows assessment in terms of likelihood. What if a suspect who is not detained re-offends before trial? This outcome has a lot of negative utility: such costs concerning public safety are, of course, vital considerations for a prosecutor who represents the public interest in criminal law. However, an assessment of the likelihood that a particular suspect will re-offend is not an easy matter. It should be added, however, that while an assessment of the likelihood that a suspect will re-offend is extremely difficult, in practical terms, it is more important for prosecutors to estimate the likelihood that an application for detention in custody will be granted.

5. *Long-term versus short-term consequences.* The consequences of a decision may become manifest in the short term or in the long term. Some decisions may require a focus on short-term consequences while other problems can be more appropriately dealt with if the long-term consequences are taken into account. For example, temporary prison overcrowding can be a short-term argument for a less frequent use of pre-trial custody.

6. *Choosing between alternatives.* Finally, a decision has to be made. If a decision can have different possible consequences, their likelihood and utility judgements will have to be weighed; judges often refer to a necessary balancing operation, which is quite apt in this context. Thus a very valuable but highly unlikely outcome may have an insignificant effect on the outcome of the decision process, and so may a rather likely but highly inconsequential outcome. A measure, or decision criterion, is needed to decide which option to choose. In the legal context some decision criteria are explicitly stated. The concept 'probable cause' as used in the United States is such a criterion; it refers to the degree of certainty that is needed for a police officer to make an arrest. Likewise, the Dutch Code of Criminal Procedure states specific decision criteria for the appropriateness of arrests and pre-trial custody, and for a court to convict.

In normative terms one would expect decision-makers to behave optimally at every step in the decision-making process. The next part of the chapter relates, descriptively, how people actually carry out these steps.

Problem Representation

Legal problems can be stated in a very clear or in a highly unstructured fashion. The exact formulation of the problem or, in cognitive terminology, the representation of the problem will impose constraints on the options to be considered. When, in a problem definition, a criminal action is perceived as attempted murder rather than intentional grievous bodily harm the option of pre-trial custody will probably be considered more readily. Moreover, if the charge is attempted murder, the seriousness of this offence is by itself enough to warrant pre-trial custody, on the formal ground that the legal order is 'shocked' by the offence. Thus, the formulation of a problem will affect the number of available options as well as the likelihood and utility of their consequences.

Assignment of Likelihoods

Actions may have all sorts of consequences. A consequence is relevant if the utility of the consequence occurring and the utility of its non-occurrence are sufficiently different, and second, if, with a certain likelihood, the consequence can be expected to occur as a result of some choices but not of others.

How are likelihoods estimated? There is a vast body of psychological literature dealing with this question. A considerable research effort has been invested in describing and modelling typical, persistent errors that people are likely to commit when they are making such likelihood judgements (Kahneman, Slovic and Tverski, 1982; Nisbett and Ross, 1980).

Referring to our burglary case, how does the prosecutor estimate the probability that the examining judge will actually grant a request for pre-trial custody? In formal terms the examining judge will grant this demand if he or she is convinced that (a) there is a certain degree of likelihood that the suspect is guilty of committing the crime and (b) certain formal grounds apply that necessitate pretrial custody (e.g. a high probability that the suspect will re-offend, or further investigation purposes, as defined in the Dutch Code of Criminal Procedure).

Prosecutors will make these judgements in order to formulate their demands. They will also anticipate how the examining judge will evaluate a case. There are three types of reasoning that can lead to the assessment of the likelihood that such a request will be granted. First we shall describe what appears to be the most common type of reasoning, which is frequently labelled as script-based or case-based reasoning. Subsequently we describe a so-called frequentistic heuristic and the problems associated with it, and finally, a personalistic heuristic will be described.

Script-based or Case-based Reasoning

A class of action patterns can be mentally represented in a script or scenario (Schank and Abelson, 1977; Schank, 1986). A script is a generic description of a prototypical course of action. Thus, a burglar may have a 'commuter apartment with dog' script and, similarly, experienced prosecutors are assumed to be able to bring an 'attempted murder script' to mind. They can compare the case at hand with what they know is a typical attempted murder case. This type of reasoning can be described in three steps:

1. the current case is compared with the script (in terms of *modus operandi*, motive, strength of the evidence).

2.. it is decided whether the current case can be considered 'typical'.

3. if the current case is a typical attempted murder case and if the examining judge usually grants demands for pretrial custody in such cases, it is judged likely that in this particular case the demand will be granted as well.

Case-based reasoning involves a comparison between the current case and a *specific* case of which the decision-maker has knowledge. This knowledge can be personal (he or she may have handled a similar case), but may be analogous as well (the current case may resemble a well-known case). Case-based reasoning of this type proceeds as follows:

1. the current case more or less resembles a case I dealt with, or learned about, in the past

2. the application for pretrial custody for that particular case was granted

3. therefore I expect this request to be granted as well.

In cognitive science, legal reasoning systems that incorporate these reasoning types are currently being developed. Usually these systems operate within small, highly context-specific areas of the law. The system HYPO (Ashley, 1990) for instance, operates in the area of intellectual property law. These two reasoning strategies obviously rely on previously acquired knowledge. This knowledge has to be used appropriately in order that good likelihood estimates are made. If non-optimal comparisons between the current case and previous cases (whether they are condensed and abstracted in scripts or kept in memory as specific cases) are made, the estimated likelihood may easily be in very serious error (Neustadt and May, 1986).

Frequentistic Estimates of Likelihood

If there is no relevant case available to which the current case can be compared, decision-makers have to rely upon other heuristics to estimate their chances. They may take frequencies into account. For example, they may consider that in their experience, some four out of five applications for pretrial custody are granted. So, without any further knowledge, they may conclude that the odds are that this particular demand will also be granted. However, decision-makers are likely to become victims of the 'base-rate fallacy' (Kahneman, Slovic and Tverski, 1982). The fact that 80 per cent of all demands are granted does not imply that any particular request to a judge has an 80 per cent chance of being granted. Not known is the probability that applications which the judge could be asked to make, but actually are not, would be granted. Assume that half of the cases in which pre-trial custody could be sought actually do go before the judge. Of this half, 80 per cent is granted. Thus, 80 per cent of half of all the eligible pre-trial custody cases is actually granted. Since the percentage of cases in which no demand is made—but which would be granted if demanded—is unknown, it is difficult to make an estimate about the base rate of granted demands. However, it will be significantly lower than the 80 per cent most people seem to think, according to Kahneman, Slovic and Tverski (1982).

Another frequentistic heuristic is the 'availability heuristic'. In contemplating the chances of a request for pre-trial detention, the decision-maker may think about cases he or she has handled in the past. If the first case that comes to mind (the first case, in other words, that becomes available to the decision-maker) has the desired outcome, namely detention, then the estimated likelihood that the current request will also be granted will be relatively high. Conversely, when the case that is most easily remembered had the undesired outcome of the request being refused, then the assigned likelihood of a positive outcome will be relatively low. The availability heuristic can be viewed as a time and energy saving substitute for an exhaustive memory search.

Frequentistic or probabilistic estimates are more error-prone than script- or case-based methods. This is not surprising since they involve the use of less specific knowledge (in the case of the base rate estimate), or a non-systematic use of knowledge (in the availability heuristic). These strategies are often applied when case-based or script-based methods fail (Hendrickx, 1991).

Personalistic Estimates

When cases have unique elements, it is difficult to use prior knowledge in order to estimate the chances of a demand being granted. In such cases a personalistic heuristic has to be applied. Estimated likelihood is defined here as the degree to which the decision-maker is convinced the outcome will ensue. Given a case with unique features, the best a decision-maker can do is make his or her 'best personal bet'.

In summary, the psychological process of likelihood estimation is inherently imperfect. It depends on the information available and on its use. When the available knowledge is poor, different strategies are afforded than when the available knowledge in long-term memory is rich, detailed and organised in either scripts or cases. This allows for personal differences in the estimation of likelihood. In her dissertation, Malsch (1990) found that lawyers predicting the outcome of cases tend to make use of simplified prediction models, thereby ignoring more specific information. This was found to impair their predictions. She also found that more specialised lawyers were more accurate in their predictions. This can be explained by the availability of better, more appropriate, scripts or more appropriate cases in long-term memory.

Assessment of Utility Values

A consequence is relevant when the decision-maker is not indifferent to it. Furthermore, it must have a marginal likelihood of occurring: a highly attractive consequence with only a remote theoretical chance of actually occurring will often not be considered at all.

In our example regarding the decision concerning the prosecutor's request for pre-trial custody in an attempted murder case, the utility of the decision depends on how necessary it is judged that the suspect be held in custody. This necessity has to be formulated in terms of applicable legal grounds. The more grounds apply (e.g. if the suspect is likely to re-offend, if he or she is likely to impede the criminal investigation process or to evade trial) the higher the utility of granting the demand, and therefore, of making the demand itself. Placing a suspect in pretrial custody has inevitable costs. One cost, or negative utility consequence, is the fact that prison cell capacity (in The Netherlands, as in most Western countries) is rather limited. Furthermore, taking a suspect's freedom before conviction is a serious matter, no matter how necessary it may seem. Thus, taking someone's freedom when presumed innocent is considered a very strongly negative utility consequence.

This brings us to the concept of 'multi-attribute utility'. One single consequence such as, for instance, granting pre-trial detention, has several attributes. Some of these attributes have high utility (for instance, keeping a possibly dangerous offender off the street), while others have low utility, for instance locking up an—as yet—innocent person. A decision procedure is needed to tackle the problem of weighing and summing the various attribute utilities. Such a procedure typically identifies the most important utility attributes and provides for a weighing or integration rule. It also provides a manner in which the utilities of the attributes can be added so that an overall utility value for the consequence in question can be computed. Another complication in multi-attributive utilities is that trade-offs are often involved. This is the case when more of one attribute is inevitably accompanied by less of another. An optimum then has to be found that provides an acceptable level of both attributes.

Making the Decision

One would want an optimal decision procedure to yield results that are 'perfect' in the sense that every suspect who will eventually be found guilty and whose detention is indeed necessary is placed in pre-trial custody and that every suspect who will turn out to be innocent will never be placed in pre-trial custody.

However, as Wagenaar, Van Koppen and Crombag (1993) argue, such a method is impossible given the fact that fixed decision criteria have to be applied. They demonstrate their point with a so-called performance table. In a performance table, four values are depicted, as in Table 6.2.1. We follow their example and elaborate the argument for the judge's decision whether or not to convict a defendant. Thus we have two possible outcomes: either a conviction or an acquittal. Furthermore, the suspect can be 'really guilty' or 'really innocent'. Ideally, the output of any criminal law system would only yield correct decisions. These are called 'hits' (convictions of guilty defendants) and 'correct rejections' (acquittals of innocent defendants). Incorrect decisions are called 'false alarms' (convictions of innocent people) and 'misses' (acquittals of guilty defendants), respectively.

In The Netherlands, about 90 per cent of all defendants going to trial are convicted (Van de Boor, 1991). According to Wagenaar, Van Koppen and Crombag (1993), it may be assumed that about 95 per cent of all defendants are actually guilty. Huff, Rattner and Sagarin (1986) estimate that the percentage of suspects convicted for serious crimes while innocent is of the order of 1 per cent. They claim that this is a rather conservative estimate and that for less serious crimes the percentage of innocent defendants actually convicted is distinctly larger.

These assumptions lead to an estimated output of the Dutch Criminal Justice System as shown in Table 6.2.2.

Table 6.2.1 The possible outputs of a criminal justice system

The suspect is:	The verdict is 'guilty	The verdict is 'not guilty'
really guilty	hit	miss
really innocent	false alarm	correct rejection

Table 6.2.2 Estimated output of the Dutch Criminal Justice System

The suspect is:	The verdict is 'guilty'	The verdict is 'not guilty'	
really guilty	89%	6%	95%
really innocent	1%	4%	5%
	90%	10%	

One may argue whether the percentage of innocently convicted defendants is relatively high or low; more interesting, however, is the question if this percentage can possibly be reduced to zero. The answer is that it cannot. This is best explained by relating the strength of the evidence to guilty and innocent subjects brought to trial. Consider Figure 6.2.1.

Let us, for now, assume that the strength of the evidence against a defendant for a population of guilty suspects is distributed as depicted in Figure 6.2.1. Some guilty defendants will have an overwhelming amount of evidence

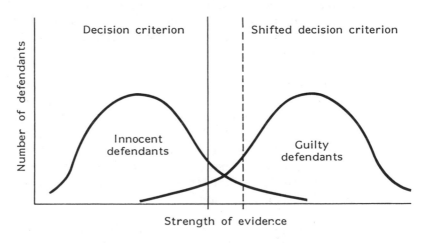

Figure 6.2.1

against them, leaving no room for any doubt whatsoever concerning their guilt. Other guilty defendants will have so little evidence against them that a conviction is out of the question. However, it is assumed that for most guilty defendants the evidence is so strong that a conviction is warranted. For innocent defendants the evidence is assumed to be similarly distributed but the average strength of the evidence against innocent suspects is considerably lower. Most innocent defendants are acquitted, but occasionally an innocent suspect will be convicted because the evidence against this defendant (e.g. as a result of a mistaken eye-witness recognition) is such that a conviction is warranted. As can be seen, the two distributions overlap to some degree. This means that for any given decision criterion, one will find innocent (however few) as well as guilty defendants. The strength of the evidence does not allow a judge or jury to discriminate perfectly between innocent and guilty suspects. Nevertheless the strength of the evidence is the decisive factor in the decision whether or not to convict a defendant.

The decision criterion is represented by the solid vertical line in the figure. In all cases to the right of this line the strength of the evidence is such that a conviction is deemed warranted. As can be seen, most defendants who are convicted given this criterion, are indeed guilty. Yet a number of innocent defendants will inevitably be convicted as well.

Is there a remedy against the conviction of innocent defendants? The most obvious thing is to change the decision criterion. If the line is placed more to the right in the figure (the dotted line), the number of innocent defendants that will be convicted decreases. However, the number of guilty defendants that will not be convicted increases dramatically when the decision criterion is shifted in this way.

Thus, changing the decision criterion will always influence both the number of false alarms *and* misses. Both cannot be excluded at the same time. Of course, theoretically, a legal system could place the decision criterion to the far right, to make sure that no innocent defendants are to be convicted. This, however, would have the unwanted consequence that a lot of guilty defendants will escape conviction. Conversely, when the objective is that no guilty defendant will slip through the net, the decision criterion should be placed to the far left. The unfortunate consequence of this policy is that most innocent defendants will be convicted as well, since virtually all trials will result in a conviction.

Thus, given these assumptions, the conviction of innocent suspects as well as the acquittal of guilty suspects is inevitable. The design of a decision procedure that entirely eliminates both 'false alarms' and 'misses' is therefore a vain enterprise. This is a typical trade-off problem. A positive outcome (more convictions of guilty defendants) is always accompanied by a negative outcome (more convictions of innocent defendants). An obvious solution would be to improve police investigations so that better evidence is gathered on guilty defendants and evidence exonerating innocent defendants is not ignored by them. The effect of this would be to reduce the overlap between both distributions, which means an increase in the discrimination between guilty and innocent defendants.

According to Wigmore's (1937) *adagium*, it is better to acquit 20 guilty defendants than to convict one innocent defendant. This means that one false alarm should be compensated by at least 20 misses. This gives an indication of where to place the decision criterion so that we satisfy a more or less general feeling of justice being done.

This does not, however, affect the conclusion that incorrect decisions will be made irrespective of the rationality of the decision procedure adopted.

Strength of Evidence

One key factor in the criminal justice procedure is the assessment of the 'strength of evidence'. Traditionally this has been a major topic in legal psychology (Pennington and Hastie, 1981; Holstein, 1985; Hastie, 1993). Strength of evidence is obviously involved in assessing likelihoods of the outcome of criminal trials and demands for pre-trial custody.

Several models have been proposed for describing how judges and jurors represent and evaluate the complex and often ambiguous information that is presented in a criminal trial. Although a complete overview of this area would go well beyond the scope of this chapter, a description of some of the most important concepts is appropriate.

A useful distinction can be made between bottom-up and top-down approaches. Bottom-up approaches take the evidence as piece-by-piece information. Each piece of information may cause the decision-maker to adjust his or her belief in the guilt or innocence of the suspect. In this case judgement formation is treated as a discrete, step-by-step process that can be logically described. Several models of this sort have been proposed (Schum and Martin, 1980, Thomas and Hogue, 1976). They can be characterised as 'fact-driven' because the actor in these models is supposed to be passive when it comes to the structuring and interpretation of the information presented. The actor performs a series of belief adjustments on the basis of factual information alone. In contrast, top-down models can be characterised as 'hypothesis-driven'. In the latter models, the decision-maker attempts to build a cognitive representation of what happened. This representation is assumed to have the structure of a narrative (Bennett and Feldman, 1981). Pieces of evidence are selected and weighed in such a fashion that they support the most likely scenario of what may have actually happened. Judgements in these models are not formed by weighing each piece of information separately, but come about when a substantial proportion of all the evidence is processed and represented in a coherent explanatory framework (Schank, 1986). The judgement is then based on this representation of the body of evidence as a whole.

A major example of the bottom-up or fact-driven approach is the Bayesian framework. Hastie (1993), in his overview of the Bayesian approach, states that the basic dimension of thought in judgement is subjective probability. This means that all information concerning a judgement about the guilt or innocence of a suspect is evaluated by the juror on a unitary dimension representing the strength of belief that an event or condition has occurred or is true. This implies that the reasoning process can be described by logical rules. A decision-maker starts out with a prior probability that a certain event— a criminal action by a certain defendant—occurred. This probability is expressed as a likelihood ratio—that is, the ratio between the likelihood that the suspect is guilty divided by the likelihood that the suspect is innocent. When a new piece of evidence is presented, it may alter the prior likelihood ratio into a posterior probability concerning the event. When all the information is processed, a final likelihood concerning the occurrence of the event is obtained. The Bayesian approach is one particular instance of a class of belief updating models. Other models of this kind use weighed averages which determine the impact of pieces of evidence. Each new piece of evidence is assigned a value. The sign of this value is dependent on whether it implies guilt or innocence of the suspect and its weight is dependent on how much importance the piece of evidence is given. The main difference between Bayesian models (such as Schum and Martin, 1980) and weighed average models is that in the Bayesian approach the revision of beliefs is modelled by a multiplicative computation. In the weighed average models, this computation is additive. Both models have been criticised as incomplete and incorrect (Pennington and Hastie, 1981; Einhorn and Hogarth, 1985). Both have, however, inspired a great deal of research concerning judgement formation in social and cognitive psychology, not only in the legal context but in many other contexts as well.

Crucial to these models, irrespective of exactly how their belief revisions are computed, is how pieces of evidence are weighed. This evaluation determines the change in beliefs under the influence of new information. Wagenaar, Van Koppen and Crombag (1993) describe this as the assessment of the diagnostic value of pieces of evidence. What a piece of evidence tells you about the guilt of a suspect can be derived from a performance table. In Wagenaar and Veefkind (1992) the diagnostic value of line-ups for person identification is assessed. We use this as an example. In Table 6.2.3 the findings of their experiment are presented. Diagnostic value is the ratio of hits and false alarms which in this case is 75 per cent divided by 5 per cent equals 15. This means that if a suspect has been recognised in a line-up, he or she is 15 times more likely to be guilty than innocent. This value can be used in the computations concerning guilt or innocence.

Table 6.2.3 The diagnosticity of line-up recognitions

The suspect is:	The suspect is recognised	The suspect is not recognised	
guilty	75%	25%	100%
innocent	5%	5%	100%

Source: Wagenaar and Veefkind, 1992

The empirical assessment of the diagnostic value of certain pieces of evidence does not imply that naive decision-makers will give a positive identification in a line-up the appropriate weight. In the cases they analysed Wagenaar, Van Koppen and Crombag (1993) claim that they found several instances in which judges under or over-valued certain pieces of evidence in spite of sound empirical findings concerning the value of that evidence.

Top-down or narrative models differ from these fact-driven approaches in several respects. For one, the unit size upon which judgements are made and adjusted is different. For instance, in Pennington and Hastie's (1986, 1992) Story Model for juror decision-making a cognitive representation of what allegedly happened is the unit upon which decisions are made. This representation contains: (a) evidence given in the proceedings of a criminal trial; (b) inferences about the evidence presented; (c) elements from the decision-maker's knowledge concerning human motivation and action. This mental representation is decisive in jurors' decision-making, the Story Model claims.

Another difference is the role of the decision-maker. In the bottom-up type model, the decision-maker is treated as a rather passive recipient of information who deals with every bit in a step by step fashion. In the top-down approach, the decision-maker is expected to play an active role in the interpretation and selection of information encountered during the decision-making process (Homel and Lawrence, 1992). He or she can ignore information and exhibit biases that invite certain interpretations of facts and disallow others (Nisbett and Ross, 1980; Kahneman, Slovic and Tverski, 1982). It is argued (Pennington and Hastie, 1981) that the Bayesian approach is of a more normative nature; it describes how evidence should be weighed, while narrative models are more descriptive since they describe how evidence evaluation is actually carried out by the human decision-maker.

A problem with the latter type of model is that such models are difficult to put to a stringent empirical test, although Pennington and Hastie have conducted a considerable amount of research on their Story Model (Pennington and Hastie, 1988, 1992, 1993).

JUDICIAL DECISION-MAKING: RATIONAL OR IRRATIONAL?

In conclusion, human decision-makers are able to perform the complex task of judicial decision-making quite well, although the methods they use are rather different from what normative models would prescribe. This is a somewhat milder claim than Kahneman and Tverski's (1973) who hold that: 'In making predictions and judgement under uncertainty, people do not appear to follow the calculus of chance or the statistical theory of prediction. Instead, they rely on a limited number of heuristics which sometimes yield reasonable judgements and sometimes lead to severe and systematic errors' (p. 237).

Do we have to qualify human decision-making as irrational? Before this question can be discussed properly, a definition is in order. Rational, in an economic sense, is an actor who (a) has perfect knowledge concerning available options and their consequences; (b) has a perfect sensitivity for differences in relevant variables such as utility and likelihood; (c) is coherent in rank-ordering of preferences (assigned utility) for consequences of decisions; (d) is perfectly capable of computing utility values for complex decisions, and (e) always tries to realise his or her maximum expected gain.

Humans cannot be rational in this demanding 'pure' sense. They do not take every conceivable option into consideration. They may overlook the best option, and may easily overlook certain consequences of the options they do consider. Furthermore, humans are quite error prone in estimating likelihoods and utilities, and the human capacity for computing complex utility outcomes is rather limited. These limitations, in combination with the fact that judicial decision-makers usually operate in a setting in which time pressure and information overload are the rule, make it inevitable that strategies are used that save time and effort and that usually but not always lead to acceptable decisions. In short, actors tend to satisfice, instead of striving for perfect rationality.

Simon's principle of bounded rationality is applicable to this state of affairs (Simon, 1955). Herbert Simon was one of the first to recognise that non-trivial decision-making often does not follow the rules of economic rationality. This, however, is far from a disqualification of human reasoning. Human thought exploits mechanisms that work extremely well given limited knowledge, limited attention, and limited computational capacities (Gingerenzer, 1993).

How often do they fail? Disturbingly often, according to Wagenaar, Van Koppen and Crombag (1993), if one takes the defendants' perspective: when judges and prosecutors deal with complex cases, they are bound to make errors. However, more detailed knowledge is needed to establish exactly what the conditions are under which such errors occur, and then how they can be prevented as much as possible. Prevention can take place at two levels in the criminal justice system. One level involves the education of individual decision-makers in the system. Knowledge of the errors that may occur is expected to decrease the likelihood of these errors actually occurring. The second level involves the system as a whole. The criminal justice system should always be (re)designed so as to ascertain that decision-making is conducted as thoroughly as possible. Whether jurisdictions achieve this goal is a not a question to be answered in this chapter. Our aim has been to make the case for psychology as the discipline which offers the knowledge as well as the tools for tackling that question. This is perhaps the most important area where cross-fertilisation between psychology and the law is to be found.

REFERENCES

Ashley, K. (1990). *Modeling Legal Argument.* Cambridge, MA: MIT Press.

Bennett, W.L. and Feldman, M.S. (1981). *Reconstructing Reality in the Courtroom.* London: Tavistock.

Coombs, C.H., Dawes, R.M. and Tverski, A. (1970). *Mathematical Psychology: An Elementary Introduction.* Englewood Cliffs, NJ: Prentice Hall.

Einhorn, H.J. and Hogarth, R.M. (1985). Ambiguity and uncertainty in probabilistic inference. *Psychological Review,* **92**, 433–61.

Gingerenzer, G. (1993). The bounded rationality of probabilistic mental models. In K.I. Manktelow and D.E. Over (Eds), *Rationality: Psychological and Philosophical Perspectives.* London: Routledge, pp. 284–313.

Hastie, R. (1993). *Inside the Juror: The Psychology of Juror Decision Making.* Cambridge, MA: Cambridge University Press.

Hendrickx, L.C.W.P. (1991). How versus how often: the role of scenario information and frequency information in risk judgment and risky decision making. Dissertation, University of Groningen.

Holstein, J.A. (1985). Jurors' interpretation and jury decision making. *Law and Human Behavior,* **9**, 83–100.

Homel, R.J. and Lawrence, J.A. (1992). Sentencer orientation and case details. *Law and Human Behavior,* **16**, 509–37.

Huff, C.R., Rattner, A. and Sagarin, E. (1986). Guilty until proven innocent: wrongful conviction and public policy. *Crime and Delinquency,* **32**, 518–44.

Kahneman, D. and Tverski, A. (1973). On the psychology of prediction. *Psychological Review,* **80**, 237–51.

Kahneman, D., Slovic, P. and Tverski, A. (Eds) (1982). *Judgment under Uncertainty: Heuristics and Biases.* New York: Cambridge University Press.

Nisbett, R.E. and Ross, L. (1980). *Human Inference: Strategies and Shortcomings.* Englewood Cliffs, NJ: Prentice Hall.

Malsch, M. (1990). Lawyers' predictions of judicial decisions. A study on calibration of experts. Dissertation Leiden University.

Michon, J.A. (1971). Psychonomie onderweg. Inaugural lecture University of Groningen. Groningen: Wolters Noordhoff.

Michon, J.A. (1985). A critical view of driver behavior models: what do we know, what should we do? In L. Evans and R.C. Schwing (Eds), *Human Behavior and*

Traffic Safety. New York: Plenum Press, pp. 485–520.

Neustadt, R.E. and May, E.R. (1986). *Thinking in Time: The Use of History for Decision Makers*. New York: Free Press.

Pennington, N. and Hastie, R. (1981). Juror decision-making models: the generalization gap. *Psychological Bulletin*, **89**, 246–87.

Pennington, N. and Hastie, R. (1986). Evidence evaluation in complex decision making. *Journal of Personality and Social Psychology*, **51**, 242–58.

Pennington, N. and Hastie, R. (1988). Explanation-based decision making: effects of memory structure on judgment. *Journal of Experimental Psychology: Learning, Memory and Cognition*, **14**, 521–33.

Pennington, N. and Hastie, R. (1992). Explaining the evidence: tests of the story model for juror decision making. *Journal of Personality and Social Psychology*, **62**, 189–206.

Pennington, N. and Hastie, R. (1993). The story model for juror decision making. In R. Hastie (Ed.), *Inside the Juror. The Psychology of Juror Decision Making*. Cambridge, MA: Cambridge University Press, pp. 192–221.

Schank, R.C. (1986). *Explanation Patterns: Understanding Mechanically and Creatively*. Hillsdale, NJ: Erlbaum.

Schank. R.C. and Abelson, R.P. (1977). *Scripts, Plans, Goals and Understanding*. Hillsdale, NJ: Erlbaum.

Schum, D.A. and Martin, A.W. (1980). Formal and empirical research on cascaded inference in jurisprudence. *Law and Society Review*, **17**, 105–51.

Simon, H.A. (1955). A behavioral model of rational choice. *Quarterly Journal of Economics*, **69**, 99–118.

Thomas, E.A.C. and Hogue, A. (1976). Apparent weight of evidence, decision criteria, and confidence ratings in juror decision-making. *Psychological Review*, **83**, 442–65.

Van de Boor, L.E.C. (1991). *Over getuigen, confrontaties en bewijs* [Concerning witnesses, confrontation and evidence]. The Hague: Ministry of Justice, Research and Documentation Centre.

Vlek, C.A.J. and Michon, J.A. (1980). Beslissen, wat is dat voor een proces? [Deciding, what kind of process is that?]. *Gedrag*, **8**, 355–61.

Wagenaar, W.A. and Veefkind, N. (1992). Comparison of one-person and many-person line-ups: a warning against unsafe practices. In F. Lösel, D. Bender and P.T. Bliesener (Eds), *Psychology and Law: International Perspectives*. Berlin: De Gruyter.

Wagenaar, W.A., Van Koppen, P.J. and Crombag, H.F.M. (1993). *Anchored Narratives: The Psychology of Criminal Evidence*. Hemel Hempstead, UK: Harvester Wheatsheaf.

Wigmore, J.H. (1937). *The Science of Judicial Proof as Given by Logic, Psychology, and General Experience*. Boston, MA: Little, Brown.

Chapter 6.3

Jury Decision-making in Complex Trials

Larry Heuer
Barnard College
and
Steven D. Penrod,
University of Minnesota

CRITIQUES OF THE JURY AS A RATIONAL DECISION-MAKER

Throughout its history the jury has been the target of both high praise and pointed criticism. Supporters praise the jury for enhancing the legitimacy of government authority; serving as a catalyst to legal reforms; individualising the administration of justice; and serving as a balance to the special interests of judges (see, e.g. Van Dyke, 1977; Rembar, 1980; Lempert, 1981; Sperlich, 1982; Hans and Vidmar, 1986; Landsman, 1993). Critics argue that the jury has difficulty understanding both the law and the evidence and the harshest of these critics call for the end of the jury. Less harsh critics are more inclined to offer reforms that they believe will assist the jury (e.g. Royal Commission on Criminal Justice, 1993; Schwarzer, 1991).

As Landsman (1993) documents, attacks on jury inefficiency and incompetency have been popular since the turn of the century and it is not difficult to find disparaging characterisations of the jury by thoughtful and responsible critics. Judge Jerome Frank, for example, complained, in (*Skidmore v. Baltimore and Ohio Railroad,* 167 F.2d 54 [2d Cir. 1948]). 'While the jury can contribute nothing of value so far as the law is concerned, it has infinite capacity for mischief, for twelve men can easily misunderstand more law in a minute than the judge can explain in an hour.'

Since Judge Frank's condemnation, a considerable body of research has accumulated concerning the jurors' understanding of the law, and rhetoric

Handbook of Psychology in Legal Contexts
Edited by R. Bull and D. Carson. © 1995 John Wiley & Sons Ltd

aside, the jury has not fared much better in the eyes of the research community. For example, Reifman, Gusick and Ellsworth (1992) observe that research suggests that jurors understand less than half of the judge's instructions.

Juries are also under fire for their incompetence at dealing with the evidence, particularly in complex litigation. Consider, for example, the following observations. Dean Griswold of the Harvard Law School: 'The jury trial is the apotheosis of the amateur. Why should anyone think that 12 persons brought in from the street, selected for their lack of general ability, should have any special capacity for deciding controversies between persons?' (cited in Kalven and Zeisel, 1966); the English legal scholar Glanville Williams: '... it is an understatement to describe a jury ... as a group of twelve men of average ignorance' (cited in Hans and Vidmar (1986). And even a Chief Justice of the United States Supreme Court, Warren Burger (1981), has questioned whether juries are competent to handle the technical matters that arise in modern trials.

While there is considerable consensus regarding the jury's struggle with the law (see, e.g., Charrow and Charrow, 1979; Elwork, Sales and Alfini, 1982) there is little agreement regarding its ability to deal with the evidence, and systematic investigation of jury performance in complex cases has been undertaken only quite recently (see, e.g. Bourgeois, Horowitz, and ForsterLee, 1993; ForsterLee, Horowitz, and Bourgeois, 1994; Horowitz and Bordens, 1990). A number of researchers have given the jury high marks for their performance with the evidence (e.g. Kalven and Zeisel, 1966; Hastie, Penrod and Pennington, 1983; Hans and Vidmar, 1986; Cecil, Lind and Bermant, 1987; Visher, 1987; Guinther, 1988). However, as Cecil, Hans, and Wiggins (1991) point out, most of these studies have focused on quite ordinary trials, and there is ample reason to suspect that juries might struggle in longer, more complex trials. However, in England, the Roskill Committee (which commissioned some psychological research) recommended that juries be retained in (complex) fraud cases.

Whatever their abilities, many juries are confronted with a challenging task. For example, in 1991, in the federal courts of the United States, 217 871 civil cases were filed. Of the 20 433 trials held in the 12-month period ending 30 June 1990, 11 502 were civil trials, 4765 of which were tried to juries. Many trials were quite lengthy: 85 lasted more than 20 days, 347 lasted between 10 and 19 days, 2393 required between four and nine days (Administrative Office of the Courts, 1990). All told, nearly 60 per cent of these civil jury trials lasted four or more days.

Unfortunately, our understanding of the jury's ability to comprehend the evidence in complex trials is based more on speculation and anecdote than systematic inquiry. Among the notable exceptions, one of the most impressive investigations of jury performance in complex cases was conducted by Cecil, Lind and Bermant (1987) (see also Cecil, Hans and Wiggins, 1991). These researchers interviewed 180 jurors out of target population of 400 who had served in 29 lengthy (more than 20 trial days) civil trials, and compared their responses to jurors from a matched set of shorter trials. The study focused on jurors' reports of: (a) the burdens imposed on them by these trials; (b) their grasp of the trial evidence and the judge's instructions; (c) their interest in the trials; and (d) the benefits of procedural aids, such as juror note-taking. Though the jurors found the lengthy and shorter trials similarly interesting, 46 per cent of jurors in long trials rated the evidence as difficult or very difficult compared to 29 per cent in short trials. In addition, 30 per cent of long-trial and 8 per cent of short-trial jurors rated the instructions as difficult or very difficult to understand. These jurors' self-reports indicate that jurors do find the evidence more difficult as trial length increases, but most jurors assert they are able adequately to comprehend the evidence.

The Cecil, Lind and Bermant (1987) study provides some valuable insights, yet it leaves many questions unanswered. In part these unanswered questions stem from methodological limitations discussed in their report, but more importantly these questions stem from a broader set of problems. Most of the scholarly discussion, and virtually all of the empirical investigations of jury performance in complex trials, suffer from the lack of a clear (and well-operationalised) definition of the problem. We suspect that consensus about the jury's performance cannot emerge before there is increased sensitivity to two major issues: the multiple dimensions of trial complexity and the multiple effects that complexity can have on jury performance.

MULTIPLE DIMENSIONS OF COMPLEXITY

Despite considerable discussion of the jury's ability to cope with complex litigation, relatively little attention has been given to the problem of what makes a trial complex. There are sound reasons to suspect that trial complexity is not a unitary construct and if it is not, any discussion of threats to jury performance (and potential remedies) should start with general agreement about what complexity is, or what forms it might take. Explicit attention to a definition of trial complexity can have a number of benefits. Perhaps the most important benefit is that sound definitions will facilitate the comparison of research findings. So, for example, if one study operationalises complexity as trial duration, and finds that jurors do not seem intellectually overburdened in lengthy trials, while another operationalises complexity according to the judge's judgement that the case included complicated evidentiary issues, and finds the jurors struggling, these apparently contradictory findings are more easily reconciled.

A second, potentially more important advantage of considering trial complexity as a multi-dimensional construct is that it underscores the possibility that variations in different dimensions of complexity might have considerably different implications for jury performance. If, for example, legal complexity and evidence complexity impact jury decision-making in different ways, one might find that legal complexity sharply differentiates judge and jury verdict preferences as, presumably, juries apply a flawed standard and judges apply the correct one. On the other hand, judges may have little advantage over juries in dealing with complicated evidence—if both comprehend the evidence, their verdict preferences might look quite similar. If both fail to comprehend, the variability in their decision patterns might increase—though possibly with little effect on their central tendencies, which would produce decision patterns that look quite similar on average.

Third, if complexity is multi-dimensional, discussions of procedural reform must be tailored to the type of complexity being targeted. So, for example, permitting jurors to take notes might be particularly helpful with lengthy trials; giving jurors written and preliminary instructions might be particularly helpful with trials involving complicated legal issues; and permitting jurors to question witnesses might be particularly helpful with trials involving complicated and technical evidence.

MULTIPLE EFFECTS OF COMPLEXITY

The second major issue to be addressed in future studies is the variety of potential consequences of trial complexity. Previous discussions have focused almost exclusively on the impact of trial complexity on rational/consistent decision-making. However, there might be basic and applied benefits from consideration of a broader set of consequences. Additional outcome measures might include, for example, measures of the perceived fairness of complex trials, the cost and efficiency of complex trials, and the extent to which decision-makers in complex trials represent a cross-section of the community. In contrast to the negative consequences of complexity that have been assumed to result when the dependent measure is rational decision-making, it is possible there might be benefits to jurors' fairness perceptions resulting from increased complexity. So, for example, if quantity of information is a dimension of complexity, we might find that additional information, in addition to adding to the jurors' challenge, would enhance the appearance (and even the reality) that the jury has conducted a thorough evidence search and this might enhance fairness perceptions. Although rational decision-making is of obvious importance, it is unlikely to be an exclusive concern to anyone interested in fostering the legitimacy of government institutions.

An additional consideration is the relative cost (in time and money) of complex trials conducted with and without innovative procedural accommodations to complexity. A lengthier set of criteria by which jury performance might be evaluated has been advanced by MacCoun (1987), who suggests such additional criteria as fact-finding competence, legal competence, impartiality, decision accuracy, and decision consistency (see also Kalven, 1964; Lempert, 1981; Hastie, Penrod and Pennington, 1983; Heuer and Penrod, 1994a, b; Tidmarsh, 1992).

DEFINING TRIAL COMPLEXITY

In his summary and critique of prior efforts to define complexity, Tidmarsh (1992) notes that the *Manual for Complex Litigation* (1985), and a leading casebook on complex litigation (Marcus and Sherman, 1985) do not offer a definition of complexity, yet the casebook devotes 450 pages to remedies for its symptoms.

Tidmarsh summarises other efforts to define trial complexity, and suggests that they fall into several categories. Among the sets of definitions he describes are those that define complexity according to the substance of the case (e.g. antitrust, securities and takeover litigation; commercial disputes, and products liability torts). A second set of definitions include those that define complexity according to procedural features (e.g. complexity during the pre-trial phase, complexity during the trial, complexity in the implementation or administration of remedies, and complexity arising from the number of parties). Tidmarsh is critical of both the substantive and procedural definitions. He observes that they have a tendency to be both under-inclusive (for example, breach of contract cases, or other substantive areas not commonly listed under such definitions can also pose challenges to reasoned decision-making) and over-inclusive (e.g. not all products liability torts are complex).

A third set of definitions identified by Tidmarsh, includes 'laundry list' definitions. These definitions have included the following as factors promoting trial complexity: the number of parties; the presence of a class action; the existence of a products liability claim; the presence of related cases involving multiple or complex factual or legal issues; the extent of discovery; and the number of parties and witnesses. In addition to sharing the problems of other categories described above, Tidmarsh argues that such definitions appear somewhat arbitrary and fail to specify the relationships among the various components.

Legal scholars are not alone in their efforts to define trial complexity. Whatever the associated problems, the 'laundry list' approach has been employed by appellate courts considering a complexity exception to the right to a jury trial. So for example, since the 1970 Supreme Court decision in *Ross v. Bernard* (396 U.S. 531), in which the court stated that it is appropriate to consider whether the contested issue exceeded the practical abilities and limitations of the jury when deciding about the right to a jury trial, numerous other decisions have suggested factors that might push a case beyond the jury's ability. In both *In re Boise Cascade Securities Litigation* (420 F. Supp. 99 (1976)) and *In re*

United States Financial Securities Litigation (609 F.2d 411 (1979)), US courts cited trial duration and case complexity as factors limiting the jury's ability to decide capably. In *In re Japanese Electronic Products Antitrust Litigation* (631 F.2d 1069 (1980)), the court ruled that the appellants should have the opportunity to show that the particular case is too complex for a jury, on the basis of three indicators of complexity: (1) the overall size of the suit; (2) the conceptual difficulties of the suit; (3) the difficulty of segregating the various aspects of the case. (Additional examples of the court-generated 'laundry lists' of complexity factors are provided by Tidmarsh, footnotes 133–6 and accompanying text.) Sperlich (1982) points out that lower courts have likewise unsystematically applied a variety of criteria (including number of issues to be decided, volume of information, technical nature of the evidence, number of parties, complexity of the law, length of the trial, and lack of jury representativeness).

SOLUTIONS TO THE PROBLEMS OF TRIAL COMPLEXITY

Generally, critiques of jury performance in complex litigation are followed by proposed remedies. The list of suggested remedies is lengthy, and need not be reproduced in its entirety here (interested readers may wish to consult the references in Tidmarsh, 1992). However, we will suggest one way of organising potential remedies, which, when considered in combination with the multi-dimensional definition of trial complexity discussed above, may prove useful. Generally, the remedies might be organised according to whether they are aimed primarily at assisting the jury with problems stemming from complicated evidence, complicated law, or voluminous evidence. Table 6.3.1 lists some examples of possible remedies, drawn from the sources listed above, along with an indication of which of these complexity dimensions they might assist.

AN EMPIRICAL INVESTIGATION OF THE MEANING AND CONSEQUENCES OF TRIAL COMPLEXITY

Although each of the complexity definitions described above has obvious limitations, we believe that a thoughtful 'laundry list' approach can minimise the problems of over-inclusion, under-inclusion, and the lack of any obvious relationships among the items on such lists. In a recent study (Heuer and Penrod, 1994b) we have taken an exploratory step toward the development of a definition of complexity that began with a 'laundry list'. In addition, we have examined the impact of complexity on several outcome measures, and the costs and benefits of several potential remedies for the challenges introduced by trial complexity.

Table 6.3.1 Remedies on three dimensions of trial complexity

| Remedies | Dimensions of complexity | | |
	Complex evidence	Complex law	Voluminous evidence
Better organisation of voluminous evidence	✓		✓
Explain complex legal issues more clearly		✓	
Limit the volume of evidence	✓		✓
Limit the time for presentation of evidence	✓		✓
Stipulate to facts before the trial	✓		✓
Allow fewer trial interruptions			✓
Provide jury notebooks including pictures and information about witnesses and exhibits	✓		✓
Allow juror note-taking	✓	✓	✓
Allow jurors to question witnesses	✓		
Instruct the jurors prior to the evidence	✓	✓	
Provide jurors written copy of judge's instructions		✓	
More thorough responses to juror questions during deliberations	✓	✓	✓
Specially qualified (Blue ribbon) juries	✓	✓	✓
Special masters (neutral experts to assist jury)	✓	✓	✓
Special verdict forms with detailed questions for jury to answer		✓	
Judge commenting or summarising of evidence	✓		✓
Greater reliance on summary judgement	✓	✓	✓
Bifurcation of issues	✓		✓
Bifurcation of parties			✓

This study of complexity was conducted as part of a larger experimental investigation of the consequences of allowing jurors to take notes and to ask questions of witnesses. The experimental design was a two [note-taking allowed versus not allowed] times two [juror questions to witnesses allowed versus not allowed] randomised factorial. In order to investigate the effects of these trial procedures in actual trials, written invitations to participate were mailed to state and federal court judges throughout the United States. Each letter of invitation included a brief overview of the study and a description of what would be required of judges who agreed to participate (i.e. their agreement to allow us to assign their trials randomly to experimental conditions, and their agreement to complete a questionnaire after the trial, and to ask the jurors and attorneys to do the same). In order to assure the presence of complex trials in the data set, judges who agreed to contribute more than one trial were asked to include an additional trial that they expected to last longer than one week, or that they expected to be a complex trial (involving moderately to very complex issues or many witnesses).

At the end of each trial, questionnaires were distributed to the jurors, both lead attorneys, and the judge. All respondents were asked to provide demographic information. In addition, all respondents were asked a series of questions regarding their general evaluations of the trial, the actors in the trial, and the experimental procedures employed. There were contributions of one or more trials from 103 judges from 33 states, totalling 160 trials (75 civil, 85 criminal). Completed questionnaires were received from 94 per cent of the judges and 81 per cent of the jurors who participated in these trials.

A Working Definition of Trial Complexity

Judges were asked to provide information about a number of trial variables related to trial complexity. Four of these variables were measured using nine-point bipolar adjective response scales. Compared to the average case:

a. How complex was the evidence?
b. How complex was the law?
c. How complex were the prosecution's (plaintiff's) arguments?
d. How complex were the defence's arguments?

Additional measures required judges to make quantitative estimates of:

e. number of witnesses
f. duration of the trial
g. number of charges (claims)
h. number of pages of documents
i. number of parties.

A principal components analysis was conducted on this set of variables. (This type of analysis is used to reduce a large set of interrelated measures to a smaller set of measures that are distinct from one another. The reduction takes place through the combining of measures that are correlated with one another and appear to measure the same, underlying phenomena.) The analysis revealed three components of trial complexity which we labelled: complexity of the evidence; complexity of the law; quantity of information. These results support the argument that, at least from the judges' perspective, trial complexity is not a unitary construct. While the method we employed has certain limitations, which we will discuss below, it is less likely to result in a definition of complexity that is more over-inclusive, under-inclusive, or arbitrary than the simple laundry list approach critiqued by Tidmarsh (1992). In suggesting a definition of complexity in which each subtype has multiple indicators, there is less risk of over-inclusion, since the definitions do not presume that, for example, a particular trial has complex evidence just because the judge in that trial thinks the evidence is complex; rather, additional factors should also be present, such as multiple witnesses, multiple claims, and a lengthy trial.

Similarly, under-inclusion is unlikely to be a problem associated with this approach, since the list of potential indicators to be examined can quite easily include virtually all the substantive or procedural variables that might reasonably be expected to be related to trial complexity. However, the three dimensions of complexity identified in this study are still subject to concerns about under-inclusion due to the fact that numerous variables that have been suggested as indicators of trial complexity were not among those rated by the judges in this study. For example, measures of the quantity and difficulty of scientific and statistical evidence were not included as indicators to be rated.

Finally, the use of principal component analyses of the indicators of complexity reduces problems of arbitrariness. In this study, indicators were assembled on the basis of their actual interrelationships based on the ratings and responses of the judges who provided the feedback on each of the 160 trials included in this design and were not based on *a priori* assumptions about the ways in which the indicators might fit together.

The Effects of Trial Complexity

In order to assess the impact of trial complexity on the trials in the experimental study we employed analyses that examined the effects of each of the three trial complexity components on jurors' satisfaction with the trial, with their own performance in the trial and with the lawyers' assessments of jury performance. We also examined the effects of each type of trial complexity on the judges' evaluation of the jury's performance, and on the rate at which juries and judges agreed on the appropriate verdict.

These analyses revealed numerous significant effects of trial complexity, which differed according to the type of complexity under consideration. These relationships indicate that as the quantity of information increased, the jurors reported greater difficulty reaching a verdict, and were less confident that their verdict reflected a proper understanding of the judge's instructions. As the complexity of the evidence increased, the jurors reported that they experienced greater difficulties deciding how to vote. And, as the legal complexity increased, the jurors found the defence attorney less helpful, and again reported lower confidence that their verdict was based upon a complete and proper understanding of the judge's instructions. A particularly noteworthy finding, which speaks to the value of employing multiple dependent measures, is that the effects of trial complexity are not all negative. For example, as evidence complexity increased the jurors reported greater confidence that they were well informed by the trial, and as the quantity of information increased the jurors reported the prosecuting/plaintiff's attorney had been more helpful.

Our data do not support the proposition that judges and juries decide cases differently, nor was any form of complexity related to the rates of judge–jury agreement. Similarly, there was no evidence that the procedural innovations of jury questioning and note-taking affected either the fairness of the jury's decisions or the rationality of those decisions, *if* judicial decision-making is the standard of rationality employed. Furthermore, while the jurors acknowledged that trial complexity imposed some difficulties, these difficulties did not affect their (quite high) satisfaction with the trial, their perception of the fairness of their verdict, or their confidence that their verdict was correct. The judges' satisfaction with the jurors' verdicts was also quite high, and not directly affected by trial complexity.

The Effects of Trial Procedures Intended to Assist the Jury in Complex Cases

Although there were no significant relationships between judge–jury disagreements and either the measures of complexity or the manipulated procedural variables, that does not mean that complexity and procedures did not influence decision-making or jury performance. When we expanded our inquiry to include judge and juror assessments of jury performance, there was evidence that both trial complexity and trial procedures matter. Most importantly, there was evidence that a full appreciation of the effects of trial complexity and of the benefits of new trial procedures requires consideration of particular procedural and complexity effects interacting with each other.

One of the advantages of recognising the multi-dimensionality of complexity is that it permits testing of alternative remedies designed to reduce the negative influence of complexity on jury decision-making. In addition to measuring the effects of complexity on our outcome variables, we also tested whether any of those complexity effects were qualified by interactions with the following trial procedures:

- allowing the jurors to take notes during the trial

- allowing the jurors to direct questions to witnesses

- judges' comments on the evidence and/or the credibility of witnesses or summaries of the evidence (judicial comments and summaries were infrequent, therefore this procedure was coded as being present if the judge in any trial commented or summarised)

- the use of any special juror orientation programmes

- the use of special verdict forms (written questions to be answered by the jury).

Among the significant interactions we observed, the following general conclusions emerged: juror questions were rated most helpful when there were high levels of evidence or legal complexity. The interactions between complexity and juror questions even revealed that questions sometimes changed the effects of complexity from a liability to an advantage. Thus, as evidence complexity increased, jurors in non-question-asking trials reported less confidence that their verdict was correct, whereas jurors in question-asking trials reported greater verdict confidence. Our interpretation is that questions do not so much 'get to the truth', but rather they help to clarify complicated testimony or legal issues. It is consistent with this reasoning to expect that the benefits of juror questions should be the most prominent in those cases where the evidence or the law was particularly complicated, which is the pattern observed. Juror questions had the consistent effect of reducing the harms of the complexity variables and enhancing the benefits of complexity.

On the other hand, the relationship between juror questions and quantity of information was different. Information quantity was less beneficial, or even harmful, in those trials where question asking was permitted. Thus, in trials where questions were allowed, as the quantity of information increased, jurors reported feeling less well informed by the trial. In trials where questions were not allowed, as information quantity increased, the jurors report feeling better informed.

Juror note-taking effects were less frequent, and interactions between note-taking and trial complexity were not straightforward. First, there were no significant interactions between note-taking and quantity of information, which is where the procedure would be expected to be most helpful. Furthermore, the pattern of interactions between note-taking and legal complexity were complicated. Note-taking jurors reported they were able to understand the law better and found the defence attorney more helpful, but they were less satisfied with the prosecuting (or plaintiff's) attorney, and less confident that they had reached the correct verdict.

Of the non-experimental procedures, the use of special verdict forms was most consistently beneficial. In trials where special verdict forms were used the jurors reported feeling better informed, more satisfied, more confident that their verdict was correct, more confident that their verdict reflected a proper understanding of the judge's instructions, and more satisfied with the prosecutor. Furthermore, examination of interactions with the complexity measures revealed that jurors found the special verdict forms most helpful in cases with large quantities of information.

Judges' comments were less helpful to the jurors. By several measures, the jurors report less satisfaction in those trials where the judges either commented on the weight of the evidence, on the credibility of witnesses, or summarised the evidence. Furthermore, interactions between commenting and complexity suggest that the judges' efforts were least helpful when the evidence was particularly complex. Because this variable was not manipulated, and because judges rarely intervened, any interpretations must be advanced very cautiously. With that caveat, several possibilities are reasonable. One possibility is that judges are quite astute at identifying those trials in which the burdens of complexity are especially pronounced, and they are commenting in those trials but not fully achieving the effects they intend. The use of standardised pattern instructions had few direct effects on the jurors' perceptions of their performance. However, there were a number of significant interactions among pattern instruction use and the measures of trial complexity. Of these, the most consistent trend involved interactions with legal complexity: pattern instructions were least helpful in cases involving complex legal issues. One interpretation of these findings is that jurors are not well served by general instructions in legally complex cases, but rather need instructions specifically tailored to the particular issues involved in their trial.

Overall, by the measures employed, juror questions and special verdicts appear most promising for assisting jurors in complex cases. However, given the paucity of systematic studies (particularly field experimentation) involving special verdicts, judges' comments, and pattern instructions, these findings should be interpreted cautiously. None the less, they can serve to identify areas for future investigation.

FUTURE RESEARCH

The Heuer and Penrod (1994b) study of trial complexity has two advantages over prior discussions of trial complexity and its effects on jury decision-making. First, the study has generated an empirically derived definition of trial complexity. Based upon responses from the judges surveyed in the study, trial complexity has three dimensions: complex evidence, complex law, and voluminous evidence. Furthermore, because of the use of principal components analysis to define its dimensions these dimensions avoid the arbitrary quality that Tidmarsh (1992) is critical of in other definitions of complexity. Second, in examining the effects of complexity (with or without the use of procedural remedies), the study considers such consequences as jurors' satisfaction with the fairness of trial procedures, in addition to considering a variety of measures of the quality of jury decision-making.

However, there are clear limitations to the Heuer and Penrod (1994b) study that must be addressed in future investigations of the effects of trial complexity. One limitation is that the definition of trial complexity is derived from judges' rather than jurors' perceptions of the trial. Although it is important to understand what complexity means to judges (especially because they are the most commonly suggested alternative to the jury in complex trials), judges and jurors might not view complexity in the same fashion. If not, it is critical to understand what makes a trial complex from the jurors' perspective. Second, other commentators on trial complexity have identified complexity factors that are poorly captured in the limited set of measures employed by Heuer and Penrod. For example, MacCoun (1987) suggests indicators such as the number of issues in dispute, inconsistencies in evidence and among witnesses, unreliability of witnesses and evidence, conceptual difficulty (and presence of) technical and scientific testimony, clarity of legal principles, difficulties in applying law to the facts, presence of conflicting normative principles, employment of statistical and probabilistic evidence, and need for higher order chains of inference.

As noted at the outset of this chapter, commentators, scholars, and judges have long complained about problems of jury competence. In recent decades, as trials have grown increasingly complex, these complaints have focused on jury performance in complex cases. It is noteworthy that critics have identified a host of possible complexity factors that might pose difficulties for juries in complex cases and it is equally noteworthy that commentators, scholars, and judges have expended great energy in devising remedies for these problems. But, it is *most* noteworthy that both these enterprises have proceeded in nearly total ignorance of how juries actually perform in complex cases. This situation is beginning to change and we believe that studies such as the one discussed in this chapter open a promising new avenue of research that will ultimately allow us to identify the strengths and weaknesses of jury decision-making in complex cases and allow us to identify procedural reforms and decision aids that will optimise jury performance in complex cases.

REFERENCES

Administrative Office of the Courts (1990). Annual Report of the Director of the Administrative Office of the US Courts.

Bourgeois, M.J., Horowitz, I.A. and ForsterLee, L. (1993). The effects of technicality and access to trial transcripts on verdicts and information processing in a civil trial. *Personality and Social Psychology Bulletin,* **19**, 220–7.

Burger, W.A. (1981). Is our jury system working? *Reader's Digest,* **118**, 126–30.

Cecil, J., Hans, V.P. and Wiggins, E.C. (1991). Citizen comprehension of difficult issues: lessons from civil jury trials. *American University Law Review,* **40**, 727–74.

Cecil, J.S., Lind, E.A. and Bermant, G. (1987). *Jury Service in Lengthy Civil Trials.* Washington, DC: Federal Judicial Center.

Charrow, R.P. and Charrow, V.R. (1979). Making legal language understandable: a psycholinguistic study of jury instructions. *Columbia Law Review,* **79**, 1306–74.

Elwork, A., Sales, B.D. and Alfini, J.J. (1982). *Making Jury Instructions Understandable.* Bobbs-Merrill.

ForsterLee, L., Horowitz, I.A. and Bourgeois, M.J. (1994). Juror competence in civil trials: the effects of preinstruction and evidence technicality. *Law and Human Behavior,* **18**, 567–78.

Guinther, J. (1988). *The Jury in America.* New York: Facts on File Publications.

Hans, V. P. and Vidmar, N. (1986). *Judging the Jury.* New York: Plenum Press.

Hastie, R., Penrod, S.D. and Pennington, N. (1983). *Inside the Jury.* Cambridge, MA: Harvard University Press.

Heuer, L.B. and Penrod, S. (1994a). Juror note-taking and question asking during trials: a national field experiment. *Law and Human Behavior,* **18**, 121–50.

Heuer, L.B. and Penrod, S. (1994b). Trial complexity: a field investigation of its meaning and its effects. *Law and Human Behavior,* **18**, 29–52.

Horowitz, I.A. and Bordens, K.S. (1990). An experimental investigation of procedural issues in complex tort trials. *Law and Human Behavior,* **14**, 269–85.

Kalven, H. (1964). The dignity of the civil jury. *Virginia Law Review,* **50**, 1055–75.

Kalven, H. and Zeisel, H. (1966). *The American Jury.* Boston, MA: Little, Brown.

Landsman, S. (1993). The civil jury in America: scenes from an unappreciated history. *Hastings Law Journal,* **44**, 579.

Lempert, R. (1981). Civil juries and complex cases: let's not rush to judgment. *Michigan Law Review,* **80**, 68–132.

Litigation Management Manual (1992). Federal Judicial Center.

MacCoun, R. (1987). *Getting Inside the Black Box: Toward a Better Understanding of Civil Jury Behavior.* Santa Monica, CA: The Rand Corporation.

Manual for Complex Litigation (2nd edn) (1985). St Paul, MN: West Publishing.

Marcus, R.L. and Sherman, E.F. (1985). *Complex Litigation: Cases and Materials on Advanced Civil Procedure.* St Paul, MN: West Publishing.

Reifman, A., Gusick, S.M. and Ellsworth, P.C. (1992). Real jurors understanding of the law in real cases. *Law and Human Behavior,* **16**, 539–54.

Rembar, C. (1980). *The Law of the Land.* New York: Simon & Schuster.

Roskill Committee (1986). *Report of the Departmental Committee on Fraud Trials.* London: HMSO.

Royal Commission on Criminal Justice (1993). *Report* (Cm 2263). London, HMSO.

Schwarzer, W.W. (1991). Reforming jury trials. *132 Federal Rules Decisions 575.* Minneapolis: West.

Sperlich, P.W. (1982). The case for preserving the trial by jury in complex civil litigation. *Judicature, 65,* 395–419.

Tidmarsh, J. (1992). Unattainable justice: the form of complex litigation and the limits of judicial power. *George Washington University Law Review, 60,* 1683.

Van Dyke, J.M. (1977). *Jury Selection Procedures.* Cambridge: Ballinger Publishing.

Visher, C.A. (1987). Juror decision making: the importance of evidence. *Law and Human Behavior,* **11,** 1–18.

Chapter 6.4

Advocacy

Dean Bartlett
University of Southampton
and
Amina Memon
University of Southampton

INTRODUCTION

The *Oxford Companion to Law* (Walker, 1980) defines advocacy as:

> The art and science of pleading cases on behalf of parties, particularly orally, before courts and juries. It requires a thorough appreciation of the relevant facts, a good knowledge of the law, persuasive presentation and argumentative powers.

This chapter will be concerned largely with the contribution psychology has to make in illuminating our understanding of the latter two of these, persuasion and argumentation. However, before discussing these two aspects of advocacy, we would like to explain why psychologists, in particular, are qualified to inform us about the processes involved in advocacy.

In attempting to persuade a juror or magistrate to believe a certain version of events one needs to make that version seem credible and any alternative version proffered by the opposition seem less credible. This is achieved by manipulating the way jurors or magistrates process, organise and evaluate the information presented to them. In a court setting this objective lends itself uniquely to the socio-cognitive approach used in psychology (for a general account of the socio-cognitive approach see Fiske and Taylor, 1984). Indeed, in their classic book *Social Psychology in Court*, Saks and Hastie (1978), commented that:

> Trial lawyers are, to a remarkable degree, professional applied social psychologists. Much of their work directly parallels the traditional major research interests of social psychology, and they are daily in a position to

manipulate key variables of social influence: they control information, manage impressions, influence attributions ... and so on. (Saks and Hastie, 1978, p.100)

A fundamental assumption of the socio-cognitive approach is that we, as organisms, are subject to information overload from our environment due to our limited processing capacity (about seven 'chunks' of information in short-term memory, or STM). Thus in order to function effectively we need some way of filtering out those pieces of information that are not relevant to us. According to this 'constructionist' approach to the study of human thought we each formulate our view of reality according to our individual wants and needs. This provides a viable framework within which to study psychology in applied settings and it is able to account for social, cultural and individual differences.

THE CONTEXT AND NATURE OF COURTROOM DISCOURSE

The importance of advocacy in court is a consequence of the trial system, particularly in adversarial proceedings which dictate that the parties are in opposition to one another: the defence seeks an acquittal; the prosecution proposes conviction. In a civil case the plaintiff seeks compensation or a special order and the defence seeks to avoid this and/or make counter-claims. In an investigatory trial system the importance of advocacy is considerably reduced but, still, different parties have competing goals. Each party attempts to achieve its desired outcome by encouraging the jurors to interpret the information presented to them and construct the events as offered by each side, in a particular way. In their seminal work, *Reconstructing Reality in the Courtroom*, Bennet and Feldman (1981) argue that in order to understand and communicate about criminal trials people transform evidence obtained into stories about the alleged criminal activities. They undertook an ethnographic study of criminal trials in Seattle. In the first year they observed more than 60 trials including drug offences, prostitution, rape and burglary. The researchers would arrive early at the court house to observe the *dramatis personae* assemble, to catch bits of conversation about the case and listen to the banter of lawyers and clients. They sat in doorways, hallways, in interviews and in the trial. Information was obtained from clerks, judges and lawyers and through a study of the transcripts of video and audio-taped recordings. They proposed that it is through the use of 'stories' that information is updated and rearranged, comparisons are made and information is interpreted.

Demographic variables constitute an important contextual factor in the consideration of courtroom interaction. Bennet and Feldman (1981) argue that the cultural and educational experiences of various cultural groups (e.g. the upper and middle economic strata) may equip them with more and greater skills in communication: 'What may surface in quantitative research as weak statistical links between variables like race and class and case outcomes may be a much broader and more subtle bias based upon communication styles' (p. 173). Factors such as race, age, class, education and other socio-economic variables are often weighted heavily in favour of barristers or judges and against witnesses thereby amplifying the status and power differentials set up by the physical arrangements of the court, such as the position and spacing of furniture. Thus it can be seen that, even before anyone has spoken, the courtroom constitutes a social situation which is both different from the normal context of social discourse and which affords ample opportunity for the manipulation of both witness accounts and juror interpretations according to the purpose of the lawyers (Carlen, 1976; McBarnet, 1983).

Structural constraints upon the way in which evidence is presented in court include the types of information that may be introduced, the method of presenting information and the order in which speeches are made (Drew, 1990). The types of information that may be introduced are determined by the rules governing the presentation of evidence and cross-examination; for example questions must be relevant and specific to the case and questions relating only to issues raised in cross-examination may be asked during re-examination. The method of information presentation consists largely of the one-way question–answer adjacency pair in which only questions and answers (as opposed to any other type of utterance) are permitted. Only the barrister or judge asks questions and the witness is under strong obligation not only to answer questions, but to answer them in a particular way (Evans, 1992). (The question of whether such constraints are appropriate, given the purpose and function of the courts, falls outside the scope of the current chapter and the reader is referred to Hayden (1987) for an interesting cross-cultural discussion of the issue.)

There is a considerable body of research concerned with the effects on jurors of the order in which speeches are made. Lind and Ke (1985) present a comprehensive review of the psychology of opening and closing statements. While there is, as yet, no strong consensus between researchers there appear to be two effects of note: the primacy effect is said to benefit the prosecution as they speak first, while the recency effect, it is claimed, benefits the defence as they speak last. Both effects have been found, but it appears that one factor responsible for determining which of them prevails is the length of time between the opening speech and summing up. A long trial brings recency effects to the fore, as the 'availability heuristic' dictates that we are more likely to utilise this more recent information in our decisions about the case as they are more easily available to our immediate or short-term memory. Primacy effects on the other hand prevail over short intervals because once a sequence of events has been interpreted in a particular way and the necessary conceptual and explanatory schemata invoked then, according to the principle of cognitive conservatism, they tend to be reinforced and maintained while any change is resisted. Also, by presenting your argument first, you are given the opportunity to prime jurors, introducing and thereby making available ideas and sequences of events (in the form of frames, scripts, or stories) which support your argument while inoculating them against your opponent's argument by presenting alternative explanations (Lloyd-Bostock, 1988).

STRATEGIES USED TO DISCREDIT WITNESSES AND PERSUADE JURIES

What constitutes a persuasive oral presentation by a lawyer? There appear to be three major factors: the person presenting, the arguments used and the evidence marshalled to support those arguments. In the words of Levi (1990), 'The outcome of virtually all dimensions of the judicial process in its day-to-day applications is at least in part a function of what is said, by whom, and how' (p. 1). Thus the successful advocate needs to appear competent, honest and above all correct. This may be achieved by using impression management tactics to enhance one's appearance to the jury, persuasive presentation and argumentation to support your case and refute the opponent's and, finally, by making your witnesses seem credible and your opponents seem untrustworthy.

Persuasive Presentation and Argument

A number of strategic devices may be used by lawyers to persuade judges and juries of their case. Aside from appearing credible, which is covered below, the key witness must have an impact on the jury. Such an impact can be achieved by the use of particularly vivid language and descriptions; for example, the sentence 'He lunged at me with flashing eyes and a contorted grimace on his face' encourages far deeper mental processing and complex imagery than the rather bland alternative 'He came towards me'. Such wording increases the saliency of key pieces of testimony thereby increasing their impact on beliefs, attributions and inferences (Nisbett and Ross, 1980). Such testimony is therefore far more likely both to influence decisions as to the accuracy and importance of the testimony and to facilitate its recall. The saliency of particular pieces of information may also be increased by repetition, that is, by encouraging witnesses to repeat particular parts of their testimony or by calling different witnesses who reiterate certain key facts (Loftus, 1979). Similarly, when it comes to instructing the jury, there is some evidence to suggest that repetition aids comprehension and improves verdict accuracy (Tanford, 1992).

Other linguistic devices used in advocacy rely on everyday strategies for interpreting discourse; for example, the use of questions involving some sort of direct or indirect presupposition causes certain inferences to be made. So, for example, the question 'Did you see the broken window?' implies, from our experience of normal conversation, that the window was indeed broken. Such questions have a biasing effect on both the witness' answer and the jurors' construction of the situation. Similarly, certain words and phrases have connotations which are not necessarily part of their literal meaning. As Lakoff (e.g. 1987) has pointed out, words do not have meanings, they invite them. This poses a special problem when interviewing child witnesses (as will be discussed briefly later in this chapter). Let us now consider an actual example of courtroom dialogue taken from a rape trial:

Counsel: And you went to a bar in Boston, is that correct?
Witness: It's a club.
Counsel: It's where girls and fellas meet, isn't it?
Witness: People go there.
Counsel: And during that evening did Mr Smith come over to sit with you?
Witness: He sat at our table.
Counsel: You had some fairly lengthy conversations with the defendant didn't you?
Witness: We were all talking.
    (taken from Drew, 1990)

In this example the questions are implying one sequence of events while the answers imply another. Which of the two options is preferred depends to some extent on the script which has been invoked to account for the sequence of events. Thus by choosing carefully selected phrases, for example 'sit with you' as opposed to 'sit near you', the questioner can attempt to invoke the script which best suits his or her version of events.

Other ways of invoking particular scripts, or explanatory schema, depend on the connections and inferences we habitually make in producing and comprehending coherent discourse. Bennet and Feldman (1981) described four types of connections which we make in our everyday use of language—empirical, categorical, logical, and aesthetic—each of which may be profitably utilised by the clever formulation of certain questions. Such effects have an even more pronounced impact when they are implicit and when placed in the context of the procedural constraints of courtroom dialogue, as in the following example, again taken from Drew (1990):

Counsel: Now, subsequent to this you say you received a number of phone calls?
Witness: Yes.
Counsel: From the defendant?
Witness: Yes.
Counsel: And isn't it a fact, Miss Jones, that you have an unlisted telephone number?
Witness: Yes.
Counsel: And you gave the defendant your telephone number didn't you?

Witness: No, I didn't.
Counsel: You didn't give it to him?
Witness: No.
   (after a long pause Counsel then goes on to a different topic).
   (from Drew, 1990)

Thus according to our everyday interpretation, the sequence of questions leads us to make the logical connection that the witness may have given the defendant her telephone number and when this is refuted a puzzle is created but left unresolved by the advocate. Because the witness is only 'allowed' to answer the questions which she is asked, she is not given an opportunity to explain how the defendant got her number and the long silence at the end of the sequence of questions amplifies the effect by giving the jury time to note and reflect upon the implications of the contrast which has been drawn between the two stories. Not only are such implications invariably biased against the witness but, by leaving the puzzle unresolved, any conclusions that are made appear to have been drawn by the jurors themselves rather than having been suggested directly by the barrister. This further increases the likelihood of acceptance by the juror (Drew, 1990).

Other linguistic strategies used in advocacy rely upon the primacy of knowledge and context in our attempts to interpret witness accounts; the same actions take on very different meanings according to the context in which they occur. The power of context in aiding comprehension and memory have been demonstrated in a series of classic experiments by Bransford and Johnson (1972). They asked subjects to recall and rate for ease of comprehension a passage of instructions concerning the operation of a washing-machine. They found that subjects could only understand and recall the passage if they knew the context, i.e. that the passage was a set of washing instructions. As witnesses inevitably give testimony in retrospect, the advocate is able to manipulate how jurors interpret and remember such testimony by setting up contextual information which influences the way in which the words of the witness are processed and stored.

Legal rhetoric constitutes an integral part of the overall strategy used by the advocate (Goodrich, 1986) and the above examples have highlighted the importance of psycholinguistic research in helping to elucidate these strategies. But not all attempts at persuasion rely exclusively on language. Kaplan and Schersching (1981) for example, showed how it was possible to influence jurors' verdicts based on assumptions about their socio-moral norms and belief systems, and to make predictions about their behaviour according to equity theory. This theory postulates that during the social exchange in court the juror attempts to see that justice is done by ensuring an equitable outcome for both defendant and prosecution. Thus by the barrister painting as sorry a picture as possible from the defendant's point of view, she or he is more likely to induce a verdict of 'not guilty' in the jury's attempt to restore equity.

Other non-linguistic strategies focus on the structuring of the case and the nature of persuasive argumentation. Perhaps the most prolific writer in the field of persuasive argumentation is Stephen Toulmin. (See Wangerin (1990) for an excellent review of Toulmin's and other research in the area.) One important point that Toulmin makes is that once people have formed an attitude or opinion on a particular matter they tend to resist change (the principle of cognitive conservatism). Resistance is, however, proportional to the degree of change required and individuals tend to have a limited latitude of change beyond which persuasion is impossible. Stating the case in probabilistic terms requires less change in opinion than an absolute statement of guilt or innocence and thus probabilistic statements of guilt tend to be more persuasive in that they confirm the opinion of those who already agree and require less change in the opinion of those who initially disagreed.

Many of the strategies used to persuade juries to accept certain versions of events also serve to discredit opposition witnesses. For example, in the rape trial questioning sequence presented above, the questions asked lead the listener to expect a certain answer so when the barrister says 'You gave the defendant your telephone number, didn't you?' and the witness replies 'No', we are automatically lead to question the truth of her response. Similarly, the use of persuasive argumentation serves to enhance source credibility and thus we see that although persuasion and credibility are treated separately here, there is in fact a complex interaction between the two.

Manipulating Witness Credibility

In a study on the credibility of expert witnesses, Hurwitz, Miron and Johnson (1992) found that subjects' ratings of credibility were determined by their judgements of expertise and trustworthiness. These two factors apply not only to the expert witness but to any witness and constitute the two primary methods by which credibility is challenged; either the witness is incompetent and therefore likely to be mistaken, or he or she is lying. The distinction between each of these is quite important; lying in court is much more damaging than merely being mistaken, both for the witness and for the case. This is because lying tends to be viewed as far more generalisable; everybody can make a mistake but the purposeful liar can never be trusted. A lie therefore reduces the reliability of the whole testimony rather than just an isolated part of it. This effect has been reported by Kelly and Sagarin (1988) who also make the point that such a distinction is often ambiguous, as illustrated by the example of an Eskimo who, when asked if he would tell the truth, the whole truth and nothing but the truth, talked at length with the court translator who turned to the judge and said 'He does not know whether he can tell the truth. He can tell only what he knows.' Lawyers have therefore been advised to play on the somewhat blurred distinction between a lie and a mistake (e.g. Clitheroe, 1980) as by doing so, the advocate may, in the eyes of the jury, be able to transform one into the other thereby influencing the generality and stability of jurors' attributions and inferences of credibility.

Many of the strategies already discussed which the advocate uses to make him or herself appear trustworthy and competent may simply be used in reverse on witnesses and thus make them appear untrustworthy and incompetent. A more subtle impact on credibility comes from variations in linguistic styles in the courtroom as documented by the Duke University Law and Language project. This was made up of an interdisciplinary research team (lawyers, social psychologists, an anthropologist and a linguist) who together have made a major contribution to research in this area. In the early stages of the research, 150 hours of criminal trial proceedings, which took place in North Carolina, were recorded and analysed to identify language variations in lawyers' and witnesses' speech. These differences in style were correlated with different social variables (perceived trustworthiness, competence, attractiveness). The hypotheses generated from the data were tested by conducting simulated jury studies using undergraduate students as 'mock jurors' (O'Barr, 1982). A distinction was made between 'powerful' versus 'powerless' speech styles, said to be stereotypically associated with American white men and American white women respectively (based upon the writings of Lakoff, 1975, cited in Lakoff, 1987). Powerless speech is marked by the frequent use of intensifiers such as 'so', 'very' and 'surely' and there are also many hesitation forms such as 'uh', 'well' and 'you know'. It is also characterised by the use of polite forms (e.g. 'please', 'thank you so much') and empty adjectives such as 'fabulous', 'horrible' and 'adorable'. Powerful speech by contrast is direct, straight-forward, assertive and rational.

The court statements obtained from tape recordings were rewritten for the purposes of the research to create a powerful or powerless version of the same testimony (i.e. the basic content was the same). When male and female mock jurors rated male and female actors reading the same testimony using powerful and powerless speech styles, the credibility of men using the powerless language was rated as much lower than that of men using the powerful style. This is also true for women speakers, with some exceptions—for example, female subjects rated women using the powerless style much lower than did the male subjects. This is compatible with research on student perceptions of male and female university professors conducted in California where it was found that females experienced the weaknesses of other females as threatening and responded with hostility towards them (Winkler, 1993).

Another area of research which has implications for credibility assessment stems from the development of sophisticated accounts of the active nature of perception and constructive nature of memory and the application of these models to eyewitness testimony (e.g. Wells and Loftus, 1984). Strategies using information gained from this type of study rely on making the witnesses appear incompetent by raising questions about their ability to correctly perceive, encode, store and retrieve information. One striking example comes from a series of studies conducted by Elizabeth Loftus (originally reported in Loftus and Palmer, 1974) in which she showed subjects a film of a car crash and then asked them to estimate the speed at which the car was travelling by using a number of alternative questions of the form 'About how fast were the cars going when they hit / smashed / collided / bumped / contacted?' The results showed that significantly different estimates of speed were given as a function of the word used with the word 'smashed' yielding the highest average of 41 m.p.h. and 'contacted' the lowest at 32 m.p.h. Loftus went on to show that after being questioned in the manner outlined above, subjects who had been given the word 'smashed' were far more likely to say that they had seen broken glass (when there had been none) than those who were questioned using the word 'hit' or a control group who were not previously questioned about the speed of the car. The implication was that the earlier questioning technique influenced the memory of the event and this hypothesis has been confirmed in several subsequent studies (Loftus, 1979). In another study Bell and Loftus (1989) demonstrated that even if the details reported were irrelevant to the case, inferences about witness credibility and attention to detail were made on the basis of the level of detail a witness was able to report. Thus by asking your own witnesses to recount any details they can remember you make them appear credible and conversely by asking the opposition witnesses questions about specific details which, in all probability they are unlikely to remember, you make them appear less credible.

THE CHILD WITNESS

Research on children's speech in naturalistic contexts, such as in the home, tells us two things. Firstly, that adults rarely tell children when they cannot understand what the children have said and secondly, that children are rarely asked to reformulate what they have said if their message was not clear (for a comprehensive review see Durkin, 1986). Where children were asked for clarification the speaker and listener found it beneficial (Robinson and Whittaker, 1986). Telling children explicitly that the speaker did not understand them was an effective way of promoting understanding about communication in real life as well as in experimental settings. The findings of child language researchers are of great importance in the legal context, where the credibility of a witness is at issue and this information is clearly not presently being transferred to the questioning of child witnesses as the examples below illustrate.

Walker (1993) reports a qualitative study of court transcripts where the aim was to see if the children had the necessary linguistic or communicative competence to understand and respond to the questions put to them. Taking a transcript of a five year old, it is clear from the point of view of production that the child met the test of legal competency. The child demonstrated competence at deciphering questions and showed adult level conversation skills. Looking at the adult who was doing the questioning, it was apparent that the examiner herself was not clear about what was being asked. The language and grammar were complex and number of age inappropriate words and expressions such as 'opportunity', 'amplified', 'depicted' and 'included' were used. In adult conversation there is a reciprocal obligation towards clarity but children don't necessarily know this. Long strings of questions are a case in point. Walker noted that as long as a child's response was 'yes' the lawyer took it for granted that the child understood the question. Once in a while a hidden misunderstanding popped to the surface but this was more often than not by accident. Walker concluded the following: 'Adults, judges, prosecutors, defence counsel, police and therapists, simply do not know enough about children's capabilities cognitively or linguistically. The lack of knowledge presents the opportunity for untold mischief' (p. 79).

Brennan (1992) argues that we need to make an appeal to meanings other than those contained within spoken discourse otherwise no sense can be made of the discourse. He details the treatment of sexually abused children in court as they are examined and cross examined. The children in the cases were between ages of 6 and 15 and the following examples show that prosecutors, magistrates and judges used language which did not enable children to present evidence in a most convincing way. The first one is where a string of words is uttered but no request is made for a response. In this example, an eight-year-old is confronted with the following statement: 'I put it to you that you are telling a lie.' The child does not know that a response is required. A second example involves the use of multifaceted questions. A seven year old is confronted with the following: 'So the first time you got smacked for telling stories you still told stories and got smacked again. So it didn't make any difference to you whether you told stories did it?' Such questions tend to elicit an 'I don't know' response as the child is unsure what question should be answered.

Another potential pressure operating in interview situations is the wish to be viewed favourably by the questioner, which leads those who are in fact able to recall correctly what they have witnessed, to report misleading information (Zaragoza, 1987) or to change their answers under repeated questioning. Real examples of this are given in court cases, for example in *People of Texas v. Marcias* (a sexual abuse case where the girl's testimony proved critical to the defendant's conviction and death sentence) the girl later stated that 'I answered questions I wasn't certain about because I wanted to help the adults'. In a sexual abuse case in Minnesota the boy later claimed that he had fabricated the stories of abuse because 'I could tell what they wanted me to say by the way they asked the questions' (Benedek, 1989, p. 915, cited in Zaragoza, 1987).

In the words of Brennan (1992): 'The extent to which truth is prejudiced by the use of these language tactics is a question to which the legal system must address itself.'

CONCLUSION

The legal domain offers psychologists, linguists, sociologists and other social scientists a unique cultural setting in which to conduct research. Levi and Walker (1990) maintain that social science research is needed to identify and test unexamined or unwarranted assumptions about language that underlie the principles and practices of our legal system and that this constitutes an important research effort in helping to further our understanding of the psychological processes involved in advocacy. By developing greater collaboration with legal scholars and practitioners, psychologists and other social scientists are able to conduct research in legal contexts and develop its application to the legal system in order to elucidate our understanding of that system and remedy its defects.

REFERENCES

Bell, B.E. and Loftus, E.F. (1989). Trivial persuasion in the courtroom: the power of a few (minor) details. *Journal of Personality and Social Psychology*, **56**, 669–79.

Bennet, W.S. and Feldman, M.S. (1981). *Reconstructing Reality in the Courtroom*. New Brunswick: Rutgers University Press.

Bransford, J.D. and Johnson, M.K. (1972). Contextual prerequisites for understanding: some investigations of comprehension and recall. *Journal of Verbal Learning and Verbal Behaviour*, **11**, 717–26.

Brennan, M. (1992). An abuse of privilege: cross examining child victim witnesses. Paper presented at the NATO Advanced Study Institute on The Child Witness, Il Ciocco, Italy.

Carlen, P. (1976). *Magistrates' Justice*. London: Martin Robinson.

Clitheroe, J. (1980). *A Guide To Conducting a Criminal Defence*. London: Oyez.

Drew, P. (1990). Strategies in the contest between lawyer and witness in cross-examination. In J.N. Levi and A.G. Walker (Eds), *Language in the Judicial Process*, volume 5 in the series *Law, Society and Policy*. London: Plenum Press.

Durkin, K. (Ed.) (1986). Language and social cognition during the school years. In K. Durkin (Ed.), *Language Development in the School Years*. Kent: Croom Helm, pp. 203–33.

Evans, K. (1992). *Advocacy at the Bar*. London: Blackstone.

Fiske, S.T. and Taylor, S.E. (1984). *Social Cognition*. New York: Random House.

Goodrich, P. (1986). *Reading the Law: A Critical Introduction to Legal Methods and Techniques*. Oxford: Blackwell.

Hayden, R.M. (1987). Turntaking, overlap and the task at hand: ordering speaking turns in legal settings. *American Ethnologist*, **14**, 251–70.

Hurwitz, S.D., Miron, M.S. and Johnson, B.T. (1992). Source credibility and the language of expert testimony. *Journal of Applied Social Psychology*, **22**, 1909–39.

Kaplan, M.F. and Scherching, C. (1981). Juror deliberation: an information integration analysis. In B.D. Sales (Ed.), *The Trial Process*. New York: Plenum.

Kelly, R.J. and Sagarin, E. (1988). Criminal justice and the cretan liar: unmasking strategies of dissimulation and deception. *Journal of Criminal Justice*, **16**, 61–72.

Lakoff, G. (1987). *Women, Fire and Dangerous Things*. Chicago: University of Chicago Press.

Levi, J.N. (1990). The study of language in the judicial process. In J.N. Levi and A.G. Walker (Eds), *Language in the Judicial Process*, volume 5 in the series *Law, Society and Policy*. London: Plenum Press.

Lind, E.A. and Ke, G.Y. (1985). Opening and closing statements. In S.M. Kassin and L.S. Wrightsman (Eds), *The Psychology of Evidence and Trial Procedure*. London: Sage.

Lloyd-Bostock, S. (1988). *Law in Practice: Applications of Psychology to Legal Decision Making and Legal Skills*. Leicester: British Psychological Society.

Loftus, E.F. (1979). *Eyewitness Testimony*. Massachusetts: Harvard University Press.

Loftus, E.F. and Palmer, J.C. (1974). Reconstruction of automobile destruction: an example of the interaction between language and memory. *Journal of Verbal Learning and Verbal Behaviour*, **13**, 585–9.

McBarnet, D.J. (1983). *Conviction: Law, the State and the Construction of Justice*. London: Macmillan.

Nisbett, R.E. and Ross, L. (1980). *Human Inference: Strategies and Shortcomings of Social Judgement*. Englewood Cliffs, NJ: Prentice Hall.

O'Barr, W.M. (1982). *Linguistic Evidence: Language, Power, and Strategy in the Courtroom*. New York: Academic Press.

Robinson, E.J. and Whittaker, S.J. (1986). Learning about verbal referential communication in the early school years. In K. Durkin (Ed.), *Language Development in the School Years*. Kent: Croom Helm, pp. 155–71.

Saks, M.J. and Hastie, R.H. (1978). *Social Psychology in Court*. London: VanNostrand Reinhold.

Tanford, J.A. (1992). The law and psychology of jury instructions. In J.R.P. Ogloff (Ed.), *Law and Psychology: The Broadening of the Discipline*. Durham, North Carolina: Academic Press.

Walker, A.G. (1993). Questioning young children in court: a linguistic case study. *Law and Human Behaviour*, **17**, 59–82.

Walker, D.M. (1980). *The Oxford Companion to Law*. Oxford: Clarendon Press.

Wangerin, P.T. (1990). A multidisciplinary analysis of the structure of persuasive arguments. *Harvard Journal of Law and Public Policy*, **16**, 195–239.

Wells, G.L. and Loftus, E.F. (1984). *Eyewitness Testimony: Psychological Perspectives*. Cambridge: Cambridge University Press.

Winkler, N.J. (1993). Credibility in the courtroom: does gender make a difference? Unpublished manuscript, Faculty of Sociology, University of California.

Zaragoza, M.S. (1987). Memory, suggestibility and eyewitness testimony in children and adults. In S.J. Ceci, M.P. Toglia and D.F. Ross (Eds), *Children's Eyewitness Testimony*. New York: Springer.

Expert Evidence

Hans Nijboer
University of Leyden

'Expertise' suggests special qualities which are contrasted with the 'general'. It suggests quality and reliability. 'Expertise' can be relied upon. It is the result of special education, experience, or training. Arising from developments in information technology 'expert systems' have been developed. However, in legal contexts 'expertise' is restricted to human activity, to humans' expertise, although this may involve the use of instruments and measures.

Two preliminary remarks should be made. First, in legal contexts, terms such as 'expertise', 'expert', or 'expert witness' are normally used to refer to specialist topics and specialists from disciplines and professions other than the law. The law is a specialist topic. (Lawyers can be called to give evidence as an expert witness on the law of another country.) So lawyers might be expected to appreciate the importance of specialist knowledge and to be aware of the problems in protecting that specialist knowledge base from misuse by 'charlatans'. Thus the extent to which many judges and lawyers regard themselves as able to represent other disciplines' knowledge base, for example as being 'common sense' or as unreliable, is rather surprising and ought to be unexpected (Freckelton, 1987; Smith and Wynne, 1989; Nijboer, 1992a; Nijboer, Callen and Kwak, 1993; Runciman, 1993).

Second, modern legal systems in the Western cultural tradition rely upon a principle of rationality in fact-finding by independent free evaluation of (relevant) information. (This is the ideal of 'free proof'.) This principle assumes, *inter alia*, that sound decisions about a factual dispute can be made by any unbiased person, or group of people (i.e. a jury) without particular skills or experience (Twining, 1990). This assumption highlights the contrast, and tension, between fact-finding as a general, lay, activity and the specialist character of expert evidence. This tension is often reflected in discussions about, and the actual assessment of, expert evidence. The tension is most prominent in legal systems which have an emphasis on oral proceedings. There, as in the English criminal jury trial, 'expertise' is represented by the expert witness. This contrasts with the 'mere' witness as to facts. It also contrasts with the lay jury, who have to make the decision, even though that will often involve an assessment of contrasting and competing expert witnesses.

Non-expert witnesses can only testify about their observations, about matters of fact deriving from their direct sensory observations. The non-expert witness should not express an opinion, although this may prove impractical and is permitted in certain ways, such as when trying to describe a lot of information in a short manner. Another manifestation of this tension is the continuing debate, in several countries, over the advantages and disadvantages of jury decision-making, otherwise described as lay decision-making versus specialists' decision-making. At the heart of most of these arguments lies the nature and quality of 'expertise' (Duflor-Favori, 1988).

The importance of expert evidence has developed during the last century, particularly in recent years (Saks and Van Druizend, 1983). Its role, and importance, is not limited to the settlement of disputes in the courts. It is increasingly called upon by official inquiries, often chaired by or involving lawyers as key members, into particular topics or incidents. It is also increasingly important in informing new legislation. And it has a major, unfortunately frequently overlooked, role in the pre-trial investigation and settlement of disputes. Civil disputes may be resolved, without a court hearing ever being necessary, because of the evidence of an expert. However the rules regulating experts' evidence are, anachronistically perhaps, made with regard only to courtroom deliberations (Carson, 1992). Especially in some key areas, such as professional malpractice or professional negligence, it has become an indispensable part of the legal landscape (Freckelton, 1987).

This chapter is concerned with 'expertise' and 'expert' in the determination of courtroom-based legal disputes. Forensic expertise is expertise from non-law disciplines which is applied to the concrete facts of cases (Nijboer, 1992a). Those cases can, however, involve very different areas of law: civil, criminal, administrative. Legal proceedings vary between different countries so that the exact roles of expertise and of experts vary (Van Den Wyngaert, 1994). While most fields of expertise concern one or more fields of science or scholarly activity, forensic expertise can be based upon merely practical experience. One example is the use of dogs and their trainers in the identification of suspects, although this and other examples do not go unchallenged (De Doelder and Hielkema, 1993). Reliance upon experience and practical skills is likely to reduce as the law, reflecting a broader societal tendency, increasingly recognises the importance of professionalism and science in modern society.

While expertise, *inter alia*, covers a range of subjects, activities, techniques, the expert is an individual fulfilling a role. Who is to be recognised as an expert? Who, in legal proceedings, may be called to act as an expert witness to be involved in the preparation of reports, to advise lawyers and, possibly, to give evidence in the proceedings? Most countries' legislation does not include a statutory definition of, or procedure for determining who is an expert. For the Federal Courts, in the United States, there is a provision in the Federal Rules of Evidence concerning the admissibility of expert witness testimony. Rule 702 defines the expert witness as a witness 'qualified as expert by knowledge, skill, experience, training or education.' He or she is allowed to testify upon 'scientific, technical or other specialised knowledge.'

In a less articulated, more latent way, other jurisdictions presume a similar set of requirements. Western legal systems rely heavily upon the discretion of the courts to decide in actual cases whether or not someone is capable of giving expert testimony. Recognition is not restricted to professional or academic leaders. Practitioners with sufficient experience and knowledge can, and have been, recognised as expert witnesses. The legal requirements for recognising someone an expert remain rather vague. However, the legal framework is usually supported by the professional rules and norms of the field of expertise in question. For example a chartered psychologist, in the UK, giving expert evidence outside of his or her area of expertise could be disciplined by the British Psychological Society. And in most Western jurisdictions there are special topics where legislation prescribes the nature of the expert evidence required, for example the taking of blood samples in drunk driving cases or certification that a prisoner is fit to be interviewed.

It is important to relate the expert's contribution, both to the admission and to the assessment of the evidence, to his or her field of expertise. The selection, admission and evaluation of the expert evidence needs to be considered within the scientific, methodological and professional standards of the relevant discipline. The expert witness owes duties both to his or her discipline and profession as well as to the case that he or she is called to give evidence upon (Phillips and Bowen, 1985; Gee and Mason, 1990; Nijboer, 1992a, b; Eisenberg, 1993;).

Comparing legal systems will demonstrate that the role of experts, and who may involve them in a case, differs considerably (Terré et al., 1969). In England and Wales and other 'common law' countries experts are invariably called to work for one of the sides or parties to the litigation. Although legislation permits it, the court appointed 'neutral' expert is an exception in those courts. This is clearly a consequence of, or indeed even a feature of, the adversarial system of court procedure.

In marked contrast in continental European jurisdictions the situation is the reverse. Not only in criminal procedure, where the parties are not dominant, but also in civil procedure (where the parties litigate in a way that is not very dissimilar from the adversarial procedure in this respect), the court appointed expert is the norm (Terré, 1969), and any expert appointed by one of the parties is generally considered to be an inferior kind of expert. This difference applies to the handling of cases within the courts and it also impacts upon the manner in which both the investigation and trial preparation are organised (Nijboer, 1994; Twining, 1990).

The contrast between the Common Law and the Continental countries is less striking at the preparation for trial stage. In the preparation of a case each party can have his or her own consultants and use them to assist preparation of the case. Pre-trial rules and procedures vary considerable between countries and, indeed, within countries depending upon the type of proceedings involved. These rules cover such issues as when and what information shall be disclosed to the other parties and how. Cases often do not reach the trial stage; they end at the 'preparatory' phase, such as through a settlement between the parties or the withdrawing of a claim.

In continental European countries (as in Latin American countries) there is usually a greater difference between the rules of evidence in civil and in criminal cases than there is in common law countries. The 'expert', on the continent, is principally considered to be an aide or assistant to the court. In England and Wales the expert is primarily seen as an aide to the party who has organised that he or she should come to court. Experts from forensic science laboratories play a particularly important role in criminal cases. Their (growing) primary product, in all legal systems, is to provide reports to investigating authorities. However, they can also be called to the witness stand at the trial stage. The use of experts, by the police or by an investigating magistrate, is subject to limited regulation in the investigation of a case or its preparation for trial. There are, for instance, rules about time limits and access for certain people to the work of the expert. Nevertheless, in practice, a broad discretion is left to those authorities as to how they guide the expert's work on a case. One of the principal concerns behind the establishment, in the UK, of a Royal Commission on Criminal Justice, was a concern that forensic science laboratories and other services had become too identified with the prosecution and insufficiently independent. Their failure to acknowledge and disclose alternative interpretations and findings was a factor in a number of cases of wrongful conviction. The Royal Commission's report (Runciman, 1993) made a number of recommendations to enhance the independence and quality of those experts' evidence.

Expert evidence given during the trial is subject to several rules. Here the law of evidence is relevant; it also differs between legal systems. The emphasis, or focus for the rules, can be put on the admission of evidence, as in England and Wales. Alternatively the focus can be placed on the evaluation or assessment of evidence which has been admitted, as in the criminal courts in The Netherlands (where the judges decide issues of fact and proof without any form of jury or other lay participation). Depending, again, on the country and on the kind of trial, expert evidence can be admitted in an oral or in a written form. Where the culture or tradition of the legal system is an oral one then the dominant form will be oral testimony by the expert. Where the culture or tradition is a written one, such as in The Netherlands, then the dominant form will be the expert's written report which may be supplemented by graphics, displays and other explanatory and informative devices. Naturally different rules for the introduction, presentation and assessment of the expert evidence are applicable to both the oral and written form of expert evidence.

Experts' reports that are helpful to the pre-trial investigation are not necessarily important, as evidence, at later stages. That initial work may have been the key to the obtaining of further and better factual evidence. Such expert reports demonstrate their value although they also, subsequently, render the expert redundant! (Perhaps rules of evidence ought to ensure that there are no financial disincentives which might, or might be thought to, influence the opinions of expert witnesses, such as to prolong an investigation or trial.)

During pre-trial investigations and preparations the parties, and sometimes the court, will need to consider whether expert evidence needs to be obtained. The expert called for at this stage should remember that the results of his or her work in written or oral form may be relied upon and used in different ways at later stages. The expert's report may became important in other ways than those originally considered. Indeed it may become an embarrassment to the party that commissioned it.

As they prepare for a trial lawyers often develop clearer ideas about the kind of evidence that they will need. Expert evidence may be sought at this stage. At the trial a number of legal issues will arise. For which purposes can expert evidence be introduced? Legal texts list different purposes including commenting upon (and giving an opinion about) data or facts before the court, explaining technical matters, reporting special inquiries, tests, and experiments that the experts have undertaken, commenting upon the quality of the work of other experts involved or cited in the case.

All those who seek to introduce expert evidence, or who have to make decisions based upon it, must consider both its admissibility and its probative value. The basic test of admissibility concerns whether there are matters in issue which require expertise for their observation, analysis or description (Hodgkinson, 1990). Countries in the continental European legal tradition, such as The Netherlands, Belgium, Germany, France and Switzerland, tend to set very low thresholds for the admissibility of expert evidence. They prefer to regulate how the expert evidence, which is admitted, is assessed. The converse applies in some common law countries. England and Wales appears to be an intermediate, if not rather novel, position. These countries restrict the role of expert witnesses in some ways, for example they may not comment on issues which the judges declare to be common sense or within the knowledge or experience of ordinary people (*Turner*, [1975] Q.B. 834), but there is a much lower threshold for the admission of novel scientific evidence than exists in other common law countries such as the USA (Freckelton, 1993). Generally the introduction of expert evidence during the trial, as a surprise to the other parties, will not be permitted. (This can be done, however, by the defence in criminal cases, in The Netherlands.) In the USA some jurisdictions (for example Missouri State) have 'trials-before-the-trial' where a judge, sitting without a jury, eliminates elements of surprise from the presentation of both the prosecution and defence. Similar enhanced judicially supervised pre-trial procedures have been recommended for major trials, for England and Wales, by the Royal Commission on Criminal Justice.

In England and Wales Rules of Court and statutory provisions (including Civil Evidence Act 1968, the Police and Criminal Evidence Act 1984 and the Criminal Justice Act 1988) provide a body of rules regulating the admission of expert evidence. A court may be involved—for example, when a party has asked for directions about how the trial is to be managed. This can involve a limit being placed upon the number of experts that are to be called as witnesses. The rules of disclosure are basically based upon a principle of mutuality (Hodgkinson, 1990, p. 43). Disclosure can be limited by rules protecting certain data or by certain professional privileges.

Rules regulating expert evidence in criminal trials clearly indicate a preference for oral evidence. However, under various conditions expert' written reports can be admitted (Hodgkinson, 1990, pp. 57–9). Once admitted expert evidence is not restricted to the benefit of the party which called it. At this stage there are no 'property rights' in the expert evidence. The competence and compellability of an 'expert witness' are subject to the same rules that apply to witnesses as to fact. The expert witness will be called by his or her 'side'. For court-appointed expert witnesses the situation is different. Furthermore a court can decide to call an expert witness, who has not been called by the parties, in the interests of justice.

An expert witness is subject to the same procedures of examination and cross-examination as other witnesses. It is good practice for expert witnesses, in England and Wales, to gives an overview of their experience and qualifications once they have been sworn in. (For descriptions of the rules and procedures surrounding expert evidence and witnesses in England and Wales see, generally, Graham Hall and Smith (1992) and Reynolds and King (1992).) The Americans here speak of the experts' 'credentials'. As well as providing information to assist when it becomes necessary to evaluate the expert evidence, this practice helps to establish the extent to which the expert represents a discipline, or a field of expertise, with a reliable scientific base. Admissibility and relevance of the field is part of any decision about expert evidence.

Novel scientific evidence presents special problems. In the USA there was a long-standing debate about the decision laid down in *Frye v. United States* (293 Fed. 1013 (D.C.Cir., 1923). The decision, basically, decided that novel scientific evidence could only be admitted into the federal courts if it had gained general acceptance in the field in which it belongs. This relatively high standard is not applied in English (or continental European) proceedings (Freckelton, 1993). However, in the *Daubert v. Merrell Dow Pharmaceuticals, Inc.* (113 S.Ct. 2786 (1993)) the US Supreme Court decided that the *Frye* test had not survived the adoption of the Federal Rules of Evidence in 1975. The Supreme Court decided that the criteria for admissibility had to involve a legal test. That requires an examination of whether the evidence is 'scientific', which will involve an inquiry into the methodology involved and other indications such as publication in peer-review journals, and whether it is relevant to the issue under dispute.

The *Daubert* test is more demanding than the informal position adopted in England and Wales, which comes closer to the continental jurisdictions than to the United States position. The admissibility of expert evidence in England and Wales depends substantially upon the courts' discretion. The 'classical' common law offers some general rules which can serve as practical guidelines for deciding on the admissibility of expert evidence:

1. While a 'normal' witness only can testify about facts an expert can give an opinion. However, that opinion must be within the limits of his or her field of expertise.

2. Information that the judge considers to be within the general knowledge and experience of ordinary people, and which thus does not require expertise, cannot be given as expert evidence.

3. Expert witnesses must not usurp the role of the judge and jury. They must not give evidence on the 'ultimate' issue, that is the very issue which the trial is concerned with. This can include the credibility of witnesses but, somehow, in England and Wales at least, excludes opinions about whether the defendant was mentally disordered at the time he or she committed the crime.

4. The expert should only state opinions upon information, facts or research results which are themselves admissible evidence. (Nijboer, 1992b, p. 271)

Continental European countries consider the expert, when testifying, not as a special kind of witness but rather as just a witness. They tend to be much more lenient or open towards the admissibility of evidence in general. Their rules of evidence primarily apply to the weight or evidential value of the evidence presented. In such countries court-appointed experts are much more common than in common law systems such as England and Wales. Where the parties are responsible for calling their own expert witnesses a 'battle' of experts can result. This can sometimes be avoided by pre-trial disclosure of the experts' evidence, by pre-trial agreements about the number of experts to be called, and pre-trial meetings of the experts. In England and Wales it is not unknown for the experts of both sides to come to court with a joint statement (Hodgkinson, 1990, p. 52).

Once the expert's evidence has been given the issue becomes how much weight or evidential value it should be given. The assessment of the weight of evidence, whether by a jury or by a judge, is very complex. It is not a simple question of deciding which pieces of evidence to believe and which to reject.

The role of the standards of proof should not be underestimated. In civil cases the court's ultimate decision should only be in favour of the person bringing the case (the plaintiff in England and Wales), only if the court is satisfied, on the balance of the probabilities, that his or her case is more likely to be true than the defendant's. In criminal cases the prosecution must prove their version of events beyond reasonable doubt.

> There is no direct method of correlating the standard of proof in criminal and civil cases to the varying degrees of certainty which scientists and other experts ascribe to their findings. The criminal standard is susceptible of no precise mathematical description, such as a 99 per cent. probability, and although the civil standard can be meaningfully described as 51 per cent. probability this is often difficult to translate into term equivalent to those of scientific results or estimates. (Hodgkinson, 1990, p. 204)

The argument is not that the kind of expressions used by experts are irrelevant but the legal standards cannot easily be included in those expressions. This is a source of problems between experts and the lawyers.

Lawyers are, naturally, more accustomed to expert evidence from certain disciplines. They are, for example, less knowledgeable about the kind of questions that can meaningfully be asked of psychologists. Many lawyers are poorly informed about subdisciplines within psychology. They may not distinguish, for example, between psychologists, clinical psychologists working in a therapeutic milieu work, and forensic psychologists who specialise, and are therefore more likely to be aware of the specialist literature, on psychology in legal contexts. There are no discipline-specific procedural and evidential rules of law for psychologists. But every expert witness should be careful to ensure that he or she is sufficiently experienced or qualified to give that evidence. They should also be careful in presenting findings, clearly distinguishing between fact and opinion and acknowledging differences of opinion within his or her own discipline. Professional standards are relevant. If there is a convention—for example, to use a particular psychological test in a particular context—then that convention should be adhered to unless there are good and sufficient reasons for a different approach being taken.

Experts who are not experienced in trial work often undergo a very unpleasant experience when they are first examined in court. They may be asked questions about why they made particular decisions—for example, chose particular tests—when they are so used to making those decisions that they no longer recall the initial rationale for the choice. They may feel that they are not as trusted as the lawyers. Their only remedies are to prepare their reports and other evidence well and, perhaps, to undertake some training to prepare themselves for lawyers' questions which may distort their evidence and damage their reputation (Carson, 1990).

Psychologists are increasingly asked questions about defendants' or other peoples' states of mind. They need to be sure that they do not leave their own area of expertise and trespass into areas where psychiatrists should be called as witnesses. Other special areas for psychologists' evidence concerns the interviewing of child witnesses (Hodgkinson, 1990). Psychologists may also be very helpful at the sentencing stage of criminal trials.

Legislation prescribing the role of psychologists as expert witnesses—for example, specifying when reports must be sought—might appear attractive but could also create a number of problems. The vagueness of the present law may actually be advantageous. Practical progress may best be achieved by the psychological professions being increasingly explicit about the assumptions and conventions within their discipline. Relevant professional bodies could also develop ways in which the 'credentials' of individual experts might more easily and accurately be established. At the moment there is too much reliance upon 'good practice' by the experts and assumptions being made about the quality and relevance of the field of expertise. Being explicit and open is desirable in order to facilitate sensible and rational discussions about the facts that have to be established both in individual trials and in trial processes, such as judicial inferences about causation and 'common sense'. How far we may progress, through greater co-operation, both in individual trials and more generally in law and psychology, must remain an open question (see generally Nijboer, Callen and Kwak, 1993).

REFERENCES

Alsberg, M, Nüse, K. and Meyer, K. (1993). *Der Beweisantrag im Strafprozess.* Cologne: Heymans.

Brodsky, S.L. (1991). *Testifying in Court.* Washington, DC: American Psychological Association.

Carson, D. (1990). *Professionals and the Courts.* Birmingham: Venture Press.

Carson, D. (1992). Beyond the ultimate issue. In F. Lösel, D. Bender and T. Bliesener (Eds), *Psychology and Law: International Perspectives.* Berlin: De Gruyter.

De Doelder, H. and Hielkema, J. (Eds) (1993). *Goed gezien? Problemen bij Identificatiemethoden in Strafzaken.* Arnhem: Gouda Quint.

Duflor-Favori, C. (1988). *Le psychologue expert en Justice.* Paris: Presses Universitaires de France.

Eisenberg, U. (1993). *Persönliche Beweismittel in der StPO.* Munich: Beck.

Freckelton, I. (1987). *The Trial of the Expert*. Melbourne: Oxford University Press.

Freckelton, I. (1993). Science and the legal culture. *Expert Evidence*, **2**, 3, 107–14.

Gee, D.J. and Mason, J.K. (1990). *The Courts and the Doctor*. Oxford: Oxford University Press.

Graham Hall, J. and Smith, G.D. (1992). *The Expert Witness*. Chichester: Barry Rose.

Hodgkinson, T. (1990). *Expert Evidence: Law and Practice*. London: Sweet & Maxwell.

Nijboer, J.F. (1992a). *Forensische Expertise*. Arnhem: Gouda Quint.

Nijboer, J.F. (1992b). De positie van de deskundige in het Amerikaanse strafprocesrecht, *Recht en Kritiek*, **18**: 259–74.

Nijboer, J.F. (1992c). Forensic expertise in Dutch criminal procedure. *Cardozo Law Review*, **14**, 165–91.

Nijboer, J.F. (1994). *Stratrechtelyk Bewysrecht*. Nijmegen: Ars Aequilibri.

Nijboer, J.F, Callen, C.R. and Kwak, N. (Eds) (1993). *Forensic Expertise and the Law of Evidence*. Amsterdam: Edita/North-Holland.

Phillips, J.H. and Bowen, J.K. (1985). *Forensic Science and the Expert Witness*. Sydney: Law Book Company.

Reynolds, M.P. and King, P.S.D. (1992). *The Expert Witness and his Evidence*. Oxford: Blackwell.

Runciman (Lord) (1993). *The Royal Commission on Criminal Justice*. London: HMSO. (Cm 2263.)

Smith, R. and Wynne, B, (Eds) (1989). *Expert Evidence*. London: Routledge.

Terré, F. et al. (1969). *L'expertise dans les principaux systèmes juridiques d'Europa*, Paris: Univ.

Saks, M.J, Van Druizend, R. (1983). *The Use of Expert Evidence in Litigation*. Washington, DC: National Centre for State Courts.

Van Den Wyngaert, C. (Ed.) (1994). *Criminal Procedure Systems in the European Community*. London: Butterworth.

Twining, W.L. (1990). *Rethinking Evidence*. Oxford: Blackwell.

Evidence Evaluation in Jury Decision-making

Ramón Arce
University of Santiago de Compostela.

INTRODUCTION

As we proceeded to the deliberation room, the judge's insistence on a unanimous verdict led to a fellow juror asking me for my verdict. While I pondered I realised that by not deciding I had already made a decision. This highlights the complex cognitive processes underlying each individual's decision which, subsequently, must be pooled with those of the other jurors in order to reach a group decision.

The participation of lay people in the administration of justice has been recorded since ancient times, and the debate regarding the function, *modus operandi* and capacity of lay people in relation to the administration of justice has been endless. The contributions of psychology to the improvement of the jury system have been substantial. This chapter will review these contributions and evaluate the jury's competence, as well as embarking on the journey which will take us from the mental (psychological) mechanisms involved at the level of the individual juror through to the jury's collective decision. Finally, the optimum conditions under which the jury may perform its duties will be considered.

IN SEARCH OF JUROR BIAS

For many years the literature has focused on jurors' bias in making judgements. The fact that juries rarely walk into the deliberation room with a unanimous verdict has been well documented (Kalven and Zeisel, 1966; Hans and Vidmar, 1986). The cause was believed to lie in underlying factors, which were identified as bias. The search for the bias that could explain the differences in the individual judgements was not very fruitful. Thus, while some studies reported that in some cases men differed from women (Efran, 1974), other studies found that there were no gender differences (Griffitt and Jackson, 1973). Alternatively, some studies concerned with the comparison between authoritarian versus non-authoritarian jurors revealed that the former are more inclined to offer a guilty verdict (Bray and Noble, 1978), whereas other studies have observed no differences (Vidmar and Crinklaw, 1973). In view of such findings several authors concluded that there was an absence of bias in the formation of the jury's judgements (e.g. Gerbasi, Zuckerman and Reis, 1977; Hastie, Penrod and Pennington, 1983). However, these studies used a great variety of case types, including rape, murder, criminal negligence, robbery and many others, which has not been taken into account. Instead of concluding that the inconsistencies between the results are due to the absence of any real, pronounced, predictable influence of psychosocial variables, it seems simpler to suppose that the inconsistencies are due to the disparity among the case materials used (Bem and Allen, 1968). Even when similar cases have been used in different studies, the cases themselves have been different so that the kind and amount of evidence presented has differed. This makes direct comparison of the results of questionable validity. In this connection Dane and Wrightsman (1982) and Vidmar (1979) found, perhaps not surprisingly, that certain kinds of bias disappeared in cases in which the evidence clearly favoured one side or the other.

A possible explanation of why the influence of psychosocial variables is affected by case type can be sought in the theory of the integration of information (Anderson, 1974). Specifically, it seems possible that psychosocial factors act not so much by imposing biases directly on a verdict, but rather as filters biasing the comprehension of the evidence presented in court. Thus evidence still plays a fundamental role in juror decisions—and if strong enough will outweigh any psychosocial bias—but psychosocial variables can have significant effects when the evidence is finely balanced and therefore requires interpretation by the juror (Malton and Davis, 1986; Vishert, 1987). It should be borne in mind that cases in which the evidence is clear, one way or the other, do not often reach trial by jury, especially when plea-bargaining occurs.

The final conclusions came in the form of multivariate statistical studies. These studies (Saks, 1977; Feild, 1978; Penrod, 1980; Hepburn, 1980; Hastie, Penrod and Pennington, 1983) found statistically significant predictors, but the variance percentages in decisions explained by their variables was small, with the exception of Feild who found that his attitudinal variables explained, on average, 26 per cent of the variance.

Arce (1989) undertook a statistical study under similar circumstances but with two modifications. The type of case was monitored and the variables that had already provided data concerning possible bias were reassessed. Under these conditions, sets of variables emerged, that is to say, profiles that were predictors of bias in juror decision-making. However, as in the previous cases, the variance that was explained was small, between 10 per cent and 15 per cent. These profiles corresponded to two sets of variables that have been well documented in the literature: (i) ideology (i.e. progressive versus conservative) and (ii) attribution (e.g. internal versus external). As was to be expected, these profiles led to significant differences in some cases, but not in others.

ROLE CHARACTERISATION IN JURY DECISION-MAKING

During the deliberation, some jurors have greater influence than others (i.e. Strodtbeck, James and Hawkins, 1957; Hastie, Penrod and Pennington, 1983). Traditionally, two mediators have been attributed to the individual's influence on jury decision-making, i.e. location and status. The jurors located at the head or end of the deliberation table are responsible for one-quarter or third of the discussion during the deliberation. Moreover, only a few jurors play a decisive role in the jury in terms of debating the issues, the figure being approximately three jurors (when working with groups of 12 members) who are responsible for 50 per cent of the discussion. Furthermore, it has also been reported that some jurors, about two to four, are responsible for only 5 per cent of the discussion, or even less in the case of other jurors who account for only 1 per cent of the discussion (Kessler, 1973; Saks, 1977; Hastie, Penrod and Pennington, 1983; Arce, Sobral and Fariña, 1991). Their active role as jurors is basically limited to voting. One hypothesis suggests that most jurors are not responsible for the deliberation because their points of view are already represented by the other jurors given that there are usually only two possible verdicts, guilty or not guilty. This seems plausible if one considers that as juries get larger so does the number of jurors that do not actively participate in the proceedings (Kessler, 1973; Saks, 1977). From these findings it was deduced that the jurors with a greater degree of participation had a greater influence on the final decision. However, whether the quantitative impact involved qualitative consequences remained unclear. We have carried out a study in order to determine, through an analysis of the content of the deliberations, whether these numerical results imply qualitative consequences.

In quantitative terms, our data supported the following three findings: (1) only a few jurors were responsible for most of the utterances; (2) the foreperson was systematically responsible for the largest number of utterances; (3) the others rarely intervened (Arce, Sobral and Fariña, 1991). The qualitative impact was assessed using regulating messages (i.e. messages governing the start and finish of the deliberation, the ballots, the changing of subject, giving either instructions or orders to jurors, etc.). (For further topics regarding the qualitative impact of regulating messages in group discussions see Rogers and

Millar, 1980.) While the percentage of random utterances was calculated to be 11 per cent, the range of utterances on behalf of the foreperson oscillated from 30 per cent to 100 per cent (the average being approximately 50 per cent) thus enabling the foreperson to dominate the deliberation. This qualitative impact, when translated in terms of group decisions, illustrates that the majority of deliberations conformed with the foreperson's initial decision.

Our findings agree with several studies concerning the role of 'non-active' jurors. In the USA the interpretation of these data has served to justify the elimination of 'non-active' jurors through the reduction in the jury size, on the grounds that this does not alter the deliberation (Apodaca, 1972; Johnson, 1972). Strikingly, however, our findings indicate that 'non-active' jurors do play a significant role in the jury since they accept arguments contrary to their initial position (pro guilty or pro not guilty) which in turn produces disequilibriums in the jury by finally swaying the more active members of the group towards a consensus (the active members being more reluctant to change after having defended and argued in public to a greater or lesser extent their position). In addition, we have observed that the 'non-active' jurors, rather than explaining or justifying their changes in judgement, limit themselves to accepting counter-arguments without any justification of their decision, thus bestowing a considerable degree of importance to their contributions as well as leading to the disintegration of the in-group. In terms of content analysis (Rogers and Farace, 1975), we observed that the 'non-active' jurors almost exclusively used the support category, i.e. approving the counter arguments to their faction. In contrast, the active jurors mainly used the categories of opposition and extension, i.e. to argue in favour of their position and to disapprove the counter-arguments. The evidence suggests that 'non-active' jurors play a more decisive role in the dynamics of the jury (or the decision-making of small groups) than is commonly perceived at first sight. Thus, great care must be taken at the time of assessing and interpreting the true role of apparently 'non-active' jurors, in particular when attempting to establish the optimum jury size.

PRELIMINARY QUESTIONS: PHENOMENOLOGY OF THE JURY AND VERDICT TYPE

There are two sets of variables that modulate the jury's deliberations and which can to some extent influence the decision. The first set of variables refers to the phenomenology of the jury: the decision rule and the jury size. The second group encompasses the 'variables under consideration': homogeneity (which we shall deal with at a later stage since its effects become manifest during the deliberation) and the type of verdict. Whereas phenomenology has been well documented in the literature (i.e. Hastie, Penrod and Pennington, 1983), the 'variables under consideration' are a subject of recent concern that can generate, just as the first set, decisions that do not take into account all of the evidence.

Juries often reach unanimous verdicts, but a two-thirds majority or even a simple majority, have been accepted as a decision rule in some countries. The 'inconvenience' of a unanimous decision can be calculated by the number of trials that conclude in a hung jury. Field studies have revealed that under requirements of unanimity, 5.6 per cent of trials lead to hung juries (Kalven and Zeisel, 1966), which involves a repetition of the hearing and thus increased social and economic costs. A possible alternative to be considered, which has already been put into practice in some jurisdictions on some occasions in order to reduce costs, is to record the trial on videotape so that it may be shown to another jury (Sobral and Arce, 1990). Nevertheless, the problem itself is not eliminated by simply reducing the criteria of decision from a unanimous verdict to a two-thirds majority; given that Kalven and Zeisel found that using the two-thirds decision rule led to 3.1 per cent hung juries. Historically, the simple majority decision rule has been applied, as in the case of the Spanish II Republic among others where the jury is responsible for carrying out the task of fact finding (Gisbert, 1990). Nowadays, we are unaware of any instance where the rule of a simple majority is still applied. Bearing this in mind, it is advisable that jurors enter the jury room with a minimum of a two-thirds majority as a decision rule. Because of the possible consequences the decision rule may have on the deliberation, Hastie, Penrod and Pennington (1983) have undertaken the most detailed study regarding this issue. Their analysis of jury deliberations revealed that in comparison to the unanimous juries, the two-thirds majority juries deliberated for a shorter period of time. However, this is not simply a matter of a longer or shorter deliberation. Unanimity leads to the greater involvement of minorities, increased juror satisfaction (which has been assessed by self-report) with regard to their final verdict, and a more detailed appraisal of both the law and the evidence as can be seen from deliberation content analysis (Hastie, Penrod and Pennington, 1983). Thus, the most representative and objective decision is to adopt the rule of the unanimous decision. In other words, once the majority required has been reached, the arguments of the minority, whether they are correct or not, are no longer considered by the majority as of significant weight.

A further phenomenological variable to be considered is the size of the group. Though there is no hard and fast rule, the countries with the longest traditions have opted for 12-member juries. Proposals have been made in the USA to reduce the jury to a minimum of six members (Van Dyke, 1977). Those in favour of the reduction have stressed the savings in social and economic costs, and that a 12-member jury does not ensure a better trial. Opponents, however, have argued that a jury should be representative of the different social groups in the community. Thus, for example, the point of view held by a minority group which represented 10 per cent of the population would be represented, with a 12-member jury, with one member in 72 per cent of juries, whereas with a six-member jury the figure would drop to 47 per cent of juries (Zeisel, 1971). Furthermore, a larger jury diminishes the margin of error, thus different 12-member juries are more likely to reach the same decision than different six-member juries (Hans and Vidmar, 1986). (For further information on the debate concerning the optimum jury size refer to Sobral and Arce, 1990.)

The above findings suggest that the larger the number of jurors the greater the quality and the representativeness of the decisions, but also the higher socioeconomic costs and frequency of hung juries. To determine the optimum number that can combine both needs seems an almost impossible task. However, we should emphasise that with small juries justice seems left to chance or to less representative decisions. We are also aware, through the study of organisational decision-making, that in large groups some individuals do not simply limit their efforts to voting but do not even follow the discussions (i.e. Koopman and Pool, 1991). This suggests that in all likelihood their votes rest on conformity, obedience, compliance, normativity or other explanatory factors rather than on informational influence.

The type of verdict, whether it be a dichotomous or multiple verdict, may also moderate the juror and jury decisions. The requirement of a guilty or innocent verdict encourages juries not to be willing to take risks and thus to become, on certain occasions, lenient (Kalven and Zeisel, 1966). To this effect we have observed (Arce, 1989) a relatively small correlation between the verdicts reached and the sentences given by jurors dealing with the same case (the correlations oscillated between .71 and .88). Specifically, in cases where jurors consider that mitigating circumstances should be taken into account, but are unable to reflect this view in the sentence given that this function pertains to the judge, they tend to transform what they believe should be a reduced sentence into an innocent verdict in order to avoid passing undue harsh or heavy sentences. The possibility of the jury being confronted with various options in terms of the verdict (i.e. innocent, manslaughter, second or first degree murder, etc.) appears to transform the process of deliberation into a negotiation in which the verdict of the jury is based not so much on the evidence but rather on the need to reach a consensus. This particular process may be said to be the following: initially all those who defend the guilty verdict would come together in opposition to the not guilty jurors, and if the outcome is innocence the deliberation would terminate. But if the decision is guilty the next step would be to negotiate the degree of guilt through a series of allegiances of the closest positions. In this way the extreme options (innocent or guilty) would hardly ever predominate, ensuring that the intermediate options would prevail since they would be represented after every fusion of majorities. In fact, the number of not guilty verdicts is very low (Hastie, Penrod and Pennington, 1983; Cowan, Thompson and Ellsworth, 1984). Consequently, the jury's final decision does not entirely emerge from informational influence but rather it is arrived at through alliances.

Bearing in mind that the jurors' estimations of sentences in criminal cases closely approximate the legal ones, any attempt to install a lay person's system of administering justice should consider a division in terms of (i) verdicts and (ii) sentencing in order to ensure the broadest of safeguards. Under these circumstances the lay person will decide on innocence or guilt. Once the verdict has been reached, both lay people and experts will pass sentence, or alternatively the experts will pass their sentence and the lay people will have the opportunity to revise it if there is a wide discrepancy with their initial assessment. This procedure would ensure not only that the administration of justice was more in line with current social thought, but it would also, to a certain extent, avoid leniency. As Kalven and Zeisel (1966) have pointed out, one of the causes of leniency among lay people is the lack of control they have over the consequences of their verdict. The data obtained in several studies support this view (Kaplan and Krupa, 1986; Arce, 1989). Both procedures have already been put into practice. The lay people's decision concerning the facts and joint sentencing has been applied in some states in the USA as well as in Austria. The jury's control on sentencing (following the verdict) was adopted during the second Spanish Republic.

In conclusion, in as far as the characterisation of the jury is concerned, an optimum performance of the jury requires unanimous decisions, and no reduction in group size. Moreover, further studies are required to determine the impact of type of verdict (dichotomous or multiple), joint sentencing, and the jury's control over sentencing.

DYNAMICS IN GROUP DECISIONS

Two sources of influence on group decisions have been identified in the literature, i.e. normative and informational influences. In terms of legal implications the most important objective lies in maximising the informational influence and minimising the effects of the normative influence. In this section we shall evaluate the anomalous effects that normative influences have on deliberations as well as dealing with the procedures designed to curb these influences. Finally, we shall examine the role that the deliberation plays in controlling juror bias through informational influences.

Leniency and the Asymmetry Effect

In 1966 Kalven and Zeisel carried out the most prominent study of jury behaviour and compared the decisions of actual juries with those that judges would reach. Of a total of 3576 criminal cases, the total number of agreements was 78 per cent (64 per cent for guilty verdicts and 14 per cent for not guilty). Curiously, successive interpretations of the above findings have emphasised the divergences. Of the remaining 22 per cent of cases, 19 per cent of the juries reached a not guilty verdict whereas the judges favoured a guilty verdict.

Similar results have been observed in several countries (e.g. Baldwin and McConville, 1979; Gisbert, 1990). This jury tendency towards not guilty verdicts is known as leniency and various hypothesis have been put forward to explain this phenomenon: different standards of proof (Kalven and Zeisel, 1966), different value scales (Champagne and Nagel, 1982), previous experience as a predictor of guilty verdicts and the lack of experience as a predictor of innocence (Werner et al., 1985), etc. Though all of these hypotheses have found data to support their assertions, other alternative explanations have been proposed. Some studies (Kaplan and Krupa, 1986; Arce, 1989) have shown that the type of response, that is the verdict (as opposed to the sentence), makes a jury inclined to favour innocence. Nevertheless, it seems evident that this is a function of group dynamics, since individual jurors are more inclined to reach guilty verdicts than are judges (Tanford and Penrod, 1986). In addition, the asymmetric effect has been observed; that is to say, juries with an equal number of jurors in favour of innocence as for guilt are inclined, following the deliberation, to favour innocence (MacCoun and Kerr, 1988). On the other hand, it could be argued that asymmetry is but a manifestation of the principle of *in dubio pro reo*, in which case the net leniency is reduced.

Though the existence of leniency has been well documented, the exact extent of its effects is difficult to determine given that there are no objective parameters with which to gauge jury performance. In fact, a 30 per cent discrepancy rate has been observed among judges (Diamond and Zeisel, 1975). Thus efforts should be made to determine the mechanisms that lead to leniency and the procedures that may limit its effects. We shall now examine how the jury's decisions tend to favour innocence due to conformity.

Conformity

We are unaware of any studies designed to compare the jury verdict with the individual post-deliberation verdicts. It has been suggested that the jurors may undergo a process of conversion, that is to say they change their verdicts only due to personal conviction. With a unanimous decision rule, we measured (Arce, Fariña and Sobral, 1992) these post-deliberation decisions and found that, though the main process was conversion, more than 10 per cent of the jurors were victims of a process of conformity. In other words, despite giving into group pressure at the post-deliberation stage, they still individually maintained their initial verdicts. This tendency was almost exclusively to conform in favour of innocence— that is, an initial individual verdict of guilt followed by a group verdict of not guilty, and thereafter an individual post-deliberation verdict in favour of guilt. This could be one of the reasons why leniency is observed among juries and not among jurors. Nevertheless, it would be convenient to examine ways to control conformity by giving *ad hoc* instructions to the jury. Given that conformity has an anomalous effect in the deliberation process, it should be controlled (minimised).

Obedience

A further normative pressure prevalent in group decisions derives from the formation of a jury of equals (with equal voting rights) who are unequal in origin (some are lay people with regard to the law but others have legal knowledge). We are obviously referring here to escabinate or mixed juries, i.e. juries formed of lay people and involving the participation of judges in the deliberation stage. Though there is no fixed formula for such mixed juries, more often than not they include more lay people than legal experts and they normally decide by majority; these measures are designed to reduce the influence of experts. The advantage is that mixed decisions offer a possible solution to the lay people's inefficiency in dealing with judicial matters. This procedure avoids the problems inherent in the division of matters of fact from judicial matters since the judge is responsible for sentencing (for further details see Soriano, 1985). However, several studies have demonstrated that group decisions made in situations where a different status is assigned to each member, produces in its lay members a process of obedience (Torrance, 1959) which has been calculated to be in the order of 65 per cent. With reference to judgements, Kirchler and Davis (1986) found that the probability of altering a judgement is strongly linked to the status of the member holding the opposing view, the higher the status the more probable that the decision will be accepted. Consequently, the results of mixed juries seem to be predetermined by the decisions of the experts (Palmer, 1987). Palmer reported that with lay juries there was a 65 per cent change in verdicts in favour of innocence, whereas with mixed juries, with law students as experts, the changes tended to be towards guilt (59 per cent) with the lay people being most of those who changed their position.

In an attempt to recreate the real-life conditions of a mixed jury, we designed a study in which the juries were composed of eight lay-people and a judge, who viewed actual trials that had been recorded on videotape. The judge was placed in the most adverse of working conditions, i.e. a unanimous verdict was required and the verdict maintained by the judge was always that of the minority. Having viewed each case on video, the jurors had to complete a questionnaire. They were asked about their individual verdicts; if the majority were in favour of innocence the judge had to maintain the opposite verdict, that of guilt, or vice versa. Subsequently, we observed a change in the jurors' initial verdict which eventually corresponded with the verdict maintained by the judge. Under these peculiar conditions we did not witness any changes in the lay people's verdicts which was in the direction of opposition to the verdict held by the judge. Nearly all the jurors were in agreement with the judge's verdict. The only possible course of action for an opposing juror was to block the jury, thus, leading to a hung jury. In all the deliberations the judges managed to sway jurors towards their own decision. A detailed analysis of the deliberation and sociograms (for further details see Moreno, 1975) provide some insight into the mechanisms involved in the judge's influence over the group. Thus, it seems reasonable to believe that the role of the lay person in a mixed jury is that of controller rather than decision maker. There is a conversion from a jury *par inter pares*; that is among peers, to a jury *primus inter pares*, i.e. a high status member among peers, and this has several implications. Thus, in France, the mixed jury system has supplanted the lay jury system with a significant reduction in the number of cases heard by a jury (see Gisbert, 1990). The similarity in results between expert and mixed juries may be the cause for the semi-disappearance of the jury. Several authors have suggested the mixed jury is but the first step towards the process of jury self-eradication (i.e. Gisbert, 1990).

Homogeneity

The existence of disagreements among jurors and juries has encouraged us to undertake a detailed analysis, which otherwise would not have been carried out if all the members had shared the same opinion about the issue in question (Hans and Vidmar, 1982). In fact, it has been observed that heterogeneous juries solve problems better than do homogeneous ones (Zeisel, 1971; Lempert, 1975). Bearing this in mind, and taking into account our work concerning statistical predictions of bias in the decisions of jurors, we assessed the impact of bias in homogeneous juries by forming ideologically homogeneous juries (only conservatives or progressives) and attributionally homogeneous juries (only subjects with internal or external attribution) which were then shown different cases on video. With this procedure we found that in some criminal cases the conservative and progressive juries differed significantly in post but not pre-deliberation verdicts (Arce, Sobral and Fariña, 1992). The bias seemed to be derived from the deliberation of homogeneous groups. Thus, homogeneity was found to precede bias at the level of the content which was dealt with in the deliberations. That is to say, since only a certain part of the whole evidence was discussed (Arce, Fariña and Sobral, 1995), the deliberation styles were controlled (Arce, Sobral and Fariña, 1990a), which led to more rigid and redundant 'cognitive deliberations' (Arce, Sobral and Fariña, 1990b).

It may be argued that juries do not correctly remember the whole evidence. This does not seem to be the case given that juries are estimated to recall 90 per cent of the evidence. However, with homogeneous groups, in certain cases, the content of the deliberation is predetermined, and so part of the evidence is ignored. Likewise, this occurs with reference to certain facts in the reconstruction of the events by jurors. Evidence which is not congruent with their decision concerning the verdict is not equally considered (Pennington and Hastie, 1986; Alonso-Quecuty and Arce, 1992). For this reason if we analyse the typical jurors' recall of evidence, their response will consist of a broad appreciation of the evidence. On the other hand, in cases where the group is biased, such as in homogeneous groups, the appreciation of the evidence during the deliberation is selective or driven to confirm their bias. Therefore, they either avoid using certain information which is not congruent with their bias or they interpret it according to their bias (e.g. they may consider the information in terms of being admissible or non-admissible, believable or unbelievable, etc.). Hence, individual bias is magnified in the deliberation under homogeneous conditions. Other authors who have examined the attitude of homogeneous groups towards the death penalty have reported similar findings (Cowan, Thompson and Ellsworth, 1984).

The Deliberation as a Controller of Dispositional Effects

One of the central assumptions in the performance of the jury is that the deliberation will act as a control mechanism by counter-balancing the individual's bias. This seems to be the case with dispositional bias. By dispositional factors we mean transitional dispositions generated during the trial. If these dispositional states provoke individual bias, and if the deliberation fails to eradicate this bias, this would seriously undermine the principles and thus the very existence of the jury system. To this effect Kaplan and Miller (1978), with a two [evidence: high versus low incrimination] x four [dispositional state: straightforward manner; negative emotional/dispositional state generated by the judge in question; negative dispositional state stemming from the prosecution; negative dispositional state deriving from the defence] design, found that the negative states produced by the prosecution did not affect the judgements of the jurors. In contrast, when the source of negativity was neutral (the judge) or the defence lawyer, the rating of the defendant's guilt rose independently of the amount of evidence that was presented. However, deliberation by the jurors eliminated the dispositional bias. Thus, one of the most popular arguments formulated against the jury system has been undermined, and the role of the deliberation has gained strength as a valuable and essential duty of the jury.

CONCERNING THE COMPETENCE OF THE JURY

Juries have often been described as incompetent, inept, and ill prepared to exercise the functions bestowed on them as part of the judicial apparatus. The label of incompetence (for an example refer to Soriano, 1985) has been used as a justification for not adopting the jury system or, in cases where it has been adopted, at least to ensure that it is mixed. However, the data obtained from several studies do not seem to support such views. One example is the work of Kalven and Zeisel (1966) who, using the opinion of judges, classified cases that had previously undergone trial by jury into easy, difficult, and very difficult. If the jury was incompetent then we would expect to find divergences between the judges and jurors regarding the verdict in the difficult cases and, in particular, in the very difficult cases. This hypothesis is not supported by the data that indicate quite the opposite; divergences are the same in all three cases. Therefore, it can not be suggested that the jury does not understand the evidence. In an attempt to repeat the earlier work of Kalven and Zeisel (1966), Baldwin and McConville (1979) undertook a study in which they observed that on some occasions the judges believed that the jury had decided what was 'just' rather than what was 'legal'. Likewise, Myers (1979), having examined 201 criminal cases in Indiana, reported similar findings that juries rarely strayed from the law, and when they did so it was because it was in line with their notion of what was 'just' and 'right' and not due to incompetence. None the less, these cases are the exception rather than the rule. Horowitz (1985) has demonstrated that juries applied the law even under conditions where juries were instructed not to do so if they felt it was unjust. The only exceptions to this were certain cases involving issues like euthanasia. Moreover, even when juries did not receive these instructions to 'nullify' they still applied the legal precepts. In more recent studies, MacCoun and Kerr (1988) have shown that judges and jurors differ since judges tend to reach a guilty verdict in cases of reasonable doubt whereas jurors are more inclined to favour a verdict of not guilty in such circumstances.

Similarly, Hastie, Penrod and Pennington (1983), working with mock juries, found that the recall of each individual juror was not always optimum, but in a group they remembered 90 per cent of the evidence (including the main evidence) and 80 per cent of the judge's instructions which were very complex. Hence, it appears that the group was able to fulfil its duties.

One may make a valid accusation of incompetence in jurors' understanding of instructions (Hans and Vidmar, 1986). Quite simply, as Judge Frank stated, the jurors may not understand the law because not even many lawyers are capable of such a feat (Skidmore, 1948). However, when the legal instructions were 'translated', the jurors had no difficulty performing competently (Elwork, Sales and Alfini, 1977; Charrow and Charrow, 1979).

In many countries the role of the jury is circumscribed to criminal cases where the sentence requires a minimum 'quantum' punishment. In other countries the jury also deals with civil cases. However, certain civil cases (i.e. litigation between large companies) may become so complex that even experts find them too difficult to follow. Hence, it is advisable that juries should not intervene in very complex civil cases (Ross, 1970). (British judges are authorised to eliminate the jury from specific cases (Kirst, 1982).) None the less, in ordinary civil cases, which are the vast majority, the jury's performance is explained by the evidence and the deliberation (Walter, 1987).

In short, the claims of jury incompetence or irrationality have not been substantiated by the evidence (Hans and Vidmar, 1986).

DISCUSSION

The present review of the literature concerning the jury system has revealed that the performance of the jury may be improved by manipulating certain conditions; for example, unanimous verdicts improve the jury's performance, legal instructions can be translated to aid the jury's comprehension, etc. The list of improvements is too numerous to mention in this brief review. Nevertheless, we would like to propose a new area of debate. Though further studies are required, we have seen that psychosocial profiles may influence the verdicts reached by individual jurors. Moreover the predictive value of these factors is small and their influence is neither exerted in all cases nor always in the same direction (guilty or not guilty).

The deliberation process in psychosocially homogeneous juries appears to be cognitively rigid and stereotyped, makes insufficient use of the available information, and the deliberation is short. These effects compound the influence of shared ideological or attributional prejudices in the production of biased verdicts. The decision process in homogeneous juries, in fact, appears to exhibit many of the characteristics of 'group think' (i.e. Janis and Mann, 1977): the illusion of group invulnerability, belief in a shared morality, pressure to conform, etc. Consequently, the decisions of homogeneous juries are likely to suffer from the same defects as 'group think': incorrect appreciation of risks and alternatives, due largely to the consideration of insufficient information.

However, we should bear in mind that totally random juror selection does not guarantee the socio-demographic heterogeneity of juries, and neither do the standby nor voir dire systems (Van Dyke, 1977). Though some countries, among them France and the USA, have taken steps to ensure that the principle of social representativeness is respected, as regards the proportional representation of women, young people, blacks and other minorities, there are at present no safeguards against psychosocial homogeneity. Since psychosocial variables seem often to act by influencing the subjective standard of proof, one step towards correcting psychosocially originated bias might be to ensure that jurors understand and use the standard of proof required by law, which recent studies have shown to be misunderstood by many jurors (Kagehiro, 1990). A second measure, suggested by 'group think' theory, is to ask jurors to set down their pre-deliberation opinions in writing, so that they are more committed to these opinions and less likely to give way to group pressure. This procedure, however, seems to be ineffective. In experiments with single-sex juries, we have observed that, although the verdicts and versions of the case given by individual jurors were often unaffected by group deliberation, their votes yielded to group pressure, that is, to conformity. In our opinion, there is a third possibility that is worth considering. This is that a pool of jurors chosen by stratified sampling procedures to eliminate bias as regards sex, religion, etc., be further examined by a panel of experts who would evaluate their psychosocial characteristics. The expert evaluation would then be used in a second stratified random selection procedure. We point out that this kind of expert evaluation would differ in character very little from what is already standard practice in many countries, i.e. the pretrial examination of jurors by the judge to prevent jury bias.

REFERENCES

Alonso-Quecuty, M. L. and Arce, R. (1992). Jurados mentirosos: análisis de la reconstrucción de la evidencia. Unpublished paper, Universidad de La Laguna.

Anderson, N.H. (1974). Cognitive algebra. In. L. Berkowitz (Comp.), *Advances in Experimental Social Psychology*. New York: Academic Press.

Apodaca, Cooper and Madden, v. Oregon, 406 U.S. (1972).

Arce, R. (1989). Perfiles psicosociales, veredictos y deliberación en jurados legos. Unpublished doctoral thesis. University of Santiago.

Arce, R., Fariña, F. and Sobral, J. (1992). From juror to jurydecision making. A non model approach. Paper presented at the Third European Conference on Law and Psychology, Oxford.

Arce, R., Fariña, F. and Sobral, S. (1995). Análisis de contenido en la interacción de jurados legos. *Análisis y Modificación de Conducta* (in press).

Arce, R., Sobral, J. and Fariña, F. (1990a). Attribution and deliberation style. Paper presented at the Second European Conference on Law and Psychology, Nürnberg.

Arce, R., Sobral, J. and Fariña, F. (1990b). Intensidad de control, dominancia, sumisividad y redundancia: su rol en la deliberación de jurados. Paper presented at the III Congreso Nacional de Psicología Social, Santiago.

Arce, R., Sobral, J. and Fariña, F. (1991). Acerca de la participición de los jurados en las deliberaciones y sus implicaciones legales. *Análisis y Modificación de Conducta*, **17**, 51, 71–83.

Arce, R., Sobral, J. and Fariña, F. (1992). Verdicts of psychosocially biased juries. In F. Lösel, D. Bender and T. Bliesener (Eds), *Psychology and Law*. Berlin: De Gruyter, pp. 435–9.

Baldwin J. and McConville, M. (1979). *Jury Trials*. London: Oxford University Press.

Bem, D.J. and Allen, A. (1968). On predicting some of the people some of the time. *Psychological Review*, **81**, 506–20.

Bray, R.M. and Noble, A. (1978). Authoritarianism and decisions of mock juries: evidence of jury bias and group polarisation. *Journal of Personality and Social Psychology*, **36**, 1424–30.

Champagne, A. and Nagel, S. (1982). The psychology of judging. In N.L. Kerr and R.M. Bray (Eds), *The Psychology of the Courtroom*. New York: Academic Press, pp. 257–83.

Charrow, R. and Charrow, V. (1979). Making legal lenguage understandable: a psycholinguistic study of jury instructions. *Columbia Law Review*, **79**, 1306–74.

Cowan, C.L., Thompson, W.C. and Ellsworth, P.C. (1984). The effects of death qualification on jurors' predisposition to convict and on quality of deliberation. *Law and Human Behavior*, **8**, 1/2, 53–79.

Dane, F. and Wrightsman, L. (1982). Effects of defendants' and victims' characteristics on jurors' verdicts. In N.L. Kerr and R.M. Bray (Eds), *The Psychology of the Courtroom*. New York: Academic Press, pp. 88–115.

Diamond, S.S. and Zeisel, H. (1975). Sentencing councils: a study of sentence disparity and its reduction. *University of Chicago Law Review*, **43**, 109–49.

Efran, M.G. (1974). The effect of physical appearance on the judgment of guilt, interpersonal attraction and severity of recommended punishment on a simulated jury task. *Journal of Research in Personality*, **85**, 395–461.

Elwork, A., Sales, B.D. and Alfini, J. (1977). Juridic decisions: in ignorance of the law or in light of it? *Law and Human Behavior*, **1**, 163–90.

Feild, H.S. (1978). Juror background characteristics and attitudes toward rape: correlates of jurors' decisions in rape trials. *Law and Human Behavior*, **2**, 73–93.

Gerbasi, K.C., Zuckerman, M. and Reis, H.T. (1977). Justice needs a new blindfold: a review of mock jury research. *Psychological Bulletin*, **84**, 323–45.

Gisbert, A. (1990). *El futuro tribunal popular español*. Barcelona: PPU.

Griffitt, W. and Jackson, T. (1973). Simulated jury decisions: the influence of jury defendant attitude similarity-disimilarity. *Social Behavior and Personality*, **1**, 17.

Hans, V.P. and Vidmar, N. (1982). Jury selection. In N.L. Kerr and R.M. Bray (Eds), *The Psychology of the Courtroom*. New York: Academic Press, pp. 41–82.

Hans, V.P. and Vidmar, N. (1986). *Judging the Jury*. New York: Plenum Press.

Hastie, R., Penrod, S. and Pennington, N. (1983). *Inside the Jury*. Cambridge, MA: Harvard University Press.

Hepburn, J.R. (1980). The objective reality of evidence and the utility of systematic jury selection. *Law and Human Behavior*, **4**, 89–102.

Horowitz, I.A. (1985). The effect of jury nullification instructions on verdicts and jury functioning in criminal trials. *Law and Human Behavior*, **9**, 25–36.

Janis, I.J. and Mann, L. (1977). *Decision Making*. New York: Free Press.

Johnson v. Louisiana, 406 U.S. 356 (1972).

Kagehiro, D.K. (1990). Defining the standard of proof in jury instructions. *Psychological Science*, **1**, 3, 194–200.

Kalven, H. and Zeisel, H. (1966). *The American Jury*. Boston, MA: Little Brown.

Kaplan, M.F. and Miller, J.H. (1978). Reducing the effects of juror bias. *Journal of Personality and Social Psychology*, **36**, 1443–55.

Kaplan, M. and Krupa, S. (1986). Severe sentences under the control of others can reduce guilt verdicts. *Law and Psychology Review*, **10**, 118.

Kessler, J.B. (1973). An empirical study of six and twelve-member jury decision-making processes. *University of Michigan Journal Law Reform*, **6**, 712–34.

Kirchler, E. and Davis, J.H. (1986). The influence of member status differences and task type on group consensus and member position change. *Journal of Personality and Social Psychology*, **51**, 1, 83–91.

Kirst, R.W. (1982). The jury's historic domain in complex cases. *Washington Law Review*, **58**, 138.

Koopman, P. and Pool, J. (1991). Organisational decision making: models, contingencies and strategies. In J. Rasmussen, B. Brehmer and J. Leplat (Eds), *Distributed Decision Making: Cognitive Models for Cooperative Work. New Technologies and Work*. Chichester: John Wiley.

Lempert, R.O. (1975). Uncovering 'non-discernible' differences: empirical research and the jury-size cases. *Michigan Law Review*, **73**, 643–708.

MacCoun, R.J. and Kerr, N.L. (1988). Asymmetric influence in mock jury deliberation: jurors' bias for leniency. *Journal of Personality and Social Psychology*, **54**, 1, 21–33.

Malton, R.J. and Davis, J.H. (1986). Factors affecting jury decision making. *Social Action and the Law*, **12**, 41–8.

Moreno, J.L. (1975). *The Sociometric Reader*. Illinois: Illinois University Press.

Myers, M. (1979). Rule departures and making law: juries and their verdicts. *Law and Society Review*, **13**, 781–98.

Palmer, A.L. (1987). Modelos matemáticos del proceso de decisión en Jurados e influencias de su composición sobre el veredicto. Doctoral thesis. Barcelona: Servicio de Publicaciones de la Universidad Autónoma de Barcelona.

Pennington, N. and Hastie, R. (1986). Evidence evaluation in complex decision making. *Journal of Personality and Social Psychology*, **51**, 242–58.

Penrod, S. (1980). Evaluating social scientific methods of jury selection. Paper presented at the Meeting of the Midwestern Psychological Association, St Louis.

Rogers, L.E. and Farace, R.V. (1975). Analysis of relational communication in dyads. new measurements procedures. *Human Communication Research*, **1**, 222–39.

Rogers, L.E. and Millar, F.E. (1980). A holistic description of transactional patterns in marital dyads: focus on redundancy. Paper presented at the Meeting of the Speech Communicational Association, New York.

Ross v. Bernhard, 369 U.S. 531 (1970).

Saks, M. J. (1977). *Jury Verdicts*. Lexington, MA: Heath.

Skidmore v. Baltimore and Ohio, R.R. (1948) at 64.

Sobral, J. and Arce, R. (1990). *La psicología social en la sala de justicia. El jurado y el testimonio*. Barcelona: Paidós.

Soriano, R. (1985). *El nuevo jurado español*. Barcelona: Ariel.

Strodtbeck, F.L., James, R.M. and Hawkins, C. (1957). Sociological status in jury deliberations. *American Sociological Review*, **22**, 713–9.

Tanford, S. and Penrod, S. (1986). Jury deliberations: discussion content and the influence processes in jury decision making. *Journal of Applied Social Psychology*, **16**, 4, 322–47.

Torrance, E.P. (1959). The influence of experienced members of small groups on the behavior of inexperienced. *Journal of Social Psychology*, **49**, 249–57.

Van Dyke, J.M. (1977). Jury Selection Procedures. Cambridge, MA: Ballinger Publishing Company.

Vidmar, N. (1979). The other issues in jury simulation research: a commentary with particular reference to defendant character studies. *Law and Human Behavior*, **3**, 95–106.

Vidmar, N. and Crinklaw, L. (1973). Retribution and utility as motives of sanctioning behavior. Paper presented at the Midwestern Psychological Association Convention, Chicago.

Vishert, Ch.A. (1987). Juror decision making. the importance of evidence. *Law and Human Behavior*, **11**, 1, 117.

Walter, B. (1987). When do jurors make up their minds? Paper presented at the Law and Society Meeting, Washington, DC.

Werner, C.M., Strube, M.J., Cole, A.M. and Kagehiro, D.K. (1985). The impact of case characteristics and prior jury experience on jury verdicts. *Journal of Applied Social Psychology*, **15**, 409–27.

Zeisel, H. (1971). ... And then there was none: the diminution of federal jury. *University of Chicago Law Review*, **35**, 228–41.

Judges' Decision-making

Peter J. van Koppen,
Netherlands Institute for the Study of Criminality and Law Enforcement

INTRODUCTION

In each trial two main decisions are taken. In civil cases the decision concerns the liability of the defendant and, if liable, the compensation (or special order) to be awarded. In criminal cases the decision concerns the guilt or innocence of the accused and the sentence if guilt is sufficiently proved. This chapter deals with the decision on guilt or innocence in criminal cases.

In many countries criminal procedure is modelled on a trial in which a jury decides on guilt and a judge decides on the sentence. A jury trial, however, is comparatively rare and usually both decisions are left to the judge or magistrate, as occurs in most other countries. This chapter assumes that the decision is always made by a judge or a panel of judges. But it should be kept in mind that these models, *mutatis mutandis,* apply to jury decision-making.

DESCRIPTIVE AND PRESCRIPTIVE

Psychological models of decision-making in criminal cases share a characteristic that is peculiar in the field of psychology: all are both descriptive and prescriptive in nature. The mixed nature of these models derives from the mixed nature of law itself. Law is a 'social system created with a view of regulating the conduct of members of a community' (Blackman, Müller and Chapman, 1984, p. 3). Thus law is a behavioural technology and both the law and the legal system can be judged by the extent to which they serve that purpose successfully (Crombag and Van Koppen, 1991). At the same time, however, the law is an expression of a social philosophy in which, depending on place, time and circumstances, an ideal state of affairs is described which society at large should strive for (Crombag, 1982; Van Koppen and Hessing, 1988). As a consequence, the study of decision-making in criminal cases has always been a mixture of prescriptive and descriptive theories. This has been most prominent in research on the decision of guilt or innocence of the suspect—the subject of this chapter—but also in research on sentencing. In sentencing studies the assumption always has been that disparity between sentences in comparable cases is evil and should be removed as much as possible (see for instance Homel and Lawrence, 1992; Berghuis, 1992).

This mixture of prescription and description stems from the mixed nature of the law and thus cannot be avoided. In each legal system the decision on guilt or innocence, for instance, is governed by a set of legal rules which prescribes how the fact finder—judge or jury—is to handle the evidence. These rules appear to emerge from the common understanding that without them too many innocent citizens might be convicted or too many guilty suspects might be acquitted. That, in itself, is an understanding which is descriptive in nature. But, the social philosophy character of law is also reflected in rules of evidence. Some of these rules, for instance, may serve to control police behaviour, by declaring evidence inadmissible if it is generated by police practices which are unwanted for whatever reason. Other pieces of evidence are inadmissible because they are considered biased against the defendant, even though they might be highly relevant for the decision on guilt or innocence; for example, in some legal systems, the prior criminal record of the defendant.

The standard of proof is another area where the mixture of description and prescription is profound. At various stages in criminal procedure, the evidence available must amount to a particular level of certainty to warrant a decision. 'Probable cause', necessary to arrest and for searches and seizure, requires 40–50 per cent of certainty (Melton et al., 1987, p. 27). In *Nugent v. Superior Court for San Mateo County* (254 C.A.2d 420, 62 Cal.Rptr. 217, 221), however, probable cause justifying an arrest without warrant is defined as a situation where the arresting officer has more evidence favouring a suspicion than against it, constituting a percentage of more than 50. For a conviction 'beyond a reasonable doubt' 90–95 per cent certainty seems to be required (Melton et al., 1987, p. 125). American jurors apparently consider around 90 per cent enough to convict (Hastie, Penrod and Pennington, 1983, p. 11).

Where do these percentages come from? They are not given by nature, because there were times when a suspicion was enough to convict (see Langbein, 1977). Indeed, in too many countries such a low standard of proof is still applied. Juries seem to use a standard as 'reasonable doubt' because they are instructed to do so (Kagehiro, 1990); judges probably do so because they have been taught that way.

What do such percentages mean? One manner in which this percentage can be interpreted is that American jurors consider it acceptable that of the convicted

Table 6.7.1 Estimated performance of juries

Reality	Jury verdict		Total
	Guilty	Not guilty	
Guilty	60.3	29.7	90.0
Not guilty	6.7	3.3	10.0
Total	67.0	33.0	100.0

defendants, 90 per cent are guilty and 10 per cent innocent. Given the base-rate of guilty and innocent defendants who appear at trial—which is highly skewed towards guilt because of the filtering done by police and prosecution—that is an amazing percentage. The standard that jurors say they apply would amount to a huge number of miscarriages of justice. A fair estimate might be the following. Kalven and Zeisel (1966) found that the jury convicts in 67 per cent of the criminal cases that come up for jury trial in the USA. Then, jurors apparently deem it acceptable that in 6.7 per cent of all cases an innocent defendant is convicted. If we assume that only 10 per cent of the defendants coming up to trial are innocent, still this juror attitude causes 3.3 miscarriages of justice in every 100 cases, while innocent defendants have only a 33 per cent chance of coming out acquitted (see Table 6.7.1). Is this the reason why so many miscarriages of justice are reported from the USA and the UK (see Borchard, 1932; Gardner, 1952; Frank and Frank, 1957; Hale, 1961; Hill, Radin, 1964; Zimmermann, 1964; Brandon and Davies, 1973; Young and Hill, 1983; Young and Sergeant, 1985; Bedau and Radelet, 1987, 1988; Gross, 1987; Woffinden, 1987; Rattner, 1988; Waller, 1989; Fletcher, 1992)?

The above analysis, however, is based on the assumption that the strength of the evidence is 'normally' distributed among guilty and innocent defendants respectively. That is not a realistic assumption, at least at the start of the trial. Under the (admittedly unrealistic) assumption that the 'evidence' which the police use for search and seizure is unrelated to the evidence presented at trial by the prosecution, it can be assumed that the strength of the evidence is distributed normally among guilty and innocent defendants respectively at the time of their arrest (see Figure 6.7.1).

Not all of these cases reach trial. The cases with too little evidence—in the judgement of police or prosecution—are dropped somewhere along the line. Under a system of plea-bargaining, the cases in which the strength of the evidence is overwhelming may not be decided by juries either. Figure 6.7.1 probably is not completely realistic, because the selection of cases which are left for a full trial depends on the policy of police and prosecution and estimates made by the defendants during plea-bargaining. The effect of the selections made prior to trial, however, is that the cases which go to trial resemble each other much more in a system with plea-bargaining than in systems without.

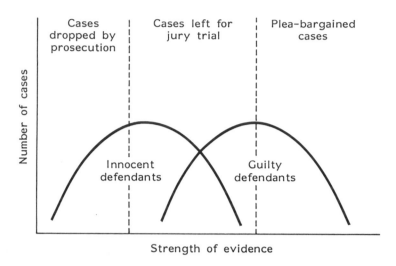

Figure 6.7.1 Hypothetical distribution of strength of evidence among guilty and innocent defendents

This example might be developed much further, but is used here to show that both descriptive and prescriptive elements play a role. Such an analysis might be used in a descriptive sense to compare inquisitorial to accusatorial systems by studying the effects of, for instance, plea-bargaining or a jury-system; but such an analysis is meaningless if the end results and the percentage of resulting miscarriages of justice are not taken into account.

The above discussion was necessary to argue that a valid theory of decision-making in criminal cases needs to account both for the empirical reality and for the normative elements involved. This chapter discusses the two kinds of models which are most widely used in the psychological study of decision-making in criminal cases: the hypothesis testing model and the so-called story model. The discussion is mainly based on the work undertaken by Crombag, Wagenaar Van Koppen (Crombag, Van Koppen and Wagenaar, 1992; Wagenaar, Van Koppen and Crombag, 1993) and will favour a story model. Before discussing the models, I will try to describe the decision-making problem faced by the fact finder in a criminal trial.

THE PROBLEM OF GUILT OR INNOCENCE

The finder of fact in a criminal trial is faced with the problem of distinguishing guilty from innocent defendants. In more general terms, that is a problem handled by signal detection theory (Green and Swets, 1966) which deals with distinguishing signals against a background of 'noise'. Distinguishing guilty defendants against the background of innocent ones is such a decision problem.

Figure 6.7.2 Confidence dimension with decision criterion for criminal cases, according to signal detection theory

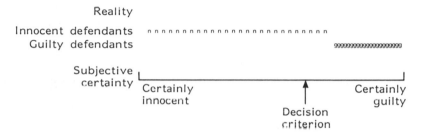

Figure 6.7.3 Decision criterion for criminal cases with perfect discrimination between innocent and guilty defendants

An essential element in the theory is the level of confidence of the decision-maker. After evaluating all the evidence, the decision-maker has a level of confidence in the guilt of the defendant. The levels of confidence can be depicted on a continuous dimension, going from 'certainly innocent' to 'certainly guilty'. On the same dimension a decision criterion can be depicted. If the level of confidence in the guilt of the defendants surpasses the decision criterion the defendant is found guilty (see Figure 6.7.2). Where a particular defendant falls on this dimension, depends on the subjective evaluation by the decision maker.

The 'true' state of affairs can be depicted on the same dimension, as is done in Figure 6.7.3: guilty defendants with a 'g', not guilty defendants with an 'n'. Truth is a relative subject in criminal cases, but for the sake of the present discussion let us assume that defendants fall into one of two classes (the guilty ones and the innocent ones) and that the evidence presented against them has some relation to their guilt. In Figure 6.7.3 a few innocent defendants are convicted, because they fall above the decision criterion. This problem, however, can be amended easily if the decision-maker only slightly adjusts his or her decision criterion. If a higher standard of proof is required, and thus the decision criterion is shifted slightly to the right in Figure 6.7.3, all innocent defendants are acquitted, while still all guilty ones are convicted.

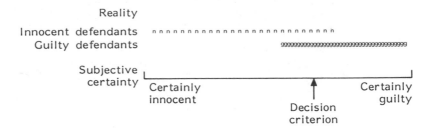

Figure 6.7.4 Decision criterion for criminal cases with imperfect discrimination between innocent and guilty defendants

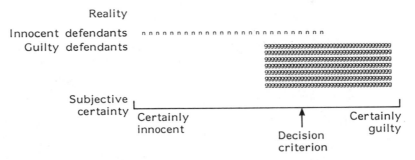

Figure 6.7.5 Decision criterion for criminal cases with imperfect discrimination between innocent and guilty defendants under a 95 per cent base-rate of guilty defendants

In reality, however, there are innocent defendants who *appear* to be guilty and there are guilty defendants who *appear* to be innocent (because too little evidence has been found against them). Figure 6.7.4 is more realistic in that sense, and shows that no shift of the decision criterion to either the left or the right can discriminate between guilty and innocent defendants without making errors.

Figure 6.7.5 is even more realistic for decision-making in criminal trials, introducing base-rate information into the decision problem. In most criminal trials the defendant is guilty of the crime charged. Crombag, Van Koppen and Wagenaar (1992) estimated that about 95 per cent of Dutch defendants are guilty (there is no reason to expect other percentages in other countries). If the judge simply convicted every defendant without further investigation then only in 5 per cent of the cases an error would be made; a rate that is considerably less than in many other areas of decision-making. Of course, there are many good reasons not to proceed in that manner, one of them being that it would leave the behaviour of the police and the prosecution completely unchecked. But it should be realised that judicial decision making must be of considerably high quality to beat a base-rate of 95 per cent guilty defendants.

There is no way in which the decision criterion can be set such that the evidence perfectly discriminates between guilty and innocent defendants, but Figure 6.7.5 also shows that a shift of the decision criterion has unequal effects on conviction rates of guilty and innocent defendants. A shift to the left—to a more lenient position—causes many more guilty defendants to be convicted, but also leads to the conviction of some innocent defendants. Likewise, a shift to higher standards of proof—when the decision criterion moves to the right—will save innocent defendants from being convicted, but causes an acquittal for many more guilty defendants.

Signal detection theory predicts that the precise placing of the decision criterion on the dimension—that is the level of confidence required for a conviction—is influenced by the utility of wrong and right decisions. And, indeed, the relation between the number of wrongful convictions and unjust acquittals has long been recognised in the legal community. Wigmore (1937), for instance, argued that avoiding one wrongful conviction is worth 20 unjust acquittals. Others have argued for other levels (see Williams, 1963, chapter 7). Apparently the costs of the suffering inflicted upon the convicted innocent is considered more grave that the hazards for society if a guilty person is turned loose.

The risks and costs involved in decision-making in criminal cases are not invariant across types of crimes. For minor crimes, the risks for society of acquitting a guilty defendant are not very large, while a wrongful conviction may cause much suffering for the defendant. For a serious crime like rape, however, the risks involved with an unjust acquittal may outweigh the costs for the innocently convicted defendant. Signal detection theory, then, predicts something which Crombag, Van Koppen and Wagenaar (1992, ch. 5) called the 'conviction paradox': for serious crimes where a true perpetrator is likely to repeat the crime, the decision criterion moves to the left—a lower standard of proof—while for minor crimes the decision criterion is moved to the right. In countries with a jury system the seriousness of the offence charged may have a counter effect: the more serious the offence, the more likely it is that the defendant is tried before a jury, which in turn makes it more likely that the defendant will be acquitted (Kalven and Zeisel, 1966).

THE LOGIC OF EVIDENCE

It would be most appealing if the evaluation of evidence in a criminal case could lead to a decision through a strictly logical process of consecutive steps. Such a process would require that the facts presented as evidence to the court or jury can be established in some objective manner. Then some inferential process almost automatically and inescapably would lead to the conclusion on guilt or innocence of the defendant.

The possibility of such a process is debatable, both on philosophical and practical grounds. It assumes that there are facts 'out there' which can be known with certainty if we just look hard enough. It has long been established that each of these individual steps in such a logical process needs some form of interpretation (in law, for instance, by Cuenta-Rua, 1981, pp. 113 ff.; Scholten, 1974, pp. 11 ff.). At the same time, lawyers behave as if such a process is possible. Wigmore (1937), for instance, described this process as a regression by which the *probandum* is specified into a large number of *facta probanda*, which are at some point matched with *facta probantia*. He appears to assume that the *probandum* can be specified as much as we want, which implies that legal proof can attain any required degree of precision. This conclusion does not follow. The regression to conditions of conditions postpones the problem without solving it. In the end the evidence must be matched with conditions and it is far from obvious that any degree of specification will make this matching unproblematic. Only a solid match would allow a perfectly safe conclusion that the condition is met. Such a conclusion can only be safe when the evidence allows just one interpretation. In reality there are always more interpretations.

Not only are the individual steps to be taken in such a logical process impossible; also the structure of the process as a whole poses problems. Any process of logical inference is a bottom-up process: one starts with the facts—the evidence—and infers conclusions from these facts. But how do we know which facts are relevant for the decision and which not? We only know which facts are relevant if we anticipate the decision. But, at the same time, we only know which decision is anticipated, if we know the facts of the case. This circular problem can only be solved by taking a decision first and working back to the facts. Such a decision need not be final but can take the shape of a working hypothesis. This working hypothesis is splendidly provided for by the prosecution.

Together, these problems shape the manner in which the decision is made into a top-down process, in which the hypothesis (the allegation of theft, rape or murder) comes first, and the fact-finding is derived from it. Intent is not inferred from facts that happened to be presented, but the other way around: certain facts are sought and presented because they may serve to prove intent. This way of describing the process comes closer to what appears actually to be happening during the trial. The trial starts with a presentation of the indictment, i.e. before facts are presented. The charge is not inferred by the judge or jury from the evidence, but the other way around. Basically, this is a process in which the evidence is used to verify the indictment; not one in which the innocence of the defendant is falsified. This problem will be looked at further below.

HYPOTHESIS TESTING

If decision-making in criminal cases is not a logical bottom-up process, one might turn to Hart's (1963, p. vii) conclusion that courtroom decision-making comes closer to rhetoric than to reason. In psychology two alternative paths have been chosen to model judicial decision-making. One draws upon the analogy to typical scientific top-down reasoning: a hypothesis is tested against evidence, as is done in most empirical sciences. The Reverend Thomas Bayes gave a mathematical formulation for this process which has become quite popular as a means of modelling decision-making in criminal cases (Kaplan, 1968; Finkelstein and Fairly, 1970; Tribe, 1971; Schum, 1979; Goldsmith, 1980; Saks and Kidd, 1980; Edwards, 1988). The principle is simple. It is assumed that the decision-maker has a certain prior belief in the truth of the hypothesis. This degree of belief is mathematically expressed by odds, i.e. a number between zero and infinity. These odds are obtained by dividing the probability that the hypothesis is true, p_{true}, by the probability that it is false, p_{false}. The prior belief, or the prior odds, then, are expressed by:

$$\text{prior odds} = \frac{p_{true}}{p_{false}} \tag{6.7.1}$$

For instance, when p_{true} is .80, and p_{false} is .20 (the hypothesis is either true or false), then the prior odds are .80/.20 = 4.0. In a criminal trial the two mutually exclusive hypotheses are 'guilty' or 'innocent'. New evidence offers the opportunity to revise the prior belief, and turn it into a *posterior* belief. This is achieved by multiplying the prior odds by the diagnostic value (*D*) of the evidence:

$$\text{posterior odds} = \text{prior odds} \times D_i \tag{6.7.2}$$

The diagnostic value of evidence is obtained from a performance table. An example is given in Table 6.7.2, showing the performance of the so-called Dolls test which is used in sexual abuse cases to establish the truthfulness of

Table 6.7.2 Performance of the Dolls test ($n = 20$)

The child was:	Results of the Dolls-test	
	Positive	Negative
Sexually abused	Hit .9	Miss .1
Not sexually abused	False alarm .2	Correct rejection .8

Source: Based on Jampole and Weber, 1987

the child's account. (Whether the Dolls-test has a diagnostic value which is high enough to make it admissible is not without debate. The Dutch Supreme Court (HR 28 February, 1989, *Nederlandse Jurisprudentie* 1989, no. 748) considered the Dolls-test so unreliable, that it decided that a court cannot ignore counter-arguments by the defence. By this Supreme Court decision the test was, in practice, abolished in The Netherlands. In the USA the Dolls-test is the most commonly used tool in the validation of sexual abuse allegations (Skinner and Berry, 1993). However some US courts have ruled that evidence based on Anatomically Correct Dolls is inadmissible because the test does not meet basic psychometric criteria (*In re Amber B. and Tella B.*, 191 Cal. App.3rd 682, 1987; *in re Christine C. and Michael C.*, 191 Cal. App.3rd 676, 1987).)

The diagnostic value (*D*) of the Dolls test is the ratio of hits and false alarms; in the table: 0.9/0.2 = 4.5, meaning that a positive test makes it 4.5 times more likely that the child was sexually abused. After this piece of evidence the prior odds—whatever they were—are adjusted to become posterior odds which may serve as prior odds for the next piece of evidence. With *N* pieces of evidence, the initial prior odds are turned into final posterior odds as follows:

$$\text{final posterior odds} = \text{prior odds} \times D_1 \times D_2 \ldots \times D_1 \times \ldots \times D_N \qquad (6.7.3)$$

If the final posterior odds surpass a pre-set level of confidence, the defendant can be convicted. This Bayesian approach thus seems an elegant model of decision-making. This chapter argues, however, that modelling decision-making in criminal cases as hypothesis testing is the right solution to the wrong problem. There are four defects of this approach: (1) setting the initial probability; (2) determining the diagnostic value of evidence; (3) revision of the probability; and (4) taking the final decision (the arguments advanced here are more fully discussed in Wagenaar, Van Koppen and Crombag, 1993).

Prior Probability

The presumption of innocence assumes that the defendant is innocent until proven guilty. This would require the decision maker to give a prior probability of zero to the hypothesis that the defendant is guilty. Then, of course, evidence of whatever quality cannot change the odds to anything higher than zero—the result of a multiplication with zero is, of course, always zero—and the Bayesian model would be useless. A solution might be to keep the initial probability 'very, very low' (proposed by Wagenaar, 1988, p. 149), say at 0.0001, or give it the value of the base-rate of guilty defendants, say 0.95. For both levels—and many more levels—arguments can be given. This problem is avoided in a variation of the model, proposed by Goldsmith (1980). He suggests that it is possible to leave the prior odds of guilt before the presentation of evidence undetermined. But his 'evidentiary value theory' still suffers from the drawbacks listed below.

On a theoretical level the initial probability of guilt is not of overwhelming importance, since it can be shown that during the process of adjustment of odds the influence of the initial value becomes less and less. In practice, however, the initial probability of guilt can be of decisive importance to the final decision as Schünemann and his co-workers demonstrated (Schünemann and Bandilla, 1989; Schünemann, 1983). In one of their experiments professional judges who had read the file of the case before the trial all convicted the defendant, while only 27 per cent of the judges who had not read the file beforehand convicted. Reading the file before the trial—as is common in most inquisitorial systems—apparently introduces a prior belief in guilt of the defendant which subsequently requires less evidence to come to a conviction at trial. Schünemann's results are confirmed in research by Koehler (1991), who concluded that '[a]ny task that prompts a person to temporarily accept the truth of a hypothesis will increase his or her confidence in that hypothesis' (p. 502).

Diagnostic Value of Evidence

In the Bayesian model—or in any quantitative approach to evidence in criminal cases for that matter—it is a *conditio sine qua non* that the value of evidence can be quantified in some way. Sometimes this can be done. An example is the Dolls test, given in Table 6.7.2. If a Dolls tests in a case proved positive, the diagnostic value of such evidence is known. That is, it is known if certain conditions are met. We at least must have empirical facts or research, before we can give a fair estimate of the diagnostic value of some specific piece of evidence, provided that the research is of decent quality and the facts are close to the evidence at hand. But, usually research is scarce and the facts are difficult to assess. Research on identification line-ups, for instance, has shown that the diagnostic value of a splendidly performed line-up is about 15 (Wagenaar and Veefkind, 1992), but what if not all the requirements are met to call it a very good line-up? And even then, some argue, the present tradition of laboratory research does not apply to forensic practice (Bekerian, 1993; Egeth, 1993; Wells, 1993; Yuille, 1993). Another example is DNA-profiling, where it remains unclear which population must be taken as the reference group to determine the probability of a match (see Easteal, McLeod and Reed, 1991; Roberts, 1991) and thus some argue that the probability of a match is at best unknown (see for the softness of other kinds of 'hard' forensic evidence Saks, 1989; Saks and Koehler, 1991). So, even with well researched kinds of evidence we usually know much about what problems and pitfalls can be encountered, but the effect on the diagnostic value of such evidence remains an enigma. With other kinds of evidence, we are much more in the dark. How to assess, for instance, the diagnostic value of the testimony of a witness who might have an interest in the outcome of the trial?

In the absence of robust figures on the diagnostic value of pieces of evidence, judges and juries cannot but step in and guess. It would be most appealing if they could be helped in decision-making with at least some indication of the lower and upper limit of the diagnostic value of evidence. The theory of anchored narratives, discussed below, provides for such a decision aid.

Revision of Probability

The process of revision, as described by the Bayesian model, assumes a number of properties that are, in fact, quite unrealistic. One of these properties is compensation: one very diagnostic piece of incriminating evidence can be cancelled out by a number of facts that point in the opposite direction through the multiplication operation. Then, a very strong piece of evidence favouring the defendant—for instance, he was in prison at the time of the crime—can be compensated by a large number of fairly weak pieces of evidence against him. Or the other way around: the fingerprints of the defendant found at the scene of the crime—often decisive evidence for a conviction—can be cancelled out by a good explanation which places the defendant at the scene at some other time. A sufficient number of 'facts' of low diagnostic value may, in the end, compensate for a fact that might be considered as decisive evidence.

Another problem is the independence of the supposed diagnostic values. All sorts of interactions cannot be represented in the Bayesian model. The same is true for contradictions. The Bayesian model, however, has no provision for such dependencies among pieces of evidence and would lump their diagnostic values together (see Cohen, 1977; Wagenaar, 1991).

The Decision Criterion

Finally there is the problem of the decision criterion. When are the odds in favour of guilt high enough to convict? The model does not explain how such a criterion is chosen, nor even whether the criterion is constant or variable. For instance, should the criterion be the same in the case of a traffic violation for which only a fine is given, as in the case of a capital crime? One could argue that the judge should take fewer risks in the latter case. Should a judge in a case of multiple rape put the criterion on a lower more risky level because after a wrongful acquittal the criminal may rape again? Does consideration of consequences justify variations in the decision criteria? The Bayesian model does not answer such questions.

Conclusion

Taken together, the problems posed by the Bayesian model of legal decision-making are overwhelming. The most important argument against the use of models of hypothesis testing for decision-making in criminal cases, however, is that judges and juries do not argue and decide in that way. In fact, hypothesis testing is so far off what actually happens in court that it is not only unsuccessful as a descriptive model, but also too alien to the legal tradition to be of use as a prescriptive model either. That does not mean that models of hypothesis testing might not be useful to discuss certain pieces of evidence or might not apply to some—but atypical—cases. The Collins case (*People v. Collins*, 68 Cal.2d 319, 1968) is such a case and has been analysed many times (for instance Edwards, 1991). But, the hypothesis testing models will not hold in most cases—and indeed in most cases with problems of evidence—for the reasons stated above. Thus, these models are the right solution to the wrong problem.

ANCHORED NARRATIVES

Alternatively, I will argue that a narrative model comes closer to a description of what judges and juries in fact do and at the same time gives a base for grounding prescriptions for evaluating evidence. A narrative is, as Bruner (1984) puts it, 'concerned with the explication of human intentions in the context of action'.

Story Context and Facts

The theory of anchored narratives (Crombag, Van Koppen and Wagenaar, 1992; Wagenaar, Van Koppen and Crombag, 1993), discussed here, is not entirely original. Others have proposed similar ideas and prepared the way. Bennett and Feldman (1981) begin their book *Reconstructing Reality in the Courtroom* by stating that 'the criminal trial is organised around story telling'. The idea is that the work of the judge or jury consists of determining the *plausibility* of the stories presented by the prosecution and the defence. Narrative theories, which have a long history in cognitive psychology (cf. Bartlett, 1950; Rumelhart, 1975), hold that evidence derives its meaning from a story context. Detached from a story, facts do not prove anything; a court cannot decide on mere facts, only on a story. Two aspects of a story may determine its believability: the 'goodness' of the story in itself (to be defined later), and the degree to which it is supported by facts (not *the* facts, which means something vastly different).

The derivation of meaning from story contexts is a well-known and easily illustrated effect. Consider the following story.

> I brought my daughter Vere to Jan's birthday party. Upon arrival I got coffee and Vere lemonade. We sang for Jan, after which he blew the candles. I left, to pick Vere up at the end of the afternoon.

This story strongly suggests a number of things that remain implicit, and that may not even be true. For instance, it is suggested that more children were at the party; and most of the readers will have imagined a cake. People will automatically fill in gaps in stories, and in doing so, give meanings to statements which maybe were never intended. On the other hand, one may re-word stories carefully, with the intention of suggesting inferences that cannot be proved by the facts.

The Quality of Stories

Researchers in many disciplines, such as literature, anthropology, and artificial intelligence, have tried to answer the question of what constitutes a good and plausible story. Rumelhart (1975), Robinson (1981), and Van Dijk (1980) have all designed story grammars: sets of rules to which a well-formed story must conform. Among the story grammars which have been proposed, Bennett and Feldman's (1981) was specially designed for judicial contexts (cf. Jackson, 1988). The manner in which they obtained their grammar is quite interesting. They asked 58 students to tell a story; half of them were asked to tell a *true* story, the other half to *invent* a story. Every time a story had been told, the others were asked to guess whether this was a true or an invented story. The guesses were not better than chance. But stories that were *accepted* as true shared some properties that the rejected stories were lacking. These properties were: a readily identifiable central action, and a context (setting) that provides an easy and natural explanation of why the actors behaved in the way they did.

In a good story all elements are connected to the central action. The context provides a full and compelling account of why the central action should have developed in this particular manner. If the context does not achieve that effect, then the story is said to contain ambiguities. There are two types of ambiguities: missing elements and contradictory elements.

The analysis of what makes stories plausible was extended by Pennington and Hastie in a series of subsequent publications (1986, 1988, 1991). Without going into too much detail, it can be said that, according to them, in good stories all actions are explained by factors of three kinds: physical conditions, psychological conditions, and goals. Each of these can influence the other two, and is also determined by the general setting. Given the goals of the actors and the situation they found themselves in, a good story makes it 'logical' that a psychological condition developed that made the crime a 'logical' outcome.

Pennington and Hastie's story grammar, and their thesis about the importance of stories, is supported by empirical research. In one study (Pennington and Hastie, 1986) they presented over 200 prospective jury members with a filmed documentary of a criminal trial. The possible verdicts were: first-degree murder, second-degree murder, manslaughter, and self-defence. On the basis of the evidence presented in the film all options were chosen by a reasonably large number of subjects. Next they were asked to explain what they thought had happened. All story structures conformed to the postulated story grammar; but different judgements were based on different selections of facts. In the authors' words: 'variability in the story construction stage is systematically related to verdict choice' (p. 253). But the variety of stories was not based upon an extremely rich and multi-interpretable set of evidence. The differences were mostly brought about by inferences about what people did, thought, felt, wanted. Inferred facts which were not present in the film constituted 45 per cent of all story components. If people are allowed to 'invent' 45 percent of the evidence, it is not surprising that they can construct different stories about what happened and reach different conclusions. (See also Hogarth (1971) who found that disparity among judicial decision of magistrates vanishes if they agree on the facts of the case.)

In another study, Pennington and Hastie (1986) showed that the order in which evidence is presented has a major influence on the judgement (which is in conflict with predictions of Bayesian theory). Both the prosecution and the defence could present their evidence in a random order, or in story order. The combination of these two variables results in four groups. The dependent variable was whether the subjects thought that the defendant was guilty of first-degree murder. The results of the study indicate that the party who presents the evidence in story order was believed more readily, even though the evidence itself was exactly the same in both conditions. The effect can be as large as changing a 31 per cent chance of conviction (when the defence presents its evidence in story order and the prosecution in random order) into a 78 per cent chance (when the prosecution presents evidence in story order and the defence in random order). Clever presentation of the story is half of the work! What is the other half?

Anchoring

Stories told in a criminal court must not only be good, they must be considered true before a conviction can follow. The truth of a story is established by means of evidence. In and of itself, however, evidence does not prove anything at all. Any piece of evidence only proves something if we are willing to believe in a general rule which we hold to be true most of the time. For instance, the testimony by two eye-witnesses will only prove something, i.e. support the story, if it is assumed that, generally, eye-witnesses do not lie or make mistakes; the post mortem report can only prove something as long as the pathologist does a good job.

Such general rules, however, are seldom true without exception. Witnesses sometimes err or lie, and experts occasionally do make mistakes. The rules that make evidence prove something should more accurately be phrased: witnesses speak the truth *most of the time*, and pathologists *almost* never make mistakes. The possibility of exceptions to rules means that, on a particular occasion, we must show that a possible exception does not apply. This argument calls on the general rule that it is very improbable that two lying eye-witnesses come up with the same lie. But, of course, this rule allows exceptions: if witnesses have had the opportunity to confer before testifying, they can easily lie and be mutually consistent at the same time. Hence the prosecution must prove that this exception does not apply, for instance by showing that the two witnesses had no opportunity to confer, or if they had, did not do so.

In a similar manner every piece of evidence needs further support, until it can be safely anchored in a general rule that cannot be sensibly contested because all parties acknowledge it to be true in the given case. These general rules are usually common-sense facts of life. We often accept an argument because we unwittingly believe the underlying rule which gives it an anchor, even though an explicit formulation of the rule would cause us to protest or even reject it. Cohen (1977) calls these generally accepted rules 'common-sense presumptions, which state what is normally to be expected but are rebuttable in their application to a particular situation if it can be shown to be abnormal in some relevant respect' (p. 247). I shall qualify the role of general rules later but for the time being define them as 'common knowledge of the world in the form of rules which are usually valid'. A pictorial representation of the anchoring heuristic is presented in Figure 6.7.6.

At the top of Figure 6.7.6 there is the story of the original indictment, of which the soundness has already been judged satisfactorily. Next comes an ordering of the evidence in such a way that it forms anchors between the story and a 'ground' of generally accepted common-sense rules. For three details evidence is offered, but each piece of evidence forms a sub-story in itself, which needs an anchor in the form of further evidence, which in turn forms a sub-sub-story in need of an anchor. Whether a sub-story is safely anchored depends on our willingness to accept as true the common-sense rule of which the sub-story is an instance.

For the first detail of the original story the anchoring is quite complicated, constituting a long anchor chain. Two pieces of evidence are offered, which apparently cannot be safely anchored as such in safe common-sense rules. Hence more evidence is sought, constituting sub-sub-stories. The first of these is anchored on to the ground through a sub-sub-sub-story; the second one is not anchored at all. Hence the anchor chain as a whole is ineffective. The second point in the story is directly anchored on to the ground of some common-sense rule. That could have been a statement such as: 'A man who runs into a bank with a mask on and a gun in his hand, has the intention to rob the bank.' There is no point in doubting this rule to be generally true and hence no reason to probe deeper for a safer anchor. The third point is anchored through one intermediate story; a police officer's sworn testimony is an example of that sort of anchoring.

Evaluating the story of the indictment and the evidence might seem to be a deductive process: it appears as if the individual case is brought under the general common-sense rule and the reasoning departs from the general rule. It is not. The point of departure is the individual case from which a

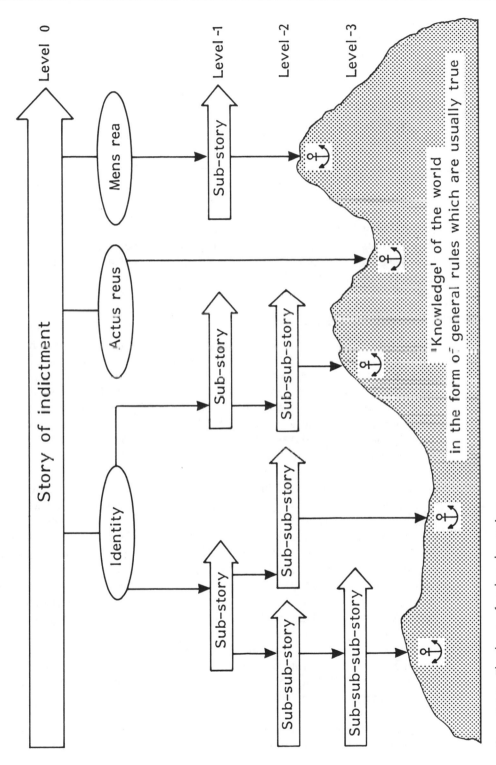

Figure 6.7.3   The theory of anchored narratives

generalisation is sought to explain the individual story (see Cohen, 1977, p. 247 ff.). It is a basic human need to explain the world around us and we are proficient in explaining odd or unexpected occurrences by generating general rules which might explain them (see Semin and Manstead, 1983).

ANCHORED NARRATIVE MODEL OF DECISION-MAKING

The model of decision-making in criminal cases, encompassed in the theory of anchored narratives, provides a means of describing these decisions, but also can serve as a vehicle to show on what points decisions based on evidence went wrong or are about to go wrong. A detailed analysis of such errors in Dutch cases was presented in Crombag, Van Koppen and Wagenaar (1992) and Wagenaar, Van Koppen and Crombag (1993). These points are discussed in more general terms below.

A Description of Courtroom Behaviour

The first task of the prosecutor is to tell a good story; a story with a central action and a context that makes the central action—the crime—so plausible, that judge and jury will react with 'Aha, of course'. At this point the defence has already half lost the case. And indeed, our study of Dutch cases showed that with a very good 'story' the prosecution can get defendants convicted, even when solid evidence is virtually absent. It is a good 'story' because it readily makes sense and fits expectations. Being a good story is independent of the quality of the evidence.

In most cases, however, the prosecutor's narrative needs anchoring in common-sense rules through chains of embedded sub-stories, i.e. pieces of evidence. Every sub-story is itself a piece of evidence that needs further anchoring, either in another sub-story or in generally accepted common-sense rules. If a court or jury accepts a piece of evidence without further sub-stories, it can only do so if it accepts one or more common-sense rules as valid and applicable to the specific case. Although such acceptance almost always remains implicit, the common-sense rules can usually be reconstructed with some knowledge of the case. If a defendant is convicted on, among others, the eye-witness testimony of his neighbour without further evidence, the following common-sense rules may implied: 'witnesses under oath usually do not lie; neighbours have little interest, most of the time, in the conviction of each other; neighbours usually know each other well enough to recognise each other under bad lighting conditions.

The role of the defence is threefold. First, the defence can challenge the story itself. The defence can either try to introduce information that makes the prosecution's narrative less plausible, or it can try to come with a better, more plausible story. A solid alibi falls in the latter class. Showing that the defendant, accused of armed robbery, has a weapon-phobia falls in the first class.

The second role for the defence—anticipating that attacks on the narrative (the prosecution story) itself almost always fail—is to attack the evidence, the sub-stories. The defence must try to show that acceptance of a specific sub-story proposed by the prosecution would involve the acceptance of a common-sense rule which is silly, not commonly accepted or simply not true. In the latter, expert witnesses sometimes play a role, to demonstrate that commonly held beliefs are wrong. The defence can also try to argue that, although the (implicitly) accepted common-sense rule is true, this case falls under the exceptions. Each common-sense rule knows exceptions, but some have more than others. Identification evidence, for instance, is relatively often not valid, while we know that as a general rule the Dutch National Forensic Laboratory makes few mistakes.

The third tactic of the defence is to come up with sub-stories that falsify the prosecutor's narrative. As noted above, the way evidence is evaluated in court is most consistent with a system of verification: evidence is used to verify the narrative told by the prosecution. This is at odds with 'beyond a reasonable doubt' standard, as Allen (1991) noted. If the 'beyond a reasonable doubt' standard is taken literally, the doubt should be the focus of attention at trial and the State should suffer the burden of demonstrating that there is no plausible account consistent with innocence (see also Zuckerman, 1989, pp. 122 ff.). This would mean the prosecution should demonstrate in court that it undertook serious attempt to falsify its own narrative, and that all attempts have failed. The practice in court is, however, that the prosecution only brings forward verifying evidence and the defence is given an opportunity to bring forward falsifying information. If the defence fails to do so, it is generally seen as evidence that supports the prosecutor's narrative, probably under the general common-sense rule that it is usually easy for innocent defendants to produce exculpatory evidence.

How Decisions Go Wrong

The model we propose, and daily practice in court, does not guarantee that the decisions of the court or the jury are logically sound. At the same time it must be recognised that the rules of criminal evidence in most civilised countries *usually* produce sound decisions. Judicial errors, wrongful convictions and miscarriages of justice are more interesting to study, because these failures of the system give much more insight into how decision-making operates. A good model of decision-making must therefore provide a framework which can be used to point out where and why decisions in the more 'difficult' cases go wrong. I will discuss some rules that can be derived from the theory of anchored narratives are discussed below.

Table 6.7.3   Ten universal rules of evidence

	Rule
1	The prosecution must present at least one well-shaped narrative
2	The prosecution must present a limited set of well-shaped narratives
3	Essential components of the narrative must be anchored
4	Anchors for different components of the charge should be independent of each other
5	The trier of fact should give reasons for the decision by specifying the narrative and the accompanying anchoring
6	A fact finder's decision as to the level of analysis of the evidence should be explained through an articulation of the general beliefs used as anchors
7	There should be no competing story with equally good or better anchoring
8	There should be no falsifications of the indictment's narrative and nested sub-narratives
9	There should be no anchoring onto obviously false beliefs
10	The indictment and the verdict should contain the same narrative

The prosecutor's narrative can take quite complicated shapes, especially when the defendant is charged with a prolonged or complicated crime. It would be practically and presumably also in principle impossible for the prosecution to offer evidence for each and every element in its narrative. Legally, the prosecution is not obliged to do so. Under Anglo-Saxon law there are, generally, no minimum requirements for evidence; a single piece of evidence is enough to convict. Dutch law specifies, with some exceptions, that at least two pieces or sources of evidence are necessary to convict. This so-called *unis testis*-rule—one witness is not enough—however, does not say anything about the quality of these two pieces of evidence. Somewhere between the legal requirements and a full burden of proof for the prosecution, the level of evidence can be found which is necessary for sound decision-making.

One requirement which can be imposed on the court or jury is that each piece of evidence which it uses to convict, should be anchored in common-sense rules which are held to be true by most people. To establish whether or not the evidence used is indeed anchored adequately requires that decision-makers cite the evidence used and the anchorings chosen. Juries are required to do neither. Under Dutch law an essential element of criminal procedure is that the court must justify its sentence. In practice, courts mention the evidence which convinced them, but they never discuss the anchors used and rarely explain *why* evidence listed in the opinion supports the decision.

A further requirement that can be imposed on decision-making in criminal cases is that at least the who-what-why in the prosecution's narrative —depicted in Figure 6.7.2 as identity, *actus reus* (including causation and absence of defence) and *mens rea*—are supported with evidence. Often it is rather easy to prove two of the three, but problems surround proving the third. The prosecution, for instance, will have no problem—using the testimony of the bank tellers—in proving that a bank was robbed and that this constitutes an offence. *Mens rea*, then, can be proved with the common-sense rule that people seldom, by accident, run into a bank with a gun in their hand demanding the contents of the safe. In these kinds of cases proof that the defendant was the perpetrator usually poses the problem.

Using this example we can take the analysis one step further to set conditions on a sound decision. The bank robbery example shows that often the same evidence is used to prove more than one component of the who-what-why. In this instance, the story told by the witnesses is used both for proving *actus reus* and *mens rea*. In some cases, their story can also be used to prove identity; for instance when they described the tattooed butterfly on the robber's cheek. It can hardly be expected of the prosecutor in each case to offer separate evidence for each of the three (or five) central elements. What can be asked, however, is that the prosecutor offers separate anchorings for identity, *actus reus* and *mens rea* which must pass the 'beyond a reasonable doubt' test for each of the three separately. The quality of anchors is looked at again below.

Rules of criminal procedure have been made to facilitate decisions without errors. Most rules, however, do not touch upon the content of the evidence and how evidence should be evaluated. From the theory of anchored narratives these rules can be derived and, because they should hold for every judicial system, we called them universal rules of evidence. They are more fully explained in Wagenaar, Van Koppen and Crombag (1993, ch. 12). Here, we will look at only one procedural requirement.

Many of the rules of criminal procedure are concerned with the selection of evidence. In countries with a jury system this is accomplished with extensive rules for the admissibility of evidence. Some of these rules are not aimed at facilitating sound decision-making but are, for instance, aimed at checking police behaviour. Most, however, are designed to withhold evidence from the jury that may unduly bias them against the defendant or evidence that is too unreliable to be of any use. After the admissible and inadmissible evidence is separated, it is left to the judge's instructions and the wisdom of the jury to give a further unchecked decision.

In continental Europe another path is chosen. Since the courts decide both on the admissibility of evidence and give the verdict, a refined tradition of rules on the admissibility of evidence never emerged. Rather, all evidence is presented to the court and only afterwards does the court decide which evidence it will or will not use in support of the decision. Of course that removes the check on the evidence to another part of the trial. Dutch judges, therefore, are obliged to render a reasoned opinion in which the evidence used is at least listed. For the same reason, both the facts of the case and the legal arguments are fully reconsidered on appeal by the Court of Appeal.

The workload of Dutch courts has recently changed this tradition dramatically and the change is soon going to be legalised by a Bill which is pending in the Dutch Parliament. Starting at the Amsterdam Trial Court the habit has grown of rendering so-called head-tail opinions. In these opinions only the formal steps taken in the procedure are listed (the head) and the sentence is given and defended (the tail). The middle part, where the evidence should be discussed, is only written if, and after, one of the parties appeals, often many months later. Anyone who has ever tried to write down an argument that seemed perfectly sound at the time knows that confiding it to paper provides a thorough check on the soundness of the argument—as is asking colleagues for comments. If such checks are missing, the carefully balanced criminal procedure may fall apart because a decision, which already has been announced publicly, will of course not be withdrawn by the court many months later if the evidence turns out to be weaker than was believed at the time of the decision. Some of the recent opinions of trial courts I have seen provide evidence which seemed rather meagre to support the decision.

Thus writing down the evidence and specifying why it supports the decision is essential for sound decision-making under an inquisitorial system. The interesting question then is whether the finely tuned rules on the admissibility of evidence under a jury system might compensate for the lack of such an essential part of criminal procedure. I doubt it.

The above does not imply that no selection of evidence is necessary. In almost every case there is at least some conflicting evidence, so courts and juries would be unable to render a verdict without at least some selection. But, they should always explain why evidence which is not used to support a decision has been ignored.

THE QUALITY OF ANCHORS

All evidence must be anchored on to common-sense rules that are safe enough to serve as anchors. In fact, the strength—that is, the diagnostic value—of evidence wholly depends on the rules chosen as anchors. As discussed above, sometimes a fair estimate of the diagnostic value of a piece of evidence can be given on the basis of empirical research. For most types of evidence that is not possible, and an impression of the diagnostic value must be obtained by scrutinising the anchors used. As noted earlier, both courts and juries leave the common-sense rules used as anchors implicit, but with some knowledge of the case, the rules can usually be reconstructed. Such a reconstruction might produce the following rule: if evidence is anchored on to rules which are silly or simply not true the diagnostic value of the evidence can be estimated at zero. If a court, for instance, was willing to accept the testimony of a witness who says he recognised the defendant as the perpetrator, while he saw the perpetrator at night, at a distance of about 100 metres, then the court has implicitly accepted as true the general rule that recognition under these circumstances is possible. However, we know that a valid recognition in this situation is virtually impossible and thus the general rule the court accepted is silly.

In less extreme cases, the exceptions possible under the common-sense rule can give a rough—but hardly quantifiable—estimate of the diagnostic value of the evidence. It is, for instance, less safe to use evidence which is anchored onto the rule that *most* allegations of sexual abuse are true, than evidence which is anchored onto the rule that 'the Dutch National Forensic Laboratory makes *few* mistakes'.

A discussion in court of anchors rather than evidence has the advantage that it points the court or jury to the most important issue. When I appear as an expert witness in court on, for instance, line-up recognitions, the court always wants to know whether it is possible that the witness made a valid recognition. The answer is yes; but that is not the issue. The discussion should focus on the question how much risk the court takes if it accepts this recognition as evidence and that can only be derived from an explicit discussion of the general rule, which might be something like 'after witnesses saw a perpetrator under the conditions that were present in this case, identifications of the defendant by witnesses are often wrong'. A court must only use evidence which is anchored onto rules that are safe enough to pass the criterion of beyond a reasonable doubt.

Discussing anchors will also expose general rules which have been shown to be not true or which leave too much room for doubt. One such rule, for instance, is 'Sound stories are more likely to be true than weak stories' (Bennett and Feldman, 1981). Another one is 'witnesses under oath rarely lie'. That may not be true. One can consider the oath in two ways. First the oath is the title under which a witness can be prosecuted for perjury if it turns out he lied. Second, this threat can be used to deter a witness from lying. But a witness may have all sorts of reasons to lie anyway. Possibly, the likelihood of lying by a witness is *reduced* by the oath and the threat of prosecution upon perjury, but without considering all other circumstances and interests of the witness, his or her testimony should not be assumed to be true under such a rule. Courts, however, do assume this.

A third example is the rule 'confessions are usually true'. That rule may also be invalid; Gudjonsson and Sigurdsson (1993) found that an astounding 12 per cent of inmates in Iceland made a false confession. Nevertheless, English defendants are commonly convicted on the basis of their confession alone, even when it is disputed at trial (Gudjonsson, 1992).

ALL EVIDENCE IS WITNESS EVIDENCE

There are many technical resources available to the police in investigations. However, in the vast majority of cases technical evidence plays no role whatsoever and most convictions are based solely on witness testimony. With few exceptions, we know little of the validity of witness testimony. How often do witnesses err; under what circumstances do they lie? In most cases we can only find out by thoroughly questioning witnesses and by comparing their statements with statements made by others or with other kinds of evidence. That tradition is highly developed in the USA and England and Wales, but little developed in The Netherlands. If witnesses appear in Dutch courts—and they seldom do, as most cases are decided on the statements written down by the police—a typical question is: 'You made such a statement to the police. Do you stick to that?' Most Dutch judges and attorneys seem to believe that a deep look into the witness' blue eyes is enough to judge whether he or she is lying or not (see for instance Mols, 1989); or they believe that the confidence of the witness is a good indicator of whether the witness is erring (it is not; see Deffenbacher, 1980).

Only on rare occasions do Dutch courts and attorneys call on expert witnesses to provide a sub-story to support or refute the witness' narrative. Ideally, an expert should be called in when the court or jury is unsure of the rules which underlie certain pieces of evidence, or are unsure of the exceptions the general rule allows (see Crombag, 1992). It should be realised that expert testimony is always anchored on to the reputation of the expert. This is returned to below.

It may be argued that all evidence becomes witness evidence if one probes deep enough into the anchoring structure. An example of sturdy evidence is a match of the fingerprints of the defendant with prints found on the murder weapon (there is doubt about the sturdiness of fingerprint evidence too; see Saks and Koehler, 1991). The relevant witnesses here are, for instance, a police officer who examined the scene of the crime, a bullet expert and a dactylographer (i.e. the fingerprint expert). They come into play as soon as a sub-story for the fingerprint evidence is sought and the question is asked of how we know the prints form a match. Although this question is almost never asked and fingerprint evidence is taken for granted, the method used to match the prints leaves room for some doubt (Macalister, 1989), if it is no more than that the expert making the match might have had a bad day. Whether or not the method is reliable enough can be established only by questioning an expert; whether or not the police officer who made the match knows his or her job can only be established by questioning that police officer. If one of the participants in court is not satisfied with the officer's testimony, one or more steps can be taken into the potentially endless regression of sub-sub-...-sub-stories. One might seek evidence to establish the quality of the police officer's training; one might examine the teachers or even the quality of the teachers, and so on for ever. At some point the court or jury has to accept somebody's word and reputation as good enough or not to use the fingerprint evidence.

Continuing the example, one might ask how we can be sure that the fingerprints indeed come from the weapon and how we can be so sure it was the *murder* weapon. We can only find out by questioning the police officer who was at the scene of the crime. Assuming that police officers have a reputation for truthfulness, we may accept the officer's testimony that bullets shot from the gun with the fingerprints matched the bullet recovered from the victim's body. This testimony will, if the court probes deeper into the structure of sub-stories, lead to the bullet expert who compared the bullets and the pathologist who cut open the corpse. Pressing on, we again arrive at a consideration of their or other people's reputations.

COMMON-SENSE RULES AND REPUTATION

The arguments advanced above support the thesis that all evidence is witness evidence; that is, as long as one probes deep enough into the structure of embedded sub-stories. The analysis also seems to imply that all evidence—again if probed deeply enough—is grounded on somebody's reputation. Before this conclusion can be drawn, a further discussion of the process of probing and anchoring is needed.

A sub-story is as much a message as any other and thus has two aspects: the message and the messenger. The diagnostic value of a sub-story can be established by anchoring the message, or by anchoring the messenger (again, either to a sub-story one level deeper or to a general rule). In general, however, the message, the testimony by a witness, cannot be evaluated without taking the credibility of the witness into account. That is not a practical constraint, but one of principle: why else question the witness? In practice, the testimony of many witnesses is accepted as valid without questioning the credibility of the witness, most of the time because the story told by the witness fits in very nicely with what the court knows about the crime from other sources. If five independent witnesses all tell more or less the same story, there is no reason to question the credibility of each individual witness. Evaluating evidence in this manner nevertheless bears a small risk. Gross (1987) reports a miscarriage of justice which occurred after 17 independent witnesses had identified the innocent defendant. Apart from this kind of exceptional cases, there seems no practical reason to probe any further if a number of witnesses confirm most of each other's stories. Then the stories are anchored onto the general rule that if independent witnesses give testimony that support one another, they almost always speak the truth. If the defence accepts anchoring to this rule and does not challenge the independence of the witnesses, the decision is going to be a sound one. If, however, the defence wants to probe deeper, the credibility of the witnesses comes into play and the trial goes into a probing of sub-stories which always ends at somebody's reputation.

The common-sense general rules which serve as anchoring grounds in the theory on anchored narratives seem to serve practical purposes. Without them, trials would go on almost for ever and probably would raise questions about many well kept reputations.

COMPARING MODELS

Why, then, does the theory of anchored narratives form a better model of decision-making than the Bayesian model? Anchored narratives are a better vehicle for prescription for courtroom behaviour and decision-making because they are less alien to the tradition in law and to what actually happens in court than the Bayesian model. In a descriptive sense this theory is better because it predicts instances of courtroom behaviour and decision making which cannot be predicted by the Bayesian model. I refer to the extensive analysis of Dutch cases in Crombag, Van Koppen and Wagenaar, 1992; Wagenaar, Van Koppen and Crombag, 1993). Here are just a few examples.

Sometimes the defence introduces a piece of evidence which at once destroys what seemed until then an iron-clad case for the prosecution. Although the fictional Perry Mason comes up with such a defeating piece of evidence in each and every case, this is a rather rare occasion in reality. In a Bayesian model a very strong piece of evidence favouring the innocence of the defendant would not destroy the prosecution's case completely; it would just adjust the odds of guilt downward. Under a story model it can easily be demonstrated how a single piece of evidence destroys a case.

With the theory of anchored narratives it can also be demonstrated how evidence that is hardly quantifiable contributes to the decision of judge or jury. In the Bayesian model that is impossible.

Most important is that the theory of anchored narratives provides for a more complete model of decision-making and what goes on at trial. It can be used to show why prosecution and defence fail or succeed in making their case; it can show how the selection of evidence operates; it can also show why some evidence is taken for granted, and other evidence is scrutinised and requires a deep descent into anchoring structure of embedded sub-stories.

ACKNOWLEDGEMENT

Steven Penrod and David Carson gave most useful comments on an earlier draft of this chapter.

REFERENCES

Allen, R.J. (1991). The nature of juridical proof. *Cardozo Law Review*, **13**, 373–422.

Bartlett, F.C. (1950). *Remembering: A Study in Experimental and Social Psychology* (2nd edn). Cambridge: Cambridge University Press. (1st edn, 1932.)

Bedau, H.A. and Radelet, M.L. (1987). Miscarriages of justice in potential capital cases. *Stanford Law Review*, **40**, 21–179.

Bedau, H.A. and Radelet, M.L. (1988). The myth of infallibility: a reply to Markman and Cassell. *Stanford Law Review*, **41**, 161–70.

Bekerian, D.A. (1993). In search of the typical eye-witness. *American Psychologist*, **48**, 574–6.

Bennett, W.L. and Feldman, M.S. (1981). *Reconstructing Reality in the Courtroom*. London: Tavistock.

Berghuis, A.C. (1992). De harde en de zachte hand: Een statistische analyse van verschillen in sanctiebeleid. Trema, **15**, 84–93.

Blackman, D.E., Muller, D.J. and Chapman, A.J. (1984). Perspectives in psychology and law. In D.J. Müller, D.E. Blackman and A.J. Chapman (Eds), *Psychology and Law*. New York: John Wiley.

Borchard, E.M. (1932). *Convicting the Innocent: Sixty-Five Actual Errors of Criminal Justice*. Garden City, NJ: Doubleday.

Brandon, R. and Davies, C. (1973). *Wrongful Imprisonment: Mistaken Convictions and their Consequences*. London: Allen & Unwin.

Bruner, J. (1984). Narrative and paradigmatic modes of thought. Invited address, Division 1 of the American Psychological Association, Toronto, August 25, 1984.

Cohen, L.J. (1977). *The Probable and the Provable*. Oxford: Clarendon.

Crombag, H.F.M. (1982). Wat is rechtspsychologie? *Ars Aequi*, **32**, 237–40.

Crombag, H.F.M. (1992). Expert witnesses as vicarious anchors. *Expert Evidence*, 1, 127–31.

Crombag, H.F.M. and Van Koppen, P.J. (1991). Praktische bezwaren: Psychologie voor juristen. In P.J. Van Koppen and H.F.M. Crombag (Eds), *De Menselijke Factor: Psychologie voor Juristen*. Arnhem, The Netherlands: Gouda Quint.

Crombag, H.F.M., Van Koppen, P.J. and Wagenaar, W.A. (1992). *Dubieuze Zaken: De Psychologie van Strafrechtelijk Bewijs*. Amsterdam: Contact.

Cuenta-Rua, J.C. (1981). *Judicial Methods of Interpretation in Law*. Baton Rouge: Louisiana State University, Paul M. Herbert Law Center.

Deffenbacher, K.A. (1980). Eye-witness accuracy and confidence: can we infer anything about their relationship? *Law and Human Behavior*, **4**, 243–60.

Easteal, S., McLeod, N. and Reed, K. (1991). *DNA Profiling: Principles, Pitfalls and Potential*. Chur: Harwood.

Edwards, W. (1988). Summing up: the Society of Bayesian Trial Lawyers. In P. Tillers and E.D. Green (Eds), *Probability and Inference in the Law of Evidence*. Dordrecht, The Netherlands: Kluwer Academic.

Edwards, W. (1991). Influence diagrams, Baeysian imperialism, and the Collins case: an appeal to reason. *Cardozo Law Review*, **13,** 1025–79.

Egeth, H.E. (1993). What do we not know about eyewitness identification? *American Psychologist*, **48**, 577–80.

Finkelstein, M.O. and Fairly, W.B. (1970). A Bayesian approach to identification evidence. *Harvard Law Review*, **83**, 489–517.

Fletcher, H. (1992). Supplementary evidence from the National Association of Probation Officers. Paper for the Royal Commission on Criminal Justice.

Frank, J.N. and Frank, B. (1957). *Not Guilty*. New York: Doubleday.

Gardner, E.S. (1952). *Court of Last Resort*. New York: Sloane.

Goldsmith, R.W. (1980). Studies of a model for evaluating judicial evidence. *Acta Psychologica*, **45**, 211–21.

Green, D.M. and Swets, J.A. (1966). *Signal Detection Theory and Psychophysics*. New York: John Wiley.

Gross, S.R. (1987). Loss of innocence: eyewitness identification and proof of guilt. *Journal of Legal Studies*, **16**, 395–453.

Gudjonsson, G.H. (1992). *The Psychology of Interrogations, Confessions and Testimony*. London: John Wiley.

Gudjonsson, G.H. and Sigurdsson, J.F. (1993). How frequently do false confessions occur? An empirical study among prison inmates. *Psychology, Crime, and Law*, **1**, 1, 21–26.

Hale, L. (1961). *Hanged in Error*. Harmondsworth: Penguin.

Hart, H.L.A. (1963). Introduction In C. Perelman (Ed.), *The Idea of Justice and the Problem of Argument*. London: Routledge.

Hastie, R., Penrod, S. and Pennington, N. (1983). *Inside the Jury*. Cambridge, MA: Harvard University Press.

Hill, P., Young, M. and Sergeant, T. (1985). *More Rough Justice*. Harmondsworth: Penguin.

Hogarth, J. (1971). *Sentencing as a Human Process*. Toronto: University of Toronto Press.

Homel, R.J. and Lawrence, J.A. (1992). Sentencer orientation and case details. *Law and Human Behavior*, **16**, 509–37.

Jackson, B.S. (1988). *Law, Fact and Narrative Coherence*. Liverpool: Deborah Charles.

Kagehiro, D.K. (1990). Defining the standard of proof in jury instructions. *Psychological Science*, **1**, 194–200.

Kalven Jr., H. and Zeisel, H. (1966). *The American Jury*. Boston, MA: Little, Brown.

Kaplan, J. (1968). Decision theory and the fact finding process. *Stanford Law Review*, **20**, 1065.

Koehler, D.J. (1991). Explanation, imagination, and confidence in judgment. *Psychological Bulletin*, **110**, 499–519.

Langbein, J.H. (1977). *Torture and the Law of Proof: Europe and England in the Ancien Régiem*. Chicago: University of Chicago Press.

Macalister, P. (1989). From fingerprints to genetic codes: indisputable evidence? *Law Society Journal*, **27**, 43.

Melton, G.B., Petrila, J., Poytress, Jr, N.G. and Slobogin, C. (1987). *Psychological*

Evaluation for the Courts: A Handbook for Mental Health Professionals and Lawyers. London: Guilford.

Mols, G.P.M.F. (1989). *Staande de zittng: Een beschouwing over het onmiddelijkheidsbeginsel*. Arnhem: Gouda Quint (oratie RU Limburg).

Pennington, N. and Hastie, R. (1986). Evidence evaluation in complex decision making. *Journal of Personality and Social Psychology*, **51**, 242–58.

Pennington, N. and Hastie, R. (1988). Explanantion-based decision making: effects of memory and structure on judgment. *Journal of Experimental Psychology: Learning, Memory, and Cognition*, **14**, 521–33.

Pennington, N. and Hastie, R. (1991). A theory of explanation-based decision-making. In G. Klein and J. Orasanu (Eds), *Decision-making in Complex Worlds*. Hillsdale, NJ: Ablex.

Radin, E.D. (1964). *The Innocents*. New York: Dell.

Rattner, A. (1988). Convicted but innocent: wrongful conviction and the criminal justice system. *Law and Human Behavior*, **12**, 283–93.

Roberts, L. (1991). Fight erupts over DNA fingerprinting. *Science*, **254**, 1721–3.

Robinson, J.A. (1981). Personal narratives reconsidered. *Journal of American Folklore*, **94**, 58–85.

Rumelhart, D.E. (1975). Notes on a schema for stories. In D.G. Bobrow and A. Collins (Eds), *Representation and Understanding: Studies in Cognitive Science*. New York: Academic.

Saks, M.J. (1989). Prevalence and impact of ethical problems in forensic science. *Journal of Forensic Science*, **34**, 772–93.

Saks, M.J. and Kidd, R.F. (1980). Human information processing and adjudication: trial by heuristics. *Law and Society Review*, **15**, 123–160.

Saks, M.J. and Koehler, J.J. (1991). What DNA 'fingerprinting' can teach the law about the rest of forensic science. *Cardozo Law Review*, **13**, 363–72.

Scholten, P. (1974). *Mr C. Asser's Handleiding tot de Beoefening van het Nederlands Burgerlijk Recht* (3rd edn, revised by G.J. Scholten). Algemeen Deel. Zwolle, The Netherlands: Tjeenk Willink.

Schum, D.A. (1979). A review of the case against Blaise Pascal and his heirs. *Michigan Law Review*, **77**, 446.

Schünemann, B. (1983). Experimentelle Untersuchungen zur Reform der Hauptverhandlung in Strafsachen. In H.J. Kerner, H. Kurry and K. Sessar (hrgb.), *Deutsche Forschungen zur Kriminalitätsentscheiden und Kriminalitätskontrolle*. Köln: Heymanns.

Schünemann, B. and Bandilla, W. (1989). Perseverence in courtroom decisions. In H. Wegener, F. Lösel and J. Haisch (Eds), *Criminal Behavior and the Justice System: Psychological Perspectives*. New York: Springer.

Semin, G.R. and Manstead, A.S.R. (1983). *The Accountability of Conduct: A Social Psychological Analysis*. London: Academic.

Skinner, L.J. and Berry, K.K. (1993). Anatomically detailed dolls and the evaluation of child sexual abuse allegations: psychometric considerations. *Law and Human Behavior*, **17**, 399–421.

Tribe, L.H. (1971). Trial by mathematics: precision and ritual in the legal process. *Harvard Law Review*, **84**, 1329–93.

Van Dijk, T.A. (1980). *Macrostructures: An Interdisciplinary Study of Global Structures in Discourse, Interaction, and Cognition*. Hillsdale, NJ: Erlbaum.

Van Koppen, P.J. and Hessing, D.J. (1988). Legal psychology or law and psychology.

In P.J. Van Koppen and D.J. Hessing (Eds), *Lawyers on Psychology and Psychologists on Law*. Amsterdam: Swets and Zeitlinger.

Wagenaar, W.A. (1988). *Identifying Ivan: A Case Study in Legal Psychology*. New York: Harvester Wheatsheaf.

Wagenaar, W.A. (1991). Waar logica faalt en verhalen overtuigen: Een beschouwing over het strafrechtelijk bewijs. *Onze Alma Mater*, **45**, 256–78.

Wagenaar, W.A. and Veefkind, N. (1992). Comparison of one-person and many-person lineups: a warning against unsafe practices. In F. Lösel, D. Bender and T. Bliesener (Eds), *Psychology and Law: International Perspectives*. Berlin: de Gruyter.

Wagenaar, W.A., Van Koppen, P.J. and Crombag, H.F.M. (1993). *Anchored Narratives: The Psychology of Criminal Evidence*. New York: Harvester Wheatsheaf.

Waller, Sir George (Chair) (1989). *Miscarriages of Justice*. London: Justice.

Wells, G.L. (1993). What do we know about eyewitness identification? *American Psychologist*, **48**, 553–71.

Wigmore, J.H. (1937). *The Science of Judicial Proof as Given by Logic, Psychology and General Experience* (3rd edn). Boston: Little Brown.

Williams, G. (1963). *The Proof of Guilt: A Study of the English Criminal Trial* (3rd edn). London: Stevens.

Woffinden, B. (1987). *Miscarriages of Justice*. London: Hodder & Stoughton.

Young, M. and Hill, P. (1983). *Rough Justice*. London: British Broadcasting Corporation.

Yuille, J.C. (1993). We must study forensic eye-witnesses to know about them. *American Psychologist*, **48**, 572–3.

Zimmermann, I. (1964). *Punishment Without Crime*. New York.

Zuckerman, A.A.S. (1989). *The Principles of Criminal Evidence*. Oxford: Clarendon.

Part 7

Group Behaviour

Chapter 7.1

Public Law Decisions

David Carson
University of Southampton

INTRODUCTION

A distinction can be drawn between private law and public law. Most of the earlier chapters of this book have been concerned with private law issues. Basically, private law concerns relationships between individuals and/or organisations. Public law involves cases where the powers and responsibilities of the government, and governmental bodies such as health and education authorities, are in issue. Suing a health, social services or education authority for the negligence of one of their employees, involves private law. Asking the courts to overturn a decision made by one of those authorities, or asking the courts to declare what those authorities' legal responsibilities are, involves public law.

The distinction is not very neat. For example, in *E. (A Minor) v. Dorset County Council,* ([1994] 3 W.L.R. 853) parents sought compensation from education authorities for the negligence of educational psychologists in not diagnosing a learning difficulty promptly, and for breach of a statutory duty to provide suitable education for a child with dyslexia. One court decided that there was no case to answer and dismissed the claims before a hearing on the merits of the case took place (*Lexis,* 7 April, 1993). The Court of Appeal, however, has decided that the parents cannot sue for breach of a statutory duty but *may* be able to sue for negligence. The judgment indicates how private law issues, such as compensation for alleged professional negligence, can become entangled with public law issues.

The case also indicates how public law issues are more likely to be perceived as 'political'. A decision for the parents, allowing them to sue for breach of the duties stated in the Education Acts, could have proved expensive for local and national government. This can, however, be overstated because the parents could only succeed if they could prove negligence.

The courts have an important role in declaring the responsibilities of government, the limits of their legitimate power and their responsibilities. Different jurisdictions and traditions lead to different approaches. For example the Constitution of the USA is central to the relationship between the legislative, executive and judicial arms of government and to the rights of individuals *vis à vis* the government. The UK, lacking a comparable written constitution, has developed a set of rules and principles through individual cases that have been taken to the courts. (It is known as judicial review and as administrative law.) This rather piecemeal approach has led to criticisms of lack of consistency (see De Smith and Brazier, 1989). In France there is a separate system of courts, with separate judges with greater experience of administrative matters, to administer *droit administratif*. Individuals may present their case to a Tribunal Administratif and there is provision for appeal to the Conseil d'Etat (Neville Brown and Garner, 1983). Where countries have adopted it their national legislation can be found to conflict with the European Convention on Human Rights.

So public law is politically sensitive. The reputation of the courts can be at stake. On one interpretation they may be protecting the individual citizen against an overbearing and intrusive government which is ignoring the law. But, on another interpretation, unelected judges may be seen as interfering with the rights of a democratically elected and accountable government. In the UK the courts manage this tension by concentrating upon the manner in which decisions are made rather than by directly challenging or examining the merits or the contents of the decisions. The courts, it is said, are neither competent nor authorised to make such decisions as how resources should be allocated, say between hospitals and missiles. But the courts are competent to check that the decisions are made in an appropriate manner. This distinction, between the merits of a decision and the merits of the way in which it is made, is also imprecise and problems can arise. But the focus is the quality of decision-making. If the courts do decide that a public law decision is improper then they so declare it, but they do not replace it with a decision of their own. The decision has to be made afresh. Psychological and related research has a great deal to say about decision-making but it has made little impact in legal contexts, to date. This chapter will consider the potential contribution of psychology to the illumination of disputes in public law.

ACTORS, ORGANISATIONS AND GAMES

Allison (1971) developed a three-part typology of government decision making. The rational actor model is subscribed to by most people, professional and lay. It assumes that decisions are the rational product of a consensus government or similar. The objectives of governments' decisions may be discovered by reasoning backwards from their actions. The organisational process model suggests that, instead of looking 'outside' to the consequences of the decisions, we should consider the extent to which the decision is the product of the internal needs of the organisation, such as for stability and continuity: 'Goals are dominated by the need to maintain the health of the organisation and to avoid threats to it' (Hall, 1980). The third model proposes that decisions should be analysed in terms of bargaining games: 'Predictions are generated by identifying the game in which an issue will arise, the relevant players, and their relative power and skill' (Allison, 1971). So a government minister's decision might be taken at face value; its objective is to implement the declared or implicit policy. Alternatively it might be seen as part of a continuing process concerned more with its symbolic significance to an electorate than for its actual instrumental effect. But, also, it might best be understood as a temporary trade-off between competing interests.

The courts, concerned with public law issues in the UK, have implicitly adopted a rational actor model of decision-making. They have overturned ministerial and other decisions by public authorities on the grounds that they are manifestly unreasonable. The rules, allowing some prediction of how the courts will decide, are drawn from a sequence of decisions which began with *Associated Provincial Picture Houses Ltd. v. Wednesbury Corporation*, ([1948] 1 K.B. 223). Decisions can also be reviewed, and declared invalid if necessary, on the grounds of illegality, irrationality or procedural impropriety (*Council for the Civil Service Unions v. Minister for the Civil Service*, [1985] A.C. 374). This is *not* the same as a test of negligence. For a decision to be found invalid it needs to be one which no reasonable or properly advised minister, or whatever, would have made. The courts seek to avoid accusations of party political bias or interference by concentrating upon the quality of the decision, and decision-making process, irrespective of the merits of the issue in question.

There appears to be no overwhelming obstacle to the courts taking account of analyses of decisions which suggest that an organisational process or games bargaining model provides a better, or more complete, explanation of a particular decision. It could be very appropriate to take into account the internal needs of an organisation when making a particular decision. The representation of a decision as the product of a 'game' between competing power interests will tend to be prejudicial. The label is, in that sense, unfortunate. Similarly the label 'rational' may be too complimentary about decisions analysed in terms of the rational actor model (Hall, 1980). But it is not the label but rather the process for arriving at a decision that matters. Balancing competing interests, trading one proposal for another, taking account of the need to maintain a majority in parliament to get legislation enacted, may be seen as a very rational, indeed necessary, approach. Where these alternative models may prove to be most valuable is in challenging the readiness to adopt a rational actor model. Events and arguments may be reassessed from the different perspectives. These are, certainly, not the only alternative models that can be considered. For example the significance of indecision could be investigated. But these alternative insights provide an opportunity to 'look beneath' the rationalisations and they remind us that decisions can also be the product of factors of which the actors were not but should have been aware at the time of decision-making.

DECISION ERRORS

Extensive psychological research has been undertaken on decision-making. This has provided some counter-intuitive information and demonstrates that we frequently make mistakes; indeed it suggests that we are poor decision-makers. How might this information be utilised by the courts in their public law roles? They have to review others' decision-making, for example the granting of planning permission to build a factory. They could investigate whether these forms of error have been made or, at least, whether good practices in decision-making, designed to avoid the errors, have been adopted. However, as the courts are also decision-makers, they will need to assure themselves, and others, that their procedures are also designed to avoid such errors.

Before deciding that someone has made an erroneous decision it is necessary to determine what a correct decision would be. Individuals have different views and preferences. Just because we would not make that decision it cannot, properly, be concluded that the decision is erroneous. Some assumptions have to be made. Thus researchers have assumed that we would, being rational and other things being equal, prefer to improve our position. If offered a 50 per cent chance of winning £10 or a 50 per cent chance of winning £100, we would prefer the latter chance. (That is a simple example; the problems begin when we start to alter the figures.) This assumption is often referred to as 'subjective expected utility'. It assumes that we should wish to maximise that which we value. Where choices can be translated into monetary values then it can be assumed that we should, and predicted that we would, seek to gain the larger sum and the smaller loss.

Subjective expected utility is a normative theory; it concerns how we should behave. Acting against it may suggest irrational behaviour. It was also expected to be a good theory for predicting people's choices. But extensive research indicates that, in a variety of ways and on a range of issues, we do not seek to maximise our gains or minimise our losses. This led H.A. Simon (1978, 1979) to argue that, in practice, we do not seek to maximise or optimise but rather to 'satisfice'. Our cognitive systems lead us, when faced with particular problems, not to seek the outcome that would be most advantageous to us but a compromise or sufficiently satisfactory substitute.

Should the courts be satisfied with satisficing? The ideal result may not be possible; we have to compromise. A politician is expected to balance objectives and, perhaps, to achieve goals in small steps. That should not, by itself, be a basis for attacking the decision. It would not be an example of 'satisficing'. That would be a case of, rationally, seeking the most advantageous outcome. 'Satisficing' refers to a human inability to manage certain problems or a proneness to particular forms of error in assessing issues. In this sense it is submitted that the courts should not be satisfied with satisficing because that would involve adopting errors. Researchers must develop theories, such as satisficing, in order to improve the prediction of human behaviour. But when it comes to the quality of a decision it is submitted that the courts should look to 'objective' expected utility as an ideal against which to assess decisions. The standard of care, in the law of negligence, refers to the standards of a responsible body of co-professionals. Responsible professionals, just like responsible government ministers, may regularly make decision errors. That may prevent claims of negligence succeeding, at least until contemporary standards of decision-making improve by the incorporation of good practice. But that, it is submitted, should not prevent the courts, in their public law roles, overturning a minister's decision when it is shown to have been so erroneous as to be manifestly unreasonable. The focus is the quality of the decision and decision-making process rather than the qualities of the decision-maker.

The ground-breaking research on decision errors has been undertaken by Kahnemann and Tversky (1972, 1973, 1984), sometimes with others (e.g. Kahneman, Slovic and Tversky, 1982). The implications of this work have been making their way into management science books (e.g. Russo and Schoemaker, 1989; Cooke and Slack, 1991). Fitzmaurice and Pease (1986) have considered some of the implications for judges' sentencing practices.

REASONING FROM DATA

Several of the decision errors are relevant to issues of probability, and thereby directly relevant to legal issues. For example, we tend, unless sensitised to the issues, to expect greater variation from the mean in larger than in smaller populations. The converse is actually the case for, in a random situation, the larger the sample or population the less deviation there will be from the mean or most probable event.

We also tend to underestimate the importance of base rates, background information which is not usually case specific. For example, there is a base rate likelihood of an adverse reaction to certain drugs. This is independent of the particular patient. The clinician needs to consider both this rate and the significance of particular features of the patient—for example, age. The problem is that the importance of this 'background' base rate information is regularly treated as less important and predictive than the individualistic information about the particular participants or clients. Special steps have to be taken to encourage clinicians to assess the likelihood data appropriately (see generally Dowie and Elstein, 1988). That example may involve private law issues but the same issues can arise in public law contexts—for example, safety consideration in planning appeals or reviews of the professional assessments of the continuing dangerousness of prisoners (*R. v. Parole Board, ex parte Telling*, 1993, *Lexis*, 6 May). The courts, in their public law role, could review the quality of decision-making by examining whether such problems have been avoided.

It must be recognised, however, that many lawyers are very reluctant to adopt statistical tests of probability (Eggleston, 1983). Indeed some legal systems have 'adopted' base rate errors. For example, such background or base rate information as prior criminal convictions is, particularly in comparison to other information, highly predictive of re-offending. But, in the UK and many other countries, information about prior convictions is excluded from court, except in very special circumstances, until a verdict has been reached. It has been noted that lawyers tend to individualise where other disciplines seek to generalise. The distinctive features of clients and fact situations are emphasised rather than the similarities (Aubert, 1963). Lawyers for the detained prisoner or patient will argue about his or her dangerousness, emphasising particularistic information, rather than noting the greater predictive value of such 'background' information as age, gender and index offence. Research on dangerousness used to concentrate upon identifying risk factors. Increasingly it is focusing upon decision-making, by people other than the patient or prisoner, about risk (Steadman, et al., 1993). Thus there is a coming together in the focus of the courts, on the quality of decision-making, with the research on decision-making.

MAKING QUALITY ASSURED JUDGEMENTS

A prerequisite of a quality decision is a fair and appropriate procedure for collecting information and arguments about the issues involved, assessing them and making the decision. Courts can review and insist upon the quality of these procedures without being perceived as interfering with the merits of the decision. Thus, as in the UK, the courts can require public bodies and officials to act 'judicially'. Some judges emphasise that this duty involves obeying the rules of natural justice whilst others emphasise a more general duty to act fairly.

> Often the terms are interchangeable. But it is perhaps now the case that while a duty to act fairly is incumbent on every decision-maker within the administrative process whose decision will affect individual interests, the rules of natural justice apply only when some sort of definite code of procedure must be adopted, however flexible that code may be and however much the decision-maker is said to be master of his own procedure. (De Smith and Brazier, 1989, p. 557)

The rules of natural justice require that decision-makers are not biased and that thcy act in good faith. They must not have a financial interest in the outcome. They must not be open to reasonable suspicion of bias. They must provide a fair hearing. There must be notice of the hearing and the issues in question. The parties must know what they must answer. They must have a fair opportunity to put their case. If, such as in planning appeals, one person or body hears the evidence but another person or body makes the decision, then those who collect and hear the evidence must provide the decision-makers with sufficiently detailed reports that will enable them to be regarded as, effectively, having heard the evidence.

These rules focus on the preparation for decision-making. Psychological research, for example on bias, might be of assistance to the courts (see Eiser and van der Pligt, 1988). Research on the process of decision-making may, however, be of greater potential. This work suggests that we, consciously or unconsciously, adopt a number of aids or 'heuristics' in order to help us make our decisions. Unfortunately these heuristics can lead us into error (Kahnemann and Tversky, 1972, 1973, 1984; Rachlin, 1989). We tend to use the information that is available to us. That appears perfectly natural. But we can forget to compensate for other information which might be available and might be more significant. For example, we recall information about people who have committed offences while on bail more readily than information about those who do not, about safety problems in factories rather than safety successes. We may have read or heard a lot about prison escapes but we should not generalise from that information—for example, that more escapes are taking place—without relevant quality comparative information. Note that our legal systems ensure that judges receive an unrepresentative view of human behaviour; they deal with breakdowns in relationships or acceptable behaviour which is comparatively rare. Added to that is our tendency to treat the information available as representative: '[W]e may buy a car on the basis of a test drive, we elect officials on the basis of their ability to campaign, and we get married on the basis of our experiences during a brief courtship' (Rachlin, 1989, p. 59). That information may not be representative. People working, for example in health and social services, need to take decisions involving risk. Ask them about their success rate and, usually, they will have difficulty in telling you. They can remember, often vividly, cases where harm resulted. But, in order to make any judgement about success in taking risk decisions, there ought to be information about successes as well as failures. Where a risk is proposed, say the siting of a nuclear installation, then past success in predicting risk could be important.

There are limits to the amount of information and the number of issues, considerations and arguments, that we can deal with 'in our heads' at one time. Court proceedings implicitly exaggerate the capacity of jurors and judges to cope with all the information. In practice, the research suggests, we develop techniques or methods to help us cope. There is no assurance that we are aware of the methods we adopt. Indeed, given that it may appear that our 'intellectual virility' is being challenged, we may be very reluctant to admit that we are adopting decision aids. One approach, when hearing a number of arguments, is to adopt a provisional point of view. Then each further argument is assessed in terms of the extent to which it supports or challenges the preliminary point of view. But this approach has problems. The provisional point of view involves one theory or possible explanation. But there will regularly be several alternative explanations. The potential of these alternatives does not get assessed when only one hypothesis is being considered.

Heuristics and decision aids are human responses to complexity and uncertainty. Their adoption cannot be prevented. The role of the courts, it is submitted, is to review how different people and bodies make their decisions and to encourage good, or at least better, practice.

MONITORING QUALITY

The role of the public law courts is restricted, in part, because the judges recognise that they often lack the expertise necessary to make particular kinds of decisions. For example, the Discretionary Lifers Panel of the Parole Board is empowered to require the immediate release of a prisoner who was previously regarded as so dangerous and unpredictable that he or she was given a discretionary life sentence. The public law courts are entitled to review the Panel's decisions but they are not entitled to substitute their own decision. They can require that the decision be taken again with the law and procedure followed properly but they do not decide the substantive issue themselves. One member of each Panel is a judge who will have greater awareness of the issues, through membership of the Parole Board. The decision, on the merits of the case, is for the Panel. The public law courts can only intervene where the Panel has misinterpreted the law, reached an 'irrational' decision, breached a procedural requirement or similar. Their task is to assure the quality of the decision-making procedures.

The role of the courts, when deciding public law issues, is substantially one of monitoring. They do not tackle issues that they perceive as being beyond their competence or role. Instead they emphasise the decision-making process and require a reconsideration of the case where significant errors have been, or may have been, made. This contrasts with their role in other types of cases, such as professional negligence. There the courts recognise their limited competence on the technical issues but go on and determine the case by relying upon expert witnesses. Particularly where there is competing expert evidence the courts go beyond reviewing the quality of the experts' data, and the process by which they reached their conclusions, in order to choose between them.

But this focus on litigation is 'false'. It is an atypical minority of legal disputes that ever get to the courts. Courts have, at least in terms of numbers, a much more important role in the way that they influence (a) the settlement of the legal disputes that never reach them, and (b) the standards of officials and experts which in turn affects whether disputes arise. By highlighting the factors that ought to be taken into account, for example in decision aids, the courts could have a much greater influence than they would have in determining a relatively narrow point of law in an individual case.

With the increasing complexity of modern society the role of experts, generally and as witnesses, must be expected to increase. The final decision in a trial may be reserved for a judge or a panel but, in reality, an increasing number of cases will turn upon the nature and quality of the evidence collected and assessed by particular experts. For example, the decision whether to require the Home Secretary to release a discretionary life sentence prisoner is made by the Discretionary Lifers Panel. But they depend upon the evidence placed before them. The prisoner may have a right to commission independent expert evidence but, particularly with pressure on expenditure, it is the evidence of those working for the Prison Service that matters. Pre-trial procedures and processes are at least as important as—and regularly more significant—than the trial process. Emphasising that it is the judge's or Panel's decision—for example, to order the release of a prisoner—allows those collecting and presenting the evidence to argue that they do not have responsibility for the decisions which the Panel makes. That, it is submitted, is casuistry and does not encourage high standards! In such cases the courts are, substantially, monitoring the quality of the work undertaken by the experts, by psychologists, prison officers, probation officers and others in release of prisoners cases (Carson, 1990). Noting the point does not, in any way, diminish the importance of the courts' role. But recognising it, and consciously developing the role, would permit the courts to have a much more effective and appropriate role directly influencing the disputes that do not, as well as do, reach the courts.

CALCULATED JUDGEMENTS

As has been emphasised, the courts, in their public law roles, avoid deciding disputes, such as the allocation of resources or the siting of planning zones, which are beyond their technical competence. They prefer to concentrate on ensuring that a proper decision could be made. They are, however, prepared to intervene when decisions are excessive in the sense that no responsible minister would have made a particular decision. Although such decisions are described, after having been invalidated, in quite extreme terms as 'irrational' the test is vague, making it quite difficult to predict what the courts will decide. Could psychology contribute by indicating the basic requirements of good quality judgements?

Extensive work has been undertaken on the perception, assessment and management of risk (see, for example, Gould et al., 1988; Rodricks, 1992;

Yates, 1992). Such issues arise when, for example, ministers have to decide whether and where dangerous industries should be sited. But many of the ideas can be utilised in other contexts because decision-making can be analysed as risk-taking since harm may result if an inappropriate decision is made.

Although a defining feature of risk-taking is uncertainty it is possible to increase our understanding of the issues, particularly likelihoods (Moore and Thomas, 1976). The values that are to be attributed to different outcomes—for example, public safety versus contribution to economy—may best be decided by politicians, in the last resort, because there are no inherently correct values to apply. But it would still be appropriate to inquire whether appropriate approaches had been adopted. Multi-attribute utility analysis, for example, breaks choices into their key parts and enables a series of questions to be posed so that real preferences can be determined. Trade-offs between objectives are negotiated (Keeney and Raiffa, 1976; Edwards and Newman, 1982). 'The major advantage to decision analysis is that it provides a systematic procedure for helping decision makers think about all relevant concerns' (Pitz, 1992, p. 309). Should a minister, or similar public official or body, particularly where the decision is very significant, be regarded as acting 'irrationally', or in a way that no responsible minister would act, if such analytical aids to quality decision-making were not utilised?

Risk assessment, particularly where technology is involved, often involves failure mode effect and criticality analysis (Abbott, 1987). Every juncture where the product, process or system could break down, and the possible causes, are identified. The likelihood and the seriousness, or criticality, of each potential failure is assessed. Ways of correcting the failure, or reducing the risk of its occurrence, are identified. Such an analysis, on its own, is likely to identify ways of making failures less likely. The appeal for lawyers lies in its potential for identifying where safety and other interventions should be invested. Would it not be appropriate to describe someone as 'irrational' who invested time, effort and resources in a low likelihood and/or low criticality possible failure to the exclusion of high likelihood and/or serious possible failures? The amount of resources, that are to be made available for prevention or safety, may involve a political judgement beyond judicial intervention. But how the resources that are made available are invested is, it is submitted, an appropriate consideration for the courts because it goes to the quality of decision-making.

Failure mode effect and criticality analysis could be applied to decision-making. Some parts of the process are much more important and liable to error than others. If the quality of decision-making is to improve then appropriate attention needs to be paid to those parts, in particular. Psychology, it has been argued, has a great deal to offer in this regard.

REFERENCES

Abbott, H. (1987). *Safer by Design: The Management of Product Design Risks under Strict Liability*. London: Design Council.

Allison, G.T. (1971). *Essence of Decision: Explaining the Cuban Missile Crisis*. Boston, MA: Little, Brown.

Aubert, V. (1963). The structure of legal thinking. In J. Andenas (Ed.), *Legal Essays: A Tribute to Fride Castberg on the Occasion of his 70th Birthday*. Boston, MA: Universitetsforlaget.

Carson, D. (1990). Reporting to court: a role in preventing decision error. *Journal of Social Welfare Law*, 151–163.

Cooke, S. and Slack, N. (1991). *Making Management Decisions* (2nd edn). Hemel Hempstead: Prentice Hall.

De Smith, S. and Brazier, R. (1989). *Constitutional and Administrative Law*. London: Penguin.

Dowie, J. and Elstein, A. (Eds) (1988). *Professional Judgment: A Reader in Clinical Decision Making*. Cambridge: Cambridge University Press.

Edwards, W. and Newman, J.R. (1982). *Multiattribute Evaluation*. Newbury Park, CA: Sage.

Eggleston, R. (1983). *Evidence, Proof and Probability*. London: Weidenfield & Nicholson.

Eiser, J.R. and van der Pligt, J. (1988). *Attitudes and Decisions*. London: Routledge.

Fitzmaurice, C. and Pease, K. (1986). *The Psychology of Judicial Sentencing*. Manchester: Manchester University Press.

Gould, L.C., Gardner, G.T., DeLuca, D.R., Tieman, A.R., Doob, L.W. and Stolwijk, J.A.J. (1988). *Perceptions of Technological Risks and Benefits*. New York: Russell Sage.

Hall, P. (1980). *Great Planning Disasters*. London: Weidenfield & Nicholson.

Kahnemann, D. and Tversky, A. (1972). Subjective probability: a judgment of representativeness. *Cognitive Psychology*, **3**, 430–54.

Kahnemann, D. and Tversky, A. (1973). On the psychology of prediction. *Psychological Review*, **80**, 237–51.

Kahnemann, D. and Tversky, A. (1984). Choices, values and frames. *American Psychologist*, **39**, 341–50.

Kahnemann, D., Slovic, P. and Tversky, A. (Eds) (1982). *Judgment under Uncertainty: Heuristics and Biases*. New York: Cambridge University Press.

Keeney, R.L. and Raiffa, H. (1976). *Decisions with Multiple Objectives*. New York: John Wiley.

Moore, P.G. and Thomas, H. (1976). *The Anatomy of Decisions: An Analytical Approach to the Consideration of Risk in Management Decisions*. Harmondsworth: Penguin.

Neville Brown, L. and Garner, J.F. (1983). *French Administrative Law* (3rd edn).

Pitz, G.F. (1992). Risk taking, design, and training. In J.F. Yates (Ed.), *Risk-taking Behavior*. Chichester: John Wiley.

Rachlin, H. (1989). *Judgment, Decision and Choice: A Cognitive/Behavioral Synthesis*. New York: W.H. Freeman.

Rodricks, J.V. (1992). *Calculated Risks: Understanding the Toxicity and Human Health Risks of Chemicals in our Environment*. Cambridge: Cambridge University Press.

Russo, J.E. and Schoemaker, P.J.H. (1989). *Confident Decision Making: How to Make the Right Decision every Time*. London: Piatkus.

Simon, H.A. (1978). Information-processing theory of human problem solving. In W.K. Estes (Ed.), *Handbook of Learning and Cognitive Processes* (vol. 5). Hillsdale, NJ: Erlbaum.

Simon, H.A. (1979). Rational decision making in business organizations. *American Economic Review*, **69**, 493–513.

Steadman, H.J., Monahan, H., Clark Robbins, P., Appelbaum, P., Grisso, T., Klassen, D., Mulvey, E.P. and Roth, S. (1993). From dangerousness to risk assessment: implications for appropriate risk strategies. In S. Hodgins (Ed.), *Mental Disorder and Crime*. Newbury Park, CA: Sage.

Yates, J.F. (Ed.) (1992). *Risk-taking Behavior*. Chichester: John Wiley.

Chapter 7.2

Psychological Insights into Managerial Responsibility for Public and Employee Safety

Ian Donald
University of Liverpool

INTRODUCTION

Public and employee safety issues touch on almost all aspects of everyday life. Potentially, therefore, consideration of the psychological issues involved can cover a vast area. It may include the design of children's toys, food hygiene, or at other extremes, radioactive contamination and disease epidemics. In each of these areas psychology has a contribution to make. Most of these contributions are likely to have legal implications. To narrow the field a little, in this chapter the focus will be on two broad areas around which there has been a growing concern. The first of these is risk from industry and the related area of accidents at work, and the second is safety in public places.

From the industrial revolution onwards the possibility of accidents visiting harm on large sections of the community has greatly increased. The potential scale of such events was clearly and dramatically demonstrated by the nuclear accident at Chernobyl that brought the issue of industrial risk to an international level. The 'near miss' at Three Mile Island, a nuclear reactor in the USA, showed that such events, while rare, are neither one-off unrepeatable incidents nor are they confined to the more primitive versions of nuclear reactors found in the former USSR. The accidents at chemical factories such as Serveso in Italy, Bohpal in India and Flixborough in the UK demonstrated that the potential for industrial accidents to do great harm to the public is not confined to one special sector. In the broad area of safety in public places other incidents, not related to industry, have also shown the consequences that accidents can have for large groups of the public. The Clapham rail crash,

Handbook of Psychology in Legal Contexts
Edited by R. Bull and D. Carson. © 1995 John Wiley & Sons Ltd

Zeebrugge ferry capsize, King's Cross underground station fire, and the crowd disaster at Mecca are all testimony to the importance of safety in public places.

The regulatory and legislative context which surrounds risk, safety and accidents are complex. For instance, some bodies are responsible for bringing prosecutions for safety violations and for framing and enforcing legislation, while others have no input to the development of regulations but may have a role to play in prosecution. For example, in the UK the Health and Safety Executive (HSE) has both a policing and regulatory role, as well as a part to play in bringing prosecutions against the transgressors of those regulations. When there has been a breach of safety, perhaps resulting in fatalities, the line between the HSE's role and that of the police is often rather fine. This can lead to ambiguities over who should, in legal terms, do what in the event of an incident. However, despite these complexities there are some basic and fundamental concerns that have wide implications and for which psychology can have an important role to play. The question of blame and responsibility is one of these. It is important in, for example, compensation litigation, and also decisions about prosecution or a company's continued operation. The concept and apportioning of blame and responsibility have never been simple. Recent developments within general psychology, and in particular in relation to safety, have added to that difficulty raising many intriguing questions.

Decisions about the siting of potentially hazardous industrial installations can also benefit from an understanding of the psychological factors involved in accidents. The area of land use planning is currently based on risk analysis techniques, such as the HSE's RISKAT (Hurst, Nussey and Pape, 1989). Unfortunately such methods as these do not explicitly include measures of social psychological factors in their calculations. Rather, they rely instead on generic failure rates in which these factors are assumed to be reflected. Thus a factor increasingly recognised as a major contributor to accidents and disasters is not included in land use planning risk assessment. It is important to note, however, that the HSE, as well as the European Commission, is trying to rectify this shortcoming.

Another area is the provision of regulations themselves. Often the regulatory and legal requirements for the design and management of public buildings are based on rather simple 'mechanistic' models of behaviour, if indeed explicit models of behaviour have played a role at all. Yet research has shown that many of these may fail to address and take into account the reality of people's behaviour and the psychological factors that can contribute to a disaster (e.g. Canter, 1990; Donald and Canter, 1990). Consequently, psychology has a role also to play in the formulation of the regulations and statutory requirements that currently might be inadequate.

In this chapter some more recent developments in understanding the role of psychological factors in safety, accidents and risk that clearly have legal implications will be described. The examples used to illustrate some of these will be drawn from two main areas. The first is industrial safety. This includes accidents that harm individuals, but, and perhaps more importantly, which also harm communities. Most often this area is considered in the form of risk assessment. The second example is in the arena of disasters that involve members of the public. In particular attention will be paid to research on behaviour in fires that challenges many often held assumptions about the nature of people's behaviour during emergencies.

INDUSTRIAL ACCIDENTS AND RISK

That there is a relationship between the context in which people work and the likelihood that they will either be involved in an accident or play a significant role in its aetiology has been widely recognised for at least a century. Consequently when there is an industrial accident or incident one central question is about causation, about whom or what was to blame for the accident. However, our understanding of the complexities of the relationship between context and safety has not only provided challenges for psychologists, but also made it an increasingly demanding area for the legal professions for whom it seems difficult to consider anything other than first order direct causal relationships (Wells, 1993).

When the accidents and injuries found in the factories of the industrial revolution had become a source of concern, ways of thinking about safety were relatively simple and straightforward. Factories were seen as, and in fact were, dangerous places. They were so poorly designed and protected that injury to individuals or surrounding communities was a likely consequence. Blame could relatively easily be put on the environment and those who were responsible for it. One advantage of the naïveté of this time was that the causal component in an accident usually had a very real, tangible and concrete existence. It is possible, for example, to see a dangerous machine. The responsibilities of companies to ensure that they complied with the appropriate regulations were relatively simple, as it was also to detect when they were transgressed. Though this is not to say that companies consequently either complied with regulations or were prosecuted for not doing so.

Within this context the traditional approach to safety focused on changing design to make environments, technology and industrial processes safer. It was, almost literally, a nuts-and-bolts approach. To some extent much modern thinking about safety has continued to be in this mould. However, there has been an important increase in sophistication and the input of psychology. More recently, for instance, particular attention has been paid to the physical and cognitive limitations and characteristics of operators.

Within this general framework there has been greater attention directed to cognitive error, particularly in the form of mental slips and lapses (Reason and Mycielska, 1982). In this case it has been recognised that people make unintentional errors due to the characteristics of the tasks they are required to do, particularly if these are relatively simple or repetitive tasks. Again the focus of solutions to these problems has been in the area of system design where there has been the development of highly defended systems that are tolerant of error, and allow recovery if an error is made.

As industries have become more complex, and their potential for causing damage to surrounding communities has increased, greater effort has been directed towards assessing risk. This has been an area that also has focused on engineering processes and ergonomic issues. More recently, however, a management factor has been incorporated into discussions of safety and accidents (e.g. Powell and Canter, 1985). The focus of this work is on, for instance, the existence of documentation and procedures, making sure that they exist, and are followed. While not an industrial accident, the Zeebrugge tragedy revealed the importance of management factors. In this case the company, P&O, was severely criticised for failing to provide safe operating systems.

Despite the success of the application of ergonomic methodology and principles to industrial safety, major incidents resulting in injury in communities surrounding major hazard sites continue to happen. Consequently there has been a search for new methods and approaches to improving safety and reducing and assessing risk. Out of this has grown an interest in social psychological factors and in particular safety attitudes and climate (e.g. Canter and Donald, 1990a; Cox and Cox, 1991; Donald and Canter, 1993; Zohar, 1980). If attributing cause to the objective conditions of an organisation is troublesome, the more subjective social psychological factors are fraught with problems and unanswered questions for their legal context. However, as it is now possible to empirically measure these social psychological factors, they can no longer be ignored (Donald, 1994).

ATTITUDES AND ACCIDENTS

Fifteen years ago Zohar (1980) argued that the safety climate of an organisation, the way it is perceived by those who work within it, is important for safe operation. Unfortunately this was never empirically demonstrated by Zohar except in terms of the judgements of safety experts. However, a series of studies carried out since the late 1980s, looking at safety attitude, has taken this further and convincingly shown the importance of these less tangible contributors to accidents.

At the foundation of the attitudinal approach is the argument that many of the actions that people perform that lead to an accident are under their direct control; they are intentional acts (Canter and Donald, 1990b; Donald and

Canter, 1993, 1994). This is in direct contrast to the notion of accidents being due to some momentary lapse of concentration or slip; a cognitive error. This is not to say that they intend to have an accident, but they do intend the action that leads to that accident.

The evidence that people do behave in ways that have the potential to result in an accident, and that they are aware of this, is strong. For example, in a questionnaire survey of 819 workers at a large steel producing site participants were asked whether they had had an accident in the last twelve months (Donald and Canter, 1993). Of those answering 'yes', almost 90 per cent thought the accident was preventable. When asked who was to blame for the accident, 50 per cent saw it as the fault of management, 23 per cent blamed their workmates, and around a third thought it was their own fault. It is worth noting that there is no evidence to suggest that the proportion of people blaming management did this due to factors such as compensation claims. If people hold the view—after the event—that the accident was preventable, and are sufficiently clear as to its cause that they can attribute blame, it is apparent that they are very much aware of the context in which they are working. If this were not the case, then they would not be in a position to point to the factors and people that played a role in the accidents. While this study was confined to a steel plant, research by the same authors in other industries suggests that the results are generalisable.

To understand why people carry out intentional actions that, unintentionally, can lead to accidents, rather than their intended outcomes, it is useful to look at the nature of these intentions and how they come about. At the centre of this is the concept of attitudes.

Attitudes and Groups

When looking at accident causation, it is important to understand whether the aetiologies of the causal factors lie within the individual or the context within which they work. While attitudes may at first be seen, particularly by people outside the psychological professions, to belong to the individuals who hold them, within psychology it has for many years been clearly shown that attitudes are developed and most readily changed in relation to the social context or milieu in which they exist (e.g. Lewin, 1947). In the case of industrial safety the context is provided by the work environment in its widest sense. People's attitudes towards safety and the safe operation of technology are a function of the attitudes of those with whom they work. These are in turn shaped by their perception of the organisation and its norms or rules.

As with many areas of psychology, there is much debate about the details of any model that is proposed to explain psychological and behavioural phenomena. Attitude research is no exception. However, while argument over the detail of the model exists, one of the most influential models of the relationship between attitudes and behaviour, that proposed by Ajzen and Fishbein (1980), provides an example of the importance of context that serves well the present purpose.

Essentially the Ajzen and Fishbein (1980) model views behaviour as mediated by intentions, which are a function of subjective norms and attitudes. The attitudes are seen as a person's beliefs that given behaviours will lead to particular outcomes, and her or his evaluations of those outcomes. Subjective norms are the person's beliefs about other individuals' or groups' views of whether he or she should carry out the particular behaviour. Also of importance is the value the person puts on the views of others.

The preceding line of argument in relation to safety can be summarised thus. People's safety behaviour, whether they perform actions that can lead to accidents that consequently lead to harm to themselves and the wider community, is a function of their attitudes. These people's attitudes are shaped by the people with whom they work. The immediate work group's attitudes are in turn likely to be shaped by its wider context; the organisation.

What this points to is the importance of organisational norms in shaping safety behaviour. These norms are the responsibility of the management of the organisations. Consequently the argument could be made, based on psychological theory, that as attitudes are shaped by the organisation, then the same organisation could be held responsible for them and for the actions that follow from those attitudes.

To date there has been little research that has attempted to show the relationship between workforce safety attitudes and their safety performance. However, a series of studies carried out by the Safety Research Unit in the Department of Psychology at the University of Surrey (now at Liverpool) has directly addressed this issue. The work has been carried out in the steel, chemical and electricity generating industries in the UK and other European countries and provides further evidence for the importance of management in people's attitudes and subsequent safety performance (Donald and Canter, 1993).

The Structure of Safety Attitudes and the Centrality of Management

Knowing the structure of safety attitudes provides useful information about how people experience and think about safety. In particular it can show what aspects of safety experience are central to attitudes. The structure of safety attitudes was empirically examined as part of the research described above.

If attitudes are thought of as comprising a system of interlinked components, then some of those components are likely to be more central to the overall system than others. Consequently any change in the aspects of people's attitudes at the centre of the system is likely to have the greatest overall impact on the way in which people think and feel about safety. The results of empirical research looking at this system of safety attitudes (Donald and Canter, 1993) show that at the core of people's attitudes is the encouragement and support they receive from management. This is important as it suggests that change in people's perceptions of management support is likely to have the greatest and most wide-ranging impact overall on people's attitude.

Another aspect of attitudes that was found to be central is concerned with shop floor appraisal of the safety system. Not only does this reveal that this is, as would be expected, important in terms of safety attitudes, but also that it is closely linked to management support.

The Relationship Between Safety Attitudes and Safety Performance

Further evidence for the importance of safety attitude for safety performance and the role of the management context is derived from looking at the correlations between the two. Using a 16-scale Safety Attitude Questionnaire Donald and Canter (1993, 1994) examined the relationship between their safety attitude scales and various indicators of safety performance. The average company scores of fourteen companies on the attitude scales were correlated with their accident rates. As accident rates are notorious for being unreliable indicators of safety performance, checks were made to ensure that those used were acceptably accurate. Further, the results reported here show that the relationship between attitudes and lost-time accident (LTA) rates, which are less open to distortion than, for example, all accident (AA) rates. With the interesting exceptions of a scale measuring 'safety representatives' practice', and another measuring attitude to 'safe working procedures' all the attitude scales correlated with LTA rates at a statistically significant level. For example, the scale that measures 'management support and encouragement' correlated 0.71, the scale 'shop floor training' 0.76, a scale measuring 'shop floor satisfaction' 0.70, and finally the scale addressing 'management support for meetings' correlated 0.66. (Similar, as yet unpublished, analysis using a population of 80 companies for the calculation of the correlations shows basically the same relationships.)

These correlations are interesting from a number of perspectives. First, they clearly demonstrate that there is a strong relationship between attitudes and safety performance as measured by accident statistics. Second, they show that the perceived support given to the workforce by management is highly predictive of their propensity to have accidents.

Not only do the results of this and other research raise questions about the culpability of organisations, they also emphasise the need to take into account attitudinal factors in risk assessment. In particular the risk to surrounding communities from proposed industrial installations, or the siting of, for example, schools and housing around those installations, may benefit from assessing social psychological factors. Planning inquiries that do not take them into account could well be open to accusations of falling short of their duties.

ATTITUDES AND LATENT ERRORS

The work on safety attitudes also fits well within, and clarifies, other approaches to human and psychological factors in accidents, one of the more cited of which is that proposed by Reason (1990). Basically, Reason makes a distinction between active and latent failures or errors in a safety system. Active failures are the direct causes of an accident, 'those errors and violations having an immediate adverse effect' (Reason, 1990, p. 28). Latent failures, by contrast, are described as 'decisions or actions, the damaging consequences of which may lay dormant for a long time, only becoming evident when they combine with local triggering factors (... active failures ... etc.) to breach the system's defences. Their defining feature is that they are present within the system well before the onset of a recognisable accident sequence' (Reason, 1990, p. 28). In describing latent failures Reason also uses the biological metaphor of 'resident pathogens' that exist within an organism, and when coupled with an external condition will result in disease.

Three general sets of latent failures are identified by Reason. These are the fallible decisions of high-level decision makers, line management deficiencies, and psychological precursors to unsafe acts. Unsafe acts are, then, active failures that result in an accident if there is a local trigger, and if local conditions have inadequate defences and thereby provide a window of opportunity for the accident to take place. Within this framework, attitudes can broadly be seen as psychological precursors, and the latent failures within senior and line management being the context in which attitudes are developed.

Whether or not Reason's (1990) concepts of latent and active failure are seen as tying into Donald and Canter's (Canter and Donald, 1990a; Donald and Canter, 1994) work on safety attitudes and climate, what is important is that the conclusions are similar in terms of responsibility. Both approaches see the psychological precursors, or attitudes, as being the appropriate focus for reducing accidents, rather than the host of immediate and specific unsafe acts. Further, while both approaches see some responsibility for accidents being with the immediate actors in the event, they point to line and senior management as the creators of the conditions in which the events take place. It is line and senior management that is also seen, therefore, as having a, if not *the*, major responsibility for accidents.

RISK-TAKING BEHAVIOUR

Wagenaar (1992; Wagenaar and Groeneweg, 1987) also comes to the conclusion that there is a need to address senior strategic management levels of an organisation to improve safety. However, he comes to this conclusion from the associated but different area of risk-taking behaviour. Wagenaar argues that those people who are engaged in behaviour that, in Reason's terminology, results in active errors are not involved in a process of assessing the risks of their actions. Therefore, by definition, they are also not involved in risk-taking, although objective risk may exist. However, at the strategic level in an organisation, Wagenaar argues, the risks associated with various actions and policies are assessed. Consequently, those involved in decision-making at that level do engage in risk-taking. It is this risk-taking that results in what Reason (1990) would see as latent errors.

The argument made by Wagenaar, that people do not assess the risk of their actions resulting in an accident, may at first appear contradictory to the position taken in here. That position, to recap, is that the actions people take that lead to an accident are under their control and are intentional. Further, people are aware that they behave in ways that have the potential to result in an accident. However, this view does not mean that people are assessing the risks of particular behaviours, although when questioned they may acknowledge that some risk was involved.

To explain all the psychological issues here would require a lengthy discussion. However, it may be possible to address the central point by briefly discussing a concrete example. Below is a quotation from an interviewee who took part in the attitude research described earlier. He relates that: 'My supervisor gets behind the machinery. I stop it at any time and he could walk into it. I could've killed him five times last week alone.' In some senses the assessment that he could have 'killed him five times last week alone' may be thought to be risk-taking. Before getting on to the main point, it can be noted that, in a sense, it is not the interviewee who is taking the risk, but his supervisor. Moreover, saying that he could have killed his supervisor is not an assessment of the probability that he would be killed.

The actions described by the interviewee, and those that result in an accident, are often routine, everyday behaviour. Wagenaar (1992) argues that such everyday behaviour is carried out automatically under action schemata and not consciously processed unless there is an obvious problem that requires deviation from the schema. As a consequence, there is no process of risk assessment prior to that behaviour. The same argument is made by Donald and Canter (1992) in their discussion of intentional behaviour in emergencies. In this case they use the similar concept of scripts as an explanation for predefined action sequences. Again, scripted behaviour does not require conscious processing, even though scripts are engaged in order to fulfil people's intentional goals. Consequently both the perspectives of Donald and Canter (1992) and Wagenaar (1992) share, at least in part, a common view regarding the psychological processes that underlie people's everyday behaviour.

It has already been noted that Wagenaar (1992) argues that risk-taking is present at a strategic management level, and therefore it is at this level responsibility for accidents rests. However, this can be taken further. In addition to using the idea of scripts, Donald and Canter (1992) introduce the concept of place rules and place schema to help explain behaviour. Place rules are internalised aspects of a person's ways of dealing with a place based on what she or he perceives to be the actions that are appropriate for that place. They argue that place rules 'do not only include formally prescribed rules and legal requirements, but also the informal and conventional rules that evolve for the use of particular types of place and which guide behaviour' (p. 205). One of the sources of these rules is the organisation that is responsible for a place. In the case of industry, this will be the directors, senior and line management. While formal rules may insist that people follow the appropriate procedures, for instance, informal rules may evolve that are contrary to these. It is these informal rules that are often related to unsafe acts, and inappropriate safety attitudes. This perspective is echoed, though in other terms, by Wagenaar (1992) when discussing the Zeebrugge tragedy. The quotation above shows the routine unsafe actions of a supervisor. Such behaviour implies the condoning of unsafe activity in that workplace. In a sense, the worker is describing something that boils down to 'this is the way we do things around here'. The people responsible for the evolution of these rules, which could also be seen as latent failures, are again the managers of an organisation.

From this discussion then, it is apparent that the perspectives of Donald and Canter (1992, 1993), Reason (1990), and Wagenaar (1992), are compatible. Further, these various positions emphasise the responsibility of management for the actions that result in accidents and disasters, even though the actions of those managers may, in both space and time, be some distance removed from those actions. A question, for inter-disciplinary discussion, is whether this managerial responsibility can and should lead to legal, corporate, responsibility.

SAFETY IN PUBLIC PLACES

It is not just in relation to industrial accidents that intention is relevant. Whether a dangerous situation turns into a disastrous one is often a function of how people behave under the circumstances, and the understanding they have of the setting. In this part of the chapter the focus will be on the nature of behaviour in public places during emergencies, in particular, fires.

Random Behaviour in Emergencies

In many disasters fatalities and injuries are often said to be a consequence of people panicking. Even a cursory glance at news reports of disasters confirms the pervasivity of this view. While there is some confusion about what is meant by panic, an extensive review of the use of the term by Sime (1990) reveals that it usually implies that people behave in a manner over which they have little or no control. Panic behaviour also shows no continuity to the usual behaviour and social psychological structures and processes that exist under normal circumstances, including those immediately prior to the emergency (Donald and Canter, 1992). As it is not structured, in many ways such behaviour can be thought of as random and therefore unpredictable. Because panic behaviour can not be understood within the social and psychological frameworks that guide normal behaviour, it is very difficult to plan for in a way that would draw upon people's cognitive understanding of the emergency. As panic is also seen as automatic and beyond the control of the individual, the possibility of changing someone's behaviour while they are panicking does not exist (Donald, 1993). Further, panic is often considered more of a threat to life than the original threat itself—for example, the fire. The assumption that panic is likely to occur in an emergency, and the reliance on it as an explanation of people's behaviour, has important implications and consequences.

Under the 'panic model', as behaviour is uncontrolled and so difficult to plan, train and prepare for, the body responsible for the place in which a disaster takes place, may not be seen as being responsible for the injury and death caused by it. What they can do is attempt to reduce the likelihood of panic. This, it may be claimed, can be achieved by, for example, reducing the sense of danger people experience, and related to this, reducing the amount of information given to the public who are threatened. This may provide a possible legal defence for the action or inaction of an organisation. If panic is accepted as a likely behaviour then actions aimed at avoiding that panic can be seen as reasonable and appropriate.

Also, in terms of preparing for possible emergencies, an organisation may be required to provide an environment that can deal with panic (for example, ensuring that the exits are located at regular intervals in the building, or that panic bolts are fitted to exit doors). Beyond this, in environmental terms, there is little they can do.

Interestingly, while blame for the death and injury of individuals is shifted to their behaviour, because panic is seen as a particular automatic response to environmental stimuli over which a person has no control, panicking becomes an involuntary and mysterious force that is to blame, rather than the individuals over which it has a hold. Thus the conclusion can be reached that death was a consequence of panic for which neither the victim nor the organisation can be seen as being to blame.

While panic is a convenient and often powerful explanation as to why people are injured during an emergency, belief in it as an explanation is based on assumption rather than empirical evidence. Empirical research has consistently shown a clear and predictable structure to people's behaviour (Canter, Breaux and Sime, 1980). Further, it has also shown that it is shaped by the particular place a person is in and the rules of use associated with that place (Donald and Canter, 1992). Moreover, the role the person occupies, and her or his prior intentions and goals are also of great importance in shaping behaviour in emergencies (Donald and Canter, 1990).

As an alternative to the 'panic model' the 'structured behaviour' shifts thinking about the contributory factors involved in turning an emergency into a disaster. Rather than planning for uncontrolled, random behaviour, the focus moves to understanding how people interpret, make sense of, or understand and use the setting, under both normal circumstances and emergencies. Moreover, it calls into question the use of panic as an explanation or defence for what happens in a disaster.

Structured Behaviour in Emergencies

Psychological research that has shown empirically that the nature of behaviour in emergencies such as major fires has many implications. In the remainder of this chapter other implications will be considered. In looking at these it is useful to have in mind a summary of the basic structure of behaviour under these circumstances.

Essentially, as Canter, Breaux and Sime (1980) identified, behaviour moves through three stages; interpretation, preparation and action. During the interpretation stage people decide what to do. They make sense of the situation around them based on the information they have. At this stage they decide whether the events surrounding them are in some way special and so require different action. In the second stage, once they have defined the situation as an emergency, they decide what they should do and prepare to carry out that behaviour. During the final stage the actions are performed.

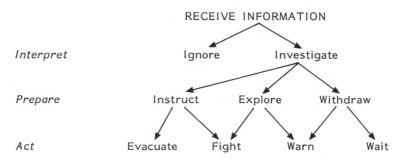

Figure 7.2.1   The structure of behaviour in fires

There are many influences that guide the detail of each of these stages; for example, people's prior expectations, the normal activities they associate with the place in which the emergency occurs, their role in that place, and the rules they associate with the use of the place. This in turn happens within the context and framework provided by the organisation that governs the place. Of crucial importance is the information people have that they can use in decision-making.

Interpretation and Information

The early stages of an emergency are characterised by ambiguity. People need to make sense of this ambiguity. In doing so they draw on the cues around them, and actively interpret these cues. Of importance is the length of time taken to establish that there is a problem. This time factor is very important in emergencies as they tend to develop rapidly and, in the case of fire, exponentionally. Delays can therefore be deadly.

As people need to go through this interpretation stage in an emergency, it is clear that, as with other similar tasks, they need as much accurate information as possible and as rapidly as possible. This then puts an onus on those responsible for managing the emergency to provide that information. Consequently, if an organisation argues that it reduced or failed to provide information so as to avoid panic, it is in fact arguing that it failed to provide the basic conditions necessary to facilitate people's escape.

Preparing to Act

Once people have reached the interpretation that there is an emergency the next stage is to decide what to do, and in the case of deciding to evacuate, for instance, to prepare for the evacuation. Again this is not automatic and assistance needs to be given. However, time-consuming actions can take place at this stage with people, for example, locking doors, collecting belongings and fulfilling the normal responsibilities of their role.

Again there is a need to provide people with clear instructions on what to do in the event of an emergency, and for it to be made clear that the responsibilities which people are expected to fulfil under normal circumstances are not the same as those in an emergency. In the case of the King's Cross fire this was clearly crucial for some of the victims. For instance, evidence from statements made to the inquiry suggests that a male toilet attendant killed in the fire died as a result of fulfilling his everyday responsibilities (Donald and Canter, 1992). The decision to carry out the activities that he did may have been at least in part shaped by what he interpreted as the expectations upon him. These expectations to some degree were likely to have been generated by the organisation for which he worked.

Action Intentionality and Evacuation

Once people have reached the conclusion that they are involved in an emergency, and have decided what to do and prepared for it, they reach the final stage in their behaviour. The actions people take can be varied at this stage. They may, for instance, attempt to fight the fire. One of the most common and effective actions in emergencies in public places is to attempt to evacuate. Again information at this stage is important. For example, the directions and movements of people need to be managed. This is perhaps a more involved task than may often be provided for. A quotation from a witness at King's Cross is useful here in providing an illustration of this. Of course, the body of research evidence comes from an analysis of the behaviour of a large number of people in different places, and not just from this one instance. A barrister in describing his actions during the disaster relates:

> This police officer said words to the effect 'Could you all please get off the platform, there is a fire on the station.' Upon hearing this I picked my bag up and left the platform ... While walking across the ticket hall I felt large gusts of heat although the heat was not immense. There were a lot of people both in front and behind me. Whilst in this passage I picked up one of the wall phones intending to phone my wife. I put a 10p piece into the slot but left the phone because the smoke became thicker. The visibility became like dense fog.

As can be seen from this account, the witness had been evacuated from a part of the station, but after walking across the ticket hall felt sufficiently out of danger to stop to make a telephone call. This not only demonstrates that full instructions are necessary, and that they need to be reinforced along the evacuation route, but also, in keeping with the behaviour of many other people and incidents studied, there is no evidence of panic. In fact the opposite of panic behaviour is clearly in evidence.

Exits and Exit Choice

An important aspect of evacuation is exit availability and exit choice. Sime (1990) provides several examples of evacuations in which people have failed to evacuate a public place because they have only used a single or small number of the exits available. Further, the use of the limited number of exits has sometimes resulted in crush injury and death. The blame for these casualties has most often been panic. However, when people's exit route choice is examined in detail there is a clear pattern to it, as well as a logic for the individuals involved. Many factors involved in exit choice have been identified by psychologists' research. These have implications for design and emergency training, planning and management. Failure to take these into account is possibly more likely to lead to casualties than not providing the legally required number of exits. Unlike the provision and accessibility of exits, these other factors are, currently, not considered in legal action following an emergency, nor are they part of the regulations governing the use of public places.

People's choice and use of exits in an emergency is complex. Research has shown that people do not distribute themselves evenly across exits, as may be the case if behaviour is random or if behaviour is manifested as panic (e.g. Donald and Canter, 1990; Sime, 1983). Instead they select exits based on their intentions and their experience of the normal use of exits in that place. So, for example people will tend to use the exits that they would use under normal circumstances. This is usually the place where they entered. Further, if under normal circumstances particular places or exits are forbidden, then people will be reluctant to use them in an emergency. This can include, for example, going on to a football pitch. Behaviour such as this is evident even when people realise that they are involved in a serious emergency.

The importance of the previous intentions of people in determining their exit choice was dramatically demonstrated by research carried out looking at the King's Cross fire (Donald and Canter, 1990) as part of the invited evidence to the Fennell Inquiry (1988). Of particular significance was work that examined the prior intentions of those who died in the fire (Donald and Canter, 1992). This was the first study in which the intentions of people who died in a disaster could so clearly be pieced together. The research used statements of people involved in the disaster, interviews with those who had travelled with some of the victims, forensic statements, and details of the locations of the bodies to put together a picture of the victims' actions and intentions. Of the 31 victims it was possible to establish the intentions of 26 of them. A small number had died in the course of their work or in their place of work. This included a fire chief, the toilet attendant, and the person from the Bureau de Change. Of the others almost all had attempted to leave via their previously intended route, or via the route they had entered the station. Most of the routes chosen were not the most effective or appropriate choices in terms of ease and distance. Although the results of this research are perhaps surprising in their strength, they are what would have been expected from other recent psychological research.

BUILDING REGULATIONS

Although the regulatory framework that governs the design and use of public places, and the role of the bodies that enforce the regulations, may not be given extensive coverage here, they are none the less part of the legal context of psychology. They do also play an important role in emergencies, and do have a place within the legal system. One area of regulation that provides a useful example of some of the implications of the research carried out on human behaviour in emergencies is concerned with design regulation regarding building exits.

Building regulations clearly specify the number of exits that there should be in a building of a particular type and capacity. If the occupants are allowed to exceed that capacity, or if insufficient exits are available there is a likelihood that a building licence, for example as a place for dancing, will be withdrawn or not granted. If a place has insufficient exits and some of those that do exist are blocked or locked it is a moderately simple matter when apportioning blame in the event of a disaster.

If the importance of use under normal circumstances was recognised, the owners and managers of public places would be under an obligation to ensure that the ways they were used under normal circumstances were such that they would facilitate escape in the event of an emergency. Thus for example, if an organisation did not ensure that exits were also used for entry, they would be open to the charge that they had contributed to evacuation difficulties.

The implications of the research that has shown the factors involved in exit choice are many. They apply both to the use of places under normal conditions and for building regulations themselves. Indeed they call into question the adequacy of the regulations and, as this knowledge has been in the public domain for more than a decade, open questions about whether the regulatory bodies themselves are not open to the accusation of failing to provide adequate guidelines.

CONCLUSIONS

There is considerable evidence that many accidents, whether they are of the scale of a major catastrophe or involve just one individual, have their primary cause in the inappropriate actions of people interacting with the social and organisational environments within which they occur. Dismissing these actions as ill-informed or unintended would undermine the possibility of understanding the framework of objectives that make accidents possible. Accepting their importance has wide implications in many legal areas. For example, it suggests that as well as a company being held responsible for its technology and safety procedures, it also be responsible for the attitudinal factors that form its safety climate. It also highlights inadequacies in risk assessment methods and the related need to take social psychological factors into account when important land use planning decisions are being made.

Behaviour during emergencies in public places has not been found to manifest in panic. Rather it shows a structure, central to which is the need for information. Failure to provide information because of concerns about panic contributes to the endangering of people in public places and so cannot be considered any form of defence.

The use of exits in public places is determined by the way in which a place is usually used and what people are trying to achieve there. It would seem that these factors are more important then the actual number of exits provided for escape. Consequently it could reasonably be asked whether the everyday management of the place and the public who use it should be seen as something for which an organisation should be held responsible. It is also something that the public have a right to expect would be taken into account in building regulations.

While these findings are gradually becoming part of the discourse on emergency behaviour, it is likely that it will be a long time before they are fully covered by regulations and even longer before they fully enter as part of legal debate and litigation. Central to many legal issues that ensue from the preceding discussion is the notion of blame, and consequently causation. In assessing the likelihood that blame will go beyond the unfortunate individuals whose final actions led to catastrophe and disaster, it is perhaps appropriate in a cross disciplinary volume such as this for a psychologist to leave the last word to a lawyer:

> One of the reasons that traditional accounts of causation are unhelpful in this context is that their starting-place is often that of the individual defendant facing a charge: did this person contribute causally to this result? That particular person's causal contribution is then all that matters; whether the result might additionally have been caused by someone else is not a relevant issue. (Wells, 1993, p. 47)

REFERENCES

Ajzen, I. and Fishbein, M. (1980). *Understanding Attitudes and Predicting Social Behaviour.* Englewood Cliffs, NJ: Prentice-Hall.

Canter, D. (1990). An overview of human behaviour in fires. In D. Canter (Ed.), *Fires and Human Behaviour* (2nd edn). London: Fulton.

Canter, D. and Donald, I. (1990a). Accident by design: environmental, attitudinal and organizational aspects of accidents. Proceedings of Culture Space History, 11th International Conference of the International Association for the Study of People and their Physical Settings. Ankara, Turkey. July 8–12, 1990.

Canter, D. and Donald, I. (1990b). Accident by Intention. Paper presented at the Annual Conference of the British Association for the Advancement of Science. Swansea, August 20–24.

Canter, D., Breaux, J. and Sime, J. (1980). Domestic, multiple occupancy and hospital fires. In D. Canter (Ed.), *Fires and Human Behaviour.* Chichester: John Wiley.

Cox, S. and Cox, T. (1991). The structure of employee attitudes to safety: a European example. *Work and Stress*, **5**, 93–106.

Donald, I. (1993). Behaviour in fires: preventing disasters. *Health, Safety and Environment Bulletin*, December, 11–14.

Donald, I. (1994). Measuring psychological factors in safety. *Safety and Health Practitioner*, March, 26–9.

Donald, I. and Canter, D. (1990). Behavioral aspects of the King's Cross disaster. In D. Canter (Ed.), *Fires and Human Behaviour* (2nd edn). London: Fulton.

Donald, I. and Canter, D. (1992). Intentionality and fatality during the King's Cross Underground fire. *European Journal of Social Psychology*, **22**, 203–18.

Donald, I. and Canter, D. (1993). Psychological factors and breaking the accident plateau. *Health, Safety and Environment Bulletin*, November, 5–8.

Donald, I. and Canter, D. (1994). Employee attitudes and safety in the chemical industry. *Journal of Loss Prevention in the Process Industries*, **7**, 203–08.

Fennell, D. (1988). *Investigation into the King's Cross Underground Fire*. London: HMSO/ Department of Transport.

Hurst, N., Nussey, C. and Pape, R. (1989). Development and Application of a Risk Assessment Tool (RISKAT), in the Health and Safety Executive. *Chem Eng Res Des*, **67**, 362–72

Lewin, K. (1947). Group decision and social change. In T. Newcomb and E. Hartley (Eds), *Readings in Social Psychology*. New York: Holt.

Powell, J. and Canter, D. (1985). Quantifying the human contribution to losses in the chemical industry. *Journal of Environmental Psychology*, **5**, 37–53.

Reason, J. (1990). The contribution of latent human failures in the breakdown of complex systems. In D. Broadbent, J. Reason and A. Baddeley (Eds), *Human Factors in Hazardous Situations*. Oxford: Clarendon Press.

Reason, J. and Mycielska, C. (1982). *Absent-Minded: The Psychology of Lapses and Everyday Errors*. Englewood Cliffs, NJ: Prentice-Hall.

Sime, J. (1983). Affiliative behaviour during escape to building exits. *Journal of Environmental Psychology*, **3**, 21–41.

Sime, S. (1990). The concept of panic. In D. Canter (Ed.), *Fires and Human Behaviour* (2nd edn). London: Fulton.

Wagenaar, W. (1992). Risk taking and accident causation. In F. Yates (Ed.), *Risk-Taking Behaviour*. Chichester: John Wiley.

Wagenaar, W. and Groeneweg (1987). Accidents at sea: multiple causes and impossible consequences. *International Journal of Man-Machine Studies*, **27**, 587–98.

Wells, C. (1993). *Corporations and Criminal Responsibility*. Oxford: Clarendon Press.

Zohar, D. (1980). Safety climate in industrial organizations: theoretical and applied implications. *Journal of Applied Psychology*, **65**, 96–102.

Part 8

Conclusions and
Future Directions

Chapter 8.1

Psychology and Law:
Future Directions

David Carson
University of Southampton
and
Ray Bull
University of Portsmouth

It is no longer a question of whether psychology has a contribution to make to
the law and its practice: psychology is making a significant contribution in a
number of different ways. This volume has, surely, demonstrated the range and
depth of that contribution. It has also indicated some of the potential for further
contributions and developments. The important questions now concern how
the relationship will flourish. Will mutual antagonisms and misunderstandings
continue? Will procedures and processes be found so that the contribution can
be maximised and yet the fears and concerns can be addressed?

Neither as editors nor as individuals do we believe that a development
programme can, or should, be prescribed. Diversity and openness are to be
valued. The relationship between law and psychology has been one of
challenge; so it should be. The lawyer's desire for a firm 'answer' or prediction
to a particular question about human behaviour must be expected to cause
problems to the psychologist who appreciates the impossibility, and
inappropriateness, of making a statement of such specificity. Equally, the
pragmatic needs of lawyers involved in particular litigation must be expected
to vary from the needs of those lawyers involved in drafting legislation or
making judicial pronouncements. It is not a simple question of how
psychological research and insights can be fed into some kind of machine that
provides 'answers' for the legal system and its many parts. It is more a question
of finding ways in which psychology's product can—appropriately and always
questioningly and critically—aid, and question, legal processes and goals.

We foresee, and would like to encourage, certain developments in the

Handbook of Psychology in Legal Contexts
Edited by R. Bull and D. Carson. © 1995 John Wiley & Sons Ltd

relationship between law and psychology. However we hope that dispute and dissention will never be closed off for a vigorous debate excites and facilitates the imaginative and critical thinking that must motivate and guide developments in all disciplines.

LEGAL PSYCHOLOGY OR LAW AND PSYCHOLOGY

We are, however, firm on at least one issue! The relationship between law and psychology must never be allowed to become one of 'employer' and 'servant'. Psychology—and psychologists—should never be seen as a resource for satisfying law's and lawyers' wishes for easy solutions to complex issues. We fear that such a status and dependence relationship is developing between lawyers and psychologists in the USA. The wider relationship between law and psychology developed earlier and has developed more in the US than in the rest of the world. Lawyers and the courts there, along with legal education, have been more welcoming than in other countries. The impression gained is that in the USA psychologists perceive it as their duty to provide expert evidence, and other forms of assistance to the legal system, at the times, in the formats and for the purposes of lawyers. Without denying that there have been and continue to be problems over the admissibility of psychological evidence in the USA, the focus has been placed on the reliability of psychological and other sciences rather than the competence and reliability of the legal system to know when to seek such evidence, how to assess its admissibility as being scientific and how to evaluate its application to the instant case. Because of the constitutional and decision-making roles of the courts we tend to focus upon what they say about other disciplines rather than review their competence to make those comments. The judges of the Supreme Court, for example, in their decision in *Daubert v. Merrell Dow Pharmaceuticals, Inc.*, (113 S.Ct. 2786 (1993)) disagreed on whether judges were competent to assess the scientific status of competing theories and findings.

An emphasis upon 'legal psychology', rather than 'law and psychology' (the ordering of the words is unimportant), creates similar impressions and concerns. 'Legal psychology' suggests a sub-specialism whose limits and roles are determined by the law and legal system. As this volume has demonstrated, psychologists from the wide range of specialisms, clinical, educational, occupational and forensic, not just 'legal psychologists', have much to contribute to the legal system. It would be most unfortunate if a sub-specialism developed which saw its role as simply to service the needs of lawyers and the legal system. So much of the potential contribution lies in encouraging lawyers to rethink issues, to challenge existing rules and practices. Neither discipline, let alone the public or the interests of justice, would be served by such a development.

Just as psychologists need to appreciate the pragmatic imperatives of lawyers so do lawyers need to appreciate that psychologists can contribute more than partial answers to their questions. For example, if psychologists are only asked for a rule or test which will define when people with mental disorders or learning disabilities are incapable of making contracts, or when an offender is 'dangerous', then we will all be poorer. We need to be open to different approaches; lawyers need to be prepared to rephrase the question, legislators need to be prepared to adopt entirely different approaches so that psychologists and others can use their sciences to answer more appropriately and reliably. Open and critical attitudes are essential. That is not possible where one discipline adopts a service or compliant attitude to the other.

EDUCATION AND DISSEMINATION

Open and yet critical attitudes will best be achieved through the development of education and training courses. Psychologists need to know about the legal frameworks within which many of their tasks will be performed. For example, they need to know about the legal requirements for decision-making about 'dangerous' offenders. But such courses need to go further. They will, invariably, adopt pathological rather than preventive orientations to the law. They will concentrate upon what may not be done and the likely responses of courts and other legal officials when harm results. The law of contract and traditional courses on it are, for example, substantially about the law of breach of contract. The emphasis upon case-law, upon past litigation, is artificial in that litigation is a relative rarity, not least in terms of the proportion of cases that are settled before trial, or where there are pleas of guilty. Courses should focus on the potential for prevention, on what the law permits, on good practice. Psychologists need to be encouraged to understand and appreciate, although certainly not necessarily to agree with, legal values, orientations. An appreciation of just a few key issues—for example, duty relationships and notions of causation—can prove very useful in orientating non-lawyers towards lawyers' approaches.

Lawyers need to know how and when psychologists can help them. They also need to have appropriate ways of assessing the information that is given to them, both for its relevance to the legal issues that they are dealing with and with regard to evaluating its scientific strength. University law degrees could only be improved, particularly by broadening the educational experience and extending the skills of those who achieve them (rather than just providing them with more information), by courses that explain and encourage critical assessments of research methodology. An understanding of different approaches to questions of causation, for example, is critical. But degree level courses cannot be sufficient, given the pace of developments in research and its applications.

Attention must be paid to the dissemination of information. While there are several excellent journals in the law and psychology fields, and a comparative 'explosion' of such journals is taking place in the UK and the rest of Europe, they tend to be written and read by psychologists, rather than by both psychologists and lawyers. This cannot be too surprising given that people in each discipline have enough problems keeping up to date with developments in their own subjects. So information needs to be disseminated in forms that are easily assimilated when required. Professional bodies could require their members to demonstrate their commitment to continuing education by attendance at certain courses or study of certain materials, as theLaw Society in England and Wales already does. But it is not enough just to be able to siphon off some psychological expertise when litigation requires it. There needs to be, as a minimum, centres where developments in law and psychology are monitored and which provide a dissemination service. There need to be centres where there are people able and willing to articulate the actual or potential contribution of law and psychology when others have overlooked it. The USA has a major advantage in the 'Brandeis Brief' procedure whereby interested organisations can make detailed submissions to the courts about the implications of different formulations of the law. But it would be even better if such organisations could influence the questions that are raised for answering, and could feed directly into law reform.

LAW REFORM

Ultimately it may be essential that legislation is drafted by lawyers aware of potential problems in the interpretation and application of statutes, and skilled in the means of minimising them. (The ideal law may be one that is never litigated, although that might also be the consequence of the law being ignored or referring to very rare events.) But several other disciplines, particularly psychology, could valuably feed into the processes whereby the framework, approach and basic tests and distinctions are created. Several contributors to this volume have, for example, demonstrated the potential for psychological insights into decision-making to assist legislators and judges.

Several countries have Law Commissions, or similar bodies, which are charged with reviewing the law and recommending changes. Generally they eschew involvement with controversial 'political' changes, although this can only be a distinction of degree rather than of kind. The Law Commissioners for England and Wales are all lawyers. Can this be justified? It is not just that having at least one Law Commissioner who is a behavioural scientist would have considerable symbolic significance as a statement about the law's openness to ideas from other disciplines. But such a commissioner could provide an invaluable role in encouraging, if not commissioning, empirical research on key issues relevant to law reform and in critically assessing the research findings submitted to the commission as grounds for law reform. This is not a challenge to the 'lawyers' agenda' of the Law Commission. It is suggested as a means of enabling the Law Commission to adopt perspectives to law reform which could make the process so much more productive.

No challenge to the legal hegemony is necessarily involved by such suggestions as the appointment of psychologists to training programmes for judges. Indeed the potential problem is that those psychologists will begin to identify too closely with the immediate needs of judges and the legal system and overlook more radical, but ultimately more valuable, strategies. The key feature is an openness to the contributions that others can make within an appreciation of the values and pragmatic imperatives that others must, at least until there is change, work within.

EXPERT EVIDENCE

It is particularly important that a more open, but yet critical, attitude is developed towards expert evidence. The problems, such as in deciding what is admissible evidence and how it should be evaluated, are clear. For example concern is often expressed about the frequency with which expert psychological evidence on eyewitness testimony is admitted in the US courts while it is only beginning to be admitted, even though there is case-law to suggest that it ought not to be admitted, in the UK. Further, many of the current rules governing expert evidence will, increasingly, bring the law into disrepute. The ultimate issue rule, for example, needs to be withdrawn. Allowing experts to give evidence on a wide range of issues, except the critical question that will be the essence of the court's decision, is misconceived. The question is not whether we have trial by experts or trial by judge and any jury. That is a false dichotomy. (Anyway litigants might like to be offered the choice of trial by expert.) The judge and jury will always have to decide whether they accept the expert's evidence. In adversarial trial systems they will still have to make choices between competing experts' interpretations. The significance of disallowing expert evidence on an ultimate issue such as the credibility of vulnerable witnesses such as children or adults with learning disabilities, needs to be appreciated. Those witnesses will, regularly, be almost the only evidence against defendants. Alleged victims also have interests. It is not just a simple question of principle or value involving the relative value of wrongful convictions versus wrongful acquittals. Other procedures, for example rigorous—but appropriate—examination of expert witnesses giving evidence about credibility could be investigated.

Equally, the rule that expert witnesses may not give evidence on any topic which is within the skills or knowledge base of judges and jurors, needs to be abolished. It is fundamentally anti-intellectual. It avoids judges and jurors learning about their ignorance. It encourages judges and juries to utilise beliefs and inductions that may have been, or be, refutable by research. It is perfectly understandable that judges wish to discourage the wasting of time, such as when expert witnesses tell courts things that they already know. But, surely, there are other ways of achieving those goals than by implying, falsely, that 'common sense' is commonly held and accurate.

But, if judges and other lawyers are to become more open to scientific evidence then they need greater assurance as to the quality of that evidence and those witnesses. Many experts condemn their experiences of being examined and cross-examined in a court. Many of these criticisms, particularly those which relate to questions which are designed to have a dramatic rather than intellectual effect, are well made. But those experts should consider what they could do, outside and before court appearances, to make their evidence more credible. Professional bodies should develop accreditation schemes, should undertake and demonstrate forms of responsibility for evidence provided to court.

LAW AND PSYCHOLOGY

For too long the disciplines, and professions, of law and psychology have kept their distance. They are still doing so. But for so long as they keep 'dancing' around each other, rather than being prepared to appreciate and respect differences in order to move forward (value assumptions always being made as explicit as possible), they will continue to hold each other as near antagonists. Law and psychology is not just a topic for some people to specialise in and develop into a clique. It is an area of overlapping intellectual and practical issues where it is crucial, not just for the participants' advantage, that there is respectful openness. This volume has, we hope, demonstrated through the participation of both lawyers and psychologists, how much has been achieved and how much more there is to achieve.

Table of Cases

Note: The abbreviation 'R. *v.*' is omitted from the following table.

Table of Statutes

Index

Indexes compiled by Liz Granger

Keep up to date with the latest developments in psychology and law...

Handbook of
Psychology in **Legal Contexts**

Edited by **Ray Bull** and **David Carson**

Forensic and legal psychology is a growing field and it is intended to publish supplements to this volume. These supplements will both update existing chapter content to reflect important developments, and also introduce new topics that have become important to the study and practice of psychology in legal contexts.

To register for information about these future supplements, please photocopy this page, complete the details below and return to the publishers by mail or fax.

Name: _____

Address: _____

_____

_____

Country: _____   Tel: _____

Please return to:

Tracy Clayton,
John Wiley & Sons Ltd,
Baffins Lane,
Chichester,
West Sussex,
PO19 1UD, UK   Fax: (01243) 775878

WILEY